I0759914

Praise for *A History of Christian Psalmody*

With encyclopedic thoroughness, Charles Cosgrove covers in detail every known instance of the use of psalms by early Christians. This will undoubtedly become the standard textbook on the subject.

Paul F. Bradshaw, emeritus professor of liturgy,
University of Notre Dame

The first and certainly for a long time most authoritative monograph on the topic of psalmody in the early Church: comprehensive in the coverage of material, outstanding in the depth of its reflection, and exemplary in the clarity of the exposition—certain to be a classic on the Christian reception of the Bible and on the history and understanding of singing in church.

Harald Buchinger, professor of liturgical studies,
University of Regensburg, Germany

Charles Cosgrove has produced here a much-needed definitive study of psalmody used in a variety of settings in early Christian history. Supported by the best in current scholarship on early liturgy and related fields, Cosgrove surveys the use of psalmody in what becomes the divine office, or liturgy of the hours, both cathedral and monastic, as well as domestic settings, feasts and festivals, and both anti-orthodox and anti-heretical processional contexts. This book, rich in theological insight, will have wide appeal for liturgical, biblical, and early Christian studies. At the same time, liturgical musicians will find much in this volume for their own illumination. Mandatory reading for courses in the liturgy of the hours. I highly recommend it.

Maxwell E. Johnson, emeritus professor of liturgy,
University of Notre Dame

In his *tour de force* of the use of biblical psalms in the first five centuries, Charles Cosgrove provides a first ever panorama of early Christian psalmody. Through sharp interpretations of church fathers, church orders and other patristic literature, the book offers refreshing discussions and lucid depictions of psalm singing in a great variety of settings, both private and liturgical. The book will serve as an authoritative overview for scholars and everyone interested in the topic.

Stig Simeon R. Frøyshov, professor emeritus of liturgical
studies, faculty of theology, University of Oslo

A HISTORY OF CHRISTIAN PSALMODY

A HISTORY OF CHRISTIAN PSALMODY

FROM THE PAULINE MISSION TO THE END OF THE FIFTH CENTURY

CHARLES H. COSGROVE

FORTRESS PRESS
Minneapolis

A HISTORY OF CHRISTIAN PSALMODY
From the Pauline Mission to the End of the Fifth Century

30 29 28 27 26 25 1 2 3 4 5 6 7 8 9

Library of Congress Cataloging-in-Publication Data

Names: Cosgrove, Charles H., author
Title: A history of Christian psalmody : from the Pauline mission to the end of the fifth century / Charles H. Cosgrove.
Description: Minneapolis : Fortress Press, 2025. | Includes bibliographical references and index.
Identifiers: LCCN 2024060193 (print) | LCCN 2024060194 (ebook) | ISBN 9798889836797 hardback | ISBN 9798889836803 ebook
Subjects: LCSH: Psalmody | Bible. Psalms--Liturgical use | Singing--Religious aspects--Christianity | Church history--Primitive and early church, ca. 30-600
Classification: LCC BS1435 .C67 2025 (print) | LCC BS1435 (ebook) | DDC 223/.206--dc23/eng/20250502
LC record available at https://lccn.loc.gov/2024060193
LC ebook record available at https://lccn.loc.gov/2024060194

Cover image: Floor mosaic of the basilica of Aquileia—paleochristian mosaic, 313–350 AD
Cover design: Kris E. Miller

Print ISBN: 979-8-8898-3679-7
eBook ISBN: 979-8-8898-3680-3

To Debbie, my wife of fifty happy years

CONTENTS

Illustrations ix
Preface xi
Acknowledgments xv
Abbreviations xvii

1. Jewish Customs of Psalm-Singing 1
2. The Rise of Christian Psalmody 15
3. Third-Century Developments 33
4. Psalm Lessons 53
5. Communion Psalmody 77
6. Daily Psalmody at Home and Church 93
7. Psalmody at Vigils and Occasional Services 123
8. Psalms in Monastic Life 157
9. Singing in the Streets 199
10. Formats 231
11. Antiphons and Antiphonal Singing 271
12. Melody 289
13. Purposes and Pleasures 319

Bibliography 365
Index of Ancient Sources 391
Subject Index 409

ILLUSTRATIONS

Figure 12.1. Psalm tone with the words of Psalm 138:1–2 296

Figure 12.2. 4QPs[b] col. xxi, Heb Psalm 102:17–18 298

Figure 12.3. Greek P. Add. 1287 300

Figure 12.4. Psalm 144:1 Codex Vaticanus gr. 1209, f. 710. 301

Figure 12.5. Psalm 144:1b Codex Sinaiticus Quire 63, f. 8r. 301

Figure 12.6. Psalm 144:1 Codex Alexandrinus p. 563v. 302

Figure 12.7. Psalm 144:2 Codex Alexandrinus p. 563v. 302

PREFACE

The impetus for this book was my discovery that the topic of early Christian psalm-singing could not be adequately covered in the history of early Christian music that I was then in the process of writing. It seemed wise to pause that effort and conduct a thorough examination of psalmody in early Christianity before returning to the broader topic. The result is the first comprehensive study of Christian psalm-singing in the first several centuries of the Common Era.

The subject has been treated by others, of course, but only in certain of its phases and aspects, albeit quite expertly in articles and essays by scholars such as Joseph Dyer, James McKinnon, Peter Jeffery, and Terence Bailey, not to mention the important contributions by Robert Taft in his magisterial work on the "liturgy of the hours." My debt to these and other learned investigators is evident at numerous points.

I have tackled the subject broadly, tracing its developments from the first-century Christian mission through roughly the end of the fifth century. The stopping point has been chosen for practical reasons—not only to keep the book from growing too large but also to keep me from straying into later periods for which I cannot claim competence.

By "psalms," I mean biblical psalms, specifically the poems of the Psalter. Moreover, since the book is conceived as a contribution to the study of early Christian music, I have focused on the *singing* of psalms. The many surviving ancient sermons and commentaries on the Psalter provide a wealth of evidence for such things as methods for interpreting psalms, conceptions of Christian piety, and developments in Christian theology. These worthy subjects are not the focus here, although I discuss them wherever that helps me elucidate the history of psalmody.

I proceed chronologically in the first three chapters, then shift to a more topical arrangement in order to examine specific developments, most of which occurred in (or are only documented for) the third century through the fifth. The general historical chapters treat the possible influence of Jewish song customs on early Christian psalmody and the earliest evidence for psalm-singing in the church in the second and third centuries. Chapters 4 through 9 treat the spread of psalmody to vigils, Scripture lessons, the daily office, funerals, processions, Communion, special feasts, work and leisure, and situations where a Christian turned to psalmody for comfort, encouragement, moral fortification, and protection against demonic threats. Chapter 10 discusses formats of psalmody. Chapter 11 examines the meaning of the terms "antiphon" and "antiphonal," which are associated with various sorts of psalmody in the fourth and fifth centuries. Chapter 12 considers the nature of the musical delivery of psalms, whether improvision or melodic composition or the use of formulas. And chapter 13 serves as a conclusion to the book by surveying various purposes of psalmody—compunction, moral formation and soul therapy, magical-ritual protection, ceremonial honor and liturgical praise, public speech, and last, but not least, the sensual or aesthetic pleasure of singing the psalms.

One gets the impression that ordinary Christians enjoyed singing psalms the way other people of their era enjoyed folk lays and the popular airs of the theater, songs they learned by heart and sang in various everyday settings. Most Christians saw no tension between taking pleasure in melody and being edified by words. By contrast, the elders of certain monasteries warned against singing psalms for pleasure. Moreover, some urban bishops worried that the pleasure of melody might distract their congregations from the message of a psalm, although these same bishops also concluded that melody is a divine method to make the psalms attractive to people, like honey added to a medicine or spice to a dish of food.

As far as we know, none of the worries of urban clergy about the charms of psalmody led to any significant curtailment of psalmody in church liturgies. The preachers and teachers, including bishops who had control of liturgies, were generally enthusiastic about psalmody. It was the bishops who established or otherwise blessed psalm-singing in every church venue. Thanks to these psalmody-approving divines and to all the ordinary Christians who found both pleasure and profit in psalm-singing, the practice spread to churches everywhere and found a place in numerous private and public settings. This pervasive presence of psalm-singing is celebrated in a panegyric to David penned by a late-antique Christian, whose words illustrate why a history of early Christian psalmody is worthy of a book-length study:

> When [David] plucks his spiritual lyre through the psalms, he charms the hearing and enlightens the understanding. For this reason, the grace of the Spirit dwells each day with nearly every Christian soul to sing him, so that we might gladden our hearing and benefit our soul. . . . In the churches there are vigils, and David is first, middle, and last. In the singing of early morning hymns David is first, middle, and last. In processions in the abodes of the dead, David is first, middle, and last. In the houses of virgins, there is weaving, and David is first, middle, and last. What a thing of wonder! Many who have not made their first attempt at reading have learned and

> can repeat by heart the whole of David. But it is not only in the cities and the churches that he shines forth on every occasion and with people of all ages. Even in the countryside and deserts and as far as the unsettled part of the world, he rouses sacred choirs to God with greater zeal. In the monasteries there is a holy chorus of angelic brigades, and David is first, middle, and last. In the convents there are bands of virgins imitating Miriam, and David is first, middle, and last. In the deserts there are crucified men conversing with God, and David is first, middle, and last. And when all humanity is under the rule of nocturnal physical slumber, dragged down to the depths, David alone stands by and awakens the servants of God for angelic vigils, earth being refashioned as heaven and humans as angelic-like beings.[1]

Translations and Citations

Unless otherwise indicated, all translations are my own, based on critical editions listed in the first section of the bibliography. Citations to these editions do not appear in the notes except in certain cases, as a courtesy to readers, and they are indicated simply by the editor's name and a page number (or a volume number and page number). All the critical editions are listed in the first section of the bibliography. In some instances, I cite to PG or PL in the notes, but I have not included the editions published by Migne—Patrologia Graeca and Patrologia Latina—in the bibliography. Sometimes I give the page number of a critical edition, where lack of editorial section numbers might make it difficult to locate. In the case of the *Didascalia*, I give the parallel in the *Apostolic Constitutions*, not because the same content is always found there but as a location help (as Alistair Stewart-Sykes and Hugh Connolly do in their respective translations). Unless noted otherwise, all references to psalms follow the Septuagint numbering (which is also that of the Vulgate), not the Masoretic Hebrew text, a procedure that accords with patristic custom.

To avoid constant repetition of the adjectives "biblical" and "Davidic," I use the terms "psalm" and "psalmody" exclusively for the poems of the Psalter, and I avoid using the word "hymn" as a synonym for a psalm, except when reflecting an ancient writer who uses the underlying Greek *hymnos* or its Latin transliteration. Occasionally I use the word "psalm" as a verb (a usage not recognized by Webster's dictionary), doing so in cases where *psallein* in Greek (or as a loanword in Latin or Coptic) might mean "deliver a psalm" but not necessarily sing it.

---

1. John Chrysostom (dub.), *Poen.* PG 64:11, 12–13.

ACKNOWLEDGMENTS

I am grateful to three libraries whose extensive resources made this book possible, notably Styberg Library of Garrett-Evangelical Seminary, the library of Northwestern University, and the University of Chicago's Regenstein Library. I was also ably served by numerous librarians, in particular by Mary-Carol Riehs, who has been a constant help over many years. Several scholars were also kind enough to assist me through correspondence about various matters—Zlatko Pleše, David Brakke, Joseph Dyer, and Stig Frøyshov. Members of the Problems in the Early History of the Liturgy, a standing seminar of the North American Academy of Liturgy, read portions of this book and offered valuable comments and bibliographical suggestions.

ABBREVIATIONS

AAA — *Acta Apostolorum Apocrypha*, ed. Richard A. Lipsius and Maximilian Bonnet. 3 vols. (1, 2/1, 2/2). Leipzig: Mendelssohn, 1891–1903. Reprint Darmstadt: Wissenschaftliche Buchgesellschaft, 1959.

AL — Armenian Lectionary

AC — *Apostolic Constitutions*

ApTrad — *Apostolic Tradition*

CIL — Corpus Inscriptionum Latinarum, ed. Augustus Mau et al. Berlin: Reimer, 1871–.

CCG — Corpus Christianorum Series Graeca

CCL — Corpus Christianorum Series Latina

CPT — Cambridge Patristic Texts

CSCO — Corpus Scriptorum Christianorum Orientalium

CSEL — Corpus Scriptorum Ecclesiasticorum Latinorum

ET — English translation.

FS — Fontes Christiani

FGrH — Jacoby, Felix (ed.). 1923–58. *Die Fragmente der griechischen Historiker.* Berlin: Weidmann.

GCS — Die Griechischen Christlichen Schriftsteller.

GMW — *Greek Musical Writings*, ed. Andrew Barker. Volume 1: *The Musician and His Art.* Cambridge: Cambridge University Press, 1984. Volume 2: *Harmonic and Acoustic Theory.* Cambridge: Cambridge University Press, 1989.

GNO — Gregorii Nysseni opera.

HA — Historia Augusta

LDAB — Leuven Database of Ancient Books

LSJ — *A Greek-English Lexicon*, 9th ed., compiled by Henry George Liddell and Robert Scott, rev. Henry S. Jones with Robert McKenzie. Oxford: Clarendon, 1940. LSJSuppl: *Greek-English Lexicon Revised Supplement*, ed. P. G. W. Glare with A. A. Thompson. Oxford: Clarendon, 1996.

LXX — Septuagint

MECL — James McKinnon, *Music in Early Christian Literature.* Cambridge: Cambridge University Press, 1987.

MT	Masoretic Text of the Hebrew Bible
NPNF	Nicene and Post-Nicene Fathers
OLD	*Oxford Latin Dictionary*. 2nd ed., ed. PO. G. W. Glare. 2 vols. Oxford: Oxford University Press, 2012.
OTP	*The Old Testament Pseudepigrapha*, ed. James H. Charlesworth. 2 vols. Garden City, NY: Doubleday, 1983 and 1985.
PG	Migne, Jacques-Paul (ed.). Patrologia cursus completes. Series Graeca. 161 vols. Paris: Migne, 1857–1866.
PGL	Lampe, G. W. H., ed. *Patristic Greek Lexicon*. Oxford: Clarendon, 1961.
PGM	Preisendanz, Karl, ed. *Papyri Graecae Magicae: Die griechen Zauberpapyri*. 2 vols. Rev. ed. A. Henrichs. Stuttgart: Saur, 1973.
PL	Migne, Jacques-Paul (ed.). Patrologia cursus completus, Series Graeca. 221 vols. Paris: Garnieri Fratres et al., 1844–1891.
PSI	Papiri della Società Italiana
SC	Sources Chrétiennes
SEG	Woodhead, A. G. et al. *Supplementum Epigraphicum Graecum*. Leiden: Brill,1923–.
TLG	Thesaurus Linguae Graecae

CHAPTER ONE

Jewish Customs of Psalm-Singing

ACCORDING TO A theory of Christian liturgical origins that remained influential throughout most of the twentieth century, the earliest church adopted the custom of psalmody directly from the Sabbath services of the Jewish synagogue. Many Christian historians embraced this view, which one writer described as "too well known to need many words."[1] A number of Jewish scholars also accepted it.[2] Not everyone agreed, however, and several decisive challenges were mounted.[3]

The contention that Jewish followers of Jesus brought psalmody from the Sabbath synagogue service to their gatherings as churches assumes that psalm-singing was an established part of regular Sabbath synagogue meetings. There is, in fact, no convincing evidence of that in Second Temple sources and early rabbinic literature. The available information suggests that Sabbath gatherings

1. Louis Duchesne, *Origines du culte chrétien: étude sur la liturgie latine avant Charlemagne*, 3rd ed. (Fontemoing, 1902), 47–48; Adrian Fortescue, "Gradual," in *The Catholic Encyclopedia*, vol. 6, ed. Charles G. Herbermann (Encyclopedia Press, 1913), 715; William O. E. Oesterley, *The Jewish Background of the Christian Liturgy* (Clarendon, 1925), 25, 73 ("too well known to need many words"), and passim; Armand Machabey, *Histoire et évolution des formules musicales du 1er aux XVe siècle de l'ère chrétienne* (Payot, 1928), 5–6; Clifton W. Dugmore, *The Influence of the Synagogue upon the Divine Office* (Oxford University Press, 1944); 7–8, 71, and passim; Gregory Dix, *The Shape of the Liturgy*, 2nd ed. (Dacre, 1945), 37–39; Carl H. Kraeling and Lucetta Mowry, "Music in the Bible," in *Ancient and Oriental Music*, ed. Egon Wellesz (Oxford University Press, 1957), 304; Egon Wellesz, *A History of Byzantine Music and Hymnography*, 2nd ed. (Clarendon, 1961), 34–37; John A. Lamb, *The Psalms in Christian Worship* (Faith, 1962), 11, 19–21.

2. Abraham Z. Idelsohn, *Jewish Music in Its Historical Development* (Holt, 1929), 60–61; Eric Werner, *The Sacred Bridge: The Interdependence of Liturgy and Music in Synagogue and Church during the First Millennium*, vol. 1 (Dobson, 1959), 2, 8, 26, and passim.

3. Louis Rabinowitz, "Psalms in Jewish Liturgy," *Historia Judaica* 6 (1944): 109–122; Johann Maier, "Zur Verwendung der Psalmen in der synagogalen Liturgie (Wochentag und Sabbat)," in *Liturgie und Dichtung: Ein interdisziplinäres Kompendium I: Historische Präsentation*, ed. Hansjakob Beker and Reiner Kaczynski (St. Ottilien: EOS, 1983), 55–90; James W. McKinnon, "On the Question of Psalmody in the Ancient Synagogue," *Early Music History* 6 (1986): 159–191; John A. Smith, "The Ancient Synagogue, the Early Church and Singing," *Music and Letters* 65 (1984): 1–16.

were devoted to the reading and exposition of Scripture.[4] The sources are silent about song at regular Sabbath meetings, as well as at daily synagogue services, until the eighth century CE, when a rabbinic tractate refers to seven psalms of the daily service.[5] It may be telling that Philo, who goes into great detail about the singing of the Therapeutae at their festive meal and all-night songfest, does not mention any song at all when he describes their Sabbath meetings.[6]

Festival Psalmody

Although the ancient Jewish people did not sing psalms or other hymns at their regular Sabbath services, they did sing on other occasions. The sources mention song during festivals, when people sang in homes, synagogues, processions, and probably in large open-air gatherings. The evidence in Second Temple writings is confined to a handful of passages in 1, 2, and 3 Maccabees and the works of Philo and Josephus, which describe festive music using general expressions: "hymning and blessing," "songs and citharas and kinnors and cymbals," "hymns," "psalms," "giving thanks to God with melodious hymns," "hymns and psalms," and "singing hymns and starting up paeans."[7]

The Mishnah and Tosefta are more specific in identifying certain psalms as festival hymns. At some point during the Second Temple era, the Levitical singers began performing a set of six psalms called the Hallel[8] as part of Passover liturgies of the temple. According to the Mishnah, while the Passover lambs were being slaughtered, the Levitical singers sang the Hallel over and over, evidently so that the songs accompanied the slaughter from beginning to end.[9] The Mishnah, together with the Tosefta, also refers to Passover performances of one or more psalms at domestic seders[10] and at concurrent liturgies in the synagogue for those

---

4. An interpretive address followed the reading, which was usually from the Torah. The lesson may have been framed by opening and closing blessings, as the Mishnah specifies in *m. Meg.* 4.1 and 4.2.

5. *Soferim* 18.1, referring to "the people's" adoption of the Levitical daily cursus specified in *m. Tamid* 7.4. On the subject as a whole, see the studies cited in n. 3.

6. Philo, *Contempl.* 30–33.

7. 1 Macc 4:24 and 4:54; 2 Macc 10:7; 3 Macc 6:35 and 7:16; Josephus, *Ant.* 12.323; Philo, *Flacc.* 121 and 122.

8. Only the rabbinic writings refer to the Hallel by that name and specify its psalms.

9. *m. Pesaḥ* 5.7.

10. *m. Pesaḥ* 9.3D–E; 10.5E (which refers to the Hallel as the "Hallelujah"); 10.6; and *t. Pesaḥ* 10.8. According to Smith, because the word "Hallelujah" at the end of *m. Pesaḥ* 10.5 lacks a definite article, it must refer to the word as a refrain, not to the Hallel as a whole. Yet "Hallel"

who had no one to lead the Hallel at their household celebrations.[11] The Mishnah says that the singing of the Hallel is to frame the consumption of the Passover lamb.[12] These rabbinic discussions reflect Palestinian custom, not necessarily practices elsewhere. Moreover, it is often difficult to say how far the customs that the rabbis describe and prescribe were typical outside their own learned circles and families. That said, the Palestinian rabbis in the Mishnah also place the Hallel at other occasions: people's celebrations of the feasts of Booths[13] and Hanukkah,[14] and morning prayer in the synagogue during Rosh ha-Shanah.[15] Moreover, the Tosefta implies that the Hallel was taught in school.[16]

Other sources also suggest that at least one of the Hallel psalms was a traditional hymn of the feasts of Booths and Hanukkah during the Hellenistic period. Writing in Palestine in the early days of the Hasmonean kingdom (probably toward the end of the second century BCE), the author of 1 Maccabees describes the triumphal return of Jewish troops under Judas Maccabeus following a military victory. "On their return," the author writes, "they hymned and glorified Heaven 'because he is good and his mercy is forever.'"[17] This victory song is a precursor of the liberation celebrations the author places a year later, festivities that culminate in the rededication of the temple and the establishment of a new festival—Hanukkah.[18] The author probably relied on his own experience of that festival in imagining what the original marchers sang. A *ḥesed* formula in the author's characterization of the song echoes the openings of Psalms 118, 136, and two other psalms (MT numberings). Each of these psalms begins with the words, "O give thanks to the Lord *because he is good, for his steadfast love (ḥesed) endures forever.*"[19] In Psalm 136, the words shown in italics are repeated three times at the beginning and then after every line, which marks them as a refrain. Psalm 118 begins with a variation of the *ḥesed*-opening of Psalm 136 and uses the

---

also lacks the definite article in *m. Pesaḥ* 9.3, where Hallel psalms, not refrains, are clearly meant. John A. Smith, *Music in Ancient Judaism and Early Christianity* (Ashgate, 2011), 119.

11. *t. Pesaḥ* 10.8.

12. *m. Pesaḥ* 10.6–7. The food is blessed and the meal ends with the conclusion of the Hallel (7).

13. *m. Sukk.* 3.9.

14. *m. Taʿanit* 4.5K (the first of Tevet is a reference to Hanukkah).

15. *m. Rosh ha-Shanah* 4.7.

16. *t. Soṭa* 6.3B.

17. 1 Macc 4:24.

18. 1 Macc 4:52–59.

19. The other two psalms are 106 and 107 (MT).

formula again at the very end. Moreover, this same *ḥesed* refrain also appears in characterizations of praise-song at ceremonies held for the postexilic dedication of the rebuilt temple, according to 2 Chronicles.[20]

The association of the *ḥesed* refrain with a thanksgiving chant sung by the Maccabean troops on their homebound journey suggests that one of the psalms with that expression may have been this marching song, as the author imagined it. There is a further clue in a passage that was probably added to 2 Maccabees in the mid-second century BCE as part of a final editing that transformed the book into a foundational account of the origin of the Feast of Hanukkah.[21] Although 2 Maccabees should not be treated as reliable history, it does contain valuable information about the festival's liturgy, given that the editor who sought to anchor the feast in history knew Hanukkah as it was celebrated in his own day. As the Maccabean war neared its conclusion, the editor writes, Judas Maccabeus gained control of the temple and cleansed it. Then the people celebrated "in the manner of the Festival of Booths," which inspired the establishment of a new feast.[22] Readers would have recognized this feast as the first Hanukkah:

> They celebrated it for eight days with rejoicing in the manner of the Festival of Booths, remembering how not long before, during the Festival of Booths, they had been wandering in the mountains and caves like wild animals. Therefore, carrying ivy-wreathed wands and beautiful branches and also fronds of palm, they offered hymns of thanksgiving to him who had given success to the purifying of his own holy place.[23]

The reference to branches is significant. Psalm 118 MT, a Hallel psalm that begins with a call for thanksgiving with the *ḥesed* formula, also includes internal references to processing, as well as an invitation that appears to imply that people carried branches: "Bind the festal procession with branches, up to the horns of the altar."[24] This does not mean that Psalm 118 was originally composed for Booths, only that the use of branches in the Booths procession would have made Psalm 118 a particularly fitting song for both that festival and Hanukkah as well, for which Booths was the template. Hence, it is not

---

20. 2 Chron 5:13; 7:3, 6; Ezra 3:11 (which introduces the expression as a people's *response*).

21. See Daniel R. Schwartz, *2 Maccabees* (De Gruyter, 2008), 7–16.

22. 2 Macc 10:1–8 (cf. 2 Macc 1:9).

23. 2 Macc 10:6–7 NRSV.

24. Ps 118:27 (MT) NRSV.

surprising that the Mishnah assigns Hallel psalms to Booths in a context where it discusses the branches carried by the people and that the Mishnah, as already noted, associates the Hallel with liturgies of Hanukkah.[25] Moreover, if Hanukkah, modeled on Booths, included Psalm 118 as a people's chant during the procession, that would explain why 1 Maccabees has Israel's victorious army marching home after a Maccabean battle singing "for he is good and his mercy is forever." Taken together, all these clues make it likely that Psalm 118 was one of the "hymns of thanksgiving" sung by the Jewish people in their Booths and Hanukkah processions.[26]

The Question of Jewish Sectarian Psalmody

References to song in the writings of the Qumran community and in Philo's account of the Therapeutae have occasionally been cited as evidence of psalmody in Jewish sectarian settings. These writings pose a number of challenges for historical reconstruction. It is not always clear from the language about song whether biblical psalms are meant. Nor is it always easy to distinguish the figurative from the literal. And in the case of Philo's *On the Contemplative Life*, there is the possibility that the work is a piece of pious fiction or at least contains a good deal of invention.[27]

The singing prescribed in the Qumran *Community Rule* and extolled in the sect's *Hodayoth* (1QH) is probably figurative. An exemplary statement in the *Community Rule* proclaims, "I will sing with knowledge; and for the glory of God shall all my music be, the playing of my harp according to his holy order; and the whistle of my lips I shall tune to its correct measure. At the onset of day and night I shall enter the covenant of God; and when evening and morning depart,

---

25. See notes 13 (Booths) and 14 (Hanukkah).

26. Based on the quotation of the *ḥesed* formula in 1 Macc 4:24, S. Stein concludes that the author may have had Psalm 118 (MT) *or* Psalm 136 (MT) in mind and that a statement in 2 Macc 1:11—ἐκ μεγάλων κινδύνων ὑπὸ τοῦ θεοῦ σεσῳσμένοι μεγάλως εὐχαριστοῦμεν αὐτῷ—may be a reference to Psalm 136. The wording of 2 Macc 2:11 is not, however, a verbal quotation or echo of any line in the Greek version of Psalm 136 (135 LXX). S. Stein, "The Liturgy of Hanukkah and the First Two Books of Maccabees—II," *Journal of Jewish Studies* 5 (1954): 154.

27. Scholars who argue that the Therapeutae are a Philonic invention include Roland Bergmeier, "Der Stand der Gottesfreunde: Zu Philos Schrift 'Über die kontemplative Lebensform,'" *Bijdragen: International Journal in Philosophy and Theology* 63 (2002): 46–70; and Troels Engberg-Pedersen, "Philo's De vita contemplativa as a Philosopher's Dream," *Journal for the Study of Judaism* 30 (1999): 40–64. An argument in favor of the basic historicity of *De vita contemplativa* is set forth in Joan E. Taylor, *Jewish Women Philosophers of First-Century Alexandria: Philo's 'Therapeutae' Reconsidered* (Oxford University Press, 2003), 7–12.

I shall repeat his precepts."[28] Later the *Rule* declares, "With hymns shall I open my mouth; and my tongue will continually recount both the just acts of God and the unfaithfulness of men until their iniquity is complete."[29] The archeological finds at Qumran do not support the conclusion that any harps were used there, much less that each resident had a harp; in fact, no musical instruments have been found at Qumran.[30] "Harp-playing" and "whistling" are probably figures of speech. And the reference to continual hymning, too, may mean continual praise and attunement to God, not literal singing.

The idea of praise as a continual disposition of the mind is more explicit in the Qumran collection of poems or stylized prayers that a modern scholar labeled *The Thanksgiving (Hodayoth) Scroll*. In no. XIX of this collection, the speaking persona addresses God with the words, "You have put thanksgiving into my mouth, praise on my tongue, the utterance of my lips in a place of jubilation. I will chant your kindness; I will ponder your might the whole day; I will bless your name continually; I will recount your glory."[31] Here, continual chanting and blessing is not likely to mean constant singing out loud all day long but mindful devotion to God in thought and deed throughout the day. If there were times for personal and corporate daily song, these lines would certainly have evoked those life moments. But references to singing at certain times or in particular liturgies are not clearly attested in the Qumran literature, which leaves the whole subject in something of a fog.

As for biblical psalms, the fragmentary remains of various psalms scrolls found at Qumran, some of which are probably collections of psalm excerpts, give no clear indication of their purpose and may have been created for pedagogical use or private meditation.[32] If some were used liturgically, nonlyrical reading is as likely as singing.

---

28. 1QS X:9–10; translation from *The Dead Sea Scrolls: Study Edition*, vol. 1, ed. Florentino García Martínez and Eibert J. C. Tigchelaar (Brill, 1997), 95.

29. 1QS X:23 (= 4Q260 V:5–6); tr. from *The Dead Sea Scrolls: Study Edition*, vol. 1, 97.

30. In an exhaustive study of music in ancient Israel and Palestine, based on archeological and literary records that include the Hellenistic and Roman eras, Joachim Braun makes not a single reference to archeological evidence for music-making at Qumran, evidently because he was aware of none. Joachim Braun, *Music in Ancient Israel/Palestine: Archeological, Written, and Comparative Sources*, trans. Douglas W. Stott (Eerdmans, 2002).

31. $1QH^{a}$XIX:5–6; tr. from *The Dead Sea Scrolls: Study Edition*, vol. 1, 189.

32. $11QPs^{a}$ (11Q5), $11QPs^{b}$ (11Q6), $11QPs^{c}$ (11Q7), and $11QPs^{d}$ (11Q8). See Johann Maier, "Zu Kult und Liturgie der Qumrangemeinde," *Revue de Qumrân* 14 (1990): 581–583; Emanuel Tov, "Excerpted and Abbreviated Biblical Texts from Qumran," *Revue de Qumrân* 16 (1995): 594–595 and 598–599.

Song is described by Philo in his account of a festival observed by a Jewish community called the Therapeutae. Philo does not name the festival but says that it takes place every seven times seven (forty-nine) days, a symbolic number representing the utmost in perfection. Philo implies that this feast was the group's own peculiar celebration, a detail that is only one of several features of the book that raise the suspicion that Philo means for his account to be taken as an ideal and largely fictional representation, not a historical account.[33]

Philo describes the Therapeutae's festival as a song-filled event with singing by individual members at a community meal and group singing at an all-night vigil. The president of the Therapeutae is the first to sing at the banquet, and he performs either a new song that he himself composed "or something ancient by one of the poets of old."[34] A song "by one of the poets of old" is as close as Philo comes to mentioning a Scripture song at the Therapeutae's festival. It is true that in describing the group's choral songs, he uses the term "hymns," which could be psalms; but he applies the same term to songs composed by individual members of the community.[35] Philo also compares the choral singing of the Therapeutae to the choral singing of the Israelites under Moses and Miriam in Exodus 15, although he does not say that they sang the Song of the Sea.

Jewish Song in Household, Recreational, and Work Settings

Some have argued that domestic psalm-singing had a fixed place in Jewish life during the Second Temple period and that this custom was carried directly into the house-based worship of Jesus's followers.[36] A number of Second Temple writings are indeed suggestive of private Jewish music-making, including biblical psalmody.

To begin with a fictional example, a morning practice of devotional song is described in *Testament of Job*. The book retells the biblical story of Job in the

33. See n. 27.

34. Philo, *Vit. contempl.* 80.

35. Philo, *Vit. contempl.* 29 and 80. Notker Füglister overlooks or discounts these passages when he argues from Philonic usage that the "hymns" of the vigil are probably biblical psalms. Notker Füglister, "Die Verwendung und das Verständnis der Psalmen und des Psalters um die Zeitenwende," in *Beiträge zur Psalmenforschung: Psalm 2 und 22*, ed. Josef Schreiner (Echter, 1988), 347.

36. Christopher Page, *The Christian West and Its Singers: The First Thousand Years* (Yale University Press, 2010), 73, 137; Smith, "The Ancient Synagogue," 10; Andrew B. McGowan, *Ancient Christian Worship: Early Church Practices in Social, Historical, and Theological Perspective* (Baker Academic, 2014), 115.

voice of Job himself and makes Job a king, not merely a wealthy man. It also turns Job into a musician who plays the psaltery and lyre, both of which were understood to have been instruments that David played. These embroideries suggest that King Job is like King David.

In one passage Job declares, "And I used to have six songs (*psalmous*) and a ten-stringed lyre. I would awaken daily after the feeding of the widows, take the lyre, and play for them. And they would sing hymns. And with the psaltery I would remind them of God, so that they might glorify the Lord."[37] The purpose of this depiction is probably to answer one of the charges against Job in the biblical book of Job—that he failed to care for the widows. The singing in this scene is literal, but it is not representative of anything typical, since a morning feeding of widows in the house of a rich man, who entertains them with song, is exceptional and has no known social parallels.

A set of admonitions in the Hebrew book of Sirach addresses "sons," urging them to sing hymns of praise with the *kinnor*.[38] In preparing a Greek version, Sirach's grandson simply transliterated the term (which he might have translated as "lyre").[39] The envisioned setting for this musical praise is not stated in either the Hebrew or the Greek version. Since the words are part of the opening section of a thanksgiving poem about the goodness of God's created works, the invitations to sing hymns to the accompaniment of the *kinnor* are tropes for praising God. In other words, the music-making is figurative.

Better evidence for domestic customs of song is found in other passages from Jewish and Hellenistic Jewish-Christian literature. One of the Jewish poems included in the *Sibylline Oracles* declares, "Let us delight God the begetter with hymns in our homes."[40] According to the *Testament of Joseph*, the patriarch sang when he found himself in chains.[41] So did the three young men in the furnace, according to the Greek version of Daniel.[42] And so did Paul and Silas, two Jewish followers of Jesus, when they found themselves in prison, according to a story

37. *T. Job* 14.1–3.

38. Sir 39:13, 14–15.

39. The *kinnor* was a string instrument played with a plectrum, like a lyre, not plucked like a harp.

40. *Sib. Or.* 3.726. The *Psalms of Solomon* pictures a righteous man's morning and evening prayer: "When he rises from his sleep, he blesses the name of the Lord; when his heart is at rest, he hymns the name of his God" (*Pss. Sol.* 6.4). The word "hymns" could certainly refer to song but might be simply a synonym for praise.

41. *T. Jos.* 8.5.

42. Dan 3:24, 51, 91 LXX and Theodotion. Poetic texts are given as the content of what they uttered.

preserved in the book of Acts.[43] The Letter of James, which clearly stems from an early Jewish follower of Jesus, instructs those who are happy to sing.[44] The nonfictional examples refer to literal singing, and the fictional examples do so as well, perhaps reflecting customs of singing to express one's faith and fortify one's spirit in situations of extremity. Taken together, the passages imply that Jews were accustomed to sing in a variety of settings and situations, including their homes. Unfortunately, the types of songs are not specified.

In the wider culture, it was common for ordinary people to sing popular theater songs at home, at festivals, and during their daily routines.[45] Jews, too, attended the public theater. No doubt some of them liked stage songs and sang them for recreational purposes or to pass the time as they worked or journeyed, just as nonJews did. We know that Jews also sang traditional Israelite odes, not only in mass choirs at festivals but in private settings as well. The rabbis preserve an interesting testimony about this. According to the Tosefta, Rabbi Akiba (c. 50–135 CE) warned that "whoever shakes his voice in the Song of Songs in a banquet hall and treats it like a common song has no share in the world to come."[46] The verb "shakes" refers to some kind of expressive effect, perhaps vibrato.[47] Akiba's concern is not merely performance style but the use of Song of Songs as a source of amatory party songs, which had apparently entered the repertoire of Judean men's drinking-odes at some point.

What remains uncertain, despite all these bits of evidence for song in everyday life, is whether Jews of the Second Temple period sang biblical psalms

---

43. Acts 16:25.

44. Jas 5:13.

45. Ovid describes plebs reclining on the grass at countryside picnics during the festival of Anna Perenna and singing "whatever they learned in the theater" (Ovid, *Fast.* 3.535). Further evidence is found in the later church fathers. Writing in the early fourth century, Asterius the Sophist of Cappadocia (a Christian) draws a contrast between holiday feasting in a proper way and spending the day singing theater songs (*Comm. in psalm.*, Hom. 18.20). John Chrysostom implies that the young men of Antioch roared out theater songs at night in the streets, no doubt after their home drinking parties or in the course of bar-hopping (*De terrae motu* in PG 50.715). During their work, Augustine complains, laborers devote "their hearts and tongues to the vanity and even to the filth of the theatre-plays" (*De opere monachorum* 17.20 in PL 40.565).

46. *t. Sanh.* 12.10a. Akiba treats the שיר השרים ("Song of Songs") as a kind of זמר. The expression בבית המשתה, referring to the location, is clarified by its use in the sense of "house/hall of feasting" in *m. Ter.* 11.10 and in one of the Jewish accounts of Alexander, a medieval recension preserved in MS London 145. See *A Hebrew Alexander Romance according to MS London, Jews' College no. 145*, ed. Wout J. van Bekkum (Leuven: Peeters, 1992), 44 (5.19–20); 98 (29.11); 100 (29.16).

47. See the examples of the term's use in a musical sense in Marcus Jastrow, *Dictionary of Targumim, the Talmud Bavli, and Yerushalmi, and the Midrashic Literature*, vol. 2 (London: Luzac, 1903), 888 (*s.v.* נויע).

on a regular basis in household, recreational, and work settings. The only direct suggestion is a passage in *4 Maccabees*, which describes a mother speaking to her martyred seven sons about their martyred father's devotion to educating them in Scripture.[48] The father taught them "the law and the prophets," pointing out biblical stories of faithfulness under trial and words of encouragement to the suffering righteous. Eleven examples follow. Each one mentions a book of Scripture and one of its sayings, including the book of Psalms. The example from Psalms reads as follows: "He used to sing to you the hymnographer David, who says, 'many are the tribulations of the righteous.'"[49] It may have been only an interest in stylistic variation that led the author to choose a verb for music-making in this statement, inasmuch as the writer takes pains to change verbs from one example to the next. Moreover, the passage, with its eleven quotations, suggests a practice of memorizing selected sayings of Scripture as practical words for life.[50] Hence, the verb "sing," used in view of the genre, could be a figure of speech. That said, in an earlier description of the torturing of one of the sons, the author has the victim refer to song as he cries out to Antiochus IV, "But God will go after you quickly, for you are cutting out the melodious tongue of divine hymns."[51] This sounds like a straightforward reference to a habit of singing. Perhaps, then, it was not unusual for pious Israelite households to engage in family rituals of hymnody, including the singing of biblical psalms. Moreover, to the extent that *4 Maccabees* means to depict the father and his sons as exemplary, worthy of imitation, the reference to their practice of psalmody would have been an encouragement to readers to do the same.

Philo may have had such a practice in mind when he referred to "hymns and thanksgivings" of the virtuous life, which are superior to animal sacrifices, whether said silently or out loud. Philo does not specify the setting(s), but personal piety, not corporate worship, better fits a kind of singing that is just as effective when it is silent as when it is voiced.[52]

There is a further hint about personal devotional use of psalms in Philo's account of the Therapeutae. It pertains not to their festival but to their daily

---

48. *4 Macc.* 18.10–19.

49. *4 Macc.* 18.15.

50. Various scriptural passages were assembled by ancient Jews in "special use texts," most of them from the Torah. See Julie A. Duncan, "Excerpted Texts of 'Deuteronomy' at Qumran," *Revue de Qumran* 18 (1997): 43–62; Tov, "Excerpted and Abbreviated Biblical Texts from Qumran."

51. *4 Macc.* 10.21.

52. Donald Binder refers to Philo, *Spec.* 1.272 as evidence of private psalmody in the synagogue. I am not sure why he is confident about this identification of the setting. See Donald D. Binder, *Into the Temple Courts: The Place of the Synagogues in the Second Temple Period* (Scholars, 1999), 407–408.

practice. The community members have private rooms, Philo says, where individuals spend time alone, occupied with "laws, oracles declared through the prophets, and hymns, and the other things by which knowledge and piety are increased and perfected."[53] The association of the "hymns" with the law and the prophets suggests that they were biblical psalms. Philo gives no hint, however, that the Therapeutae *chanted* the hymns during their periods of individual meditation.

The rabbis quoted in the Mishnah and Tosefta say nothing about daily lay practices of psalmody, their own or those of other people, whether at home or in the synagogues. They do discuss daily prayer, which shows that they were indeed interested in lay devotional practice.[54] As for daily psalmody, they ascribe it only to the *temple* liturgy, outlining what was sung each day.[55] Although some interpreters have imagined that the rabbis adopted this temple psalmody as their own practice, the sources give no hint of that.[56]

There was one particular occasion when it was customary for families to sing certain biblical psalms at home—their annual Passover seder, where the Hallel psalms were traditional. According to Philo, Passover diners keep "paternal custom with prayers and hymns."[57] The Gospel of Mark contains further evidence, when it has Jesus and his disciples conclude their Passover meal by singing a hymn before going out.[58] It is significant that the author of Matthew took over Mark's words about this,[59] for it shows that a Hellenistic Jew who believed that the Last Supper was a Passover meal thought it perfectly natural for the diners to have sung at the end of their supper. None of these sources identifies the hymn(s), but rabbinic rules for the seder, set forth in the Mishnah and assumed by the Tosefta, show that the Hallel had a fixed place in the seder by at least 200 CE.[60] The question is whether the rabbis of this period were seeking to standardize certain details of an existing custom or were innovating by advocating an incorporation of the Hallel into the meal as part of liturgical changes made in the

53. Philo, *Vit. contempl.* 25.

54. This point is made by A. J. Berkovitz, *A Life of Psalms in Jewish Late Antiquity* (University of Pennsylvania Press, 2023), 77.

55. Daily song in the temple is described in a section at the end of the Mishnah tractate *Tamid*.

56. This is correctly emphasized by Berkovitz, *A Life of Psalms in Jewish Late Antiquity*, 78.

57. Philo, *Spec. leg.* 2.148.

58. Mark 14:26.

59. Matt 26:30.

60. See the references above in the discussion of festival song.

aftermath of the two Jewish wars, when it was clear that the temple would not be rebuilt in the foreseeable future.

A clue is found in a debate between the House of Shammai and the House of Hillel about just what the Passover seder signifies. The original biblical Passover meal is situated on the eve of the Israelites' departure from Egypt. The Shammaites make this detail the basis of an argument that Psalm 114 (MT), a Hallel psalm, should not be sung at the seder, as the Hillelites taught. Given that the original Passover meal took place before the exodus, they argue, Israel's commemorative reenactment of that meal should not include an exodus psalm that refers to events that occurred after the people's departure.[61] Since the houses of Hillel and Shammai were active before the first Jewish war with Rome, the very fact of their debate suggests that Hallel psalms had a place at the meal before 70 CE in the practice of certain Palestinian rabbis.[62] Passover Hallel-singing by Palestinian Jews more widely is suggested by the rabbis' reference to Hallel rituals in synagogues for those who had no one to lead the singing at their home seders (see above).

Levitical Psalmody

Before concluding this survey of ancient Jewish music, I will say a word about Levitical psalmody. What the Levitical singers performed at the temple did not embrace the entire Psalter. John Smith points out that in the Septuagint, the superscriptions for five psalms assign them to days of the week and that the Mishnah assigns the same five psalms as the Septuagint's to the same days of the week and also specifies that Psalm 82 MT is the psalm for the third day and that Psalm 81 MT is for the fifth day.[63] It is clear, then, that by at least the second century BCE, the Levitical singers had a repertoire of fixed daily psalms for the twice-daily sacrifices. Moreover, in addition to mentioning the priestly singing of the six Hallel psalms for the sacrifice of the lambs at Passover (see above),[64] the Mishnah reports that the Levites sang Psalm 30 MT for the presentation of

61. *m. Pesaḥ.* 10.6, explained in *t. Pesaḥ.* 10.9.

62. Joseph Tabory points out this debate and its relevance for the question of when the Hallel was introduced to the domestic Passover meal. See Joseph Tabory, *The JPS Commentary on the Haggadah: Historical Introduction, Translation, and Commentary* (The Jewish Publication Society, 2008), 50. Moreover, Tabory also infers that the debate was merely academic and that the Hallel was not a novum at the meal but was already well established when the Shammaites raised questions about Psalm 114.

63. Psalms 23, 47, 93, 92, and 91, in that order, for the first, second, fourth, sixth, and seventh days of the week; *m. Tam.* 7.4. See Smith, *Music in Ancient Judaism and Early Christianity*, 89.

64. *m. Pesaḥ.* 5.7.

the first fruits at the temple.[65] Smith concludes that these psalms—the five, the two, the six, and this last one—constituted the core sacrificial repertoire of the Levites, fourteen psalms in all.[66] Finally, the Levitical singers also performed at nonsacrificial celebrations in the temple. All told, their temple repertoire may have included as many as eighty-four psalms, at least "theoretically."[67] But since the Levitical singers were not professional musicians and since a given singer typically served in the temple only briefly during his lifetime, the Levitical repertoire may not have been quite so large.[68]

As long as there was hope for the rebuilding of the temple, Levitical families had an incentive to preserve the musical traditions entrusted to them, which included competence on the traditional musical instruments of the temple. Smith surmises that following the establishment of the Roman city Aelia Capitolina on the ruins of Jerusalem and the failure of Judean Jews to thwart this effort by going to war against the Romans in 132–135 CE, Levitical families, who had not served the cult since the destruction of the temple in 70 CE, lost all hope that the temple would be rebuilt. Their commitment to maintaining their musical heritage dwindled away, so that "by the beginning of the third century CE, if not earlier, the musical traditions of the Jerusalem Temple had perished irrevocably."[69] Although there is no explicit evidence that Levitical families ceased to cultivate their musical traditions, there is also no evidence that any of the music of the temple was preserved.

There are no hints of any influence of Levitical song on church song in any case. Although one might imagine an early Christian thinking that Levitical songs for various sacrifices were appropriate for Christian Communion services, once the Eucharist was conceived as a cultic sacrifice, only one author from the first several centuries seems to suggest that, although not explicitly and not with reference to temple psalms.[70] Moreover, the Communion psalms mentioned in Christian literature do not correlate to Levitical sacrificial songs[71] and there are no references to Communion song being a kind of Levitical service.

---

65. *m. Bik.* 3.4. The superscription for Psalm 30 MT (29 LXX) in both the Septuagint and the Hebrew assigns it to the dedication of the temple, which reflects an earlier conception of its use.

66. Smith, *Music in Ancient Judaism and Early Christianity*, 89.

67. Smith, *Music in Ancient Judaism and Early Christianity*, 97 (referencing his table on p. 93).

68. See Smith, *Music in Ancient Judaism and Early Christianity*, 101–105.

69. Smith, *Music in Ancient Judaism and Early Christianity*, 116.

70. See the discussion of a Communion scene in the *Apocalypse of Paul*, as discussed in chapter 5.

71. Regarding Christian Communion psalmody, see chapter 5. John Chrysostom implies that Psalm 117 (118 MT) was a Communion psalm. Although this is one of the Hallel psalms, sung

Conclusion

There is no evidence for regular psalmody in Sabbath synagogue services of the Second Temple period and only modest explicit evidence for psalmody as a Jewish domestic practice in that era, specifically, a lone passage in *4 Maccabees*, which describes one model family's practice, and a somewhat vague reference in the *Sibyllene Oracles* that may not refer to biblical psalms. The only evidence for psalmody as a widespread popular practice are references to occasional psalmody at festivals, which included song at special synagogue services, home banquets such as the Passover seder, and mass outdoor gatherings. Whether Jewish customs of household psalmody or the better-documented festival psalmody were adopted by the early church is a question for the next chapter.

by the Levites and the people at Passover, it is not a sacrificial song. The same goes for Psalm 22, which John Chrysostom also implies was used at Communion. The fifth-century Armenian lectionary assigns Psalm 22 (23 MT) to the Holy Thursday Communion service. While this psalm, long interpreted by Christians as a prophecy of Christ's passion, is called a "song" of David in its superscription, it is not characterized as a song of sacrifice and is not part of the Levites' core sacrificial repertoire (see Smith, *Music in Ancient Judaism and Early Christianity*, 89). The standard Communion psalm, Psalm 34 (33 LXX), is not associated with sacrifice or with singing in its superscription or in other Jewish sources.

CHAPTER TWO

The Rise of Christian Psalmody

A FRUSTRATING OBSTACLE to determining the extent to which early Christian writings refer to biblical psalm-singing by Jesus's followers is ambiguity in the terminology. No single word was used to designate biblical psalms, and every word used for them was also applied to other types of speech and song.

The earliest evidence of Hebrew titles for the biblical psalms appears in the Dead Sea Scrolls. The *War Scroll* speaks of the *Sofer Tehillim*, "Book of Praises."[1] *Tehillim*, "Praises," is also the title that the Masoretes assigned to the book of Psalms, undoubtedly relying on tradition. *Tehillim* is a masculine plural noun, cognate to the feminine singular form *tehillah*. The masculine plural seems to have been coined as the title for the collection.[2] Hence, it is surprising to discover that the word *tehillah* is used internally as a title for an individual psalm only once, in the prescript for Psalm 145, which reads, "A praise [ascribed] to David." The Septuagint translates accordingly, using a Greek word for praise (*ainos*). The Septuagint uses the expression "hymn" (*hymnos*) in a few psalm superscriptions, a word that a number of Hellenistic-Jewish writers also apply to the psalms of David.[3] Significantly, the summary conclusion in Ps 71:21 LXX states, "The hymns (*hymnoi*) of David, son of Jesse, are concluded," where the MT has *tehillim*. In other words, the Greek translators found it natural to use the word "hymns" for *tehillim*.

In view of the traditional Hebrew title for the Psalter, Hellenistic Jews may sometimes have meant biblical psalms when they referred to "praises" (*ainoi* and *epainoi*), but the existing evidence shows no clear example of that (outside the superscriptions in the LXX Psalter), nor any clear instances of *psalmos* as a designation for a biblical psalm by Hellenistic Jews (outside the superscriptions). Philo never uses the word *psalmos* at all in his many surviving writings.

1. ספר התהלים in 4Q491(4QM[a]), fr. 17.4. It is possible, however, that this expression refers not to a biblical book but to a collection of compositions by the Qumran sectarians. See Peter W. Flint, *The Dead Sea Psalms Scroll and the Book of Psalms* (Brill, 1997), 23 n. 56 (citing personal correspondence from Florentino García Martínez). The Qumran *Psalms Scroll* states that David composed 3,600 תהלים (praises) along with 446 songs (11Q5[11QPs[a]], col. 27).

2. See Flint, *The Dead Sea Psalms Scroll and the Book of Psalms*, 22; also Hans-Joachim Kraus, *Psalms 1–59: A Commentary*, tr. Hilton C. Oswald (Augsburg, 1988), 11.

3. See below.

He invariably calls biblical psalms "hymns" (*hymnoi*) and "songs" (*asmata*).[4] Josephus does happen to use the word *psalmos* but never expressly for a biblical psalm. He calls them hymns and odes; he refers to Levitical singers as *hymnōdoi*, a generic term for cult singers.[5] Similarly, the author of *4 Maccabees* calls David a "hymn-writer."[6]

The earliest extant use of the term *psalmoi* for the biblical psalms appears in early Christian writings. Luke quotes words of David "in the Book of Psalms" (20:42), and he has Jesus speak of "everything written in the law of Moses and in the prophets and the psalms concerning me" (24:44). Acts continues this usage when it uses the formula "for it is written in the Book of Psalms" (Acts 1:20). These are the only places where biblical psalms are designated by their book title in the early Christian writings that later Christians assigned to the apostolic age and regarded as Scripture. In other words, Luke and Acts gave a scriptural imprimatur to "psalms" as a designation for the hymns/praises of David. That said, for all the reasons I have stated, it should not be assumed that when the Greek term *psalmos* or the Latin *psalmus* appears in ancient Christian sources, it always refers to a biblical psalm. Often it does not.

David the Psalmist as a Prophet of the Gospel

Despite the variety of authorship assignments in the superscriptions of the Psalter, ancient Jews regarded David as the author of the Psalter,[7] a view that Jewish Christians took for granted. Hence, it became conventional to refer to any poem of the Psalter as David's.

Some Jews also regarded David's poems as prophecy,[8] an opinion that was even more pronounced in the early church, where David was esteemed as the

---

4. Philo refers to biblical psalms as ὕμνοι or ὑμνῳδία in *Plant.* 29 and 39; *Agr.* 50; *Somn.* 2.245; *Conf.* 39 and 52; *Migr.* 157; *Mut.* 115; and note the description of the biblical psalmist as ὁ ὑμνῳδός in *Deus* 74 and the biblical psalms as ᾄσματα in *Mut.* 115; *Gig.* 17; *Somn.* 2.246.

5. Josephus speaks of biblical psalms as ὕμνοι and ᾠδαί in *Ant.* 7.305 and *Ap.* 1.40. He refers to Levitical singers as ὑμνῳδοί in *Ant.* 7.364 and 8.94. David soothes Saul with his "harp song (τῷ ψαλμῷ) and hymns (ὕμνοις)" (*Ant.* 6.214).

6. *4 Macc* 18:15 (ὑμνογράφος).

7. Note 2 Macc 2:13 ("the writings/books of David"). *Pirq. Avot* 6.9 also assumes that David is the author of the *Tehillim*.

8. David seems to be numbered with the prophets in 4Q397, frs. 14–17, col. 1 (= 4QMMT[d] = 4QHalakhic Letter[d]). On this topic, see Esther M. Menn, "Sweet Singer of Israel: David and the Psalms in Early Judaism," in *Psalms in Community: Jewish and Christian Textual, Liturgical, and Artistic Traditions*, ed. Harold W. Attridge and Margot E. Fassler (Society of Biblical Literature, 2003), 61–74.

chief prophet of the gospel.[9] Paul and other early Christian writers treated the psalms as David speaking about Christ, or alternately as Christ himself speaking in the first person.[10] Indeed, in the New Testament, the Psalter is the most oft-quoted book of Scripture.[11] Not surprisingly, this high regard for the psalms as messianic prophecy influenced the way later Christian apologists and teachers viewed the psalms.[12]

The most frequently cited psalm in the New Testament is Psalm 109 (110 MT). This psalm appears to have been part of the earliest church's traditional missional-apologetic preaching, which explains why it is quoted so often by New Testament authors. A writer such as the author of the Third Gospel would have noticed that the Greek superscription of Psalm 109 calls it a "psalm" and ascribes it to David. Perhaps these details led Christians to call the "hymns" or "praises" or "odes" of David "psalms," even though Hellenistic-Jewish authors such as Philo, Josephus, and the author of *4 Maccabees* call David's poems hymns.

It has been suggested that Paul's special interest in psalms that refer to Christ as a "rock," according to his messianic reading of them, implies that those psalms were sung in the churches of the Pauline mission.[13] This speculation exceeds the evidence. Paul explicitly quotes some seventeen biblical psalms in his letters, and he makes additional unmarked allusions to many psalm verses. In none of these references does he associate the psalm with church singing. This applies even to the quotations from the psalms in Romans 15, which are sometimes interpreted as reflective of Christian liturgy: "Therefore I will confess you among the gentiles; I will sing to your name" (Ps 17:50) and "Praise the Lord all you gentiles; give praise to him all you peoples" (Ps 117:1). These quotations are prooftexts, and

---

9. See, for example, Matt 22:41–46 and Acts 1:16. See also Harold W. Attridge, "Giving Voice to Jesus: The Use of the Psalms in the New Testament," in *Psalms in Community*, 101–112; Diana M. Swancutt, "Christian 'Rock' Music at Corinth?" in *Psalms in Community*, 125–143.

10. Harold Attridge treats the variety of these New Testament uses of the psalms with reference to Jesus in "Giving Voice to Jesus." Attridge shows that certain New Testament authors appear to treat particular psalms as the voice of Jesus himself, notably in Heb 2:12–13; Rom 15:3; and Rom 15:9.

11. According to Attridge, based on the Nestle-Aland 27th edition of the Greek New Testament, wording from at least 129 of the 150 canonical psalms appears in the New Testament ("Giving Voice to Jesus," 101).

12. Justin Martyr, for example, cites Ps 3:5 as Jesus speaking in the first person about his own death and resurrection (*Dial.* 97.1).

13. Swancutt, "Christian 'Rock' Music at Corinth?" 137 (referring to Deut 32 and 1 Sam 2, along with Pss 18, 19, 89, 94). Toward the end of her article Swancutt says that "it may well be that rock psalms were among the traditions Paul passed on to the Corinthians to be sung" (140). Two pages later, she is less tentative: "This essay has demonstrated that Paul "encourage[ed] psalm-singing in his churches" (142).

the proof-texting includes quotations from Deuteronomy and Isaiah as well.[14] Paul understands them as "prophecy" about what the followers of the Messiah would one day do—what the church in his own time was doing in fulfilling these prophecies. He does not present the prooftexts as examples of words that Christians sing in church.

More suggestive is the fact that in 1 Corinthians 14 Paul characterizes the songs of the church as thanksgivings.[15] Had he quoted a thanksgiving formulation from one of the biblical psalms in this context, we would have reason to think that he had taught the Corinthians to sing biblical thanksgiving psalms. But he does not. It is also worth noting that Psalm 117 LXX / 118 MT, which begins with a thanksgiving formula and was very probably a standard Jewish festival hymn, does not, in its Septuagint version, use Paul's word for giving thanks.[16] Moreover, it happens that verse 22 from this psalm—"The stone that the builders rejected has become the head of the corner"—is quoted by several early Christian writers, but *not* by Paul, despite his interest in other "rock" psalms.[17]

When psalms are quoted in early Christian writings of the first and second centuries, the purpose is always apologetic or didactic. Nothing is said or implied in any of these citations that either increases or diminishes the possibility that the quoted psalms were also sung at church meetings. Moreover, references to *song* in first-century Christian literature—in Acts, 1 Corinthians, Ephesians, Colossians, and James—give no hint that biblical psalms were part of anyone's song repertoire.[18] The deutero-Pauline letters Colossians and Ephesians instruct churches to engage in musical activities, which they characterize as "psalms, hymns, and spiritual songs."[19] To the extent that Christian leaders were influenced by the

14. Rom 15:9–12. The series of quotations is meant to show that the Scriptures prophesied the gentile mission. Those who see liturgical implications in the passage infer that the words "sing" and "praise" refer not only to *literal* singing and praising by gentiles but to gentiles singing the *very psalms* quoted here. Neither is implied.

15. 1 Cor 14:15–17.

16. Paul uses the verb εὐχαριστέω and its cognate noun εὐχαριστία (1 Cor 14:16-17). The Septuagint's translation of Psalm 118 MT uses the verb ἐξομολογέομαι (LXX 117:1), which generally means "confess" or "declare" but seems to mean "declare praise" and/or "give thanks" in the Septuagint.

17. Construed as prophecy by Christians, Ps 117:1 was understood to mean that Jesus is the rejected stone that has become the cornerstone. The earliest quotations of this verse are in the Synoptic gospels and 1 Peter. Other verses from the psalm are also quoted by later Christian authors. None hint at any use of the psalm as a church song.

18. 1 Cor 14:13–18, 26; Col 3:16; Eph 5:19; Jas 5:13; and Acts 16:25.

19. Col 3:16; Eph 5:18–19.

promulgation of these instructions, they had reason to encourage song at church meetings. But what church members sang in the late first and early second centuries is not documented, and the expression "psalms, hymns, and spiritual songs" is widely interpreted by modern commentators as a pleonasm, not a specification of three genres.[20] Of course, biblical psalms might have been included under so broad a description. Yet there is no reason to be confident that they were, given the absolute silence about biblical psalmody as a Christian practice in all extant Christian literature prior to *Acts of Paul*.

What interest in David as a prophet clearly shows is that from the very beginning, Christian leaders fostered an understanding of the Psalter as a book about Christ, which gave the psalms a central place in Christian teaching and preaching. As Tertullian would later put it, "the most holy and most accepted prophet David . . . sings to us about Christ," and "through him Christ has sung about himself."[21] Hence, it was only natural that the followers of Christ eventually began singing the psalms. In fact, some of them probably did so in Tertullian's day (see below).

A "Last Supper" Christian Hallel Tradition?

In the preceding chapter, I noted a debate between the Hillites and the Shammaites about whether a certain Hallel psalm, Psalm 114 MT, should be sung at domestic Passovers. This debate implies that during the Second Temple period, the Hillites sang Psalms 113 and 114 at Passover, while the Shammaites stopped at the end of Psalm 113. Moreover, the Tosefta says that synagogues provided Hallel liturgies on Passover eve for families who had no one to lead the Hallel at their domestic meal. While these two bits of evidence do not prove that the special format of the Passover Hallel as prescribed by the rabbis was followed by the general populace in Palestine, they do suggest that the general populace sang one or more Hallel psalms at their Passover seders or attended a synagogue Hallel liturgy. Furthermore, the Hellenistic-Jewish author of the Matthew refers to Jesus and his disciples "hymning" at the close of their Passover meal and probably believed that they sang the Hallel. Without corroborating evidence, however, this detail falls short of proving that Jewish-Christians sang the Hallel at Passover or at eucharistic gatherings modeled on the stories of the Last Supper.

---

20. See, for example, Joachim Gnilka, *Der Epheserbrief* (Freiburg: Herder, 1971), 270 (calling the language "plerophorisch"); Peter T. O'Brien, *Colossians, Philemon* (Waco, TX: Word, 1982), 209–210; James D. G. Dunn, *The Epistles to the Colossians and to Philemon: A Commentary on the Greek Text* (Eerdmans, 1996), 237-239.

21. Tertullian, *Carn.* 20.3.

No Hallel psalm is mentioned as either a Communion psalm or an Easter psalm in extant Christian literature of the first three centuries. The earliest specification of psalmody for a service commemorating the Last Supper is found in the Armenian Lectionary, which takes its cues from Jerusalem liturgy and is thought to reflect the liturgy of the Holy City in the fifth century. The AL prescribes that at the seventh hour on Thursday of Holy Week, the people are to assemble at "the Martyrium in the city," a propos of Jesus's words to his disciples about wishing to eat the Passover meal with them.[22] This service would have been an appropriate occasion for one or more Hallel psalms, had singing the Hallel been an ancient tradition inherited from the church of the first century. But the AL gives no hint of that. It specifies a service of the word (with Scripture readings and a homily), then Communion, with readings that describe the Last Supper (1 Cor 11: 23-32 and the account in Matt 26).[23] Before these readings, Psalm 22 is sung with verse 5 as the response: "You have prepared a table before me in the presence of those who oppress me." Psalm 22 is not a Hallel psalm, and the AL does not assign any Hallel psalms to this service.

Of course, there could have been an unrecorded Christian tradition of singing the Hallel at Pascha. One might imagine that Quartodecimans, for example, since they kept the Jewish Passover as a Christian Passover, sang a Hallel psalm at their evening Paschal supper. But there is no explicit evidence of that.[24]

The Earliest References to Christian Psalmody

Christian writings dating to roughly the last decades of the second century and the first decades of the third provide us with sufficient evidence to conclude that Christian psalmody was common during this period across a somewhat wide geography and among both Greek and Latin speakers. In the *Acts of Paul*, which was probably composed toward the end of the second century, we find a scene in which the author imagines Paul and the Corinthians singing "psalms of David" at an after-supper celebration. In a set of instructions about how to behave at Christian dinner parties, Clement of Alexandria extols the singing of psalms of David and interprets the word "psalms" in Col 3:16 as a reference to David's poems. And in a defense of the Christian church addressed to the elite citizens of Carthage, Tertullian refers to Christians singing "from Scripture"

22. AL 38. Regarding the expression, "the Martyrium in the city," see Athanase Renoux, *Le codex arménien Jérusalem 121*, vol. 2: *Édition comparée du texte et de deux autres manuscrits* (Brepols, 1971), 193–194 [55–56].

23. AL 39. The gospel reading is given as Matt 26:17–30 in mss. JE, as 26:20–30 in ms. P.

24. On the Quartodeciman customs, see chapter 3.

at community suppers, which would almost certainly have included psalms.[25] It should not go unnoticed that the setting for the singing in all three cases is some form of Christian social meal.

Psalmody at a Christian Community Supper in *Acts of Paul* 12

Acts of Paul is a Christian romance that traces the mission of Paul through various cities. At the close of its account of Paul's stay in Corinth, the *Acts* depicts a farewell community supper where the church sings "psalms of David." The most well-preserved version of the text reads as follows:

> Each one shared in the bread and feasted according to [. . .] among (?) them with psalms of David and songs, and Paul too enjoyed himself. On the following day, after they had spent the whole night according to the will of God, Paul said, "Brothers, I shall set out on Friday and sail for Rome that I may not delay what is commanded and laid upon me, for to this I was appointed." They were greatly distressed when they heard this, and all the brothers contributed according to their ability so that Paul might not be troubled, except that he was going away from the brothers.[26]

The lacuna [. . .] can perhaps be partially completed as "according to the custom of thanksgiving," that is, the Eucharist.[27] The reference to "psalms of David *and*

---

25. Tertullian, *Apol.* 39.18.

26. Fr. 7 in Carl Schmidt and Wilhelm Schubart, eds., *Πράξεις Παύλου. Acta Pauli nach dem papyrus der Hamburger Staats- und Universitäts-Bibliothek* (Augustin, 1936), 50. See the Coptic text in Carl Schmidt, ed. *Acta Pauli aus der Heidelberger Koptischen Papyrushandschrift Nr. 1* Hinrichs, 1904), 44*–45.* My translation is based in part on J. K. Elliott, *The Apocryphal New Testament* (Oxford University Press, 1993), 383. Modern editors and translators order and number the extant pages of P. Hamburg differently. The passage about singing is in ch. 9 in Elliott, *The Apocryphal New Testament*, 383; and in ch. 12 in Willy Rordorf's translation in François Bovon and Pierre Geoltrain, eds. *Écrits apocryphes chrétiens*, vol. 1 (Gallimard, 1997), 1168; also in ch. 12 in Pervo, *The Acts of Paul*, 283.

27. Schmidt and Schubart read συνήθ̣ι̣α̣[ν] and [νη]σ̣τίας, supplementing as follows, based on their opinion that νηστίας was inadvertently written twice (dittography): μετα̣λ̣αβ̣ῖ̣ν [ἕκαστον το]ῦ̣ [ἄ]ρτου καὶ εὐωχεῖσθαι αὐτοὺς κατὰ τὴν συνήθ̣ι̣α̣[ν] τῆς] νη[. . .νη]σ̣τίας (ms. p. 7 in Schmidt and Schubart, 50). Fasting is indeed mentioned in the very fragmentary parallel text in the Coptic (P. Heid. p. 52, line 16 [Schmidt, 44*]), but Schmidt and Schubart's reconstruction seems doubtful, since the supplements do not fill the gap and because it is not altogether clear what the text so reconstructed means. See Wilhelm Schneemelcher, "Acts of Paul," in Edgar Hennecke, *New Testament Apocrypha*: vol. 2: *Writings Relating to the Apostles, Apocalypses and Related*

songs" makes clear that the Davidic psalms were sung, not used in some other way. While the story is fictional, it probably projects onto the mission of the historical Paul a practice that was typical of Christian community suppers known to the author when the story was composed. The references to Christian psalmody in Clement of Alexandria and Tertullian strengthen this inference.

Another thing to notice is that the gathering in *Acts of Paul* assumes the character of a vigil, since it lasts all night and is done in accord with "the will of God." Here, too, the author probably modeled the scene on something familiar to him—all-night Christian gatherings with psalmody. Church leaders must have discovered early on that an extended prayer meeting of this sort required structure to keep people from nodding off. Singing offered such a structured activity.

The author and place of composition for *Acts of Paul* cannot be established, but the work must stem from circles dedicated to preserving the memory of Paul's mission and teaching. Its place of composition could have been almost any Greek-speaking ecclesial center in Asia Minor or Achaia, even Rome.[28] External evidence dates *Acts of Paul* to the late second century.[29] The text known to modern scholarship is an edition produced circa 300 CE and represented in its earliest witness by P. Hamburg, a Greek manuscript that was copied sometime early in the fourth century.[30] The original editors concluded that besides P. Hamburg, another fragmentary manuscript represents part of the story—the sixth-century Coptic Heidelburg papyrus. Although Paul's location is not preserved at the purported parallel point in the Heidelberg narrative,[31] there are striking similarities in certain details, notably the prophecy of one Cleobius, followed by a prophecy by a certain Myrta, and then a community meal with what appears to be a reference to psalms of David.[32] The fact that the story appears in two fragmentary manuscripts that appear to reflect somewhat different editions of *Acts of Paul*

Subjects, ed. Wilhelm Schneemelcher and R. McL. Wilson; tr. Ernest Best et al. (Westminster, 1963), 380 n. 2.

28. Tertullian, whose information may or may not be accurate, states that the author was a presbyter of Asia Minor (*Bapt.* 17.5).

29. *Acts of Paul* is mentioned by Tertullian (*Bapt.* 17.5), used as a source by Hippolytus (*In Dan.* 3.29.3), and quoted several times by Origin. See Richard I. Pervo, *The Acts of Paul: A New Translation with Introduction and Commentary* (Clarke, 2014), 43–46.

30. The quotation from *Acts of Paul* given above is translated from this manuscript.

31. See the citation in n. 26. To achieve a plausible correlation of narrative sequence with P. Hamburg, the pages of P. Heidelberg have to be reordered to make pp. 41–52 immediately precede pp. 71ff.

32. P. Heid., 51–52 (Schubart, 44*–45*).

encourages the conclusion that the farewell supper was not an interpolation into the final edition made around 300 CE but was part of the late second-century original.

Tertullian's Description of Christian Community Symposia

The works of Justin Martyr and other second-century writings besides *Acts of Paul* are silent about biblical psalmody.[33] Chronologically, the next witnesses to the practice are Tertullian and Clement of Alexandria.

In *On Spectacles*, Tertullian insists that Christians possess a sufficient supply of their own "verses, sentences, songs, [and] proverbs" to compensate them for giving up the winsome "teachings of the stage."[34] These verses and songs must be biblical poetry, since the church had no other shared body of literature other than the Bible, certainly none that Tertullian would have endorsed in an unqualified way. Since he refers to songs, not simply poems, he must mean that Christians should *sing* this biblical poetry. In his *Apology*, Tertullian describes a Christian custom of after-supper song where the diners take turns singing "from Scripture or their own invention."[35] "From Scripture" must refer to biblical psalms and canticles. And that suggests that his reference in *On the Soul* to *psalmi* sung at Christian services probably includes biblical psalms.

The mentions of Christian song in *On Spectacles*, the *Apology*, and *On the Soul* increase the likelihood that in a passage in Tertullian's treatise *On Prayer*, where he explicitly mentions responsorial performance of certain psalms, he means that they were *sung*. "During prayer," he writes, "the more diligent are in the habit of adding to their prayers an 'Alleluia' *et* that kind of psalm to which those present respond at (or "with") the endings."[36] I have left the particle *et* untranslated for the moment and will return to it shortly.

The Latin word *Alleluia* derives from the Psalter. Tertullian and his fellow Christians would have found it in the Old Latin Bible, based on a Greek version[37] that used *Allēlouia* to translate the Hebrew *Hallēluyah*. The Hebrew

33. Justin describes a eucharistic communal meeting for the newly baptized and a weekly eucharistic church service on Sunday (*1 Apol.* 65 and 67). In neither description does he mention singing, much less psalmody. Nor does this topic appear explicitly in his few references to hymns/hymning elsewhere in his writings.

34. Tertullian, *Spec.* 29.4.

35. Tertullian, *Apol.* 39.18.

36. *Diligentiores in orando subiungere in orationibus alleluia solent et hoc genus psalmos quorum clausulis respondeant qui simul sunt.* Tertullian, *Orat.* 27.

37. The question of old Latin translations of biblical books, including some or all of the Psalter, is unresolved, but it is likely that they were available in the second century and were based on

book of psalms, as represented by the Masoretic text, shows ten psalms with an initial *Hallēluyah* (or *Hallēlu Yah*) that functions as a heading or an opening exclamation.[38] The Septuagint uses Alleluia at these same points and also at the head of other psalms. Moreover, the Septuagint does *not* use Alleluia to render the Hebrew *Hallēluyah* and related forms within the body of a psalm. In these instances, it uses expressions with the verb *aineō* (praise).[39] The Septuagint also lacks Alleluia where the MT has Hallelujah at the end of a psalm (as a closing exclamation), except for the appearance of Alleluia after Psalm 150. Altogether, twenty psalms in the Septuagint carry the Alleluia heading.[40]

Hence, Tertullian and other educated Christians who read the Psalter in Latin translations based on Greek translations, whether the Septuagint or versions that treated Alleluia in a similar way, would have encountered the term "Alleluia" at the beginning of various psalms and not as exclamations in the middle of any psalms. This might have encouraged them to think of Alleluia as a heading or designation for a certain kind of psalm. They may also have known that at two other points in the Septuagint (outside the Psalter), Alleluia is used as an exclamation, namely, in Tobit and 3 Maccabees.[41] Moreover, the author of an anonymous *Homily on the Psalms*, a Greek Christian sermon that stems from roughly the same period as Tertullian's *On Prayer*, pictures David and his fellow singers *responding* to psalms by singing Alleluia.[42] In view of the evidence as a whole, and given that Tertullian's comment in *On Prayer* mentions both Alleluia and responding, the simplest way to interpret his formulation is to understand Alleluia as a psalm that carries that word in its superscription, which was understood as an indication that Alleluia should be sung as a response. If this

---

Greek versions, not Hebrew ones. See Benjamin Kedar, "The Latin Translations," in *Mikra: Text, Translation, Reading and Interpretation of the Hebrew Bible in Ancient Judaism and Early Christianity*, ed. Martin J. Mulder (Van Gorcum, 1988), 299–313. I will note that Origen's *Hexapla* does not have psalm headings.

38. Psalms 106, 111–113, 135, and 146–150 MT.

39. Where Ps 22:27 MT has יהללו יהוה, Ps 21:27 LXX translates αἰνέσουσιν κύριον. Where Ps 135:1b MT has הללו את שם יהוה, 134:1a LXX translates αἰνεῖτε τὸ ὄνομα κυρίου; where Ps 135:3 MT has הללו יה, 134:3 LXX translates αἰνεῖτε τὸν κύριον. See further examples in Ps 146:1b MT // 145:1b LXX; Ps 147:1a MT // 147:1b LXX; Ps 149:1a MT // 148:1b LXX.

40. Psalms 104–106, 110–118, 134–135, and 145–150. Ancient Christian divines were also interested in this subject. Athanasius counts eighteen, since he does not include Psalms 110 and 116 (*Ep. Marc.* 25). And in remarks on the Psalter that precede his commentary on the psalms, Eusebius gives a count of fifteen: τῶν εἰς τὸ Ἀλληλούϊα ιε′ (PG 23: 68).

41. Tob 13:18; the "Hanukkah" Alleluia of 3 Macc 7:13 (where τὸ ἀλληλούϊα might designate the Hallel, in view of *m. Pesaḥ* 10.5E; see chapter 1 n. 10).

42. This homily is discussed in chapter 3.

is correct, the particle *et* in Tertullian's sentence does not introduce a reference to an additional and different kind of prayer-ending but clarifies what adding an Alleluia means: "During prayer, the more diligent are in the habit of adding an Alleluia [psalm] to their prayers, *specifically* that kind of psalm to which those present respond at the endings [with 'Alleluia']."[43]

Christopher Page opines that in the remarks about Alleluia psalms added to prayers, Tertullian had in mind urban ascetics who kept hours of prayer at home.[44] He draws his picture of these ascetics based on the rigorous ideals of piety that Tertullian promotes in *On Prayer* and his *Exhortation to Chastity*. In the former writing, Tertullian argues that Christians should go beyond the obligatory observance of morning and evening prayer by adopting, as a rule of life (*quasi lege*), the third, sixth, and ninth hours for prayer, along with moments of prayer before meals and before going to the baths. At least they should pray no less than three times a day, like Daniel.[45] In *An Exhortation to Chastity*, he urges Christians not to marry so that they can devote themselves single-mindedly to the Lord; and he advocates celibacy not only for single persons but for married couples. These clues lead Page to conclude that "there was an *horarium* of domestic psalmody amongst house-ascetics a hundred years or more before anyone thought of going into the desert as a monk."[46] It was *their* psalmody that sometimes took the responsorial form that Tertullian mentions as the habit of the "more diligent."

The household is certainly the most likely setting for group prayer in this period.[47] By "more diligent," however, Tertullian means "more devoted," not "more rigorous" in ascetic discipline, as his ensuing explanation shows. Adding

43. See n. 36. The particle *et* usually means "and," but sometimes it introduces a clarifying amplification, the way the Greek καί sometimes means "even." See *OLD* 1: 682 (no. 6); also Charlton T. Lewis and Charles Short, *A New Latin Dictionary* (Oxford: Clarendon, 1879), 660 (II.A).

44. Christopher Page, *The Christian West and Its Singers: The First Thousand Years* (Yale University Press, 2010), 137–138 (see also 83–84).

45. Tertullian, *Orat.* 25. The fivefold cursus exceeds the norm followed elsewhere. The *Didache* calls for three times of prayer (8.3). Clement of Alexandria also mentions three traditional prayer times, although he, too, advocates a higher ideal: the truly devoted "gnostic" Christian prays at other times as well, even continuously, which probably refers to mental attitude (*Str.* 7.7.40 and 7.7.49). Similarly, Origen comments that "what is usually called prayer" is done three times a day, although one also prays continuously by leading a virtuous life (*Orat.* 12.2).

46. Page, *The Christian West and Its Singers*, 138.

47. In a copious survey of the evidence for daily prayer in the first three centuries of Christian history, Paul Bradshaw observes that there is little evidence of daily corporate prayer and "much which would suggest the opposite, that daily prayer, at least as a general rule, was made by individuals in private." Bradshaw concludes that prior to the fourth century, corporate prayer tended to be conducted in private "by a family together or a small group of friends." Paul F. Bradshaw,

an Alleluia psalm to a prayer extends the prayer in a particular way, making it *saturatam*, that is, "full," like a "fat sacrificial victim" (*opimam hostiam*).[48] "This (victim), devoted from the whole heart (*de toto corde devotam*), fed by faith, cared for by truth, completely innocent, pure in chastity, crowned with love, we should lead to the altar of God with a procession (*pompa*) of good works, amid psalms and hymns, to obtain all things for ourselves from God."[49]

Although this comment interprets the significance of extending one's prayers through Alleluia psalms, it does not explain how the custom itself arose. The reason for the practice must have had something to do with the fact that the twenty Alleluia psalms of the Psalter are all praise and thanksgiving hymns. This made them especially suitable conclusions to prayers by Christians who had been taught to praise and thank God in all circumstances, according to a Pauline dictum in 1 Thessalonians, especially since this apostolic teaching is echoed in Ephesians as part of an instruction to sing.[50] Moreover, in explaining why it is proper to pray in public in certain circumstances, even though Jesus taught that one should pray in secret, Tertullian adduces the examples of Paul and Silas offering hymnic prayers in jail and Paul making a "thanksgiving" to God on a ship.[51] These biblical stories were very well-known and must have exerted a significant influence on Christian understandings of prayer. The description of Paul's prayer in the second passage, together with many similar associations of prayer with thanksgiving in the Pauline corpus,[52] would have taught Christians that thanksgiving should be an integral part of their prayers. The syntax in the passage about Paul and Silas would have encouraged them to think of singing to God as a form of prayer,[53] as would Paul's characterization of singing in church as

---

Daily Prayer in the Early Church: A Study of the Origin and Early Development of the Divine Office (Oxford University Press, 1982), 65–66.

48. Tertullian, *Orat.* 27.

49. *Orat.* 28.4. The language is clearly figurative, but the mention of psalms and hymns echoes the literal reference to Alleluia psalms as conclusions to prayers.

50. 1 Thess 5:18; Eph 5:20.

51. Tertullian, *Orat.* 24, referring to Acts 16:25 and 27:35. Regarding Acts 16:25, see n. 53.

52. The letters attributed to Paul associate praying with thanking: (1) in Paul's descriptions of his own practice (1 Cor 1:4; Phil 1:3–5; Col 1:3; 1 Thess 1:2 and 3:9; 2 Thess 1:3 and 2:13; Phlm 1:4) and (2) in his instructions about prayer (Phil 4:6; Eph 5:4 and 5:20; Col 1:12; 2:7; 3:17; 4:2; 1 Thess 5:17–18; 1 Tim 2:1), together with (3) his references to the regular custom of giving thanks at meals (Rom 14:6; 1 Cor 10:30; 11:24) and for specific things (2 Cor 1:11 and 8:16 etc.).

53. "At midnight, Paul and Silas, praying (προσευχόμενοι), were singing hymns to God (ὕμνουν τὸν θεόν)" (Acts 16:25). The participle "praying" modifies the main verb "hymning," implying

"thanksgiving."[54] Hence, it would have been natural for Christians who regarded the Psalter as a book of songs to have sung the book's psalms of thanksgiving in devotional settings. It is not surprising, then, that in Carthage, where the church's community suppers included singing "from Scripture," some of the city's Christians, when they gathered for prayer, added psalms of thanksgiving and praise to their prayers, namely, Alleluia psalms.

The addition of Alleluia psalms to prayers is the first known instance of a pairing of psalms with prayers. Whether the convention of intercalating prayers and psalms as documented for the late fourth century is a direct development from a continuous tradition inaugurated around the time of Tertullian cannot be proven, however, since there is silence about this format in the literature of the intervening decades (more than 150 years). The two customs may not be related historically, especially since the psalmody of the West does not appear to have been a model for psalmody in the East but rather the reverse. Moreover, developments in church song were not necessarily linear. Similar practices may have arisen in a variety of times and places for similar and dissimilar reasons, flourishing and fading, without being part of any evolutionary chain.

I have already mentioned an additional reference to song in Tertullian's corpus. In *On the Soul* he gives a description of activities "in church during the Lord's solemnities (*in ecclesia inter dominica solemnia*)," where a woman with prophetic gifts receives revelations "while Scripture is read, psalms are sung (*psalmi canuntur*), discourses (*allocutiones*) are given, or prayers are made."[55] Although the expression "Lord's solemnities" is unusual, it could refer to the regular community supper[56] or, more generally, to any meetings where any of the activities Tertullian mentions took place.

Did the *psalmi* at the *dominica solemnia* include biblical psalms? James McKinnon thinks not, because he takes the gathering to be a Montanist service and reads the passage in the light of a passage in Tertullian's tractate against Marcion, where Tertullian challenges Marcion to produce a "psalm" (or a "prayer" or "vision") while in a state of prophetic ecstasy, as a manifestation of the gifts of

---

that hymning is a form of the praying. On hymnody and in particular psalmody as prayer in Christian conception, see "Psalmody as Prayer" in chapter 6.

54. 1 Cor 14:15-17. See above with n. 16.

55. Tertullian, *An.* 9.4.

56. This assumes that Tertullian's references to Christian instruction in *Apol.* 39.1–4 pertain to the community meal described in 39.16–19. That is not certain, of course, but see an argument for it in Charles H. Cosgrove, "Word and Table: The Origins of a Liturgical Sequence," *Vigiliae Christianae* 74 (2020): 359–360.

the Spirit, the way certain members of Tertullian's own Montanist circle do.[57] This leads McKinnon to conclude that the *psalmi* mentioned in *On the Soul* were probably ecstatic songs, not biblical psalms.[58]

It is indeed clear from the passage in *Against Marcion* that Tertullian sometimes used the term *psalmus* for songs composed by Christians, including heretics. In fact, he used it for both those types of songs and biblical psalms, drawing a contrast in *On the Incarnation* between the "psalms" of Valentinus and those of David.[59] But if Tertullian and his fellow Montanists continued to attend "catholic" services, which is likely,[60] and if a catholic service was the setting of the woman's prophetic visions, which also seems likely (since she explains her vision only *after* the meeting),[61] then the *psalmi* were not songs of a Montanist gathering. Hence, they probably included biblical psalms, such as the psalms that some Carthaginian Christians sang "from Scripture" at community suppers.

Psalmody at Christian Dinner Parties in Clement's Alexandria

Around 200 CE—either near the end of Clement's time in Alexandria, where he served as a presbyter, or not long after 202, when he fled that city—Clement

57. Tertullian, *Adv. Marc.* 5.8.12.

58. See McKinnon's headnotes to nos. 81 and 82 in *MECL*.

59. Tertullian, *Carn.* 20.3.

60. Tertullian composed *On the Soul* during what has been called his "Montanist" period (the years 206–212); it reflects his commitments to the New Prophecy. See Timothy D. Barnes, *Tertullian: A Historical and Literary Study* (Oxford University Press, 1971), 55. It is now generally agreed by Tertullian specialists that during this phase of his life, he did not leave the "catholic" church and join a separate communion. Hence, the meeting was probably a regular liturgy of the majority church and not a separate Montanist synaxis. See Douglas Powell, "Tertullianists and Cataphrygians," *Vigiliae Christianae* 29 (1975): 33–38 (33–54); David Rankin, *Tertullian and the Church* (Cambridge University Press, 1995), 27–41; Christine Trevett, *Montanism: Gender, Authority and the New Prophecy* (Cambridge University Press, 1996), 73–76; Eric Osborn, *Tertullian: First Theologian of the West* (Cambridge University Press, 1997), 176–177; Geoffrey D. Dunn, *Tertullian* (Routledge, 2004), 6–7.

61. Tertullian does not suggest that the occasions for the woman's visions were other people's ecstatic utterances. His description implies that ordinary prayer, song, preaching, and Scripture-reading prompted her visions, which she shared with other Christians (perhaps with the Montanist members of the congregation) only after the service: *post transacta sollemnia dimissa plebe, quo usu solet nobis renuntiare quae uiderit* (*An.* 9.4). McKinnon's translation of the description of the woman's visions interprets *medicinas desiderantibus sumit* as "applies remedies to those who need them," as if she did so by speaking to particular church members during the meeting (*MECL* no. 82); but *sumo* has a broad semantic range and probably means "receives" in this context.

composed a practical tract on Christian behavior called *Paedagogus*. Whatever the precise date of the work, it stands in close temporal proximity to Tertullian's corpus but represents a different part of the Christian world.

At one point in *Paedagogus*, Clement discusses proper conduct at social meals. He begins by focusing on musical enjoyments at drinking parties. Christians should reject the usual pagan entertainments, he advises, especially those that entail erotic songs and musical instruments that stimulate licentious desires. Instead, they should use their own minds and voices to praise God. To make this point from Scripture, Clement quotes various psalms that command praise with musical instruments, interpreting the instruments as parts of the human body—voice, mouth, skin, nerves, and tongue. These are peaceable instruments, he says, unlike the musical instruments used by various nations for battle. At Christian dinner parties,[62] he urges, the duty of peaceable guests is to fulfill the double love commandment by showing love for one another through proper decorum and love for God through "thanksgiving and psalmody."

By "psalmody" Clement probably means—or at least means to include—the singing of biblical psalms. Here is the passage in full, with topical numbers[63] added:

> (1) Let our friendly feeling at a drinking party be in accord with the double law. For "if you love the Lord your God," then (also) "your neighbor." And let your friendly feeling be first of all toward God through thanksgiving and psalmody, second, toward your neighbor through decorous conversation. For the apostle says, "Let the word of the Lord dwell among you richly." And this word adapts and adjusts to occasions, persons, places, and is now sympotic. For the apostle again declares, "teaching and admonishing one another in all wisdom with psalms, hymns, spiritual odes, with thanksgiving, singing with your heart to God. And everything, whatever you do in word or deed, do all in the name of Jesus, giving thanks to God the Father." This is our thanksgiving revel. (2) And if you want to sing to and play the lyre or cithara, it is no disgrace, for you would imitate a righteous Hebrew king, who is thankful to God. "Rejoice in the Lord, you righteous. Praise suits those who do right," says the prophecy [Psalm 32:1]. "Give thanks to the Lord with the

62. Clement has in view private social gatherings, not community suppers. He uses a traditional Greek term, συμπόσιον, which by his time often meant a social meal with socializing and drinking, not exclusively a drinking party. He also calls the Christian social meal a "revel" (κῶμος), another traditional Greek word for a party.

63. The topical numbers are for convenience of reference in the discussion that follows and do not reflect the paragraph numbers in the critical edition.

> cithara; sing (or "play") to him with the ten-string psaltery; sing to him a new song." Does not the ten-string psaltery signify the word, which is Jesus, revealed in the element of the decad? (3) And inasmuch as it is fitting, before partaking of nourishment, to bless the maker of all things, so, too, it suits a symposion for those who partake of his created things to sing to him. For a psalm is a melodious and temperate blessing. And the apostle has called a psalm a spiritual song.[64]

This is a rich and dense discussion. In (1), Clement uses Colossians 3:16 as a prooftext for his instruction that Christians should engage in "thanksgiving and psalmody" at their drinking parties. In (3), he reveals how he interprets the word "psalms" in Colossians 3:16. In Clement's era, the word "psalms" had both a generic sense and a special narrow Christian sense. In the generic sense the word meant songs of any type, including Christian hymns. In the narrow sense, it meant biblical psalms. Significantly, in interpreting the nouns in the musical list of Colossians 3:16—"psalms, hymns, spiritual songs"—Clement takes the third as a synonym for the first, commenting that "the apostle calls a psalm a spiritual song." Here he also states that a "psalm is a melodious and temperate blessing." Together, these interpretations of "psalms" in Colossians 3:16 show that he does not treat the word as a generic term for song, even generic Christian song, since he would not have assumed that every song or even every Christian composition was, by definition, spiritual and conducive to a temperate lifestyle. Hence, he must have understood the word "psalms" in Colossians 3:16 to mean biblical psalms, which he would have regarded as categorically spiritual and temperate. As it happens, Clement elsewhere uses the noun *psalmos* only of biblical psalms and, in one place, of the songs that Christians should sing at supper and before bed (in *Stromata*),[65] never in reference to "pagan" song.[66] Hence, it is possible that not only in his discussion of Colossians 3:16 but also in his other reference to psalm-singing, he means biblical psalms. Perhaps Clement had gotten into the habit of calling only biblical poems "psalms." But that is only a guess. In any case, Clement's interpretation of Colossians 3:16 implies that he believed that biblical psalms had been part of the church's song repertoire during the time of Paul.

In (2), Clement defends the use of the lyre or cithara to accompany Christian song, arguing that David's use of stringed instruments justifies it. Later he compares Greek song-passing to a custom of Hebrew psalmody. These details, too,

64. Clement of Alexandria, *Paed.* 2.4.43.1–2.4.44.1.

65. *Str.* 7.7.49.4.

66. When Clement speaks of nonbiblical songs, he uses the terms "ode" (ᾠδή), "hymn" (ὕμνος), and "song" (ᾆσμα).

suggest that Clement is thinking of biblical psalms as *songs*, not exclusively as sources of divine teaching and, moreover, that he regards them as ideal songs for Christians to sing at social meals when they express their "friendly feeling . . . toward God through thanksgiving and psalmody" (2).

A remark in *Stromata* fills out the picture of Christian singing at dinner parties in Clement's social environment by giving us a clue about its format:

> We must attend to music for the grooming and dressing-up of our manners. For instance, while drinking, we toast (our) singing to one another, subduing our appetite through song and glorifying God for the abundant gift of human enjoyments.[67]

The statement, "we toast our singing to one another," is meant to recall one form of the long-standing Greek custom of wine toasting at symposia. Ancient Greek toasts differed from the modern toast, where a person says a few words and then "drinks to" someone. In an ancient Greek toast, the one toasting offered his or her cup to another diner or to the whole dining group. In the latter case, the cup was passed around the couches. Significantly, during the classical era, the cup receiver sometimes sang.[68] This explains Clement's expressions, "passing around toasts of song" (in *Paedagogus*) and "toast our singing to one another" (in *Stromata*), which hark back to what he regarded as venerable customs of the old Greek symposion.[69] When Christians toast their singing, they take turns, each offering a song to the other diners.

Conclusion

We find only a relatively small number of references to song by the followers of Jesus in the New Testament. They appear in very brief passages in seven books of the New Testament—Matthew, Mark, Acts, 1 Corinthians, Ephesians, Colossians, and James. It cannot be determined whether any of these refer to Christian psalm-singing. In other surviving literature of the church from its

67. Clement, *Str.* 6.11.89.4–90.1.

68. See Charles H. Cosgrove, *Music at Social Meals in Greek and Roman Antiquity: From the Archaic Period to the Age of Augustine* (Cambridge University Press, 2023), 314.

69. In *Paedagogus*, Clement also adduces the old Greek custom of song-passing, drawing a parallel to Hebrew customs and implying that Christians in his day follow a style of singing that goes back to the Israelites, from whom Greeks learned the custom. See *Paed.* 2.4.44.3. For a detailed discussion of all these matters, see Cosgrove, *Music at Social Meals in Greek and Roman Antiquity*, 314–316.

beginnings through the early third century, Christian song is mentioned only by the author of the *Acts of Paul*, Clement of Alexandria, and Tertullian. Although this evidence is somewhat meager, its paucity has to be put into perspective. As it happens, we possess precious little information about Christian worship and devotional practices in this era, although these things were ubiquitous. Incidence of mention is no reliable guide to incidence of their practice. Hence, the limited evidence for psalmody is probably not fully representative of the extent of the practice. While it would be imprudent to assume that all the churches of this period had adopted psalmody, it stands to reason that a significant number of Christians in various places had done so, especially since the existing evidence shows that psalmody was practiced in both Greek-speaking and Latin-speaking communities.

Finally, it can be no coincidence that to the extent that the references to Christian song in the literature from this period speak about the formats, they describe individual singing, not unison choral song. It was the individual Christian who memorized a psalm and sang it in private or in a communal setting, whether a community supper, a dinner party, or a prayer gathering. In after-dinner settings, such as those described by Clement and Tertullian, it was common for Christians to sing by turns.

CHAPTER THREE

Third-Century Developments

After the references to psalmody in the turn-of-the-century writings of Clement of Alexandria and Tertullian, explicit and implicit evidence for the practice appears in three pieces of third-century literature and in two places in Eusebius's *Church History* that bear on third-century practice. Cyprian places psalmody at a private Christian dinner party. The author of a Christian homily appears to have been familiar with a practice of singing Alleluia as a response to psalms. An instruction to traveling ascetics in the pseudo-Clementine *Letters to Virgins* concerns occasions when it is proper for them to sing Scripture songs. A statement in an episcopal letter, quoted by Eusebius, refers to Paschal psalmody at Antioch under Bishop Paul of Samosata. And Eusebius claims that the Therapeutae described by Philo were Christians, whose Paschal song, Eusebius believed, was the same as the traditional Paschal song familiar to Eusebius himself, which he would have known from the time of his adolescence in the latter part of the third century. The geographical distribution of this evidence for psalmody ranges from Palestine to Rome to Carthage. It is a pity, although not a surprise, that Origen does not describe Christian social meals where the after-supper song discussed by Clement of Alexandria might still have been a pious Christian recreation.

Melodic Reading of the Psalter?

The preceding list of references to psalmody does not include a passage about the psalms as "songs" that leisured Christians ought to read at home. The *Didascalia apostolorum*, a Greek "church order" composed around 230,[1] recommends biblical literature as an alternative to the pagan literature they enjoy. The passage appears in a Syriac version of the *Didascalia*, in the Greek form that was incorporated into the *Apostolic Constitutions*, and in a collection of Latin fragments. The Syriac, Greek, and Latin versions all place the Psalter in the category of songs, distinct from other forms of biblical poetry. The author of the *Apostolic*

1. This is the standard opinion. See, for example, Paul F. Bradshaw, *The Search for the Origins of Christian Worship: Sources and Methods for the Study of Early Liturgy*, 2nd ed. (Oxford University Press, 2002), 79; cf. also the more recent discussion by Stewart-Sykes, who agrees that the book was composed in the early third century but opines that it contains redactions made in the early fourth. Alistair Stewart-Sykes, *The Didascalia Apostolorum: An English Version with an Introduction and Annotation* (Brepols, 2009), 49–54.

Constitutions had a copy of the (now lost) Greek original in front of him. Hence, his wording probably reflects the Greek of his exemplar at many points:

> If you are rich and have no need to make a living by working at a trade, do not wander here and there and hang around aimlessly, but at all times go among the faithful and those who are of one mind with you, meditating and learning together with them through the living words. Otherwise, if you are sitting at home, read the law, the books of kings, the prophets; sing the hymns . . . If [you desire] sophistical and poetical things, you have the prophets, Job, the author of the proverbs, in which you will find greater wisdom than in those of all poetry and sophistry, for they are the voices of the Lord, the only wise God. If you are enamored of lyrical things (*asmatikōn*), you have the Psalms.[2]

As we have seen, Christians in various cities had begun singing psalms by this time—at domestic prayer gatherings and social meals, both private dinner parties and community suppers. The *Didascalia* is the first Christian writing to mention a wealthy person's private leisure as a setting for reading psalms. Moreover, writing in an era when educated people distinguished poetry meant for declamation from poetry meant to be sung, the author calls the biblical psalms "songs." The *Apostolic Constitutions* understands this to mean that one should read the psalms at home by singing them, for it says, "If you are sitting at home . . . sing the hymns." If this instruction was part of the author's Greek exemplar, then it may well have been original to the third-century *Didascalia*. It is more likely, however, that the *Apostolic Constitutions* added the instruction, since it is absent from the Syriac version of the *Didascalia*.

Cyprian's *Letter to Donatus*

Cyprian's *Letter to Donatus* reflects something of developments in Carthage between the time of Tertullian and the mid-third century, when Cyprian was the bishop of Carthage. At the close of what purports to be a personal letter to a fellow Christian named Donatus, composed in the year 246 or thereabouts, ostensibly at the time of the wine festival, Cyprian mentions an evening banquet where he, Donatus, and a few other friends will dine together. Donatus will recite psalms.

Certain features of the letter's construction reveal it to be a piece of fictional epistolary literature.[3] At the beginning, Cyprian writes as if he and Donatus were

2. *Const. ap.* 1.5-6 // *Didasc.* 2.

3. See Jakob Engberg, "The Education and (Self-)Affirmation of (Recent or Potential) Converts: The Case of Cyprian and the Ad Donatum," *Zeitschrift für Antikes Christentum* 16 (2012):

meeting together in a secluded grape arbor to spend the day in conversation. The body of the letter is the purported conversation of that meeting, in which Donatus is pictured listening attentively: "your eye is now fixed on me. In your gaze, your thought, you are completely a listener."[4] Then, at the close of the letter, where Cyprian describes the end of the day, he suggests that Donatus should perform psalms at a supper with friends. Cyprian paints an idyllic picture of this imagined scene:

> Since this is a holiday rest and time of leisure, let us pleasantly spend what remains of the day, as the sun dips toward evening, not letting even the hour of supper lack heavenly grace. Let the temperate meal resound with psalms (*psalmos*); and since your memory is tenacious and your voice sonorous, take up this duty yourself as a matter of custom. You will serve something better to your dearest friends if, while we have something spiritual to listen to, a religious sweetness charms our ears.[5]

A generation earlier, Tertullian had described how Christians at suppers in Carthage took turns singing from Scripture or from their own invention.[6] Cyprian describes a gathering where only one person takes up the "customary duty" of song. Since the trait that qualifies Donatus for this task is his good memory, a capacity associated with learning Scripture by heart, the implication is that he has committed to memory some number of biblical psalms and will sing from that repertoire. It is possible that this kind of psalmody entailed responses by the rest of the diners, but Cyprian does not say.

There is also a difference in setting between what Tertullian describes and what Cyprian envisions. Between the times of Tertullian and Cyprian, the church at Carthage had abandoned the community supper, there being too many church members to accommodate at community meals.[7] The morning service, which had already been established in Tertullian's time as an additional eucharistic gathering,[8] was now the main occasion for plebs to receive the Eucharist.

129–144. Engberg, who does not doubt that Donatus is a real person, sees the letter itself as contrived, fashioned to influence other recent and potential converts through the example of Donatus and of Cyprian himself (136–138).

4. Cyprian, *Don.* [= *Ep.* 1] 1.

5. Cyprian, *Don.* 16.

6. The passage in *Apol.* 39 is discussed in chapter 2.

7. Cyprian, *Ep.* 63.16.1. See Andrew McGowan, "Rethinking Agape and Eucharist in Early North African Christianity," *Studia Liturgica* 34 (2004): 172–174.

8. Tertullian, *Cor.* 3.3 and *Orat.* 19.1–4. See McGowan, "Rethinking Agape and Eucharist in Early North African Christianity," 169–172.

Yet elite Christians such as Cyprian continued to dine with men of their own class.[9] The remarks in the *Letter to Donatus* about the evening supper and its psalmody are a bit of advice about how a company of upper-class Christian friends should conduct their private dinner parties.

An Anonymous *Homily on the Psalms*

A Christian account of the compositional process used by David and his fellow psalm-singers appears in an anonymous Greek *Homily on the Psalms.* Although the homily offers no independent evidence of Christian psalmody, it does show how Christians of the third century imagined the inspiration of the psalms and the original psalmodic practice of David and his fellow singers. The author's description of that practice was probably based on church psalmody. The passage also sheds light on Clement of Alexandria's claim that the ancient Hebrews originated a custom of song-passing that was imitated by Greeks of the classical era and adopted by Christians in his own day.[10]

The *Homily on the Psalms* carries no attribution, but a Syriac fragment names Hippolytus as the author. On the basis of that assignment and certain linguistic parallels in several works of Hippolytus of Rome, Pierre Nautin accepts the ascription to Hippolytus and dates the homily to the early third century.[11] There is uncertainty, however, about whether the Hippolytan works in which Nautin finds linguistic parallels were all composed by Hippolytus of Rome, although a rough early third-century dating is generally accepted for them.[12] Allen Brent has made out a plausible case that the author of the *Homily*, whoever he was, belonged to the church of Rome as part of a circle or "school" devoted to Hippolytus and his teachings.[13]

---

9. In a letter to Caecilius, bishop of another city in the Roman province of northwest Africa, Cyprian explains, "When we dine, we cannot gather the people to our supper so that we might celebrate the truth of the sacrament in the presence of all the brotherhood." Evidently, Cyprian and the others he includes in this "we" were still gathering for "our supper," but the whole church was no longer invited. Cyprian, *Ep.* 63.16.1.

10. See chapter 2.

11. Pierre Nautin, *Le dossier d'Hippolyte et de Méliton dans les florilèges dogmatiques et chez les historiens modernes* (Éditions du Cerf, 1953), 103–105.

12. Many of the parallels are to the *Refutation of All Heresies*; some are to the *Commentary on Daniel* and *On Christ and Antichrist.* Regarding debates about the authorship of these works, see in particular Allen Brent, *Hippolytus and the Roman Church in the Third Century: Communities in Tension before the Emergence of a Monarch-Bishop* (Brill, 1995); and J. A. Cerrato, *Hippolytus between East and West: The Commentaries and the Provenance of the Corpus* (Oxford University Press, 2002).

13. Brent, *Hippolytus and the Roman Church in the Third Century*, 332–341.

The subject of the anonymous homily is the book of Psalms. According to the homilist, David chose four singers by lot, whose names were Asaph, Heman, Ethan, and Jeduthun. These men served as leaders of Levitical choruses.[14] They were also psalm composers, the homilist says, which explains why the superscriptions of the Psalter assign individual psalms to different persons or groups of singers. While all the psalms go back to David as the leader of psalm production,[15] the superscriptions refer to the work of David and the psalm leaders as composers of particular psalms or parts of psalms. Hence, when a superscription says "a psalm of Asaph," then Asaph was the composer. When a superscription says "a psalm for the sons of Korah," the composers were Asaph and Heman, and so on. As for the process, the homilist imagines that the psalms were composed during the singing, that is, as composition-in-performance. The Holy Spirit prompted a given psalmist to start singing, then at a certain point withdrew to bring that singer's contribution to an end. When that occurred, the rest of the singers, together with their choruses, responded with Alleluia.[16] None of these details are mentioned or even hinted at in the Psalter itself or in the biblical accounts of David and the Levitical singers. The author of the homily, however, and his audience presumably, found it plausible that David and his fellow psalmists proceeded in the way described.

A short essay titled "Eusebius of Caesaria Concerning *Diapsalma*" (included among the introductions to Eusebius's *Commentary on Psalms*) presents a similar picture. The essayist refers to "five leaders, who interpreted," that is, five song-leaders who received communications from the Spirit that they interpreted in song. These were "the ones chosen by David the King from the tribe of Levi, being by name Asaph [and] his sons, Korah, Heman, Ethan, Eduthun."[17] Like the homilist, the essayist describes choral Alleluias after each singer's performance, and he adds an additional idea when he connects these with the occasional appearance of the word *diapsalma* in the Psalter. "Where the grace of the Spirit is absent for a moment, the rest of the [musical] instruments not being moved, then they probably wrote *diapsalma*." The word *diapsalma* is a Greek translation of the Hebrew *selah*. There is reason to believe that the Greek translators interpreted *selah* as

14. *Hom. Pss.* 3.

15. In *Hom. Pss.* 6, the homilist says that all the psalms ἀναφέρονται τοῦ Δαυίδ. This somewhat vague locution is varied in §7, where he says that the psalms ἀναφέρεται εἰς τὸν Δαυίδ. They are attributed to David, the homilist goes on to explain, in the sense that he is the reason for their existence.

16. *Hom. Pss.* 5.

17. "Eusebius of Caesarea concerning *Diapsalmatos*" in *Comm. in psalm.* (PG 23: 76). Curiously, the author implies that the last three are not sons of the second, Korah, but that Korah is also one of the sons, perhaps of Asaph. Hence, he counts five psalm leaders instead of four.

a signal for a musical interlude on strings.[18] The essayist, however, interpreted *diapsalma* as an indication of the Spirit's movement in directing the compositional singing. Although the title of the essay assigns its views to Eusebius, the essay's content does not jibe with the remarks about *diapsalma* in the body of Eusebius's commentary, a sign of the essay's secondary character. Moreover, the essay contains language that is very similar to that of the *Homily*, at points even identical, which suggests that the essayist used the *Homily* as a source, or that both relied on an earlier third source. The two passages compare as follows:[19]

Anonymous *Homily on the Psalms*	"Eusebius of Caesaria Concerning *Diapsalma*"
These stand before the sanctuary praising God, one with cymbals, another with a psaltery, another with a harp, another with a cithara, another with a horn...	These stood before the sanctuary of the Lord, praising the ruler of all. One has cymbals, another a psaltery, another a harp, another a horn, another a cithara.
In their midst stands David, leading the leaders of the hymns himself...	In their midst stood David. Thus, they were leading the singers, holding the instruments in their hands.
And each, when moved by the Holy Spirit, hymns God. When, therefore, the Spirit fell on the blessed Asaph, all [the others] observed silence, submitting to a quiescent moment, being kept in order by the Spirit. And afterward they responded to the one singing in a hymn to God, saying, "Alleluia."	And each, when moved by the Spirit, hymns God; and all respond with "Alleluia" to the one singing.
	Whenever the grace of the Spirit withdrew for a while, the rest of the instruments not being moved, then, it seems, they wrote *diapsalma*.

18. See Albert Pietersma, tr., *A New English Translation of the Septuagint and Other Greek Translations Traditionally Included Under That Title: The Psalms* (Oxford University Press, 2000), xxiv.

19. *Hom. Pss.* 4; "Eusebius of Caesarea concerning *Diapsalmatos*" (PG 23: 76).

Both the homilist and the pseudo-Eusebian essayist assume that David and his fellow singers used "Alleluia" as a response. This detail also appears in another preface to Eusebius's commentary on the psalms, this one most likely by Eusebius himself, although exact parallels in wording show that he drew on the anonymous homily.[20] Eusebius describes "four harpers leading the songs," whom "David, having brought [the ark] to Jerusalem, selected by lot from the tribe of Levi" (namely, Asaph, Heman, Ethan, and Eduthun):

> Standing before the Ark of the Covenant of the Lord, they played and sang to the Lord, one with a harp, one with cymbals, one with a cithara, one with a psaltery. And the blessed David was standing in their midst, leading the leaders of the odes himself, holding a psaltery in his hands. Each sang and played, hymning God by the Holy Spirit in an orderly way. When, therefore, the Spirit fell on one of those leading the psalmody, the others observed silence, standing by and responding harmoniously with "Alleluia" to the one singing.[21]

Since none of the biblical stories of the singers of David's court and none of the psalms themselves imply this kind of compositional process or a responsorial format with Alleluia, the descriptions in the three Christian accounts must have been influenced by some other source or practice. There is a clue in the homilist's comment that the apostle Paul made use of the same turn-taking pattern when he instructed the Corinthians about the exercise of their spiritual gifts, the implication being that Christian liturgical order, rightly conducted, follows the procedure of David and his fellow singers, an order that Paul laid down as a rule for the church.[22] This raises the suspicion that Christian psalmodic practice influenced the picture of psalmody found in the three accounts about David and his

20. The following phrases of the homily are found nearly verbatim in Eusebius's remarks: ὧν μέσος ἵστατο Δαυίδ, αὐτὸς ἄρχων ἀρχόντων ᾠδῶν, κρατῶν ἐπὶ χεῖρα τὸ ψαλτήριον and Ἡνίκα τοίνυν ἐσκίρτα τὸ πνεῦμα ἐπὶ . . . ἡσυχίαν ἦγον. Slight differences are that Eusebius modifies the name Δαυίδ as ὁ μακάριος and that he uses the plural χειρᾶς instead of the singular χεῖρα. Eusebius, *Comm. in psalm.* (PG 23: 73).

21. Eusebius, *Comm. in psalm.* (PG 23: 73).

22. "Paul the apostle, making use of this rule (λόγῳ) and wanting to soundly establish the church in the way that Israel in the beginning behaved in good order, teaches as follows: 'If a revelation is given to one [prophet], let the other be quiet. For you can all prophesy one by one. For the Spirit of the prophets is subject to the prophets." *Hom. Pss.* 5 (quoting 1 Cor 14:30–32 in a somewhat condensed fashion).

co-psalmists.[23] Since the use of Alleluia refrains in Christian psalmody goes back to at least the time of Tertullian,[24] it is conceivable that Christian practice inspired the idea that David and his co-singers intoned Alleluia as a psalm response.

This possibility gains strength from the absence of any Jewish tradition about the use of Alleluia/Hallelujah as a response. First of all, in the Greek Bible, none of the psalms with *diapsalma* carry the Alleluia superscription. Hence, it was not a correlation of *diapsalma* and Alleluia in the Greek Psalter that led the pseudo-Eusebian essayist to imagine that *diapsalma* marks a moment for a group Alleluia. Second, in the Hebrew Bible (MT), "Hallelujah" stands at the beginning of two Hallel psalms (113 and 117) and it appears at the close of four (113, 115, 116, and 117).[25] It is very uncertain whether these Hallelujahs were meant to designate a refrain, or even whether they were later construed that way in Jewish tradition. In most instances, Hallelujahs are praise statements internal to their psalms. In several places in the Psalter, however, some pairs of "*Hallēl**" stand in succession in a way that could suggest that the first (in the form *Hallēlu Yah*) is a superscription (Psalms 113, 135, 146, 148, and 150) and the second an exclamation. In these cases, the Septuagint transliterates the first *Hallēluyah* as *Allēlouia* and renders the second with a Greek verb for praise. This shows that the translator(s) of the Septuagint Psalter construed the initial "Hallelujah" as a superscription. Moreover, the Septuagint also multiplies the number of Hallelujah/Alleluia superscriptions. Yet this multiplication appears to be motivated by exegetical-historical interests, not by an influence of liturgical practices.[26] Hence, there is nothing in the psalm inscriptions of the MT or the LXX suggesting that Hallelujah or Alleluia was a common response to a biblical psalm at any point in ancient Jewish history, although there is evidence that it was used as an exclamation of rejoicing in personal devotion and at Jewish festivals.[27]

The rabbis tell us how the Hallel was recited by Jews of the Roman era. In a discussion about the manner in which the Israelites performed the Song of the

23. So Harald Buchinger, "Die älteste erhaltene christliche Psalmenhomilie: Zu Verwendung und Verständnis des Psalters bei Hippolyt (Zweiter Teil)," *Trierer Theologische Zeitschrift* 104 (1995): 272–275.

24. Tertullian, *Orat.* 27 (discussed in chapter 2).

25. In the set of Hallel psalms in the MT, Hallelujah is found at the head of Psalm 113. Psalm 117:1 has a variation. Psalms 115–117 close with Hallelujah. Psalms 114 and 118 lack a Hallelujah at both places.

26. This is demonstrated in Albert Pietersma, "Exegesis and Liturgy in the Superscriptions of the Greek Psalter," in *Proceedings of the Xth Congress of the International Organization for the Septuagint and Cognate Studies, Oslo July-August 1998*, ed. Bernard Taylor (Scholars Press, 2001), 99–138.

27. See n. 32.

Sea (Exodus 15), the Mishnah quotes R. Akiba's opinion that they "responded word by word after Moses, as they do when they read the Hallel psalms."[28] A parallel passage in the Tosefta is more explicit. Akiba is now said to refer to the reciting of the Hallel in school by children in the following form: Moses said A and the people responded with A; Moses said B and the people responded with B; and so forth.[29] Rabbi Eleazar ben Yose offers a different opinion. The Israelites followed the pattern of response to an adult's reading of the Hallel in the synagogue: Moses said A and the people responded with A; Moses said B, and the people again responded with A.[30] In this form, the opening line is used as a refrain. Hence, the synagogue practice, which would have been conducted at Passover and certain other festivals, was for a leader to sing each line, and the people to sing the first line as a recurring refrain.[31] This means that the refrain for Psalm 113 was Hallelujah, probably also for Psalm 117, but that the other Hallel psalms were performed with different refrains, since their first lines are different.

The word "Hallelujah" or "Alleluia" appears in several other works, four of which antedate the passage in Tertullian's *On Prayer* and the anonymous *Homily on the Psalms.* Three are Jewish. One is Christian. In the Jewish writings, the word is an exclamation of praise or exultation.[32] In the Christian book of Revelation, Alleluia appears four times as a shout or word of praise, once being paired with "Amen."[33] None of these examples concern psalms, much less responses to psalms, and it is obvious that the author of Revelation got his understanding of Alleluia from Jewish tradition.[34]

---

28. *m. Soṭa* 5.4d–e. Translation from Jacob Neusner, *The Mishnah: A New Translation* (Yale University Press, 1988), 455.

29. *t. Soṭa* 6.2–3.

30. *t. Soṭa* 6.3.

31. Occasions for adults to read/sing the Hallel in the synagogue included Passover (see chapter 1) and certain other festivals, perhaps occasional ad hoc weekday gatherings as well. See Charles H. Cosgrove, *Music at Social Meals in Greek and Roman Antiquity: From the Archaic Period to the Age of Augustine* (Cambridge University Press, 2023), 265–305. The regular Sabbath service does not appear to have included a psalm liturgy until centuries later (see chapter 1 of the present book).

32. Tobit 13:18; 3 Macc 7:13 (unless τὸ ἀλληλούϊα here means "the Hallel;" see chapter 1 n. 10); *Vit. Adae et Ev.* (a.k.a. *Apoc. Mos.*) 43.4.

33. Rev 19:1, 3, 4, 6.

34. The picture does not change if the Christian examples in *Quaest. Barth.* 4.69 and 4.70 are included, since the *Questions of Bartholomew*, which is almost impossible to date, represents Alleluia as a one-word declaration. It is not a psalm response in either context. Christian Alleluia responses in the first several centuries are discussed more fully in chapter 10.

Silence in the Jewish sources about Alleluia as a psalm response encourages the conclusion that the anonymous homilist's account of Davidic psalm composition projects a Christian practice onto David and his fellow singers. It appears that the custom of singing an Alleluia response to a psalm was a distinctively Christian custom, not something that Christians learned from Jewish writings or from personal acquaintance with Jewish singing conventions.

Traveling Ascetics

Scripture song was also a practice of traveling ascetics, according to the pseudo-Clementine *Letters to Virgins.* Most scholars who comment on this work tentatively accept Harnack's judgment that it was penned in Syria or Palestine in the middle of the third century.[35] Originally composed in Greek, the book is most completely preserved in a Syriac manuscript. This Syriac version includes instructions about how wandering ascetics should behave when they cannot find Christians to take them in and have no choice but to seek hospitality from non-Christians. As guests of pagan householders, they should refrain from "casting their pearls before swine,"[36] for "we neither sing nor read Scriptures before gentiles, that we might not be like pipers or singers or soothsayers, the many who act this way and do these things to satisfy themselves with a mouthful of bread, and, for a little wine, 'sing songs of the Lord in the foreign land of the gentiles,' which is not permitted."[37] This implies that the usual practice of wandering ascetics, the one the author approves, was to lodge with Christians, which the author deemed an appropriate setting for Scripture songs, which the wandering ascetics performed in return for hospitality. Their Scripture songs must have included biblical psalms and canticles.[38]

---

35. Adolf von Harnack, "Die pseudoclementinischen Briefe de virginitate und die Entstehung des Mönchtums," *Sitzungsberichte der königlich-preussischen Akademie der Wissenschaften zu Berlin* 21 (1891): 363–373; Hugo Duensing, ed., "Die dem Klemens von Rom zugeschriebenen Briefe über die Jungfräulichkeit," *Zeitschrift für Kirchengeschichte* 63 (1950/1951): 168; Arthur Vööbus, "Ein merkwürdiger Pentateuchtext in der pseudo-klementinischen Schrift De virginitate," *Oriens Christianus* 43 (1959): 54–58 (arguing for a Syrian provenance); Alfred Adam, "Erwägungen zur Herkunft der Didache," *Zeitschrift für Kirchengeschichte* 68 (1957): 24 (1–47) (proposing a second-century date, ca. 170).

36. Ps.-Clement, *De virg.* [*Ep. virg.*] 2.6.1–2.

37. Ps.-Clement, *De virg.* [*Ep. virg.*] 2.6.3–4. I have relied on the Latin translation of the Syriac in the Pseudo-Clementine *Letters to Virgins* in Franz Diekamp, ed. *Patres apostolici*, vol. 2 (Tübingen: Laupp, 1913), 39.

38. The admonition says nothing about composed Christian hymns but may not have been comprehensive in describing the repertoires of the wandering ascetics.

Psalmody at Paschal Gatherings

The earliest Christian Paschal observance was "Quartodeciman," a term that refers to the focal date of the observance, 14 Nisan, the date of the Jewish Passover, which the Quartodecimans regarded as the date of the crucifixion. The Jewish Passover seder took place, according to the Jewish divisions of days, after sunset, which was the beginning of 15 Nisan. This domestic meal included Hallel psalms, but there is no evidence that Christians adopted this custom for their own Christ-focused Pascha. Third-century Christians did sing psalms as part of their Paschal liturgies. Understanding the place of Christian Paschal psalmody requires a reconstruction of the history of the feast.

The Quartodeciman Pascha was established in Asia Minor in the second century. It is very likely that Easter evolved from it or, in some places, in reaction to it. The *Didascalia*, composed in the early third century, reflects this evolution and was itself probably Quartodeciman in an earlier form or in some of its source material.[39] I will focus on the evidence in the *Didascalia* that suggests that Quartodecimans and the churches addressed by the *Didascalia* not only included readings of psalms at their Paschal vigils but celebrated with a fast-breaking supper where they sang psalms of joy and thanksgiving. Tracing out this evidence requires close examination of a text whose layering complicates historical reconstruction of the practices reflected in the work.

Language in the *Didascalia* suggests that its purpose may have been to transform a Quartodeciman observance of Pascha into an Easter celebration; or else the *Didascalia* took such a transformation for granted and meant only to provide its own regulations for Easter. In any case, the *Didascalia* contains clear traces of a Quartodeciman framework, elements that have been incorporated into a celebration of a Sunday Easter.[40] It quotes from the Mosaic law of the Passover and instructs that because Moses commanded that the Israelites observe the Passover "from the tenth until the fourteenth," the church is to "fast in the days of the Pascha from the tenth, which is the second day of the week."[41] The appeal to Moses for a date-span of the 10th through the 14th of Nissan clearly derives from a Quartodeciman version or source, but the dates have been reinterpreted

39. The earliest information about the Quartodeciman Pascha is given in Eusebius, whose sources include a letter by Bishop Polycrates (*H.E.* 5.23–24). *Peri Pascha* by Melito of Sardis (circa 160–190) is a sermon preached at a Quartodeciman service, but it contains no liturgical information.

40. Gerard Rouwhorst's assiduous analysis of these matters, in several publications, has been met with a general consensus regarding the Quartodeciman heritage of the *Didascalia*'s Easter. For the present discussion, see principally Gerard A. M. Rouwhorst, *Les hymnes pascales d'Ephrem de Nisibe: Analyse théologique et recherche sur l'évolution de la fête pascale chrétienne à Nisibe et à Edesse et dans quleques églises voisines au quartrième siècle* (Brill: 1989), vol. 1: 162–193.

41. *Didasc.* 21 // *Const. ap.* 5.18.

so that they no longer specify the dates of a liturgical calendar for keeping the Paschal fast but serve as "historical" warrants for beginning the Paschal fast on Monday of a Holy Week that concludes with Easter Sunday.

Speaking in the voice of the apostles and weaving liturgical directives into a description of Jesus's final week in Jerusalem, the *Didascalia* sets forth and explains the requirements for its fasts and vigils as follows ("parallel" section numbers in the *AC* provided for convenience of location):[42]

1. The church is to fast from the second day of the week through the end of the week; and on Friday and on Saturday, they are to keep vigil "for the entire night . . . reading the prophets and with the Gospel and with the psalms with fear and trembling and constant supplication" until the third hour of the night, when the fast is broken. *Didasc.* 21 // *Const. ap.* 5.18.
2. "The fast of the Friday and of the Sabbath is especially binding on you, as is the vigil and the watching of the Sabbath, and the reading of the Scriptures and the psalms, and prayers and intercession on behalf of those who have sinned, and the watching and the hope of the resurrection of our Lord Jesus, until the third hour in the night which is after the Sabbath. And thereafter, offer your offerings, eat and be merry, rejoice and be glad, because Christ, the pledge of our resurrection, is risen." *Didasc.* 21 // *Const. ap.* 5.19.6–7
3. "For this reason [the suffering of the messiah and the ruination of the people of Israel who opposed him], you are to mourn on their behalf on the Sabbath day of the Pascha until the third hour of the night following. And then, at the resurrection of Christ, rejoice and be glad on their behalf, and break your fast." *Didasc.* 21 // *Const. ap.* 5.20.9

In these passages, the *Didascalia* states rules for the fasts and vigils that conclude on Easter Sunday. Its statements about the vigils mention the reading of the Scriptures, including psalms (nos. 1 and 2). Were these psalm lessons sung? Perhaps. The distinction between *Scripture* readings and *psalm* readings places psalms in a special category. Moreover, in a different context (although unrelated to Pascha or liturgy), the *Didascalia* speaks of psalms as *songs*.[43] That

42. The following translations are from Stewart-Sykes, *The Didascalia Apostolorum*, 220–222 (with slight alterations of capitalization and punctuation, none affecting the sense).

43. See *Didasc.* 2 (and see the paraphrase in *Const. ap.* 1.5–6), discussed above under "Melodic Reading of the Psalter?"

said, melodic reading of psalm lessons is not explicitly documented until the fourth century.

Eusebius also mentions song at Paschal vigils. Writing nearly a hundred years after the *Didascalia*, he claims that the Therapeutae described by Philo in *On the Contemplative Life* must have been Christians of the apostolic age because their customs so closely resemble those of the church in Eusebius's time, including their singing at a certain feast.[44] This implies a continuous tradition from the era of the apostles to Eusebius's own day. His comparison must have been based on his own first-hand experiences of Paschal psalmody since his teenage years (perhaps the 280s), that is, as far back as he could recall. Otherwise, he would not have believed—and could not have imagined that he could plausibly claim—that the Easter song-style of churches in his day was a continuation of a song-style already in use among Christians in the first century.

Eusebius's comparison does not claim that the Therapeutae celebrated an annual Pascha; the festival Philo describes took place every seven weeks. Nor does Eusebius claim that the *ordo* of the Therapeutae's feast was the same as that of the Christian Pascha in his own time. Instead, he singles out certain customs of their celebration that were typical at the church's Pascha in his day: (1) fastings, (2) all-night vigils, (3) "attention to the word of God," and (4) songs.[45] Philo himself does not specifically mention fasting in his account of the Therapeutae's feast, but he does say (and Eusebius notes) that the Therapeutae fasted every day and consumed food only in the evening.[46] At the festal supper, Philo says, the community president gives a Scripture-expounding address; individual singing with group responses follows; next the Therapeutae consume a modest meal; after which they spend the entire night engaged in choral song.[47] The gathering begins and ends with prayer. In his rehearsal of the Therapeutae's holiday, Eusebius does not mention the meal, and the parallel he draws to the Therapeutae's singing summarizes Philo's description of their opening ritual of responsorial song, ignoring their after-dinner song or perhaps conflating it with the presupper singing.[48]

In another passage, Eusebius mentions the prayers of the church at the Easter vigil.[49] It is possible that "prayer" was sometimes a shorthand for "prayers and

44. Eusebius, *H.E.* 2.16–17. See also my discussions of the Therapeutae and their song in chapter 1.

45. Eusebius, *H.E.* 2.17.21–22.

46. Philo, *Contempl.* 34; Eusebius, *H.E.* 2.17.16.

47. Philo, *Contempl.* 64–89.

48. Eusebius, *H.E.* 2.17.22.

49. Eusebius, *H.E.* 6.34.

psalms" in fourth-century liturgical references,[50] which would make sense here, inasmuch as the parallels Eusebius saw between the Christian Pascha of his day and the feast of the Therapeutae included "the hymns which are customarily sung by us."[51] Greek-speaking Christians often used the term "hymns" for biblical psalms. Eusebius himself does so in each instance in his church history where, formulating in his own words, he uses the term "hymn" in a way that implies its type; he clearly means a biblical psalm.[52] In the one place where he describes songs composed by Christians, he calls them "psalms and odes," not hymns.[53] It is particularly telling that in his paraphrase of Philo's descriptions of the Therapeutae's festal song, he omits Philo's reference to songs both old and new, the new ones being composed by members of the sect. He does not claim that the Therapeutae composed hymns to Christ. Nor does he mention the Therapeutae's custom of dividing into two choirs for their after-supper song. Eusebius reduces Philo's lengthy descriptions of the Therapeutae's festive musical activities to "the hymns which we are accustomed to recite and how, while one chants with regular rhythm, the others, listening to the hymns in silence, join in by sounding forth the endings."[54] Hence, when Eusebius claims that the hymns sung responsorially by the Therapeutae in Philo's era were the same hymns that Christians of Eusebius's own time sang at Paschal vigils, he probably means biblical psalms.

In describing the vigil prescribed by the *Didascalia*, I passed over the question of the timing of the fast-breaking and its association with a festive supper that probably included singing. Variations in timing from one Christian group to the next included fast-breaking as early as the evening. Hence, some Christians may have terminated their fast by holding a community supper with the usual post-supper song. Passages in Eusebius's corpus show that even in his day, the dominical Easter celebration was observed according to somewhat diverse customs of fast-breaking. In *Gospel Questions*, he mentions an ambiguous passage in Matthew that might encourage breaking the fast on the Sabbath evening, a few hours before midnight, "if the evangelist meant that." Nevertheless, he adds, "we

50. See Juan Mateos, "La vigile cathédrale chez Égérie," *Orientalia christiana periodica* 27 (1961): 299–301.

51. Eusebius, *H.E.* 2.17.22. Eusebius paraphrases loosely. According to Philo, the Therapeutae sang newly composed hymns and hymns by various "poets of old," by which he probably meant biblical songs, psalms and perhaps canticles (*Contempl.* 80).

52. These are *H.E.* 1.2.5; 10.3.3 (see the discussion of this passage in chapter 6); and two instances in 10.4.5–6 (where he quotes someone's oration in words that he almost certainly composed for his representation of the speech).

53. *H.E.* 5.28.6.

54. Eusebius, *H.E.* 2.17.22.

are accustomed to ending the fast not in the evening of the Sabbath but when night has begun—at midnight or cockcrow or near dawn."[55] The *Didascalia* instructs that the fast is to be broken in "the third hour of the night" (nos. 1–3 in the passages listed above), but it also says that the people are to keep vigil for "the entire night" (no. 1).

At one point at least, the hours of the Paschal instructions of the *Didascalia* are reckoned according to Jewish custom. On Friday, the day of the crucifixion, there were three hours of darkness, the *Didascalia* says, "from the ninth hour until evening . . . and afterwards the night of the Sabbath of the passion." The *Didascalia* next quotes or paraphrases a version of the Gospel of Matthew as follows: "'On the evening of the Sabbath as the first day of the week was dawning came Mary and the other Mary, Magdalene, to see the tomb.'"[56] These time references reflect the Jewish custom of marking the beginning of a day at sundown. Hence, if we assume that the *Didascalia* operates with a Jewish conception of the hours in its instructions for the fasts and vigils, then "the third hour of the night which is after the Sabbath" means three hours after sunset on Sunday, around 9 p.m.[57] It is possible, however, that this time-scheme reflects a Quartodeciman layer of tradition in the *Didascalia*, a tradition that the author-redactor of the final edition has revised, although not without leaving traces that create certain tensions or contradictions.[58] An example is the instruction that the vigil is to last "the entire night" (see no. 1 above). Following this line of reasoning, we might infer that the final redactor revised the time-length of the vigil without correcting or dropping the expression "third hour in the night."[59] It is also possible that the vigil pertained to Friday night, not Saturday night, for there are

55. Eusebius, *Quaest. ev. ad Marinum* 2.2 (PG 22: 941; SC 523: 204). This valuable clue to the history of the Easter fast is pointed out by Harald Buchinger, "Breaking the Fast: The Central Moment of the Paschal Celebration in Historical Context and Diachronic Perspective," in *Sanctifying Texts, Transformative Ritual: Encounters in Liturgical Studies: Essays in Honour of Gerard A. M. Rouwhorst*, ed. Paul van Geest, Marcel Poorthuis, and Else Rose (Brill, 2017), 196.

56. *Didasc.* 21 // *Const. ap.* 5.14. Tr. from Stewart-Sykes, *The Didascalia Apostolorum*, 214.

57. This is the interpretation of Rouwhorst, *Hymnes*, vol. 1, 174; also Stewart-Sykes, *The Didascalia Apostolorum*, 220 n. 44; and Buchinger, "Breaking the Fast," 198.

58. The likelihood that the *Didascalia*'s instructions for Pascha reflect two or more layers of text, the earliest being thoroughly Quartodeciman, has been shown by Rouwhorst (see n. 40).

59. Bradshaw assumes that the third hour refers to Roman time. But that does not remove the apparent contradiction, since a fast broken at 3 a.m. does not satisfy the instruction that the church should fast the entire night. Nor does Bradshaw claim that it does. See Paul F. Bradshaw, "The Origins of Easter," in *Passover and Easter: Origin and History to Modern Times*, ed. Paul F. Bradshaw and Lawrence A. Hoffman (University of Notre Dame Press, 1999), 88.

confusions about this in the manuscript tradition.[60] Assuming that the vigil was to begin at the close of Saturday (the Sabbath), the text in its final form may not, in fact, contain a contradiction. If the vigil and the fast overlapped but did not precisely coincide in time-length, the tension evaporates. The vigil was to last until dawn, but it was divided into two phases: a fasting mourning phase and a fast-breaking celebratory phase.

Those who broke their fast before sundown must have held a community supper, and those who postponed the breaking of their fast until 9 p.m. probably also held a supper. In both cases, any singing would have been a species of the usual song at church suppers in this era, bearing a resemblance to the pattern described in the apocryphal *Acts of Paul*, where the church fasts, breaks its fast with a supper, then spends the night singing psalms and hymns until dawn.[61] As pointed out in chapter 2, although the story in *Acts of Paul* is fictional, it probably reflects church customs known to the author, since neither the Pauline letters nor the book of Acts describes song-filled after-supper vigils.

A late-night Paschal supper followed by a vigil appears in the second-century *Epistula apostolorum*, in an account in which the resurrected Jesus instructs his disciples to keep "the remembrance of his death, which is the Passover." In this story, Jesus goes on to refer to this remembrance as an "agape," a term for the Christian community supper. Moreover, in a prophecy about Peter's arrest before Passover during the early years of the Christian mission, Jesus declares that "when you complete my agape and my remembrance at the crowing of the cock, [Peter] will again be taken and thrown in prison for a testimony."[62] Assuming that the Paschal narrative in *Epistula apostolorum* was patterned on liturgical practice or sought to prescribe a pattern for it, the procedure it describes is to celebrate a Passover supper that extends deep into the night. This supper breaks the usual fast.

The custom of holding a Paschal community meal is one of two factors that would help explain why some Christians of Pentapolis in Cyrenaica celebrated Easter by breaking their fast "in the evening," according to Dionysius, patriarch of Alexandria from 248–264.[63] If Dionysius refers to a Quartodeciman custom or survival,[64] then the Christians of Pentapolis timed their fast-breaking

60. See Buchinger, "Breaking the Fast," 198 n. 29 (opining that the textual uncertainty is an important argument for the "quartodeciman pedigree of the dominical paschal vigil").

61. *Acts of Paul* 12.

62. *Ep. ap.* 15 (26) (Ethiopic and Coptic). The translations are from C. Detlef G. Muller, tr. "Epistula apostolorum," in *New Testament Apocrypha*, vol. 1, rev., ed. Wilhelm Schneemelcher, tr. R. Mcl. Wilson (Clarke, 1991), 257–258.

63. Dionysius of Alexandria, *Ep.* 14.1.

64. This is the opinion Paul F. Bradshaw and Maxwell E. Johnson, *The Origins of Feasts, Fasts and Seasons in Early Christianity* (SPCK, 2011), 53. See further Buchinger, "Breaking the Fast," 195–196.

in relation to the Jewish Passover meal. That is, the church's community supper remained customary for their annual Pascha even in an era when the regular celebration of the Eucharist had been—or was in the process of being—shifted to the morning. This shift may explain why Dionysius himself endorsed a breaking of the Easter fast at cockcrow, which people associated with the approach of morning, and why this was also the custom of the church at Rome.[65] An Easter morning Eucharist could have taken place at an early morning hour. Or else it was deemed acceptable to take food before the morning service. In either case, the fast was seen as a preparation for the celebratory morning Eucharist.

According to Dionysius, the fast should be broken "after the time of our Lord's resurrection," but he also points out that the gospels say nothing definite about the hour of the resurrection.[66] Hence, Christians in the see of Basilides, his correspondent, who celebrated the dominical Easter by breaking their fast in the evening (before midnight) could have reasoned that Jesus rose shortly after the first day of the week began, according to Jewish reckoning. In any case, given the uncertainty about the hour of the resurrection, Dionysius's own preference for a fast-breaking shortly before dawn was probably influenced by the new custom of celebrating the Eucharist at an Easter morning service. Yet that preference did not hold sway in Alexandria during the ensuing decades. Rather, Alexandrians of the fourth century broke their Easter fast in the evening. This is evident from the formulas used by Athanasius at the close of his festal Easter epistles, which suggest that the church in his time followed a Quartodeciman custom with respect to the hour of the fast-breaking, although they did so within the framework of the dominical Easter.[67]

I have taken the time to describe the evidence for Paschal fast-breaking because I assume that *celebratory Paschal suppers* would have included song. Yet all the evidence is circumstantial. In a nutshell, the clues suggest that those who held a Paschal community supper during the evening at the end of 14 Nisan (which, post-sundown, was the beginning of 15 Nisan in Jewish time-reckoning), as well as those who celebrated the dominical Easter as a community supper in

---

65. People relied on the cock's cry to wake them in time for their morning responsibilities. It is not altogether clear whether the cock typically crowed shortly before dawn or nearer to 3 or 4 a.m. Modern observations of the time of the cockcrow in spring in Jerusalem are set forth in Richard Bauckham, *The Jewish World around the New Testament* (Mohr Siebeck, 2008), 412–417. There is also a clue in Ambrose's hymn, *Aeterne rerum conditor*, where the cockcrow heralds the onset of dawn. The same implication is found in a poem about a cock in *Greek Anthology* 7, no. 202.

66. Dionysius of Alexandria, *Ep.* 14.1.

67. See the references in Harald Buchinger, "Die Bedeutung der Auferstehung für Termin, Gestalt und Gehalt der ältesten Osterfeier," in *"If Christ has not been raised. . .": Studies on the Reception of the Resurrection Stories and the Belief in the Resurrection in the Early Church*, ed. Joseph Verheyden et al. (Vandenhoeck & Ruprecht, 2016), 183–184 n. 89.

the evening hours before Easter Sunday began (the hours before midnight), would have sung psalms and hymns of joy and thanksgiving as a natural part of their after-supper celebration. But the closest thing to a reference to sympotic music-making at a Paschal supper is a single expression in the *Didascalia* in an instruction that Connolly translates, "eat and make good cheer" and Stewart-Sykes renders "eat and be merry."[68] The statement comes after a reference to offering the gifts of the Eucharist, and it is followed by a further reference to the mood of joy in celebrating the resurrection. It would be odd if a joyous Paschal meal featured only festive eating and drinking but no after-supper song. Assuming that there was song, it probably included psalm-singing, psalms having been singled out in the immediately preceding description of the fasting Christians' vigil as readings additional to "Scripture" readings ("the reading of Scripture and the psalms").[69]

To the extent that the *Didascalia* reflects longstanding Paschal customs, it almost certainly attests a festive meal that was originally a social meal and not a liturgical ceremony. But in a Christian text composed in the 230s, the contemporary sense of words about eating and merrymaking need not be taken to mean that the church reclined and dined as in the old days. The traditional language of feasting could have been retained as part of a description of gatherings that took a more ceremonial liturgical form, with people standing to receive Communion and sing. Yet if spatial accommodations were large enough to permit them to sit, perhaps they enjoyed more of a regular meal and continued drinking after their meal as they engaged in song, just as the Christians at Carthage had done at their agapes only a few decades earlier.

Since the Quartodecimans adhered to some aspects of Jewish custom, they may have sung Hallel psalms at this supper, since the Hallel was probably traditional at Jewish Passover suppers in the second century.[70] Moreover, the Hallel psalms are celebratory and would certainly have been suitable as gladsome song at an Easter supper among those who made the adjustment encouraged by late second-century bishops and church councils to orient the timing of their Paschal fast so that they held their feast on Easter Sunday. If Hallel psalms were part of Quartodeciman suppers, however, it is doubtful that they were also adopted for Easter suppers by a significant number of nonQuartodeciman Christians, since no Hallel psalm is mentioned as either a Communion psalm or an Easter psalm in extant Christian literature of the first three centuries.

---

68. *Didasc.* 21 // *Const. ap.* 5.19; *Didascalia Apostolorum: The Syriac Version Translated and Accompanied by the Verona Latin Fragments*, ed. and tr. R. Hugh Connolly (Clarendon, 1929), 190; Stewart-Sykes, *The Didascalia Apostolorum*, 221.

69. *Didasc.* 21 // *Const. ap.* 5.19 (Stewart-Sykes, *The Didascalia Apostolorum*, 221).

70. See chapter 1.

Easter psalmody is also mentioned in a synodal letter concerning Paul of Samosata, bishop of Antioch from 260 to 268. Eusebius quotes the letter, which accuses Paul of banning Christ-hymns at Antioch when he was the bishop there and instructing a choir of women to "sing to him" at a Paschal service.[71] Since Paul rejected Christ-hymns on the grounds that they were recent Christian compositions, it is doubtful that he redressed this "problem" by commissioning new hymns in his own honor. Nor does the bishops' letter say that he did. Instead, the implication is that the songs were old and traditional, the offense or blasphemy being that they were sung "to" him as he sat on an ostentatious throne. Hence, it is likely that he had his choir sing biblical psalms to him.[72]

Since Paul also refused to confess that "the Son of God descended from heaven" but claimed that Jesus was "from below" (a mortal), and since some of Paul's supporters "who sang to him and praised him among the people" claimed that Paul himself was an angel descended from heaven,[73] the bishops could well have alleged that Paul intended to be hymned with biblical psalms as a divine person. Perhaps Paul meant to imply that he himself was in some way a messianic subject of the psalms. Or perhaps his intent was a more modest desire to be honored by ceremonial psalmody during the service.[74]

The bishops' letter does not claim that psalms had not been sung at Easter or other services prior to Paul's interventions in the liturgy, only that Paul banned Christ-hymns and organized a choir of female devotees to sing psalms to him. As for the implication that Antioch had a tradition of Christ-hymns at Easter, this does not fit very well with Eusebius's account of Paschal song. Eusebius, confronted with Philo's references to the Therapeutae's custom of singing songs that they themselves had composed, chose to omit that detail when he equated their hymnody with the Paschal hymnody of the church in his own day (see above). Yet Eusebius was familiar with composed Christian hymns, for he mentions them at a later point in his history.[75]

---

71. Eusebius, *H.E.* 7.30.10.

72. This is also the conclusion drawn by Martin Hengel in his article, "The Song about Christ in Earliest Worship," in idem, *Studies in Early Christology* (T. & T. Clark, 1995), 247 n. 48.

73. Eusebius, *H.E.* 7.30.11.

74. On the honorific function of psalms in certain situations, see chapters 9 and 13.

75. Eusebius, *H.E.* 28.5 (in his own criticism of Paul of Samosata).

CHAPTER FOUR

Psalm Lessons

THE EVIDENCE FOR psalmody progressively increases in the fourth century, and new occasions are mentioned. One of these is the reading from Scripture that precedes the homily in services of the word.

Scholars of an earlier era assumed that the sung psalm lesson of the fourth-century West was the Gradual psalm or its precursor.[1] They knew that Augustine sometimes preached on the sung psalm.[2] They also knew that in Augustine's church, this psalm was performed by the lector. They assumed that the singing of one or more psalms in the service of the word was a custom that the primitive church adopted from the synagogue.[3] Hence, they did not ask why it was a *lector* who sang the psalm or why the *singing* of a psalm was placed among the readings.

In the mid-1980s, James McKinnon, having discovered that psalmody was not a fixed part of Sabbath services in the ancient synagogue,[4] recognized that if the synagogue was not the model for the church's sung psalm lesson, some other explanation of its origin was needed. McKinnon astutely reasoned that the placement of a sung psalm among the readings and its delivery by a lector argued for its origin as an ordinary nonlyrical reading.[5] This persuasive analysis leads us back into the history of the lessons as the setting in which the sung psalm arose.

The History of Sung Psalm Readings

The question of the origin of the sung psalm lesson entails two questions. First, what is the earliest evidence for a psalm lesson as part of the Scripture readings

1. See, for example, *The New International Encyclopedia*, ed. Daniel C. Gilman, Harry T. Peck, and Frank M. Colby (Dodd, Mead and Co., 1906), 98 (*s.v.* "Gradual").

2. See Hugh Pope, *Saint Augustine of Hippo: Essays Dealing with His Life and Times and Some Features of His Work* (Sands and Co., 1937), 52–53.

3. This opinion is expressed by Peter Wagner in the 1901 edition of his introduction to Gregorian chant. Peter Wagner, *Einführung in die gregorianischen Melodien: Ein Handbuch der Choralwissenschaft*, vol. 1, 2nd ed. (Universitäts-Buchhandlung, 1901), 84.

4. James W. McKinnon, "On the Question of Psalmody in the Ancient Synagogue," *Early Music History* 6 (1986): 159–191. On this subject, see chapter 1.

5. James W. McKinnon "The Fourth-Century Origin of the Gradual," *Early Music History* 7 (1987): 91–106.

in a service of the word? Second, what is the earliest evidence for the singing of such a lesson? The question is complicated by the fact that references to lyrical readings of psalms in church do not always make clear whether a prehomily lesson, a psalm read lyrically at the daily office, or a vigil is meant.

In Justin Martyr's Greek-speaking congregation of Syrian Christians at Rome in the mid-second century, one or more persons read from "the memoirs of the apostles or the books of the prophets" at the beginning of each service.[6] A sermon ensued, then prayer; after that, Communion. To what extent this order was followed elsewhere is unknown. A generation later, in Tertullian's Carthage, there may have been Scripture reading and instruction before the consumption of the community meal, then song afterward.[7] As we have seen, Tertullian also lists Scripture readings, sung *psalmi*, discourses, and prayers as characteristic activities at "the solemnities of the Lord," an expression that could refer to a particular type of church meeting or to church gatherings of various sorts.[8] The *psalmi* probably included biblical psalms or psalm excerpts, but Tertullian's list does not purport to be a service order. Nor is it clear that the psalms were lessons, read before homilies.

In one of his sermons on the book of Numbers, Origen comments on how listeners receive different Scripture lessons, presumably before the sermon. "When the gospels or the apostle or the psalms are read," he observes, they are received gladly (unlike readings from Numbers, he adds).[9] This suggests that in early third-century Alexandria, Scripture lessons regularly included readings from the book of Psalms. But Origen does not imply that psalm readings were sung.

Among the earliest pieces of evidence for lyrical renderings of psalm readings at church services are some canons promulgated by the Council of Laodicea. This synod probably took place sometime between 345 and 381,[10] and one of

6. Justin Martyr, *1 Apol.* 67.3.

7. Tertullian, *Apol.* 39. For a discussion of the structure of this chapter of the *Apologeticum* and an argument that 39.2–4 pertains to instruction at the beginning of the community meal, whose after-supper song is described in 39.17–18, see Charles H. Cosgrove, "Word and Table: The Origins of a Liturgical Sequence," *Vigiliae Christianae* 74 (2020): 359–360.

8. Tertullian, *An.* 9.4. See the discussion of this passage in chapter 2.

9. Origen, *In Num.*, Hom. 27.1.4.

10. Regarding the date of the council, see the summary of the evidence in F. J. E. Boddens Hosang, *Establishing Boundaries: Jewish-Christian Relations in Early Council Texts and the Writings of Church Fathers* (Brill, 2000), 91–92; see also Ulrich Huttner, *Early Christianity in the Lycus Valley* (Brill, 2013), 294–295. Note that Canons 1 through 19 show one form of wording for introducing their rules (περὶ τοῦ), while Canons 20 through 59 exhibit a different form (ὅτι οὐ δεῖ). This may imply that the latter derive from a different and later conciliar source than the former, although that is far from certain.

its canons shows that the bishops of this synod favored the assignment of psalm readings to singers, instead of leaving that duty to the regular readers. Canon 15 directs "that no other persons should sing a psalm (*psallein*) in church except the canonical singers, who ascend the platform and sing from the parchments [a fine vellum copy of Scripture]." The issuance of this rule implies that not all churches restricted the readings of psalms to canonical singers, whether it was because they did not ordain singers or because they sometimes permitted a lector to sing a psalm when a singer was not available. A distinction between readers and singers is assumed in Canon 23, which instructs that "neither the reader nor the singer should wear a scarf (or "stole") and thus read or sing." Canons 15 and 23 do not specify the setting(s) they mean to regulate, but the language of Canon 17 implies the daily office when it demands that "the psalms should not be consecutive in the service; instead, between each psalm there should be a reading."[11] Hence, it is possible that none of the three rules has prehomily lessons in view.

Athanasius drops a remark about liturgical psalm reading in his *Letter to Marcellinus*, which cannot be dated except to say that it was probably written between 328, when he became bishop of Alexandria, and his death in 373. The *Letter* is mostly concerned with private reading of the Psalter, but one passage mentions how psalm readings are appropriated by hearers: "the one who hears the one who is reading as concerning himself receives the spoken song."[12] Where did this take place in the Christian community at Alexandria? A setting that Athanasius mentions explicitly in another writing is the vigil he describes in *On His Flight*. On this occasion, the deacon read a psalm, and the people responded with one of the verses as a refrain.[13] An anecdote about Athanasius, told by Augustine, mentions sung psalm lessons, claiming that Athanasius demanded a reduced lyricism from the reader. This suggests that readers in Alexandria sang psalms melodically, *too* melodically in Athanasius's opinion.[14]

11. According to Taft, the urban daily office did not typically feature Scripture readings, besides psalmody. But he finds exceptions in sources from Egypt and Cappadocia. See Robert Taft, *The Liturgy of the Hours in East and West: The Origins of the Divine Office and Its Meaning for Today* (Liturgical, 1986), 32–33, 34–36, and 39. For Egypt, he cites the *Canons of Hippolytus* (canons 21, 26, and 27) and Paphnutius's *History of the Monks of the Egyptian Desert*; for Cappadocia he cites Socrates's *Church History*. He does not happen to mention Canon 17 of the Council of Laodicea. I also note a reference to Scripture readings at the daily office in *Const. ap.* 8.34.8–10. Taft's remarks may not have the urban West in view, but I will mention a further reference in Augustine, *Ep.* 29.10–11.

12. Athanasius, *Ep. Marc.* 11 (PG 27: 21).

13. Athanasius, *Apol. pro fug. sua* 24.4.

14. Augustine, *Conf.* 10.33.50. Not everything about this anecdote is plausible. Writing in his own words, Athanasius himself emphasizes that "the Lord has ordained" that psalms should be

References to sung psalms among the lessons also appear in the *Apostolic Constitutions*, where we find the following instruction:

> Let the reader, standing in an elevated place in the middle, read the books of Moses and of Joshua, son of Nun, and of Judges and Kings, and of Chronicles and of the return from exile; after them the books of Job and Solomon and the six prophets. These readings being done, two by two, let someone else sing the hymns of David, and let the people sing the endings in response.[15]

Like the canons of the Council of Laodicea, the *Apostolic Constitutions* distinguishes the reader from the one who sings. The setting is a pre-eucharistic service of the word, and the plural "hymns of David" does not necessarily imply that more than one psalm was to be sung at such a service, since the expression is probably a book title.

John Chrysostom occasionally mentions a sung psalm as one of the Scriptures delivered before he preached.[16] In a sermon on 1 Corinthians, for example, he differentiates between the reader and the singer, observing that "because there must be one voice in the church, therefore only the reader speaks, and he who holds the office of bishop sits and keeps quiet; and only the singer sings, and when all respond, the voice goes forth as from one mouth. And only the preacher preaches."[17]

The earliest evidence for sung psalm lessons in the West may be some late fourth-century references to the office of "singer." In a treatise composed between 388 and 394, Ambrose refers to the *psaltae*.[18] Writing in 393 to a presbyter in

---

"read *with song*" and speaks of "the melodic reading of the Psalter" (*Ep. Marc.* 28; PG 27: 40). See the discussion of the anecdote in chapter 12.

15. *Apost. const.* 2.57.5–6.

16. John Chrysostom, *In psalm. 41*, 1; *In psalm. 117*, 1; *In psalm. 150*, 1; *In 1 Cor.*, Hom. 36. 6. It is not certain in any of these references whether the sermon was delivered when John was a presbyter in Antioch (386 to early 398) or when he was bishop in Constantinople (398 to June of 404). I base this on Wendy Mayer's cautious criteria for assigning provenance to the sermons. See Wendy Mayer, *The Homilies of St. John Chrysostom—Provenance: Reshaping the Foundations* (Pontificio Istituto Orientale, 2005).

17. John Chrysostom, *In 1 Cor.*, Hom. 36.6 (PG 61: 315; Field, *Interp. in. ep. Paul.* 2: 461).

18. Ambrose, *Interpel. Job et Dauid* 4.6.24 (PL 14: 821; CSEL 32/2: 284). On the dating of this treatise to between 388 and 394, see the summary of discussion in Giuseppe Visonà, ed., *Cronologia Ambrosiana, Bibliografia Ambrosiana (1900–2000)* (Biblioteca Ambrosiana, 2004), 120–121.

Italy, Jerome distinguishes cantors from readers in a way that assumes the familiarity of his correspondent with these offices.[19] One of the canons of the Third Council of Carthage, held in around 397, also makes this distinction.[20] The office of cantor in the West probably presupposes the influence of the East and the Eastern development of sung psalm lessons that were originally delivered by readers but were eventually assigned to designated singers.

Finally, Augustine's sermons show that in Hippo during his episcopate (391-430), there was always a prehomily psalm lesson (which would have been given between the gospel and the epistle).[21] In quite a few of his sermons, Augustine mentions that the congregation had sung a response to the psalm lesson.[22] Although few of these sermons can be dated with confidence, at least one was probably preached between 396 and 400.

Psalms "Before the Sacrifice"

A further stage in the history of the sung psalm readings is reported to have been reached in the Mass of the Roman church during the papacy of Celestine I (d. 432). The report is found in the ancient compilation of papal biographies called the *Liber pontificalis*, compiled during the papacy of Pope Hormisdas (514–523) and subsequently revised in a second edition during the papacy of Vigilius (537–555).[23] The first edition includes the following statement about Celestine I: "he decreed that the one hundred fifty psalms of David be sung before the sacrifice (*ante sacrificium*), which had not been done before; only the Epistle of the Apostle Paul and the Holy Gospel had been recited—and in this way were Masses celebrated."[24] Specialists remain divided about the meaning of *ante sacrificium*. There are two plausible possibilities. One is that *ante sacrificium* means "before the service," in which case Celestine introduced a custom of introit

---

19. Jerome, *Ep.* 52.5.6 (PL 22: 532; CSEL 54: 424).

20. Council of Carthage, Canon 21 (*Sacrorum conciliorum*, vol. 3: 884). Further details about these references are given in chapter 5.

21. Geoffrey G. Willis, *St. Augustine's Lectionary* (SPCK, 1962), 21.

22. See James W. McKinnon, "Liturgical Psalmody in the Sermons of St. Augustine: An Introduction," in *The Study of Medieval Chant: Paths and Bridges, East and West: In Honor of Kenneth Levy*, ed. Peter Jeffery (Boydell, 2001), 7–24; see also my own discussion in chapter 10.

23. See McKinnon, *Advent Project*, 79 with n. 7.

24. *Hic constituit ut psalmi CL Dauid ante sacrificium psalli, quod ante non fiebat, nisi tantum recitabatur epistola Pauli apostoli et sanctum evangelium, et sic missae celebrabantur. Lib. pont.* 45 (Duchesne, I: 89). The second edition adds the phrase *antephanatim ex omnibus* after *psalli* (Duchesne I: 89 [Variantes XLV 2] and 230).

psalmody. This interpretation was adopted by medieval interpreters of the passage, beginning with Amalar in the ninth century.[25] In modern scholarship, it has received its most erudite defense from Joseph Dyer.[26] A second possibility, set forth by Peter Jeffery in an equally careful study, is that *ante sacrificium* means "before Communion" and concerns the introduction of psalm lessons to the readings that precede the homily.[27]

In favor of the first possibility (introit psalmody) is the fact, thoroughly established by Dyer, that in ancient Christian liturgical usage, the term *sacrificium* almost always refers to the whole service, not to the eucharistic rite more narrowly.[28] This would explain why medieval interpreters, who were familiar with introit chants in their own times, gravitated to the introit as the subject of Celestine's innovation. Yet there are no references to introit song in fourth- and fifth-century Christian sources. Perhaps there was simply no occasion to mention that custom. Or the introit itself may have been a Roman innovation, undocumented for the early centuries because homilies and other writings by bishops of Rome and others who knew its liturgy have not survived. The earliest evidence for introits in the Roman Mass dates to the eighth century, although they must have been introduced earlier, since the eighth-century evidence shows a well-developed stage of the introit repertoire.[29] Some educated conjectures suggest that the introit may have been introduced at Rome in the late fifth to mid-sixth century.[30] If so, the introduction of the introit to the Mass would have

25. Peter Jeffery surveys the medieval interpretation of the passage in his seminal article, "The Introduction of Psalmody into the Roman Mass by Pope Celestine I (422–432): Reinterpreting a Passage in the *Liber Pontificalis*," *Archiv für Liturgiewissenschaft* 26 (1984): 148–153.

26. Joseph Dyer, "*Psalmi ante sacrificium* and the Origin of the Introit," *Plainsong and Medieval Music* 20 (2011): 91–121; see also Dyer's first and much shorter statement of his view in "The Introit and Communion Psalmody of Old Roman Chant," in *Chant and Its Peripheries: Essays in Honour of Terence Bailey*, ed. Bryan Gillingham and Paul Merkley (The Institute of Medieval Music, 1998), 110–113.

27. Jeffery, "The Introduction of Psalmody into the Roman Mass by Pope Celestine I (422–432)." Jeffery's interpretation is also defended by James McKinnon, *The Advent Project*, 79–80.

28. Dyer, "*Psalmi ante sacrificium* and the Origin of the Introit," 94–103.

29. The evidence is found in the *Antiphonal Missarum Sextuplex*, which contains "the mature Gregorian repertoire" and "reflects the liturgical calendars of Gregory II (725–731) and Gregory III (731–741)." Christoph Tietze, *Hymn Introits for the Liturgical Year: The Origin and Early Development of the Latin Texts* (University of Chicago Press, 2005), 47 (citing Alberto Turco).

30. Tietze, *Hymn Introits for the Liturgical Year*, 42–81, esp. 46 (summarizing recent studies that suggest, respectively, time ranges of 492–525, the sixth century, and the seventh century) and 52–81 (setting forth his own arguments for an introduction of the introit before the mid-sixth century). Dyer opines that the expression *hymni ante oblationem* in Augustine's quarrel with a certain Hilary "might well have been an introit procession" ("*Psalmi ante sacrificium* and the

occurred by the time of the first edition of the *Liber pontificalis*, but even then, if the first edition had introit psalmody in view, it projected onto Celestine's time, in the earlier decades of the fifth century, an innovation that took place a generation or so later.

An objection to the claim that introit psalmody is in fact the subject of Celestine's innovation is the phrasing "before the *sacrificium*." If *sacrificium* is taken as a reference to the service as a whole, why would introit psalmody have been described as taking place "before" the service and not "at the start," say, with an expression such as *in ingressu sacrificii/missae*? At first glance, this objection appears quite persuasive. Yet it loses much of its force when the work of the editors of the *Liber pontificalis* is closely examined. For at one point in its biography of Pope Telesphorus, the second edition rephrases language of the first edition by replacing the words *in ingressu sacrificii* (regarding the placement of the *Gloria in excelsis*) with *ad sacrificium*.[31] Was this a correction of substance or of style? In other words, did the editor conclude that an assignment of the *Gloria* "at the beginning" of the *sacrificium* had to be a mistake and therefore fixed the language? Or did he think that the first edition's *in ingressu* meant "before" and could be better expressed by *ad*? In either case, we would need to know the exact sense of *sacrificium* in the context, and that is not clear. What is clear is that "the place of the *Gloria* in the Roman Mass has not changed since the sixth century," that is, since the time of the compilation of the *Liber pontificalis*, when it stood, as it still does, "close to the beginning of the Mass and before the readings."[32]

Favoring the possibility that Celestine's new custom was the introduction of psalms to the prehomily Scripture lessons are the biographer's explicit reference to Scripture readings as the locus of the innovation and the fact that prehomily lessons were a well-established part of the service of the word in churches East and West.[33] An additional reason for thinking that Celestine introduced psalmody to the prehomily lessons is said to be the use of the word *sacrificium* very explicitly for Communion in another passage in *Liber pontificalis*. According to Jeffery, in the three applications of *sacrificium* to Christian rites within the first edition of *Liber pontificalis*, the word is ambiguous in two places (including the Celestine passage) but unambiguous in its third instance,

Origin of the Introit," 97). This would push the origin of the introit into the early fifth century, although not necessarily at Rome.

31. *Lib. pont.* 9 (Duchesne, vol. I: 57 and 129).

32. Dyer, "*Psalmi ante sacrificium* and the Origin of the Introit," 98.

33. This association is one of the considerations emphasized by Peter Jeffery, "The Introduction of Psalmody into the Roman Mass by Pope Celestine I (422–432)," 159–162.

where it must refer to the Communion phase of the Mass.[34] This putatively unambiguous use of *sacrificium* is found in a decree attributed to Pope Sylvester "that the sacrifice of the altar (*sacrificium altaris*) be celebrated not with silk or dyed cloth."[35] Sylvester's rule is intended to regulate the type of cloth placed on the altar or used for the veils of the altar, and it is phrased as a celebration of the *sacrificium* because its rationale is that "the body of our Lord Jesus Christ" was buried in a linen shroud. Hence, in this instance the word *sacrificium* might certainly refer to Communion.[36] It may go too far, however, to rule out the alternative by inferring that *sacrificium* clearly does not refer to the Mass as a whole here but must refer narrowly to Communion. To sum up, none of the three instances of *sacrificium* in the first edition of the *Liber pontificalis* is an unambiguous reference to Communion, although it is *possible* that one or two of them have that sense.

The biographer's statement that prior to Celestine's innovation, "only the epistle of the Apostle Paul and the Holy Gospel had been recited," is an important clue to the topic but not a determinative one. Like the new psalmody, these readings belonged to the time *ante sacrificium*. If that means that they were Scripture lessons before the sermon, how is it conceivable that they were restricted to Paul and the gospel, when already in Ambrose's Milan and Augustine's Hippo the lessons were drawn from the whole Bible? As for the possibility that they were introit texts, it has already been noted that the earliest direct evidence for the introit does not appear until the eighth century and that efforts to reconstruct its prior history do not demonstrate that it was probably current in Celestine's time.[37]

Finally, there is a significant clue adduced by Jeffery from the pseudonymous correspondence of Jerome and Pope Damasus, a set of letters invented by a sixth-century forger who used the Celestine passage as his source for a comment he places in the mouth of Damasus regarding the state of Scripture use in the late

34. Jeffery, "The Introduction of Psalmody into the Roman Mass by Pope Celestine I (422–432)," 154–156. The other two instances of *sacrificium* are found in *Lib. pont.* 9 (Pope Telesphorus; Duchesne I: 57), which I have already cited, and *Lib. pont.* 34 (Pope Sylvester; Duchesne I: 77). Jeffery adds that the term "Mass" (expressed by the plural noun *missae*) is the usual designation for the service as a whole in *Liber pontificalis*, but that fact carries no clear implication for the question of whether *sacrificium* was a synonym for *missae* or a term with a narrower meaning.

35. *Lib. pont.* 34 (Pope Sylvester; Duchesne I: 77 and 171).

36. Although the sentence is followed by "thus should the Mass be celebrated (*sic missas celebrarentur*)," this statement does not refer narrowly to the rule about the altar cloths but concludes a series of Sylvester's liturgical prescriptions. Hence, as Jeffery points out, there is no implication that *sacrificium* and *missas* [= *missae*] are synonyms here. Jeffery, "The Introduction of Psalmody into the Roman Mass by Pope Celestine I (422–432)," 154 n. 46.

37. See above with n. 30.

fourth-century Roman liturgy.[38] The forger's Damasus tells Jerome that due to the "simplicity" of his church, "only one epistle of the apostle is recited on Sunday, and one chapter of the gospel is said, while no voice resounds with singing, nor is the hymnodist [David] known to our mouth."[39] It is clear that the forger did his work between the first and second editions of the *Liber pontificalis* (which were separated in time by less than a generation), since the second edition's entry for Damasus incorporates the forger's "information" about that pope, while the first edition does not.[40]

The forger used the Celestine passage to describe Pope Damasus's frustration about the unhappy state of Scripture use in his church. Hence, any differences between the forger's phrasing and that of the biographer are clues to the forger's interpretation of the passage. Those differences include a reframing of the passage in order to reproduce its information in first-person speech by the pope himself and from the pope's perspective prior to his promulgation of his decree (which necessitated different grammar in the verbs and other syntactical adjustments). With respect to the language about the liturgy, the forger paraphrased as follows:

1. He rendered *epistola Pauli apostoli* as *apostoli epistula una*.
2. He turned *et sanctum euangelium* into *et euangelii capitulum unum*.
3. He used two verbs for the recitation of the apostle and the gospel (*recitetur* and *dicatur*, respectively), where the *Liber pontificalis* lets a single verb (*recitabatur*) do double duty.
4. Where the *Liber pontificalis* uses the expression *ut psalmi CL Dauid ante sacrificium psalli* in stating the decree that remedies the absence of psalm-singing, the forger used this thought to describe the absence itself, writing *nec psallendo uox ululatur nec hymnidicus in nostro ore cognoscitur*.
5. The forger did not use the source's expressions *ante sacrificium* and *sic missae celebrabantur*.
6. The forger situated the subject *in die dominico*, which is not an expression used by the source.

Paraphrases 1–3 look like efforts to match the sense of the source without giving the appearance of copying. Paraphrase 4 shows that the forger understood *psalli*

38. That the forger used the Celestine passage as a source is definitively shown by Jeffery, "The Introduction of Psalmody into the Roman Mass by Pope Celestine I (422–432)," 156–159.

39. *Ps.-ep. Damasi ad Hieronymum*, ed. Donatien de Bruyne, *Préfaces de la Bible latine* (Godenne, 1920), 65.

40. *Lib. pont.* 39 (Pope Damasus; Duchesne I: 85 and 213). See Jeffery, "The Introduction of Psalmody into the Roman Mass by Pope Celestine I (422–432)," 158.

to mean singing. His wordier description was surely meant to insinuate verisimilitude by putting into the pope's mouth a heartfelt expression of lament about the sad state of his congregation's acquaintance with psalmody. The forger's decision not to use the expressions listed in no. 5 (again, probably so as not to give the appearance of copying) would have made the setting vague, but the forger avoided that by substituting an expression that, while not a synonym for either expression, must have been intended to serve the same setting-fixing purpose: *in die dominico*. In other words, when the forger read *sic missae celebrabantur*, he took it to be obvious that the Sunday eucharistic service was meant. More significantly, he assumed that referencing Sunday eliminated any need for further specification, such as adding the source's expression *ante sacrificium* or its equivalent. Moreover, that assumption implies that the forger and his readers knew that in their time—and, they would have inferred, in Celestine's time as well—readings from the gospel and Paul took place at only one point in the service. In other words, the forger's paraphrase does not contemplate two points for such readings, necessitating a further specification that the readings occurred *ante sacrificium*. The Damasus-letter forger assumed that it was enough for him to refer to readings on "Sunday," since he had no reason to imagine that there could be confusion about the locus of the singing in connection with the Mass. As a contemporary of Celestine's biographer, he knew that there was only one locus.

The preceding analysis justifies the following conclusion by way of reductio ad absurdum. In the mid-sixth century, the only time during the Roman Mass when one heard the gospel, the apostle, or a psalm was the moment when sections of Scripture were read before the homily, not when an introit was recited or intoned. For it is inconceivable that while the rest of the Christian world heard Scripture lessons before the homily, the churches of Rome heard sermons without lessons. Therefore, the forger must have understood the reference to readings *ante sacrificium* as prehomily lessons. Moreover, he is our best guide to what other sixth-century readers of the passage would have understood *ante sacrificium* to mean in that context and what the sixth-century biographer himself meant by it.

To summarize, a forger's use of the Celestine passage—to shape a representation of Pope Damasus—helps us determine what Celestine's biographer meant by *ante sacrificium*: the service of the word that preceded Communion. Assuming that the preceding reasoning is sound, it does not, unfortunately, answer the question of whether Celestine's biographer had accurate information about Celestine's purported innovation. One has to wonder about the claim in the *Liber Pontificalis*, since it is difficult to imagine that when Celestine assumed the episcopate of Rome, the prehomily readings were restricted to Paul and the gospels, to the neglect of Old Testament texts and the rest of the New Testament. That would have meant that the primary texts for all the regular Sunday sermons were gospel texts and passages from Paul's letters. Although Celestine's sixth-century biographer had no reason to doubt that, based on the information he had, we have reason to doubt it, based on period evidence available to us. Given what we know about prehomily readings in Eastern and Western churches in the late fourth and early fifth centuries, it is almost inconceivable that psalms did not feature among the Scripture lessons at Rome in Celestine's day (just as it is hard to imagine that other books of the Old Testament were not read). More likely, Celestine's biographer relied on a faulty source or misinterpreted his source. For example, if the lessons at Rome always included readings from the gospel and Paul in Celestine's time, readings from other books being *variable*, and if Celestine made a psalm mandatory, perhaps a tradition about that became distorted in transmission and ended up in the implausible form we find in *Liber pontificalis*. But that is merely a guess.

Clerical Readers and Cantors

The preceding examination of the history of lyrical reading of psalms mentions two ways in which those who performed these readings were designated. Sometimes they were called readers, sometimes singers. It is difficult to determine when the clerical office of reader was first established, since there are relatively few unambiguous references to such an office in the early centuries. Even more obscure is the development of the clerical office of cantor as distinct from that of the reader.[41] The difference between the ad hoc recruitment of literate persons to read Scripture and the appointment of persons to an office of reader are difficult to discern. The canons of the Council of Laodicea are exceptional in their specific reference to a "canonical" singer, which at the very least implies some kind of office.

The earliest reference to the office of reader may be Tertullian's use of the term "lector" in describing disorderly heretics, whose churches have "one bishop today and tomorrow a different one, a deacon today who is a lector tomorrow, a presbyter today who is a layman tomorrow."[42] A generation later, in Rome, a letter of Bishop Cornelius quoted by Eusebius lists the ministerial offices of his church in the early 250s. In addition to the bishop, he specifies "forty-six presbyters,

41. This subject is carefully examined in Edward Foley, "The Cantor in Historical Perspective," *Worship* 56 (1982): 194–213; revised under the same title in idem, *Ritual Music: Studies in Liturgical Musicology* (The Pastoral Press, 1995), 65–87 (esp. pp. 77–80). See also the various discussions of the topic in Christopher Page, *The Christian West and Its Singers: The First Thousand Years* (Yale University Press, 2010); also Kaija Ravolainen, "The Singer in the Ecclesiastical Hierarchy: The Early History of the Order" (Doctoral diss.; University of the Arts Helsinki, 2014).

42. Tertullian, *Praescr. haer*. 41.8 (CCL 1: 222).

seven deacons, seven subdeacons, forty-two acolytes, fifty-two exorcists, readers, and doorkeepers."[43] About the same time, Cyprian refers to particular readers by name.[44] The next reference in chronological order is a comment by Athanasius about a vigil in Alexandria in 356, where he told "the reader" to deliver a certain psalm, to which the people responded.[45] This may be the earliest explicit reference to reading a psalm by singing it, and the duty fell to a lector on this occasion, not to a "singer."[46] Whether the lector was a member of the clergy is unclear.

The earliest reference to the office of a singer is Canon 15 of the Council of Laodicea, which I have already quoted. It permits no one except "canonical singers" to stand on the platform and sing from Scripture. This rule cannot be dated precisely, since the council's exact date is unknown. It took place sometime between 345 and 381.[47] Near the end of the fourth century, the editor-compiler of the *Apostolic Constitutions* also distinguished the one who reads the lessons from the one who delivers the psalms.[48] Where the canons of the Council of Laodicea consistently use the noun *psaltēs* for the singer in each canon in which the singer is mentioned,[49] the terminology of the *Apostolic Constitutions* varies. The *AC* refers to "the one singing" (*tou psalontos*);[50] it uses the term "singers" (*psaltai*) when it mentions various clergy;[51] and it speaks of a "psalm-singer" (*psaltōdos*)[52] and "singers" (*ōdoi*) in other passages.[53] The *AC* reflects a combination of literary traditions and a history of redaction, which explains the variety

43. Eusebius, *H.E.* 6.43.11.

44. See below with n. 74.

45. Athanasius, *Apol. pro fug. sua* 24 (SC 56: 234) (discussed in chapter 7).

46. Henri Leclercq draws attention to a memorial inscription for an eighteen-year-old man, who died in the city of Hadriani in Bithynia. The inscription describes him as one who "[uncertain verb] all in the holy psalms and in the readings." Leclercq dates the inscription to the second or third century, but Merkelbach assigns it to the fourth or fifth century. It is not, in any case, unambiguous evidence of the office of cantor. See Henri Leclercq, "Chantres," in *Dictionnaire d'archéologie chrétienne et de liturgie*, 3/1, ed. F. Cabrol and H. Leclercq (Letouzey et Ané, 1913), 344–345; Reinhold Merkelbach, ed., *Steinepigramme aus dem griechischen Osten*, vol. 2: *Die nordküste Kleinasiens (Marmarameer und Pontos)* (Saur, 2001), 125.

47. Regarding the date of the council, see above with n. 10.

48. *Const. ap.* 2.57.5–6.

49. Canons 15, 23, and 24.

50. *Const. ap.* 8.14.1.

51. *Const. ap.* 8.13.14; 8.28.7–8; 8.47.26.

52. *Const. ap.* 2.28.5 and 6.17.2.

53. *Const. ap.* 2.26.3.

in terminology. An office of singer is implied when the word *ōdoi* appears in a list of clerical offices: "These [the bishops] are your high priests—and your priests are the presbyters, and your Levites are now deacons and those who read for you and singers (*ōdoi*) and doorkeepers." Another passage in the *AC* classifies singers with lesser orders of clergy (*klērikois*): "We do not permit any of the rest of the clergy to baptize, whether readers or singers (*psaltais*), or doorkeepers or subdeacons (helpers), but only presbyters and bishops."[54] The use of nouns for singers and the appearance of these terms in lists of clerics probably reflect the era of the *AC*'s final redaction. A reference to cantors is also found in a list of greetings in one of the Pseudo-Ignatian letters: "Greet the subdeacons, readers, cantors (*psaltas*), doorkeepers, laborers, exorcists, and confessors."[55] These letters date to the late fourth century. Moreover, close terminological, stylistic, and theological affinities between them and the *Apostolic Constitutions* strongly suggest that the author-editor of the *AC* composed these letters, as well as a commentary on Job.[56]

If we assume a Greek-speaking Syrian provenance for the *Apostolic Constitutions* and the Pseudo-Ignatian letters, it is surprising to discover that in the one passage in which John Chrysostom happens to refer to the one who delivers the psalm lesson, he uses a substantival participle (*ho psallōn*), not a noun (such as *psaltēs* or *psaltōdos* or *ōdos*).[57] Sozomen describes Marcianus as "a *psaltēs* and reader" who was active in the church of Constantinople in the 350s,[58] implying that the same person read the lessons and sang the psalms, which fits the lector's time period. When Egeria visited Jerusalem, sometime in the late fourth century, those who recited the psalms at the Sunday morning vigil were "a presbyter," "a deacon," and "one of the other clergy."[59] Clearly, in the development of the role of psalm singer, the nature of the assignment and the

---

54. *Const. ap.* 3.11.1. Other passages in the *AC* also imply that singers are lower-order clergy (8.28.7–8; 8.47.26).

55. Ps.-Ignatius, *Ep.* 9(*Ad Antioch.*)12.2 (Diekamp and Funk, 222; PG 5: 908).

56. See especially Dieter Hagedorn, *Der Hiobkommentar des Arianers Julian* (De Gruyter, 1973), XXXVII–LVII; Marcel Metzger, "La Théologie des Constitutions apostoliques par Clement," *Revue des Sciences Religieuses* 57 (1983): 29–49, 112–122, 169–194, 273–294. See also the summaries of research in Bart D. Ehrman, *Forgery and Counter-Forgery: The Use of Literary Deceit in Early Christian Polemics* (Oxford University Press, 2013), 460–466 (with 394–395).

57. John Chrysostom, *In 1 Cor.*, Hom. 36.6 (PG 61: 315; Field, *Interp. in. ep. Paul.* 2: 461). No forms of ψάλτης, ψαλτῳδός, or ᾠδός turned up in my search of John Chrysostom's works in the TLG.

58. Sozomen, *H.E.* 4.3.1.

59. Egeria, *Itin.* 24.9.

terminology for it evolved and also varied from one church center to the next, even in the same general region.

Kaija Ravolainen draws attention to evidence for psalm singers in the *Canons of Athanasius*.[60] This work is partially preserved in a medieval Coptic version believed to be a translation of an original Greek document. An Arabic translation of the Coptic gives the full version.[61] The collection was likely formed from a variety of sources, and even those that go back to the fourth century may not all derive from Athanasius. Moreover, the Arabic version shows traces of contemporizing in choice of words, for there is a reference to Muslims in Canon 11. This may be one of the "many passages" that Eusèbe Renaudot detected (but did not identify) that he thought could not have come from the time of Athanasius.[62] Reference to the Meletians in Canon 12 and Canon 18 (which mention singers) and the presence of an instruction in Athanasius's *Festal Letter* 39 (of 367) that uses language close to the framing of Canon 11 seem to favor Athanasian authorship of at least certain canons, even if some of them were subsequently updated.[63] Perhaps various instructions were culled from Athanasius's writings after his death and supplemented by additional canons over the ensuing decades.

According to Canon 18, the singers (as well as the readers) are to read only from the catholic (or perhaps "canonical") books. Canon 12 states that they must sing only "in the Spirit" and not perform the writings of Meletius or other ignorant persons. Singing in the Spirit evidently refers to singing the biblical psalms, and the reference to heretical songs by Meletians suggests a late fourth-century date for the canon.[64] Canon 78 prescribes that "the readers" shall repeat the word of God or recite the psalms before the altar during Communion.[65] This

60. Ravolainen, "The Singer in the Ecclesiastical Hierarchy," 125–126.

61. See Wilhelm Riedel and W. E. Crum, eds., *The Canons of Athanasius of Alexandria: The Arabic and Coptic Versions* (Williams and Norgate, 1904).

62. Eusèbe Renaudot, *Historia Patriarcharum Alexandrinorum Jacobitarum* (F. Fournier, 1713), 97 (quoted in Riedel and Crum, *The Canons of Athanasius of Alexandria*, XV).

63. See Athanasius, *Ep. fest.* 39 (Joannou, 2: 75–76); Riedel and Crum, *The Canons of Athanasius of Alexandria*, XV–XVI.

64. Meletius, bishop of Lycopolis, was excommunicated in 311 by Peter of Alexandria; the Meletians were later readmitted into the church, at the Council of Nicea; Athanasius disagreed with that decision. See Athanasius, *Contr. Ar.* 71 and the discussion in Riedel and Crum, *The Canons of Athanasius of Alexandria*, xvii–xviii. Although the Meletians are also mentioned by authors of the fifth and sixth centuries, a rule about singers performing heretical compositions in church better fits the fourth century, for which we have parallel legislation in the Canons of Laodicea (Canon 59).

65. *Canons of Athanasius*, Canon 78 (quoted more fully in chapter 5). See the translation in Riedel and Crum, *The Canons of Athanasius of Alexandria*, 49.

presupposes no distinction between reader and singer. None of these canons supplies any information about church psalmody not already known from other fourth-century sources, and the use of both "singer" and "reader" for psalm performers is also consistent with the same variety in fourth-century sources.

Evidence for the West in the late fourth century also shows diversity. Jerome, writing to a Western presbyter named Nepotian, advises him that if his duties should take him to the house of a widow or a virgin, he should bring along "a reader (*lector*) or an acolyte or a psalm-singer (*psaltes*)."[66] This shows that by 393, Jerome could assume that the church in a coastal town in northeastern Italy (Altinum) distinguished the one who intoned the psalms from the reader who delivered the other scriptural lessons. The grouping of the *psaltes* with the reader and the acolyte also strongly suggests that this psalm-singer was not simply a lay person with vocal skill but a member of the lower echelon of clerics.[67] Moreover, in his commentary on Ephesians, Jerome refers to the boys whose duty it is to sing the psalms in church, a clear allusion to cantors.[68] The Third Council of Carthage (circa 397) distinguishes readers (*lectores*) from psalmists (*psalmistae*), terming both "clerics."[69] And Ambrose may have had an office in view when he referred to the *psaltae* ("singers" or "psalm singers") in a treatise composed sometime between 388 and 394.[70]

By contrast, Augustine refers to "the one singing" (*psallenti*) as the reader (*lector*) when he graciously glosses a mistake by this lector, who had not sung the psalm that Augustine had chosen. God inspired "the reader," he suggests, to sing a different psalm.[71] In other places, too, Augustine refers to the psalm-singer

---

66. Jerome, *Ep.* 52.5.6 (PL 22: 532; CSEL 54: 424). Regarding the date and destination of the letter, see Andrew Cain, *Jerome and the Monastic Clergy: A Commentary on Letter 52 to Nepotian, with an Introduction, Text, and Translation* (Brill, 2013), 2.

67. Christopher Page sets forth evidence that in the Vulgate, completed circa 405, Jerome shows a consistent preference for *cantor* as the word for the office of Levitical singer (where the Old Latin shows more variety in translation terms), which is perhaps a further hint of his familiarity with this clerical office. See Christopher Page, *The Christian West and Its Singers: The First Thousand Years* (Yale University Press, 2010), 99.

68. *audiant haec adolescentuli: audient hi quibus psallendi in ecclesia officium est.* Jerome, *Comm. in ep. ad Eph.* 3 (on Eph 5:19) (PL 26: 528). McKinnon's headnote in *MECL* no. 333 points out the implicit reference to the office of cantor.

69. Council of Carthage, Canon 21 (Mansi, 883–884).

70. Ambrose, *Interpel. Job et Dauid* 4.6.23–24 (PL 14: 821; CSEL 32/2: 284).

71. Augustine, *Serm.* 352: "The penitent's voice is heard in the words we say in response to the singer (*psallenti*), 'Hide your face from my song and wipe away all my sins' [Ps. 50:11]" (PL 39: 1549–1550). Augustine goes on to say that he did not order this psalm "to be sung by the reader (*cantandum lectori*)."

as the reader.[72] Hence, lectors, not cantors, must have been singing the psalm lessons in Hippo during at least the early years of Augustine's episcopate, which began in 395.[73]

The Age of the Clerical Singer

The Western sources, from as early as the mid-third century, give the impression that the singer was typically young, probably because the office evolved out of that of the reader, who was also typically a youth. Referring to lectors named Aurelius and Celerinus, Cyprian describes the one as an "adolescent," "new in years," and says that neither was yet "advanced in years."[74] Ambrose mentions the boy (*parvulus*) who delivered the psalm lesson at the funeral of Ambrose's brother Satyrus.[75] The word *parvulus* was typically used of boys in their primary school years.[76] Since Ambrose had in mind a functioning reader and not a child with an honorific title, one can assume that the boy cantors in his church were younger than twelve, but probably not much younger. Another factor to consider is that some readers and singers who assumed these roles as children did not advance to higher office, whether owing to their personal abilities or their social status, but remained in their lowly posts well into their twenties.[77]

Page reports inscriptional evidence for Roman lectors who died before turning twenty-five. The inscriptions are from the fourth through the sixth century and somewhat beyond. Five lectors under twenty-five died before the year 423,[78] and their ages at death ranged from eighteen to twenty-four. Inscriptions

72. See McKinnon, "Liturgical Psalmody in the Sermons of St. Augustine," 15 with n. 28. In addition to the foregoing example, McKinnon cites a number of additional instances, among them *In psalm. 40* (CCL 38: 447); *In psalm. 84* (CCL 39:1163); *In psalm. 138* (CCL 40:1990); *Serm.* 15 (Mai) (= PLSupp 2: 452); *Serm.* 352 (PL 39: 1550).

73. Only a sermon series on the Psalms of Ascent has been roughly dated, and none of the references to the congregation's singing appear in these sermons. On the matter of dating Augustine's sermons, see the summary of research in J. Patout Burns, "Situating and Studying Augustine's Sermons," *Journal of Early Christian Studies* 26 (2018): 309–310.

74. Compare the following: Cyprian, *Ep.* 27.1.2; 38.1.2; 39.4.3; and 39.5.2.

75. *per vocem lectoris parvuli*. Ambrose, *Exc. frat. Satyr.* 1.61 (CSEL 73: 240–241).

76. Page, *The Christian West and Its Singers*, 115. Boys typically moved on from their primary education to the next stage under a grammarian, at about age twelve. See M. L. Clarke, *Higher Education in the Ancient World* (Routledge and Kegan Paul, 1971), 12 (giving the standard scholarly opinion about the age when a boy was entrusted to a grammarian).

77. Canon 18 of the *Breviarium Hipponense*, which dates to 393, instructs the post-pubescent reader to marry (and live chastely) or adopt celibacy (CCL 149: 38).

78. A few others may have died in the fifth century, but the dating is very uncertain.

datable to the sixth century or later show age ranges from six to sixteen. Of these, two of uncertain date are for children who died at age five (one from the fifth or sixth century and the other probably from the Byzantine era).[79] Slim as the evidence is, it suggests that in the fourth and early fifth centuries, lectors tended to be young men who had finished their schooling; while in later centuries some were much younger. Yet Ambrose's reader must have been under twelve, and Jerome's advice to readers that they should not behave like stage actors probably fits teenagers who were still in school and had not yet assumed the weighty responsibilities of adulthood.[80]

Page comments about the five-year-old that he was "perhaps too young to have begun his studies with a grammarian but not necessarily too young to have learned to read."[81] But is it conceivable that five-year-olds were ascending the *ambo/pulpitum* to read gospel passages or intone psalms with the lexical precision expected for the delivery of sacred Scripture? Much more likely is the theory that the very young children of well-to-do families were given clerical titles before they were able to perform the duties of the office and that some were awarded honorific titles postmortem.[82]

Literary evidence from the East for the age of lectors and singers is very meagre. The *Apostolic Constitutions* prescribes that lectors and singers must be married only once, allowing that if they are not married when they assume their position, they may marry after assuming it.[83] This implies that readers and cantors were sometimes in their marrying years, but it is possible that most started out younger and got married in their twenties if they continued in their service beyond their teens. The qualifications for the reader stipulated by the *Apostolic Church Order* (fourth century?)[84] do not include anything about marital history

79. Table 5.2 in Page, *The Christian West and Its Singers*, 126–127.

80. Jerome, *Comm. in ep. ad Eph.* 3 (PL 26: 528) (see the further discussion in chapter 13). Jerome addresses these singers as *adolescentuli*. But this does not tell us much, since *adulescentulus*, *adulescens/adolescens*, and *adulescentia* specified a broad age range (when used outside of law), covering ages from two to twenty-six and perhaps meaning simply "under thirty." Writing about the time when he moved to Milan, when he was just entering his thirties, Augustine says, "My evil and unspeakable adolescence (*adulescentia*) was dead" (*Conf.* 7.1.1).

81. Page, *The Christian West and Its Singers*, 106–107.

82. G. W. Clarke, "An Illiterate Lector?" *Zeitschrift für Papyrologie und Epigraphik* 57 (1984): 103–104 (adducing two such cases—five-year-old lectors—mentioned in CIL XI 1709 and CIL VIII 453). Page also mentions a purely honorific title as a possibility in the case of the five-year-old reader (*The Christian West and Its Singers*, 106).

83. *Const. ap.* 6.17.2.

84. Most scholars date the work to the fourth century. See Bruno Steimer, *Vertex Traditionis: Die Gattung der altchristlichen Kirchenordnungen* (De Gruyter, 1992), 65. Stewart-Sykes proposes

or managing one's own children, whereas the order's qualifications for deacons presuppose that deacons, as a rule, were married men.[85] A certain Porphyrios from Pisidia, who is called a singer of antiphons,[86] is a member of an association that dedicated a church to St. George in 365 or, more probably, in 419.[87] He is obviously an adult, but we do not know how old he was when he began his service. Finally, some decades later, in Vandal Africa, the banishment of Catholic clerics from Carthage in 484 caught up a number of lectors, some of whom were singers and some of whom were also children (*infantuli*).[88]

Inscriptional evidence from the East provides more information and also suggests that the reader of tender years—the term "singer" is rare—may not have been the norm in Greek-speaking regions. Of some thirteen Christian inscriptions that refer to readers and are datable to before 600—none can be ascribed to the fourth century—eleven mention adult readers. The other two are not clear about the age of the person, although a piling up of character traits in one of them gives the impression of an adult.[89] Two Christian inscriptions datable to

---

a date in the early third century. Alistair Stewart-Sykes, *The Apostolic Church Order: The Greek Text with Introduction, Translation, and Annotation* (St. Paul's, 2006), 78. The expression "the offering (τῆς προσφορᾶς) of the body and the blood" in § 25 favors a later dating. See R. H. Connolly, "The Use of the *Didache* in the *Didascalia*," *Journal of Theological Studies* 24 (1923): 155–156 and cf. Paul Bradshaw's comments in his review of Stewart-Sykes' book in *Journal of Theological Studies* 60 (2009): 273.

85. *Apostolic Church Order* 19 (readers) and 20 (deacons).

86. The title ἀντιφωνάρις must mean a singer of antiphons. Had Porphyrios been a composer of antiphons, his title would have ended with -γραφος, which was standard in forming words for composition, even when they did not entail writing.

87. Porphyrios 1. Sylvain Destephen, *Prosopographie chrétienne du bas-empire*, vol. 3: *Prosopographie du diocese d'Asie* (Association des amis du Centre d'histoire et civilisation de Byzance, 2008), 817.

88. Victor of Vita describes a lector who sang an Alleluia, which shows that the duties of lectors included chanting (*Hist. pers. Afr. prov.* 1.41 [1.13]; CSEL 7: 18). Victor also mentions that among the exiles were *lectores infantuli* (3.34 [5.9]; CSEL 7: 89).

89. Of the thirteen Christian inscriptions, twelve are very explicitly Christian (as indicated by crosses and/or explicit Christian language). One is probably Christian, since the name of the reader's wife is Thekla. The eleven inscriptions that refer to adult readers are as follows, with information suggesting maturity by marital status or occupation etc.: IG II^2 13547 (5th/6th) (married); IvO 657 (early 5th) (μαρμαραρίῳ: marble worker); IG VII 2692 (Roman period) (deacon); ArchEph (1929) 151, 6 (5th?) (married); SEG 39: 515 (5th/6th) (married); IG X, 2 1 1030 (6th) (πακτωτής: tax collector?); RIChrM 242 (5th/6th); IG X, 2 2 151 (5th/6th) (χαρτουλάριος: archivist?); SGLIBulg 223 (5th) (40 yrs. old); IC 489 (5th/6th) (χαρτουλάριος: archivist?); IGLSyr2 270 (506/507) (ἐπιτρόπου: trustee?). The two where the age of the reader is uncertain are RIChrM 225 (5th/6th) and SEG 49: 728 (5th).

this era mention Christian singers whose ages, although not stated, are clearly implied. Both are adults.[90]

The evidence for both the East and the West suggests that lector-singers varied in age. Children were appointed to the office, but adults also served. While it is possible that in some churches, only children or only adults were recruited, the available information does not tell us that. An educated, but tentative, guess would be that in the late fourth century and the fifth, it was typically children of a certain age who were trained for the task, some of whom continued in the role after they reached adulthood and married.

Training

Direct information about the training of reader-singers/cantors is entirely lacking for the first four centuries. Yet we can draw a few inferences from circumstantial evidence. As a corollary of the establishment of sung psalm lessons for various liturgies, decisions had to be made about procedures for selecting reader-singers. The *Apostolic Tradition* envisions no ordination ceremony for readers but says that they enter their position when the bishop hands them the book.[91] The nature of the *Apostolic Tradition* as a source that went through multiple revisions makes it impossible to date this custom. Canon 15 of the Council of Laodicea implies that somewhat informal processes of selection prevailed in certain churches in the middle of the fourth century, a situation the council sought to remedy by requiring that only "canonical" singers perform the duty of singing from the Bible. "Canonical" as applied to the term "singers" implies approval by authorities and perhaps ordination.[92] Whatever the nature of the approval, official selection would have entailed some sort of screening process. The Council of Laodicea specifies only moral-spiritual requirements for readers and singers, yet at least some determination must have been made about how well the prospective readers could deliver a text and which of them could sing from the Psalter,[93] or they had to be trained in those skills. Already in Carthage a century earlier, the bishop himself initially examined the readers before assigning them.[94] This probably included having them sight-read and perhaps perform psalm texts with song.

90. FGLIBulg 243 (6th) (married) and IGChEg 2 (530) ("the blessed Abba Theodorus").

91. *Trad. ap.* 11.

92. Note that the *Apostolic Constitutions* classifies both lectors and singers as lower-order clergy. See *Const. ap.* 6.17.2 and 8.47.26; cf. 8.13.14.

93. Council of Laodicea, Canon 24.

94. Cyprian, *Ep.* 29 (CSEL 3/2: 548). This is pointed out by Page, *The Christian West and Its Singers*, 93.

The secular education of readers would have varied considerably, and practical training in music was not part of a typical education. Advanced students in some schools learned special techniques for reciting Homer and the old lyric poets.[95] Whether they were also taught to sing lyric poems melodically, according to a dictum laid down in the school-text *Ars grammatica*,[96] is possible but not well documented. References to instruction in singing are rare in the texts that inform us about schools in late antiquity.[97] That said, the inclusion of some elements of musical training as part of the education in oratory (as evidenced at least for the late republic and the Augustine age) and the publication of handbooks on music suggest interest, both intellectual and practical, among the educated.[98] While this does not mean that the average lector acquired practical school instruction in singing, it may mean that some well-educated Christians, including bishops, regarded themselves as good judges of singing and wanted lector-singers to receive vocal training. Moreover, Jerome's insistence that a good voice is not necessary for good singing betrays the fact that most people thought the opposite.

Jerome's reference to cantors who smear their throats implies that some church singers received formal instruction from professional singers or at least from amateurs who knew the standard training methods. The maintenance of church choirs is further evidence of interest in good singing, since choirs had to

95. See Charles H. Cosgrove, "Semi-Lyrical Reading of Greek Poetry in Late Antiquity," *Harvard Studies in Classical Philology* 111 (2021): 463-482.

96. Dionysius Thrax, *Ars gramm.* 1.1.

97. I note that apart from a reference to the pedagogic use of songs (singing the alphabet) and a slave girl on her way to a singing lesson (P. Oxy. 3555), the topic of singing in school appears nowhere in what Raffaella Cribiore has described of education in late antiquity based on papyrological and other evidence. See Raffaella Cribiore, *Writing, Teachers, and Students in Graeco-Roman Egypt* (Scholars Press, 1996) and *Gymnastics of the Mind: Greek Education in Hellenistic and Roman Egypt* (Princeton University Press, 2001). Nor are there references to singing in the model conversations about school in the colloquia, although recitation of old poetry may be in view at points. See the colloquia collected, edited, and translated in Eleanor Dickey, *The Colloquia of the Hermeneumata Pseudodositheana*, 2 vols. (Cambridge University Press, 2012 and 2015); on hints regarding poetry recitation in the colloquia, see Cosgrove, "Semi-Lyrical Reading of Greek Poetry in Late Antiquity," 474–475. Girls of well-to-do families probably learned music at home from a music teacher, as described in a second-century CE novel by Achilles Tatius (*Leuc. et Clit.* 2.1.1) and depicted in a domestic painting from Pompeii (British Museum 1867.0508.1353), which is reproduced in Charles H. Cosgrove, *Music at Social Meals in Greek and Roman Antiquity: From the Archaic Period to the Age of Augustine* (Cambridge University Press, 2023), 184 (Fig. 5.2).

98. See Stefan Hagel and Tosca Lynch, "Musical Education in Greece and Rome," in *A Companion to Ancient Education*, ed. W. Martin Bloomer (Wiley, 2015), 408–411; Massimo Raffa, "Music in Greek and Roman Education," in *A Companion to Ancient Greek and Roman Music*, ed. Tosca A. C. Lynch and Eleonora Rocconi, eds. (Wiley, 2020), 318–319.

be trained. The earliest mention of a choir is the women's chorus of the notorious Paul of Samosata in the third century.[99] A children's choir served the liturgy of the church of Jerusalem when Egeria paid her visit there.[100] The *Apostolic Tradition* calls for a vesper choir composed of virgins and children.[101] *Testamentum Domini* mentions a vesper boys' choir,[102] and the *Syrian Chronicle* attributed to Zachariah of Mitylene describes regular choral concerts at the orphanage of Constantinople in the mid-fifth century. According to the *Chronicle*, the presbyter Acacius, who was head of that orphanage, had a brother named Timocletus, who composed songs, "which they sang," the *Chronicle* reports, "and the people enjoyed [them] and they flocked in crowds to the orphanage."[103] Choral singing at an orphanage would most likely have been a performance by a children's choir, and it happens that a boys' choir is well documented as an institution of the orphanage of Constantinople in later centuries.[104]

The first explicit references to Christian instruction in singing for lector-cantors and choirs concern a priest of Vienne (in Gaul) named Mamertus Claudianus and a onetime lector of Carthage named Theucarius, both of whom were active in the latter half of the fifth century. Claudianus, who died in 473, was a learned priest of some reputation whose older brother was the bishop of Vienne (southern Gaul).[105] Sidonius Apollinaris describes Claudianus as "an orator, logician, poet, interpreter, geometrician, musician," as well as a "psalm singer" (*modulator psalmorum*) and "voice teacher" (*phonascus*). He served his brother the bishop in various ways, including teaching the *classes* ("divisions") that sang "before the altar."[106] Sidonius does not use the word "choirs" here, and the Latin word *classes* is not associated with music except in a few patristic descriptions of the "ranks" of the Levitical temple singers. Hence, it is unclear what the term's referent is and what kind of singing the

99. Eusebius, *H.E.* 7.30.10.

100. Egeria, *Itin.* 24.5.

101. *Trad. ap.* 25/29C 11.

102. *T. Dom.* 2.11.

103. Ps.-Zachariah Rhetor, *Chron.* 4.11; tr. from *The Chronicle of Pseudo-Zachariah Rhetor: Church and War in Late Antiquity*, ed. Geoffrey Greatrex, tr. Robert R. Phenix, Cornelia Horn, Sebastian P. Brock, and Witold Witakowski (Liverpool University Press, 2011), 152.

104. See Timothy S. Miller, *The Orphans of Byzantium: Child Welfare in the Christian Empire* (The Catholic University of America Press, 2003), 212–214.

105. See Christopher Page, "The Magnificence of a Singer in Fifth-Century Gaul," in *Magnificence in the Middle Ages*, ed. C. Stephen Jaeger (Palgrave MacMillan, 2010), 35–49.

106. Sidonius Apollinaris, *Ep.* 4.11.6.

members of these divisions performed. Presumably, youthful lector-cantors were among them, who may have formed the sorts of choirs we hear about in other sources.

After describing Claudianus's role as vocal instructor, Sidonius mentions that he also prepared lectionaries, which probably means that he selected the psalms and canticles to be paired with readings for various services, along the lines of what we see in the Armenian Lectionary, which was derived from the church of Jerusalem in the same era.

Theucarius of Carthage is mentioned in a history of Carthage under the rule of the Vandals because he succeeded in keeping "twelve"[107] boys from exile during the purge of Catholics from that city, which occurred in 484. Theucarius was a former lector, which may mean that he began his clerical career as a cantor in North Africa, where those who sang the psalm lessons were still called readers, at least in Hippo, as late as Augustine's episcopate (396–430).[108] Theucarius, who had been the boys' instructor, apparently had influence with certain Vandal authorities, perhaps even with the royal court, for he managed to get the boys called back after they were already on their way into exile, arguing to the authorities that the boys had "voices that were strong and suited for melodic song."[109] Upon their return, the boys "lived together, ate together, and sang together,"[110] presumably under Theucarius's continuing tutelage.[111] Victor does not describe Theucarius as a monk or suggest that the boys were taken in by a monastery. It is possible that they were orphans. Since they had been slated for exile when the Catholic clergy were expelled and were brought back because of their musical abilities, they were presumably clerical reader-cantors. They may have returned to their liturgical duties under the auspices of the newly ascendant "Arians." Page opines that their corporate living arrangement could suggest that they were adopted by a bishop or other wealthy person as a trained choir to perform choral hymns on various occasions.[112]

107. The figure "twelve" should not be taken too literally, since the account goes on to compare them to the twelve apostles.

108. When Augustine mentions the psalm performer, he calls him a lector, not a cantor. See above with notes 71 and 72.

109. *vocales strenuos atque aptos modulis cantilenae.* Victor of Vita, *Hist. pers. Afr. prov.* 3.39 [5.10] (CSEL 7: 91).

110. Victor of Vita, *Hist. pers. Afr. prov.* 3.40 [5.13] (CSEL 7: 91).

111. According to Victor, the boys were mistreated upon their return, when they refused to accept Arian doctrine. He does not say expressly that Theucarius himself tried to beat them into theological submission, but that may be implied.

112. Page, *The Christian West and Its Singers*, 222.

Children's choral song, as well as lectional psalmody by boys and young men, would not have been possible without training. Lectors stood in need of initial training at the very least. It is possible that they also received ongoing guidance from liturgists like Claudianus, who was active in Vienne in the mid-fifth century, if not earlier, and probably had predecessors. Choirs had to be both organized and regularly rehearsed. Senior cantors or music masters who selected psalms and canticles for various services may also have been responsible for training the choirs.

The Melodic Aspect

How did it happen that palm readings came to be sung? James McKinnon has proposed that the "inherent lyrical characteristics" of the psalms inspired readers to render them "in a more musical fashion," which eventually led to singing the psalm lessons, with congregational responses.[113] This reasoning seems to imply that the development was an organic one within the confines of Scripture lessons, uninfluenced by the fact that singing psalms had been established at church suppers long before the earliest evidence for sung psalm lessons.

In any case, the evolution of lyrical psalm reading is not likely to have resulted from the inherently lyrical quality of the psalms. Psalm texts were not inherently lyrical in either Greek or Latin. They had no meter, varied in line lengths, and must have looked like prose hymns or prose prayers to ancient Christians, possibly with features that somewhat resembled the so-called Asiatic prose-style of Late Antiquity. Hence, already-established psalm-singing customs in other settings—domestic prayer, community prayer, vigils, and the daily office—are more likely to have been the primary source of influence on the evolution of the sung psalm lesson than the literary character of the psalms themselves.

113. James McKinnon, *The Advent Project: The Later-Seventh-Century Creation of the Roman Mass Proper* (University of California Press, 2000), 47.

CHAPTER FIVE

Communion Psalmody

THE CHRISTIAN COMMUNITY meal was an ancient institution, the earliest form of the Eucharist, going back to the apostolic age. It is doubtful that Christians of the first two centuries divided their community meals into eucharistic and noneucharistic types, distinguishing Eucharists from agapes.[1] The practice that led eventually to the concept of the discrete eucharistric rite was originally the sharing of a meal with thanksgiving for God's saving grace in Jesus Christ. The food elements varied, as did the prayers. Hence, when Christians in Tertullian's Carthage sang from Scripture at their community suppers, when Clement of Alexandria and his friends sang David's poems at their private dinner parties, and when the *Acts of Paul*'s fictionalized Paul and the Corinthians shared a meal and sang psalms and odes deep into the night, we might say that they engaged in the earliest form of "eucharistic" psalmody. This did not mean, however, that they sang during a ritual action of breaking and sharing bread with appropriate eucharistic prayers. The psalm-singing took place after supper.

Now, Tertullian had a concept of the food consumed at these suppers as "the sacrament of the Eucharist," which he elsewhere calls simply "the Eucharist," also "the body of Christ."[2] The Eucharist in this sense was a transferable entity. Tertullian refers to a morning distribution of the Eucharist by the bishop, apparently as an adjunct to the community supper and an accommodation to those who had been unable to attend the community supper.[3] The food of this Eucharist had probably been blessed at the community meal the night before. Some Carthaginian Christians also reserved the Eucharist, whether from a supper or a morning distribution, and kept it for home consumption.[4] Whether similar customs of episcopal distribution or lay reservation were common

1. See Paul F. Bradshaw and Maxwell E. Johnson, *The Eucharistic Liturgies: Their Evolution and Interpretation* (Liturgical, 2012), 12–13.

2. Tertullian, *Cor.* 3.3 (*eucharistiae sacramentum*); *Orat.* 19.1–4.

3. Tertullian, *Cor.* 3.3. I am persuaded by Andrew McGowan's interpretation of this morning rite. See McGowan, "Rethinking Agape and Eucharist in Early North African Christianity," *Studia Liturgica* 34 (2004): 169–172.

4. Tertullian, *Cor.* 3.3; *Ux.* 2.5.

elsewhere in Tertullian's era is unknown.[5] Moreover, there is no information about which *other* practices of the Carthaginian community supper, besides the sacrament, may have been incorporated into the morning distribution or the domestic consumption of reserved sacramental bread. Tertullian says nothing about song or even prayers at morning distributions. Of course, those who sang at home, as Tertullian elsewhere urges, may have incorporated their home consumption of reserved bread into a ritual framed by song and prayer. But Tertullian says nothing about that either.

A generation later, Cyprian explains to the bishop at Biltha that it has become unfeasible in Carthage to hold community meals for the whole church; the eucharistic food is now being distributed to the people only at a morning liturgy.[6] Cyprian does not say whether the tradition of song, which had been a characteristic feature of community suppers in Tertullian's day, was incorporated into the morning rite that replaced the supper in Cyprian's time.[7]

The Sunday morning service of word and table, which evolved in both the East and the West,[8] eventually did incorporate psalmody into its Communion rite. The earliest explicit evidence does not appear until the latter half of the fourth century. Moreover, all the fourth-century evidence for Communion psalmody is from the East. The *Mystagogical Catecheses* attributed to Cyril of Jerusalem tells catechumens that during their first Communion, they will hear Psalm 33: "After these things [the sanctifying prayers over the gifts], you hear the singer urging you with a divine melody into the communion of the holy mysteries, and saying, 'Taste and see that the Lord is good.'"[9] This is probably a sung prompt, giving the congregation the pattern of the psalm response. If the *Mystagogical Catecheses* was composed by Cyril, which is more likely than not, then the passage about Communion psalmody dates to his episcopate, which

---

5. On the subject of Communion in the third century, see Bradshaw and Johnson, *The Eucharistic Liturgies*, 30–36.

6. Cyprian, *Ep.* 63.16.1.

7. On the transition from community suppers to morning Eucharists in Carthage, see chapter 3.

8. "Word" and "Table" were already joined in the Syrian-Roman community of Justin Martyr (*1 Apol.* 65–67), and both probably had a place in the community supper described by Tertullian (*Apol.* 39; see Charles H. Cosgrove, "Word and Table: The Origins of a Liturgical Sequence," *Vigiliae Christianae* 74 [2020]: 359–360). Origen, who provides evidence for both, nowhere explicitly connects the two, although there are circumstantial clues in his writings that the two were indeed joined in Alexandria in his day. See Harald Buchinger, "Early Eucharist in Transition? A Fresh Look at Origin," in *Jewish and Christian Liturgy and Worship: New Insights into Its History and Interaction*, ed. Albert Gerhards and Clemens Leonhard (Brill, 2007), 207–227.

9. [Cyril of Jerusalem], *Myst. cat.* 5.20.

extended from c. 350 to 387. If it was composed by Cyril's successor, John II of Jerusalem, then it reflects practices in the years that followed but almost certainly not as late as the fifth century.[10]

Further evidence for Psalm 33 as a Communion psalm appears in the *Apostolic Constitutions*. Following a set of instructions for how the bread and the cup are to be received, the *AC* dictates that Psalm 33 is to be sung during the distribution:

> Let the bishop offer the sacrifice, saying, "The body of Christ." And let the one who receives say "Amen." And let the deacon take the cup and, when he gives it, say, "Blood of Christ, cup of life." And let the one who drinks say, "Amen." And let the thirty-third psalm be said while all the rest are partaking. And when all the men have partaken and all the women, let the deacons carry the leftovers into the sacristy. And when the singer has finished, let the deacon say [a prayer].[11]

There is no specific reference to a congregational response here. It was probably taken for granted.

James McKinnon has suggested that the singing of Psalm 33 at Communion is also implied by Jerome in a homily on Isaiah that Jerome preached to the monastic community at Bethlehem: "Each day, filled with the heavenly bread, we say, 'Taste and see how sweet is the Lord' [Ps 33:9]."[12] Although the Eucharist was not celebrated liturgically each day at the monastery in Bethlehem,[13] Jerome could have had in mind a practice of receiving consecrated bread each day or reserving it for daily consumption.[14] It is equally possible that he meant daily spiritual nourishment through the words of Scripture, inasmuch as an exegetical tradition had already connected Psalm 33 with the discourse about bread from heaven in John 6, Psalm 33:9 being interpreted as a reference to life in Christ.

---

10. See the assessment of current scholarship on authorship and dating in Maxwell Johnson, *Lectures on the Christian Sacraments: The Procatechesis and the Five Mystagogical Catecheses Ascribed to St. Cyril of Jerusalem* (St. Vladimir's Seminary Press, 2017), 35–55.

11. *Const. ap.* 8.13.15–8.14.1.

12. Jerome, *Comm. in Esai.* 2.5.20 (CCL 73: 77; PL 24: 86); tr. from *MECL*, 144 (no. 331). See McKinnon, *The Advent Project*, 43.

13. See Daniel Callam, "The Frequency of Mass in the Latin Church Ca. 400," *Theological Studies* 45 (1984): 621.

14. According to Jerome, Communion (at least the bread) was taken every day in the church at Rome, whether he means at church or at home, perhaps by reservation. See Jerome, *Ep.* 21.26–27; *Ep.* 71.6.

For example, in comments on Psalm 33:9, Eusebius says that the shewbread symbolizes the "bread of life" that came down from heaven, an allusion to John 6.[15] And Athanasius remarks, also without any reference to receiving Communion, "'Taste and see that the Lord is good.' Taste the true bread, it says, which has come down from heaven," another allusion to John 6.[16] Certainly, both John 6 and Psalm 33 were widely regarded as interpretations of Communion, but that in itself does not prove that Jerome, or Athanasius for that matter, referred to Psalm 33 as a Communion hymn.

Meanwhile, in Antioch, Psalm 144 was used for Communion, with verse 15 as a response: "The eyes of all look hopefully to you, and you give them their food at the right time." According to John Chrysostom, this psalm contains the words that "the initiated continually sing in response."[17] Was Psalm 144 peculiar to Communion at Easter, as a hymn for the newly baptized, or did John mean "initiated" in a more general sense as a synonym for Christians? There is no reference to Psalm 144 as a Communion hymn in other writers of the time. That said, John nowhere mentions Psalm 33 as a Communion psalm. He does speak of Psalm 117:24 as a verse that "the people are accustomed to say in response at that spiritual assembly and heavenly banquet."[18] It was this verse that "the fathers ordained" to be sung by the people, he says, which implies that at the end of the fourth century, Psalm 117 was a well-established Communion (or Easter-Communion) psalm in the Antiochene liturgical tradition.

In some places, different Communion services had different traditional psalms. Where Psalm 33 was traditional at the Easter morning service in Jerusalem (as Cyril says), Psalm 22 was a Communion psalm of Holy Thursday in the fifth-century liturgy stemming from Jerusalem, as attested by the Armenian Lectionary. This psalm may have been used as a Communion psalm already in late fourth-century Jerusalem, since verse 5 was interpreted as a reference to the Lord's Supper/Last Supper by a number of late fourth-century Eastern fathers. Eusebius, for example, interprets Psalm 22:5 as a prophecy of the Eucharist: "And having received a memorial of this offering to perform on a table through symbols of the body and salvific blood, according to the bonds of the new covenant, we are taught again by the prophet David to say, 'You prepared a table before me in the presence of those who oppress me; you anointed

---

15. Eusebius, *Comm. in psalm. 33* (PG 23: 296).

16. Athanasius, *Expos. in psalm. 33*, (PG 27: 168).

17. John Chrysostom, *In psalm. 144* 1 (PG 55: 464).

18. *Expos. in psalm. 117* 1 (PG 55: 328).

my head with oil; and your cup intoxicates me as the finest.'"[19] The *Mystagogical Catecheses* also connects Psalm 22 with Communion:

> When a person says to God, "You prepared a table before me" [Ps 22:5a], what else does this signify but the mystical and spiritual table, which God prepared counter to the opposite, that is, resistant to the demons? . . . "And your cup intoxicates me as the finest" [Ps 22:5c]. You notice, then, the cup that is mentioned, about which Jesus, having taken it with his hands and having given thanks, said, "This is my blood, which is poured out for many for the forgiveness of sins."[20]

A eucharistic interpretation of Psalm 22:5 is also given by John Chrysostom. Commenting on the admonition in Ephesians not to get drunk with wine but to be filled with the Spirit, he tells his audience:

> There is for you a good cup of intoxication. It is a cup of intoxication that works prudence, not dissipation. What sort is it? It is the spiritual cup, the undefiled cup of the blood of the Lord. . . . See how David speaks about this spiritual cup, which lies on this table. "You have prepared a table before me in the presence of those who oppress me."[21]

These remarks are from an Easter homily, and John's reference to "this spiritual cup which lies on this table" must refer to the chalice on the Communion table.

The evidence from Eusebius, the *Mystagogical Catecheses*, and John Chrysostom reveals a common interpretive tradition of Psalm 22. Eusebius's remarks come the closest to suggesting that this psalm was used in Communion liturgies. The other two authors are vaguer, and none of the three clearly states or implies that the people sang Psalm 22 as a Communion hymn. As noted, however, the Jerusalem-derived fifth-century Armenian Lectionary specifies Psalm 22 as a Communion psalm for Holy Thursday at Jerusalem. Hence, it is conceivable that Psalm 22 was already being sung at one of the two evening Communion services of Holy Thursday that Egeria mentions in her late

---

19. Eusebius, *Dem. ev.* 1.10.28. The Septuagint at 22:5c is rather different from the MT.

20. [Cyril of Jerusalem,] *Myst. cat.* 4.7.

21. John Chrysostom, *Adv. ebr. et de res. dom.* 2 (PG 50: 436).

fourth-century journal,[22] especially since the *Mystagogical Catecheses*, which gives the psalm a eucharistic interpretation, stems from Jerusalem and was also composed in the late fourth century.

Three books of canons mention Communion psalmody but without specifying particular psalms. One is the *Canons of Hippolytus*, which seems to reflect Syrian practice and was written sometime during the first half of the fourth century, the years 336–340 being a widely accepted date range for its composition.[23] Canon 29 instructs that when the priests go "behind the veil" at Communion,[24] they are to sing psalms—probably biblical psalms[25]—doing so "each time they enter, because of the powers of the holy place."[26] This takes place at the altar, where the clergy watch over the cup to ensure that no insect or anything else falls into it. The *Canons of Athanasius* prescribes that "the readers" shall "sing in the word of God or shall repeat from the psalms" before the altar during Communion.[27] This rule, which is numbered §78 by modern editors, presupposes no distinction between reader and singer. The plural term "readers" and the statement that they sing "in the word of God or repeat from the psalms" might suggest that during a given Communion more than one person assumed the task of singing and that more than one hymn was sung. Or else the canon speaks generally. The theological rationale for this Communion singing is that the Lord should be continually praised when he is present in the mystery. The authorship and date of the *Canons of Athanasius* are unknown. The work was

22. Egeria, *Itin.* 35.1, describing a Communion service from the eighth to the tenth hour in the Martyrium and a shorter one afterward at Behind the Cross.

23. Regarding the date and provenance of the canons, see chapter 6 with n. 82.

24. Regarding altar veils, see Robin M. Jensen, "Altar Veils Concealing or Displaying the Holy in Church Architecture," in *Why We Sing: Music, Word, and Liturgy in Early Christianity*, ed. Carl J. Berglund, Barbara Crostini, and James A. Kelhoffer (Brill, 2023), 409–432. The few bits of evidence for how altar veils were used in the fourth century suggest that they were open(ed) for Communion. Yet this passage in *Canons of Hippolytus* (apparently overlooked by Jensen) seems to imply that they remained closed during at least part of the Communion ritual.

25. In a fourth-century document of this type, the term "psalms" most likely means biblical psalms. Moreover, they are given an apotropaic function against demons, which better fits biblical words than composed Christian poetry.

26. Canon 29. See Carol Bebawi's translation in Paul F. Bradshaw, ed., *The Canons of Hippolytus*, with an English tr. by Carol Bebawi (Grove Books, 1989), 30; cf. Coquin's translation: "qu'ils psalmodient chaque fois qu'ils entrent . . . que les psaumes remplacent pour eux les clochettes qui étaiens sur le vêtement d'Aaron." Georges Coquin, *Les canons d'Hippolyte* (Firmin Didot, 1966), 401 [133].

27. *Canons of Athanasius*, Canon 78; tr. from Wilhelm Riedel and W. E. Crum, ed. and tr., *The Canons of Athanasius of Alexandria: The Arabic and Coptic Versions* (Williams and Norgate, 1904), 49 (slightly altered for style).

almost certainly composed in Alexandria before 500 CE, probably closer to the latter half of the fourth century or the early fifth century than to the late fifth, although it contains both earlier and later material.[28] Since §78 refers to the psalm-performers as readers, not cantors, this canon probably belongs to earlier, fourth-century, material.

The evidence from the fourth century shows the beginnings of liturgical coalescence around the Communion use of Psalm 33. In later centuries, when mentioned as a Communion psalm, Psalm 33 was designated not by its number or its first words but by the initial words of its traditional response, verse 9, even by no more than the first word of that verse. The Liturgy of Saint James, for example, prescribes, "The psalm-singers begin the *Taste*."[29] (The reference to a choir of psalm-singers in this directive reflects a Byzantine development.)

Further clues to Communion psalmody in the fourth century appear in two books of the Christian apocrypha. One is the *Passion of Matthew* (or *Matthias*), which is based in part on the second- or third-century Greek *Acts of Andrew and Matthew*.[30] Richard Lipsius concludes that the Greek *Passion of Matthew* reflects fifth-century "Catholic" redaction of a late third-century edition.[31] After telling how a certain king of Myrna put Matthew to death and buried him in the sea

28. For a late fourth-century dating and a sourcing of the contents to Athanasius himself, although not necessarily verbatim, see Riedel's discussion in Riedel and Crum, *The Canons of Athanasius of Alexandria*, XII–XXVI. The absence of mention of Christmas supports a dating prior to the fifth century or at least before 432, according to René-Georges Coquin, "Canons of Pseudo-Athanasius," in *Coptic Encyclopedia*, vol. 2, ed. Aziz Suryal Atiya (Macmillan, 1991), 458–459. A fifth-century date is defended by Hans Förster, *Die Anfänge von Weihnachten und Epiphanias* (Mohr Siebeck, 2007), 75–78. Regarding the composite nature of the work and its incorporation of fourth-century material, perhaps even some teachings culled from the writings of Athanasius, see Riedel and Crum, *The Canons of Athanasius of Alexandria*, XV–XVI.

29. Ἄρχονται δὲ οἱ ψάλται τὸ Γεύσασθε. Liturgy of Saint James in Codex Rotulus Messanensis (10th-11th cent.). The statement is formulated a bit differently but with the same sense in Codex Rossanensis (= Vatican gr. 1970; 13th cent.). See the texts in Charles A. Swainson, ed., *The Greek Liturgies, Chiefly from Original Authorities* (Cambridge University Press, 1884), 316; Henri Leclercq, "Communion ("Rite et antienne de la)," in *Dictionnaire d'archéologie chrétienne et de liturgie*, vol. 3, part 2, ed. Henri Leclercq and Fernand Cabrol (Letouzey et Ané, 1914), 2428–2429.

30. Aurelio de Santos Otero, "Later Acts of Apostles," in *New Testament Apocrypha*, vol. 2: *Writings Relating to the Apostles, Apocalypses, and Related Subjects*, rev. ed., ed. Wilhelm Schneemelcher, English translation ed. R. Mcl. Wilson (Clarke, 1992), 459; Richard A. Lipsius, *Die apokryphen Apostelgeschichten und Apostellegenden: Ein Beitrag zur altchristlichen Literaturgeschichte*, vol. 2/2 (Schwetschke, 1884), 109–141.

31. Lipsius, *Die apokryphen Apostelgeschichten und Apostellegenden*, 121–122. As far as I can discover, Lipsius's discussion of the *Passion of Matthew* remains the standard account and the only one that includes an effort to date the work.

in a lead coffin, the narrator in the Greek *Passion* describes a vigil, followed by a dawn Communion conducted by a bishop named Plato, who proceeds according to a heavenly command:

> "Bishop Plato, take the Gospel and the Psalter of David, together with the crowd of faithful brothers and sisters, and go to the east side of the palace; and sing Alleluia and read the gospel and offer the holy bread. And having pressed three clusters from the vine into the cup, commune with me, as the Lord Jesus revealed the offering above on the third day, when he rose from the dead." And the bishop, hurrying into the church and taking the Gospel and the Psalter of David, and gathering the presbyters and the crowd of brothers and sisters, went to the side east of the palace at the hour of the sun's rising, ordering the singer (*ton psallonta*) to go up on a high rock and start singing to God in hymns of the ode:[32] "Precious before the Lord is the death of his holy ones" (Ps 115:6). "I went to bed and slept; I rose because the Lord will help me" (Ps 3:6). And they were answering the hymn(s)[33] of the ode of David. "Surely the sleeper will not contribute to rising up?" (Ps 40:9). "'Now I will rise up,' says the Lord" (Ps 11:6). And everyone cried, "Alleluia!" And the bishop read the Gospel, and everyone cried out, "Glory to you, the one who is glorified in heaven and on earth." And they made offerings[34] for Matthias, and having partaken, they glorified God.[35]

This is not a typical Eucharist but a special sunrise gathering to conclude a vigil and to witness the transformation and assumption of Matthew. The statement that "they made offerings for Matthew" reflects a Christian custom of making offerings for the dead, which clearly refers to the Eucharist here and probably carries that sense in other early references to Christian offerings for the departed.[36]

32. The expression ὕμνοις ᾠδῆς must mean simply "psalms," as a synonym for one of the Septuagint's expressions in the psalm titles—ψαλμὸς ᾠδῆς.

33. The text reads ὕμνος, which Tischendorf corrects to the accusative. Bonnet suggests ὕμνοις or ὕμνους (*AAA* 2/1: 253).

34. Another scribal slip: προσήνεγκας should be προσήνεγκαν (or -εν).

35. *Pass. Matth.* (*Mart. Matth.*) 25 PF text. The UVF text is slightly longer at this point and is printed separately by the editor. *AAA* 2/1: 252–254.

36. See, for example, Tertullian, *Cor.* 3; *Didasc.* 6.22; and Cyprian, *Ep.* 1.2; 12.2; 39.3. These and other passages on the topic are cited by Bradshaw and Johnson, who were apparently unaware of *Pass. Matth.* 25 (*The Eucharistic Liturgies*, 56–57).

The author has chosen psalms that fit the occasion, and the quotations of individual psalm verses may refer to the responses. Although the story is apocryphal, it takes certain liturgical customs for granted. The type of psalmody—a singer and not a clerical cantor—better fits fourth-century custom than fifth.[37] Perhaps more than one psalm was sung at Communion in large churches. What about the "Alleluia" that concludes the psalmody?

It happens that the singing of Alleluia at Communion is also described in a scene in the *Apocalypse of Paul* (*Visio Pauli*). This book is a somewhat rambling narration of the heavenly excursions of the apostle when he was caught up to heaven (2 Cor 12:24). At one point, an angel shows Paul a liturgy in the heavenly Jerusalem, where David sings "Alleluia" and everyone on the towers and gates of the city answers with "Alleluia." The angel explains that "when Christ the King of Eternity shall come with the assurance of his kingdom, he shall again go before him that he may sing, and all the righteous at the same time shall sing by responding with Alleluia."[38] When Paul asks why David has this role, the angel explains that it is "because Christ the Son of God sits at the right hand of his Father, and this David sings before him in the seventh heaven, and as it is done in heaven so also below, because a sacrifice may not be offered to God without David, but it is necessary that David should sing in the hour of the oblation of the body and blood of Christ: as it is performed in heaven, so also on earth."[39]

The *Apocalypse of Paul* was originally composed in Greek, perhaps in the third century or even the late second. But the only extant Greek version is a late epitome, and the opening of the long Latin version makes clear that this Latin version (or its source) was published no earlier than 388. The language about the offering may offer a clue to the date of the passage about David and the heavenly liturgy. The Latin uses the expression "oblation of the body and blood of Christ," and the Greek epitome phrases this as "offer . . . the sacrifice even in the hour of the sacrifice of the precious body and blood." It is difficult to discover when the idea first developed that the church (or bishop) *offers* the body and blood of Christ as a *sacrifice*. From an early period, the church spoke of its prayers as a

37. The author uses a substantival participle (τὸν ψάλλοντα) and not the noun ψάλτης (psalmer/cantor) for the one who delivers the psalm (*AAA* 2/1: 253.8).

38. *Apoc. Paul* 29; tr. J. K. Elliott, tr., *The Apocryphal New Testament: A Collection of Apocryphal Christian Literature in an English Translation Based on M. R. James* (Oxford University Press, 1993), 632. I have slightly modified Elliott's translation of the Latin and Greek verbs for singing, which are in each instance a form of *psal**.

39. *Apoc. Paul* 29; tr. Elliott (slightly modified; see n. 38). The key language is found in various versions, including the Latin: *non licet sine Dauid ostiam offerre Deo set necesse est ut psallat Dauid in hora oblacionis corporis et sanguinis Christi* (James, 27); and the Greek epitome: οὐ γὰρ ἐξὸν χωρὶς τοῦ Δαυὶδ ἀνενεγκεῖν θυσίαν καὶ ἐν τῇ ὥρᾳ τοῦ θυμιάματος τοῦ τιμίου σώματος καὶ αἵματος τοῦ Χριστοῦ (Tischendorf, 56).

sacrifice of praise, and this idea found expression in eucharistic prayers. At the same time, it became common to speak of the eucharistic elements themselves as offerings to God, an idea found as early as Justin Martyr and Irenaeus.[40] This way of speaking reflects the view that the elements, as gifts of the people, constitute a particular type of sacrifice, namely, a thank-offering. Justin and Irenaeus refer to the bread and the cup as the offering. They do not say that the church offers the *body and blood of Christ* as a sacrifice, but that idea is asserted by Cyprian, who was either the first to make this connection or else the first to make explicit what was already implicit in the minds of many when they heard or uttered eucharistic prayers.[41]

Cyprian reflects Western sensibilities. His conception of Communion as a liturgical act of sacrificing Christ's body and blood is not found in the Eastern church of the second or third century. Even in the fourth century, it is more common for Eastern ecclesiastics to speak of "sharing" in the sacrifice of the body and blood. Yet one third-century passage has been adduced as an indirect indication of the currency in the East of something like Cyprian's idea. In the *Martyrdom of Polycarp*, Polycarp is depicted making a final prayer in which he speaks of giving himself as an offering by willingly dying for his faith. Specialists in eucharistic liturgy have noted that the form of Polycarp's prayer resembles eucharistic anaphoras.[42] It is not clear, however, that the borrowing of the anaphora form for a martyr's final prayer of self-offering relies on the assumption that the church (or bishop) offers Christ's body as a sacrifice in the Eucharist. After all, Polycarp offers himself in imitation of Christ's willing offering of himself, which is a theme of eucharistic anaphoras. This association is sufficient to explain the martyrdom's adoption of the anaphora form. Hence, although it is possible that the oblation language in the liturgical scene of the *Apocalypse of Paul* is original to the work as a third-century composition, the absence of any clear evidence that the scene's conception of the eucharistic offering was current in the East in the third century makes it more likely that the scene entered the *Apocalypse* at a later date.

---

40. Justin Martyr, *Dial.* 70.4; Irenaeus, *Adv. haer.* 4.17.5 (extant only in Latin translation). Bradshaw and Johnson point out that although Justin uses ποιεῖν in 70.4, a common verb for "do" or "make," it can have cultic overtones and probably does so here, especially in the light of the use of προσφέρειν and θυσία in *Dial.* 41.3 (*The Eucharistic Liturgies*, 52–54, including n. 39).

41. Cyprian, *Ep.* 63.9 (see Bradshaw and Johnson, *The Eucharistic Liturgies*, 57). Tertullian uses the expression *sacrificium offertur* but does not explain it. Tertullian, *Cult. fem.* 2.11.2.

42. *Mart. Polycarp* 14. Regarding the anaphoral form of the martyr Polycarp's prayer, see the studies cited in Bradshaw and Johnson, *The Eucharistic Liturgies*, 55 n. 46. On the dating of the work, see the survey of evidence and scholarly opinions in Bart D. Ehrman, *Forgery and Counterforgery: The Use of Literary Deceit in Early Christian Polemics* (Oxford University Press, 2013), 493–502.

Moreover, if the scene is a fourth- or fifth-century invention, that would make better sense of the idea that David is indispensable to a sacrifice. The dictum that "it is not permitted to offer a sacrifice without David" is unparalleled in the literature of late-antique Christianity, but it fits the ubiquity of psalms in Christian liturgy in the late fourth century and after, a prevalence that was sometimes described as the presence of David in the life of the church. As an anonymous fourth- or fifth-century Christian author wrote, "David is first, middle, and last" in morning hymns, funeral processions, the households of female ascetics, and the nocturnal song of angel-like choirs of monks.[43] This author celebrates the pervasiveness of psalmody in the life of the church and in effect declares that David is indispensable to every phase of liturgical devotion—*de facto* if not *de jure*. (Although the author's list does not mention psalmody at Communion or even at the service of the word, for that matter, these omissions are incidental, since the panegyrical piling up of examples is merely illustrative, not comprehensive.)

Despite the liturgical rule stated by the angel in the *Apocalypse of Paul*, the Communion scene of the *Apocalypse* does not fit neatly with the information about Communion psalmody found in patristic sources. The *Apocalypse* says that David sings Alleluia in heaven when the oblation is made on earth, and it implies that the church also sings (or should sing) Alleluia in response. In addition to suggesting this by declaring that a sacrifice cannot be made without David, the Latin version implies the participation by the church in David's song by citing a dominical rule derived from the Lord's Prayer: "as it is performed in heaven, so also on earth."[44] The Greek epitome includes this same rule and also states more explicitly the implication for church liturgy by adding that "it is necessary to sing the Alleluia with David."

What sort of song is this singing of Alleluia in response to Alleluia? At the risk of trying to explain the obscure by the more obscure, I will mention one more anecdote that may be connected to the practice described in the *Apocalypse of Paul*. According to Victor of Vita's history of the Vandal persecution of the church in Africa, composed in 487, a contingent of Vandals led by an "Arian" priest attacked a Catholic congregation during a worship service, entering the church with swords and mounting the roof to send arrows through the upper windows. "A lector," writes Victor, "standing in the pulpit singing an 'alleluiatic melody', was shot in the throat by an arrow, while the people of God were listening and singing."[45] The reference to the liturgical activity of the people as both

43. Ps.-Chrysostom, *Poen.* (PG 64.12–13), which I quote fully in the preface.

44. The rule does not quote the Lord's Prayer verbatim but is obviously adapted from a petition in the Matthean version of the prayer: γενηθήτω τὸ θέλημά σου ὡς ἐν οὐρανῷ καὶ ἐπὶ γῆς (Matt 6:10c).

45. Victor of Vita, *Hist. pers. Afr. prov.* 1.41 [1.13] (CSEL 7: 18) (*alleluiaticum melos*).

listeners and singers makes clear that this Alleluia song was performed responsorially. Since Victor does not call the song an Alleluia "psalm" (or "hymn") but speaks of it as an alleluiatic "*melos*," it may have been a melismatic Alleluia, that is, the singing of the word "Alleluia" in an extended form, to which the people responded with Alleluia. Victor places the event at an Easter celebration in the time of the Vandal King Gaiseric's long campaign to subdue the Roman province of Africa, which he carried out between 422 and 448. We know from Augustine that Alleluia was sung as a response in the African city of Hippo, for he refers to Alleluia responses; and in one sermon he associates them with the joyous fifty days of Easter. During this season, he says, the church sings Alleluia just as the angels do, with whom the church will one day sing Alleluia in heaven.[46] Augustine does not say, however, that the lector sang the Easter Alleluia as a melismatic intonation of the word.[47]

The *Apocalypse of Paul*'s picture of an Alleluia—where the only thing the heavenly David is said to sing is Alleluia, with the responders intoning Alleluia in response—could have been modeled on an Eastertide Alleluia sung melismatically by a lector with the congregation making Alleluia responses, a type of singing that was conceived as imitating the angels, even joining them in song. This last idea is also mentioned in the story in the *Apocalypse of Paul*, which explains that Alleluia is a Hebrew word, the language of "God and angels,"[48] hence an expression that angels and Christians sing together, blessing God/Christ in a common liturgical song during the oblation.

No other Christian author of the fourth or fifth century mentions Alleluia as a Communion song. Does this mean that the scene in the *Apocalypse of Paul* tells us nothing about actual Communion practice in the church? The fact that not one but two fictional scenes in late-antique Christian apocrypha depict the

---

46. Augustine, *Serm.* 252.9.

47. Writing on a different topic, Michel Huglo happens to quote Victor's story about the unfortunate lector and translates *alleluiaticum melos* as "jubilus." See Michel Huglo, "The Cantatorium: From Charlemagne to the Fourteenth Century," in *The Study of Medieval Chant: Paths and Bridges, East and West: In Honour of Kenneth Levy*, ed. Peter Jeffery (Boydell, 2001), 96. In medieval liturgy a jubilus was a melismatic intonation of the final syllable ("a") of Alleluia. Augustine writes about "jubilation" (*iubilatio*) in sermons on Psalms 32 (CCL 38: 254) and 99 (CCL 39: 1394), but he does not associate it with Alleluia. Nor does he say that jubilation was a type of liturgical chant. On the distinction between Augustine's "jubilation" and the Alleluia, see James McKinnon's headnote to *MECL* no. 356. On the format of the medieval Alleluia, see David Hiley, *Western Plainchant: A Handbook* (Clarendon, 1993), 130–139.

48. The author has the angel tell Paul that "Alleluia is Hebrew, the language of *God and angels*, for the meaning of Alleluia is this: *tecel cat marith macha*" (*Apoc. Paul* 30). The last four words are not from a known ancient language, but perhaps the author thought they were Hebrew and expressed the sense of Alleluia. The author's main interest is to declare that God and angels speak Hebrew. "Alleluia" is a word of their language.

singing of Alleluia suggests that this was indeed a practice, whatever its exact form, in at least some churches during this period.

Aside from the reference to a Communion Alleluia of angels and the church in the Latin recension of the *Apocalypse of Paul*, the earliest hint of Communion psalmody in the West is a remark by Augustine in his *Retractions*, composed in 427.[49] Summarizing a tract he had written on behalf of the church of Carthage against a certain layman named Hilary, he explains that Hilary had objected to "the custom that had then begun in Carthage . . . of reciting hymns from the Book of David at the altar, whether before the oblation (*ante oblationem*) or while what had been offered was distributed to the people."[50] The second phrase is clear enough and implies that psalms were sung while the consecrated elements were given to the congregants. The meaning of "before the oblation" is uncertain, however, since "oblation" could mean the service of word and table as a whole, the second half of the service (following the dismissal of the catechumens), or the Communion ritual more narrowly in the second half of the service. Hence, depending on the meaning of oblation, the issue could have concerned an introit psalm, a sung psalm lesson, or an offertory chant.[51]

The first possibility, taking *oblationem* to mean the whole service and the hymns to be introit psalms, suffers from the fact that introit hymns are not attested, at least not unambiguously, for the fourth or fifth century.[52] Moreover, the introit did not take place "*before* the service;" it was the opening liturgical event of the service.

As for the second possibilty, psalms sung in the first part of the service (the service of the word that preceded the Mass proper),[53] it is difficult to imagine that Hilary objected to psalms being included among the lessons. Was it the *singing* of the psalm lesson that provoked his criticism? If singing had been the issue, Augustine would surely have used a verb for singing, not the imprecise

49. Although Ambrose cites Ps 33:8 in a eucharistic context, he does so without speaking of Communion hymnody (*Myst.* 58).

50. Augustine, *Liber retractionem* 2.11.37 in PL 32: 634; CCL 57: 98.

51. The possibilities are judiciously surveyed in Joseph Dyer, "Augustine and the 'Hymni ante oblationem': the Earliest Offertory Chants?" *Revue des études Augustiniennes* 27 (1981): 85–99.

52. Dyer makes this point but suggests that an introit psalm has at least some support from another debated passage, a decree by Pope Celestine I recorded in the *Liber Pontificalis*. See Dyer, "Augustine and the 'Hymni ante oblationem'," 96; also the discussion of the Celestine passage in chapter 4. Dyer concludes that the loss of Augustine's *Contra Hilarum* is "an insurmountable barrier" to determining the meaning of the expression *hymni ante oblationem* ("Augustine and the 'Hymni ante oblationem'," 98).

53. McKinnon contends that the most obvious referent for "hymns before the oblation" is the psalm lesson (*The Advent Project*, 41 and 299–300).

dicerentur ("were said"). Moreover, "before the oblation" is an odd way to speak of the temporal location of a psalm lesson in the liturgical sequence. If a psalm lesson was the focus, why was Augustine not more specific? Why did he not use an expression such as "between the Gospel and the Apostle"? That degree of specificity would have been comparable to his other phrase—"or while what had been offered was distributed to the people."

By contrast, the phrase "before the oblation" is very precise if Augustine meant an offertory psalm, the third possibility, so long as we assume the following: that he used *oblatio* to designate the Communion rite proper, whose beginning point he understood as the liturgy of the bread and cup conducted at the altar.[54] According to a traditional interpretation of Augustine's language, the elements were carried to the altar in a procession accompanied by an offertory psalm.[55] Nevertheless, a procession of this sort is not attested by patristic sources. Communion included so-called pre-anaphoral rites, among them the conveyance of the gifts to the altar, a task that was performed by laity or deacons. But none of the sources mention a procession with song or even a procession.[56] Granted, an innovation might not have had contemporary attestation outside the *Retractions*. Yet the conjecture also lacks any subsequent corroborating evidence until the medieval period in the West and the Byzantine era in the East.[57]

---

54. Dyer observes that *oblatio* was used in both a broad sense and a narrow one during the early centuries of the church. In its narrow sense it meant "the objects (bread and wine) offered" or "the act of presenting the bread and wine for the Eucharist," usages attested for the African church by Tertullian, Victor of Vita, and Augustine himself in *Ep.* 111.8 (CSEL 34/2: 655) and *Conf.* 5.9.17 (CSEL 33: 104) (Dyer, "Augustine and the 'Hymni ante oblationem'," 92–93). It was typically the laity who brought an "*oblatio*" to the altar.

55. The history of this traditional interpretation is summarized in Dyer, "Augustine and the 'Hymni ante oblationem'," 92.

56. Of course, the gifts were brought to the presider before or during the service, but there are no references to a ceremonial style of transfer. According to Justin Martyr, in his descriptions of the practices of small house churches, the gifts "are brought" (by whom is not stated) to the president at the time for the blessing and distribution (*1 Apol.* 67.5). The *Apostolic Tradition* states that deacons bring the gifts at this point in the liturgy (*Trad. ap.* 21.27; cf. 4.2). The *Didascalia* prescribes that the deacons guard the gifts when the people are entering, which implies that the deacons convey the gifts to the bishop at some appropriate moment (*Didasc.* 12.6 // *Const. ap.* 2.57; Stewart-Sykes, *The Didascalia Apostolorum*, 175). According to the *Apostolic Constitutions*, the deacons bring the gifts to the bishop at the altar (8.12.3) and then the bishop begins the anaphoral ritual (8.12.4).

57. The first specific Western reference to an offertory chant is in *Ordo Romanus I* (reflecting the early eighth-century development of the liturgy). According to *Ordo Romanus I* 85 (Andrieu 2: 95), the pope, after the oblations have been placed on the altar, is to signal the choir (*scola*) to stop singing. On the origins of the Roman offertory chant, see Joseph Dyer, "Offertory Chant of the Roman Liturgy and Its Musical Form," *Studi musicali* 11 (1982): 3–20. In the Byzantine

Besides an offertory psalm, there is another possibility, which has not been considered in previous studies of the question. Canon 29 of the *Canons of Hippolytis* 29 (see below) and Canon 78 of the *Canons of Athanasius* 78 (discussed earlier in this chapter) speak of psalmody at the altar during Communion. Hence, if the preposition *ante* is locative, not temporal, then *ante oblationem* could refer to psalmody in front of the oblation, that is, in front of the gifts on the altar. In that case, Hilary could have objected to the introduction into the Latin church of the Eastern custom of Communion psalmody, performed as a rite of sanctification at the altar in preparation for the rituals of consecration (see below) and perhaps while the consecrated elements were being distributed to the people.

The Purposes of Communion Psalmody

The purpose of psalmody varied according to its occasions. Yet reflection about that, like so many aspects of liturgical conventions, is often left unremarked in the sources. Occasionally, however, someone states the reason for a practice, whether a shared understanding of the rationale or an idiosyncratic explanation.

In the case of Communion psalmody, the choice of psalms is usually obvious from the words of their refrains. But these choices according to theme do not tell us why psalms were sung at all at Communion. One possible reason is a practical consideration. Bishops probably thought it useful to keep people engaged throughout the service. The Communion rite was participatory, but it did not keep the individual church member fully occupied throughout the somewhat time-consuming distribution. Responsorial psalmody provided an edifying activity for that interval.

Three of the passages mentioned in the preceding discussions happen to state explicit reasons for Communion psalmody. Rule 29 of the fourth-century *Canons of Hippolytus* calls for the clergy to sing when they go behind the veil "because of the powers of the holy place." The author compares this psalmody to the bells on the robe of Israel's high priest, which suggests that the psalms served an apotropaic function.[58] The canon does not say what the priests do at the altar while they sing. Obviously, they cannot sing and offer prayers at the same time. Perhaps the psalmody is an act of apotropaic cleansing before they proceed to the rituals of consecration.

East, the offertory chant was the Cherubic Hymn. This hymn of the pre-anaphoral procession ended with a threefold Alleluia. According to Brightman, citing the eleventh-century Byzantine historian Cedrenus, it was introduced in the time of Emperor Justin II (565– 578 CE). See Frank E. Brightman, *Liturgies Eastern and Western*, vol. 1: *Eastern* (Clarendon, 1896), 532 n. 9.

58. See the further discussion of this in chapter 13.

Canon 78 of the late fourth-century/early fifth-century *Canons of Athanasius* prescribes that "the readers" shall "sing in the word of God or shall repeat from the psalms" before the altar during Communion, adding that "because it is [the Lord's] body and blood, they shall not cease praising him until the place is cleansed." The author appends a scriptural prooftext, Isaiah 62:6, which speaks of "sentinels" who "shall never be silent, remembering the Lord" as they guard the city of Jerusalem and, with the city itself, await God's vindication of Jerusalem among the nations. As quoted by the *Canons of Athanasius*, this seems to imply that "the place," the altar on which the Lord is present in the elements, is effectually the spiritual Holy of Holies in the temple of Jerusalem and that the psalm-singers are like the sentinels as they sing about the Lord on the altar, calling him to mind. In other words, the author interprets Communion psalmody as both honorific and anamnetic, like the eucharistic prayer. The reference to cleansing probably refers to the expectation that the holy place in Jerusalem, desecrated by gentiles, will be cleansed when God creates the new heavens and earth. It is difficult to date Canon 78. Some of the material collected in the Canons of *Athanasius* probably goes back to fourth-century sources; other parts were added later. Since Canon 78 refers to "readers" as singers, it probably belongs to earlier rather than the later material.[59] The plural "readers" probably does not refer to a choir of reader-singers but to liturgical readers as a class. The placement of the singing reader before the altar is unusual. It is not clear whether it is significant that the canon does not mention congregational responses to the singing.

The *Apocalypse of Paul*, whose description of Communion psalmody in heaven cannot be taken as directly reflective of a corresponding earthly liturgy of the church, nonetheless states two rules as grounds for Communion psalmody. One is a general rule derived from the Lord's Prayer, which states that "as it is performed in heaven, so [it is to be done] on earth." By itself, this rule does not implicate psalmody or any other aspect of Christian liturgy. But the rule of sacrifice is very specific: "a sacrifice may not be offered to God without David." This must be an inference from the fact that the Levitical priests sang psalms during the sacrifices in the temple. The author presumably reasoned as follows. Since the atoning death of Christ is a sacrifice that replaces and perfects all prior sacrifice, the oblation of Christ's body and blood in Communion must be accompanied by psalmody.

---

59. See the discussion in chapter 4.

CHAPTER SIX

Daily Psalmody at Home and Church

DAILY PRAYER WAS a custom of pious Jews that many Jewish followers of Jesus kept as well. Acts depicts instances of it at certain traditional hours; the Lord's Prayer in both its Matthean and Lukan versions implies that it will be said daily; and Paul's letters contain references to his own habit of regular prayer, as well as an instruction that became a rule of the monastic life—"pray without ceasing."[1] Most of the references to prayer in sources emanating from the first and second generations of the Christian movement make no mention of song, but one speaks of hymning as a form of prayer and another pairs praying and singing as activities of a community gathering, probably a supper.[2] Moreover, the personal and household singing that later Christian writings encourage would have been natural in settings of prayer, even if not confined to them.

Individual and household prayer, with or without song, was well-established by the time churches began hosting regular corporate prayer meetings. From a very early period, Christians sometimes met not to share a meal but only to pray (and perhaps to listen to teaching).[3] These prayer gatherings could well have included song, even if there are no mentions of that in the earliest Christian literature. Eventually, churches developed daily liturgies of prayer and psalmody, the earliest clear mention of which is in Eusebius. He marvels at the daily psalmody found in churches far and wide in the aftermath of the Edict of Milan, but it is doubtful that daily church psalmody was a pure novelty in this era. Moreover, Eusebius does not say that daily prayer at church was invented after the Edict, only that it became universal in a time when churches were being built and

1. Acts 3:1 and 10:9 (Peter prays at the ninth hour and the sixth hour); 10:2 and 10:30 (Cornelius, a man who prayed "constantly," keeps the ninth hour of prayer); Matt 6:9–13 and Luke 11:2–4 (imply daily prayer); 1 Thess 5:17 ("Pray without ceasing"). On personal and corporate habits of prayer in the first two generations of the early church (including Jewish antecedents), see Paul F. Bradshaw, *Daily Prayer in the Early Church: A Study of the Origin and Early Development of the Divine Office* (Oxford University Press, 1982), 1–46.

2. Acts 16:25 (see n. 117); 1 Cor 14:13–18.

3. See Acts 1:14, which describes Christian devotion to corporate prayer in terms that seem to distinguish these prayer gatherings from community meals, which Acts describes as "the breaking of bread" and which also featured prayer, as well as teaching (Acts 2:42). A spontaneous prayer gathering is described in Acts 12:5.

rebuilt all over the empire and the stream of converts to the now protected faith had become something of a flood.

The relation between the establishment of the ecclesiastical daily office and lay practices of prayer and psalm-singing is an important, if somewhat elusive subject; but it is likely that lay practices gave birth to the daily church prayer in certain influential churches, whether sometime during the late third century or in the early fourth.

Lay Psalmody

As noted in chapter two, Tertullian describes two settings for group prayer, a meeting where some attendees add Alleluia psalms to their prayers (to which the group responds) and domestic prayer, where husbands and wives sing psalms and hymns together.[4] He also urges the keeping of five hours of prayer—the two obligatory morning and evening hours, as well as the third, sixth, and ninth, for which he finds precedents in exemplary biblical figures.[5] It is reasonable to infer that Tertullian and his own wife kept these five hours of prayer and that they sang psalms and hymns at one or more of these prayer times. While he does not tell us how prevalent these customs were among other wealthy Christian households of Carthage, it is probably fair to assume that he and his wife were not completely exceptional.[6] It is also conceivable that at least some nonelite Christian families, whose work hours did not afford them the luxury of keeping as many as five hours of prayer at home, observed morning and evening prayer in some form.

Disciplines of daily household prayer were cultivated not only by husbands and wives but also by wealthy widows and unmarried women of independent means. Moreover, some of these women took in other unmarried women who wished to lead lives devoted to prayer, psalmody, Scripture-reading, works of mercy, and ascetic discipline of the body. Certain married couples also embraced celibacy as part of an ascetic lifestyle.

Direct references to ascetic households first appear in fourth-century literature, but hints in earlier fictional and nonfictional Christian literature suggest that they existed in the second and third centuries. Thecla, the encratic

4. Tertullian, *Orat.* 27 and *Ux.* 2.8.8.

5. Tertullian, *Orat.* 25.

6. "Shortly after 200," Christopher Page writes, "it is possible to isolate, at least in the Christian communities of Carthage, a prosperous kind of ascetic householder, still regulating the affairs of the domus with its slaves and menial tasks to be supervised, but now living a life of sexual continence, seeking a singleness of purpose without distractions, and following an *horarium* of prayer, scriptural study and psalmody, quite possibly sung, that was sometimes responsorial." Christopher Page, *The Christian West and Its Singers: The First Thousand Years* (Yale University Press, 2010) 138.

female heroine of *Acts of Paul*, is adopted by an older wealthy convert named Tryphaena.[7] The *Acts of Thomas* extolls the encratic way of life, expressed in both spiritual marriage[8] and unilateral renunciation of the marriage bed, the latter lifestyle being embraced by the women Mygdonia and Tertia, whose husbands let them "live according to their own will."[9] A pastoral encyclical published in the 260s denounces Paul of Samosata on the charge that he and members of his clergy at Antioch had young women living with them, probably in spiritual marriages.[10] In the 270s, there was at least one community of virgins in Lower Egypt; and the famed Antony, on the cusp of embracing the life of a solitary, was able to entrust his younger sister to a community of ascetic women so that she, too, would lead a life of virginity. This sister eventually became a leader of the community.[11] Also during the latter part of the third century, a virgin woman named Tekousa began taking in virgin girls to live with her and a young man named Theodotus, to whom Tekousa was a spiritual mother. This story is told in *The Martyrdom of Saint Theodotus of Ancyra and the Seven Virgins with Him.*[12]

The sources do not describe the daily routines of these ascetic households, but there is at least an indirect hint that psalmody was part of the household of Paul of Samosata, who was criticized not only because he and his clerics lived with women in spiritual unions but also because he organized a female choir to sing psalms to him at Easter. Paul reportedly preferred psalms to Christ hymns because psalms were old, which probably means that they were traditional and scriptural, while Christ-hymns were "new."[13] The two charges about his lifestyle and his choir combine as strong circumstantial evidence that Paul had formed an ascetic community of men and women who kept a routine of prayer and psalmody similar to what is described for ascetic households a century later.

The Women's Monastery at Annisa

One of those later households is the community of women led by Macrina the Younger, sister of Gregory of Nyssa and Basil of Caesarea. Macrina was born

7. *Acts Paul* 4.2 (Pervo numbering = *Acts Paul and Thecla* 27 in Elliott, *The Apocryphal New Testament*, 369).

8. The bridal couple in *Acts of Thomas* 9–15; probably Siphor and his wife in 130–132.

9. *Acts of Thomas* 169.

10. Episcopal letter quoted in Eusebius, *H.E.* 7.30.12.

11. Athanasius, *Vit. Ant.* 3 and 54.

12. See Susanna Elm, *'Virgins of God': The Making of Asceticism in Late Antiquity* (Clarendon, 1994), 52–59.

13. See the discussion of Paul and his detractors in chapter 3.

to wealthy Christian parents in Caesarea around 327. According to Gregory, she was devoted to psalm-singing from childhood. Psalmody was an integral part of the pious education her mother ensured that she received at home.[14] Macrina's namesake grandmother, Macrina the Elder, was probably also a spiritual influence, although there is no direct evidence in the scant bits of biography about Macrina the Elder (born before 270) that she and other pious women of Neocaesarea in her day practiced daily psalmody.[15]

As for Macrina the Younger, her brother Gregory reports that she embraced a celibate life, doing so of her own accord around 345, following the death of the man whom her father had selected as her husband-to-be.[16] Macrina declared herself a "widow" and persuaded her mother Emmelia (who by this time was a widow in fact[17]) that the two of them should organize themselves, together with Macrina's siblings and the house's female servants, into an egalitarian community committed to virginity, poverty, and a life of prayer and psalmody.[18] The family sold off its properties, retaining only its country estate.[19] There, by degrees, Macrina and her mother established a community. As Gregory tells the story, no bishop played any role in these developments; nor did he or their brother Basil have a hand in the organization. As Gregory characterizes the family relationships, he and Basil were their older sister Macrina's pupils in the faith, a hagiographic exaggeration perhaps but one that nonetheless reflects his respect for his older sister's spirituality.[20]

The women of the household monastery at Annisa filled their days with manual labor, prayer, and psalmody, pursuing the mystic path to communion

---

14. Gregory of Nyssa, *Vit. Macr.* 3.

15. In his letters, Basil praises both Macrina the Elder and his mother as his own nurturers in the faith. See *Ep.* 223.3 and 204.6. In the second of these letters, written to the church at Neocaesarea, where his grandmother grew up, Basil refers to her as a famous person, who had absorbed the teachings of Gregory Thaumaturgis (bishop of Neocaesarea until his death in 270) and had passed them on to her family, including Basil when he was just a boy.

16. On the dating, see Anna M. Silvas, *Macrina the Younger: Philosopher of God* (Brepols, 2008), 28–29.

17. Basil the Elder died around 344 or 345. See Silvas, *Macrina the Younger*, 31 with n. 99.

18. Gregory of Nyssa, *Vit. Macr.* 5, 7, 11.

19. Regarding the family estate at Annisa (which became the site not only of Macrina's monastery but of a monastery established by her brother Naucratius, which her brother Basil used as an ascetic retreat), see Anna M. Silvas, *The Asketikon of St. Basil the Great* (Oxford University Press, 2005), 45–48; also Silvas, *Macrina the Younger*, 9–12 (and passim).

20. See, for example, *Vit Macr.* 6 (on Macrina and Basil) and Gregory's treatise *The Soul and the Resurrection* (a representation of a dialogue with his sister in which she is the primary instructor).

with God through simplicity, bodily rigor, and constant spiritual devotion.[21] Gregory describes "unceasing prayer and uninterrupted hymnody extending to every moment throughout the whole of night and day."[22] Of specific hours, Gregory mentions evening prayer and morning prayer. Vespers was held in the monastery's church, and morning prayer may have been held there too.[23] At one point during his last visit to his sister, Gregory heard the sound of the psalmody, which signaled vespers.[24] This may imply that he heard the women on their way to the chapel. They may also have sung at their work, as the men of the other monastery at Annisa did.[25] That was typical of monastic life and fits Gregory's idealized description of the teenager Macrina's devotion to psalmody. She knew the whole Psalter by heart, Gregory says, and "went through each part of the psalmody at its own time—when rising from sleep, taking up her duties or resting from them, taking nourishment or leaving the table, going to bed or rising for prayers. She always had psalmody like a kind of good travelling companion that never left her at any time."[26] This description of a pious ascetic woman's daily cursus jibes with Basil's words to a virgin who had violated her vows, telling her to recall her former "days free of upheaval, illuminated nights, spiritual songs, resounding psalmody, holy prayers."[27] And the daily psalmody that an ascetic woman should practice is also described in the Greek tractate, *Discourse on Salvation to a Virgin*, which was probably composed in the fourth century.[28]

The "Protest" Psalmody of an Ascetic Female Household

The church historian Theodoret of Cyr tells a story about a widow named Publia, a deaconess at Antioch in the mid-fourth century who took a number of celibate women into her home, presumably both widows and virgins. According to

21. Their practices, based on the rules and ideals established by Macrina, are mentioned at various points by Gregory of Nyssa in *Vit. Macr.* 11–35.

22. Gregory of Nyssa, *Vit. Macr.* 11.

23. Gregory refers to the community observing vespers at the church (*Vit. Macr.* 22) and also to *orthros* (morning prayer) following the special funeral vigil for Macrina (33).

24. Gregory of Nyssa, *Vit. Macr.* 22.

25. Basil, *Ep.* 2.2, describing the daily cursus of his life in retreat in 358 at what must have been Annisa.

26. Gregory of Nyssa, *Vit. Macr.* 3.

27. Basil, *Ep.* 46.2.

28. Ps.-Athanasius, *Virg.* 20. On the dating and authorship of the writing, see David Brakke, "The Authenticity of the Ascetic Athanasiana," *Orientalia* 63 (1994): 44–47.

Theodoret, Publia and her household used psalmody to protest Emperor Julian's promotion of pagan religion during the year he spent in Antioch preparing to launch his campaign against the Persians (361–363). It seems that when Julian's regular transit through the city brought him past Publia's house, she and her housemates expressed their opposition to him by singing psalms very loudly.[29]

Although psalm-singing was probably a regular part of the women's daily routine, the implication is that they altered their routine to sing when Julian passed, whether it was the hour for their psalmody or not, selecting psalms with anti-idolatry themes and raising their voice so that he would hear them. It is possible that they even went outside to sing at him.

On the first occasion, Theodoret says, the women sang the following words from a psalm: "The idols of the nations are silver and gold, the works of human hands."[30] Since group psalmody in this era was typically responsorial, this line was probably the women's refrain verse. Julian reacted by demanding that they stop singing at him. Publia ignored his order and urged her group to confront the emperor again the next time he appeared. On this occasion, she sang Psalm 67, and the women blasted the emperor with the refrain, "Let God arise and his enemies be scattered," an even more direct assault.

At this point, an angry Julian "demanded that the leader of the chorus be summoned." It is not clear whether he issued his order on the spot or later in the day. In any case, one of Julian's soldiers reddened (or bloodied) Publia's cheeks, and after this, she "made it a habit to attack [the emperor] with spiritual songs, just as the composer and teacher of that chant" [meaning King David] stopped the evil spirit that was troubling Saul." Since Publia suffered no further discipline from the emperor, he must have resigned himself to ignoring her.

The story about Publia is found in a single source, a church history composed in the latter 440s, decades after the event. While it is true that the author of the history was born and educated in Antioch and could well have heard the story from Antiochene contacts, it is also possible that the anecdote was invented after Publia's death. Or else a true story, perhaps first told by Publia about how she and her household sang psalms at Julian, was embellished in posthumous retellings to feature direct interactions between Publia and Julian and to make Publia something of a martyr at Julian's hands.[31] Whatever the mix of historical memory and fictional embroidery the anecdote may contain, its unexpressed assumption is that a household of women like Publia's would have sung psalms.

---

29. Theodoret of Cyr, *H.E.* 3.19.1–6.

30. These words appear in Pss 113:12 and 134:15.

31. Teitler doubts the historicity of the story, suspecting that it is one of many tales about Julian that Christians invented to illustrate his cruelty. See Hans C. Teitler, *The Last Pagan Emperor: Julian the Apostate and the War against Christianity* (Oxford University Press, 2017), 83–84.

Psalmody at Daily Cathedral Prayer

By the 320s, city churches across the empire were holding daily services of prayer at prescribed times or "hours." In later Roman liturgical tradition, these services came to be called the *officium divinum*, "divine office," the Latin *officium* meaning "service" or "duty."

The earliest explicit evidence for the daily office as liturgies of the church is found in Eusebius. In Book 10 of his church history, which he added to the history in around 324, Eusebius describes conditions following the Edict of Milan in 313, which established the so-called "peace of Constantine." In the beginning of Book 10, Eusebius pictures a period of renewal when destroyed church buildings were reconstructed on a grander scale and services of dedication were held all over the world.[32] He also comments on the restoration of the liturgies of these churches and alludes to psalmody:

> And there was one power of the divine Spirit moving through all the members, one soul common to all, the same eagerness of faith, and one hymn of praise by all, indeed perfect worship services of those who led, holy rites of the priests, and divine rites of the church, here with psalmody and the rest of the vocal utterances given to us by God for our hearing, there with the conducting of divine and mystic services; and the ineffable symbols of the savior's passion were present.[33]

The words "here . . . there" seem to suggest different occasions, one being a gathering for psalmody and Scripture reading, the other a gathering to celebrate the Eucharist.[34]

Much clearer is Eusebius's description of services with psalms in a parallel set of remarks about the flowering of Christian worship after the Edict of Milan. In a commentary on the psalms, composed perhaps a decade after this event, he speaks of the church's morning and evening praise as a fulfillment of a prophecy in Psalm 64 (LXX).[35] This is the earliest clear evidence for the morning and evening "cathedral" office, that is, daily services of prayer at prescribed hours in urban churches.[36]

32. Eusebius, *H.E.* 10.2.1 (rebuilding of churches) and 10.3.1–4 (dedication services).

33. Eusebius, *H.E.* 10.3.3.

34. The syntax is ὧδε μὲν (the psalmody etc.) . . . ὧδε δὲ (the symbols of the savior's passion).

35. Eusebius, *Comm. in psalm. 64* (PG 23: 640).

36. See Juan Mateos, "Quelques anciens documents sur l'office du soir," *Orientalia christiana periodica* 25 (1969): 347 (347–374); Robert F. Taft, *The Liturgy of the Hours in East and West: The Origins of the Divine Office and Its Meaning for Today* (Liturgical, 1986), 33.

It is possible that in some places morning and evening hours of prayer had been held at church before the edict, but explicit evidence is lacking. Paul Bradshaw notes that despite a good deal of second- and third-century evidence for Christian prayer at various hours—three hours being the norm, although additional prayer times were also encouraged—the references in these earlier centuries suggest individual or household prayer; there are no unambiguous references to corporate prayer in churches.[37] This would explain why the mid-third-century *Didascalia*'s criticism of lay laxity in church attendance mentions only their failure to show up regularly at Sunday services, not any neglect of morning or evening prayer at church on their part, even though the criticism draws a contrast with pagans who honor their idols every morning.[38] There must not have been any daily church office in Syria at the time.

Psalm 64:6–9, Eusebius's prooftext for the universal spread of cathedral psalmody as a divinely ordained fulfilment of prophecy after the Edict of Milan, reads as follows:

> *God our Savior...*
> *preparing the mountains by his strength,*
> *girded with power.*
> *the one who stirs the hollow of the sea,*
> *the noise of its waves.*
> *The nations shall be stirred up,*
> *and those who dwell at the ends of the earth shall be put in awe by*
> *your signs.*
> *You shall gladden the early and evening outgoings.*[39]

37. See Bradshaw, *Daily Prayer in the Early Church*, 65–66. Tertullian does not mention the setting of corporate prayer that he describes, and neither does Cyprian, when he gives the following instruction about praying together and for all: "Before all else, the teacher of peace and master of unity desires that we should not make our prayer individually and alone, as whoever prays by himself prays only for himself. . . . Our prayer is common and collective; and when we pray, we pray not for one but for all people, because we are all one people together." Cyprian, *De dom. orat.* 8; tr. from Nathan Chase, "Another Look at the Daily Office in the 'Apostolic Tradition'," *Studia Liturgica* 49 (2019): 23 n. 112.

38. *Didasc.* 13 // *Const. ap.* 2.60.2.

39. Eusebius, *Comm. in psalm.* 64 (PG 23: 640). The Hebrew of the MT has a different sense in 8a—not "stir up" or "trouble" but "still" —which explains why the last line of this passage speaks of God making mornings and evenings happy. Hence, in the MT, the nations' fear seems to be a sense of wonderment, not terror. That is probably the sense in the LXX, too, in view of verse 6 LXX.

Eusebius interprets the waves of the sea as ungodly opponents of the church and sees their defeat as a universal act of salvation for the peoples of the world. He takes *terpseis* ("you shall gladden") not as a verb but as the noun "delights" (v. 9c), and he understands these delights as the "signs" that God performed, manifested in Christian psalmody.

To arrive at this interpretation, he exploits the variety of Greek translations of this verse, including those of Aquila and Symmachus (which are represented in Origen's *Hexapla*). Symmachus translates verse 9c, "The goings forth of the morning and the evening you shall make hymnologies."[40] Aquila has the word *ainopoiēseis* ("praise-makings") at the point where the Septuagint has *terpseis*. Consistent with the way Eusebius construes *terpseis*, Aquila takes *ainopoiēseis* as a plural noun rather than a verb.[41] Combining the senses of the various translation terms, Eusebius interprets the passage as follows:

> Who, having seen the arrogant pretensions of the worldly rulers and their acts of opposition to the church of God, both the persecutions and the threats of ungodly men, would not say they were a lofty mountain and a truly surging sea, a sound of waves, the blasphemies of the impious and God-denying? All these the Savior of all the ends of the earth was quite accustomed, in his power, to bring down in a single moment. How those who saw their fall and destruction quaked! They profited and recovered a fear of God, confessing the destruction of the impious to be visible signs of the divine power of the Savior. "Early outgoings and evening delights. You surveyed the earth and watered it." Next to those mentioned (the destructions) were also other signs of the power of the Savior, as he says: "Early outgoings and evening delights." Instead of this, Symmachus has translated, "[he makes] the goings forth of the morning and the evening hymnologics." For this one great sign of the Savior's power appears, the morning outgoings and vesper pleasures risen together among human beings after the downfall of the aforementioned. According to Symmachus, it is "hymnologies," according to Aquila "praise-makings." For the fact that there arose to God throughout the whole world in the churches of God, at the early risings of the sun and the vesper hours, hymnologies and praise-makings and truly divine delights, was no trifling sign of the power of God. And delights of God are taking place, the hymns sent up everywhere on earth

40. τὰς προελεύσεις τοῦ ὄρθρου καὶ τῆς ἑσπέρας ὑμνολογούσας ποιήσεις. Symmachus in Origen, *Hex.* (Field, *Orig. Hex.* 2: 196).

41. Aquila in Origen, *Hex.* (Field, *Orig. Hex.* 2: 196).

> in the church at morning and vesper times. Therefore, it is said somewhere, "Let my praise be a delight to him" and again, "Let the lifting of my hands be an evening sacrifice" [Ps 140:2b LXX] and "Let my prayer be as incense before you" [Ps 140:2a LXX].[42]

In this rehearsal of the passage, prophecies of the dawn and evening solar transitions herald times of song. Eusebius emphasizes the sudden defeat of the enemies ("in a single moment") and the universality of the morning and evening hymns ("throughout the whole world in the churches of God"). The dramatic reversal effected by the Edict of Milan and the quick spread of the custom of morning and evening song in churches far and wide struck Eusebius as a kind of miracle and led him to interpret Psalm 64 as a prophecy of these "signs." He was later echoed by Hilary of Poitiers, who, taking language from the same verse (Ps 64:9, but in the Vulgate), says that "the proceeding of the church in delightful morning and evening hymns is a great sign of God's mercy. We begin the day with prayers to God, we end the day with hymns to God." Then Hilary quotes the same verse from Psalm 140 that Eusebius does.[43] Since Hilary made these comments in a treatise on the psalms composed sometime in the 360s (when he was bishop of Poitiers in Gaul), the similarity of his remark to that of Eusebius suggests that Eusebius inaugurated an influential exegetical tradition.[44]

Perhaps the establishment of morning and evening prayer in churches after the Edict of Milan was not a complete novum. But whatever the precise history of this ecclesiastical development, it is difficult to explain why the daily office joined prayer with psalmody unless the two were already joined in the longstanding customs of daily prayer of pious families and household ascetic groups in the third century.

As for the content of the morning and evening church psalmody described by Eusebius, he does not specify particular morning and evening hymns; nor does he imply that there was any fixed set of songs. His silence is revealing. Had churches far and wide been singing the very same morning and evening psalms,

---

42. Eusebius, *Comm. in psalm. 64* (PG 23: 640).

43. Ps 64:9 in the Vulgate describes the inhabitants at the ends of the earth quaking at *signis tuis exitus matutini et vespere delectabis*. Hilary, like Eusebius, interprets this as the churches' delightful morning and evening psalmody: *progressus ecclesiae in matutinorum et vespertinorum hymnorum delectationes maximum misericordiae Dei signum est. Dies in orationibus Dei inchoatur, dies in hymnis Dei clauditur, secundum quod dictum ist* [quotations follow: Ps 103:34 and Ps 140:2]. Hilary of Poitiers, *Tract. in psalm. 64* 12 (PL 9: 420; CCL 61: 230).

44. On the date of Hilary's commentary on Psalms, see Paul C. Burns, *A Model for Christian Life: Hilary of Poitiers' Commentary on the Psalms* (The Catholic University of America Press, 2012), 22.

that fact would have provided a brilliant capstone to Eusebius's interpretation of Psalm 64:9 as the prophecy of a divinely ordained wonder. Hence, we can assume that the churches were not all singing the same songs. In fact, nothing in Eusebius's comments implies that any of the churches had traditions of fixed psalms for these offices.

Yet Robert Taft argues that when Eusebius celebrates daily church psalmody by appealing to Psalms 62 and 140, this implies that these two psalms were, respectively, widely used as the regular morning and evening hymns.[45] Before examining Taft's arguments and to preempt any possible confusion, let me point out that he cites references in Eusebius to four psalms—Psalms 62, 64, 140, and 142—to argue that two of them, Psalms 62 and 140, were traditional psalms of the morning and evening office.

On the basis of "comparative liturgy," Taft infers that when a biblical psalm known to have been a regular part of daily prayer, based on explicit evidence in certain patristic authors of the late fourth and early fifth centuries, is cited in earlier patristic literature as a prooftext for psalmody at a certain hour, that counts as tacit evidence that the psalm was sung at the gathering for which the prooftext is adduced.[46] This seems to overlook the fact that proof-texting for daily prayer and times of prayer long preceded the custom of assigning fixed psalms to morning and evening prayer. The prooftexts were taken from various parts of Scripture. Tertullian adduces exemplary moments in Acts to argue that the third, sixth, and ninth hours are especially appropriate times for prayer, in addition to the obligatory morning and evening hours.[47] He does not happen to mention Psalm 140:2, but Origen does so in offering a number of Scripture proofs that a Christian should pray three times a day.[48] Hence Eusebius was simply drawing on established tradition when he cited Psalm 140:2 in his discussions of the "signs" prophesied in Psalm 64. Tellingly, his appeal to Psalm 140:2 as a word of Scripture fulfilled in church psalmody implies that both morning and evening prayer are instances of it. Moreover, he uses quotation formulas, which suggests that he did not assume that his readers would instantly recognize the lines of Psalm 140:2 as familiar words sung every evening at cathedral prayer.

Nor is there any hint that Eusebius quotes from the liturgy when he cites two additional psalm passages many pages after his comments on Psalm 64, writing

45. Taft, *The Liturgy of the Hours in East and West*, 33–34.

46. For instances of Taft's use of the methodological principle of "comparative liturgy," established by Anton Baumstark, see *The Liturgy of the Hours in East and West*, xii, 81, 127, and 193.

47. Tertullian, *Orat.* 25. He also adduces the example of Daniel.

48. Origen, *Orat.* 12.2. When Origen cites Ps 140:2 again, later in the tract, it is to instruct about proper posture in prayer (*Orat.* 31.1). Nowhere does he imply that Psalm 140 was sung or recited by the church at prayer gatherings.

as follows in comments on Psalm 142: "'Make the hearing of your mercy early to me' [Ps. 142:8]. We ask for the mercy of God in our trials. Wherefore let it be with wakefulness in our prayers (that) we devote ourselves, and even more at the morning time, so that it is possible to say, 'Oh God, my God, I rise early to you' [Ps. 62:2]."[49] The verse from Psalm 62 serves as a warrant for early prayer. Had Eusebius meant to illustrate by quoting what the church sang at that hour, he probably would have continued with the first-person plural, not with the words "so that it is possible to say," which is his impersonal way of drawing an inference using his citation-proof.[50]

Nor is there any implication of fixed daily psalms in Eusebius's explicit discussion of daily prayer in his comments on Psalm 118:161–164. The conclusion of this passage is the statement, "Seven times a day I praised you for the judgments of your righteousness." Eusebius adds some observations about this sevenfold cursus, telling his readers the following:

> Having noted this, you will understand how, before the sun, [David[51]] rising from his bed, according to what is said—"In the night my soul rises to you, O God" [Isa 26:9b] and "Oh God, my God, I rise early to you" [Ps 62:2]—used to send up the first hymn. Then with the onset of day, at the first hour, likewise early, he brought the second sacrifice to God, similarly a third at the third (hour), and again the fourth at the sixth, the fifth at the ninth, and the sixth at the twelfth. Then at vespers, after care for the body, he used to offer the seventh hymn when he was about to turn to bed. And in this way, he used to fulfill what is said, "Seven times a day I praised you."[52]

Eusebius makes no suggestion that either Isaiah 26:9b–20, which eventually became a canticle of the church, or Psalm 62, which at some point became a morning prayer, were the very hymns that David sang, or the ones that the church

---

49. Eusebius, *Comm. in psalm. 142* (PG 24: 49).

50. ὥστε δύνασθαι λέγειν. Patristic writers use the formula to introduce Scripture quotations, for example: Gregory of Nazianzus, *In sanct. bapt.* (*Orat.* 40) 40 (PG 36: 416); Basil, *Hom. in psalm. 7* 3 (PG 29: 236); Ps.-Athanasius, *De sancte trinitate, Dial.* 1.12 (PG 28: 1136). Hence, Taft exceeds the evidence when he draws the inference that Eusebius's quotation of Ps 62:2 "implies" that "the corresponding nucleus of morning praise [for the morning office] was Ps 62" (*The Liturgy of the Hours in East and West*, 33).

51. In his opening comments on this psalm, Eusebius makes clear that he assumes that David is the author, referring to him as "the prophet." *Comm. in psalm. 118* (PG 23: 1368).

52. Eusebius, *Comm. in psalm. 118* (PG 23: 1392).

of Eusebius's time sang daily. Instead, he speaks of David offering hymns to God throughout the twenty-four-hour cycle in accordance with practices he mentions in certain psalms.

One question remains. I have been referring to the songs of the daily office as psalms. Since Eusebius never specifies any particular song that Christians sang at these hours, is it possible that he meant composed Christian hymns? That is unlikely. No subsequent fourth- or fifth-century references to the daily office mention Christian hymns. Where later writers mention specific songs of the office, they are always biblical psalms, canticles, and an expanded *Gloria*. Hence, while the use of Christian hymns cannot be ruled out (such as an early form of *Phos hilaron* at vespers), the evidence suggests that the songs of the daily office were overwhelmingly psalms. Otherwise we would have to imagine that daily hymnody was replaced within a generation by daily psalmody.

In summary, the peace following the Edict of Milan created the conditions for a massive church building program and a renewal of worship, including the widespread establishment of morning and evening cathedral hours. Eusebius provides the earliest clear evidence for these hours, noting how widespread the custom was in his day and situating it in a historical context as something new, at least in its universality. He makes it clear that song, almost certainly psalmody, was part of this office, but he does not suggest that particular psalms were fixed parts of these liturgies. Of course, a given church in a given city may have settled on its own regular psalms for the daily office. But Eusebius makes no mention of that either.

After Eusebius's remarks about the cathedral office in the East, the next references may be statements in certain canons of the Council of Laodicea; but these are difficult to date, and their references to psalmody appear in contexts that imply church services but do not specify the type of service. Canon 17 is the most suggestive because it says that "between each psalm there should be a reading." This fits the daily office or a vigil, depending on local custom. Additional evidence for morning and evening church prayer and song, along with other hours, appears in writings that date to the late fourth century, including Egeria's travel journal, the *Apostolic Constitutions*, the *Canons of Hippolytus*, the tractate *On the Faith*, which concludes Epiphanius's *Panarion*, and a baptismal catechesis by John Chrysostom, along with John's sermons.

In chapter 23 of *On the Faith*, Epiphanius writes that Christian liturgies include "morning hymns" and "morning prayers" at church, as well as "vesper psalms together with prayers."[53] In chapter 24, he says that "the holy universal and apostolic church" "ordains the sending up of prayers to God . . . at the

53. Epiphanius, *Fid.* 24 (Holl 3:524).

established hours by night and by day."[54] These passages suggest that an established ecclesiastical *horarium* prevailed in Eastern churches and consisted of song and prayer each morning and evening. The opening lines of *On the Faith* show that Epiphanius conceived *On the Faith* as a conclusion to his *Panarion*, which is where it is found. Hence, it was composed when that work was written—in the latter part of the 370s when Epiphanius was bishop of Constantia (Salamis) on Cyprus,[55] or not much later.

Egeria tells us that at Jerusalem, monks and various laypeople gathered at the Church of the Resurrection (the Anastasis) before cockcrow for song and prayer. A prayer was recited by a presbyter after each of the songs, which she terms "hymns," "psalms," and "antiphons."[56] This service took place before the bishop arrived, and it concluded with morning hymns at the first sign of day.[57] Then the bishop came, with additional clergy, and entered the cave to conduct prayer, commemorations, and the blessing of the catechumens. Egeria does not mention psalmody as part of the bishop's service. Later, at the sixth hour (roughly noon), monks and laypeople again gathered in the Church of the Resurrection for "psalms and antiphons;" they did the same at the ninth hour (roughly 3 p.m.), in both cases before the bishop arrived.[58] It is possible that prayers were recited by presbyters between the psalms at these hours, just as they were at cockcrow, although Egeria does not say. In Lent, the church also kept the third hour (roughly 9 a.m.), doing so in the same manner as the sixth.[59] Egeria notes that this third hour was a recent innovation. She probably assumed that the other hours of the daily office were very old.

Egeria has more to say about song at vespers. At the tenth hour (roughly 4 p.m.), a service of songs was conducted in the Anastasis, which was filled with light from candles and lamps.[60] "Vesper psalms and also antiphons" were recited, she says. The expression "vesper psalms" implies a more-or-less-fixed set of hymns for vespers. These may have included not only biblical psalms, such as Psalm 140

54. Epiphanius, *Fid.* 24 (Holl 3:525). The expression νύκτωρ καὶ μεθ' ἡμέραν is classical (LSJ, s.v. μετά with the acc., II.2), and the classical meaning ("by night and by day") is the only translation that makes good sense here.

55. See Frank Williams, tr., *The Panarion of Epiphanius: Book I*, 2nd ed. (Brill, 2009), xvi and xx.

56. Egeria, *Itin.* 24.1.

57. *Itin.* 24.2.

58. *Itin.* 24.3.

59. *Itin.* 27.4.

60. *Itin.* 24.5.

(which was the evening psalm at Antioch[61]), but one or more Christian hymns.[62] The psalms and antiphons are sung "for some time" before the bishop is called. Once the bishop has arrived and he and the presbyters are in their seats, more psalms and antiphons are sung. There is a commemoration of persons, conducted by a deacon, who reads out names, one by one; and after each name, a large choir of children responds by singing *Kyrie eleison*. This is the only place in Egeria's journal where such a choir is mentioned, and it does not perform psalms, at least not by itself, probably because the vesper psalmody was not unison choral singing by a choir but responsorial congregational psalmody in which the children participated along with everyone else.

The *Apostolic Constitutions* is a composite document, which has been assigned a Syrian provenance and has been dated to sometime between 375 and 380.[63] There are decisive reasons for concluding that it cannot have been earlier and less decisive reasons for thinking that it was not composed after 381 or even as late as the 390s. The considerations favoring a composition before 381 are said to be (1) that the *AC* inveighs against Christian participation in pagan rites,[64] an instruction that would have been unnecessary after the Edict of Thessalonica issued by Emperor Theodosius in 380; and (2) that the *AC* regards the Holy Spirit as a created being, which contradicts the doctrine of the Spirit approved by the Council of Constantinople in 381. As for the unorthodox doctrine of the Spirit, it is conceivable that the author was heterodox on that subject, just as he appears to have had "Arian" (or "Homoean") inclinations.[65] The proof based on imperial legislation falters on the fact that the Edict of Thessalonica, although it declared Nicene Christianity to be the official state religion, did not ban pagan rites. Bans were subsequently issued in the imperial edicts of February of 391 at Aquileia, in June of 392 at Milan, and in November of 392 at Constantinople, the last being comprehensive in scope. Moreover, it is not known how far any of these bans were

61. See John Chrysostom, *In psalm. 140* 1 (PG 55: 427), discussed below.

62. For example, at some point a hymn called *Phos hilaron* was sung at vespers in the Eastern church, although its composition and use cannot be confidently dated to as early as the fourth century. Basil's quotation of a vesper formula that closely resembles one of its lines (*Spir. Sanct.* 29 [73]) is ambiguous evidence, since the hymn may have incorporated a pre-existing vesper formula. For a full discussion of the history of the hymn, see Peter Plank, ΦΩΣ ΙΛΑΡΟΝ: *Christushymnus und Lichtdanksagung der frühen Christenheit* (Borengässer, 2002).

63. See the discussion of the provenance and date of the *AC* in Marcel Metzger, *Les Constitutions apostoliques*, vol. 1 (Cerf, 1985), 54-60; also the summary of discussion in Paul F. Bradshaw, *The Search for the Origins of Christian Worship*, 2nd ed. (Oxford University Press, 2002), 84–86.

64. *Const. ap.* 2.60.6–62.4.

65. Bradshaw, *The Search for the Origins of Christian Worship*, 85. Regarding the terms "Arian" and "Homoean," see chapter 9 n. 12.

enforced.[66] In any case, the fact of the bans suggests some continued attachment to traditional pagan rites, which could certainly have included Christian loyalty to them, especially in the countryside. Furthermore, admonitions against pagan practice were already part of one of the *AC*'s source-texts, the *Didascalia*, and that would have been reason enough for the compiler to have retained them as "apostolic" injunctions.

Book 2 of the *Apostolic Constitutions* gives instruction for the morning and evening church office and includes the earliest explicit information about specific fixed psalms for these services. The source of Book 2 is the *Didascalia*, which was composed in Greek in the early third century; but the Syriac version of the *Didascalia*, which was translated from one of the Greek editions, does not include the instruction about morning and evening prayer. That instruction, therefore, was probably added by the compiler of the *Apostolic Constitutions*:

> Since you are the body of Christ, do not "scatter" [Matt 12:30] by not gathering together. Having Christ as head, according to his promise to be with you and commune with you, do not fail to take care of yourselves; do not deprive the savior of his own members; do not divide his body; do not scatter his members; and do not prefer worldly needs to the word of God. But gather each day in the morning and evening to sing and pray in the precincts of the Lord (*en tois kyriakois*), saying Psalm 62 in the morning and Psalm 140 in the evening.[67]

This admonition is preceded by an instruction to bishops, cast in second-person singular imperatives, reminding them of their duty to see to it that the people gather at church every day, morning and evening. The succeeding words, addressed to the church as a whole, are full of arguments for attending the morning and evening services. Hence, the tenor of the passage suggests that members of the laity were not in the habit of showing up in significant numbers for daily prayer. For manual laborers and those who ran small shops, it may have been difficult to do so.[68] Since the primary readership of the *Apostolic*

66. See Alan Cameron, *The Last Pagans of Rome* (Oxford University Press, 2011), 59–70.

67. *Const. ap.* 2.59.2.

68. Even in the case of the weekly Sunday service of the word and Communion, it was mostly the wealthy Christian elite, including some prosperous artisans and small landowners and their households, who had the leisure time to regularly attend Sunday services. See Ramsay MacMullen, "The Preacher's Audience (AD 350–400)," *Journal of Theological Studies* 40 (1989): 504–506 and 510–511 (503–511); reiterated in MacMullen, *The Second Church: Popular Christianity A.D. 200–40* (Society of Biblical Literature, 2009), 14–15, 20–21; Wendy Mayer,

Constitutions would have been clergy, these admonitions are probably a bit of guidance to bishops and deacons about how to make the case to the people that they should attend morning and evening prayer at church.

The instruction that Psalm 140 should be said in the evening and Psalm 62 in the morning indicates standardization. At the same time, it implies that the recitation of these psalms at morning and evening cathedral services did not go without saying. Is that because psalmody at the daily office had been (or still was) variable in western Syria until recently and the author of the *AC* wanted to establish a custom of fixed psalms? Yet Psalms 62 and 140 must have already been the standard morning and evening psalms in Antioch, for John Chrysostom tells his congregation that Psalm 140 was selected by "the fathers" to be said every evening and Psalm 62 every morning and that they must have had good reason for making these selections besides the mere mention of times of day in these psalms.[69] The attribution of the custom to "the fathers" implies an established tradition, and John's comment shows that he had no information, firsthand or otherwise, about the reasons for the decision. Hence, the psalms must have been selected before he commenced his presbyterial service in Antioch in 381, deep enough in the past that no one was still telling stories about the fathers' decision by the time John started his ministry.[70] John's statements encourage us to think that Psalms 62 and 140 had been established as the regular psalms of the daily office in Antioch sometime in the mid-fourth century, whereas the *AC*'s late fourth-century instruction that these psalms should be sung at the morning and evening office may reflect its author's effort to get certain other Syrian churches besides Antioch to adopt the same custom.

Apart from the remarks in John's homily and the instruction in the *Apostolic Constitutions*, fourth-century sources in the East do not specify particular psalms for morning and evening church prayer or for other hours.[71] There is, however,

---

"Who Came to Hear John Chrysostom Preach? Recovering a Late Fourth-Century Preacher's Audience," *Ephemerides Theologicae Lovanienses* 76 (2000): 87.

69. John Chrysostom, *In psalm. 140* 1 (PG 55: 427). "I do not think," John remarks, "that this psalm was thoughtlessly designated by the fathers to be said every evening or because of the one word ["evening"]."

70. The homily on Psalm 140 in which John makes his remark cannot be dated with any confidence except to say that it was delivered during his years as a preaching presbyter in Antioch from 381 to 397 or as patriarch in Constantinople from 397 until his death in 407. In any case, the selection made by "the fathers," about which John had no information regarding its reasoning, must have been made well before 381. On the dating of John's homilies, see Wendy Mayer's exacting study, *The Homilies of St. John Chrysostom—Provenance: Reshaping the Foundations* (Pontificio Istituto Orientale, 2005).

71. On the basis of the evidence in *Apostolic Constitutions* and John Chrysostom that Psalms 62 and 140 were, respectively, the standard morning and evening psalms, Taft infers that such

evidence for specific fixed psalms in monastic liturgies. John Cassian's recollections of his early monastic life include the memory that Psalms 50, 62, and 89 were sung at a Bethlehem monastery in a sunrise service that was relatively new in 382–383, when a young John Cassian lived there.[72] Psalms 62, 5, and 89 were sung at matins by monks in North Africa, according to the *Ordo monasterii* (a short rule associated with the circle of Augustine).[73]

The fact that Psalm 62 was the standard hymn of the morning office in Antioch, that it was also endorsed for that role by the *AC*, and that it was one of three regular hymns of a morning office in the two monastic traditions just mentioned cannot be coincidental and raises the question of whether monks brought urban-church customs to their monastic routines or vice versa. The early-morning psalmody that Egeria ascribes to the daily office at Jerusalem takes place before the bishop arrives, and it is part of a service of monks, laity, and presbyters. The presbyters read the prayers, but Egeria does not say that they lead the psalmody. This has suggested to some liturgical historians that it was monks who brought psalmody to the urban daily office, with the result that the cathedral office of the late fourth century was a hybrid, a combination of an indigenous cathedral office, led by the local bishop and his clergy, and a monastic office at which monks played the leading role. I will say more about this in chapter 8.

As for the West, Ambrose cites some of the old prooftexts from Psalms 118 and 64 and Isaiah 26 when he refers to morning psalmody in his commentary on the psalms, composed in the 390s.[74] Significantly, when he quotes these passages, he refers to his audience as the ones who "say" the words, and at one point he makes clear that he has in mind attendance at church, not prayer at home.[75] It

---

was "probably" the case (along with other features of these offices) more or less universally in the East at the end of the fourth century (*The Liturgy of the Hours in East and West*, 55). This could be right, but these two psalms are documented as the regular fixed hymns of these offices only for Syria and perhaps Constantinople (which probably followed Antiochene custom), the evidence being the prescription in the *Apostolic Constitutions* and John Chrysostom's remark about liturgical practice.

72. John Cassian, *Inst.* 3.6, nicely explicated by Taft, *The Liturgy of the Hours in East and West*, 78–79.

73. *Ord. mon.* 2.

74. Ambrose, *Expos. psalm. 118* 19.30 (Isa 26:9) and 19.33 (and Pss 64:9 and 118:148) (CSEL 62: 437–438).

75. According to Ambrose, Christ speaks the words of Isa 26:9 to Ambrose's readers but does so in the voice of the readers: "you say" (*dices*) words of that verse, just as "you say" the words of Ps 64:98 and "you will not be hindered from saying" the words of Ps 118:148. These formulations use second-person *singular* verbs, but Ambrose has practices at church in mind. For on the way to quoting Ps 118:148, he urges, "Hurry to church (*mane festina ad ecclesiam*)." Taft quotes the relevant portions in translation. He further suspects that Ambrose's allusion to the "evening

appears, then, that the morning office at Milan differed from morning psalmody in Syria. The Milanese office had more than one fixed psalm, which did not, apparently, include Psalm 62; it also included a fixed canticle.

The late fourth-century sources make clear that biblical prooftexts, drawn from the Psalter, had in some places influenced choices about fixed psalms of the daily office, although they did not dictate the psalm choices everywhere. Only three of the five psalms variously assigned to morning prayer by late fourth-century monastic and ecclesiastical authorities contain prooftexts cited by earlier writers. These are Psalms 140, 62, and 5.[76]

Morning and evening prayer were not the only hours kept by churches in the late fourth century. While Book 2 of the *Apostolic Constitutions* seems to know only two daily hours, Book 8 refers to a sixfold cursus: "Perform prayer in the morning, at the third hour and the sixth and the ninth, and in the evening and at cockcrow."[77] After stating symbolic rationales for each of these hours, the *AC* adds the following instruction:

> And if it is not possible to gather at church because of the unbelievers, assemble at home, O bishop, so that piety might not enter an assembly of the impious. For the place does not sanctify the person, but the person the place. And if the impious hold the place, let it be avoided by you, because it has been profaned by them. For as the holy priests sanctify, the profane pollute. And if you cannot gather together in a house or in the church, let each sing, pray, and read alone or together in groups of two or three.[78]

If home prayer, as an alternative to attending church prayer, was to include song and Scripture readings, the church hours must have featured the same. The *AC*'s guidance implies that the usual places of assembly were occasionally occupied by "unbelievers," the typical word for nonChristians (not for heretics). There is no hint that these unbelievers were hostile, only that their presence polluted the locale. This might suggest that some of the churches met in public or semi-public places, not in their own church buildings, which raises very interesting questions

sacrifice" in *Expos. Ps. 118* 8.48 implies the use of Psalm 140 as a fixed vesper psalm (CSEL 62: 180). See Taft, *The Liturgy of the Hours in East and West*, 142–143.

76. Ps 140:2 is cited as a prooftext by Origen (*Orat.* 12) and Eusebius (*Comm. in psalm. 64* in PG 23: 640, quoted above); Ps 62:2 is cited as a prooftext by Eusebius (*Comm. in psalm. 142* in PG 24: 49, discussed above), Ps 5:4 by Origen (*Orat.* 12) and Cyprian (*Dom. orat.* 35).

77. *Const. ap.* 8.34.1.

78. *Const. ap.* 8.34.8–10.

about the audience and milieu of the *AC*. Perhaps the author-compiler meant to address not only urban church leaders but clergy of the countryside, where village congregations had no building of their own but met in public places.

The songs envisioned by the *Apostolic Constitutions* for all six daily prayer services must have included biblical psalms, perhaps hymns and biblical canticles as well.[79] It is uncertain to what extent this sixfold cursus reflects an already established custom in the region for which it was composed, as opposed to an aspirational vision. John Chrysostom seems to imply that the church at Antioch observed only morning and evening prayer, prayer at other times being a purely personal duty.[80] Perhaps the author of the *Apostolic Constitutions* had witnessed the daily cursus at Jerusalem and wished to promote it in Syria.

A daily morning gathering at cockcrow is mentioned in Rule 21 of the *Canons of Hippolytus*, which urges the clergy and the people "to perform the prayers, the psalms, and the reading of scripture."[81] The original Greek *Canons of Hippolytus* was composed in Egypt in around the years 336–340.[82] What it

---

79. An expanded version of the *Gloria* is quoted in *Apostolic Constitutions* but without a comment about when it was sung (*Const. ap.* 7.47–48.3). Although Vaticanus gr. 2089 calls it a "morning hymn" in the heading (see Funk's edition, 455), this is probably a later scribal addition. That said, the pairing with the *Nunc dimittis* (7.48.4) may suggest that these were already well-known as the morning and evening hymns, respectively. The fifth-century Codex Alexandrinus designates the *Gloria* as a morning hymn. And the *De virginitate* (doubtfully attributed to Athanasius) instructs celibate women to say the *Gloria* at the end of their nighttime vigil, specifically at dawn (*Virg.* 20).

80. John Chrysostom, *Cat. bapt.* 8.17–18 (SC 50: 256–257); *Expos. in psalm. 140* 1 and 3 (PG 55: 427–433); *In 1 Tim.*, Hom. 6.1 (PG 62: 530; Field, *Interp. in. ep. Paul.* 6: 48). I assume that, whether delivered in Antioch or Constantinople, these sermons and writings reflect liturgical traditions first established at Antioch. The reference to the duty of personal prayer appears in *Ann.*, Hom. 4.5–6 (PG 54: 666–668). All this evidence from Chrysostom is laid out with extensive quotation in Taft, *The Liturgy of the Hours in East and West*, 42–44.

81. Translation from Paul F. Bradshaw, ed., *The Canons of Hippolytus*, with an English translation by Carol Bebawi (Grove, 1987), 26.

82. The only extant version is an Arabic edition based on a Coptic translation of the Greek. A composition of the Greek original between 336 and 340 has been ably argued by René-Georges Coquin, *Les canons d'Hippolyte* (Firmin Didot, 1966), 324–329 [56–61]. The case he makes has been widely accepted and has convinced, for example, Bradshaw, *The Canons of Hippolytus*, 5–8. Christoph Markschies, however, makes a case for the latter part of the fourth century, probably the last quarter, based on the pneumatological tendencies he discerns in the work. And Alister Stewart contends that the document was redacted over several decades between 340 and 380 in different places. See Christoph Markschies, "Wer schrieb die sogenannte Traditio Apostolica? Neue Beobachtungen und Hypothesen zu einer kaum lösbaren Frage aus der altkirchlichen Literaturgeschichte," in Wolfram Kinzig, Christoph Markschies, und Markus Vinzent, *Tauffragen und Bekenntnis* (De Gruyter, 1999), 63–69; Alister Stewart, *The Canons of Hippolytus: An English Version, with Introduction and Annotation and an Accompanying Arabic Text* (Macquarie Centre, SCH, 2021).

commands for the liturgy at cockcrow is the same as that prescribed by the *AC* for daily services: prayer, song, and Scripture readings.

In the West, the earliest evidence for additional daily hours beyond morning and evening prayer is a statement by Augustine in a letter of 395. Speaking of daily prayer at Hippo, he mentions "divine readings and psalms" at midday and "alternating reading and psalmody" in the afternoon.[83]

Excursus

The Rhetoric of Plurals

Taft observes that "from the second half of the fourth century, sources with remarkable consistency call matins '*matutini hymni*' or some such plural name."[84] Moreover, John Chrysostom remarks that some members of his flock imagine that they have done all that is necessary for their salvation if they have sung "two or three psalms" and have performed "the customary prayers,"[85] which must refer to members of his flock who attend the morning or evening office or both. It is unclear, however, which of these services might have featured more than one psalm. Moreover, in another place, John implies that there was a single morning psalm and a single evening psalm.[86] This is also the impression one gets from the *Apostolic Constitutions*, which specifies a single psalm for morning prayer and a single one for vespers.[87]

Plurals can be tricky. When Epiphanius says that "there are continuously morning hymns in the same holy church and morning prayers, and lamp-lighting psalms and at the same time prayers,"[88] the plurals could refer to more than one psalm at each service or to a multiplicity of psalms thanks to the repetition of the services day after day. Moreover, not every plural was meant literally. Although Ambrose urges, "In the morning, hurry to church... How pleasant it is to begin the day with psalms,"[89] he also says that "the start of day echoes with a psalm;

83. Augustine, *Ep.* 29.10–11 (PL 33: 119–120; CSEL 34/1: 121).

84. Taft, *The Liturgy of the Hours in East and West*, 193.

85. John Chrysostom, *In Matt.*, Hom 11.7 (PG 57: 200; Field, *Hom. in Matt.* 1: 149).

86. John Chrysostom, *In psalm. 140* 1 (PG 55: 427) (cited above).

87. *Const. ap.* 2.59.2.

88. Epiphanius, *Fid.* 24 (Holl 3:524).

89. Ambrose, *Expos. psalm. 118* 19.32 (CSEL 62:438–439). Note that this passage is quoted in *MECL* no. 281 but without its continuation in the sentence I have just quoted (an oversight, no doubt).

sundown resounds with one."[90] Egeria uses the expression "hymns and antiphons" to describe the singing of a single hymn during a Palm Sunday procession down the Mount of Olives, namely, Psalm 117.[91] In these passages, Ambrose's and Egeria's plurals are probably rhetorical.

The rhetorical plural is first mentioned as an element of style by Aristotle in *The Art of Rhetoric*, where he encourages the use of the plural for the singular to achieve a more elevated style, "as the poets do."[92] This use of plurals remained common with later speakers and writers, being found in the Roman era in both poetry and prose, Greek as well as Latin. Ovid uses the plural *atria* instead of the singular *atrium*, where the referent is singular.[93] Dio Chrysostom speaks in the plural of emperors when he means only one.[94] The Latin historian Justin refers to Alexander's tendency to murder his "friends," meaning a single friend (Cleitus).[95] An imperial biography in the *Historia Augusta* declares that "if the senate of the Roman people had its old authority . . . the public fortunes would not have gone to the Vitelliuses or the Neros or the Domitians."[96] One did not need an advanced education to understand or use this element of style, since ordinary people heard it in public speeches.

Vigils and Prayer Meetings as Preludes to Communion

The weekly Sunday morning service at Jerusalem was immediately preceded by a resurrection vigil that commenced before cockcrow and replaced or otherwise subsumed the weekly office at cockcrow.[97] For lack of a better term, I will use the term "prelude" to suggest the immediate relation of this gathering to the morning Communion service that followed.

Outside the still-locked Anastasis, the lamp-lit forecourt was filled with people, including monks, laity, and clergy. "Hymns as well as antiphons" were

---

90. Ambrose, *Expl. psalm. 1* 9 (CSEL 64:7).

91. Egeria, *Itin.* 31.2.

92. Aristotle, *Rhet.* 3.6.4 (1407b26–35).

93. Ovid, *Met.* 4.763.

94. Dio Chrysostom, *Or.* 46.3–4, where τῶν αὐτοκρατόρων means τοῦ αὐτοκράτορος, as the next sentence shows.

95. Justin, *Epit. hist. Philipp.* 9.8.15–16, drawing a comparison between Philip's treatment of Alexander and Alexander's treatment of Cleitus.

96. *non ad Vitellios neque ad Nerones neque ad Domitianos publica fata venissent. HAClodAlb.* 13.5.

97. Egeria, *Itin.* 24.8–12 (the vigil) and 25.1 (the eucharistic service).

sung with prayers "between each hymn and antiphon."[98] (It is possible that among the psalms, hymns, and antiphons, there were both biblical psalms and biblical canticles, but Egeria does not specify what was sung.) The bishop arrived at cockcrow, the doors were opened, and the people crowded into the lighted interior. There, presbyters and deacons took turns leading responsorial psalmody, specifically, three psalms, each followed by a prayer.[99] The bishop read an account of the passion, including the resurrection, while incense filled the basilica. Then he was led "with hymns" to the Cross, a "rock" just outside the Church of the Holy Sepulcher, where he presided at a ritual consisting of a psalm and prayer.[100] After that, he and some of the lay people retired, while the monks and others returned to the Anastasis for more psalmody, which continued right up until daybreak, when the bishop returned and the morning eucharistic service commenced.

A somewhat similar prelude service is mentioned in one of the canons falsely attributed to Basil: Canon 97 prescribes that "when you begin to hold the Mysteries, you should not do it in an unruly fashion but should wait until the whole community is gathered; the psalms should be read as long as they [the people] are coming in."[101] Then, "when the congregation is assembled," the service is to begin with lessons from the epistles, Acts, and the gospels.[102]

There is speculation that in Milan, where Communion was held every day at noon, it may have been customary to hold a prayer service with song as a direct prelude to midday Mass. In comments on Psalm 118, Ambrose urges his congregation to go to church at midday, when "hymns are sung and the *oblatio* is celebrated."[103] The plural "hymns" could suggest something more than a psalm

98. Egeria, *Itin.* 24.8-9. This Sunday vigil replaced the regular daily service at this hour (see 24.1).

99. Egeria, *Itin.* 24.10.

100. Egeria, *Itin.* 24.11.

101. Ps.-Basil, *Canon* 97; my translation of Riedel's German translation, which is given more fully in n. 102.

102. "When the mysteries begin to take place, they should not behave in an unruly way but should wait until the whole congregation is assembled: as long as they are going in, they should read psalms. Then, when the congregation is gathered, there should be readings from the Apostles, then from the Acts and the Gospel. If the deacons read (out loud) well, they should read the psalms. And if the presbyters read well, they should read the Gospel." My English translation of the German translation of Ps.-Basil, *Canon* 97 in Wilhelm Riedel, *Die Kirchenrechtsquellen des Patriarchats Alexandrien* (Deichert, 1900), 273 (f. 169a). The *Canons of Basil*, which survive in Arabic and some Coptic fragments, have yet to be published in a critical edition.

103. Ambrose, *Expos. psalm. 118* 8.48 (CSEL 62: 180). See Josef Schmitz, *Gottesdienst im altchristlichen Mailand* (Hansten, 1975), 309–310. Schmitz sees a parallel between the passage in Ambrose and the one in Egeria. On the whole subject, see Ansgar Franz, "Die Tagzeitenliturgie

lesson before the sermon and might be shorthand for a service of psalms, prayers, and Scripture readings.[104]

Psalmody as Prayer

The singing of psalms at prayer gatherings is so well-known to historians of Christian liturgy that it is easy for those of us who study the subject to neglect to ask why *psalms* became a standard element of prayer services. Pagan cults offer only a limited and indirect cultural parallel. The hymns and prayers of pagan cults were performed by priests and choirs kept by the temple or organized for a particular sacrificial ritual, not by ordinary worshipers who attended the liturgies.[105]

Did Christians include psalmody at the daily office because general cultural assumptions led them to regard hymns as a form of prayer? The church's formative development took place mostly in Greek-speaking environments, where the common meaning of the word *hymnos* was "sung praise of a deity." In the Hellenic tradition, the hymn was distinguished from prayer, even though there was overlap between the two in content and often in structure.[106] From Archaic times through the first four centuries of the Common Era, verbs for singing were rarely used by Greek-speaking people to describe the performance of anything called a prayer or thanksgiving, and hymns were almost never called prayers.[107] The reason is no doubt the prevailing Hellenic conception of prayer. While moderns think of prayer as any form of address to God, ancient Greeks regarded prayers as cultic vows and petitions to a deity. The *Suda*, a Byzantine lexicon based largely on preByzantine sources, sums up these two senses as *euchē*

der Mailänder Kirche im 4. Jahrhundert: Ein Beitrag zur Geschichte Kathedraloffiziums im Westen," *Archiv für Liturgiewissenschaft* 34 (1992): 70–74.

104. Franz (see n. 103) argues that there is strong circumstantial evidence in this passage and others that such a prayer service (a "Mittagshore") held directly before the midday Mass included Ambrose's hymn *Iam surgit hora tertia* (which has a third-hour theme) and Psalm 118. If he is correct, other psalms may have been sung as well, with prayers in between.

105. See the discussion of this subject in chapter 10 under "The Wider Culture."

106. See the broader discussion of hymns and prayers in William D. Furley and Jan M. Bremer, *Greek Hymns: Selected Cult Songs from the Archaic to the Hellenistic Period*, vol. 1: *The Texts in Translation* (Mohr Siebeck, 2001), 3–4.

107. This assertion is based on proximity searches in the TLG, using grammatical and lexical forms of ἀείδειν and ᾄδειν, ἐπαείδειν, μέλπειν, and ψάλλειν in proximity to εὐχή, προσευχή, εὐχαριστία and ἐξομολόγησις. Although I would not claim that I have found every example, the results are probably generally reflective of speech conventions with combinations of these words.

(promise, vow) and *proseuchē* (petition).[108] Although this is an overly neat division of terms, since *euchē* was often used as a synonym of *proseuchē*, it is an accurate description of how prayer was generally understood. As for hymns, although they often included petitions, they were not called petitions; and it was extremely rare for them to be called prayers.[109]

As for the Romans, they had no precise Latin equivalent for the Greek word *hymnos*. They used the more general word *carmen* to designate what Greeks called a hymn. *Carmen* was used for poems generally, songs generally (including hymns), prayers (some of which may have been sung by priests), spells, oracles, and even legal formulas. The Latin church, however, used the word *oratio*, not *carmen*, for prayer; and it used the Greek loanword *hymnus*, not *carmen*, for a hymn. In other words, the Latin church took its cues from Eastern church custom.

In Hellenistic Judaism, however, the book of Psalms was often referred to as a collection of "hymns," and psalm superscriptions in the Septuagint label many of them as prayers. These superscriptions may have encouraged both Hellenistic Jews and educated Christians to think of the psalms as prayers and to use that term as a general appellation for them. Philo spoke of "someone familiar with Moses praying in the hymns," by which he meant the psalmist in Psalm 30.[110] It may have been common for Hellenistic Jews, who referred to the *Sofer Tehillim*—"Book of Praises" in Hebrew—as "the hymns,"[111] to think of these hymns as prayers.

Christians, whether influenced by Hellenistic-Jewish usage or only by the clues they found in the superscriptions of the Psalter itself, characterized psalms as prayers, examples of which are discussed below. But they also routinely distinguished psalms from prayers. Tertullian, for example, lists the elements of a certain "dominical" liturgy as readings, psalms, discourses, and prayers.[112] The *Apostolic Constitutions* advises that if a regular assembly is not possible for the hours of prayer, each person should "sing, read, and pray" alone or in a small

---

108. *Suda* E 3819, εὐχά.

109. I have discovered only three instances (outside of Jewish and Christian literature), where hymning is associated with praying. The first is a statement in an elegiac couplet by the sixth-century BCE poet Theognis: "I will sing, praying to the immortal gods" (Theognis 943–944). The second is merely figurative: an ancient scholiast calls Polyneices's shout of triumph after his military victory "a hymn and a prayer that he sings to the gods" (scholium to Aristophanes, *Sept.* 636 in *Scholia Graeca in Aeschylum* 2.2, ed. O. L. Smith [Teubner, 1982]). The third is a comment by Maximus of Tyre on Ariphron's famous paean to Health, and it probably refers not to the paean as a whole but only to the opening lines, which he quotes (Maximus of Tyre, *Diss.* 7.1).

110. Philo, *Conf.* 39 (referring to Ps 30:19).

111. See chapter 2.

112. Tertullian, *An.* 9.4.

private group.[113] Egeria distinguishes psalms (and hymns and antiphons) from both prayers and Scripture readings.[114] In view of the many examples where psalms and prayers are differentiated, Adalbert de Vogüé concludes that in the minds of fourth- and fifth-century Christians, psalmody was *not* prayer.[115] Moreover, Anselme Davril, although he cites at least one example where a desert father characterizes psalm recitation as speaking to God, as well as evidence that psalmody and prayer served similar functions for the monks, adduces many passages where the two are distinguished as a matter of course and one passage that suggests a hierarchy of the two.[116]

Yet quite a few Christians who distinguished psalms from prayers also spoke of psalms *as* prayers. The book of Acts describes the hymn-singing of Paul and Silas as "praying."[117] This is not necessarily psalmody, but it does treat song as prayer, probably meaning songs of thanksgiving and praise. Clement of Alexandria encouraged "psalms and hymns before supper and before bed, but also *prayers again* at night."[118] The "again" shows that he regarded the supper "psalms and hymns" as prayers. Origen tells his congregation that before a set of psalms is read in church, he prepares for the service by praying one of them.[119]

Eusebius's treatment of psalms is particularly revealing. He differentiates the psalms into speech-types through designations in a list of *hypotheseis*, "subjects," a kind of table of contents within the introductory material of his commentary on the psalms.[120] These summaries characterize fourteen of the psalms as prayers or petitions and describe many more psalms as thanksgivings and confessions. Eusebius calls five psalms "teaching about confession," which must mean that

113. *Const. ap.* 8.34.10.

114. To give one example, at the predawn daily service, clergy are present "to say the prayers between each hymn or antiphon" (*Itin.* 24.1).

115. Adalbert de Vogüé, "Psalmodier n'est pas prier," *Ecclesia Orans* 6 (1989): 7–32. De Vogüé granted that sometimes the word "prayer" was applied to a psalm or psalm-verse.

116. Anselme Davril, "La psalmodie chez les Pères du désert," *Collectanea Cisterciensia* 49 (1987): 135 (psalmody as speaking to God), 132 (psalmody and prayer both produce compunction), and 133 (prayer is superior to psalmody).

117. "At midnight, Paul and Silas, praying (προσευχόμενοι), were singing hymns to God (ὕμνουν τὸν θεόν), and the prisoners were listening to them" (Acts 16:25). The syntax implies that the hymning was a form of praying.

118. Clement of Alexandria, *Str.* 7.7.49.4.

119. Origen, *In psalm. 67*, Hom. 1.1 (from the authentic psalms commentary of Origen in *Codex Monacensis Graecus 314*).

120. Eusebius, *Periochae* (Bandt, 128–141; PG 23: 68–70), under the Greek heading Ὑπόθεσεις κ.τ.λ.

he regarded them as models of confession. Prayers, petitions, thanksgivings, and confessions all count as prayer in Christian understanding. But Eusebius calls Psalm 1 an "exhortation" and Psalm 10 a "victory hymn." He characterizes other psalms as topical poems, using expressions such as "of perfect divine restoration" (Psalm 14), "the election of the church and the resurrection of Christ" (Psalm 15), "teaching about God with ethical instruction" (Psalm 18), "a reproach of the wicked with teaching about God" (Psalm 35), "the manifestation of Christ the King" (Psalm 44), and so forth. He also terms many of the psalms "prophecies." Yet a revealing passage in the body of the commentary shows that he also thought of the whole Psalter as a book of prayers. The passage concerns a statement at the end of Psalm 71 that scholars, both ancient and modern, have taken as an editorial addition meant to mark off the first seventy-one psalms as a group. Here is Eusebius's opinion:

> [After the double "So be it"], it is next stated, "The hymns of David, son of Jesse, have ceased," instead of which Symmachus has translated, "The prayers of David, son of Jesse, have been completed." And Theodotion and the Fifth Edition: "The prayers of David, son of Jesse, have been summed up." Those unacquainted with exactitude in reading have not taken "The hymns of David, son of Jesse, have ceased" as part of the whole psalm but have read it as added from outside of the prophecy. But the rest of the translations and the Hebrew text clearly show that these are part of the whole psalm. For David the king made the genesis of the foretold Savior from his seed to shine forth constantly in his *prayers*. When this came to fruition, all the prophecies were about to be fulfilled. Naturally, he adds, after the completion of all the things previously said, how, therefore, the *prayers* of David are completed and fulfilled through the things previously said. It is also possible that "have been completed" or "have ceased" are spoken prophetically about a coming time. For each of the things already enumerated will take place when the "prayers of David, son of Jesse" are completed and fulfilled.[121]

Eusebius concludes that the statement in question is the last line of Psalm 71 and that David, in uttering it, is speaking within this poem, using a term, "prayers," that applies to all his poems. Moreover, in a remark in this context where Eusebius uses his own language without borrowing his terms from the translations, he speaks of David's "prayers": "For David the king made the genesis of the foretold Savior from his seed to shine forth constantly in his prayers.

121. Eusebius, *Comm. in psalm.*, PG 23: 821 (emphasis added).

When this came to fruition, all the prophecies were about to be fulfilled."[122] It is significant that he regards David's prophecies as prayers, even though prophecies are, as a matter of genre, addressed to the people, not to God. It is clear, then, that the diversity of speech-types in the Psalter did not prevent Eusebius from calling the Psalter David's prayers in a genre-transcending sense. He must have assumed that David addressed all these poems to God. (The assumption that all the psalms are addressed to God also seems to be assumed by the anonymous *Homily on the Psalms* and by a prefatory essay included in the introductory materials of Eusebius's commentary on the psalms, but not composed by him.[123] Both depict the composition of the psalms as liturgical activity that David and his fellow singers, with their choirs, performed in front of the sanctuary when they praised God.)

A differentiation of the Psalter into speech-types is also set forth by Athanasius, who likewise conceives of the Psalter as the church's prayerbook. Athanasius holds that the psalms contain all the genres of Scripture, and he enumerates many psalms that are meant, in his view, to function as prayers of the Christian, suitable to various personal situations. Presumably, he distinguishes these prayer forms from the other types he describes, such as prophetic psalms that foretell the coming of Christ, didactic psalms meant to instruct, and narrative psalms that rehearse the actions of God in creation and history. Yet he also thinks of all personal reading of the Psalter as speech offered to God. "Whatever the things are," he says, referring to what is said by a person reading the psalms, "these one lifts up to God as if one had done them oneself and as speaking from oneself."[124] And in another place, he advises, "Let one say and sing simply the things written, as they were spoken, so that the persons who rendered these words as their service"—the original psalmists—"might join us in praying, recognizing what is their own."[125] Similarly, in a sermon in which John Chrysostom declares that the psalmody of the people after an earthquake "removed" and "dissolved" God's wrath, he refers to their psalmody as "your prayers."[126]

A conception of psalms as prayers is also apparent in one of the precepts of the *Rule of Augustine*, which instructs that "when praying to God in psalms and hymns, what is offered with the voice should be turned over in the heart."[127]

---

122. Eusebius, *Comm. in psalm.*, PG 23: 821.

123. See chapter 3 for a discussion of the homily and the essay.

124. Athanasius, *Ep. Marc.* 11 (PG 27: 24).

125. Athanasius, *Ep. Marc.* 31 (PG 27: 41–44). Note, too, his remark that Habbakuk "prays with song (μετ' ᾠδῆς)" (*Ep. Marc.* 9; PG 27: 17).

126. John Chrysostom, *Terr. mot.* (PG 50: 716).

127. Augustine, *Reg.* 2.3.

Ephrem Syrus urges, "Speak often to God, infrequently to people. When you lend your hands to work, let your mouth sing a psalm, and let your mind pray. Let a psalm be always in your mouth."[128] The Christian author of the *Physiologus* (a fourth-century bestiary) describes virgins sending up "a euphonious hymn with concordant voice through prayers and psalmody to God."[129] And Basil asks, "Who can still consider one to be a foe with whom one utters the same prayer to God? Thus, psalmody provides the greatest of all goods, charity, by devising in its common song a certain bond of unity, and by joining together the people into the concord of a single chorus."[130]

We find similar understandings of psalms in monastic thought. The *Dialogues of Zacchaeus and Apollonius* treats monastic psalmody as an activity of "sacred worship" in which "the divinity is always praised or prayed to."[131] John Cassian differentiates psalms and prayers formally but equates them functionally. In his *Institutes*, he distinguishes psalms and prayers when he gives precise descriptions of the components of a given synaxis. In his *Conferences*, however, he treats psalmody as a form of prayer when he describes the use of the psalms by those who are advanced in their spirituality. "Taking into oneself the feelings of the psalms," he writes, "one begins to chant them in such a way that they draw out the deep compunction of the heart as if they were not composed by the prophet but had been produced by oneself as one's own prayer (*quasi orationem propriam*)."[132] If it was common for monks to think of psalms as prayer, meditative prayer one might say, that would also explain, at least in part, why the tradition of the Twelve Prayers evolved into a tradition of Twelve Psalms.[133]

It is not surprising that Christians who thought of psalms as prayers also differentiated the two when describing or regulating the occasions when they were used together, such as vigils and the daily office. In these settings they used the term "psalms" (or "hymns") for the poems in Scripture, and they used the term "prayers" for speech composed (or improvised) as address to God in confession and petition. Psalms in these settings were usually sung; prayers were recited. There was no convenient way to describe or instruct about a liturgical event that included the prayers of David and the prayers of the people than to

128. Ephrem Syrus, *De psalm.*, lines 5–7.

129. *Physiologus* 35a.

130. Basil, *Hom. in psalm. 1* 2 (PG 29: 212); tr. from *MECL* no. 131.

131. *Cons. Zacch. et Apoll.* 3.6.5 (SC 402: 204).

132. Cassian, *Conlat.*10.11.4.

133. See chapter 8.

call the former psalms/hymns and the latter prayers, even if the psalms were also conceived as a form of prayer.

A general conception of the Psalter as a book of sung prayers must have been one influential reason why Christians began including psalmody at prayer gatherings. Morning and evening church hours included both prayer and psalmody. Since the hours evolved from longstanding practices of private prayer, for which extensive scriptural rationales had been made, the inclusion of songs at the meetings, specifically sung psalms, is best explained by the widespread Christian conception of psalmody as a form of prayer.

At the same time, the conception of psalms as prayers also expanded the idea of what prayer is, since the psalms include not only forms of address to God such as petition, confession, thanksgiving, and praise but also instruction and other speech forms that do not take the form of prayer in the ordinary sense of the word. It is likely that many Christians regarded any speech addressed to God or "offered" to God as a form of prayer and thought of psalmody as song offered to God, hence as a form of prayer. This is not to say that the tendency to categorize psalmody as prayer was universal or that every ancient Christian who commented on the two was consistent in his or her conception.

CHAPTER SEVEN

Psalmody at Vigils and Occasional Services

IN ADDITION TO including psalmody among the prehomily lessons, Communion, and daily prayer, Christians of the late fourth century also sang psalms at annual feasts such as Epiphany, Lent, and Pascha/Easter, as well as other gatherings, some of which belonged to regular liturgical schedules and others that did not.

Paschal Vigils

Early Christians celebrated vigils of many types.[1] The earliest evidence for an annual vigil is the Paschal watch, which seems to have developed at an early date, probably as early as the latter part of the second century in Quartodeciman circles. I discussed this evidence in chapter 3, as well as Eusebius's claim that Christian vigils known to him were similar to the Therapeutae's song-filled vigils for their periodic feast—proof that the Therapeutae were Christians, according to Eusebius. Since the parallels Eusebius saw between the Christian Pascha of his own day and the feast of the Therapeutae included "the hymns which are customarily sung by us,"[2] probably biblical psalms,[3] this would imply a belief that a tradition of Paschal psalmody stretched from the apostolic age to his own time. If that is what he believed, then psalm-filled Paschal vigils were at least as old as his own memory of them, perhaps from his childhood.

A reference to Paschal psalmody is also found in the *Demonstrations* by Aphrahat (d. post 345). Aphrahat, who hailed from a region near the border of eastern Syria and Persia, mentions the following elements of Easter night: fasting, prayer, praise, "the singing of psalms in whatever manner is suitable," baptism, "the benediction of consecration" (the Eucharist?), and "all the things

---

1. The evidence for vigils has been surveyed by Robert Taft, who identifies no fewer than nine different types. See chapter 9 of Robert F. Taft, *The Liturgy of the Hours in East and West: The Origins of the Divine Office and Its Meaning for Today*, 2nd ed. (Liturgical Press, 1986), which is a detailed examination of cathedral vigils that concludes with a convenient list (pp. 166-190).

2. Eusebius, *H.E.* 2.17.22.

3. Not only the time period, the first half of the fourth century, but also Eusebius's own tendencies in using terminology for songs suggest that the Paschal hymns were predominantly psalms. See the observations in chapter 3 (with notes 52 and 53).

that are usually completed."[4] He does not clarify when the fast was broken. If the list reflects a temporal sequence, the psalmody preceded the fast-breaking Eucharist, which may have concluded the vigil.

Egeria's description of the Easter vigil at Jerusalem is rather brief. She reports that it was done "the same way as us," and she focuses on the rites conducted by the bishop with the newly baptized.[5] She says almost nothing about song. The vigil began on Saturday of Holy Week. The customary ninth hour was not observed. Instead, the Paschal vigil began at the ninth or tenth hour in the Martyrium. This could well be an echo of the old Quartodeciman resurrection vigil, a celebration that began with a supper at sundown or several hours later. Moreover, the resurrection focus of the regular Sunday vigil and its additional lighting, which made the church bright not only inside but outside in its forecourt, are reasons to suspect that when this Sunday vigil was added to the daily office in Jerusalem, it was modeled on the church's much older Paschal vigil. In any case, the lack of detail about the Easter vigil is best explained by the assumption that it was no different from the weekly resurrection vigil, except for the earlier start, which incorporated vespers, and the bishop's activities with the baptizands. The weekly resurrection vigil included extensive psalmody.[6]

An Easter vigil with bright lights symbolizing the resurrection was also customary elsewhere,[7] including late fourth-century Cappadocia. In the words of Gregory of Nazianzus, "the holy and famous Pascha" is "the queen of days, the bright night that banishes the darkness of sin, when we celebrate our salvation with bounteous light, and, having died with the light who died for us, rise with the risen one."[8] He makes this remark in an account of a resurrection vigil on the night when the bishop, Gregory's father (Gregory Sr.), was on the verge of death. The people did not know whether to celebrate the resurrection or weep for the bishop, so they ended up mixing cries of grief into their singing: "O those tears, which were shed by the people then! O the sounds and wails and hymns mixed with the psalmody!"[9]

---

4. Aphrahat, *Dem.* 12.13 (Parisot 1: 537–538; I have relied on the editor's Latin translation).

5. Egeria, *Itin.* 38.

6. See "The Sunday Vigil in Jerusalem" below and also the description of this vigil in chapter 6.

7. According to Eusebius, Constantine improved the lighting of the Easter vigil by installing wax tapers and torches throughout the city (probably Constantinople), so that the night of the Easter vigil was bright as day (*Vit. Const.* 4.22).

8. Gregory of Nazianzus, *Or.* 18(*Funebris oratio in partem*).28 (PG 35: 1017).

9. Gregory of Nazianzus, *Or.* 18.28 (PG 35: 1020). The language of "hymns mixed into the psalmody" is somewhat curious. If it is not simply a pleonasm, it could mean both psalms and canticles. If so, that would explain why Gregory goes on to mention Miriam striking her timbrel

Only John Chrysostom mentions a specific Easter psalm, assuming that it is Easter he has in mind in his remarks at the beginning of a sermon on Psalm 117: "The verse of this psalm. which the people are accustomed to sing in response, is this: 'This is the day which the Lord has made. Let us rejoice and be glad in it' (v. 24). This has roused many, and the people are accustomed to sing it above all at that spiritual festival (*panēgyris*) and heavenly banquet."[10] According to John, it was "the fathers" who established this fixed psalm and its response.

In summary, an annual celebration of a Christian Pascha had established itself in Asia Minor by the second half of the second century. It included a fast that was broken by a supper on the evening of 14 Nisan, which some may have thought of as the start of 15 Nisan (according to a Jewish division of days). By the 190s, Christians in other places had transformed this Quartodeciman Pascha into a dominical Easter, which made Easter Sunday the pinnacle of the feast. Some of them continued the custom of breaking the fast at an evening supper, others did so at midnight, and still others at cockcrow or dawn. Some who observed an evening fast-breaking continued the tradition of a supper. Those who broke their fast in the middle of the night or at or near dawn probably celebrated a ceremonial Eucharist and satisfied their hunger at a morning breakfast at home. Where the custom of an evening supper was dropped, psalmody, which in the early development of Pascha had belonged to after-supper singing, became part of the Paschal vigil. In churches where the breaking of the fast was followed by a continuation of the vigil and not a dismissal, Christians probably sang psalms during both phases of the vigil, the preCommunion phase and the postCommunion phase.

Epiphany

Clement of Alexandria reports that some followers of Basilides celebrated the baptism of Jesus on January 10 and others on January 6, with a preceding vigil that featured "readings."[11] This is the earliest evidence for Epiphany.[12] Clement

(18.28). Although this might be purely figurative, it could refer to the singing of Exod 15:20–21 or the whole victory canticle of Exod 15.

10. John Chrysostom, *In Psalm. 117* 1 (PG 55: 328). Gregory of Nyssa also interprets these words as a reference to the resurrection of Christ, which establishes a new creation; but he says nothing about their use as a psalmodic refrain. See Gregory of Nyssa, *De tridui inter mort. et res. Dom. nos. Iesu Christi spatio* (*Or.* 1) (GNO 9/1: 279).

11. Clement of Alexandria, *Str.* 1.21.146.1–3 (15th or 11th of Tubi).

12. On the origins and theological evolution of the Feast of Epiphany in early Christianity and particularly in the East, see Gabriele Winkler, "The Appearance of Light at the Baptism of Jesus and the Origins of the Feast of Epiphany: An Investigation of Greek, Syriac, Armenian, and

does not say (and may not have known) what the followers of Basilides read at their Epiphany gatherings or whether they sang.

The earliest explicit reference to psalms at Epiphany may be a description given by Gregory of Nazianzus. As part of a funeral panegyric in which he claims that the Arian emperor Valens felt intimidated by the size of the crowds that came to hear Basil, he describes an appearance of Valens at Basil's church in Caesarea during Epiphany in the year 372. When the emperor entered the church, he was taken aback by "the sea of people" and "the crashing psalmody."[13] Gregory, who was probably present,[14] does not specify the time or day of the service. Nor does he say which moment in the service had arrived when the emperor entered the church, although he implies that Communion had not yet taken place. Unless there was an entrance hymn, the singing must have been part of a responsive psalm lesson. The story illustrates the importance of popular support for a bishop when he found himself at odds with an emperor, and in this case, the thunderous psalmody of the people signified the unified orthodox voice against an Arian threat. At least that is how Gregory saw it. It is a pity that he does not happen to specify the Epiphany psalm.

There is also a reference to Epiphany song in the *Canons of Athanasius*, which was probably composed in Alexandria in the late fourth or early fifth century.[15] In a series of paragraphs concerning a bishop's obligations to the poor, the *Canons* sets forth his duties on Sundays and feast days, according to the dictum that "God has established the bishop because of the feasts, that he may refresh [the poor] at the feasts," specifically at Pascha, Pentecost, and Epiphany.[16] The instructions call Epiphany not only "the feast of [Jesus's] baptism" but also a "New Year's feast," which was celebrated in Tybi on the last day of the harvest, when the olives were gathered. On that day, "the bishop shall gather all the widows and orphans and shall rejoice with them, with prayers and hymns, and shall give unto each according to his needs."[17] This was a service of prayer and song, where the bishop

Latin Sources," in *Between Memory and Hope: Readings on the Liturgical Year*, ed. Maxwell E. Johnson (Liturgical, 2000), 291–347.

13. Gregory of Nazianzus, *Or.* 43(*In laud. Bas.*).52 (PG 36: 561).

14. See the discussion of Gregory's account of the imperial visit and its political context, including the church service, in John A. McGuckin, *St. Gregory of Nazianzus: An Intellectual Biography* (St. Vladimir's Seminary Press, 2001), 182–186. McGuckin does not happen to mention Valens's reaction to the psalmody.

15. See chapter 5 with n. 28.

16. *Can. Athan.* 16; tr. Riedel and Crum, *The Canons of Athanasius of Alexandria*, 27 (slightly altered for English style), 27.

17. *Can. Athan.* 16; tr. Riedel and Crum, *The Canons of Athanasius of Alexandria*, 27.

presided over a distribution of food to the needy.[18] The word "hymns" could include both psalms and composed hymns—psalms because they were such a ubiquitous part of Christian liturgy by this time and hymns because it would have been natural for bishops to have commissioned hymns themed to a particular feast or liturgical moment. Papyrological evidence from Egypt attests hymns that feature the topic of Jesus's baptism and other Epiphany motifs.[19] Unfortunately, none can be dated with any confidence before the late sixth century.[20]

Egeria reports on psalmody during the feast of Epiphany. The sole surviving manuscript of her account is marred by a lacuna at the point where she would have discussed Epiphany Eve.[21] The narrative picks up with a reference to a procession of monks and the bishop (perhaps others as well), who proceed to Jerusalem during the night. This detail implies that the Jerusalem church's Epiphany Eve was celebrated in Bethlehem. During the journey of five miles from there to the Holy City, the monks sang "'Blessed is the one who comes in the name of the Lord' and the rest that follows," that is, Psalm 117:26–29. Whether they repeated only this short hymn over and over or sang additional hymns and psalms, Egeria does not say. At the concluding predawn service in the Anastasis, there was a psalm, prayer, and blessings by the bishop. The monks remained to sing "hymns" until daylight.[22]

The Armenian Lectionary does not mention an Epiphany procession but does specify lessons and psalms for January 5 and 6 of Epiphany. It assigns Psalm 22 to a service held at the tenth hour in "the place of the shepherds," presumably at a shrine located somewhere in the countryside outside Bethlehem proper, where shepherds, "keeping their flocks by night," received the angelic annunciation, according to Luke 2:8-14. The AL gives verse 1 of Psalm 22 as the response: "The Lord is my shepherd."[23] And Psalm 79 is sung as an Alleluia psalm. There

---

18. A harvest service, with an implication of a distribution to the poor, is also described in Canon 36 of the *Canons of Hippolytus* but without reference to Epiphany or song.

19. The earliest is P. Berol. 16595, *editio princeps* in Kurt Treu, "Varia Christiana," *Archiv für Papyrusforschung* 24/25 (1976): 113–127. Some of the Epiphany hymns are discussed in David G. Martinez, "Epiphany Themes in Christian Liturgies on Papyrus," in *Light from the East: Papyrologische Kommentare zum Neuen Testament*, ed. Peter Artz-Grabner and Christina M. Kreinecker (Harrassowitz, 2010), 187–215.

20. The date assigned to P. Berol. 16595 by Kurt Treu (see n. 19) has been judged by some as too early. See Agnes T. Mihálykó, *The Christian Liturgical Papyri: An Introduction* (Mohr Siebeck, 2019), 76 and 327 (for P. Berol. 16595 specifically).

21. *Itin.* 25.6.

22. Egeria, *Itin.* 25.7.

23. AL 1. Athanase Renoux, ed., *Le codex arménien Jérusalem 121*, vol. 2: *Édition comparée du texte et de deux autres manuscrits* (Brepols, 1971), 210–211 [72–73].

is a second service, held at night—presumably in the church at Bethlehem[24]—where Psalms 2 and 109 are sung, the latter as an Alleluia psalm.[25] On the following day, January 6, an Epiphany service is held at the Martyrium in Jerusalem, and these two psalms are sung again.[26]

The rationale for the choice of Psalm 2 is evident from the response: "The Lord said to me, 'You are my son; today I have begotten you.'"[27] This verse is not explicitly associated with Jesus's baptism in the canonical gospels, but a widely attested "Western" textual variant to Luke's account of the voice from heaven quotes it. In addition to Codex Bezae (D) and many Old Latin versions, there is further evidence for this form of the text in quotations of the baptismal voice by Justin Martyr, Clement of Alexandria, the *Gospel of the Ebionites*, Origen's *Homilies on Ezekiel*, the *Didascalia*, and the fourth-century *Symposium* of Methodius.[28] The *Didascalia* associates this variant explicitly with Christian baptism.[29] Given the antiquity of the association of Psalm 2 with Jesus' baptism, it is reasonable to assume that it had already become central to the Jerusalem church's celebration of Epiphany by Egeria's day and probably long before.

Egeria witnessed an octave of Epiphany services, which is just what we find in the Armenian Lectionary. It is very difficult to guess which additional psalms may have been sung at vigils connected to these services in Egeria's day or at the feast's daytime services. The AL assigns Psalm 109 to four Epiphany services,[30] and the frequent use of Psalm 109 in earlier christological proof-texting might suggest that it had long been an Epiphany psalm. But when it is associated directly with Psalm 2:7 in the earliest writers, the connection does not concern baptism.[31] Moreover, in the sources that interpret the baptism of Jesus as his

24. See Renoux, *Le codex arménien Jérusalem 121*, vol. 2: 214 [76] n. 5 (which refers to the note number in the translation on p. 215). According to Luke, the reaction of the shepherds was to go to Bethlehem to see the child (Luke 2:15).

25. AL 1*bis*. Renoux, *Le codex arménien Jérusalem 121*, vol. 2, 214–215 [76–77].

26. AL 2. Renoux, *Le codex arménien Jérusalem 121*, vol. 2, 214–217 [76–79].

27. Ps 2:7 (somewhat conflated).

28. Justin Martyr, *Dial.* 88.8 and 103.6; Clement of Alexandria, *Paed.* 1.6.25.2; *Ev. Ebion.* in Epiphanius, *Pan.* 30.13.6 Holl 1: 350; *Didasc.* 9.3 (// *Const. ap.* 2.32) by implication; and Methodius, *Symp.* 8.9.

29. "In baptism through imposition of the bishop's hand, the Lord bore witness of each of you, as his holy voice was heard saying, 'You are my son, this day I have begotten you.'" *Didasc.* 9; tr. Stewart-Sykes, *The Didascalia Apostolorum*, 155.

30. AL 1, 2, 4, and 5.

31. Hebrews cites Ps 2:7 and Ps 109:1 in close proximity in a string of prooftexts about Christ's superiority to angels (Heb 1:5 and 1:13; and note the additional allusion to Ps 109:1 in 1:3). *First*

glorification and exaltation, a theme for which verse 1 of Psalm 109 is well suited, that verse is not quoted or alluded to.[32]

The AL also assigns other psalms to the days of Epiphany.[33] None of these psalms are quoted in New Testament passages about Jesus's baptism or in Christian discussions of the baptism. Most of them deal with kingship and deliverance, themes that were christologically significant for Christians and therefore pertinent to Epiphany but not peculiar to it.

Lenten Vigils

Egeria also reports on Lenten vigils but does not identify the particular psalms of these services.[34] Describing the sixth Friday vigil of the Quadragesima (Lent), she tells her correspondents that "during the whole vigil psalms and antiphons appropriate to the place and the day are always recited."[35] This suggests that psalms were chosen to fit a Lenten theme at a service held at a site with Lenten associations.

The vigil in question, held on each Friday of Lent, took place at the Anastasis in the first five weeks and at the Sion church in the sixth week. Constantine built the Anastasis over the reputed site of Jesus's tomb, the place of his burial and resurrection. Sion was believed to include the location where Jesus was scourged, as well as the place where the risen Jesus appeared to his disciples "when the doors were shut" (John 20:19), as well as the site of the original Pentecost.[36] The putative pillar to which Jesus was bound for flogging could be seen there and

---

Clement quotes them back-to-back as proofs to make the same point (*Ep. 1 ad Cor.* 36.4–5). Acts uses these verses as christological prooftexts but not in the same contexts (Acts 13:33 and 2:34–35). So does Justin Martyr but also in different contexts (e.g., *Dial.* 88.8 and 83.2; also *1 Apol.* 40.14 and 45.2).

32. I base this inference on Winkler's careful analysis of the evidence for how Jesus's baptism was understood in its earliest phases (see n. 12 above). The Armenian *Teaching of Gregory* quotes not Ps 109:1 but Isa 52:13 to say that Jesus was "lifted up and magnified and exceedingly glorified" (§416.10) (quoted in Winkler, "The Appearance of Light at the Baptism of Jesus," 334).

33. AL 1, 3, 5, 6, 7, 8, 9, specifying Psalm 79 as an Alleluia psalm; Psalm 5 (with 13b as a response); Psalm 20 as an Alleluia psalm; Psalm 131 as an Alleluia psalm; Psalm 98 (with v. 9 as a response); Psalm 29 (with v. 4 as a response); Psalm 39 as an Alleluia psalm; Psalm 95 (with v. 2b as a response); Psalm 71 as an Alleluia psalm; Psalm 97 (with v. 2 as a response); and Psalm 84 as an Alleluia psalm.

34. Egeria, *Itin.* 27.7–8 and 29.1–2.

35. *Itin.* 29.2; translation from McGowan and Bradshaw, *The Pilgrimage of Egeria*, 165.

36. *Itin.* 37.1 (the pillar in the Sion church); 39.5 (Sion as site of post-resurrection appearances); Cyril of Jerusalem, *Cat. ad illum.* 16.4 (and cf. Egeria, *Itin.* 25.6 and 43.2–3 for a Pentecost

was an object of devotion. On the morning of Good Friday, Egeria says, many of the faithful went to Sion to pray at this pillar.[37] It was located within the church itself, where a pilgrim named Theodosius saw it in the sixth century.[38] Hence, in addition to its resurrection association, the place was connected to the passion, just as there was a connection of both with the Anastasis, where the same Friday vigil was held during the other four weeks. The pillar and the tomb might well have been suitable foci for Lenten devotion, signifying testing and death. Of course, neither church was the site of Jesus's fast in the wilderness; hence, suitability of "place" in Egeria's conception of Lenten services did not always mean a liturgy at the corresponding biblical event-site.

Holy Week, the Easter Octave, and the Fifty Days of Easter

In the time of Egeria, the daily office in Jerusalem was modified for Holy Week, which comprised Palm Sunday through Easter Sunday. We have already seen a small part of that modification in the absorption of vespers into the Easter vigil.

Egeria is very specific about the liturgical times, places, and movements of Holy Week, which in Jerusalem was called "the Great Week."[39] Yet she speaks only vaguely about "psalms, hymns, and antiphons" and, with one exception, does not identify any particular psalm(s). The exception appears in her description of an evening service on Palm Sunday, when the people, having celebrated on the Mount of Olives, processed down at the eleventh hour singing Psalm 117 with verse 26 ("Blessed is the one who comes in the name of the Lord") as the response.[40] This late-afternoon procession and its psalm re-enacted the gospel story of the "Triumphal Entry," with the bishop being led like Jesus by the palm-carrying throng.[41] Perhaps to avoid any overly close equation, the bishop

---

Sunday Mass at Sion). On the church at Sion, see McGowan and Bradshaw, *The Pilgrimage of Egeria*, 59–60.

37. *Itin.* 37.1.

38. Theodosius, *De situ terrae sanctae* 7 (CSEL 39: 141). Theodosius places the scourging at the house of Caiaphas and says that the pillar was later moved into the church on Sion. The gospels speak only of a scourging ordered by Pilate.

39. Egeria, *Itin.* 30.1.

40. Regarding the similarities and differences between AL and Egeria concerning the Mount of Olives liturgy(ies), see McGowan and Bradshaw, *The Pilgrimage of Egeria*, 168, note on 31.1.

41. Egeria thinks that it was children who greeted Jesus with palm branches (*Itin.* 31.2), probably on the basis of church teaching that read Matt 21:8 in the light of Matt 21:15.

did not ride an ass into the city. He went on foot. The Armenian Lectionary, which has the same evening service and procession, also assigns Psalm 117.[42]

As I have said, Egeria does not name any of the other psalms for the services of Holy Week and the Easter Octave; but the Armenian Lectionary does, and there is good reason to believe that a significant number of the psalm choices current in the time of Egeria were still current when the AL was composed. I will show this by comparing Egeria's and the AL's information regarding a Good Friday service.

According to Egeria, one of the Good Friday services commenced at the sixth hour. It featured readings from the prophets, epistles, Acts, and the gospels, the selections being taken from descriptions of the passion in those Scriptures, with prayers interspersed, and readings "from the psalms wherever they speak of the passion."[43] These Good Friday readings about Christ's sufferings caused the people to groan in commiseration, Egeria says, and we can imagine that the congregation wailed the psalm responses, perhaps in the manner of funeral dirges.

The ordering of psalms, lessons, and prayers for Good Friday, as Egeria reports it, resembles the scheme in the Armenian Lectionary, which also has psalms and prayers intercalated with readings for what appears to be the same service, one that started at the sixth hour.[44] Egeria says that the service took place "before the cross" and clarifies that this means the courtyard between the cross and the Anastasis, which is probably where the AL locates the service.[45] Of the eight psalms designated by the AL for the main Good Friday service, the responses of three of them are also quoted or clearly paraphrased in the gospel lessons themselves, which are all passion texts.[46] Additionally, traditions of interpretation, well established by the latter part of the fourth century, interpreted the responses for another three of the Good Friday psalms of the AL as prophesies

42. AL 34 *bis*.

43. Egeria, *Itin.* 37.5. The assumption, of course, is that certain biblical psalms and other passages in the Old Testament describe Jesus's sufferings prophetically.

44. AL 43.

45. Egeria, *Itin.* 37.4; AL 43. See Renoux, *Le codex arménien Jérusalem 121*, vol. 2, 281 [143] n. 3.

46. The psalms with their responses are as follows: 34 (v. 11), 37 (v. 18), 40 (v. 7b), 21 (v. 19), 30 (v. 6), 68 (v. 22), 87 (v. 5b), 101 (v. 2). See Al 43 (Renoux, *Le codex arménien Jérusalem 121*, vol. 2, 281–293 [143–155]). The gospel lessons are Matt 27:1-56; Mark 15:1-41; Luke 22:66–23:49; and John 19:16b-3 (with some variations in P but from these same passages). These lessons are all from gospel passion accounts. Ps 21:19 is paraphrased in Matt 27:35; Ps 68:22 is paraphrased in Matt 27:48; and Ps 30:6a is quoted in Luke 23:46.

of moments of Jesus's passion as described by the gospels.[47] Hence, six of these eight psalms would have had clear passion associations in Egeria's day.[48]

Egeria is the earliest witness for the liturgies of the Easter Octave and the Fifty Days of Easter. She calls the Easter Octave (Easter day through the following Sunday) "The Eight Paschal Days" in distinction from Holy Week, "the Great Week." Her focus is on times and places. The liturgical activities on various days were "observed in the same way as with us."[49] She mentions songs as she goes through the days and states three times that they were "appropriate to the day and the place."[50] This is a formula with Egeria. She had the impression that all the readings and hymns of liturgies conducted in Jerusalem were chosen in view of the time and place, as defined by the moments of sacred history they honored.[51] But she names no specific psalms of the Easter Octave.

The Easter Octave was the start of the fifty nonfasting days of the Easter season, which culminates with Pentecost.[52] In describing the liturgies of this period, chiefly of Pentecost Sunday, Egeria mentions songs occasionally, twice commenting on their appropriateness to the time and place,[53] noting at one

---

47. For Psalm 34, response verse 11 (AL 43, Renoux 2: 283 [145]), see Eusebius, *Comm. in psalm.* (on v. 11) (PG 23: 305); [Origen, dub.], *Frag. in psalm. 34:11* (Pitra 3: 7); Cyril of Alexandria, *Expos. in psalm.* (PG 69: 901); Athanasius, *Expos. in psalm.* (PG 27: 172). For Psalm 40, response v. 7b (AL 43; Renoux 2: 285 [vol. 147]), see Eusebius, *Dem. ev.* 10.1.25; Athanasius, *Expos. in psalm.* (PG 27: 197); Didymus the Blind, *Comm. in psalm. 40* 7 (Gronewald 5: 293); Theodoret of Cyr, *Interp. in psalm. 40* 7 (PG 80: 1165). For Psalm 87, response verse 5b (AL 43; Renoux 2: 289 [151]), see Origen, *Comm. in ev. Joann.* 1.31.220 (SC 120: 166); Eusebius, *Comm. in psalm.* (PG 23: 1056); Athanasius, *Expos. in psalm.* (PG 27: 380); Cyril of Jerusalem, *Myst. cat.* 14:8; Didymus the Blind, commenting on the passage in his discussion of Psalm 35:9, *Comm. in psalm.* (Gronewald 4: 238); Gelasius of Caesarea Maritima, *H.E.* 2.31.7.

48. As for the other two psalms, several fathers construe the AL's designated refrain-verse of one of them (Psalm 37, response verse 18; AL 43; Renoux 2: 283 [145]) as a reference to God's corrective discipline, applicable to David or God's people when they sin and repent. See Eusebius, *Comm. in psalm.*, commenting on Ps 37:18 in a discussion of Psalm 38 (PG 23: 349); Athanasius, *Expos. in psalm.* (PG 27: 185); Cyril of Alexandria, *Expos. in psalm.* (PG 69: 967–968); Basil, *Hom. in psalm. 37* (PG 30: 101). The AL may have assigned it as a psalm of confession appropriate to a passion setting. Regarding the other psalm (Psalm 101, response verse 2; AL 43; Renoux 2, 291 [153]), patristic writers do not give its refrain-verse a christological interpretation, and its pertinence to the Good Friday liturgy is unclear.

49. Egeria, *Itin.* 39.1.

50. *Itin.* 39.5; 40.1 and 2.

51. *Itin.* 47.5.

52. *Itin.* 41–43.

53. *Itin.* 43.5 and 6.

point that the songs, readings, and prayers were intercalated.[54] This was probably typical.[55] But again, she does not specify any particular psalms.

It is possible that certain educated guesses about the Easter Octave and Pentecost could be made by examining the relevant parts of the Armenian Lectionary, as I have illustrated for the Good Friday service, but I will not undertake that task here.

Christmas Psalmody

A celebration of the day of Jesus's birth became its own feast in the fourth century, distinct from Epiphany. Just when and where is uncertain, since the computations of the date of Jesus's birth in various authors are not themselves proof of the existence of a feast day. Nor is the reference in a Roman calendar of 336 to Jesus's birth having occurred on December 25, although it is suggestive of the possibility that the day was celebrated liturgically.[56] Still less is known about the liturgy of Christmas day. The *Apostolic Constitutions* witnesses its spread to Syria by the end of the fourth century but specifies no elements of its observance.[57] Meanwhile, in Jerusalem, Epiphany continued to be the liturgical setting for commemorating Christ's birth, witness the Armenian Lectionary (see above).

A surviving sermon by John Chrysostom on a new Feast of the Nativity mentions no psalm lesson.[58] The earliest reference to psalmody at Christmas appears in a sermon by Augustine, who declares, "If Mary is of the earth, let us recognize what it is that we sing": the words of Psalm 84:12: "Truth is sprung out of the earth."[59] Augustine quotes this verse in six of his fourteen surviving Christmas sermons, and in three instances they are cited in the sermon's opening.[60] In an era when it was still common for the preacher or local bishop to assign the lessons for his sermon, Augustine himself probably selected Psalm

---

54. *Itin.* 43.5.

55. In addition to *Itin.* 43.5, see 31.1; 32.1; 35.3; and 37.6.

56. *Natus Christus in Betleem Judeae*, one of two entries for December 25 in the Philocalian Calendar (Chronograph) of 354.

57. *Const. ap.* 5.13.1.

58. John Chrysostom, *Hom. in diem nat. Jes. Chr.* (PG 49: 351–362).

59. Augustine, *Serm.* 189 (*In nat. dom.* VI) (PL 38: 1005) as cited and translated by James McKinnon, *The Advent Project: The Late-Seventh-Century Creation of the Roman Mass Proper* (University of California Press, 2000), 78.

60. Augustine, *Serm.* 184.1 (PL 38: 905); 185.1 (PL 38: 907); 189.2 (PL 38: 1005–1006); 191.2 (PL 38: 1010); 192.1 (PL 38: 1011); 193.2 (PL 38: 1014).

84 as the lesson for his Christmas sermons. But he was not the first to identify it as a prophecy about Christ. Eusebius, in his commentary on Psalm 84, gives that interpretation. Although he does not mention "Christmas" themes or equate "the earth" with Mary's womb,[61] his Cappadocian contemporary Asterius the Sophist (d. circa 341) makes the connection, construing "from the earth" to mean "from the virgin."[62] A Christmas sermon falsely attributed to John Chrysostom also quotes the verse, explaining that "from the earth" means "from the virgin according to the flesh."[63] These clues suggest that Psalm 84 had become a Christmas Day psalm in both the East and the West by the early fifth century, verse 12 being the likely refrain verse.

Three other psalm verses are quoted in Augustine's Christmas sermons. Sun and light imagery became associated with Christmas because December 25 was the *dies natalis Solis Inviciti*, "the birthday of the Unconquered Sun." Psalm 18:6, which compares the sun to a bridegroom, appears in six of Augustine's Christmas sermons as a description of Christ in his movement into the world through his human birth.[64] As Augustine puts it, "faith" believes that it was indeed possible for God to be born "in flesh" and "for the infant 'bridegroom' to come forth 'from his chamber', that is, from the virgin's womb." He quotes the verse more fully in other Christmas sermons and once in *Confessions*, declaring that Christ came from the virgin's womb "'like a bridegroom going forth from his chamber, and leaped like a giant to run his course.'"[65] In the psalm, this bridegroom is the sun, which comes forth from his chamber every morning. Augustine interprets the bridegroom as Christ, one might say as "Christ the Sun" born on December 25.

Psalm 18 also had a prior exegetical history as a prophecy of Christ. Justin Martyr quotes verses 3 to 6 as a messianic proof concerning Christ's appearance in history, although he does not focus on the bridegroom image or interpret the "chamber" as Mary's womb.[66] Hermogenes, whose teachings are summarized by Hippolytus, interprets the verse as a reference to a phase of Christ's ascension.[67] The author of a homily attributed to Epiphanius says that Mary is

---

61. Eusebius. *In psalm. 84* (PG 23: 1021–1024).

62. Asterius soph., *In psalm.*, Hom. 25.24.

63. John Chrysostom, *In nat. Jes. Chr.* (PG 61: 766).

64. Augustine, *Serm.* 187.4 (PL 38: 1002); 188.2 (PL 38: 1004, without an editor's ref.); 191.2 (PL 38: 1010); 192.3 (PL 38: 1013); 194.4 (PL 38: 1017); 195.3 (PL 38: 1018).

65. Augustine, *Conf.* 4.12.19.

66. Justin Martyr, *1 Apol.* 40.1–4.

67. Hippolytus, *Ref.* 8.17.3–4.

the "bride and chamber" and that Christ goes forth "from her."[68] The homily might be as early as Augustine's era, but that is not certain.[69] It is worth noting that a significant number of fourth- and fifth-century Greek commentators on the psalms—Asterius, Cyril of Jerusalem, John Chrysostom, Diodorus, and Theodoret—do *not* give the verse a christological interpretation.[70]

Augustine also quotes Psalm 117:24, "This is the day that the Lord has made etc.," in two of his sermons.[71] This verse had a long and diverse history in Christian interpretation and was construed as referring to the day of the original creation through Christ (Clement of Alexandria[72]), Christ himself (Cyprian[73]), the day of Christ's resurrection (Eusebius,[74] Theodoret of Cyr[75]), the day of Christ's epiphany (Eusebius[76]), the day of Christ's future parousia (with the judgment and final resurrection) (Cyril of Alexandria[77]), the time of righteousness brought by Christ (Didymus the Blind[78]), and the time of salvation (Cyril of Alexandria[79]). Clearly, the verse was quite amenable to different interpretations, and the same author could give it more than one meaning. We might hesitate, then, to infer from Augustine's quotation that it was a Christmas Day lesson. Yet in a Nativity sermon, Gregory of Nyssa also interprets the verse as a reference to the day of Jesus's birth, and he mentions that the congregation had sung it in the service.[80]

---

68. Ps.-Epiphanius, *Hom. in laud. Mar.* (PG 43: 489).

69. The author of an Edinburgh M.A. thesis concludes that all five sermons were composed by the same person and that a fourth-century date is possible. Timotheos Zinonos, "*Homilia in divini corporis sepulturam*: An Examination of Its Language, Style and Authorship (Epiphanios of Salamis and Other Candidates)" (M.A. thesis; University of Edinburgh, 2020).

70. See their psalms commentaries.

71. Augustine, *Serm.* 184.1 (PL 38: 995); 187.4 (PL 38: 1002). There may be an allusion in *Serm.* 196.1 (PL 38: 1019).

72. Clement of Alexandria, *Str.* 6.16.145.

73. Cyprian, *Orat. dom.* 35 (CSEL 3/1: 293).

74. Eusebius, *Comm. in psalm. 91* (PG 23: 1173).

75. Theodoret of Cyr, *Interp. in psalm. 117* v. 24 (PG 80: 1816–1817).

76. Eusebius, *Dem.* 9.18.7.

77. Cyril of Alexandria, *Comm. in XII proph. minor.* 1.43.

78. Didymus the Blind, *Comm. in Zach.* 4.110.

79. Cyril of Alexandria, *Glaph. in pent.* (PG 69: 265).

80. Gregory of Nyssa, *Oratio in diem nat. Christi* (Mann, 1129).

Finally, there is Psalm 95:1–2 ("Sing to the Lord a new song etc."), which Augustine quotes in two Christmas sermons.[81] This set of verses does not appear in surviving Christmas sermons by any other patristic divines.

Community Suppers after the Shift to Morning Eucharists

One of the earliest settings of Christian psalmody, perhaps the very earliest, was the community supper. When the regular celebration of the Eucharist was dislodged from its original supper setting (which would not have occurred everywhere all at once), Christian suppers continued in both private and churchly forms, including elite Christian dinner parties and meals for the poor.

A bit of evidence for the latter appears in the *Canons of Hippolytus*, a work that was probably composed in Egypt in the 330s.[82] At the end of an ensemble of instructions for fasting and alms, Canon 32 gives the following directives for meals for the poor:

> If there is a meal or supper made by someone for the poor—it is the Lord's. The bishop is to be present at the time when one lights the lamp. The deacon is to light it, and the bishop is to pray over them and over the person(s) who invited them. It is necessary for the poor that the thanksgiving be said at the beginning of the liturgy. They are to be dismissed so that they depart before dark,[83] and they are to recite psalms before their departure.[84]

This passage is a reworking of instructions in *Apostolic Tradition* 25/29C.[85] The *ApTrad* underwent multiple redactions over the course of about two centuries,

81. Augustine, *Serm.* 189.1 (PL 38: 1005); twice in 190.4 (PL 38: 1008–1009).

82. See chapter 6 n. 82.

83. An instruction to dismiss before dark is also given in Canon 35 with reference to meals given for widows; this canon draws on *ApTrad* 30. Neither passage mentions psalms.

84. My translation is based on Carol Bebawi's translation in Paul F. Bradshaw, ed., *The Canons of Hippolytus*, with an English translation by Carol Bebawi (Grove, 1987), 32, with minor modifications based on the translation in Georges Coquin, *Les canons d'Hippolyte* (Firmin Didot, 1966), 405 [137] and the translation and notes in Alister Stewart-Sykes, *An English Version, with Introduction and Annotation and an Accompanying Arabic Text* (SCH, 2021), 139.

85. What editors originally labeled chapter 25 was subsequently identified as material that belonged later in the book and was designated as 29C. See Paul F. Bradshaw, Maxwell E. Johnson, and L. Edward Phillips, *The Apostolic Tradition: A Commentary* (Fortress, 2002), 141.

and it survives in several incomplete versions in different languages.[86] The directions for the liturgy of the vesper supper are preserved only in the Ethiopic manuscript tradition, the earliest form of which is an Aksumite tradition now known as Ethiopic I. The later form, Ethiopic II, was probably completed in the late fourth century.[87] Under the heading "Concerning bringing in lamps at the supper of the congregation,"[88] *ApTrad* 25/29C gives directions for prayer, reception of bread, and the use of psalms. Some parts of the meeting's *ordo* are implied or mentioned only in passing. The liturgy unfolds as follows in the Ethiopic witnesses, although some parts are absent from Ethiopic I (specifically §§10–15, which include directives for psalms to be sung by a choir of children and virgins):

An opening thanksgiving is led by a deacon, with the bishop present, when the lamps are brought in (§§1–10). This liturgy is not eucharistic: "But he shall not say 'Lift up your hearts', because it is said in the offering" (§6).[89]

The supper follows (implied by the expression "after supper" in §11).

An after-supper liturgy is conducted (§§11–16 of Ethiopic II; §§10–15 are absent from Ethiopic I):

- Psalms are sung by a choir of children and virgins.
- An Alleluia[90] psalm is said by a deacon holding "the mixed cup of oblation."
- There is an optional reading, by a presbyter, from the Alleluia psalms.

---

86. See the discussion in Bradshaw, Johnson, and Phillips, *The Apostolic Tradition: A Commentary*, 1–17. An effort to reconstruct something approaching the original Greek core of the *Apostolic Tradition* and the development of its traditions from the second through the early fourth century can be found in Paul F. Bradshaw, *The Apostolic Tradition Reconstructed: A Text for Students* (Alcuin Club and the Group for the Renewal of Worship, 2021).

87. The Ethiopic versions of the *Apostolic Tradition* are eight Ethiopic manuscripts edited by Hugo Duensing (now labeled Ethiopic II) and one earlier Ethiopic version manuscript in an Aksumite Ethiopic collection of texts edited by Alessandro Bausi (now labelled Ethiopic I). See the bibliography.

88. Translation from Bradshaw, Johnson, and Phillips, *The Apostolic Tradition*, 156.

89. Ethiopic I; my translation of the Italian translation in Bausi, 51; the other Ethiopic mss. say essentially the same thing.

90. The translation in Bradshaw, Johnson, and Phillips uses "Hallelujah" for this word. I use "Alleluia" simply to remain consistent with my discussion of Alleluia psalms, as designated by superscriptions, in the Septuagint and Vulgate, which differ from the MT.

After the bishop has "offered the cup," he says "the psalm that is appropriate for the cup."[91] To this psalm and perhaps the others, the people respond with "each Alleluia."[92]

The presbyter then gives thanks for the cup and distributes crumbs of the bread to the diners.

The believers each receive a morsel of bread from the hand of the bishop before breaking their own bread "because it is a blessing and not the Eucharist like the body of our Lord."[93]

The repeated clarification (in §6 and §11) that the gathering should not be treated as eucharistic implies that the meal was originally understood as a eucharistic supper. These clarifications appear in both Ethiopic I and Ethiopic II.

It is difficult to date the redaction that introduced the instructions for psalmody—a set of psalms by a choir of children and virgins, followed by an Alleluia psalm said by a deacon, and then, at the presbyter's discretion, a responsorial Alleluia psalm led by him. There are very few references in Christian literature of the first several centuries to discrete liturgical choirs distinguished from a congregation that sings as a responding chorus. The earliest mention is a synodal letter's reference to an Easter women's choir, organized by Paul of Samosata when he was bishop of Antioch in the 260s.[94] After that, no more references appear until Egeria's comment that a group of children sang *Kyrie eleison* at vespers in Jerusalem, which would have been in the late fourth century at the earliest.[95] The *Testament of the Lord* calls for a choir of boys to sing "psalms and hymns" at vespers, but it is a fifth-century rewriting of the *Apostolic Tradition*.[96]

---

91. Translation from Bradshaw, Johnson, and Phillips, *The Apostolic Tradition*, 156.

92. The references to the deacon's and presbyter's psalms do not mention a response. But after the instruction for the bishop's psalm for the cup, the *ApTrad* dictates that "when they read the psalms they are all to say Alleluia." Translation from Bradshaw, Johnson, and Phillips, *The Apostolic Tradition*, 156 (slightly altered).

93. Translation from Bradshaw, Johnson, and Phillips, *The Apostolic Tradition*, 156.

94. Eusebius, *H.E.* 7.30.10 (discussed above).

95. Egeria, *Itin.* 24.5.

96. *T. Dom.* 2.11. A late fifth-century dating is defended by some scholars but may be a bit too late, given that the oldest fragment of a copy of *Testamentum Domini* dates to the late fifth century. See Simon Corcoran and Benet Salway, "The Newly Identified Greek Fragment of the Testamentum Domini," *Journal of Theological Studies* 62 (2011): 118–135; also Michael Kohlbacher, "Wessen Kirche ordnete das *Testamentum Domini Nostri Jesu Christi*? Anmerkungen zum historischen Kontext von CPG," in *Zu Geschichte, Theologie, Liturgie und*

The choir mentioned by Egeria is the closest parallel to the choir in *ApTrad*, since the Jerusalem boys' choir also sang at vespers. Hence, although one cannot exclude a third-century dating for the layer of redaction about psalmody in Ethiopic II, it is more likely that this editing was done in the late fourth century.[97]

Funerals

By the latter half of the fourth century, psalmody had replaced traditional dirges at funeral rites for monks and bishops. The extent and history of a more general Christian embrace of funeral psalmody is difficult to establish.[98] Based on what he judges to be an absence of instructions in writings by bishops and other influential Christian leaders about how a funeral should be conducted—whether clergy should preside, whether the Eucharist should be celebrated, which symbolic items and gestures should be included, and whether dirges should be replaced by psalms—Éric Rebillard concludes that "in the fourth and fifth centuries there was no 'Christian ritual' that the church attempted to impose for lay Christians: the family remained the principal player in funerals."[99] If this was generally true, there were certainly clerical efforts in late fourth-century Syria to influence funeral rites and mourning practices. The *Apostolic Constitutions* gives instructions for the third day of mourning and the funeral procession,[100] and John Chrysostom urges his congregations to give up traditional mourning customs as incompatible with Christian faith.[101] Yet it is unclear how many

Gegenwartslage der syrischen Kirchen, ed. Martin Tamcke and Andreas Heinz (LIT, 2000), 55–137.

97. Bradshaw's reconstruction, which covers the evolutions of the traditions incorporated into the *ApTrad* from the second century into the early fourth century, omits the material regarding psalmody altogether as a later interpolation that falls outside this date range. See Bradshaw, *The Apostolic Tradition Reconstructed*, 29.

98. On the topic of psalmody at Christian funerals, see Johannes Quasten, *Music and Worship in Pagan and Christian Antiquity*, tr. Boniface Ramsey (National Association of Pastoral Musicians, 1983), 160–167; Reiner Kaczynski, "Die Psalmodie bei der Begräbnisfeier," in *Liturgie und Dichtung: Ein interdisziplinäres Kompendium*, vol. 2, ed. Hansjakob Becker and Reiner Kaczynski (EOS, 1983), 795–831; Ulrich Volp, *Tod und Ritual in den christlichen Gemeinden der Antike* (Brill, 2002), 140–148; passim references in Éric Rebillard, *The Care of the Dead in Late Antiquity*, tr. Elizabeth Trapnell Rawlings and Jeanine Routier-Pucci (Cornell University Press, 2009), 128–139.

99. Rebillard, *The Care of the Dead in Late Antiquity*, 139.

100. *Const. ap.*, 8.42.1 and 6.30.2.

101. John Chrysostom's preaching on the subject of mourning is described below.

Christians heeded such clerical guidance about how they should express their grief and honor their dead.

The earliest known instance of psalmody in funeral rites may be the ministrations accorded to a monk named Paul the Hermit, who died in 342. According to Jerome, the famed Antony hurried to Paul's desert cave to perform the necessary funeral ministrations, including carrying Paul's body out for burial while "chanting hymns and psalms the whole time, according to Christian custom."[102] This correlates well with evidence in the *Life of Pachomius* that in the 340s and perhaps earlier, the brothers of Pachomian monasteries chanted psalms when they conducted their dead to the cemetery.[103] Of course, it is possible that Jerome's account of Paul, which was composed a generation after Paul's death, reflects only later Christian custom. And although the *Life of Pachomius* was written not long after Pachomius's death in 346, it is possible that the extant editions of that life reflect somewhat later funeral practice.

Given these uncertainties, the earliest securely datable evidence of psalmody in a Christian funeral procession is found in Gregory of Nazianzus's account of his brother Caesarius's funeral in 368/369.[104] Not long after, in Umbria in 373, a Christian funerary memorial was inscribed with the words, "We say psalms to you, Aurelia Yguia."[105] Although this example does not specify the setting, it implies that at least some Latin-speaking Christians, too, had adopted funeral psalmody. So does a Roman inscription, vaguely dated to the fourth century, which reads, "With hymns (*hymnis*) is she conducted (*translata*) by us to the quietude of peace."[106] And when one of Augustine's stenographers, Armenus,

---

102. Jerome, *V. Pauli* 16 (PL 23: 27). A passage in the *Acts of Cyprian* (part of the *Acta proconsularia*) mentions psalmody in the funeral procession for Cyprian in 258. But the *Acts of Cyprian* was probably composed in the fourth century, precisely when is unknown. Pontius's *Life of Cyprian*, which was written not long after Cyprian's death, does not describe his funeral. On the dating of these works, see Éric Rebillard, The *Early Martyr Narratives: Neither Authentic Accounts nor Forgeries* (University of Pennsylvania Press, 2021), 10–11.

103. *Pach. vit. Boh.* 93, 123, 205, 207; *Pach. vit.*, Greek[1] 103, 116, 117. According to John Chrysostom, the monks of the Syrian desert also sang psalms when they conducted the body of a deceased brother to the grave. *In 1 Tim. 5*, Hom. 14.5 (PG 62: 577; Field, *Interp. in. ep. Paul.* 6: 124).

104. Gregory of Nazianzus, *In laudem Caesarii fratris* (*Or.* 7) 15.5. Gregory refers to "hymns" during the funeral procession, and he remarks that his mother sang psalms to suppress her urge to sing dirges.

105. *Salmos tibique dicamus Aurelia Yguia.* CIL XI 4629, cited in Ulrich Volp, *Tod und Ritual in den christlichen Gemeinden der Antike* (Brill, 2002), 142.

106. ILCV II 4711.

died, he made his departure with psalm verses on his lips and was honored with three days of psalms ("hymns") at his grave.[107]

All these funerals would have been handled by the families of the deceased. In two instances those families were upper-class people from whom high-ranking clergy had come. In two other cases the families had sufficient wealth to afford a sarcophagus for their loved one. While these examples imply some degree of embrace of psalmody as a funeral rite in upper-class Christian circles, an indication of reluctance to give up the old customs is the set of instructions in the *Apostolic Constitutions* that "the third day of the departed should be observed with psalms and prayers,"[108] that the Eucharist should be administered, and that psalms should be sung when the body is carried to the grave.[109] The issuance of a rule typically implies that a significant number of people are *not* doing what the rule requires.

Other signs of Christian persistence in the old funeral traditions are the remonstrations of bishops against dirges, wailing, hair pulling, beating of breasts, and weeping. In a sermon preached to his congregation at Antioch, John Chrysostom describes "the lamentations in the marketplace, the wailings performed for those who are departing life, the cries, the other disgraceful things."[110] He derides demonstrative mourning as a "disease of women." They "make a display in their laments," he says, "with wailing, baring their arms, tearing their hair, making torrents down their cheeks," doing these things "in the sight of men," and generally behaving "indecorously."[111] While "it is no surprise" that "worldly women" engage in the usual outpourings of grief, John remarks, Christian women should not mourn like those who have no hope of the resurrection.[112] Yet, "well-to-do" pagan women refrain from such low-class behaviors, John says. They do not "pull their hair or bare their arms," for they are unwilling to "humiliate" themselves.[113] A Christian woman's piety ought to be at least as decorous as an upper-class pagan woman's sensitivity to social opinion, for it is not "the nature of the circumstances that accustoms us to grieve but our choice, not the death of the departed but the weakness of those who lament."[114]

107. Augustine, *Ep.* 158.2 (CSEL 44: 489–490). Augustine does not say when Armenus died but implies that his death was not recent in 414, when the letter was composed.

108. *Const. ap.* 8.42.1.

109. *Const. ap.* 6.30.2.

110. John Chrysostom, *In Hebr.*, Hom. 4.5 (PG 63: 42).

111. John Chrysostom, *In Joann.*, Hom. 62.4 (PG 59: 346).

112. John Chrysostom, *In Hebr. 2*, Hom. 4.5 (PG 63: 43).

113. John Chrysostom, *In Joann.*, Hom. 62.4 (PG 59: 347).

114. John Chrysostom, *Laz.*, Hom. 5.3 (PG 48: 1021).

John's view represented a moralizing construal of a teaching that started out as a word of comfort, namely, the Apostle Paul's effort to console the church at Thessalonica with the reassurance that they need not mourn "as others do, who have no hope." But already by the second century, this reassurance was interpreted as a behavioral rule. Tertullian quotes Paul's words as a norm for proper Christian response to death, and Cyprian interprets them as a rebuke.[115] Similar appeals to the verse appear in the fourth century in remarks by Ambrose and John Chrysostom.[116]

For fourth-century Christian divines who regarded grief as a faithless Christian response to loss of a Christian friend or family member, the proper attitudinal alternative was joy for the deceased, and the proper behavioral alternative to wailing and dirges was psalmody, as Chrysostom explains in a series of rhetorical questions:

> Do we not glorify God and give thanks that he has finally crowned the departed, because he has set them free from pains, because he has them with himself, casting out all fear? Are not hymns for this? Are not psalmodies for this? All these things belong to one who rejoices. For it says, "If someone is glad, let them sing" [Jas 5:13].[117]

By contrast, tears of grief imply lack of belief in the resurrection, John warns in a homily on the raising of Lazarus. "For if you believed that the deceased had been taken to a better place, you would not have mourned him as if he existed no more; you would not have beaten your breasts that way; you would not have let loose such noises as these, full of unbelief."[118] In a sermon on Matthew, he urges, "If you consider these things [of Christian faith] sure, do not sing dirges. Do not weep. For if you weep, how will you be able to persuade the Greek that you believe?"[119] And while John grants that "it is not possible not to weep" when a loved one dies, for Christ himself wept at the tomb of Lazarus, he insists that Christians should imitate Christ's tears by weeping

---

115. Tertullian quotes 1 Thess 4:13 to show that even the "impatience" of grief is not permissible for a Christian (*Pat.* 9.1–3). Cyprian interprets Paul's words of comfort as a rebuke (*Mort.* 21).

116. Ambrose, *Exc. frat. Satyr.* 1.70 (CSEL 73: 245); John Chrysostom, *De Laz.*, Hom. 5.3 (PG 48: 1021).

117. John Chrysostom, *In Hebr. 2*, Hom. 4.5 (PG 63: 43). I have pluralized the objects of the verbs.

118. John Chrysostom, *In Joann.*, Hom. 62.4 (PG 59: 347).

119. John Chrysostom, *In Matt.*, Hom. 31.4 (PG 57: 375; Field, *Hom. in Matt.* 1: 438).

"gently with decorum."[120] His aristocratic sensibilities shine through quite clearly in this last remark.

John's views were shared by other Eastern divines. When Gregory's sister Macrina died at the monastery she headed on the Nyssen family estate at Annisa in 379, the virgins of her house were overwhelmed by grief and began singing a dirge.[121] Gregory himself was present, and when he gained his own composure, he reminded the virgins of Macrina's strict rule against mourning. "Look at her," he shouted to them over the din of their wails, "and remember her instructions, through which you were taught by her to be orderly and decorous in every circumstance. Her divine soul appointed one time for you to weep, commanding you to do it in the time of prayer," that is, in prayerful mourning for one's sins.[122] "What is proper for you to do now," he said, "is to turn the wailing of your dirges into sympathetic psalmody."[123] With that, he sent the virgins to another part of the house to sing psalms; and when other mourners arrived, he divided them into psalm-singing choruses of men and women.

Gregory's phrasing of Macrina's dictum implies that grief is a disordered state, which manifests itself inwardly in overwhelming emotion and outwardly in physical displays of lamentation. By contrast, the proper response to death is the ordered state of faith, manifested inwardly through calmness and apatheia, and outwardly through psalmody.[124] Like John Chrysostom, Gregory introduces notes of gender and class when he draws contrasts between traditional demonstrative mourning and a proper Christian response to loss. Calmness and orderliness express male rationality. Distress, high emotion, and lack of control express female irrationality and emotionality. He portrays his sister Macrina as the paragon of male rationality, a soul who transcends "nature."[125] Similarly,

---

120. John Chrysostom, *In Joann.*, Hom. 62.4 (PG 59: 347).

121. Gregory of Nyssa, *Vit. Macr.* 26.23–29. Gregory purports to quote the women's dirge. On its form, see Charles H. Cosgrove, "An Ancient Greek Lament Form," *Journal of Hellenic Studies* 138 (2018): 173–181.

122. Gregory, *Vit. Macr.* 27.4–9.

123. *Vit. Macr.* 27.9–11.

124. Note Gregory of Nyssa's description of how the dead Macrina's peaceful face affected him personally: "as if I was being rebuked for the disorder (ἀταξίᾳ) of those who were wailing through the dirge." He then reminds the wailing virgins that Macrina had taught them "order and decorum in everything." *Vit. Macr.* 27.3–7.

125. Compare Gregory's opening description of Macrina as one who transcended nature, someone who perhaps should not even be called a "woman" (*Vit. Macr.* 1.15–17), with his account of the way she responded to the death of their brother Naucratius by opposing rationality to passion (*Vit. Macr.* 10). Regarding Macrina's transcendence of human nature, see also *Vit. Macr.* 11 and 22. The topic of Macrina's "maleness" is discussed in Virginia Burrus, "Is Macrina a

when he praises his mother for the restraint she showed in responding to news of the death of her son Naucratius, he writes that "she did not suffer anything lowborn and womanish that would have caused her to cry out against her misfortune or rend her clothing or lament with pathos or start up dirges."[126]

There is a hint of this same association of aristocratic female bearing with devout female piety in Gregory of Nazianzus's account of how his pious mother Nonna responded when her son and his brother Caesarius died in 368/9. She put on "splendid attire," Gregory says, "defeating her tears with her philosophy, and putting her lamentations to sleep with psalmody."[127]

The mass of Christians did not restrain their grief. When Basil of Caesarea died in 379 and was borne to his grave with psalmody, masses of people came out to mourn him, and the hymns of David were soon overcome by lamentations.[128] So says Gregory of Nazianzus, not approvingly. And at Macrina's passing, when the virgins heeded Gregory of Nyssa's directive and sang psalms, they were not fully successful in restraining their emotions, with the result that "the psalmodies of the virgins, *mixing with their lamentations*, resounded throughout the place."[129]

Another indication of the persistence of traditional mourning appears in Jerome's language about the funeral for the abbess Paula,[130] who died in 404. "There was none of the hubbub of lamentation that is customary among worldly people," he observed, but only psalmody.[131] All of Palestine came to her funeral, and "swarms of monks raised a din of psalms in diverse languages."[132] In other

---

Woman? Gregory of Nyssa's Dialogue on the Soul and the Resurrection," in *The Blackwell Companion to Postmodern Theology*, ed. Graham Ward (Blackwell, 2001), 249–264; see also Hans Boersma, *Embodiment and Virtue in Gregory of Nyssa: An Anagogical Approach* (Oxford University Press, 2013), 109. Compare the comment about Melanie by her biographer, who says not that Melanie transcended nature but that because "the feminine measure in [Melanie] had perished," the desert fathers received her "as a man" (ὡς ἄνδρα) (Gerontius, *Vit. Mel.* 2.39; SC 90: 200). See Ruth Albrecht, *Das Leben der heiligen Makrina auf dem Hintergrund der Thekla-Traditionen* (Vandenhoeck & Ruprecht, 1986), 197 and the discussion that follows. Gregory's conception is that Macrina, being above the passions of the body, transcends gender and in this way approaches angelic existence.

126. Gregory of Nyssa, *Vit. Macr.* 10.6–10.

127. Gregory of Nazianzus, *Fun. in laud. Caesar.* (*Or.* 7) 15.5.

128. Gregory of Nazianzus, *Fun. or. in laud. Bas. Magn.* (*Or.* 43) 80.3.

129. Gregory of Nyssa, *Vit. Macr.* 33.

130. Paula had founded a monastery for women in Bethlehem as a companion community to the one Jerome organized there.

131. Jerome, *Ep.* 108.29 (CSEL 55: 348), cited above.

132. *Ep.* 108.29 (CSEL 55: 348).

words, while traditional rites of mourning were *typical* at funerals, in the case of an abbess, with masses of monks in attendance, a different ethos held sway.

Then there are the practices addressed by John Chrysostom in a homily on Hebrews in which he criticizes his congregation at Antioch for incongruously combining the old traditions with the new.[133] They called in a presbyter for comfort at their funerals, brought in singers to perform psalms, and joined in the psalmody themselves. But they also hired mourners to wail for the departed, and they joined the lamenting, men tearing their hair and women shrieking out their grief, as if they did not believe in the resurrection.[134] As John saw it, their behavior was contradictory and ruined the public image of the church. "For Greeks pay attention not to what is said by me but to what is done by you."[135] Evidently, those who mixed the old with the new did not see any contradiction, probably because they did not agree with John that Christians should not grieve. Annoyed that his sermons were falling on deaf ears, John threatened to discipline any members of his church who violated Christian norms, even to "exclude for a long time" anyone who hired "these mourning women."[136]

There are a few indications about which psalms were chosen for funerals. Psalm 114 was the psalm lesson for a funeral sermon delivered by Ambrose on the occasion of Emperor Theodosius's death in 395.[137] John Chrysostom cites the same psalm in a homily delivered at the feast of the martyrs Bernice and Prosdoce (circa 386–397)[138] and, in comments about proper behavior at a funeral, he asks his congregation to recall what they sing on such an occasion, namely, "Return,

133. John Chrysostom, *In Heb. 2*, Hom. 4.5–6 (PG 63: 42–44). On the question of whether the sermon was delivered at Antioch (in the years from 386 to early 398) or in Constantinople (398 to June of 404, when he was exiled), see the discussion in Pauline Allen and Wendy Mayer, "The Thirty-Four Homilies on Hebrews: The Last Series Delivered by Chrysostom in Constantinople?" *Byzantion* 65 (1995): 337–339.

134. John Chrysostom, *In Heb. 2*, Hom. 4.5 (PG 63: 43–44). John refers to funeral "hymns" and quotes from some of them, making it clear that the hymns are biblical psalms. He also distinguishes "the singers" (τοὺς ψάλλοντας), who are "called/invited" along with the presbyter, from "the (female) mourners" (τὰς θρηνούσας), who are hired. This implies that the singers are fellow Christians who perform or lead the psalms.

135. *In Heb.*, Hom. 4.5 (PG 63: 42).

136. *In Heb.*, Hom. 4.5 (PG 63: 44).

137. Ambrose, *De obit. Theodos.* 17 (CSEL 73: 380). Ambrose refers to the congregation hearing this reading. He does not mention their response.

138. John Chrysostom, *De Bernice et Prosdoce* 3 (PG 50: 634). On the date of the homily, see Wendy Mayer and Bronwen Neil, *St. John Chrysostom: The Cult of the Saints: Select Homilies and Letters* (St. Vladimir's Seminary Press, 2006), 156.

my soul, to your rest" (Ps 114:7).[139] He then adds two additional psalm-verses as further examples: "I will fear no evil, for you are with me" (Ps 22:4) and "You are the refuge from the affliction that encompasses me" (Ps 31:7).

Another traditional funeral psalm may have been Psalm 115, for the *Apostolic Constitutions* cites one of its verses (along with Ps 114:7 and other biblical passages) as grounds for psalmody in the funeral rites for the faithful: "Precious before the Lord is the death of his holy ones" (Ps 115: 6).[140] While proof-texting does not imply liturgical use, the words of verse 6 would certainly have provided a suitable refrain for a Christian funeral psalm.

Psalms 114, 22, 31, and 115 all contain words of comfort in the face of death or dire affliction. Presumably, other psalms with that theme might have been chosen for a funeral. A very differently themed psalm was sung spontaneously by Augustine's friend Evodius when Augustine's mother Monica died in Ostia in 387. Evodius intoned Psalm 100, and the whole house responded.[141] The topic of this psalm is the blamelessness of the psalmist and his constant opposition to sinners. Evodius may have chosen Psalm 100 to honor the character of Monica.

Psalmody at Feasts of the Martyrs

Martyr feasts were well-attended fair-like events that usually featured a mixture of popular "feasting with the dead"[142] and the newer rites instituted by bishops, including psalmody at a vigil held in a chapel or the open air, followed by a morning service where the local bishop preached.

A canon attributed to a synod of Elvira, which may have convened in the early fourth century, bans women from conducting vigils at cemeteries, probably including martyrs' tombs, on the grounds that they often use the pretext of praying to engage secretly in heinous acts.[143] By contrast, the *Acts of the*

139. ἐννόησον τί ψάλλεις κατὰ τὸν καιρὸν ἐκεῖνον· ἐπίστρεψον, ψυχή μου κ.τ.λ. John Chrysostom, *In Hebr. 2*, Hom. 4.5 (PG 63: 43) (pointed out by Kaczynski, "Die Psalmodie bei der Begräbnisfeier," 801).

140. *Const. ap.* 6.30.3.

141. Augustine, *Conf.* 9.12.31

142. On the musical activities at martyr feasts, see Charles H. Cosgrove, *Music at Social Meals in Greek and Roman Antiquity: From the Archaic Period to the Age of Augustine* (Cambridge University Press, 2023), 333–339.

143. Canon 35 of the Council of Elvira: *Ne feminae in cimiteriis pervigilent. Placuit prohiberi ne feminae in cimiterio pervigilent, eo quod saepe sub obtentu orationis latenter scelera conmittant.* The history of composition of the corpus of these canons, assigned to an alleged fourth-century synod at Elvira, is very difficult to establish. See Miguel J. Lázaro Sánchez, "L'état actuel de la recherche sur le concile d'Elvire," *Revue des sciences religieuses* 82 (2008): 517–546.

Martyrdom of St. Saturninus speaks glowingly of how the church honors the martyrs "with vigils, hymns, and indeed solemn sacraments."[144] If this work dates to around 300, as some have surmised,[145] it provides the earliest evidence of what was done at liturgical vigils in honor of martyrs. But the *Acts of the Martyrdom of St. Saturninus* is more likely a work of the fifth century.[146]

Theodoret of Cyr also describes a new kind of psalmody for vigils that two ardent Nicene laymen named Diodore and Flavian were said to have invented for martyr feasts. It was they, Theodoret claims, who "first taught (the church) to sing Davidic song in alternation by dividing the choirs of singers in two . . . And gathering the lovers of divine things at the tombs of the martyrs, they passed the nights with them hymning God."[147] Theodoret places these activities in the time of conflicts over Arianism in the time of Bishop Leontius (344–358), and he implies that the new alternating psalmody played a salutary role in the defense of orthodoxy.

The reference to "tombs of the martyrs" would have included the martyrium at the Antiochene suburb named Daphne that held the remains of Babylas and the three children who died with him, and perhaps other martyria as well, whether at Antioch or Daphne. According to Theodoret, the aforementioned bishop Leontius, seeing how many of the city's Christians attended the martyr vigils, urged them to move their hymn-fests from the martyr shrines to the city's church buildings, which were all in the hands of the Arians.[148] If Theodoret is correct about this, Leontius probably hoped to bring the martyr vigils into the orbit of his own authority and the influence of his clergy.[149]

Alternating psalmody with two choirs became very popular in Antioch, Theodoret writes, and spread everywhere.[150] There is indirect evidence of that spread to martyr vigils in Gregory of Nyssa's account of the funeral rites for his sister Macrina, who died in Pontus in 379. Gregory compares the psalm-sounding

---

144. *uigiliis, hympnis* [*sic*], *sacramentis etiam sollempnibus* [*sic*]. *Opusc. pass. ac transl. s. Saturn.*, 1 [Prolog.] in Patrice Cabau, "Opusculum de passione ac translatione sancti Saturnini, episcopi Tolosanae ciuitatis et martyris. Édition et traduction provisoires," *Mémoires de la Société archéologique du Midi de la France* 61 (2001): 65.

145. Taft, *The Liturgy of the Hours in East and West*, 166, citing Thierry Ruinart's 1713 edition and G. Marcora, *La vigilia nella liturgia: Ricerche sulle origini e primi sviluppi (sec. I– VI)* (Ambrosius, 1954), 61.

146. See Cabau, "Opusculum de passione ac translatione sancti Saturnini," 59 with n. 2.

147. Theodoret, *H.E.* 2.24.9 (GCS NF 5: 154).

148. Theodoret, *H.E.* 2.24.10 (GCS NF 5: 154).

149. See Mayer and Allen, *The Churches of Syrian Antioch*, 191–192, 200–201.

150. I discuss alternating psalmody as a format in chapter 10.

pannychis held for Macrina to "the panegyric for the martyrs,"[151] and he mentions that he organized the mourners into choirs of men and women. Although he does not say that they sang in alternation, the dual choir format is suggestive of that. Gregory also provides evidence that psalmody (with or without alternating choruses) had been a fixture of martyr vigils in Pontus twenty years earlier. In his second *Homily on the Forty Martyrs,* he recalls that when he was a young man, his mother insisted that he journey to the Feast of the Forty Martyrs, presumably at their shrine in Sebaste. This would have been around 360. The *pannychis* was held in a garden "and the remains of the saints were honored with psalmody."[152] Writing in the same period, probably between 362 and 379, Basil preached a sermon at a morning service following a martyr *pannychis.* "Having come to this sacred enclosure of the martyrs many hours ago," he began, "and having propitiated the God of the martyrs with hymns, you have endured until this midday hour."[153]

Pilgrim Rites at Holy Sites

Egeria reports to her correspondents that when she visited various holy sites, "it was always our custom . . . [that] first prayer was made there, then the reading was read from the codex. Also one psalm relevant to the matter was recited and prayer was made there again."[154] These practices were outside any local liturgies, although sometimes Egeria and her traveling companions were received by local monks or clergy, who may have participated in the ad hoc rites. It seems fair to infer that other pilgrims also followed customs of this sort, although Egeria does not say.

Presumably, the "one psalm" Egeria mentions was typically a biblical psalm, although a biblical canticle might have been chosen if its topic was deemed fitting. For example, when Egeria and her companions visited the Red Sea, they may have sung the Song of Moses from Exodus 15.[155]

151. Gregory of Nyssa, *Vit. Macr.* 33.6–8. Gregory's aim is to imply that his sister, although she did not suffer a martyr's death, was worthy of the veneration accorded to martyrs.

152. Gregory of Nyssa, *Encom. in xl mart. ii* (PG 46: 785; GNO 10: 167). Gregory experienced a terrifying but life-changing admonitory vision at this feast. Having fallen asleep in a garden not far from the shrine, when he should have been keeping vigil with the other faithful, he dreamed that the forty martyrs came to him. They reproved him for his lack of devotion and beat him with rods.

153. Basil of Caesarea, *Hom. in Ps. 114* 1 (PG 29: 484).

154. Egeria, *Itin.* 10.7. In reporting on visits to various places, she does not always specifically mention a psalm or hymn (see 3.6 for example); but in 10.7 she is emphatic that this was her invariable rule.

155. *Itin.* 6.3.

Unscheduled Vigils

The earliest references to Christian vigils include the story in Acts about Paul and Silas in jail and the account in *Acts of Paul* about Paul and the Corinthians holding an all-night vigil following a community supper a few days before his departure from the city. These stories probably reveal what Christians of the late first and the second century considered typical activities at a Christian vigil. Both refer to song, and *Acts of Paul* specifically mentions psalms of David.

The stories just mentioned suggest a custom of spending the night in song and prayer because a certain set of circumstances seemed to call for that kind of vigil. There are no descriptions of these kinds of occasional vigils in third-century Christian literature. In fact, the descriptions of vigils in Acts and *Acts of Paul* aside, spontaneous, situational vigils are not specifically documented until the late fourth century.

In early January of 356, a general named Syrianus arrived in Alexandria with a body of soldiers to effectuate Emperor Constantius's recent decision to expel Athanasius from his see.[156] Athanasius challenged him and demanded that the question be directly clarified through communication with Constantius. Syrianus agreed, probably because he was not acting on direct orders and Athanasius had the support of the church and most of the city. Three weeks passed; then the general again proceeded against the bishop. During the night, when Athanasius was conducting a vigil at the church of Theonas in preparation for a morning "synaxis," Syrianus's soldiers surrounded the basilica. According to Athanasius, while the soldiers were still outside, he took his seat on the bishop's throne and instructed the deacon to read a psalm and the people to answer, "For his mercy is forever."[157] Just what happened next is uncertain, but when the soldiers burst through the doors, Athanasius managed to elude capture.

A vigil, presumably with fasting, would ordinarily have been to prepare for Communion. But an encyclical letter of the Council of Alexandria, included in Athanasius's *Defense against the Arians*,[158] implies that Communion was celebrated only on Sundays in Alexandria.[159] Athanasius gives the date of the siege

156. Concerning the incident and its political circumstances, see David M. Gwynn, *Athanasius of Alexandria: Bishop, Theologian, Ascetic, Father* (Oxford University Press, 2012), 43–45; Timothy D. Barnes, *Athanasius and Constantius: Theology and Politics in the Constantinian Empire* (Harvard University Press, 1993), 118–119.

157. Athanasius, *Apol. pro fug. sua* 24 (SC 56: 234).

158. This encyclical is quoted in Athanasius, *Apol. contra Arianos* 3–19.

159. In refuting a claim that a certain Macarius had broken the mystical cup during a celebration of Communion, the defenders of Athanasius formulated an argument that seems to imply that Communion was celebrated only on Sunday: "For that place in which the cup was broken was

as 14 Mechir.[160] The *Index to the Festal Letters of Athanasius* is more precise: "the *dux* caused a lot of trouble for the church on the thirteenth of Mechir (8 February), and when on the fourteenth (9 February) at night he entered Theonas with his troops,"[161] which implies that the morning synaxis was to take place on 14 Mechir, a Thursday. Hence, the vigil was from Wednesday evening into Thursday, and it was sometime after midnight, in the wee hours, that the soldiers entered the church. The vigil was not in preparation for Sunday Communion, and the planned Thursday morning synaxis would not have been a Communion service, unless it was an exception to the usual custom.[162] Or else one could speculate that a change of custom had occurred between the encyclical letter, composed in 338,[163] and the events of February 8/9, 356. But nearly a hundred years later, the church historian Socrates could still say that Communion was restricted to Sundays in Alexandria.[164] Hence, it is not clear why Athanasius called a vigil, unless he suspected that the general meant to arrest him that night or the following morning, which might explain both the vigil and the decision to hold a morning synaxis. In any case, the singing of a psalm that was suitable to the situation would have been intended to fortify the people and probably Athanasius himself, who was not prepared to be arrested and soon fled the city.

A similarly dangerous vigil took place in Milan thirty years later during Holy Week of 386, when Ambrose and the Catholics were engaged in a contest with the fourteen-year-old Arian Emperor Valentinian II and his powerful mother,

---

not a church. There was no priest residing there. The day on which they say that Macarius did the thing was not the Lord's Day. Hence, since there was no church there, no celebrant, no day that demanded it [the Eucharist], what kind of mystical cup was it, and when and where was it broken?" This passage is from the encyclical letter, as quoted in Athanasius, *Apol. contr. Arianos* 11.5–6. This and other evidence for Alexandria is noted in Robert F. Taft, "The Frequency of the Celebration of the Eucharist throughout History," in *Between Memory and Hope: Readings on the Liturgical Year*, ed. Maxwell E. Johnson (Liturgical Press, 2000), 80–81.

160. Athanasius, *Hist. Ar.* 81.

161. *Index to the Festal Letters of Athanasius* 28 (tr. Brakke and Gwynn, 265).

162. Taft interprets this as a regular Thursday vigil in preparation for the weekly Friday morning Eucharist, which he calls "an Alexandrian peculiarity" (*The Liturgy of the Hours in East and West*, 167), although in a subsequent article he concludes that Communion was restricted to Sundays in Alexandria (see n. 159). In any case, the *Index* makes clear that the synaxis was scheduled for Thursday, not Friday, with a Wednesday vigil (see above with n. 161).

163. On the date of the council and its letter, which is not in dispute, see David M. Gwynn, *The Eusebians: The Polemic of Athanasius of Alexandria and the Construction of the 'Arian Controversy'* (Oxford University Press, 2007), 76.

164. Socrates, *H.E.* 5.22 (discussing diversity of Paschal observances among the churches and comparing it to the similar diversity of churches in other matters).

Empress Justina, over possession of certain basilicas. On Tuesday, Catholics began filling the Portian Basilica, outside the walls, having learned that soldiers had been sent to erect imperial banners inside the church.[165] Meanwhile, Catholics were also pouring into the "new church," where soldiers had also appeared. Ambrose's account is confusing as to which basilicas were involved in the events of this week and in which churches he himself presided at various points.[166] He mentions psalmody in rehearsing the events of Wednesday. At one of the churches, the imperial banners had been taken down and were in tatters, the result of playful vandalism by children, he says. Whether children were responsible or not, the shredding of the banners heightened the tension. When Ambrose arrived at this church or perhaps at one of the other churches, he found soldiers standing guard. Because of their presence, he says, he could not go home but remained there with the congregation.[167] "We said psalms with the brothers," he writes, "in the small basilica of the church."[168] Apparently, he stayed there through the night, for he makes no mention of any change of locale in referring to a church service "the next day," at which he preached on Jonah.

Augustine, who knew these events in Milan from his mother Monica, describes the psalmody and its purpose during those days of tension. According to him, "the devout people kept watch in the church, ready to die with their bishop."[169] Monica was with them. "There," he writes, "my mother, your maidservant, maintaining a principal part in the anxieties and vigils, lived in prayer." The context of these recollections is Augustine's earlier description of the impact the church's singing had on him in the period leading up to his conversion. The singing he had in mind was a recent custom in Milan and served as a "type of

---

165. Except where otherwise noted, I summarize Ambrose's account in *Ep.* 76 (Maur. 20) (CSEL 82: 108–125), a letter to his sister Marcellina.

166. Regarding current scholarly discussion of these events, see Michael S. Williams, *The Politics of Heresy in Ambrose of Milan: Community and Consensus in Late Antique Christianity* (Cambridge University Press, 2017), 226–239, including whether there was a single contest over basilicas in 386 or two contests, one in 385 and a second in 386 (pp. 227–232) and which basilicas were in dispute (pp. 233–234); also the detailed bibliographic note in Marcia L. Colish, "Why the Portiana? Reflections on the Milanese Basilica Crisis of 386," *Journal of Early Christian Studies* 10 (2002): 362 n. 2.

167. According to Ambrose's biographer, Paulinus of Milan, the soldiers permitted Catholic Christians to enter the building but would not allow anyone to leave. Paulinus, *Vit. Ambr.* 13. This probably does not give the full picture, since the soldiers were sent to seize the church. Their orders would have given them every reason to empty the basilica of Catholics, even if, initially, they sought to intimidate the Catholics by refusing to let them leave.

168. Ambrose, *Ep.* 76.24 (CSEL 82:123).

169. This statement is missing from McKinnon's translation in *MECL*, no. 351 (no doubt an oversight).

consolation and exhortation."[170] It is this remark that prompts his description of the conflict between Ambrose and the emperor "about a year earlier or not much more," a time-reference that associates the conflict with the recent introduction of consolation and exhortation through song. Then, at the end of his anecdote, he adds a further reference to the singing. "At that time, it was instituted that psalms and hymns should be sung in the manner of the eastern regions, so that the people would not be worn out by the tedium of sorrow."[171] In other words, when the people were huddled in church for hours on end with soldiers ready to seize the building by force, they were consoled and fortified by singing psalms. Moreover, Paulinus, who served as a deacon in Milan and later as Ambrose's secretary, also speaks about the place of song during this period. "At this time," he writes, "antiphons, hymns, and vigils first began to be celebrated in the Milanese church."[172]

Psalmody itself may not have been new to Milan in the mid-380s, since it could well have had a place in the daily office and services of the word.[173] But vigils with extensive psalmody and hymnody (such as the singing of Ambrose's own hymns) must have been a new thing. In other words, the extraordinary vigils of Holy Week, 386, inspired a use of psalms that afterward became a regular part of Milanese church life.[174]

Ambrose's decision to have the people sing psalms was directly related to his political-ecclesiastical aims in the power struggle with the emperor and empress. Instead of negotiating an end to the people's occupation of the basilica and persuading them to go home, he stood with them, using psalmody and at least one sermon to keep them occupied and strengthen their resolve. The act of corporate singing must have been unifying. Not many years later, in an exposition of Psalm 1, Ambrose commented that "clearly, it is a great bond of unity for the whole number of the people to unite in one chorus."[175] Perhaps this remark owed something to his observations about the social power of psalmody during the battle for the basilicas.

---

170. Augustine, *Conf.* 9.7.15.

171. *Conf.* 9 7.15.

172. Paulinus, *Vit. Ambr.* 13.3 (Bastiaensen, 70; PL 14: 31).

173. The earliest surviving references to psalmody in Milanese church liturgy all date, as far as dating is possible, to the 380s and 390s, with uncertainty about whether Ambrose's works of the 380s antedate the events of 385/386. But in a writing of the late 370s, Ambrose refers to holy virgins of Bononia who sing spiritual songs (*Virginibus* 1.60).

174. I touch on these matters in chapter 10 as well.

175. Ambrose, *Expos. psalm. 1* 9 (PL 14: 925; CSEL 64.8).

Defenses of Psalmody at Vigils by Basil and Niceta of Remesiana

In a letter written to the clergy of Neocaesarea in 375, Basil of Caesarea refers to psalmody at an unspecified type of vigil, where the people divided into two choruses. It appears that a certain teacher had convinced the Neocaesarean clergy that Basil's church had given up the traditional style of psalmody in favor of a different "kind of singing (*melōdias*)."[176] This singing was probably the two-choir format that Basil goes on to defend in his letter, explaining its spiritual utility and insisting that "the vigils, common psalmody, and prayers" of his church were customary not only in Cappadocia but also in Egypt and among "the Libyans, Thebans, Palestinians, Arabians, Phoenicians, and those who live near the Euphrates."[177]

In the same passage Basil also refers to "the psalm of confession" without specifying it by number, which implies that a certain psalm was commonly designated by his expression. A likely candidate is Psalm 50, whose LXX superscription describes it as David's confession. Didymus the Blind refers expressly to Psalm 50 as "the psalm of confession,"[178] and it happens that Psalm 50 was a fixed part of a sunrise service instituted at the monastery at Bethlehem around the middle of the fourth century.[179]

Although Basil describes the psalmody of the vigil, the nature of the vigil is otherwise unclear. His reference to "the people" (*laos*) suggests that it was a church vigil, not a monastic service,[180] which also fits with the fact that the clergy of Neocaesarea held him responsible for it. Taft terms the gathering "an

---

176. Basil, *Ep.* 207.2.

177. *Ep.* 207.3. The nature of this performance format is discussed in chapter 10.

178. ὁ πεντήκοντα ἀριθμὸς ἔχει τι ἐξαίρετον· καὶ διὰ τὰς ἀρετὰς αὐτοῦ αὐτῷ ἐπετέθη ὁ ψαλμὸς ὁ τῆς ἐξομολογήσεως. Didymus's comments make clear that by ὁ ψαλμὸς ὁ τῆς ἐξομολογήσεως he means a psalm of confession of sins. Didymus the Blind, *Comm. in psalm. 26*, ms. p. 106, 24 (Gronewald 2: 218). Compare Basil's reference to τὸν τῆς ἐξομολογήσεως ψαλμόν (*Ep.* 207.3).

179. See John Cassian, *Inst.* 3.6.

180. Some scholars opine that "the people" refers to urban ascetics/monks (so Juan Mateos, "L'office monastique à la fin du IVe siècle: Antioche, Palestine, Cappadoce," *Oriens Christianus* 47 [1963]: 85–86; Joseph Dyer, "The Desert, the City and Psalmody in the Late Fourth Century," in *Western Plainchant in the First Millennium: Studies in the Medieval Liturgy and Its Music*, ed. Sean Gallagher et al. [Ashgate, 2003], 26; James McKinnon in *MECL*, 68, no. 139). Others conclude that "the people" are a combination of regular laity, monks, and female ascetics (Taft, *The Liturgy of the Hours in East and West*, 39–40; Benoît Gain, *L'église de Cappadoce au IVe siècle d'après la correspondance de Basile de Césarée (330–379)* [Pontificium Institutum Orientale, 1985], 172–173).

occasional cathedral vigil such as we see in Alexandria and Constantinople at this time."[181]

A vigil was the occasion for a sermon by Niceta of Remesiana that came to be labeled *On the Usefulness of Hymnody*, a discourse on psalmody that Niceta called especially fitting for an occasion when "we celebrate what our sermon takes up to describe."[182] Niceta served as bishop of Remesiana from around 370 until his death not long after 414. In the opening of his homily, he refers to the participants as a *psallenti fraternitati*.[183] Hence, it is possible that he delivered his sermon at a monastic vigil. Yet it is equally possible that he means *fraternitati* in a gender-inclusive sense, in which case he preached at a cathedral vigil.

Among the subjects Niceta addresses is the deprecation of singing by some "in both our region and the east, who regard the singing of psalms and hymns as superfluous and scarcely suitable for divine religion."[184] These detractors may have been certain ascetics who thought that melody was a worldly pleasure.[185] In making his case against their opinion, Niceta enumerates various spiritual benefits of psalmody and chances to mention the placement of psalms within the *ordo* of a vigil, their intercalation between prayers and readings.[186] He also gives advice about how to sing in a properly blended manner.[187]

The Sunday Vigil in Jerusalem

I will conclude this chapter by describing a vigil observed in the Jerusalem church before the weekly Sunday-morning service. I mentioned this preCommunion vigil in chapter six. It began "officially" at cockcrow, according to Egeria, when the bishop arrived and the doors to the Church of the Anastasis were opened. But because so many people arrived early—not only monks who wished to conduct their own nocturns at the church but laity as well, and clergy—the vigil got underway in the lamp-lit forecourt, where "hymns as well as antiphons" were sung with prayers "between each hymn and antiphon."[188] When the bishop

181. Taft, *The Liturgy of the Hours in East and West*, 40.

182. Niceta of Remesiana, *Util. hymn.* 1.

183. *Util. hymn.* 13.

184. *Util. hymn.* 2.

185. In his sermon *On Vigils*, Niceta mentions people who object to psalm-filled vigils as superfluous and even unsuitable (*Vig.*1).

186. Niceta, *Util. hymn.* 12.

187. *Util. hymn.* 13.

188. Egeria, *Itin.* 24.8–9. This Sunday vigil replaced the regular daily service at this hour (see 24.1).

arrived and the doors were opened, the people crowded into the lighted interior. Presbyters and deacons took turns leading responsorial psalmody, with a prayer after each psalm.[189] The bishop read an account of the passion that included the story of the resurrection; the vigil, with its exceptional lighting inside and outside the church, was a resurrection vigil, Sunday being the day of Jesus's resurrection.[190] Moreover, Egeria calls the passion reading "the account of the Lord's resurrection."[191] After this reading, the bishop was led "with hymns" to the Cross, a "rock" just outside the Church of the Holy Sepulcher, where the service concluded with a final psalm and prayer.[192] After that, the bishop and some of the lay people retired, but the monks and other laity returned to the Anastasis for more psalmody, which continued right up until daybreak.

189. *Itin.* 24.10.

190. The Christian Sunday was traditionally understood as a celebration of the resurrection of Jesus on the first day of the week. Moreover, the instructions in the *Apostolic Constitutions* for the weekly Sunday services appear to include a service of prayer that could be a predawn "resurrection" vigil (2.59), which is what Taft infers, noting a parallel in Egeria to its three prayers (*The Liturgy of the Hours*, 44–45 and 53). At a later point in the *AC*, a daily service of prayer is specified for cockcrow (8.34.7), which corresponds to the time of the weekly vigil in Egeria.

191. Egeria, *Itin.* 24.10.

192. *Itin.* 24.11.

CHAPTER EIGHT

Psalms in Monastic Life

THE ORIGINS OF monasticism are somewhat obscure, not only because it took various forms, whose beginnings are difficult to discover, but because the earliest full-fledged account of it, Athanasius's *Life of Antony*, reveals that there were already old monks in Lower Egypt when a young Antony arrived there in the 270s or so. These were solitary ascetics living in rustic huts and pursuing holiness through constant prayer and Scripture meditation. Athanasius mentions a handful of them. Jerome's biography of Paul (the Hermit) of Thebes, who is said to have been the first monk of Egypt (a claim that cannot be treated as historical), was composed many years after Athanasius's book and makes only one mention of psalmody: when Paul died while Antony was visiting him, Antony ministered to his body and performed the customary psalmody. Athanasius's account of Antony supplies more information on the topic of psalms in Antony's practice.

Athanasius's and Jerome's biographies of their respective solitaries are hagiographic literature and not critical histories. Jerome did not interview Paul, and although Athanasius visited Antony, it is unknown whether any of the few references to psalmody in his biography derive from those conversations as opposed to second-hand sources. I will examine Athanasius's information in due course.

John Cassian's Reports about Psalmody in Eastern Monasticism

John Cassian writes copiously about Eastern monastic traditions, including those of Egypt, and he had personal experience in some of the monastic traditions he describes.

Yet he is not always a reliable reporter. For one thing, the entire program of Cassian's *Institutes* (circa 417) rests on dubious generalities about current practices and their history in the East and the West.[1] Cassian holds up Egyptian monasticism as the ideal form, the only one that preserves the original rigor of the apostles. Not only is the claim about apostolic origins the sort of pious fiction that was typical of fourth-century authors who wished to cloak the norms

1. See Richard J. Goodrich, *Contextualizing Cassian: Aristocrats, Asceticism, and Reformation in Fifth-Century Gaul* (Oxford University Press, 2007), 119–150.

they advocated in apostolic authority, Cassian's picture of Egyptian monasticism as uniform and universal, except for the Pachomians, is not supported by the evidence.[2] Nor are his claims to be relying on his own personal memories fully honest, given that source-critical analysis shows his extensive, unacknowledged borrowing from Evagrius Ponticus and other authors.[3] Hence the representations Cassian makes to his Gallic audience about what he himself learned directly about monks in Egypt, Palestine, and Mesopotamia, together with his recommendations as purportedly the most authentic monastic form of life, with just a few practical leniencies, is highly misleading, "a rhetorical construct . . . used to buttress the authority of what he prescribed for Gaul."[4] Hence, the only safe way to proceed in using Cassian's *Institutes* as a historical source is to discount his universalizing generalities and to examine each claim cautiously on its own terms.

In book 3 of the *Institutes*, Cassian introduces the topic of customs at monasteries in Palestine and Mesopotamia, then goes on to speak of Bethlehem more specifically. The monks at Bethlehem sang Psalms 148–150 at the end of nocturns, he says. Since he would have participated in nocturns when he lived at a monastery in Bethlehem in the early 380s, his report of the bare fact seems credible. The account is part of his discussion of a new morning office at Bethlehem.

> What we should also know is that no change was made in the ancient custom of psalmody by our elders, who decided that this morning service (*matutinam sollemnitatem*) should be added. But the dismissal (*missam*) was always celebrated in the nocturnal service in the same order as before. For the hymns which in this country (Gaul) are taken up at the morning service, which they are accustomed to end after cockcrow and before dawn, they [the monks of Bethlehem[5]] still sing today at the end of the nocturnal vigils, that is, Psalm 148, the beginning of which is "Praise the Lord from the heavens (*Laudate dominum de caelis*)," and the rest that follows [meaning the remainder of Psalm 148 *and* Psalms 149 and 150 as well[6]]. But Psalms 50, 62, and 89, as we know, have been assigned to this new service (*huic nouellae sollemnitati fuisse deputatos*).

2. This is widely recognized by modern scholars. See for example, Taft, *The Liturgy of the Hours in East and West*, 58; Goodrich, *Contextualizing Cassian*, 119.

3. See Goodrich, *Contextualizing Cassian*, 119–128.

4. Goodrich, *Contextualizing Cassian*, 121.

5. In *Inst.* 3.4.1, Cassian refers explicitly to Bethlehem as the place of origin for this custom.

6. Note that the expression *et reliquos qui sequuntur* probably does not refer to the rest of the words that follow the first verse, since that would have gone without saying. Hence, the phrase

> Finally, throughout Italy to this day, when the matins hymns are ended (*consummatis matutinis hymnis*), Psalm 50 is sung in all the churches, which undoubtedly was drawn from no other source.[7]

In short, the old prematins service had these *Laudate dominum* or lauds psalms. The new matins service at Bethlehem did not disturb nocturns; it was an additional service with its own psalms, namely, Psalms 50, 62, and 89. But in Gaul, the lauds psalms were sung at matins. There is direct evidence in John Chrysostom that by the closing decades of the fourth century, the monks of the Syrian desert were in the habit of singing Psalms 148–150 at the end of nocturns (see below). This correlation suggests that what Cassian reports about the singing of the lauds psalms at nocturns by the monks he knew in late fourth-century Bethlehem is accurate. The other details he gives about psalmody at the Bethlehem monastery may be historical as well.

Shortly after describing nocturns at Bethlehem and its new matins, Cassian mentions a vigil that began on Friday evening, with the start of the Sabbath, and continued through the night.[8] I will describe its format, with the proviso that the passage has been judged to be an interpolation.[9] The monks first sang three "antiphons"[10] standing. Then they sat on low benches and chanted three "psalms," responsorially, taking turns reciting the verses. They also added three lessons to the psalms while they sat, which may mean that each seated psalm was

---

probably refers to the two psalms that follow Psalm 148 to close out the Psalter, both of which also begin with the words, "Praise the Lord."

7. Cassian, *Inst.* 3.6. Some translations attach the modifier "at the end of the nocturnal vigils" to the subordinate clause, since it follows that clause; but this gives the passage a confusing impression. I follow an interpretation of the syntax that Taft defends on compelling contextual grounds: *in fine nocturnarum uigiliarum* ("at the end of the nocturnal vigil") modifies the verb whose subject is the monks at Bethlehem (*decantant*—"they chant"), not the verb whose subject is the monks of Gaul (*excepere*—"they have reserved"); since otherwise the sentence does not make its point, which is to specify the difference between the practices in these two centers (Taft, *The Liturgy of the Hours in East and West*, 99–100). The issues are also discussed in Paul F. Bradshaw, *Daily Prayer in the Early Church: A Study of the Origin and Early Development of the Divine Office* (Oxford University Press, 1982), 108–109.

8. This all-night vespers is described in *Inst.* 3.8, which is a continuation of a discussion that begins in 3.4 concerning daily matins in Bethlehem.

9. See chapter 11 with n. 68.

10. Cassian, *Inst.* 3.8.4. It is not clear how the word "antiphon" is to be understood in *antiphona tria concinuerint*. It could refer to a form of psalmody. But if the passage is an interpolation, its use of the term might differ from that of Cassian, who may use the word "antiphon" for a kind of hymn. See chapter 11.

paired with a reading or that the three readings followed the three psalms.[11] The whole pattern must have been repeated through the course of the vigil, which lasted from vespers until "the fourth cockcrow" in winter and until just before dawn in the other seasons.[12] On other days, when the monks observed nocturns, they may have performed "the twelve psalms" (see below) in a somewhat similar fashion, that is, in threefold units by alternating between standing and sitting.

If the passage is original to the *Institutes*, it may reflect Cassian's experience as a monk at Bethlehem in the 380s. If it is an interpolation, it tells us about a custom that cannot be situated in time or setting. It could reflect a practice that a fifth-century editor of the *Institutes* wished to encourage, but that is very uncertain. The earliest manuscripts of the *Institutes* date to the tenth or eleventh centuries.

In another set of guidelines in the *Institutes*, Cassian purports to rely on knowledge of monastic customs in Egypt. There is no doubt that he traveled through parts of Egypt in the 370s, visiting monasteries.[13] Less certain is how far his generalizations about Egyptian practices are accurate. The cenobitic monks of Egypt, he says, kept only two daily services, an evening synaxis and a night-time gathering at cockcrow, except on Saturday and Sunday, when they celebrated Communion at the third hour.[14] Here is Cassian's description of their daily meetings:

> Therefore, as we have said, throughout all Egypt and the Thebaid, the number of the psalms is kept at twelve in both the evening and the night-time services; strictly in this fashion two lessons follow, one from the Old Testament, of course, and one from the New. This pattern, established anciently, has for that reason continued intact for many ages in the monasteries of the provinces there, unchanged to the present time.[15]

We should be suspicious about the claims of antiquity and universality, even if we can accept that Cassian recalled the practices as common in some of the places he visited.

11. Cassian, *Inst.* 3.8.4.

12. *Inst.*, 3.8.1–3.

13. See Columba Stewart, *Cassian the Monk* (Oxford: Oxford University Press, 1998), 7–12.

14. This statement happens to appear in *Inst.* 3.2, following Cassian's account in *Inst.* 2 of the coenobitic customs in Egypt that I am about to rehearse.

15. *Inst.* 2.4.

Cassian next rehearses a myth, told in other sources as well, about how an angel appeared in the guise of a monk and modeled the correct number of psalms—twelve psalms with a closing response of "Alleluia."[16] The monks recognized the singer as an angel, because he vanished after finishing his demonstration. The ancient fathers, Cassian says, who prescribed the angel's revelation as a rule—the so-called Rule of the Angel—added the two Scripture readings, according to their own lights (with certain variations in the readings for Saturday, Sunday, Easter, and Pentecost).[17] A bit later, Cassian writes that the monks took an unhurried approach to their communal psalmody by dividing the performance of each psalm into two or three segments, with prayers in between.[18]

The Rule of the Angel

Richard Goodrich notes that the earliest reference to the Rule of the Angel is an allusion in Jerome's preface to his translation of the *Rule of Pachomius* (about 405) and that the closest version to Cassian's account is the one in Palladius's *Lausiac History* (circa 420), which has the angel reveal the rule to Pachomius. Goodrich suggests that Cassian rewrote a Pachomian version of the story and "modified it to apply to his own Egyptian patriarchs."[19] Cassian's beliefs required that the revelation had been given originally not to Pachomius but to the first generation of monks in Egypt. If Cassian modified a Pachomian version of the Rule, then he shaped his account of it to fit his description of the evening and nocturnal practice of the monks of Egypt. But since we do not know the source and form of the legend that Cassian heard or read, and since Jerome's allusion to the angel's revelation is the earliest known evidence for the Rule, there is reason for caution in drawing any inferences from Cassian about the cenobitic monks of Egypt in the 380s. For if Cassian first heard about the Rule of the Angel in the early fifth century (which is when Jerome alludes to it), then he would have wanted to believe that the Rule had been universally adopted in Egypt long before his own time, whether that agreed with his thirty-five-year-old memory of communal psalmody in Egypt or not.[20]

---

16. *Inst.* 2.5.5.

17. *Inst.* 2.6.

18. *Inst.* 2.11.1.

19. Goodrich, *Contextualizing Cassian*, 138–139.

20. Discussing the evidence in Cassian for the twelve-psalm practice, Stig Frøshov reasons as follows. According to Cassian, the monks never added "Alleluia" to a psalm that did not have that word in its title, which means that the twelfth psalm of each meeting's psalmody had to be an Alleluia psalm. *Inst.* 2.11.3 (CSEL 17: 27) ("In the response of Alleluia, no psalm is said except

The likelihood that the legend of the twelve psalms began as a story about twelve prayers adds a further complication. Book 32 of the *Lausiac History* ("Concerning Pachomius and the Tabennesiots") contains an account in which the angel commands a series of guidelines for monastic life, including instructions for the hours. The guidelines require that the monks live in cells of three. No communal hours of prayer are prescribed, although communal meals are assumed. The rule regarding daily prayer in the Greek text of *Lausiac History* Recension G, thought to be the earliest extant form of the story, can be translated as follows: "He prescribed that they perform twelve prayers through the whole day and twelve in the evening, and in the night twelve; and three at the ninth hour; and commanding as well that when the multitude was about to eat, a psalm be sung with each prayer."[21] Armand Veilleux compares the relevant wording of the angel's command about hours of prayer in the three witnesses of *Lausiac History* Recension G (mss. 30–32), the *Third Greek Life of Pachomius* (G³), the Syriac, Ethiopic, and Latin versions of the *Life*, and mss. 33 and 47 of the *Lausiac History*, which Veilleux thinks may represent a tradition independent of Recension G.[22] The shared words of Recension G agree essentially with the language of these other witnesses (for the *Lausiac History* and the *Life of Pachomius*) in specifying two sets of twelve prayers, one for the day and the other for the night.[23] The formulation for daytime prayers (*dia pasēs hēmeras*) can mean

---

one which is marked Alleluia in its title"). Moreover, since the angel is said to have added an Alleluia response after the twelfth psalm and not after each psalm, the other eleven psalms must not have been Alleluia psalms. Hence, the twelfth psalm was not sung in course (*currente psalterio*), as some have assumed, but was selected by a different logic. See Stig Simeon R. Frøyshov, "The Cathedral-Monastic Distinction Revisited, Part 1: Was Egyptian Desert Liturgy a Pure Monastic Office?" *Studia Liturgica* 37 (2007): 206–207. This could well be correct. Although Cassian's account by itself is a somewhat shaky platform on which to base conclusions about the selection of psalms for the communal synaxis in Egypt in the late fourth century, in view of Cassian's commitment to the story of the Rule of the Angel, Frøyshov, who notes this reason for caution, goes on to supplement his argument by adducing additional evidence.

21. Palladius, *Hist. Laus.* 32.6.

22. Armand Veilleux, *La liturgie dans le cénobitisme pachômiene au quatrième siècle* (Herder, 1968), 324–339. Veilleux sets forth the material for comparison (regarding the tradition of the angel's directive about hours of prayer) in two tables (*La liturgie*, 326–327). Table I reflects Recension G of the Lausiac History. Table II reflects the lives of Pachomius (G³, Syriac, Ethiopic, and Latin), and mss. 33 and 47 of the *Lausiac History* (note the erratum in line 2: "33–37" in Table II seems to be a mistake for "33–47," that is, for mss. 33 and 47).

23. The formulation in the *Third Greek Life of Pachomius* (G³) is Διὰ πάσης δὲ ἡμέρας ποιεῖν εὐχὰς δώδεκα, ὡς εἶναι τὴν εὐχὴν ἄπαυστον· καὶ ἐν ταῖς παννυχίσιν ὡσαύτως. *Vit. Pach.*, *Vit. tert.* 32 (Halkin, 276). This is the reading in Ms. 9 of the Monastery of St. John at Patmos. The formulation is also found with a slightly different syntactical order of expressions in G⁴ from Codex Monacensis gr. 3 and in Codex Athous Lavrensis E 182 (also in the edition by Halkin).

either "through every day" or "throughout the day," but the second possibility must be meant, since the corresponding expression (*en tais pannychisi*) refers to all-night activity.[24] Veilleux concludes that the twelve prayers of day and night meant continuous prayer (according to a literal interpretation of the apostolic command "Pray without ceasing"), and he notes that in the versions of the Greek lives of Pachomius the two sets of twelve prayers are explained in just this way.[25]

The "twelve psalms" may have been normative practice for some monasteries by the time Jerome alluded to an angelic revelation in his preface to his translation of Pachomius's *Precepts*. But the origin and form of the story, which Jerome does not relate, remain obscure. Neither the story of the Rule of the Angel nor the scheme of two sets of twelve prayers, much less of twelve psalms, appears in the earliest editions of the *Life of Pachomius*. The twelve psalms are not mentioned in the Coptic *Life*, whose final editing took place sometime after the death of Athanasius in 367 CE and perhaps before the death of Horsiesios (of unknown date but post 387);[26] nor are they found in the *First Greek Life*, edited after the death of Horsiesios. Hence, it is difficult to imagine that the rule that prescribed twelve prayers for day and twelve for night was followed in the Pachomian Koinonia during the last two decades of the fourth century, whatever Palladius may have thought. Moreover, the large body of surviving documents about the Pachomian communities make clear that the Rule of the Angel, which Palladius appears to have used as a source, was almost certainly not genuinely Pachomian but was composed by "someone who had only a very superficial knowledge of the Pachomian Koinonia."[27] And if Jerome's belief that the Rule of the Angel was revealed to Pachomius led him to infer that it was a Pachomian practice, he simply erred.

Veilleux leaves open the question of whether the twenty-four-hour schedule of prayers was original to the Rule of the Angel,[28] and it is unclear what

24. See n. 23. The pannychis was the all-night party of certain Greek festivals. The Christian vigil repurposed the custom and the term.

25. Veilleux, *La liturgie dans le cénobitisme pachômiene au quatrième siècle*, 324–339. The statement ὡς εἶναι τὴν εὐχὴν ἄπαυστον is explained in G^3 and G^4.

26. The Bohairic life lacks its conclusion, but the last pages tell of the death of Theodore in 368 (*Pach. vit. Boh.* 206) and the beginning of Horsiesios's leadership over the community (208–210). The final editing of the *First Greek Life* was done after the death of Athanasius in 373 and probably after the death of Horsiesios. Note the summarizing past-tense description of Horsiesios's work as head of the Pachomian brotherhood, given by this vita (*Gr.*[1] 149), which has been dated to sometime after 387.

27. Armand Veilleux, tr., *Pachomian Koinonia*, vol. 2: *Pachomian Chronicles and Rules* (Cistercian, 1982), 6.

28. Veilleux, *La liturgie dans le cénobitisme pachômiene au quatrième siècle*, 330.

connection there might have been between this schedule and the two sets of twelve psalms described by Cassian, which Cassian dubiously claims was already a universal custom in Egypt when he traveled there in the 380s.

Further clues may be present in other anecdotes from the Egyptian monastic tradition. A story in the *Lausiac History* about Antony testing the would-be monk Paul the Simple tells how Antony examined Paul by reciting a single psalm twelve times before supper and then making twelve prayers, to see whether Paul would join in. After supper, he again sang twelve psalms and made twelve prayers.[29] Similar anecdotes appear in *Apophthegmata Patrum* in its different iterations. One story concerns some brothers from a cenobitic fellowship who visit an anchorite. When evening comes, the visitors perform "the twelve psalms" and do the same at night.[30] In another story, a certain Roman monk, who has taken up residence in Scetis near a church, is visited by an Egyptian. When evening comes, the two of them perform the twelve psalms and repeat the same exercise at night.[31] Afterward, the Roman monk explains his desert ascesis to the Egyptian, remarking at one point that, "instead of musical entertainments and citharas, I say the twelve psalms."[32] Another story about the twelve psalms is told in the *Apophthegmata* of Pseudo-Macarius. Two young pilgrims visit Macarius at Scetis. During the night, after Macarius himself has retired, they stand and pray, while he secretly observes them. In the morning, they ask, "Shall we perform the twelve psalms?" When Macarius agrees, the following takes place, according to his first-person narrative:

> The smaller (pilgrim) psalms (*psallei*) five psalms of six lines and one Alleluia. With each line, a light of fire proceeded from his mouth and went up to heaven. Likewise, the other, when he had opened his mouth singing, a rope of fire went forth and was caught up to heaven. And I spoke a little by heart. And as I went out, I said, "Pray for me."[33]

29. Palladius, *Hist. Laus.* 22. The first verb used for Antony's performance of psalms is βάλλει (22.6) The verb ψάλλει is also used (22.8).

30. ὅτε ἐγένετο ὀψὲ ἔβαλον τοὺς δώδεκα ψαλμούς, ὁμοίως δὲ καὶ τὴν νύκτα. *Apoph. patr., Collectio anonyma* 229.

31. ὡς ἐγένετο ὀψὲ ἔβαλον τοὺς δώδεκα ψαλμούς, καὶ ἐκοιμήθησαν, ὁμοίως δὲ καὶ τὴν νύκτα. *Apoph. patr., Collectio alphabetica*. PG 65: 388 // and *Apoph. patr., Collectio systematica* 10.150 (SC 474: 112).

32. ἀντὶ μουσικῶν καὶ κιθαρῶν κ.τ.λ. *Apoph. patr., Collectio alphabetica* (PG 65: 388).

33. Ps.-Macarius, *Apoph.* 33 (PG 34: 256) // *Apoph. patr., Collectio alphabetica* (PG 65: 277) // *Collectio systematica* 20.3 (SC 498: 164).

This anecdote takes for granted that "the twelve psalms" are to be said at a single time.[34] The story of the two young pilgrims is also told in the Bohairic life of Macarius but with no mention of a recitation of psalms.[35] According to other traditions, the pilgrims who visited Macarius were Maximus and Domatius, monks memorialized in a hagiography that went through different recensions and language versions. The anecdote about the twelve psalms appears in only one of these, the Bohairic, a Coptic dialect spoken in Nitria.[36] This fact provides Veilleux with further confirmation of his suspicion that the custom of the twelve prayers or psalms originated in the deserts of Nitria and Scetis.[37]

The tradition preserved in the *Lausiac History* speaks of a custom of twelve prayers (not psalms) performed in the day and in the night by the monks of the Pachomian Koinonia. This ascription is not historical. Just what its relation to traditions about twelve psalms may be is uncertain. In the sources examined thus far, when "the twelve psalms" are mentioned—note the definite article—they are always a set, performed at a particular time of day. Moreover, the sources associate this custom with Scetis and Nitria and describe it as both a private discipline of the solitary in his cell and a communal monastic practice. Further evidence appears in the fifth-century Codex Alexandrinus, which contains a horologion of twenty-four psalms, one for each hour of the day and night.[38] Stig Frøyshov, who has determined which psalms made up this schedule, thinks that a twenty-four-hour horologion would have better suited a cathedral cursus than the cursus of a monk in a cell, since a monk would not have wished to interrupt his private meditation by reciting a psalm every hour according to a lectionary.[39] In any case, a cathedral setting is consistent with the fact that Codex Alexandrinus is a deluxe book, produced for a wealthy urban church, whether at Alexandria or some other city.

34. Was only a portion—six lines—of each of the five psalms recited? Compare this to the tradition about six sections, discussed below.

35. Veilleux cites to the edition and translation published by Émile Amélineau, *Histoire des monastères de la Basse-Égypte* (Leroux, 1894), 87 (Veilleux, *La liturgie dans le cénobitisme pachômiene au quatrième siècle*, 333 n. 27).

36. This, too, is pointed out by Veilleux (*La liturgie dans le cénobitisme pachômiene au quatrième siècle*, 334). He cites the passage in the Bohairic *Life of Saints Maximus and Domatius* from Amélineau, *Histoire des monastèries de la Basse-Égypte*, 299.

37. Veilleux, *La liturgie dans le cénobitisme pachômiene au quatrième siècle*, 334.

38. Codex Alexandrinus, British Library Royal 1 D VII, fol. 11v [532^{v}]. See Frøyshov, "The Cathedral-Monastic Distinction Revisited, Part 1," 209–213, 215. Juan Garcés and Scot McKendrick of the British Library examined the codex directly for Frøyshov.

39. Frøyshov, "The Cathedral-Monastic Distinction Revisited," 211.

The sources leave us with a puzzling picture and one that frustrates efforts to trace one or more of the traditions back to the fourth century. The witnesses to twelve prayers, twelve psalms, and horologia of twenty-four prayers or twenty-four psalms, distributed through day and night, are all documented by writings composed or compiled in the fifth century or later. Moreover, the producers of these writings were avid for legends, eager to edify, and had every reason to adapt anecdotes to suit their own times, settings, and interests. Hence, while some of the traditions may be considerably older than the writings in which they are found, it is not clear which, much less what their original forms and settings were. Even Veilleux's plausible suspicion that a custom of twelve prayers or psalms began with certain monks in Nitria or Scetis does not lead him to speculate about further particulars.

Another custom, only superficially connected to the twelve prayers, is the tradition of "six sections."[40] The sections consisted of parts of Scripture that monks were assigned to recite by turns at the ambo during the morning synaxis in the monastery and at the evening gatherings in the various houses, presumably with prayers. In other words, the sections were not composed exclusively of psalms but included them, according to a number of rules concerning which parts of Scripture a monk ought to learn by heart. Moreover, absence of any mention of "six sections" in the *Life of Pachomius*, together with the fact that the various collections of Pachomian rules that refer to the six sections represent the tradition as it stood at the end of the fourth century, may suggest that the six-sections custom was a development after the death of Pachomius (post the mid-340s).[41]

Psalmody in the Pachomian Community

The evidence for the Pachomian form of monasticism survives in the *Life of Pachomius*, extant in various language versions, and in the *Precepts*, *Institutes*, and *Laws* attributed to Pachomius and in the *Regulations of Horsiesios*. The *Life* was composed not long after Pachomius's death in the 340s. The books of rules represent Pachomian practice in the late fourth century or later, even if some

40. The expression is often translated "six prayers," but Veilleux points out that the Coptic probably means "six sections" (note on *Pr.* 121 in Veilleux, *Pachomian Koinonia*, vol. 2, 191). Although Jerome's translation uses the expression "six prayers and psalms" in *Inst.* 14, the Coptic has only "six sections" at this point (see the note to *Inst.* 14 in *Pachomian Koinonia*, vol. 2, 193).

41. There is no reference to the six sections in *Pr.* 1–12; they are mentioned in *Pr.* 121, which appears to elaborate the rule of *Pr.* 10, reflecting a later point in the development of the rules. This probably also applies to the references to the six sections in *Pr.* 126; *Inst.* 14; and *Leg.* 10. See Veilleux, *La liturgie dans le cénobitisme pachômiene au quatrième siècle*, 296–298.

of the material is earlier and goes back to Pachomius himself.[42] Along with an incomplete Coptic version, the *Precepts* survives in Jerome's translation (circa 404), which is based on a Greek version of a Coptic text. Comparison of Jerome's version with extant parts of the Coptic manuscript tradition reveals that he sometimes paraphrased. Some of these paraphrases may reflect his own misunderstandings, others perhaps his own adaptations.

A few of the stories in the Bohairic-Coptic *Life of Pachomius* mention psalms. This work probably draws on an original Coptic life in Sahidic, composed not long after Pachomius's death, which occurred in around 346.[43] The Bohairic *Life* mentions psalmody by angels escorting the souls of the righteous to heaven:

1. Pachomius has a vision in which a soul is carried to heaven by angels, and one of them "psalms[44] in front of the soul in a language no one knows," although Pachomius recognizes the response as "Alleluia." The narrator goes on to tell how the righteous soul "also sings and blesses the Lord" as he approaches his heavenly resting place.[45]
2. One day during a communal synaxis, Theodore hears angel voices psalming melodiously in the air.[46] Pachomius explains the significance to him: angels are conducting a soul to heaven.
3. Monks working in the open air look up and see a departing soul "before whom the angels were psalming as they brought it to its resting place."[47]

42. See Philip Rousseau's cautions about using the Pachomian writings for purposes of historical reconstruction. Philip Rousseau, *Pachomius: The Making of a Community in Fourth-Century Egypt*, rev. (University of California Press, 1999), 47 and passim.

43. On the date of this life, see Armand Veilleux, tr., *Pachomian Koinonia*, vol. 1: *The Life of Saint Pachomius and His Disciples* (Cistercian, 1980), 1–2.

44. *Pach. vit. Boh.* 82 (ⲉⲣⲯⲁⲗⲓⲛ—"to recite or sing psalms;" CSCO 89: 88.28).

45. *Pach. vit. Boh.* 82 (ϣⲁϥϩⲱⲥ—"sings;" CSCO 89: 89.29).

46. *Pach. vit. Boh.* 83. Melodious psalming is clearly implied by the double use of the verb, together with a modifier that means sweet or melodious: ⲉⲩⲉⲣⲯⲁⲗⲓⲛ ϧⲉⲛⲡⲓⲏⲣ ϧⲉⲛⲟⲩϫⲓⲛⲉⲣⲯⲁⲗⲓⲛ ⲉⲥϩⲟⲗϫ (CSCO 89: 93.17–18): "psalming in the air in an act of psalming that is sweet/melodious" (a literal rendering based on the kind guidance of Zlatko Pleše). Veilleux translates: "in the air. . . singing a melodious song" (*Pachomian Koinonia*, vol. 1, 110). Cf. Gr[1] 93: ἐν τῷ ἀέρι φωνὴν ὡς ψαλλόντων μέλος λίαν τερπνὸν καὶ εὐαίσθητον (Halkin [1982], 45).

47. *Pach. vit. Boh.* 181 (ⲉⲣⲯⲁⲗⲓⲛ; CSCO 89: 160.9). Translation from Veilleux, *Pachomian Koinonia*, vol. 1, 217 (with Veilleux's "singing psalms" changed to "psalming"). Another example can be found in *Pach. vit. Boh.* 123.

In these passages, the author uses a Coptic transliteration of the Greek *psallein*. Since his subject is angelic psalmody, he no doubt means song, not recitation. The reference to "Alleluia" is another indicator of that, as is his description of the psalming in the second passage.

The Bohairic-Coptic *Life of Pachomius* also describes psalmody by monks who escorted Athanasius to the Thebaid following his election as patriarch in 328. As the story has it, Pachomius brought a group of brothers to greet the bishop as he processed to their monastery, led by an entourage of bishops. The brothers joined this procession and recited psalms as they escorted Athanasius to the monastery.[48] The Coptic *Life* also describes a subsequent visit of Athanasius to the Thebaid in 363, when he was accompanied by lay people, bishops, clerics who carried lamps and candles, as well as monks from many places, who went ahead chanting psalms and odes.[49] Since this story concerns events closer to the time of the composition of the biography and appears in the independent *First Greek Life*, it has a claim to antiquity.[50] Similar honors were also accorded to the Pachomians' own Apa Horsiesios when he returned to the monastery at Phbow.[51] Moreover, Pachomian monks psalmed when they conducted funeral rites for departed brothers, performing psalms during the vigil and while bearing the body to the grave.[52]

In all these descriptions, the verb "psalm" is used without an object. But in a description of the monks who belonged to Athanasius's entourage, the author uses a verb for reciting/repeating with the object "psalms and odes."[53] Given the reference to odes, singing is surely meant, especially in view of the context, an

48. *Pach. vit. Boh.* 28 (ⲉⲣⲯⲁⲗⲓⲛ; CSCO 89: 28.6).

49. *Pach. vit. Boh.* 201. The monks leading the procession "were reciting (ⲉⲩⲧⲁⲟⲩⲟ) the psalms with the odes" (CSCO 89: 198.5). The brothers with Theodore eventually join these monks in their psalming (ⲉⲣⲯⲁⲗⲓⲛ) (CSCO 89: 199.9; repeated with ⲉⲩⲉⲣⲯⲁⲗⲓⲛ at 199.24–25). The *First Greek Life* also mentions psalming in its parallel account (Gr.[1] 143). The monks psalm again when they conduct Athanasius to the church of one of their monasteries (*Pach. vit. Boh.* 202—ⲉⲩⲉⲣⲯⲁⲗⲓⲛ; CSCO: 200.11). This visit is also noted in the Syriac *Index* to the *Festal Letters* of Athanasius, which states that on the 27th of Phaophi (October 24) of 363, Athanasius fled Alexandria, following a threatening decree by Julian, and went to the Thebaid (*Index* 35).

50. See chapter 9 with n. 8.

51. *Pach. vit. Boh.* 204 (the psalming to greet and accompany Horsiesios) (ⲉⲩⲉⲣⲯⲁⲗⲓⲛ / ⲁⲩⲉⲣⲯⲁⲗⲓⲛ; CSCO 89: 203.16, 18).

52. *Pach. vit. Boh.* 93, 123, 205, 207; *Pach. vit.*, Gr.[1] 103, 116, 117. Compare *Precepts* 127 and 128, which imply that funeral psalmody was usual and was performed responsorially.

53. *Pach. vit. Boh.* 201. See n. 49. In the *First Greek Life*, the descriptions of funerals use the verb ψάλλειν (*Pach. vit.*, Gr.[1] 103, where the custom is denied to a brother) and the expression μετὰ ψαλμῶν (116 and 117).

episcopal procession. Since Pachomian monks joined these processions and did so by psalming, and since they imagined that angels and even deceased human souls psalmed when the righteous were conducted to heaven, it is reasonable to infer that the Pachomians engaged in honorific *singing* when they participated in processions, even if they did not always sing when performing psalms in their private or corporate synaxes.

The *Life* characterizes the daily regimen of the Pachomian monks as unceasing prayer, vigils, reciting God's law, and performing manual labor.[54] It does not mention psalms when describing their practices, but Jerome's translation of the *Precepts of Pachomius* refers to the psalms in regulations for the morning and evening gatherings, as well as in prescriptions for the Sunday service.[55]

When the Pachomian brothers gathered for their morning and evening synaxes, they took turns reciting while plaiting ropes. One instruction in the *Precepts* implies that each recital was concluded with prayer: "When the one who stands first on the step, reciting by heart something from Scripture, claps with his hand for the prayer to be concluded, no one should delay in rising but all shall get up together."[56] A Greek excerpt happens to contain this rule, and it may preserve what Jerome found in his Greek Vorlage. Where Jerome has "reciting by heart something from Scripture," the Greek uses just one word, *apostēthizomenos*, which means "repeating from memory."[57] In neither the Greek form of this precept nor Jerome's Latin form (the Coptic not having been preserved) is there any reference to psalmody. But another precept of the Latin version implies that psalms were indeed said at these gatherings, as well as lessons from Scripture, and prayer. According to the Latin form of this precept, in an effort to curb a tendency to talk or joke during "the time of psalming (*psallendi tempore*) or prayer or the middle of the reading," the fathers specified a punishment in front of the community.[58] A Greek (but no Coptic) version of this rule happens to have been preserved, and, significantly, where Jerome's translation specifies various community activities during which unwanted joking and so forth might occur, including during psalming, the

---

54. *Pach. vit. Boh.* 35.

55. The morning and evening meetings are regulated by *Precepts* 3–14, the Sunday Eucharist by *Precepts* 15–18.

56. *Pr.* 6 (tr. from Veilleux, *Pachomian Koinonia*, vol. 2, 146). The reference to "concluding" the prayer probably means that after each recital, the monks stood for prayer, which concluded each recital + prayer unit.

57. *Exc.* 1 (Boon, 170).

58. *Pr.* 8.

Greek excerpt has simply "in the synaxis."[59] This raises the suspicion that Jerome added the reference to psalms.

According to Jerome's Latin version of the *Precepts*, the Pachomian monks also engaged in responsorial psalmody at their Sunday synaxis. One precept requires that all servers must be in attendance at the Sunday service "responding to the psalmist" (*psallentique respondens*).[60] There is no surviving Coptic or Greek version of this rule. Another precept specifies that "no one is to have the right of psalming (*psallendi*)" except the housemaster and esteemed elders at this meeting.[61] Again, none of the Coptic and Greek versions of this rule have survived. A third precept provides a sanction for any brother who leaves while one of the elders "is psalming, that is, reading the Psalter."[62] No Coptic version of this precept has been preserved, but there is a Greek excerpt. It refers to "the reading," not to psalming or to reading from the Psalter.[63]

To summarize, the only references to psalms at community synaxes in Pachomian literature are found in Jerome's Latin translation of the *Precepts*, where there are four references; in two of these four, the two for which there happens to be a version in the Greek *Excerpts*, the Greek does not refer to psalmody. This encourages the speculation that Jerome added references to psalms where his Vorlage did not have them, whether he meant to clarify on the basis of his own assumptions or to adapt the rules at these points for a different monastic setting.

That said, a regulation dealing with a monk's private synaxis, preserved in the Coptic *Regulations of Horsiesios*, implies that each monk had set pieces for his own meditation and rose at night to "recite *his psalms* and his section of texts."[64] This is consistent with another rule in the *Regulations of Horsiesios* and with two further rules in the *Precepts of Pachomius*. One states the minimum amount of Scripture for a newcomer to learn—"the Lord's prayer and as many psalms as he can learn." Another precept says "twenty psalms or two of the Apostle's epistles or some other part of the Scripture."[65] And still another sets a minimum for any monk, whether a newcomer or not, as "at least the New Testament and the

---

59. *Exc.* 2 (Boon, 170).

60. *Pr.* 15. refers to the weekly servers, seated on their mats at the Sunday service, who respond to the one psalming (*psallentique respondens*).

61. *Pr.* 16 (Boon, 17).

62. *Pr.* 17 (Boon, 16–17); tr. Veilleux, *Pachomian Koinonia*, vol. 2, 148.

63. *Exc.* 7 (Boon, 171).

64. *Reg. Hor.* 17 (tr. Veilleux, *Pachomian Koinonia*, vol. 2, 202).

65. *Pr.* 49 and *Pr.* 139 (tr. Veilleux, *Pachomian Koinonia*, vol. 2, 153, 166).

Psalter."[66] One of the *Regulations of Horsiesios* contemplates that not everyone will succeed in learning the whole Psalter by heart: "Let him who does not memorize much memorize at least ten sections along with a section of the Psalter."[67]

The rules for memorization imply that psalms were an important part of the daily routine of a monk's personal discipline. But psalms were not, apparently, the primary mode of praying without ceasing. Moreover, we cannot be confident that the directives regarding psalm memorization and recitation, all of which are found in the regulatory literature, reflect customs that were established in the time of Pachomius himself.

Another source of information about the use of psalms in desert monasticism is Athanasius's *Life of Antony*. In a summary of what Antony taught as the proper ascesis for a monk, Athanasius mentions constant prayer, singing before sleeping and upon waking, repeating the commandments of Scripture, and imitating the works of the saints.[68] In another place, he characterizes the desert monks who follow Antony's teaching and example as so many small choirs psalming, studying, fasting, praying, and working.[69] Prayer is the activity most often associated with Antony in the *Life*. Psalming is mentioned in only a handful of passages. In one story, Antony tells how he sometimes lies on his mat praying and psalming "by myself," while demons rage noisily in his cell.[70] The psalming and praying weakens and repels his attackers, but sometimes the demons imitate his discipline by "psalming and speaking from Scripture" in a wily ploy to unnerve or deceive him.[71] In one of his most detailed descriptions of these auditory assaults, Athanasius has Antony explain how the demons use the discipline itself to torment him and other monks:

> They are deceitful and ready to be metamorphized and changed in form into every sort of thing. Indeed, often, without becoming visible, they put on a show of psalming with song and they mention passages from the Scriptures. It often happens that when we are reading, they themselves immediately speak, like an echo, the very same things that were read; often, too, they arouse us to prayer when we are sleeping. And they do this constantly, almost preventing us from sleeping at all. And

66. *Pr.* 140 (tr. Veilleux, *Pachomian Koinonia*, vol. 2, 166).

67. *Reg. Hor.* 16 (tr. Veilleux, *Pachomian Koinonia*, vol. 2, 202).

68. Athanasius, *Vit. Ant.* 55.3.

69. *Vit. Ant.* 44.2.

70. *Vit. Ant.* 39–40; see also 9.3 and 13.7.

71. *Vit. Ant.* 39.5.

> it also happens when they model themselves after the form of monks, pretending to speak like the pious in order to deceive by likeness in form and finally to lead where they wish those deceived by them.[72]

The biographical accuracy of Athanasius's picture of Antony's use of psalms is difficult to judge. In his introduction to the *Life*, Athanasius mentions that he did not consult any monks who had known Antony but instead relied on his own knowledge, based on times when he himself visited Antony and on knowledge gleaned by "following" him. "Following" probably means gathering second-hand stories about Antony. These provided the basic material for the life, a hagiography that leans in the direction of a romance. The narrative is a combination of third-person narrative[73] and long quotations of Anthony, "speeches-in-character" that Athanasius composed on the basis of his recollections of his conversations with Anthony and the stories he had heard about him. The stories that circulated about Antony would have been subject to the interests of monastic oral transmission, a process in which anecdotes were modified in the retelling to serve a practical, edifying purpose, and a story about one person was sometimes transferred to the lore about another figure. The question of biography aside, Athanasius's account does provide an illuminating general picture of desert-monastic experience in the period when he gathered material for his biography.

Psalmody in Syrian Monasticism

In the early 370s, when John Chrysostom was pursuing an ascetic existence in the rugged environs of the Syrian mountains east of Antioch, he encountered coenobitic monks who observed nighttime psalmody together. In later sermons, he occasionally drew on his memories of that experience; and in a homily on Matthew 3, he described the monks' song at their communal morning office:

> These lights of the world, when the sun has risen, rather long before its rising, get up from their beds, healthy and wide awake and sober . . . And having formed one choir, they all sing hymns to God with a

72. *Vit. Ant.* 25.1–3 (ψάλλειν μετ' ᾠδῆς). Antony goes on to say that the demons assault other monks in similar ways, "so that they might bring the simple into despair and say that the discipline is useless and make people sick of it, as if the solitary life were difficult and burdensome" (25.4).

73. In only one instance does Athanasius use the narrative first-person to describe an event in Antony's life, namely, Antony's departure from Alexandria after a visit to refute the Arians. Athanasius writes, "When he was leaving and *we* were conducting him. . . ." (*Vit. Ant.* 71).

> cheerful self-awareness, harmoniously with one voice, honoring him and giving thanks to him for all things, both benefactions to oneself and those that are communal. Thus, if it seems good, let us ask, having left Adam behind, in what respect is there a difference between angels and this choir of those who sing on earth, saying, "Glory to God in the highest. . ."[74]

The closing quotation implies that in addition to psalms, the monks sang the canticle *Gloria in excelsis*, the angelic hymn of Luke 2:14.

In a homily on 1 Timothy, John repeats this characterization of the monks in their night office, calling them "truly holy, even angels among human beings" and telling how they rise at cockcrow and "stand, singing prophetic hymns."[75] The term "prophetic" is virtually a synonym for "Davidic." John goes on to cite two illustrative prooftexts for this prayer at night: "'In the night,' he says, 'lift up your hands to God' [Ps 133:2] and again, 'At night my spirit rises early to you, O God, because your statutes are a light upon the earth' [Isa 26:9]." John adds that the psalms stir up tearful love for God, which he illustrates by quoting more prooftexts from the Psalter: "And the Davidic songs provoke many fountains of tears. For when he sings, [he expresses this,] saying, 'I have become worn out with my groaning, and every night I will bathe my couch and shower my bed with my tears' [Ps 6:7]." John goes on to quote lines from ten additional psalms to illustrate how David "shows their ardent love for God." The topics range from another verse about tears (Ps 101:10) to lines that speak of the lowliness of humanity (Pss 8:5; 143:4; 48:17), solitariness (Ps 67:7), and deadly threats (Pss 22:4; 90:5–6; 43:3).

It has been argued that John's quotations refer to a fixed psalm and a fixed canticle of the nightly office—Psalm 133 and Isaiah 26:9ff., respectively, as invitatory songs.[76] Robert Taft draws the further inference that the vigil concluded with Psalms 148–150, since John quotes Psalm 148:1 at the end in a separate statement.[77] Before these conclusions are examined, an aspect of John's language needs to be clarified. In his introduction to the quotations from Psalm 133 and Isaiah 26, John uses singular verbs for saying and singing to introduce the various psalm verses he cites. He also uses a singular verb, "shows," to sum up what the various psalms signify as nocturnal prayers. The subjects of these verbs are not

---

74. John Chrysostom, *In Matt. 21*, Hom. 68.3 (PG 58: 644; Field, *Hom. in Matt.* 2: 296–297).

75. John Chrysostom, *In 1 Tim. 5*, Hom. 14.4 (PG 62: 576; Field, *Interp. in. ep. Paul.* 6: 121).

76. Notably by Juan Mateos and Robert Taft. See notes 77 and 78.

77. Robert F. Taft, *The Liturgy of the Hours in East and West: The Origins of the Divine Office and Its Meaning for Today*, 2nd ed. (Liturgical Press, 1986), 80–81 (cf. 195).

expressed; but in the next sentence, John speaks of the monks singing with the angels, and at that point he switches to a plural verb. According to Juan Mateos, this plural implies that the prior singular verbs have a collective choir of monks as their implied subject, despite the fact that for forty lines all the verbs that John uses when the monks are his grammatical subject are plural, right up to the quotations in question.[78] A simpler explanation is that the singular verbs imply that David or "Scripture" is their subject. John's verb "says" is often used by Christian writers to introduce Scripture quotations, and in those instances its subject is either a biblical speaker/writer or Scripture in an impersonal sense ("it says").[79] The following rendering gives the passage in fuller form, using "it*" as an English placeholder for grammatical subjects that the Greek does not express and may not be intended to be definite:

> These (the monks) are truly holy, even angels among human beings. And do not be surprised to hear these things. For their great fear toward God does not let itself go into the depths of their sleep to submerge their mind, but it lies on them lightly, only giving them rest. Such is sleep with them. It is necessary that their dreams also be the same, not fantasies or nightmares. But as I have said, the cock has crowed and immediately, when the leader has come and prodded the sleeper on the foot, he makes them all get up. For it is a rule there not to sleep naked. And having awakened, they immediately stand and sing prophetic hymns with much harmony, with well-crafted melodies. No cithara or pipes or other musical instrument releases such a sound, which one can hear these saints singing in the deep quiet and in the wilderness. And these same songs are suitable and full of love for God. "In the night," it* says, "lift up your hands to God" [Ps 133:2], and again, "At night my spirit rises early to you, O God, because your statutes are a light upon the earth' [Isa 26:9]." And the Davidic songs provoke many fountains of tears. For when it/he sings, saying [here the illustrative psalm quotations follow in a long string], it* shows their ardent love for God. And [it* does so] again, when they sing with the angels—for the angels also sing then—saying, "Praise the Lord from the heavens" [Ps 148:1], while

78. Juan Mateos, "L'office monastique à la fin du IVe siècle: Antioche, Palestine, Cappadoce," *Oriens Christianus* 47 (1963): 55. John does call the monks a choir in that substantially earlier context—forty lines earlier.

79. Examples of both the personal and the impersonal uses are found elsewhere in Chrysostom's quotations from Scripture, including an exact parallel to the use of φησί(ν) for what passages from different parts of the Bible "say" (in *Ad Theodor.* [2] 3; SC 117: 60).

> we are yawning, scratching, snoring, or simply lying flat on our backs calculating a thousand deceitful things.[80]

Since John's hearers were accustomed to introductory Scripture-quotation formulas that use singular verbs for "saying" with unexpressed subjects, they probably did not worry about identifying a specific grammatical subject but heard John's quotations as illustrative of the feelings that the psalms once stirred up in David and now engender in the Syrian monks.

It would be overreading to infer that John's quotations rehearse a set of fixed psalms of the monks' nightly synaxis.[81] But what about the first two citations from Psalm 133 and Isaiah 26, which John quotes before giving his longer list? Taft, following Mateos's suggestion, treats the singular verb that introduces these citations as a collective, understanding the monks as its implied subject and translating with "they": "And these same songs are suitable . . . 'In the night,' *they* say, 'Lift up your hands' to God' [Psalm 133] and again 'In the night my soul keeps vigil before you, O God [etc.] [Isaiah 26]." When John says that the monks sing these hymns, Taft concludes, as Mateos does, John means that Psalm 133 and Iasiah 26 were fixed hymns that started off the nocturnal service.[82] This inference goes beyond the evidence. There is no contextual basis for thinking that "the monks" is a collective, unexpressed grammatical subject of the singular verb in what is manifestly a citation formula. Instead, the quotations are best taken as illustrative prooftexts. Moreover, there is no direct evidence in other late fourth-century or early fifth-century sources that Psalm 133 was a fixed hymn of nocturns or that Isaiah 26:9–25 was a fixed invitatory canticle.[83]

---

80. John Chrysostom, *In 1 Tim.* 5, Hom. 14.4 (PG 62: 576; Field, *Interp. in. ep. Paul.* 6: 121–122).

81. This is also the conclusion of Mateos ("L'office monastique à la fin du IVe siècle," 56) and of Taft, who concludes that John "is just citing appropriate verses at random, not giving a set order of psalms proper to this office" (*The Liturgy of the Hours in East and West*, 81).

82. Taft, *The Liturgy of the Hours in East and West*, 81.

83. Taft treats references to Isa 26:9b in Basil (*Ep.* 207.3) and Ambrose (*Expos. psalm. 118* 19.30) as evidence that Isa 26:9–25 was a standard ode of the Cappadocian vigil and of the morning service at Milan (*The Liturgy of the Hours in East and West*, 39–41 and 142). But in both cases, they are prooftexts for the practice, not quotations of what people sang. Basil defends the vigil by observing that "among us the people 'rise early in the night' [Isa 26:9] in the house of prayer;" and after they have prayed, "they begin the psalmody." Adducing a series of scriptural grounds for prayer at sunrise, Ambrose puts Isa 26:9b in the mouth of Christ (*Expos. psalm. 118* 19.28, 30; CSEL 62: 437).

Taft's suggestion that the monks must have ended nocturns with Psalms 148–150, the "lauds" psalms, is better grounded.[84] John uses a plural subject when he quotes Psalm 148:1 at the end of his description: "when *they* sing with the angels . . . saying, 'Praise the Lord from the heavens' [Ps 148:1]." This "they" is clearly the monks.

Psalmody in Monastic Communities in Cappadocia

It was perhaps during his second Pontic retreat in the 360s that Basil conceived the ascetic cursus of prayer that he sets forth in his *Longer Rules* thought to have been composed during the 360s and 370s. In *Longer Rules* 37 he argues from Scripture for seven hours of prayer,[85] stating in his preliminary discussion that "prayer and psalmody" do not require a life of leisure because they can be performed at all times, including times of work.[86] Yet this does not mean that he prescribes no structure. He does, and Taft refers to Basil's sevenfold ascetic office as a "liturgicizing" of the ancient private hours of daily prayer, and he calls the result a hybrid "monastic-cathedral" or "urban-monastic" office.[87]

Basil, who opines that variety in psalmody is beneficial,[88] does not assign fixed psalms to each hour, except to mention that Psalm 90 is to be used at sext and compline.[89] He says that the third hour should be observed by the gathered community[90] but he does not make clear which other hours should be conducted communally. Nor does he describe the format(s) of the communal psalmody, for example, whether one recites and others respond.

The *Longer Rules* is designed to encourage and regulate ascetic communities composed of men and women, even families with children, as well as orphans. Basil envisions a secluded setting, ideally in the country, where the ascetics engage in agriculture.[91] He was preceded in his efforts at monastic organization by his elder sister Macrina, who presided over a monastery at Annisa, where there were

84. Taft, *The Liturgy of the Hours in East and West*, 81.

85. Basil, *Reg. fus. tract.* (*Asc. magn.*) 37.3–5 (Silvas, 245–247; PG 31: 1012–1016).

86. *Reg. fus. tract.* 37.3 (PG 31: 1013, with reference to the preceding discussion).

87. Taft, *The Liturgy of the Hours in East and West*, 84 and 90.

88. Basil, *Reg. fus. tract.* 37.5 (Silvas, 247; PG 31: 1016).

89. *Reg. fus. tract.* 37.4 (sext), 5 (compline) (Silvas, 246–247; PG 31: 1013, 1016).

90. *Reg. fus. tract.* 37.3–4 (Silvas, 246; PG 31: 1013).

91. *Reg. fus. tract.* 38 (Silvas, 248–249; PG 31: 1016–1017).

both men's and women's houses (although not married couples devoted to celibacy or families, as far as we know).[92]

It is unknown how many hours the community at Annisa observed. According to Gregory, Macrina had practiced psalmody since childhood.[93] Recounting the pious education she received from her mother, he writes that "of the psalmody of Scripture she was not at all ignorant, going through each part in its own time, attending to it when rising from bed, busy with work, resting, taking nourishment, leaving the table, rising for prayer, and going to bed. She always kept psalmody as a kind of good companion that never left her."[94] He also refers to the communal psalmody practiced by the monastery she founded. During one of Gregory's last conversations with her, he heard "the voice of the psalmers" on their way to vespers.[95]

Singing or Reciting?

Joseph Dyer observes that the vocalization of biblical psalms in desert monasticism was not predominantly melodic and in this respect differed from that of urban ascetics. When desert monks recited the psalms in their private discipline, they typically used a sub-vocalization, a method for meditating on a text that the monks also used for other Scriptures.[96] Dyer cites the Hebrew phrasing of Psalm 1—the wise person "mutters" Torah day and night—as evidence of a longstanding ancient Mediterranean tradition for private recitation.[97] He also notes that one of the characteristic words for monastic recitation was *meletan* (Coptic *meleta*), "meditate," precisely the activity that muttering a text was meant to serve, since muttering reduced vocalization to its minimum, so that the monk remained focused on the meaning of the words, not their sound. To illustrate, Dyer cites an early seventh-century observer who compares the sound of ruminating monks to the buzzing of bees.[98] He also stresses that although the desert monks occasionally sang in communal settings, prevailing monastic

92. The chief source of information about Macrina and her monastery at Annisa is the biography of Macrina composed by her brother Gregory.

93. Gregory of Nyssa, *Vit. Macr.* 3.

94. *Vit. Macr.* 3.19–26.

95. *Vit. Macr.* 22.

96. Dyer, "The Desert, the City and Psalmody in the Late Fourth Century," 17.

97. הגה. See Ludwig Koehler, W. Baumgartner, and J. J. Stamm, *The Hebrew and Aramaic Lexicon of the Old Testament*, vol. 1 (Brill, 2001), 237.

98. Dyer, "The Desert, the City and Psalmody," 37 n. 36, citing Arnuf of Metz (PL 137: 280).

attitudes toward both sensual pleasure and personal pride were incompatible with a concern for melodic sweetness or musical performance. To sing with skill threatened the humility of a monk; to enjoy the sound of melody contradicted his renunciation of sensual pleasure.[99]

Much of Dyer's evidence derives from sources that cannot be dated with any precision but belong to a period when "troparia" and "modes" had entered Christian vocabulary as terms for church song. Hence, some of the testimonies may reflect shifts in desert attitudes and practice that desert abbas adopted in reaction to developments in urban church song, some of which may not have occurred as early as the fourth century or even the fifth. I will concentrate on the evidence from those earlier periods, as far as dating permits.

When the monks of the Syrian desert performed their communal synaxes, they formed a choir and sang, John Chrysostom says.[100] John uses an unambiguous word for singing (*adousi*), and he is even more emphatic about the musicality of the monks' psalmody in another homily where he describes their nocturnal devotion, how they "rise and immediately stand (to pray), singing prophetic hymns with much harmony and with well-crafted melodies."[101] The Syrian monks also performed the psalms in some sort of melodic fashion when they made their annual pilgrimage to the shrine of the Maccabean martyrs at Antioch. In the words of Ambrose, "they made their way singing psalms (*psalmos canentes*) in accord with their ancient practice."[102]

When John Cassian rehearses the tradition about the angel who appeared in the guise of a monk, he says that the angel "sang eleven distinct psalms with similar pronunciation (*parili pronuntiatione cantasset*) in the successive verses, interspersed by prayers."[103] Whatever *parili* means here, *cantasset* is a common Latin word for "sing."[104] It happens that in his *Conferences*, Cassian never uses verbs for singing in describing recitation of Scripture. The distinction is

99. "The Desert, the City, and Psalmody," 21–24.

100. John Chrysostom, *In Matt. 21*, Hom. 68.3 (PG 58: 644; Field, *Hom. in Matt.* 2: 697).

101. John Chrysostom, *In 1 Tim.*, Hom. 14.4 (PG 62: 576; Field, *Interp. in. ep. Paul.* 6: 122) (ὕμνους ᾄδοντες προφητικοὺς μετὰ πολλῆς τῆς συμφωνίας, καὶ μετ' εὐρύθμων μελῶν). This description draws attention to the musical quality of the monks' psalmody, as do the remarks that precede it: "Neither cithara nor syrinxes nor any other musical instrument gives out such a sound as that of these holy ones singing."

102. *Psalmos canentes ex consuetudine usuque veteri pergebant.* Ambrose, *Ep.* 40.16 (PL 16: 1107) (in a letter to Emperor Theodosius composed in 388).

103. *Undecim psalmos orationum interiectione distinctos contiguis uersibus parili pronuntiatione cantasset.* Cassian, *Inst.* 2.5.5.

104. Regarding *parili pronuntiatione*, see below with n. 108.

illustrated in Conference 10, where we find a number of expressions for the verbal activities of monks. In a series of descriptions of "the mind's" performances of prayer, psalmody, and Scripture reading, respectively, Cassian writes "when it prays (*cum orat*)," "when it chants (*cum decantat*)," and "when it recites a lesson (*cum lectionem recitat*)." Referring to psalmody in the *Conferences*, Cassian uses the verb *decantare* and in one instance *canere*, but never *cantare* (the word he uses in the *Institutes* to describe the psalmody of the angel).[105] Of these three verbs, *cantare* and *canere* were common verbs for ordinary singing, even if they could be applied to speech-types that exhibited various degrees or sorts of melody.[106] When Cassian is not using a general word for "saying," his favorite word for monastic psalm-delivery is *decantare*, which the *Oxford Latin Dictionary* defines as "to recite through in a singing tone, to chant" and "to reel off, repeat."[107] Cassian's preference for this term suggests that monastic psalmody as he knew it was repetitive chanting with reduced melody. This might also explain his qualification of the singing of the angel who gave the monks their "rule" as *parili pronuntiatione*, which might mean "evenly pronounced," perhaps simple, "unadorned" chanting.[108]

It is instructive to note that in the Coptic Pachomian literature, the Coptic verb *meleta* is often used with no object but just as often with the Scriptures as an object and in at least one place with psalms as its object—in a description of a monk's synaxis in one of the *Regulations of Horsiesios*.[109] Moreover, a Greek

105. Cassian uses *decantare* ten times in *Conferences*, twice to introduce a prooftext (3.12.3; 11.9.2), once in referring to a psalm's original act of composition (10.11.5), and seven times in describing monastic psalmody (8.16.1; 10.10.14 and 10.10.15; 10.11.4; 10.11.5; 10.13.2; 16.15). He uses *cantare* twice, each time to introduce a prooftext (2.13.10; 9.36.1). He uses *canere* to introduce prooftexts (3.15.4), to describe a monk's psalmodic practice (23.5.9), and to speak figuratively of maturation in wisdom (14.9.2). Arguably, some of the uses of these three verbs to introduce prooftexts imply a practice of singing the psalms, where the subject is not the psalmist but a Christian fulfilling or otherwise enacting what the text says, a clear case of that being *decantans* in 11.9.2. But the two uses of *cantare* with human subjects are nonliteral. In 2.13.10, Cassian says that his reader will be able to "sing in deed and power" a verse about God's gift of compassionate speech (Isa 50:4). Here singing is a figure for action. Likewise in 9.36.1, when he says that "we will be able to sing" verse 2 of a certain vesper psalm (Psalm 141) "when we have become strong in virtue," this "singing" refers to exemplifying the verse or being worthy of it, not performing it melodically.

106. In addition to the *OLD* entries for *cano* and *canto*, see Thomas N. Habinek, *The World of Roman Song: From Ritualized Speech to Social Order* (Johns Hopkins University Press, 2005), 59–74.

107. *OLD*, *s.v.*, *decanto*, def. 1.

108. So Dyer, "The Desert, the City and Psalmody in the Late Fourth Century," 31.

109. *Reg. Hor.* 17 (CSCO 159: 86.33).

fragment that preserves a rule for newcomers, says that they must learn to meditate psalms (*psalmous . . . meletan*).[110] These tendencies of the Pachomian writings strongly suggest that when psalms were recited as part of Scripture rumination, they were not distinguished by a markedly melodic style of utterance. It is also important to keep in mind that the Coptic verb *psallei* in the Pachomian texts probably meant simply "perform a psalm," without implying a particular type of delivery, which was also true for at least some instances of late-antique Christian use of the Greek verb *psallein*.[111]

In certain settings, however, Pachomian psalm recitation was not dronelike chanting but melodic singing. *Pachomian* monks joined the lyrical psalmody of the bishops, clerics, monks, and lay people who escorted the bishop Athanasius when he visited Upper Egypt.[112] The *Life* also says that when a brother died, the angels conducted him to heaven with melodious song and that the monks "psalmed" when they escorted the body of a dead brother to the grave.[113] If the monks joined the psalm-singing of episcopal parades and held their own funeral processions with psalms, they may well have sung in the latter case, since the purpose of a procession was honorific.[114] As for the Sunday synaxis of the Pachomians, the *Precepts* refers to the monks "responding to the psalmist,"[115] which might suggest a musical delivery like the psalm-singing in urban churches. It should be kept in mind that most monks, including the leaders of monastic communities, grew up in urban churches and may have been nurtured in urban psalmody, at least after the Edict of Milan, when daily psalmody became widespread.[116] That said, as described earlier in this chapter, the two precepts about responding at the Sunday synaxis are extant only in Jerome's Latin version, and a third related precept, preserved in both Latin and Greek, is expressed with the word "psalming" in Jerome's Latin and "reading" in the Greek. Hence, the

110. ψαλμοὺς . . . μελετᾶν. *Exc.* 17 (Boon, 174). My observations about terminology are based on an examination of terms in context, guided by lists in the indices to Lefort's critical editions of the Bohairic-Coptic vita and the other Pachomian writings.

111. Note that in *Letter to Marcellinus*, Athanasius finds it necessary to modify the verb ψάλλειν with the expression "with song," which implies that there was a form of psalming without song. See *Ep. Marc.* 28 (PG 27: 40). See also the passage from the desert fathers quoted below: Vat. Grec. 1579, f. 200[r–v] (see n. 129) and Athanasius, *Vit. Ant.* 25.1–3 (quoted above with n. 72).

112. *Pach. vit. Boh.* 201. See note 49 above.

113. See the preceding discussion of Pachomian practices.

114. Regarding the honorific character of funeral psalmody, see chapter 9.

115. *Pr.* 15 (*psallentique respondens*) (Boon, 16) and cf. *Pr.* 16.

116. See below under "Monastic Use of the Psalms and the Spread of Psalm-Singing in the Wider Church."

three precepts may tell us more about performance of psalms at Sunday monastic liturgies in Jerome's monastery than in Pachomian communities.

Pachomian monks meditated on psalms and other Scriptures in their cells, psalms being only part of the Scriptures they recited by heart. They did the same in communal work settings, where meditation was done both silently and out loud, depending on a monk's personal preference.[117] This shows that there was no custom of singing corporately and responsorially at work, simply simultaneous individual recitation of psalms and other Scriptures. Jerome's translation of *Precept* 116 says that the monks "shall chant (*decantabunt*) from psalms and from [other parts of] Scripture" as they work.[118] Apparently, he thought that their psalm-recitation did not differ much, if at all, from their rendition of other Scriptures in work settings, and that they chanted everything meditatively in a drone. The Coptic version and the Greek use their respective verbs for "meditate" here.[119]

In its account of a certain monk's funeral rites, the Coptic *Life* uses the verb *meleta* for the vigil and *psallei* for the procession to the grave.[120] The *First Greek Life* describes a vigil with readings over the body, then psalming when the body is brought to the grave.[121] But in another place, the Coptic *Life* describes how, when a sister of a female monastery died, the monks *sang* at the door while her body was prepared.[122] Psalm recitation at funeral vigils may have varied over time and from one Pachomian community to another. Moreover, if individual practice ranged from silent recitation to dronelike chant to melodic singing, the leader of the psalm recitation at a funeral vigil may have dictated the performance method on that occasion.

I have already cited the earliest explicit information about the use of psalms in a monk's private devotion—earliest as a matter of both the story's time-setting and the date of the record of it. It is a passage in Athanasius's *Life of Antony*, where Athanasius has Antony tell how demons sometimes vexed him by putting

---

117. *Reg. Hor.* 45 permits reciting in one's heart in the bakery, and *Reg. Hor.* 44 forbids shouting the recitations, urging the monks to recite softly while they make bread.

118. *Pr.* 116 (Boon, 44); see the note in Veilleux, *Pachomian Koinonia*, 2: 190.

119. *Pr.* 116 Coptic ⲉⲩⲛⲁⲙⲉⲗⲉⲧⲁ (CSCO 159: 32.31); Greek μελετήσωσιν (Boon, appendix, 181). The Coptic also lacks a reference to psalms and Scriptures, although these would have been understood as the focus of the meditation.

120. Forms of ⲙⲉⲗⲉⲧⲁⲛ and ⲉⲣⲯⲁⲗⲓⲛ, respectively, in *Pach. vit. Boh.* 207, where the former word is used for psalm recitation over the body (CSCO 89: 209.25) and the latter for the procession to the grave (CSCO 89: 210.1).

121. *Pach. vit.*, Gr.[1] 147.

122. *Pach. vit. Boh.* 27.

on a show of psalming with song.[123] Is the point that they mocked him by doing something that was part of his own regular routine? Or is the idea that they sought to tempt him with melody? Whatever the exact meaning of the anecdote, there is no hint in the *Life* that a monk should not sing.

In the stories about monks in their cells conducting a solitary synaxis or a set of exercises with one or two others, the verbs that the sources use for the monks' delivery of psalms are "psalm"[124] and "cast," sometimes with a variation of verbs in the same anecdote.[125] The use of "cast" is a particularly idiomatic term for saying psalms. When two monks visit Macarius, one suggests, "Shall we cast (*balōmen*) the twelve psalms?"[126] The same verb is used in an anecdote in Palladius about Antony's performance of psalms.[127] The different verbs tell us nothing, however, about the degree of musicality or lack of it in the monks' performances.

In the *Life of Pachomius*, only one anecdote describes a monk singing in his cell, and his song is not a psalm but a biblical canticle. When Theodore seeks to correct a certain proud monk, the demon in the monk incites him to respond by trying to kill Theodore with a stone. Theodore rebukes the demon, and the demon speaks as follows:

> "Do you want to know that I am the one at work in those who sing for pleasure? If you do not believe me, listen to that brother who is singing. He is going to say that verse nine times." There was a brother in a cell, who was singing the beginning of the Song of Moses with these words, "Let us sing to the Lord, for he has been exalted gloriously."[128]

Was the error of this singing brother not simply that he repeated his lyrical rendition *for pleasure* but also that he *sang*? Since the Pachomian brothers sang psalms when welcoming a bishop and conducting funeral rites, singing itself was not proscribed. Nor is there any rule in the Pachomian legislation against singing. The matter of how to render a psalm privately was left to the discretion of the individual, and the anecdote about the singing brother who sang "for pleasure"

123. Athanasius, *Vit. Ant.* 25.1 (the account of these demonic attacks is quoted more fully above).

124. Palladius, *Hist. Laus.* 22.8; Ps.-Macarius, *Apoph.* 33 (PG 34: 256).

125. Both βάλωμεν and ψάλλει are used in practically the same breath in Ps.-Macarius, *Apoph.* 33 (PG 34: 256).

126. Ps.-Macarius, *Apoph.* 33 (PG 34: 256).

127. Palladius, *Hist. Laus.* 22.6.

128. *Pach. vit. Boh.* 64; tr. Veilleux, *Pachomian Koinonia*, vol. 1, 85–86.

is cautionary. As we have seen, however, meditative recitation and not melodic singing appears to be what was normally practiced in a monk's private synaxes.

Three stories outside the Pachomian tradition directly address the question of whether it is proper for a monk to sing.

1. A fifteenth-century miscellany quotes an exhortation in Greek attributed to Antony, in which Antony instructs an audience of monks to keep away from all worldly things. Among his remarks is the following instruction:

   "It is fitting for priests and lay people to sing troparia and modes (*ēchous*) . . . but with monks it is inappropriate and unfitting . . . . I speak of psalmody with song."[129]

2. A story about Abba Pambo, a fourth-century ascetic who lived in the mountains of Nitria, contains the following admonitory anecdote about singing:

   Abba Pambo sent his disciple to Alexandria to sell their handwork. He spent sixteen days in the city, as he told us, and slept in the narthex of the church during the nights, in the Temple of the Holy Apostle Mark. And having seen the service of the holy church, he returned to the old man (Pambo). Now, he had learned troparia. Therefore, the old man says, "I see, child, that you are unsettled. No temptation confronted you in the city, did it?" The brother says, "Naturally, father! We spend our days carelessly in this desert. And we sing neither canons nor troparia. But when I went to Alexandria, I saw the choirs of the church, how they sing. And I fell into much sorrow because we do not sing canons and troparia." And the old man said, "Woe to us, child, should the days arrive in which the monks abandon the hard way expressed through the Holy Spirit and perform a service of songs and modes (*ēchous*). For what kind of compunction is that? What sort of tears are brought forth by troparia? What kind of compunction is there for a monk when he stands in church or in his cell and makes his voice sound like cattle? For when we stand before God, we must stand with much compunction and not with elevation (pride). For the monks have not gone out into the desert in order to stand before God and elevate (themselves) and sing songs and rhythmicize modes (*ēchous*) and shake their hands and move their feet. But we must offer prayers to

129. . . . τὸ δὲ τροπάρια καὶ ἤχους μελίζειν, τοῖς ἱερεῦσιν καὶ κοσμικοῖς πρέπει. . . μοναχοῖς δὲ ἀπρεπὲς καὶ ἀνάρμοστον. . .ψαλμωδίας φημὶ τῆς μετὰ ἄσματος. Vat. Grec. 1579, f. 200^{r-v}. See Gérard Garitte, "Un fragment grec attribué à S. Antoine l'Ermite," *Bulletin de l'Institut historique belge de Rome* 20 (1939): 166–167 (f. 200v).

God with much fear and trembling, with tears and groaning, with piety and repentance and a moderate humble voice."[130]

3. An anecdote about a monk who is struggling with acedia (listlessness) and the difficulty of staying awake during his nightly recitations reports the counsel he received from Abba Silvanus, a desert father who lived in Scetis in the latter half of the fourth century:

   A brother put a question to Abba Silvanus, saying, "What should I do, Abba? How shall I acquire compunction? For I am severely attacked by acedia and sleep. I struggle a great deal. When I rise at night, I do not say a psalm without *ēchou* and I cannot overcome sleep." And the old man answered, "Child, your saying the psalms with a tune is a cardinal instance of pride and haughtiness, meaning 'I sing.' A brother does not sing (*psallei*), for song hardens and petrifies the heart and does not permit the soul to be stung with contrition. Therefore, if you want to enter into compunction, give up song. And when you stand making prayers, let your mind seek out the power of the phrase and consider that you stand in the presence of God, who tests hearts and minds. And when you rise from sleep, your mouth shall glorify God before everything else, and do not begin immediately with the canon (*tou kanonos*). But leaving your cell, recite the Creed and the Our Father in Heaven. Then, going back in, begin the canon gently, gently,[131] groaning and pondering your sins. . . ."

   And [another] brother says, "Abba, since I became a solitary, I have sung the sequence of the canon, and the hours, and the things of the eight-mode system (*oktaēchou*)." And the old man says, "For that reason compunction and grief flee from you. You know the great fathers, how they were unskilled and untrained, except in a few psalms. And they knew neither modes (*ēchous*) nor troparia. And they shone like stars in the world. Abba Paul and Abba Antony and Abba Paul the Simple and Abba Pambo and Abba Apollo and the rest, who raised the dead and received authority against demons, did not (do those things) with songs and troparia and tunes but with prayer and fasting. For the beauty of song is not the salvation of a human being. . . . For song has led many down to the base things of the earth, and it has buried not only lay people but priests in

130. See Othmar Wessely, "Die Musikanschauung des Abtes Pambo," *Anzeiger der philosophisch-historischen Klasse der Österreichischen Akademie der Wissenschaften* 89 (1952): 50–52. The story is preserved in an eleventh-century author, Paul Evergetinos.

131. ἀνετῶς, ἀνετῶς. This adverb often means "loosely" or "easily" but here perhaps "gently."

> fornications and many passions. And song, child, belongs to worldly things. For this reason, too, people gather in the churches. Know, child, how many choirs there are in heaven, and it is not written about them that they sing with the *oktaēchos*. Rather, one choir sings the 'Alleluia' without ceasing; another choir the 'Holy, Holy, Lord Sabaoth'; another choir 'Blessed Is the Glory of the Lord from His Place and House' [Ezek 3:12]. Therefore, you, child, must love the humility of Christ and pay attention to yourself, guarding your mind in the hour of prayer. Wherever you are careless, you do not prove yourself to be a wise person and a teacher. But where you are like the humble, God grants you compunction."[132]

None of these stories reflects a fourth-century or even early fifth-century framing of the question about whether a monk should sing. The musical terms *ēchoi*, *oktaēchos*, and "troparia" first entered the vocabulary of the church several generations or more after the era of the desert fathers whose teachings these stories purport to convey. Whether a given anecdote reworks an earlier version or not, the anachronisms show that in their present forms they reflect a later period, an era when the foundations of Byzantine church song were being laid, probably no earlier than the sixth century.[133]

The late fourth-century Latin *Dialogues of Zacchaeus and Apollonius*, which were probably composed around 394,[134] deals with monastic customs from a Western perspective. The work features a philosopher named Apollonius and a Christian named Zacchaeus, whom we can assume are fictional characters. One section of the *Dialogues* treats the question, "What is the custom of singing and praying and from where did the monks receive these precepts?"[135] The philosopher argues that singing is a distraction, taking a monk's mind off the words, and that "it is more fitting to honor the divine majesty with praises that are

132. In François Nau, ed., *Jean Rufus Évêque de Maïouma, Plérophories: Témoignages et révélations contre le Concile de Chalcédoine, version syriaque et traduction française* (Firmin-Didot, 1911), 180 [580]. The story is adduced by the editor to supplement the stories told about certain solitaries in the *Plerophoria* of John of Maiûma (see p. 10; the story is in ms. Paris Greek 1596). The story is not part of the *Plerophoria*, and Nau does not date it.

133. Regarding the musical terms and forms, see chapter 12.

134. On the date, see M. A. Claussen, "Pagan Rebellion and Christian Apologetics in Fourth-Century Rome: The *Consultationes Zacchaei et Apollonii*," *Journal of Ecclesiastical History* 46 (1995): 607–608; David G. Hunter, *Marriage, Celibacy, and Heresy in Ancient Christianity: The Jovinianist Controversy* (Oxford University Press, 2007), 250–256.

135. *Cons. Zacch. et Apoll.* 3.6 (SC 402: 202). Dyer draws attention to this "often overlooked" discussion of the topic in the Western sources. Dyer, "The Desert, the City and Psalmody," 23.

serious rather than merry (*facetis*)."[136] In his response, Zacchaeus agrees that one should, of course, make requests to God with seriousness,[137] but he defends singing by arguing that it aids a monk in his duty to pray often, even without ceasing. For after adducing the argument that to obtain requests, one must pray often,[138] Zacchaeus immediately explains that when a monk *chants* the psalms, "all is serious, all is dignified, so worthy of (the duty of) sacred worship that the divinity is always praised or prayed to."[139] Moreover, God in effect indulges the weakness of human nature through psalmody, "combining the soft with the sad, the agreeable with the severe," to keep the mind rightly focused.[140] Zacchaeus goes on to insist that God's "benefits are not only to be spoken, but it also delights (us) to sing them." He backs this up with numerous Scriptures in which people praise God with song, beginning with Moses's song in Exodus 15 and concluding with Paul and Silas singing in jail.[141] He concludes as follows:

> From this, you see that psalming and praying are rightly to be frequently celebrated among the duties of the saints. Free from worry, the latter expect, in such an activity, their own universal end, when it arrives; while, in this feeling of delight (*mentium oblectatione*), both the honor of their faith and the ardor of their souls grow. Meanwhile a joyful grace (*laeta gratia*) drives out the troubles of the world and of obvious disquiet, which a sorrowful discipline is not able to achieve.[142]

John Chrysostom, who had experience as a monk and celebrated the tuneful psalmody of the desert monks of Syria, would probably have agreed with this.

Evagrius Ponticus (c. 345–399) in his *Treatise to Eulogius* mentions certain challenges that monks face when reciting psalms, experiences familiar to Evagrius himself as a desert ascetic in Egypt in the environs of Nitria. At one point, he

---

136. *Cons. Zacch. et Apoll.* 3.6.2 (SC 402: 202). Lewis and Short give "merry, witty, jocose, humorous, facetious" as one sense of *facetus* as applied to speech, and this meaning fits here as the opposite of "serious" (*seriis*). Charlton T. Lewis and Charles Short, *A New Latin Dictionary* (Clarendon, 1879), 714 (II.B.2).

137. *Cons. Zacch. et Apoll.* 3.6.3 (SC 402: 202, 204).

138. *Cons. Zacch. et Apoll.* 3.6.3 (last statement) and 3.6.4 (prooftexts) (SC 402: 204).

139. *Cons. Zacch. et Apoll.* 3.6.5 (SC 402: 204).

140. *Cons. Zacch. et Apoll.* 3.6.5 (SC 402: 204).

141. *Cons. Zacch. et Apoll.* 3.6.5–9 (SC 402: 204, 206, 208).

142. *Cons. Zacch. et Apoll.* 3.6.10 (SC 402: 208).

takes up the topic of acedia as a special affliction of solitaries. "In the time of the synaxis," he observes, referring to a monk's private synaxis in his cell, "when a spirit of acedia falls over you, it tells the soul that performing psalms[143] is burdensome." Evagrius advises adaptation to the circumstances:

> Sometimes one must speak a psalm in a whisper in the synaxis, and sometimes to persevere in the psalmody is the proven method. For it is necessary to adapt ourselves in accord with the trickery of the opponent. For sometimes he teaches the tongue to drive when acedia circles the soul. And sometimes, when self-pleasure poses an impediment to the soul, he provokes (the tongue) to sing the words.[144]

Whispered recitation of psalms would have been akin to the sub-vocalization or "muttering" attributed to it by scholars who have examined the characteristic verbs used in the monastic literature for meditating on the psalms (*meletan* and *apostēthizein*).[145] In the present context, Evagrius advocates whispering as a tactic to resist a certain form of demonic attack. When lassitude is the problem, the demon tells the tongue to drive, that is, to hurry through the psalm, as if this hurrying were the right way to prove that one is not listless. Faced with this temptation, it is best for the monk to simply persevere in the regular, measured way. But when a demon senses that a monk is vulnerable to pleasure in psalmody, he provokes the tongue to sing. The best way to resist in that case is to whisper the psalm.

Evagrius clearly associates the temptation of self-pleasure (*autareskia*) with singing, suggesting that psalm-singing is a practice easily exploited by demons who are constantly trying to defeat solitaries with various lures and deceits. In another place, however, Evagrius calls for reciting psalms with "good rhythm,"

143. Evagrius uses the word ψαλμῳδία, which in Christian writings of the late fourth century did not always carry a musical sense but sometimes meant simply "performing psalms," without implying a form of delivery.

144. Evagrius Ponticus, *Eulog.* 9. Πῇ μὲν ῥοίζῳ τὸν ψαλμὸν ἐν τῇ συνάξει λεκτέον, πῇ δὲ ἐνδελεχεῖν τῇ ψαλμωδίᾳ δοκιμαστέον. . . . On the text, see chapter 13, n. 179. On the meaning of ῥοίζῳ as "in a whisper," see chapter 13 with notes 181 through 183.

145. "Half-aloud," according to Stig Simeon R. Frøyshov, "The Cathedral-Monastic Distinction Revisited, Part 1," 204. The ruminations of many monks in their cells must have made a sound like a "muted rumble or hum," according to Dyer ("The Desert, the City and Psalmody in the Late Fourth Century," 17). By contrast, John Wortley concludes that desert monks sang and did so robustly! See John Wortley, "How the Desert Fathers 'Meditated'," *Greek, Roman, and Byzantine Studies* 46 (2006), 317–318, 325–327.

an expression that other Christian writers used for melodic singing.[146] And in still another comment, he says that "melody/singing, when joined to the psalms, alters the condition of the body and drives away the demon that touches it on the back, chills its sinews, and troubles all its members." He then cites the example of David's musical treatment of Saul. Whenever an evil spirit came over Saul, Evagrius reminds his readers, David took the harp and refreshed Saul, and the spirit left him.[147] It appears, then, that Evagrius was no opponent of singing. He took for granted that melodizing was a proper mode of psalm recitation but advised that in certain circumstances of spiritual temptation, it is better not to sing.

Finally, there is Palladius's description of monastic psalmody in the Egyptian desert at Nitria, which must be based on his own experience, when he lived as a monk at Nitria and Cells in the 390s. Standing outside the cells of the monks "around the ninth hour," he says, one can "hear the psalmodies going forth from each cell and imagine that one is high above in Paradise."[148] Does the reference to heavenly psalmody suggest that the monks' psalmody was melodically beautiful? Or was it simply their devotion, exhibited by their constant recitation, that justified the comparison?

To conclude, the early sources for desert asceticism show that many of the desert monks did in fact sing. Singing was the norm at the communal synaxes of the desert monks of Western Syria but probably not the Pachomian monks of Scetis in Egypt. Some Pachomians sang in their cells but probably most chanted in a dronelike way. Monks of Jerome's community probably sang responsively at Sunday services. The imaginary Zacchaeus of the *Dialogues of Apollonius and Zacchaeus* seems to have been familiar with monastic singing. Athanasius describes Antony as singing psalms, and even if Athanasius's picture of Antony's use of psalms is not fully reliable as historical biography, its handful of references to psalm-singing can be treated as reflective of the practices of at least some solitaries of the desert in the early fourth century, when Athanasius was collecting anecdotes for his hagiography.[149]

Monks who recited meditatively instead of singing may have done so simply because they found it to be the most effective way to conduct their discipline.

---

146. Evagrius, *Orat.* 82 (PG 79: 1185). Gregory of Nyssa asserts that musical "rhythm" arises from the pitches and their durations (*Inscr. psalm.* 1.3; GNO 5:34), which implies that he can use the word "rhythm" as a synecdoche for melodic disposition of sound.

147. Evagrius, *Antirrhētikos* 4.22 (citing 1 Sam 16:23); translation from David Brakke, tr., *Evagrius of Pontus, Talking Back: A Monastic Handbook for Combating Demons* (Liturgical Press, 2009), 104. On the sense of the Syriac, see chapter 13.

148. Palladius, *Hist. Laus.* 7.5.

149. See the discussion Athanasius's *Life of Antony* given earlier in this chapter.

Occasionally, however, we hear a concern that the pleasure of melody might be a distraction or worse for a monk. This worry intensified in later centuries. The sweetness of song that certain fourth-century ascetics found worrying seemed even more troublesome to the desert fathers of the seventh and eighth centuries, when the urban churches' musical traditions had developed beyond their simpler forms.

Monastic Use of the Psalms and the Spread of Psalm-Singing in the Wider Church

James McKinnon has argued that monasticism played a decisive role in the spread of psalmody and enthusiasm for it in the fourth century, engendering its incorporation into the daily office, the pre-eucharistic service of the word, the Communion distribution, and the routines of urban monks, both men and women.[150] According to McKinnon, ideals of daily psalmody spread from desert monasticism to urban settings via urban monks and influential church leaders who had spent their early years in monasteries.[151] An important clue is said to be a distinction between monastic hours and cathedral hours in Egeria's account of the daily office in Jerusalem, where the urban church hosted monastic psalmody in which lay people participated.[152]

As we have seen, some communities of desert monks did urge memorization of psalms, and to varying degrees they incorporated psalm recitation into their private and corporate synaxes. It is less clear whether they exhibited a contagious enthusiasm for psalm recitation. One gets the impression that urban monks were more devoted to psalm-singing than desert monks were.[153]

---

150. This thesis was set forth by James McKinnon, "Desert Monasticism and the Later Fourth Century Psalmodic Movement," *Music and Letters* 75 (1994): 505-521. McKinnon repeats his views in "The Book of Psalms: Monasticism and the Western Liturgy," in *The Place of the Psalms in the Intellectual Culture of the Middle Ages*, ed. Nancy van Deusen (State University of New York, 1999), 43–58; and subsequently in a more seasoned form in *The Advent Project: The Later-Seventh-Century Creation of the Roman Mass Proper* (University of California Press, 2000), 32–40.

151. See n. 152.

152. McKinnon, *The Advent Project*, 38–39. The hybrid Jerusalem office is discussed further below.

153. Dyer may have been the first to sound a cautionary note about this aspect of McKinnon's thesis. Dyer argues that it was urban ascetics far more than desert monks who so wholeheartedly embraced psalmody and engendered its wider spread in the late fourth century (Dyer, "The Desert, the City and Psalmody in the Late Fourth Century," 11 and the discussions that follow).

Moreover, the book of Psalms was established as a Christian hymnbook in many places long before sizable numbers of Christians fled to the desert seeking to achieve greater holiness by living in a pleasure-denying, unworldly environment. Psalms and hymns were sung at Christian suppers in second- and third-century Carthage and Alexandria, at community prayer in Tertullian's Carthage, probably at Paschal vigils in the East in the third century,[154] and in private and household devotion in Alexandria and Carthage circa 200.[155] A gradual but steady spread over time best explains why psalmody is so well documented in the literature of the late fourth century, when some traditions of psalmody continued to develop and still others, more recently established, happened to be mentioned in the burgeoning production of Christian literature. The dramatic increase in Christian literature in the fourth century, its production and the amount that has survived, could account for our impression that there was a sudden increase in the spread of psalmody and not a more-or-less steady one.[156]

Whether or not the history of psalmody in the fourth century is better characterized as a "movement" or a continuation of a more-or-less gradual spread of psalms into various occasions of church life, the role of desert monasticism in fourth-century developments of psalmody is a separate question. The practice of psalmody by desert monks is said to have originated from their desire to find a satisfactory way to fulfill the apostolic command to "pray without ceasing" (1 Thess 5:17). But the claim that they sought to fulfill that command through constant repetition of psalms[157] is not supported by the evidence.

In his *Life of Antony*, Athanasius describes how, when Antony abandoned society to embrace the ascesis of a hermit's life, he did so in obedience to the

---

154. The evidence for the third century is found, indirectly, in Eusebius's discussion of the Therapeutae. See chapter 3.

155. See chapters 2 and 3. In chapter 2, I argued that Clement of Alexandria encouraged the singing of psalms and may have reserved the word "psalms" for biblical psalms (see chapter 2 with notes 65 and 66). In calling for personal psalmody at various times of day, he would have included and even preferred biblical psalm-singing. When Tertullian pictures husbands and wives singing "psalms and hymns" together (*Ux*. 2.8.8), he probably envisions that these songs typically include biblical psalms, especially given his reference to Scripture songs in *Apol.* 39.18 (see chapter 2). Christopher Page opines that "there was an *horarium* of domestic psalmody amongst house-ascetics a hundred years or more before anyone thought of going into the desert as a monk." Christopher Page, *The Christian West and Its Singers: The First Thousand Years* (Yale University Press, 2010), 138.

156. McKinnon discounts the possible objection to his thesis about a fourth-century "psalmodic movement," that it may be only an appearance, thanks to literary mentions in fourth-century literature, by contrast with "comparative silence" in earlier sources (*The Advent Project*, 36).

157. This is a basic thesis of McKinnon in "The Book of Psalms, Monasticism, and Western Liturgy," p. 9; repeated in McKinnon, *The Advent Project*, 37.

dominical injunction to "sell all"[158] and initially took up the solitary life outside an Egyptian village. During this formative period, Antony "prayed constantly, having learned that it is necessary to pray unceasingly by oneself."[159] He may have learned the importance of this discipline from the senior monks of the regions, whom he used to visit;[160] or he may have been already familiar with it, since monks were not the first to interpret Paul's encouragement to pray without ceasing as a rule of life. It had already been embraced as a spiritual ideal by earlier generations of Christians—witness the references to it in the writings of influential second- and third-century Christians, including Ignatius of Antioch, Clement of Alexandria, Origen, Tertullian, and Cyprian.[161] 1 Thessalonians 5:17 was the motto of Christians who kept times of prayer throughout the day, including those devoted to keeping prayer in one's heart at all times, a lifestyle of internality that could be practiced in the city as well as anywhere. It was not associated with psalmody. Moreover, Athanasius, who was himself a great advocate of incorporating psalmody into daily life, does not portray Antony as making psalmody the primary vehicle for his ceaseless prayer.

The lifestyle that the senior monks taught Antony consisted of working with one's hands, giving to the poor, praying constantly, absorbing all the Scripture one can, and making progress in virtuous living.[162] Antony eventually established himself in a more remote hut, out in the wilderness, where he continued his education in the ascetic way on his own.

With respect to Antony's recitation of psalms specifically, the *Life* mentions psalming in only three places. One is a set of representations of Antony fighting off demons by praying, psalming, and quoting Scripture against them.[163] A second is a representation of Antony instructing pilgrims about the life of an ascetic. A third is Athanasius's own description of the life of desert monks who

---

158. Athanasius, *Vit. Ant.* 2–3.

159. *Vit. Ant.* 3.5.

160. *Vit. Ant.* 3–4.

161. Ignatius, *Ep. Polycarp* 1.3; Clement of Alexandria, *Str.* 7.7; Origen, *Orat.* 12.2; perhaps Tertullian, *Orat.* 23 ("Concerning times of prayer, nothing has been prescribed except to pray at all times and places"); Cyprian, *Dom. orat.* 36 (adducing the example of Anna's constant prayer at the temple to round off his discussion of all the appropriate times for prayer). The history of prayer, including times of prayer, as a way of fulfilling Paul's dictum, "Pray without ceasing," has been thoroughly investigated by liturgical scholars. See especially Paul F. Bradshaw, *Daily Prayer in the Early Church: A Study of the Origin and Early Development of the Divine Office* (Oxford University Press, 1982), 47–71.

162. Athanasius, *Vit. Ant.* 3–4.

163. *Vit. Ant.* 39–40.

were inspired by Antony to embrace the solitary life. Since the first passage does not purport to describe Antony's routine but reports a few crisis moments when demons attacked him, I will focus on the other two passages:

1. Athanasius's description of the desert monks: "Their cells were in the mountains like tents filled with divine choruses, psalming, studying, fasting, praying, rejoicing in the coming hope and laboring to perform alms, having both love and sympathy for others."[164]
2. Athanasius's representation of Antony's mature teaching to pilgrims who visited him, how he instructed them that a monk ought "to pray constantly, to psalm before and after sleep, and to repeat the precepts found in the Scriptures."[165]

In neither passage is psalming treated as a form of prayer, and Antony's instruction about psalming before bed and after sleep (2) is not what one would expect to hear from someone who believed that one should psalm constantly as the way to pray without ceasing. Antony's instruction about when to psalm sounds like the incorporation of an older, well-established ideal into the monastic discipline. Indeed, if Antony sang psalms before going to sleep, he would only have been doing what the urban Egyptian divine Clement of Alexandria had advised some two generations earlier.[166] Moreover, the morning and evening psalmody taught by Antony may have been a habit he had learned growing up in a pious churchgoing family. Now, Athanasius's summary description of the activities of desert monks (1) lists psalming as one of their regular habits. Yet his biography of Antony does not otherwise represent singing or reciting the psalms as the primary form of Antony's own unceasing prayer or the chief focus of his Scripture meditation. Athanasius's own commitment to the idea that there is a psalm for every life occasion and situation (which is the message of his *Letter to Marcellinus*) gave him a reason to play up the degree of psalmody in Antony's daily routine, including singing them.[167] Yet, he was limited by his sources. It may have been his own interest in the value of psalmody that led him to place it first in his list of the activities of the desert monks. But his

---

164. *Vit. Ant.* 44.2.

165. *Vit. Ant.* 55.3.

166. Clement of Alexandria, *Str.* 7.7.49.4.

167. In *Letter to Marcellinus*, Athanasius states that "the Lord, wanting the melody of the words to be a sign of the spiritual harmony in the soul, prescribed that the canticles be sung melodically and the psalms be read with song." *Ep. Marc.* 28 (PG 27: 40).

biography, which is perhaps best treated as reflective of desert monastic experience generally in the early fourth century, suggests that reading and reciting psalms was only one part of most monks' meditation on Scripture and that individual practice varied.

Pachomius, who founded a monastery at Tabenissi sometime in the years 318 to 323, was born to pagan parents according to his biographer, but converted to the Christian faith not long after Constantine came to power.[168] Wanting to serve humanity in Christ's name he became a healer, but success brought the press of the crowds, which became too much for him. Therefore, he decided to become a monk.[169] The Coptic biography of Pachomius recounts that he sought out an esteemed ascetic named Apa Palamon, who described the monastic life for him, enumerating, among other things, the recitation of Scripture and a cursus of sixty prayers during the day and fifty at night.[170] The biographer's rehearsal of the discipline does not mention psalmody.

The *Life* was composed shortly after Pachomius's death, but the various community rules that have come down under his name and under that of his successor Horsiesios are living literature. Veilleux argues persuasively that while they may contain original rules of Pachomius, those cannot be identified; the various books of regulations reflect the developing Pachomian tradition in the late fourth century.[171] Moreover, it is only in the regulatory books, not in the *Life*, that psalms are mentioned as part of the Scripture texts that each monk should know by heart. The Pachomian monks did not meditate only on the psalms, and how much a monk should focus on psalms varied from one teacher to another, as the differences between the regulations for memorizing "sections" shows (see above).

It is true that a number of influential Eastern divines who extolled the practice of psalmody in church and personal life spent time in monasteries, including Athanasius, John Chrysostom, Basil, and Gregory of Nyssa. But the suggestion that these men and others like them were agents of an urban psalmodic movement inspired by their exposure to monastic psalm-singing is not supported by available evidence. Athanasius was a great advocate of personal psalmody; yet, to reiterate, his biography of Antony mentions psalmody only a handful of times and does not claim that Antony and other desert solitaries prayed without ceasing by psalming. Moreover, Antony's own instruction about the desert discipline, as represented by Athanasius, calls for psalmody when going to sleep and

168. *Pach. vit. Boh.* 3–8.

169. *Pach. vit. Boh.* 9–10.

170. *Pach. vit. Boh.* 10.

171. See Veilleux's discussion of the sources in *Pachomian Koinonia*, vol. 2: 7–13.

upon waking, which sounds like a practice he had learned as a boy, growing up in a pious urban household. Basil of Caesarea and his brother Gregory of Nyssa were also champions of psalmody and spent periods of their careers in monastic retreat, yet their formative exposures to personal psalmody occurred in childhood under the influence of their Christian parents and their remarkable older sister Macrina, about which I will say more below.[172]

It is not known whether John Chrysostom was nurtured in a Christian family, but he would have been exposed to the psalm-singing practiced by the churches of Antioch when he was a young man. We can be confident of this for several reasons. First, Eusebius's remark that morning and evening psalmody became universal in the decades after the Edict of Milan, while it may exaggerate, must have applied to Antioch, since it was scarcely a city that was remote from Eusebius's cosmopolitan orbit.[173] Second, John himself says that it was "the fathers," that is, men of a preceding generation, who selected the morning and evening psalms (Psalms 62 and 140).[174] Furthermore, when the relics of the martyr Babylas were translated from Daphne to Antioch in a great procession in the early 360s, a teenaged John may have participated by marching with the crowd and singing the psalms. He certainly would have witnessed the event, which he later describes in what sounds like a personal recollection.[175] Hence, when John left his lectorship in Antioch to embrace a more rigorous Christian discipline in the mountains (in the early 370s), he was already familiar with established church psalmody in Antioch.

John spent several years in the mountains,[176] and it was probably during this period that he encountered a group of coenobitic monks who practiced what struck him as beautiful communal psalmody. I have already quoted his description of it. Whether John lived with these monks is not known. But their psalmody greatly impressed him, for he draws on his memory of it in order to gently upbraid his congregation for their lack of comparable spiritual rigor, remarking that while the monks of the desert rise in the deep of night to sing psalms for hours, "we are yawning, scratching, snoring, or simply lying flat on our backs calculating a thousand deceitful things."[177] The psalmody of the Syrian

172. In addition to the discussion of Basil to follow, I describe the influences of the brothers' mother Emmelia, as well as their sister Macrina, in chapter 6.

173. See the discussion of Eusebius's comments about morning and evening psalmody in chapter 6 (under "Psalmody at Daily Cathedral Prayer").

174. See chapter 6 with n. 69.

175. See chapter 9. John gives a vivid description of this procession in *Hom. sur Bab.* 10.

176. Palladius, *Dial.* 5.

177. John Chrysostom, *In 1 Tim.* 5, Hom. 14.4 (PG 62: 576; Field, *Interp. in. ep. Paul.* 6: 122).

monks was evidently quite lyrical, but lyrical psalmody was already part of the Antiochene daily office and its liturgical processions when John went out into the mountains. In fact, he was not in any position to shape urban liturgical customs until he became the bishop of Constantinople in 397.

There must have been urban monks in Antioch in the latter part of the fourth century, although no urban monastery is mentioned in the sources. Whether city monks attended the daily office of the city churches is also not disclosed. It is not even clear that churches in Antioch observed more than two daily hours of prayer.[178] In Jerusalem, however, monks and lay people sometimes gathered at church for prayer and song before the bishop arrived to conduct a service. Extensive psalmody was an important part of these gatherings but not of the bishop-led services that Egeria witnessed, with the exception of vespers and the latter part of the Sunday vigil.[179] Apart from these exceptions and the custom of escorting the bishop with psalmody as he moved through the complex from one service to the next, Egeria's mentions of "psalms, hymns, and antiphons" are confined to her descriptions of gatherings composed of monks, ascetic virgins, and lay people: a predawn matins before lauds, a prevespers service, gatherings at other hours (terce, sext, and none), as well as a vigil that extended from Saturday night to Sunday morning and replaced, on that day, the popular psalmodic vigil.[180] Egeria mentions that lay people attended these services, and she notes the presence of presbyters and deacons at the predawn matins.[181] Moreover, it is very possible that lay people and clergy attended the other services that were conducted without the bishop, since Egeria begins her description of sext (there was no terce) by saying that "all similarly go down into the Anastasis" and because she remarks that the ninth hour "was done just as the sixth hour."[182] The services without the bishop may have been led by rotations of cathedral clergy—"in turn each day," as she puts it of clergy leadership at the predawn service. This speculation makes perfect sense. The bishop, encumbered by many responsibilities, could not attend the whole of every service; not even lower clergy were expected to do that.

178. John Chrysostom, in sermons he preached in Antioch or Constantinople, mentions only morning and evening church prayer and otherwise urges private prayer during the remaining hours of the day. See the discussion in chapter 6.

179. See Egeria, *Itin.* 24–25.

180. McKinnon adduces this evidence as a strong indication that monasticism was the chief driver of the psalmodic movement (*The Advent Project*, 38–39).

181. Egeria, *Itin.* 24.

182. Egeria, *Itin.* 24.3.

Does the fact that Egeria describes gatherings for prayer and psalmody that took place without the bishop imply that these were monastic services that the cathedral adopted as part of a late fourth-century episcopal enthusiasm for monastic psalmody? Egeria's precise wording in her first, full description of such a gathering admits more than one interpretation: "Hymns are recited and psalms are responded to, similarly also antiphons; and between each hymn a prayer is made. For two or three presbyters, similarly also deacons, are there in turn each day, with the *monazontes*, to recite the prayers between each hymn or antiphon."[183] Monks did not need clergy to offer prayers between psalms. Were clergy present because monks had begun attending an office originally established by the bishop? Or did the bishop send presbyters and deacons to these gatherings as a way of asserting episcopal authority, after the fact, over services that monks had originally introduced? Alternately, were these services the result of a collaboration between the bishop and the abbot of a local monastery? The statement that clergy "are there in turn each day with the *monazontes*" to conduct prayers seems to imply that the monks had a leadership role. But the references to singing are expressed with passive verbs, which do not reveal whether they were led by the church's ordained lector-cantors, by deacons, or by the ascetics (monks and virgins).

Similarities between monastic and cathedral prayer extended to the very division of the day into hours of prayer, some of which were conducted as liturgies in communal monasticism. Although Cassian mentions only two such hours for Egypt and the same is attested as Pachomian practice in the literature of their community, John Chrysostom mentions the little hours as part of the cursus of the monks of Syria,[184] and little hours were also part of the monastic regimen in Cappadocia, according to Basil's *Longer Rules*.[185] Taft suggests that it was monks living in or near cities who introduced the little hours to cathedral worship, filling out the daily horarium "by creating common synaxes or formal liturgical hours—the 'little' or 'day' hours of terce, sext, none—at the traditional fixed time of *private* prayer."[186] An influence of urban monasticism in the establishment of these hours is certainly possible. But if monks were the organizers, what influences led *them* to conceive schemes of daily horaria with psalmody?

---

183. Egeria, *Itin.* 24.1; tr. McGowan and Bradshaw, *The Pilgrimage of Egeria*, 150 (with a slight alteration).

184. John Chrysostom, *In 1 Tim.* 5, Hom. 14.4 (PG 62: 576; Field, *Interp. in. ep. Paul.* 6: 123).

185. Basil, *Reg. fus. tract.* 37.3–4 (PG 31: 1013–1016). Basil is vague about which of these hours were to be observed liturgically and which only personally.

186. Taft, *The Liturgy of the Hours in East and West*, 90.

To review the pertinent information about this subject as laid out in chapters two and three, the earliest references to private Christian song, almost certainly including psalmody, date to around 200 in the form of Clement of Alexandria's encouragement that the enlightened Christian sings hymns at specific times and also throughout the day and in Tertullian's advice that married Christian couples should sing together. Significantly, Tertullian also identified two scripturally mandated hours of daily prayer (upon waking and before going to bed), and he urged the keeping of three additional hours (the third, the sixth, and the ninth hours).[187] The earliest reference to daily psalmody at church is Eusebius's remark that shortly after the Peace of Constantine, morning and evening psalmody had become universal in churches throughout the empire. That custom must have evolved from the daily psalmody of pious individuals and households. And the development of such personal and household forms of piety through the course of the third century and into the fourth would explain why Gregory's and Basil's older sister Macrina, even as a child (in the 340s[188]), practiced psalmody throughout the day. Moreover, third-century customs of private daily psalmody best explain why a solitary such as Antony (b. circa 250) taught the pilgrims who visited him to recite psalms in the morning and before going to sleep. Hence, while the example of certain monastic communities' psalmody (such as that of the monks of the Syrian desert) may have influenced the development of the cathedral office, the ideal of daily psalmody exemplified by household traditions of Christian piety is likely to have been the prevenient influence on urban clergy, urban ascetics, and desert monks alike.[189]

I will conclude with some observations about Basil and his family. Before assuming the duties of a bishop in Caesarea, Basil composed his influential *Shorter* and *Longer Rules*, a monastic guide, after experimenting with the ascetic life during retreats at Annisa. He had grown up in a pious family, where he was nurtured in the faith by his parents and his grandmother. He mentions his mother and grandmother in a letter against the charismatic wandering ascetic Eustathius, referring to "the teaching about God that I received as a boy from my blessed mother and my grandmother Macrina [the Elder]."[190] There was another family influence, according to Basil's brother Gregory, namely their older sister, Macrina the Younger, who, after their father's death, convinced their mother to

187. Tertullian, *Orat.* 25.

188. For the dating, see Silvas, *Macrina the Younger*, 28.

189. Stig Frøyshov argues that desert monks most likely borrowed and adapted pre-existing cathedral-office patterns, including cathedral psalmody (Frøyshov, "The Cathedral-Monastic Distinction Revisited, Part 1").

190. Basil, *Ep.* 223.3.

embrace an ascetic lifestyle, along with the female servants of her household. In time, she persuaded her brothers to embrace the ascetic life as well. In the case of Basil, this may have occurred when he returned to Annisa upon hearing news of his brother Naucratius's death.[191] Basil was in an arrogant frame of mind, Gregory writes, thanks to his recent success in the schools of rhetoric at Athens, but Macrina "took him in hand and drew him with such speed towards the goal of philosophy that he withdrew from the worldly show . . . and went over of his own accord to the life where one toils even with one's own hands, thus providing for himself through perfect renunciation a life that would lead without impediment to virtue."[192] One must take this anecdote with a grain of salt, given Gregory's hagiographic aims in his *Life of Macrina*. That said, there is no reason to doubt that Macrina was an influential example of piety for Basil, as she was for Gregory, and that the monastery she had already established furnished him with an example of the ascetic life in which psalmody was central.

And who taught Macrina to sing psalms daily as a child, if not her mother?

---

191. See the reconstruction of the historical events in Silvas, *The Great Asketikon of St. Basil the Great*, 67–71.

192. Gregory of Nyssa, *Vit. Macr.* 6 = 8.3 in Anna M. Silvas, *Macrina the Younger: Philosopher of God* (Brepols, 2008), 117. I have used Silvas.

CHAPTER NINE

Singing in the Streets

IN THE DECADES following the Edict of Milan, the Christian church grew dramatically, and the public presence of Christians was increasingly apparent in various social settings. These included street parades such as funeral processions, episcopal advents, and martyr translations. Psalmody was a distinguishing mark of all of these, and it was also a prominent feature of certain public processions of the stational liturgy of Jerusalem, as well as occasional instances of public Christian song that fit no new custom, one-offs, as far as we know.

Episcopal Processions with Psalmody

In an oration delivered in 380 or so, on the feast day of Athanasius, Gregory of Nazianzus describes Athanasius's second return from exile in 346. Athanasius entered Alexandria riding on a colt, like Jesus entering Jerusalem. Heralds in the lead announced his coming and a chorus followed.[1] He was greeted by crowds who threw out branches, flowers, garments, and other precious things. The people shouted praises and applauded as he passed.[2] Several of these details associate the bishop's procession with an imperial adventus.[3] For centuries, rulers had been entering cities in ceremonial fashion, specifically in a procession-reception called an *apantēsis* (also *hypantēsis*) in Greek and an *adventus* in Latin, the Roman triumph being one type of the latter. In describing Athanasius's arrival

1. Gregory of Nazianzus, *In laud. Athan.* (*Or.* 21) 29 (PG 35: 1116–1117). In this context, οἱ προχορεύοντες (who follow the οἱ προβοῶντες) would have been a chorus of singers, not dancers performing in step, although there may have been individualized dancing. Regarding the historical context of Athanasius's second return from exile, see Timothy D. Barnes, *Athanasius and Constantius: Theology and Politics in the Constantinian Empire* (Harvard University Press, 1993), 87–92.

2. Gregory of Nazianzus, *In laud. Athan.* (*Or.* 21) 29 (PG 35: 1117).

3. Ammianus Marcellinus remarks that when Julian entered Sirmium in 361, a crowd, including soldiers, met him in the suburbs with flowers and lights (*Res gest.* 21.10.1). Shortly before Stilicho entered Rome in 399 to receive his consulship, his adventus was pictured by the poet Claudian, who foresaw "all the road bestrewn with flowers" (Claudian, *Cons. Stilichonis* 2.400–401). The procession and reception of Athanasius in the style of an adventus is noted in Sabine MacCormack, "Change and Continuity in Late Antiquity: The Ceremony of 'Adventus'," *Historia* 21 (1972): 747.

in Alexandria, Gregory alludes to the style of an imperial advent by suggesting that "not even [Emperor] Constantius himself" would have experienced such a welcome.[4]

Gregory's references to Constantius show that he meant the return of Athanasius from exile in the year 346. Yet in this section of his panegyric, Gregory "seems to conflate the return of 346 with those of 337 and 362."[5] It is possible, therefore, that Athanasius first adopted the mode of episcopal adventus as early as 337 or as late as 362.

Similar descriptions of processional travel by Athanasius are found in two editions of the *Life of Pachomius*. According to the *Bohairic-Coptic Life*, after Athanasius's fourth departure into exile, a group of Pachomian monks went to meet him in the northern part of the district of Šmoun in Upper Egypt and found him on his way to the city of Šmoun. He was riding on a donkey, accompanied by lay people, bishops, clerics carrying lamps and candles, as well as monks from many places, who were in front of the parade chanting psalms and odes.[6] The Pachomians entered the procession and joined the psalmody. This was in 363. A parallel account in the *First Greek Life of Pachomius* also mentions a large entourage and the detail about the Pachomian brothers singing psalms.[7] Since the *First Greek Life* is independent of the *Bohairic Life*,[8] the two accounts corroborate each other.

Whether the style of procession that Gregory and the Pachomian lives attribute to Athanasius was adopted by him as early as the 330s or only later, the advent style of entry into a city was embraced by another bishop as early as 339. That year, according to Athanasius himself, when "a certain Gregory from Cappadocia" was chosen to replace him (precipitating Athanasius's second exile), the new bishop made "a magnificent and illustrious entry into the city."[9] This can only refer to a cavalcade with all the typical regal trappings, and it shows that the adventus mode of entering a city had been adopted by at least one Greek

4. Gregory of Nazianzus, *In laud. Athan.* (*Or.* 21) 28 (PG 35: 1116).

5. Barnes, *Athanasius and Constantius*, 266 n. 27.

6. *Pach. vit. Boh.* 201. I follow the dating given by Veilleux for the parallel account in the *First Greek Life*. See Armand Veilleux, *Pachomian Koinonia*, vol. 1: *The Life of Saint Pachomius and His Disciples* (Cistercian, 1980), 400.

7. *Pach. vit. Gr.*[1] 143.

8. *The Bohairic Coptic Life of Pachomius* and the *First Greek Life* were composed independently of one another, each drawing directly or indirectly on a third and original vita composed not long after Pachomius's death in the year 346. See Veilleux, *Pachomian Koinonia*, vol. 1, 1–3. The Sahidic fragments of the *Life* do not happen to cover this episode.

9. Athanasius, *Ep. enc.* 2.2 and 4.1 (ἡ θαυμαστὴ καὶ λαμπρὰ εἴσοδος Γρηγορίου τοῦ Ἀρειανοῦ).

Christian bishop, with corresponding participation by throngs of welcoming Christians, at least as early as the late 330s.

The Pachomian accounts are very explicit that Athanasius's advent-style processions in Upper Egypt entailed psalmody, and the same feature is clearly implied by Gregory of Nazianzus when he refers to the presence of a "chorus" in the procession that brought Athanasius back to Alexandria in 346.

There are no additional mentions of episcopal advent processions in fourth- and fifth-century sources, at least as far as I have been able to discover. This silence does not necessarily imply that they were uncommon. The Christians of a city would not have received a bishop without ceremony, people of the era being habituated to receive dignitaries in certain customary ways. But biographies of bishops are rare, and the vast majority of funeral panegyrics for bishops, which typically featured biographical elements, have not survived. The only additional description I have found of a bishop's reception by a city appears in Mark the Deacon's *Life of Porphyry*, which reports that when Bishop Porphyry and his entourage disembarked from their ship, upon his return to Gaza in 402, the Christians who lived near the port greeted him with psalmody and were joined by the Christians of the city.[10] Although Mark does not mention a procession from the port to the city, he gives no hint that there was anything unusual about a popular reception with psalmody.

Translations of Martyr Relics with Psalmody

Martyr relics were "translated," that is, moved from one locale to another. These translations took the form of processions with psalmody. Funeral psalmody may have provided a model. A martyr translation was a conveyance of remains to a new place of interment, a kind of second funeral. Moreover, Christian bishops regarded funeral psalmody as an honorific act. John Chrysostom says so explicitly. The purpose of funeral psalmody is "to honor the departed,"[11] he reminds his congregation. And the monks of the Syrian desert, he says in another sermon, conduct their dead to the grave "with hymns" and call this "a *procession*, not a carrying out."[12] In other words, they treat the conveyance of the body to the grave as a ceremonial act, to be dignified by psalmody. Sozomen says the same when he describes the funeral procession for Bishop Meletius, who was "honored by turns with psalmody" as his cortege moved from city to city.[13] The same implication

10. Mark the Deacon, *Vit. Porph.* 58.

11. John Chrysostom, *In Heb.*, Hom. 4.5 (PG 63: 44).

12. *In 1 Tim.* 5, Hom. 14.5 (PG 62: 577; Field, *Interp. in. ep. Paul.* 6: 124).

13. Sozomen, *H.E.* 7.10.5.

is probably implied by a funerary inscription that declares, "We say psalms to you, Aurelia Yguia."[14]

Honorific psalmody for the deceased did not exclude the more primary purpose of psalmody as hymnody addressed to God. Augustine combines both ideas when he recounts the funeral of one of his secretaries. "We commenced the funeral with appropriate honorific acts as were fitting for so great a soul," he writes. "We praised God with hymns for three days over his grave."[15]

If Christians of ordinary status were worthy of funeral psalms, martyrs were all the more deserving when their relics were conveyed to a second grave. If psalmody was deemed a proper part of a Christian funeral procession by those who conducted the earliest martyr processions, it would have been only natural for them to have incorporated psalm-singing into the event.[16] And just as Christians saw no conflict between honoring both a deceased person and God with psalmody, they saw no conflict between honoring a martyr and praising God with psalmody. Hence Basil did not need to explain his meaning when, having arrived late to preach at a service following a vigil for the martyrs, he commended the people who had sung psalms all night and were still engaged in psalmody when he finally showed up. "Having come to this sacred enclosure of the martyrs many hours ago," he observed, "and having propitiated the God of the martyrs with hymns, you have endured until this midday hour. For you, therefore, who *esteemed honor to the martyrs*[17] and *worship of God* above sleep and rest, a reward is prepared."[18]

A martyr translation was also a public event in which Christians participated by going out to greet the martyr and join the parade. In this respect, a martyr translation resembled an adventus. This similarity is implied by Jerome in his defense of martyr feasts. "Are all the bishops to be judged as not only sacrilegious but foolish," he asks, "because they carried that most worthless thing, dust and ashes, in silk in a golden vessel? Are the people of all the churches fools, because they went to meet the sacred relics, and welcomed them . . . so that there was one united swarm of people [moving] from Palestine to Chalcedon?"[19] The language of "going out to meet" the relics and "welcoming" them suggests

14. *Salmos tibique dicamus Aurelia Yguia*. CIL XI 4629.

15. Augustine, *Ep.* 158.2 (CSEL 44: 489–490).

16. Psalmody at funerals and psalmody in martyr processions (and episcopal processions) show up in the record around more or less the same time—the middle of the fourth century. See chapters 7 and 9.

17. τὴν εἰς τοὺς μάρτυρας τιμὴν.

18. Basil of Caesarea, *Hom. in Ps. 114* 1 (PG 29: 484).

19. Jerome, *Contra Vigilantium* 1.5 (PL 23: 343). I supply "moving" on the assumption that the statement is elliptical.

an advent-like reception, and Jerome's additional remark that the people "were sounding praises in Christ with one voice" probably refers to psalmody.[20]

It was the psalm-singing of martyr parades, as much as anything else, that broadcast their Christian identity.[21] For whatever one might have been able to see of the procession, one could always hear the singing, especially the loud refrains. These refrains were probably sung after each verse or two.[22] Processions were intended to make an impression on spectators. The most effective way for a martyr procession to do that was through the refrains of its psalmody, which would have been much louder than the verses sung by the psalm-leader(s). Hence, there was a rationale for frequent repetition of the refrains. Moreover, frequent repetition would have enhanced the paraders' sense of their own importance as participants.

The Removal of the Bones of Babylas from Daphne to Antioch

The earliest known instances of martyr translations occurred in the 320s through the 360s,[23] and one of the best-documented instances is the transfer of the bones of Babylas in the early 360s during the reign of Emperor Flavius Claudius Julianus. The story begins a hundred years earlier, when an Antiochene bishop named Babylas was executed, around 250, during the Decian persecution.[24] Babylas was buried in a cemetery at Antioch, probably the city cemetery outside the walls.[25] His bones were subsequently transferred to a port suburb of

20. It is possible that *in Christi* means "to Christ," but Christian writers of the era typically spoke of praises and thanksgiving "to God."

21. Sabine MacCormack interprets the translation of Christian relics, including the translation of the bones of Babylas back to Antioch, as a type of Christian adventus, although she does not focus on the role of psalmody in translations or observe that psalmody was an element shared by the martyr translation, the funeral procession, and the episcopal adventus. (MacCormack, "Change and Continuity in Late Antiquity," 748).

22. On formats of psalmody in this era, see chapter 10.

23. Ambrose speaks of the translation of the martyrs Felix, Nabor, and Victor to Milan (Hymn. 10[*Victor, Nabor, Felix pii*].29–32), which is thought to have been accomplished under Bishop Maternus (316–328). The supposed relics of Luke and Andrew were brought to Constantinople in either 336 or 357 or perhaps in both years as a transfer and re-transfer. See Richard W. Burgess, "The Passio S. Artemii, Philostorgius, and the Dates of the Invention and Translations of the Relics of Sts. Andrew and Luke," *Analecta Bollandiana* 121 (2003): 5–36. The relics of Babylas were translated in the 350s and 360s (see below).

24. Margaret A. Schatkin, Cécile Blanc, Bernard Grillet, and Jean-Noël Guinot, ed. and tr., *Jean Chrysostom, Discours sur Babylas; Homélie sur Babylas* (Cerf, 1990), 15–18.

25. Schatkin et al., *Jean Chrysostom; Discours sur Babylas*, 18. Regarding Antioch's city cemetery (κοιμητήριον), see Wendy Mayer and Pauline Allen, *The Churches of Syrian Antioch (300–638 CE)* (Peeters, 2012), 85–89.

Antioch called Daphne, nearly a hundred years later, in around 353, when Gallus Caesar ruled the eastern provinces. It was then that the remains of Babylas and three children who had died with him were reinterred in a mausoleum near the temple of Apollo at Daphne.[26] According to John Chrysostom, it was Gallus who ordered the transfer, wishing to transform Daphne from being a pleasure resort and home for demons into a place for respectable people.[27] But Gallus may have done so at the urging of the city's Christians (see below) and of Leontius, the bishop of Antioch, who would have had his own reasons for seeing to it that Babylas was given a proper shrine.[28]

The transfer of Babylas to Daphne is not described, but it must have entailed a procession, since relics would not have been transported unceremoniously like baggage. In this period, when the style of translations was first established, decisions had to be made about how such a procession should be conducted. I have already suggested that the Christian funeral procession and its psalmody may have provided the church with an obvious model. It is unclear, however, who made the decisions about the style of transfer when this custom was first developing, since martyr veneration was a movement of popular piety, supported in some cases by aristocratic families who set up shrines on their estates.[29] Rufinus's account of the translation of the relics of Babylas speaks of what the *people* did, how "the whole church came together, mothers and husbands, virgins and youth" and conducted the relics, with psalmody, to their new place of interment.[30] Of course, it may have been clergy who took charge, organizing the march and selecting the psalm(s).

The account just mentioned belongs to the historical record of the retranslation of the relics of Babylas back to Antioch a decade after the first translation. The second translation occurred after Gallus's half-brother Julian came to power. Known to history as "the Apostate," Julian devoted his short reign to reviving Roman religion and curbing the practice of Christian faith. During a visit to Antioch that lasted from about July of 362 to March of 363,[31] he ordered that the

26. John Chrysostom, *Disc. sur Bab.* 67 (SC 362: 178); Sozomen, *H.E.* 5.19.12–13. The children are mentioned by John Chrysostom, *Pan. Juv.* 1 (PG 50: 571); Theodoret, *H.E.* 3.10.2; and other sources.

27. John Chrysostom, *Disc. sur Bab.* 67–69 (SC 362: 178–184).

28. See Susanna Elm, *Sons of Hellenism, Fathers of the Church: Emperor Julian, Gregory of Nazianzus, and the Vision of Rome* (University of California Press, 2012), 280.

29. See Kim Bowes, *Private Worship, Public Values, and Religious Change in Late Antiquity* (Cambridge University Press, 2008), 142–143, 151–152, 154–155.

30. See the full quotation below (from Rufinus).

31. Julian arrived in Antioch in July of 362, according to Ammianus Marcellinus, *Res gest.* 22.9.14; see Joseph Bidez, *La vie de l'empereur Julian* (Belles Lettres, 1965), 277 with n. 1. Julian

remains of Babylas be removed from the mausoleum at Daphne. As Christians told the story, when the emperor sought to consult the oracle at Daphne about the prospects for his upcoming military campaign against the Persians, he was told that the oracle refused to speak. Inferring that the nearby relics of Babylas were to blame, he issued an order for their removal.[32]

The transfer of the relics to the city cemetery at Antioch was a journey of about four-and-a-half miles.[33] John Chrysostom, who was an Antiochene teenager at the time, later recalled that throngs of people joined the parade.[34] An account by the church historian Rufinus, part of which I have already quoted, says that the crowds processed singing biblical psalms against idolatry:

> The whole church came together, mothers and husbands, virgins and youths, and with immense rejoicing pulled along the martyr's coffin in a long procession, singing psalms with loud cries and exultation and saying, "Let them be confounded who worship graven things and who trust in their images."[35]

The psalm verse quoted here is Psalm 96:7, probably one of the refrains, which is how Sozomen interprets it, writing that "the accomplished among them began the psalms, and the crowd came together in harmony and sang this verse in response, 'They have all been put to shame who worship what is graven and who trust in idols.'"[36]

According to John Chrysostom, when Babylas's cortege reached the sacred precinct at Antioch—perhaps the grave-site at the city cemetery where Babylas's remains had reposed before being removed to Daphne—an act of divine justice took place back in Daphne: a lightning bolt set fire to the temple of Apollo,

---

departed the city in March of 263, according to Ammianus Marcellinus, *Res gest.* 23.2.3–6; see Bidez, *La vie de l'empereur Julian*, 316.

32. John Chrysostom (b. 347), who had been a teenager in Antioch at the time of the order, was the first to float this interpretation. *Disc. sur Bab.* 80–81 (SC 362: 200–202); *Hom. sur Bab.* 5 (SC 362: 302, 304). He was followed by Socrates, *H.E.* 3.18.1–2; Sozomen, *H.E.* 5.19.12–17; and Theodoret of Cyr, *H.E.* 3.10.1–2.

33. Strabo, *Geog.* 16.2.6 ("40 stadia").

34. John Chrysostom, *Hom. sur Bab.* 10.

35. Rufinus, *H.E.* 10.36; tr. Philip. R. Amidon, *The Church History of Rufinus of Aquileia, Books I and II* (Oxford University Press, 1997), 40 (slightly altered).

36. Sozomen, *H.E.* 5.19.19. Sozomen calls the psalm-leaders ἀκριβοῦντες, which lexicons define as "exacting;" but the adjective must mean something like "expert" or "accomplished" here.

incinerating the god's image.[37] There was indeed a fire at the temple. According to the contemporary Roman historian Ammianus Marcellinus, it was caused by some ordinary accident.[38] But Julian cast suspicion on the Christians and closed the Great Church of Antioch.[39] Rufinus, who does not mention this church closing, says that in retaliation for the public translation and accusatory psalms, Julian ordered the arrest and torture of a number of the Christian participants.[40]

Both Socrates and Sozomen relied on Rufinus,[41] who composed his account in Latin in 402 or 403. It is possible that Sozomen also had additional information, derived from his contacts in Antioch. In any case, when Rufinus penned his account, a significant number of those who had witnessed the translation or had participated in it were still alive (including John Chrysostom). Rufinus could have obtained an account through one of them. If he relied instead on an existing written account, that account would have been composed even nearer in time to the event. Hence, there is no reason to doubt that the Christians of Antioch sang "protest" psalms against the emperor when they conducted the relics of Babylas to his new resting place.

It appears that interChristian politics may also have been entangled in the history of the remains of Babylas. In the early 360s, Antioch's churches were divided into Nicene and Arian, more exactly "Homoean,"[42] communions. If Leontius, bishop of Antioch and a proponent of a Homoean Christology, was the public organizer of the translation of the relics to Daphne,[43] that would have

37. John Chrysostom, *Disc. sur Bab.* 93–94 (SC 362: 218–220); *Hom. sur Bab.* 8 (SC 362: 308).

38. The account given by Ammianus Marcellinus suggests an ordinary accident (*Res gest.* 22.13.3).

39. Ammianus Marcellinus, *Res gest.* 22.13.2. Theodoret also mentions this church closing (*H.E.* 3.12.1).

40. Rufinus, *H.E.* 10.37.

41. Sozomen may have read Rufinus in a Greek translation. A clue is the departure of Sozomen's quotation from the Septuagint at one point, which seems to reflect an influence of a word in Rufinus's quotation that differs from Jerome's Latin translation of the psalms. Instead of the Septuagint's ἐγκαυχώμενοι, Sozomen has πεποιθότες, which carries the same sense as Rufinus's *confidunt* (*H.E.* 10.36), where Jerome has *gloriantur.*

42. Homoeans regarded Christ as "like" the Father but not ontologically the same, a view that fell short of Nicene christology and bore a certain resemblance to the Arian christologies of a previous era. Church historians now distinguish types of Arianism, differentiating the philosophically sophisticated Neo-Arianism of the latter fourth century from the earlier, late third-century/early fourth-century Arianism and both of these (and other types) from a mid-fourth-century Homoean type.

43. See above with n. 28.

given Babylas and his Daphnae shrine a Homoean association. Hence, it may be significant that the church that Julian closed after the second translation was the Great Church, held by the Homoeans.[44] Perhaps the city's Homoean faction also carried out the procession with its offensive psalmody[45] or at least played a prominent role in an event in which other local Christians joined as well. The sources speak of participation by everyone, not just the Arian Christians. "The whole city poured out into the road," Chrysostom recalls.[46] Rufinus speaks of "the whole church."[47] The later church historians speak in similarly broad terms, although they may only be repeating Rufinus.[48] In any case, it appears that both Homoean and Nicene Christians celebrated Babylas, and both probably wished to claim him as their own.

That is clearly implied by a third translation of Babylas, which occurred not long after his reburial at Antioch. The Nicene Christians of Antioch had become divided into two communions after Bishop Meletius returned from exile in late 362 (or early 363) and gathered the majority of Nicene Christians to himself. Meanwhile, a bishop of Carala named Lucifer, also recently returned from exile, arrived in Antioch and ordained a certain Paulinus as the Nicene bishop of Antioch.[49] Moreover, the Homoeans had their own recently appointed bishop, one Euzoeus. After Julian died in 363 and was succeeded by the Homoean emperor Valens, the Homoeans held most of the city's churches; the Nicene Christians attached to Paulinus possessed a single small church; and Meletius and his followers were meeting across the river Orontes, where the Nicene faithful had been gathering at different places, including the military drill field (*campus martius*).[50] It seems that Meletius, who had been exiled again, from about 371 to 378, returned not long after Valens came into power. Following the synod of September 379, where Meletius was recognized as the rightful bishop of

---

44. Theodoret of Cyr, *H.E.* 3.12.1.

45. Hanss Brennecke contends that the Arian faction was in control of the cult of Babylas at Daphne and that the procession from Daphne to Antioch was directed by the Arian bishop Euzoeus. Hanns Christof Brennecke, *Studien zur Geschichte der Homöer: Der Osten bis zum Ende der homöischen Reichskirche* (Mohr [Siebeck], 1988), 137–138. Mayer and Allen agree (*The Churches of Syrian Antioch*, 139).

46. John Chrysostom, *Hom. sur Bab.* 10 (SC 362: 310).

47. Rufinus, *H.E.* 10.36.

48. Sozomen, *H.E.* 5.19.17–18; Theodoret, *H.E.* 3.10.3. Participation by nonArian Christians in the procession is not excluded by Brennecke or by Mayer and Allen (see n. 45).

49. Rufinus, *H.E.* 10.28; Socrates, *H.E.* 3.5.

50. Socrates, *H.E.* 3.9; Rufinus, *H.E.* 10.31; Theodoret, *H.R.* 2.15; Mayer and Allen, *The Churches of Syrian Antioch*, 138–140.

Antioch (which did not resolve the division in the Nicene community), Meletius ordered a new church to be built across the Orontes to house the relics of Babylas, which were transferred there around 381.[51] Despite the split among the Nicene Christians, the public procession of the relics to the new shrine symbolized a Nicene appropriation of the saint.[52] The sources do not happen to mention psalmody as part of this third translation, no doubt because it did not need to be mentioned.

There is a revealing footnote to the story. Meletius died in Constantinople in May of 381 during the ecumenical council called by Theodosius I.[53] According to memories collected by Sozomen, the deceased bishop "was received, by order of the emperor, through every thoroughfare into the cities, within the walls, which is against the customs of the Romans; and, being honored by turns with psalmody in those places, he was brought to Antioch" and interred "next to the grave of the martyr Babylas."[54] The conveyance of Meletius's remains from city to city and the language of "reception" suggest that Meletius's funeral parade was conducted as a kind of episcopal adventus. This multicity cortege, carried out by order of the emperor, was another public symbol of the triumph of Nicene Christianity.

A Procession of Martyr Relics at Constantinople (circa 400)

A song-filled procession of relics is also recorded for Constantinople when John Chrysostom was patriarch there.

Constantinople was dedicated in 330 by Constantine himself as the political heart of the empire, and the Church of the Holy Apostles he built there was meant to serve as a central focus of the new imperial cult. Constantine planned

51. John Chrysostom, *Hom. sur Bab.* 10 (SC 362: 310, 312) (mentioning the new shrine and Meletius being buried next to the relics); Sozomen, *H.E.* 7.10.5 (Meletius buried next to the grave of Babylas). See also Glanville Downey, "The Shrines of St. Babylas at Antioch and Daphne," in *Antioch-on-the-Orontes*, vol. 2: *The Excavations, 1933–1936*, ed. Richard Stillwell (Princeton University Press, 1938), 47–48; Schatkin et al., *Jean Chrysostom, Discourse sur Babylas; Homélie sur Babylas* (Cerf, 1990), 21–22.

52. John Chrysostom celebrates the role of Meletius in giving Babylas a new shrine ("across the river") and his boldness in opposing the emperor (meaning Valens); he also mentions Meletius's eventual interment at the new shrine (see n. 51). See further Mayer and Allen, *The Churches of Syrian Antioch*, 138–140. "Remarketing" is their term. Regarding the political struggle between the Nicene and Arian Christians at Antioch, Mayer and Allen cite, as the "definitive" study, Ferdinand Cavallera, *Le schisme d'Antioche (IVe – Ve siècle)* (Picard, 1905).

53. Socrates, *H.E.* 5.9.3–4; Sozomen, *H.E.* 7.10.5.

54. Sozomen, *H.E.* 7.10.5; cf. Chrysostom, *Hom. sur Bab.* 10.

to have his own remains interred in the apse of the church, surrounded by tombs holding the relics of the twelve apostles.[55]

The building's splendid architecture and especially the relics it housed lent honor not only to the emperor but to the city itself, as Paulinus of Nola notes in the following verses:

> When Constantine was founding the city named after himself and was the first of the Roman kings to proclaim himself a Christian, the godsent idea came to him that since he was then embarking on that splendid enterprise of building a city which would rival Rome, he should likewise emulate Romulus's city with a further endowment—he would eagerly defend his walls with the bodies of apostles. He then removed Andrew from the Greeks and Timothy from Asia; and so Constantinople now stands with twin towers, vying to match the hegemony of great Rome, and more genuinely rivaling the walls of Rome through the eminence that God bestowed on her, for he counterbalanced Peter and Paul with a protection as great, since Constantinople gained the disciple of Paul and the brother of Peter.[56]

The putative remains of the apostolic-age saints Luke and Andrew were translated to Constantinople in either 336 or the 350s.[57] According to the medieval chronicler Georgius Cedrenus, the remains of the Palestinian martyrs Pamphilus and Theodulus, along with their companions, were translated to Constantinople and its "great church" (Hagia Sophia) in 360.[58] During the reign of Valens, the supposed head of John the Baptist, then reposing in Cilicia, was first translated to a village called Cosilaos near Chalcedon[59] and then, in 391 under Theodosius I, carried to Constantinople, where it was deposited in a church specially constructed for it at the Hebdomon, a suburb of the imperial city.[60] According to Sozomen, the intention had been to transfer the Baptist's

---

55. Pierre Maraval, *Lieux saints et pèlerinages d'Orient: Histoire et géographie des à la conqête arabe* (Cerf, 1985), 92–93.

56. Paulinus of Nola, *Carm.* 19(*Natal.* 11).329–342 (CSEL 30: 129–130). Translation from *The Poems of St. Paulinus of Nola*, tr. P. G. Walsh (Newman, 1975), 142–143.

57. See n. 23.

58. Georgius Cedrenus, *Comp. hist.* (Bekker 1: 523).

59. Sozomen, *H.E.* 7.21.1–3.

60. Sozomen, *H.E.* 7.21.4–5; *Chron. Pasch.* (Dindorf, 564); PG 92: 773–774.

head directly to Constantinople. But when the cortege reached the district of Pantichium, the mules pulling the chariot refused to go any farther. This was interpreted as a sign, and the head was deposited at nearby Cosilaos.

The mention of a chariot is significant. Literary and visual depictions of imperial advents indicate three modes of transport. On medallions, both Constantine and Constantius are shown on horseback, moving at a walk.[61] On the arch of Constantine in Rome, the emperor is ensconced in an ornate four-wheel cart, pulled by horses.[62] When Ammianus Marcellinus describes this event, he also mentions this "cart (*carpento*) shining with the brightness of various jewels."[63] A third form of conveyance appears in a scene on the arch of Galerius at Thessalonica, which shows the emperor seated on a throne in a chariot.[64] The poet Claudian's description of Emperor Honorius's entry into Rome in 404 also refers to him traveling in a chariot.[65] Hence, the Christians who decided to use a chariot to translate the casket carrying the head of John the Baptist did so to give the transfer the look and dignity of an imperial adventus.

Certain martyr relics, unnamed in the sources, were brought to the Great Church at Constantinople sometime between the 360s and the early 400s. John Chrysostom supervised their subsequent translation to the martyrium of the Apostle Thomas at Drypia, a suburb of the imperial city. This took place during the reign of the Eastern emperor Arcadius, after his wife Aelia Eudoxia had been elevated to the status of Augusta, which occurred on January 9, 400.[66]

On the day following the translation, John preached at the martyrium in Drypia, devoting the first part of his sermon to the empress. Eudoxia had participated in the procession and had put on a conventional display of imperial humility, for which John effusively praised her.[67] Implicit but obvious in the

61. MacCormack, "Change and Continuity in Late Antiquity," 729, citing Jocelyn M. C. Toynbee, *Roman Medallions* (The American Numismatic Society, 1944), pl. VIII, 4 and pl. XVII, 11.

62. This is noted by MacCormack, "Change and Continuity in Late Antiquity," 731.

63. Ammianus Marcellinus, *Res gest.* 16.10.6.

64. As described in MacCormack, "Change and Continuity in Late Antiquity," 730.

65. Claudian, *VI cons.* 551.

66. Regarding the *terminus post quem* for the *translatio*, see Kenneth G. Holum, *Theodosian Empresses: Women and Imperial Dominion in Late Antiquity* (University of California Press, 1982), 56.

67. Regarding the empress's display of humility, see Mischa Meier, "Die Demut des Kaisers: Aspekte der religiösen Selbstinzenierung bei Theodosius II (408–450 n.Chr.)," in *Die Bibel als politisches Argument: Voraussetzungen und Folgen biblizistischer Herrschaftslegitimation in der Vormoderne*, ed. Andreas Pečar and Kai Trampedach (Oldenbourg, 2007), 135–158; Peter Van

imperially sanctioned event was the ascendance of the Nicene Christians of Constantinople over "the Arians," who continued to make appearances in the city but had been deprived of their church buildings and were *personae non gratae* in the eyes of not only the church but the emperor and empress. John alludes to these imperial Christian politics when he characterizes Eudoxia as "destroying the error of the heretics."[68]

John also describes the procession, which took place at night.[69] The empress walked directly behind the "cloth-covered" casket, which may have been conveyed on a low cart, since she was able to grasp the relic box as she walked. A massive torch-carrying throng, practically the entire population, stretched out along the road in a long "river of fire." As the people processed, they sang Psalm 138:11–12. John's specification of particular verses suggests the traditional responsorial format of the era. He also mentions that this psalmody was performed in at least four languages: Latin, Greek, Syriac, and what he calls "barbarian," meaning a Gothic tongue.[70] It could be that each ethnic congregation processed as a group with its own psalm leader(s), for John speaks of multiple choruses.[71] If so, members of a given chorus would have been able to hear snatches of the singing of the other choruses. In any case, the procession was both unified and diverse, signifying a cosmopolitan solidarity, everyone "holding a single cithara, that of David," John says, yet singing in their own languages.

Whatever input the empress may have had in planning the procession, John would have selected the psalms and the refrains. He was the one who envisioned that during the nighttime procession with torches creating a long ribbon of light in the darkness, the people would repeat the refrain, "Night is light in my weakness, because darkness will not be dark by you [God], and night will be lit up as day. As the darkness of night, so the light of night." John recalled this detail in his sermon the following day. "Did not this night become brighter than any

---

Nuffelen, "Playing the Ritual Game in Constantinople (379–457)," in *Two Romes: Rome and Constantinople in Late Antiquity*, ed. Lucy Grig and Gavin Kelly (Oxford University Press, 2012), 197 (183–201); Christopher Kelly, "Stooping to Conquer: The Power of Imperial Humility," in *Theodosius II: Rethinking the Roman Empire in Late Antiquity*, ed Christopher Kelly (Cambridge University Press, 2013), 231–232.

68. John Chrysostom, *Hom. dicta post. reliq. martyr.* 3 (PG 63: 471).

69. Torches were used in both daytime and nighttime processions. In this instance, the parade took place at night. See below with n. 73.

70. John Chrysostom, *Hom. dicta post. reliq. martyr.* 3 (PG 63: 472). The Church of St. Paul in Constantinople was home to a congregation of Nicene Goths.

71. *Hom. dicta post. reliq. martyr.* 3 (PG 63: 472).

day, with such abundance of joy by all the exuberant[72] people . . . so many people pouring out, flooding the road and the marketplace?"[73]

The Discovery and Translation of the Bones of Stephen

Before turning to the West, I will mention a martyr translation that took place in Jerusalem in 415 during the episcopate of John of Jerusalem. According to first-hand accounts of the *inventio* of the relics, a certain Lucian the Priest claimed to have experienced a set of visions regarding the history of the death and burial of Stephen, the church's first martyr. The *Revelation of Saint Stephen*, as Lucian's account is called, has come down to us in two original recensions, both of which were published about the same time, circa 415, the year of the visions.[74] According to these accounts, Lucian informed John about the visions, and John ordered a recovery effort, which led to the discovery of the relics in a field of Kephar Gamala, not far from Jerusalem. A translation of the bones to Jerusalem "with psalms and hymns" was accomplished on December 26, 415.[75]

The "plot" of the narrative is that Stephen's bones had to be found because the world was in crisis and needed the miracle that only a martyr of his great stature could effect. Humanity, steeped in sin, was suffering a divine judgment in the form of a worldwide drought. When Stephen's bones were finally discovered and made their advent-like return to Jerusalem, the city of Stephen's original ministry, his presence brought salvation to the world. No sooner had the people of Jerusalem received him and deposited his remains in the church on Sion than blessed torrential rains began to fall all over the world.[76]

It is difficult to disentangle the fictional elements and embroidery from the historical facts in this story. But it is clear that John of Jerusalem was central to the events, that a translation of bones claimed to be Stephen's did take place, and that these bones were enshrined in Jerusalem and also, in bits and pieces,

72. John uses the word σκιρτώντων, which means leaping or dancing (*Hom. dicta post. reliq. mart.* 2; PG 63: 470).

73. *Hom. dicta post. reliq. mart.* 2 (PG 63: 470).

74. I rely on the editions of these two recensions, including the letter of Avitus (see below), in Vanderlinden, "Revelatio Sancti Stephani (BHL 7850–56)." *Revue des Études Byzantines* 6 (1946): 178–217.

75. Both recensions describe the translation. Recension B reads as follows: *Et ita cum psalmis et hymnis asportaverunt reliquias beati Stephani in sanctam ecclesiam Sion, ubi et archidiaconus fuerat ordinatus.* Lucian, *Revelatio Sancti Stephani*, rec. B 48 (Vanderlinden, 217).

76. See the references to the worldwide drought, the necessity that Stephen's remains be found so that he can bring God's mercy to a world suffering from drought, the discovery of the bones, healings, and the end of the drought in rec. A 5–8, 50 and rec. B 7, 18, 26, 44–47.

distributed around the world. The translation itself is described only briefly and in only one of the two Latin versions, which were prepared shortly after the transfer but for different purposes. The longer recension says that many people were present when the grave was opened and an earthquake ensued, releasing a sweet aroma, and that three bishops who had been attending a synod (John of Jerusalem, Eutonius of Sebaste, and Eleutherius of Jericho) were present, too, or arrived shortly after (there being an apparent inconsistency in the text). Miraculous healings followed, a foretaste of the saint's saving power. The bishops and the crowd of people then conducted the relics "with psalms and hymns" to the Sion church in Jerusalem.[77]

From everything we have seen thus far, the essential elements of a martyr translation were (1) the relics themselves in a proper container (such as a golden urn or fine box), (2) a suitable vehicle of conveyance (a fine cart or carriage, even the hands of a walking cleric),[78] (3) Christians in parade singing psalms, and (4) at least one bishop with his entourage of clergy. In the case of the relics of Stephen, the translation was one of the most public aspects of the first stage of publicity about them, the local phase, when Christians from the farms and towns, as well as Jerusalem itself, would have contributed one of the most important elements of the event—the processional psalmody that honored the saint in his first general public manifestation, which culminated in an advent-like entrance into Jerusalem. In the two published accounts, however, which were produced after the translation and which inaugurated the second, much wider stage of publicity, the translation itself is referenced almost perfunctorily, the role of the people not at all. With respect to living persons whose involvement in the events brought the relics and their saving benefactions to the world, the accounts credit the priest Lucian, the priest Avitus who served as Lucian's translator, and the three bishops, John of Jerusalem above all. The participation of other people is not foregrounded, much less vividly described. Except for a monk named Migetius, mentioned in what seems to be an interpolation;[79] no other person is referenced by name. Moreover, when the unfolding narratives arrive at the translation, the point where ordinary people made their most

77. *Rev. s. Steph.*, rec. B 42–48. The shorter recension also mentions the three bishops and other people ("the brothers who were present") at the opening of the grave, the sweet aroma (but not any earthquake), and the healings. It also refers to a two-day interval between the discovery and the translation, evidently a time of preparation for the transfer; but it does not describe the translation itself, focusing instead on its date (December 26) and the worldwide drought-ending rain that immediately followed. *Rev. s. Steph.*, rec. A 44–50.

78. The possibility that a bishop might on occasion carry the relic box or urn in his own hands is suggested by language in a comment by Jerome, although he may not be referring specifically to the translation parade. See Jerome, *Contr. Vigilantium* 1.5 (PL 23: 343), quoted above.

79. In both recensions at 35–41.

significant contribution, one account is brief and the other is briefer. In both statements about the transfer, the implied grammatical subject is the bishops.[80] The phrasing of the accounts is designed to put the spotlight on them, not on the layfolk and their psalmody.

For us, the paucity of details about most of the martyr translations are frustrating. The liturgical historian craves specifics. So does the music historian, who would like to know (1) whether certain psalms became standard for martyr processions; (2) how the refrain-singing marchers were able to hear the psalm leader and whether the verses of the psalm were perhaps sung by a small ensemble of singers; (3) whether the psalm leaders were the boy cantors who read psalm lessons at church services or local monks who had memorized the Psalter or even a group of trained singers who could project their voices over a considerable distance; and (4) how the singing in multiple languages (no less than four in the procession to Drypia) was done. None of these *desiderata* are satisfied by this or any other account of a martyr translation of the era.

The Translation of the Relics of Gervasius and Protasius in Milan

In 386 Ambrose had the relics of the martyrs Gervasius and Protasius brought from a cemetery outside the walls of Milan into the city to be deposited in a crypt beneath the altar of his namesake basilica, the Ambrosiana. In a letter to his sister Marcellina, composed shortly after the event, he rehearses the sermons that he gave on the day of the translation and the succeeding day of interment.[81] According to Ambrose, it was he himself who "discovered" the relics, which were reposing, without anyone's knowledge, at the burial place of three other martyrs—Felix, Nabor, and Victor—who had been translated to Milan some years prior.[82]

---

80. *Rev. s. Steph.*, rec. A 48 ("they transferred") and rec. B 48 ("they brought"). In Recension A the antecedent of "they" is a preceding "they," who kiss the relics and close the grave in preparation for the transfer. The implication is that the bishops, who had taken control of the site, gave orders for the grave to be closed until the translation could be arranged. In Recension B, the three bishops are the only ones mentioned in the context, and they effect the translation and give a small portion of the remains to Lucian (48).

81. Ambrose, *Ep.* 77.3–13 and 15–23 (CSEL 82: 128–140). *Letter* 77 in CSEL is *Letter* 22 in PL 16: 1019–1026. It is not clear that John means literal dancing here, since he uses the same word figuratively at the beginning of the homily to describe his own spiritual elation over the event.

82. Ambrose tells his sister that a strong feeling of "presentiment" (*praesagii*) came over him, which caused him to have the burial place of the martyrs Felix and Nabor opened and searched (*Ep.* 77.1–2 [CSEL 82: 127]).

In his *Life of Ambrose*, Paulinus of Milan says that once the bones of Gervasius and Protasius were discovered, they were placed on litters (*in lecticis posita*) and carried to the basilica of Fausta.[83] Ambrose mentions a brief stay of the remains at this basilica, followed by a removal to the Ambrosiana on the following day. The latter translation would have entailed the usual pomp, although the only detail Ambrose mentions is a healing that occurred along the way, when a blind man touched "the hem of the robe of the martyrs, with which the sacred relics were covered."[84] Augustine writes that the martyrs "were transferred to the Basilica Ambrosiana with fitting honor (*digno cum honore*)."[85]

Peter Kritzinger draws attention to a hymn composed by Ambrose in honor of the martyrs Felix, Nabor, and Victor. A passage in the hymn describes the translation of the bones of these saints *plaustri triumphalis modo* ("in the manner of a triumphal wagon").[86] The relics of the three men (who died in 306) were brought to Milan during the episcopate of Maternus, who served as bishop from 316 to 328.[87] Since the transfer occurred before Ambrose was born, his statement that the transfer was "in the manner of a triumphal wagon" must reflect what he had heard about it and certainly what he himself regarded as a proper way to transport martyr relics, including those of Gervasius and Protasius, whose translation to the Ambrosiana and celebration there were great public events, orchestrated by Ambrose himself.[88] Hence, the "litter" on which the remains

83. Paulinus of Milan, *Vit. Ambr.* 14.2 (PL 14: 32; Navoni, 76).

84. Ambrose, *Ep.* 77.2 and 17 (CSEL 82: 128 and 137).

85. Augustine, *Conf.* 9.7.16.

86. Ambrose, *Hymn.* 10(*Victor, Nabor, Felix pii*).32.

87. See, for example, Gillian V. Mackie, *Early Christian Chapels in the West: Decoration, Function, and Patronage* (University of Toronto Press, 2003), 125–126.

88. See Kritzinger, "The Cult of the Saints and Religious Processions in Late Antiquity and the Early Middle Ages," in *An Age of Saints? Power, Conflict, and Dissent in Early Medieval Christianity*, ed. Peter Sarris, Matthew Dal Santo, and Phil Booth (Brill, 2011), 43–47 (36–48). Kritzinger seeks to bolster and expand his interpretation of the translation of Gervasius and Protasius by noting the similarity between the poem's description of the earlier translation and a procession depicted in the Trier ivory. The latter, however, is probably not even roughly contemporary. A well-studied piece of religious artwork, the Trier ivory has been variously dated to as early as late antiquity and as late as the tenth century. A late dating is very plausible, since the style of the iconography and carving fit very well with what is known of ninth- and tenth-century medieval religious art. Moreover, it is not clear whether the picture shows a particular event or even depicts a fictional one in a realistic way. Regarding these points about the ivory, see Leslie Brubaker, "The Chalke Gate, The Construction of the Past, and the Trier Ivory," *Byzantine and Modern Greek Studies* 23 (1999): 258–285; Philipp Niewöhner, "Historisch-topographische Überlegungen zum Trierer Prozessionselfenbein, dem Christusbild an der Chalke, Kaiserin Irenes Triumph im Bilderstreit und der Euphemiakirche am Hippodrom," *Millennium* 11

of Gervasius and Protasius were initially carried to the basilica of Fausta for a brief stay was probably replaced by a more ornate wagon or even a chariot for the translation to the Ambrosiana.

Psalmody in a martyr translation was understood in the East as an act of thanksgiving that glorified God and honored the martyr(s). Without mentioning psalms or any other specific feature of the translation, Augustine refers to the honorific character of the translation of Gervasius and Protasius with his phrase *digno cum honore*. This language suggests ceremony, and we have reason to suspect that it would have included the essential elements of a martyr translation that I have already listed: the relics themselves in a proper container, a suitable vehicle of conveyance, Christians in parade singing psalms, and a bishop with his entourage of clergy.

Ambrose, expatiating on the glory of Gervasius and Protasius as victors in shedding their own blood for the faith, borrows language of the Roman triumph, referring to the martyrs as *tropaia*, monuments of a victory, "removed from an ignoble grave and displayed under heaven."[89] The people could see "the marks of the bloody triumph (*cruoris triumphalis notae*)," and it was fitting that "these triumphant victims" should be placed with Christ "beneath the altar," "where Christ is victim."[90] The idea that martyrs achieve triumph in death was an ancient Christian trope. Ambrose reinterpreted this trope by applying it to a particular, material, and public event: the transfer of the relics of Gervasius and Protasius to the Ambrosiana and the public display of these "monuments of victory" in that church, where they lay in state before their final interment in the crypt under the altar.

José San Bernardino suggests that Ambrose's homiletic phraseology about the martyrs' triumph was intended not only to celebrate them but also to evoke the bishop's own victory over the adolescent regent Emperor Valentinian II and Empress Justina, his mother, in the recent conflict over the basilicas.[91]

(2014): 261–288; Paroma Chatterjee, "Iconoclasm's Legacy: Interpreting the Trier Ivory," *Art Bulletin* 100 (2018): 28–47.

89. Ambrose to his sister, June 20, 386, *Ep.* 77.4 (CSEL 82: 129). The letter is number 61 in other collections.

90. Ambrose, *Ep.* 77.12–13 (CSEL 82: 134); cf. a remark in Ambrose's sermon for the interment the following day, when he declared that "the blood cries out by the triumph of its passion" (*Ep.* 77.23; CSEL 82: 140).

91. The conflicts over the basilicas are described in Ambrose's letters 75a(21a) and 76(20), although there has been considerable debate about the date and occasion for 76(20) and whether it responds to a law of January 23, 386 (*Cod. Theod.* 16.1.4), which granted imperial access to cathedrals. In any case, José San Bernardino cites the homiletic passages that I have quoted, which carry "un tono trionfalistico," and he associates this evocation with Ambrose's own victory over the emperor in the battle of the basilicas. See José San Bernardino, "*Sub imperio discordiae*:

The transfer of the relics was itself a politically bold act, since the movement of buried bodies, including martyr remains, had recently been banned by imperial decree (in February of 386).[92] Yet Ambrose had already demonstrated that Valentinian II and the empress could not control him. Hence, the procession of the relics, which took place not long after the battle for the basilicas, would have seemed like a triumph-parade for not only the martyrs but the bishop himself.

It goes without saying that Ambrose would have been prominent in the parade.[93] For not only was he the bishop of Milan, it was he who discovered the martyrs and arranged to have them translated to the Ambrosiana, his namesake basilica, to be interred beneath the altar there, a location that he envisioned for his own tomb.[94] In his sermon in that basilica following the transfer, he is quite explicit in highlighting his own role, telling his congregation, "I have acquired these martyrs for you,"[95] and mentioning that he had decided to share his own burial chamber with the saints.

I have suggested that church custom provides a reason for assuming that psalms were sung in the procession of Gervasius and Protasisus to the Ambrosiana. It is difficult to imagine that such a procession took place with no singing. Congregational psalmody is documented for the West at least as early as a commentary on the psalms by Hilary of Poitiers, composed in around 365, where he writes as if psalmody were a familiar and widespread custom.[96] Funeral psalmody is documented for the West as early as 373 in a Latin inscription from Umbria, as well as in another fourth-century Latin

---

l'uomo che voleva essere Eliseo (giugno 386)," in *Nec timeo mori: atti del Congresso internazionale di studi ambrosiana*, ed. L. F. Pizzolato and M. Rizzi (Vita e pensiera, 1998), 736 (709–736).

92. *Cod. Theod.* 9.7.17, ascribed to Gratian, Valentinian II, and Theodosius I. Gratian (brother of Valentinian II and his co-regent in the West) was dead by this time.

93. Inspired by San Bernardino's analysis (see n. 91), Kritzinger suggests that Ambrose used the relics translation as a vehicle for "his own triumph-parade," presenting himself as *episcopus triumphans* ("The Cult of the Saints and Religious Processions in Late Antiquity and the Early Middle Ages," 47 and 46).

94. Ambrose, *Ep.* 77.13 (CSEL 82: 134).

95. Ambrose, *Ep.* 77.12 (CSEL 82: 134).

96. Hilary of Poitiers refers to "church" psalmody at morning and evening prayer, echoing Eusebius's comments about Ps 64:9: *progressus ecclesiae in matutinum et uespertinorum hymnorum delectationes maximum misericordiae Dei signum est.* ("The going forth of the delightful morning and evening hymns of the church is a sign of the greatest mercies of God.") *Tract. in psalm. 64* 12 (on v. 9). (CSEL 22: 244; PL 9:420). Cf. Hilary's remark about Ps 64:2: *Hymnus ergo hic Deo condecet, qui sit in Sion spiritali et ecclesiastico cantico innocens et Dei laudibus dulcis.* ("Therefore, this hymn to God is fitting, which would be a sweet and pure hymn of praise to God

inscription that refers to psalmody during a funeral procession specifically.[97] Hence, it would have been fitting if the holy relics of Gervasius and Protasius were conveyed to the Basilica Ambrosiana in the Eastern manner—with psalms. That said, one has to consider the possibility that Ambrose composed a hymn for the occasion.

At first thought, a parade hymn seems quite plausible, given that Ambrose had already penned a hymn for the martyrs Felix, Nabor, and Victor. Yet no hymn for Gervasius and Protasius appears in the vast Ambrosian corpus of hymns. Furthermore, the procession took place just two days after the discovery of the relics. In such a short time, could a busy Ambrose have composed a hymn that was then learned by heart by a soloist or an ensemble of song leaders for performance in a parade? Perhaps. But the use of one or more familiar psalms would have been more expedient, and it may have been *de rigueur* to sing biblical psalms in a martyr translation.

Although Ambrose provides almost no information about the procession or its song, he does refer to the psalm lessons given at the services held in the martyrs' honor. Psalms 18 and 112 were chosen, according to a lectionary scheme.[98] As a skilled preacher, Ambrose was perfectly capable of drawing the lessons he wished from almost any predetermined lectionary reading. Commenting on Psalm 18, whose theme is the heavens declaring the glory of God, Ambrose encourages his hearers to think of the exalted martyrs as examples of this heavenly proclamation, their own witness pouring forth speech night and day.[99] In his remarks on Psalm 112—which describes how God, seated on high, "regards lowly things in heaven and on earth" and makes them sit on high with the rulers, causing "the barren woman to rejoice"—Ambrose says that God "regarded" the remains of Gervasius and Protasius, which were buried and hidden in the earth, and enrolled them among "the rulers," thus causing "the church of Milan, which was barren of martyrs,[100] to rejoice . . . in

---

in spiritual and ecclesiastical song.") (CSEL 22: 234; PL 9: 414). See chapter 6 for a discussion of Eusebius's comments on Ps 64:9.

97. CIL XI 4629 and ILCV II 4711, quoted in chapter 7 and cited in notes 105 and 106 of that chapter.

98. Ambrose refers to one of the psalm lessons as *fortuita* (*Ep.* 77.4 [CSEL 82: 129]).

99. Ambrose, *Ep.* 77.3–4 (CSEL 82: 128–129).

100. In what sense had the church been "barren of martyrs," if the bones of Felix, Nabor, and Victor had rested in a Milanese cemetery for more than a generation? The answer is probably that those relics belonged to private shrines founded by matrons, whereas Gervasius and Protasius were gifted by Ambrose to the church of Milan itself, a distinction that Ambrose would have made for his own political reasons. On matrons as founders of martyr cults and their shrines, see the following (and the literature cited there): Felice Lifshitz, "The Martyr, the Tomb, and

the public notices and examples of her own sufferings."[101] These interpretations focus on the greatness of the martyrs and the luster they bring to the church. Perhaps Ambrose's mention of their status among the "rulers" carried a veiled political message, insinuating the superiority of the church—its martyrs and its bishop—over emperors.[102]

A Comparison of the Forms and Functions of Imperial Adventus Chants with the Psalmody of Church Processions

The adventus style of procession, which martyr parades and episcopal cavalcades to some extent imitated, had its own tradition of popular speech, including acclamations and other chants. One of the few writers to characterize the style of popular Roman acclamations is Dio Cassius, who describes "what [the crowds] were accustomed to shout in a certain rhythmic manner in theaters in paying court to Commodus," which, when they turned on Commodus (in 192 CE), "they changed into the most ridiculous form and sang out" against him.[103] In addition to referencing the competence of crowds to spontaneously revise their chants, this comment indicates that the "singing" took the form of a shout and was rhythmical "in a certain manner." Surviving examples show that the acclamations shouted out in the theater, the arena, and at parades were relatively short and therefore would not have been set to melodies of any complexity.

Rome, both the republic and the imperial city, had a long history of advents with chants improvised by soldiers, who were granted great freedom to praise, jest, mock, and deride.[104] Soldiers' chants in the age of the republic used the

---

the Matron: Constructing the (Masculine) 'Past' as a Female Power Base," in *Medieval Concepts of the Past: Ritual, Memory, and Historiography*, ed. Gerd Althoff, Johannes Fried, and Patrick J. Geary (Cambridge University Press, 2002), 333–334.

101. Ambrose, *Ep.* 77.7 (CSEL 82: 130–131).

102. Peter Brown interprets the event as part of a "re-wiring" of the social institution of martyr veneration, heretofore the province of private wealthy households, so that the martyr translation becomes both a public expression of a bishop's social capital and a means of creating and reinforcing ecclesial unity. See Peter Brown, *The Cult of the Saints: Its Rise and Function in Latin Christianity*, enlarged ed. (University of Chicago Press, 2015), 37–40.

103. Εὐρύθμως πως ἐκβοᾶν. . . ἐξῇδον. Dio Cassius 74.2.3 (73.3.3 in other editions).

104. Two sources refer to these customs for the time of the republic. Livy speaks of crude verses for Valerius Portius (a fifth-century consul) (Livy, *Ab urb. cond.* 4.53.11–12). Appian mentions a chorus of citharists and pipers, along with song, dance, and mime for the general Scipio Africanus, with soldiers in the rear, alternately praising, teasing, and deriding their commanders (Appian, *Lyb.* 295 [66]).

trochaic septenarius (a meter of old Roman comedy). Suetonius quotes examples from Julius Caesar's Gallic triumph in 46 BCE. Here is one of them:

> *Urbani servat(e) uxores* | *moechum* calv(*um*) *adducimus.* ||
> – –– – – ––– | – – – – –⏑ –||
>
> *aur(um) in Galli(a) effutuisti;* | *hic sumpsisti mutuum*
> – – –⏑ –⏑⏑ –– |– – – – –⏑ –.[105]

> Romans, guard your wives. We're bringing home the bald lecher.
> In Gaul you [Caesar] f---ed away the gold you grabbed up here on loan.

Soldiers used their favorite meter flexibly and helped out the rhythm by dropping the occasional last syllable of a word. They would have chanted these words to a simple, repeated tune, if they melodized at all.

During the age of Augustus, too, Roman soldiers mocked their generals and other dignitaries during triumphs. According to Dionysius of Halicarnassus, they sang "improvised verses" of jest and satire.[106] Martial refers to soldiers chanting "jokes and trivial songs."[107] Sometimes these soldiers' chants combined praise and abuse.[108] A biography of Emperor Aurelian (270–275 CE) quotes some short praise chants uttered by soldiers during the days of Aurelian's preimperial military successes. Although they are not assigned to triumphs, most scholars assume that they reflect a type of song that soldiers intoned in various celebratory situations, including the triumph. Both examples are short. One consists of four lines, the other of two.[109]

Victory chants for Constantine are mentioned by Eusebius. After the emperor's military success at the Milvian bridge, he processed into Rome "with *epinikiōn*."[110] Epinicia in the strict sense of the Greek word were lyric poems of

---

105. Suetonius, *Div. Iul.* 51; see also 49.4. For the meter, see James W. Halporn, Martin Ostwald, and Thomas G. Rosenmeyer, *The Meters of Greek and Latin Poetry* (Bobbs-Merrill, 1963), 78.

106. Dionysius of Halicarnassus, *Ant. Rom.* 7.72.11.

107. *iocos leuioraque carmina*. Martial, *Ep.* 7.8.9.

108. See Frances Hickson Hahn, "Triumphal Ambivalence: The Obscene Songs," in *Ancient Obscenities: Their Nature and Use in the Ancient Greek and Roman Worlds*, ed. Dorota M. Dutsch and Ann Suter (University of Michigan Press, 2015), 156–157.

109. *HA Aureliani* 6.5 and 7.2. Hendrik S. Versnel, for example, cites these verses in his classic study, *Triumphus: An Inquiry into the Origin, Development, and Meaning of the Roman Triumph* (Brill, 1970), 381.

110. Eusebius, *H.E.* 9.9.9 and *Vit. Const.* 1.39.2.

the late-archaic and classical era, composed in honor of winners in the panhellenic games. This type of melic poetry was dead by the early Hellenistic period, but Eusebius could well have used the word in a looser sense for any kind of victory song, including the usual victory chants of soldiers.[111] That seems especially likely, since composed praise songs, performed by a trained choir to honor a ruler, are not otherwise attested as a feature of Roman triumph-processions in the imperial age[112] (although they may have figured in the postparade parts of the reception ceremonies).[113] Even when the imperial adventus was Christianized in late antiquity, composed song, including psalmody, was not introduced into imperial processions.[114]

Acclamations in the Greek world were likewise brief shouts. They were not metrical and may not have been sung or otherwise intoned, except perhaps in the sing-song swing of a unison chant. Greek words for acclamation suggest cries and shouts, not chanting or singing.[115] Examples of acclamations addressed

111. Eusebius knew that in Symmachus's translation of the Greek Bible, certain psalms that celebrate divine deliverance are termed "epinician" (e.g., Eusebius, *Comm. In psalm.* [on Ps. 17], PG 23: 168). Eusebius himself, using ἐπινίκιος as an adjective, invariably calls such psalms "victory hymns" or "victory odes." Among the examples, see his description of Psalm 10 as ἐπινίκιος ὕμνος (PG 23: 68), Psalm 123 an ἐπινίκιον ᾠδὴν (PG 24: 13), and, in a speech he composes in praise of Constantine and places in the mouth of a certain Christian orator, his characterization of Ps 47 as a ὕμνον ἐπινίκιον (*H.E.* 10.4.6). He does not call the praises uttered during Constantine's procession "victory songs" or "victory hymns," probably because they were shouts/chants, not full-fledged songs/psalms. Ernest C. Richardson, who translated the *Life* for the Schaff series, takes the expression μετ' ἐπινίκιων to mean simply "in triumph" (NPNF 1: 493). A few sentences later Eusebius uses a parallel expression to describe how Constantine was received—"with εὐφημιῶν (praises)"—by the senators and the crowds during the procession.

112. Dionysius of Halicarnassus, recounting a triumph of Rome's legendary first king, Romulus, describes the soldiers "hymning the gods with ancestral songs and praising the ruler with improvised verses" (*Ant. Rom.* 2.34.2). If the detail about the hymns is true, which is not at all certain, many centuries separate this event from the imperial era. But perhaps Dionysius writes anachronistically.

113. Speeches were probably more typical at these ceremonies, although choirs are sometimes mentioned. As for praise songs in advent processions, they may have been an established feature of the old Hellenistic advent. In the late 290s BCE, the City of Athens received King Demetrius Poliorcetes with "processional hymns and *ithyphalloi*" that honored Demetrius as a god alongside Demeter. See Demochares (*FGrH* 75 F 2) and Duris (*FGrH* 76 F 13) = Athenaeus 6.62–3 (252f–53f). Hellenistic praise poetry for kings is also documented for the Ptolemaic kings, although not specifically as part of a royal advent (ἀπάντησις).

114. Note, for example, the absence of any examples of lyric praise poems or other types of composed song in the comprehensive study of the late-Roman triumph by Michael McCormick, *Eternal Victory: Triumphal Rulership in Late Antiquity, Byzantium, and the Early Medieval West* (Cambridge University Press, 1987).

115. Chaniotis lists the various Greek words for the act of acclamation (in both secular and religious contexts), such as βοᾶν and its cognates, as well as κράζειν/ἀνακράζειν. See Angelos

to civil authorities and emperors from the second century CE and later show stock rhythmic (not metrical) prose formulations, such as those preserved in the following inscription from around 300 CE for a town meeting. There is no reason to think that acclamations cried out by Greek-speaking populaces, when greeting advent processions, differed in style from these town-hall acclamations:

> For all eternity the rule of the Romans! The lords Augusti! Long live the prefect, long live the Katholikos! Long live the Prytanis, bravo, glory of the city! Hurrah, Dioskoros, you foremost of citizens! Everything that is good will be increased under your administration, you initiator of good things! The Nile loves you as the blessed (Hesies) and rises! Long live he who loves his fellow citizens, long live he who loves moderation, initiator of good things, founder of the city![116]

The inscription quotes the acclamations seriatim, but they would not have been performed that way by a mass of people. We should assume that one or more leaders gave out a shout consisting of a single line or a grouping of parallel lines, which the crowd repeated some number of times before going on to the next shout as prompted by the leaders.[117]

If we compare Greek and Roman popular chants with the psalmody sung during martyr processions and the advents of bishops, we can infer certain differences of form and execution, as well as certain similarities. The Greek and Roman chants were not composed songs but short unison ejaculations in rough rhythm, improvised or adaptively reworded for each occasion and honoree. Psalms were established hymns taken from a sacred book. The Greek and Roman chants were repeated in unison; psalms were sung by a soloist (or a group of song-leaders) with unison refrains by the other participants. Greek and Roman chants varied in their purpose as speech addressed to rulers and other authority figures, ranging

---

Chaniotis, "Acclamations as a Form of Religious Communication," in *Die Religion des Imperium Romanum: Koine und Konfrontationen*, ed. Hubert Cancik and Jörg Rüpke (Mohr Siebeck, 2009), 201.

116. The first set of acclamations at a town meeting, as memorialized in P.Oxy 41 (= W. Chr. 45), as translated in Thomas Kruse, "The Magistrate and the Ocean: Acclamations and Ritualised Communication in Town Gatherings in Roman Egypt," in *Ritual and Communication in the Graeco-Roman World*, ed. Eftychia Stavrianopoulou (Presses universitaires de Liège, 2006), 300.

117. A speech of this length is implausible as the spontaneous utterance of a crowd. Kruse imagines that the people were prepared beforehand and that their utterances were "quasi conducted (in a musical sense)" by the organizers ("The Magistrate and the Ocean," 311). I am not sure what he means by "conducted." My suggestion that leaders gave out the acclamations in separate units does not require the assumption of a preparation of the crowd before the event.

from laudation to petitions and demands to joking and derision, depending on the circumstances. Although psalms varied in thematic content—and in one unusual instance a processional psalm was used as protest song against an emperor—the usual purpose of psalmody in martyr and episcopal parades was to thank and praise God; honoring the procession's focal human subjects, a saint or a bishop, was secondary.

Two similarities are also salient. First, as group speech, psalms in procession, like popular chants and acclamation, were the collective public voice of a people. Second, the unison refrains of psalmody, like the repeated unison acclamations, must have fostered a sense of solidarity and collective identity among the chanters. To repeat some words of Ambrose already quoted in chapter 7, "Clearly it is a great bond of unity for the whole number of the people to unite in one chorus."[118]

Public Liturgical Processions on Feast Days

Public liturgical processions on feast days were a fixture of medieval and Byzantine cities.[119] They are documented for premedieval times in the case of Jerusalem in the late fourth century, as described by Egeria, and perhaps Rome in the fifth century, according to a hint in the *Liber pontificalis.*

In her description of Jerusalem liturgies she witnessed in the 380s, Egeria refers to various processions with psalmody. In fact, her customary way of referring to a procession is "they go with psalms," an expression that the Armenian Lectionary uses in this way as well.[120] Processions with psalms took place during the eight days of Pascha and on certain other feast days of the liturgical year. These ceremonial movements were a unique phenomenon of the city's stational liturgy. A celebration would begin at one locale within the Church of the Holy Sepulchre—a large compound that included a courtyard—and then proceed with hymns to another part of the same church. These movements were short—from the Martyrium to the Anastasis, for example, and from the Anastasis to the Cross. Processions of this type remained within the walls of the precinct and were therefore not parades through the public streets.

118. Ambrose, *Expl. psalm. 1* 9 (PL 14: 925; CSEL 64.8).

119. For the West, see, for example, *Prozessionen und ihre Gesänge in der mittelalterlichen Stadt: Gestalt, Hermeneutik, und Repräsentation*, ed. Harald Buchinger, David Hiley, and Sabine Reichert (Schnell und Steiner, 2017); for the East, see, for instance, Albrecht Berger, "Imperial and Ecclesiastical Processions in Constantinople," in *Byzantine Constantinople: Monuments, Topography, and Everyday Life*, ed. Nevra Necipoğlu (Brill, 2001), 73–88.

120. This is pointed out by John Wilkinson, *Egeria's Travels*, rev. and corr. (Oxbow, 2002), 179.

Yet, on certain days there were movements from the main church to a church called Sion, which stood on the famous hill of that name. On the first and last Sunday of the Easter octave, following vespers at the Anastasis in the Church of the Holy Sepulchre, all the people led the bishop to Sion, a distance of some 800 meters, about half a mile.[121] And on each of the eight days of the Easter octave, the bishop conducted services after breakfast at a church at Eleona on the west side of the Mount of Olives, and subsequently at the nearby Imbomon. Then everyone—the clergy, the newly baptized, and others in attendance—processed with psalms to the Anastasis for vespers.[122] This journey was perhaps just over a mile, depending on the available route.

Although the processions during the Easter octave were public movements, they did not resemble the traditional Greco-Roman festal processions that wound with great pomp through an urban space for many blocks with crowds of citizens lining the streets. By contrast, the celebration of Epiphany entailed a five-mile public procession from Bethlehem to Jerusalem. I have already described this feast and will not repeat the details here, except to say that the procession took place at night, following a vigil in Bethlehem, attended by the bishop and monks, perhaps including brothers and sisters from the monasteries at Bethlehem. Deep into the night, the bishop and the monks departed for Jerusalem, singing a portion of Psalm 117; eventually they arrived at the Anastasis for a predawn service.[123]

On Palm Sunday, too, a public procession was staged that began outside the city walls. First there was a service at the Eleona on the Mount of Olives with many people in attendance, including families.[124] The throng of celebrators then went from the Eleona to the Imbomon for a second service, at the close of which a gospel lesson about the Triumphal Entry was read. After that, everyone processed down to the city "with hymns and antiphons," carrying palm branches and responding with the words "Blessed is the one who comes in the name of the Lord!" (Ps 117:26), the children leading the bishop "as Jesus was led then."[125] After passing through the eastern gates, the parade wound through "the whole

---

121. Egeria, *Itin.* 39.4 (Easter Sunday) and 40.2 (the Sunday after Easter).

122. *Itin.* 39.3–4.

123. *Itin.* 25.6–7. See chapter 7.

124. Egeria, *Itin.* 31.1 ("all the people;" a reference to children appears a bit later).

125. Egeria, *Itin.* 31.3. In Matthew, the people shout an adaptation of Ps 117:25–26: "Hosanna to the son of David! Blessed is the one who comes in the name of the Lord!" "Hosanna" is a transliteration of the Hebrew of Ps 118:25a. Matthew adds the words "to the son of David," then pairs the first shout with "Blessed is the one who comes in the name of the Lord!" from LXX Ps 117:26. The attribution of a special role to the children (children of Jerusalem in Egeria's time and in Jesus's time) seems to be derived by inference from the next scene in the temple, according to Matt 21:15.

city" to the Anastasis.[126] This rough imitation[127] of the Triumphal Entry, with the bishop in the role of Jesus, resembled a royal adventus, which is what the gospel stories themselves imply about the original event.

A Pentecost procession followed a similar route. On Pentecost Sunday, at the close of a morning Communion, the archdeacon would announce, "Today immediately after the Sixth hour let us all be ready on Eleona [at] the Imbomon."[128] According to Egeria, nearly every resident of Jerusalem showed up for the services on the Mount of Olives, which concluded with vespers. Then this great mass of Christians proceeded down to the city, singing "hymns and antiphons suitable to the day." They reached the gates when it was still dark, and some two hundred of them were supplied with candles. Moving on, the throng slowly made its way to the main church campus, passing through the city market, still singing, and on into the Martyrium.[129]

Public processions were also introduced to Roman church liturgy, although perhaps not as early as the fourth or fifth century. Rome developed a stational liturgy for the first Sunday in Advent through the end of Pentecost. On most stational Sundays, the people gathered at the specified church, but on weekdays during Lent, they assembled at a "collect" church for a liturgy of prayer; then they processed to the stational church. While the origins of Rome's stational liturgy are obscure, the sixth-century *Liber pontificalis* provides a hint when it states that Pope Hilarius (461–468) provided many sets of sacred vessels for the designated stational churches, including twenty-five goblets (*scyphi*), twenty-five flagons (*amae*), and fifty chalices, presumably to supply each of the twenty-five title churches in Rome.[130] Since this act of benefaction did not create the stational liturgy but only replaced the necessary Communion vessels, the liturgy itself may have predated the papacy of Hilarius. It is not known, however, whether the stational liturgy at that time included public processions through the streets

126. Egeria, *Itin.* 31.4.

127. The event is not a slavish imitation of the gospel stories, which do not precisely harmonize in any case. Morozowich argues that Egeria uses the word *typus* of the bishop's role (at 31.3, the only instance of the term in her journal), instead of saying that his role was *similiter*, because the procession was not meant to be a historical re-enactment. While this may over-read Egeria's word-choice, Morozowich's emphasis on the anamnetic purpose of the procession is well taken. Mark M. Morozowich, "Historicism and Egeria: Implications of *In eo typo*," *Ecclesia Orans* 27 (2010): 169–182.

128. Egeria, *Itin.*, 43.3 (tr. McGowan and Bradshaw, *The Pilgrimage of Egeria*, 185).

129. *Itin.*, 43.6–7. On the location, see McGowan and Bradshaw, *The Pilgrimage of Egeria*, 186, note on 43.7.

130. *Lib. pont.* 48.11 (Duchesne, I: 244).

from a collect church to a stational church on Lentin weekdays or, if so, whether these processions entailed psalmody.

Singular Instances of Spontaneous Public Christian Song

The examples of public Christian song discussed so far were institutionalized customs of the church. Occasionally, however, public Christian singing took place more spontaneously. And it could be that institutionalized customs fostered a habit among the people of taking to the streets in song in response to moments of great public trauma or joy.

After an earthquake at Antioch (or perhaps Constantinople), the people processed through the streets singing psalms, which John Chrysostom interpreted as an act of propitiation that saved the city from God's wrath.[131]

According to Eusebius, spontaneous public processions sprang up in 311 after the Edict of Recantation. This law, issued by a dying Galerius in the name of some or all the members of the imperial tetrarchy, banned state persecution of Christians.[132] As a result, those who had been sentenced to servitude in the mines were set free and allowed to return home.[133] They journeyed in masses, Eusebius says, and "praised God with songs and psalms" as they passed through the public streets and marketplaces.[134] Eusebius may have witnessed some of these parade-like returns of the liberated.

Men and women who had suffered the punishment of forced labor for refusing to betray their faith must have been especially devoted Christians. Many of them would have known at least some psalms by heart.[135] Hence, we can imagine that in addition to any improvised thanksgiving chants they might have sung, the homebound Christians engaged in responsorial psalmody. Those who knew psalms by heart would have sung the verses and their companions the refrains.

---

131. John Chrysostom, *Terr. mot.* (PG 50: 716), stating that the people's psalmody "removed" God's wrath.

132. Eusebius, *H.E.* 8.17.3–10.

133. Eusebius, *H.E.* 9.1.10.

134. Eusebius, *H.E.* 9.1.11.

135. According to Eusebius, Christians who were executed during the most severe persecutions sang hymns and thanksgivings right up to the last moments of torture (*H.E.* 8.9.5). This claim probably exaggerates, but its assumption that pious Christians could sing hymns and thanksgivings by heart must reflect what Eusebius knew about devout Christians in his day. In fact, Eusebius says that he himself witnessed some of the martyrdoms (*H.E.* 8.9.4).

At some point during John Chrysostom's tenure as bishop of Constantinople (397–404), the "Arians" of the city, who had been deprived of their church buildings, began holding open-air singing demonstrations on Saturdays and Sundays, as well as on feast days. They would stage their singing at night in public areas near the city gates. Then, in the morning, they would parade through the city streets, eventually exiting to go to their meeting places outside the walls. The sources call their singing "antiphonous" and say that they featured Arian formulas, as well as refrains that attacked the Nicene Christians.[136] In an effort to undermine the popularity of this Arian hymnody, John Chrysostom arranged for Christians of his own communion, who held the churches of the city, to form similar choirs. Backed by the Empress Eudoxia, the Nicene Christians processed through the city with greater splendor, carrying silver crosses and tapers, as they sang hymns with Trinitarian refrains.[137]

The Arian and Nicene singers inevitably encountered each other and on one occasion came to blows, which led the emperor to ban the Arians from singing publicly in the city. No similar restriction was placed on the Nicene Christians, who continued some version of their custom. This last detail is reported by Sozomen, who witnessed the practice in Constantinople in the 440s while he was writing his church history there.[138]

It is not clear whether it was psalms or hymns or both that the Homoean or the Nicene Christians sang, but the partisan nature of the singing suggests hymns composed to suit the respective propagandistic purposes of the two sides. It is also uncertain whether Sozomen's reference to the continuation of the custom in Constantinople means that the Christians there were still processing through the streets at night in Sozomen's time, carrying crosses and tapers as they sang. It is possible that he means no more than that the church continued the "antiphonous" style and used it for psalm-singing at their indoor vigils.

The Purposes and Functions of Public Psalmody

By the late fourth century, urban Christian bishops who were well educated and socially advantaged, especially those who served in cities with majority Christian populations and enjoyed considerable social authority, found themselves in a novel situation. Not only did they govern large Christian churches, they also

136. The meaning of "antiphonous" in this context is discussed in chapter 11.

137. These events are described by Socrates (*H.E.* 6.8) and Sozomen (*H.E.* 8.8), who uses Socrates as a source but may have had additional information from local tradition in Constantinople, where he lived in the 440s, when he wrote his history.

138. Sozomen, *H.E.* 8.8.5.

belonged to the ranks of "the old aristocrats, the civic officeholders, and the nouveaux riches in assuming a prominent position in society and a role of public leadership."[139] Capitalizing on popular enthusiasm for processions, they were able to use public parades as a means of displaying and reinforcing their new status,[140] pleasing the mass of Christians under their care, consolidating loyalty from them, and in some cases using parades to negotiate power relations with other Christian factions, even with emperors.

Organizing a martyr translation that had the look of an adventus afforded bishops an occasion to enhance the prestige of their city and to conduct a grand public event in which they themselves were central figures. Episcopal travel staged with the trappings of an adventus at one or more towns of the bishop's region also enhanced a bishop's public prestige. Mass psalmody in martyr processions and in episcopal advent parades was also a powerful instrument of social cohesion for the Christians who participated in them.

Bishops organized martyr translations, and Christian emperors sometimes ordered them. Yet the literary sources are mostly silent about imperial participation in martyr parades, whether by the sovereign himself, members of his family, or other imperial representatives. This is not surprising. An emperor is not likely to have participated in a martyr procession that moved over the course of many miles; he would have assigned himself a place of honor only during the final advent phase of such a translation and, even then, only when he was already in residence at the receiving city. According to the *Chronicon Paschale*, when the putative relics of the prophet Samuel were brought to Constantinople in 406, Emperor Arcadius Augustus led the way, along with other dignitaries.[141] We should probably assume that he was already in residence at the imperial city, not that he journeyed with the relics from Judea to Constantinople. Similarly, when the Empress Eudoxia participated in the translation of certain martyr relics to Drypia, a suburb of Constantinople, she was in residence at Constantinople.

The procession to Drypia afforded Eudoxia a rare opportunity to display imperial humility in a public way, and John gave her due praise for it. She was like the biblical Miriam, he says, who carried the bones of Joseph as she led the people

139. Claudia Rapp, "The Elite Status of Bishops in Late Antiquity in Ecclesiastical, Spiritual, and Social Contexts," *Arethusa* 33 (2000): 379.

140. Brown makes this observation in describing the social situation of bishops who controlled vast amounts of new church wealth in the early fifth century, particularly in the West (*The Cult of the Saints*, 40; see also n. 102 above). The situation must have obtained to some degree already in the late fourth century, given the socio-political status of bishops in cities such as Antioch and Constantinople in the East and Milan in the West, where significant power negotiations took place between bishops and emperors.

141. *Chron. Pasch.* For the year 406 (Indiction 4, year 12, in the 6th consulship of Arcadius Augustus and of Probus, following Olympiad 296) (Dindorf 1: 496).

of Israel in a procession after the exodus, while they sang a Hebrew hymn. Yet surpassing Miriam, Eudoxia "brought out innumerable choirs," which all sang the psalms of David in their own languages.[142] John does not imply that Eudoxia was a psalm leader or even that she joined in on the refrains. Instead, he interprets the psalmody as an act of homage to her, declaring that the choirs "crowned" her "with their prayers," which can only refer to the peoples' psalm-singing.[143]

Occasionally, a Christian procession broadcast a different set of relations between the church and the emperor. The translation of the relics of Babylas to Antioch, after Julian demanded their removal from Daphne, entailed a psalmodic protest against the emperor. And the translation of the martyrs Gervasius and Protasius in Milan in 386, which publicized Ambrose's success in honoring the City of Milan with newly discovered martyrs, may have symbolized, at least tacitly, his successful resistance to imperial authority in the battle for the basilicas.

The participation of monks in processional psalmody is a revealing aspect of the history of Christian psalm-singing. Many monks recited psalms in the same way that they meditated other Scriptures, without melody, perhaps in many cases using a monotonal rhythmic chant that aided their effort to concentrate on the sense of the words and maintain their rule of prayer without ceasing. But when they joined an episcopal adventus, participated in a martyr translation, or conducted their dead to the grave, they sang in a tuneful way, because on these occasions the psalms served a ceremonial role.

Processional psalmody often honored not only God but certain human beings. In a funeral procession, psalm-singing paid homage to the deceased; in martyr processions, it paid homage to the martyr; and in episcopal advent processions, it paid homage to the visiting bishop. John Chrysostom suggested that Eudoxia was "crowned" with the psalm-singing of the people.

Mass public singing in episcopal processions and martyr translations united the Christians of a city and its surrounding villages, drawing in people from multiple congregations and more than one language group. Indeed, the singing throng of a martyr parade was as large a body of Christians as one might ever have encountered at a single event. On these rare occasions, the Christians of a

142. John Chrysostom, *Hom. dicta post. reliq. martyr.* 3 (PG 63: 472). According to Exod 13:19 and Josh 24:32, at the time of the exodus, Moses and the people of Israel carried the bones of Joseph out of Egypt. John pictures Miriam carrying these bones, when she and Moses led the Israelites in a victory song (Exod 15:20–21), after the people had passed safely through the sea and the pursuing Egyptian army had drowned.

143. Καὶ διάφορα ἔθνη καὶ διαφόρους χοροὺς ἦν ἰδεῖν μίαν κιθάραν ἅπαντας ἔχοντας, τὴν τοῦ Δαυΐδ, καὶ ταῖς εὐχαῖς σε [Eudoxia] στεφανοῦντας. Although Christian writers distinguished psalms and prayers as a practical matter when describing the elements of a given liturgy, they otherwise conceived psalmody as a form of prayer. References to psalms/psalmody as prayer are found throughout the Christian literature of the first four centuries (see chapter 6).

region experienced collective identity in a vivid way, all singing the same refrains with one voice and being electrified by the heightened emotion of the occasion. Jerome describes a martyr translation as "one united swarm of people [moving] from Palestine to Chalcedon."[144] John Chrysostom pictures "a massive torch-carrying throng, practically the entire population," flowing in a long "river of fire"[145] from Hagia Sophia in Constantinople down to the martyrium of the Apostle Thomas at Drypia. These accounts give us an idea of how impressive a martyr procession appeared to its participants and any onlookers. Moreover, beyond how such a procession appeared, there was the continuous sound of the mass psalmody, the soaring high voice of the soloist[146] and the thunder of the refrains.

144. See above with n. 19.

145. See above with n. 73.

146. Adolescents typically performed psalm readings in this era. It is conceivable that for a special event, such as a martyr procession, a group of young cantors sang together, having memorized the psalm to a fixed melody, so as to ensure a beautiful unison rendering of the verses in a volume that could be clearly heard. Or urban monks might have assumed such a role.

CHAPTER TEN

Formats

ANCIENT CHRISTIAN REFERENCES to psalm-singing rarely specify the formats of performance. In modern scholarship, several expressions are used to distinguish arrangements: direct, responsorial, antiphonal, and alternating. Direct (or *in directum*) refers to singing straight through without responses, whether one person sings or a group does so in unison. Responsorial means any arrangement where a leader performs the verses and some number of others sing a response, whether a refrain or a final answer to the psalmer. Antiphonal refers to two choirs trading the verses of a song, whether lines or larger units.

Formats of Christian Psalmody in the Second and Third Centuries

The earliest hint about a format for singing at a church meeting is Paul's statement that if someone blesses in a tongue—whether in speaking or singing—and another person is not in a position to understand, the uncomprehending person will not be able to say "amen."[1] Since there is no hint that this "amen" was also sung, the sung blessing was direct solo song. It was not biblical psalmody, however, since the words were chosen by the singer, who was thought to speak under the inspiration of the Spirit.

Apart from an obscure statement about Christians in one of Pliny's letters to Trajan,[2] further information about song formats does not appear again until remarks by Clement of Alexandria and Tertullian more than a hundred years later. Both speak of individual singing by turns at Christian suppers. Christian "toasts of song," as Clement called them, included psalms,[3] and the singing "from Scripture" that Tertullian describes would also have included them.[4] Neither Tertullian nor Clement mentions responses to sympotic Christian psalm-singing,

1. 1 Cor 14:16.

2. Pliny, *Ep.* 10.96. It is not clear whether *carmen* in this passage refers to a song, an oath, or a confession. It is addressed "to Christ as if to a god," and is said or sung "by turns (*dicere secum invicem*).

3. Clement of Alexandria, *Paed.* 2.4.44.3; *Str.* 6.11.90.1. See the discussion in chapter 2.

4. Tertullian, *Apol.* 39.18.

but a response is mentioned by Tertullian when he describes the habit of some Christians to add "an Alleluia to their prayers, specifically that kind of psalm to which those present respond at the endings."[5] Just what the word "endings" refers to is unclear, whether the responders sang Alleluia as a recurring refrain or intoned it only once as a concluding response. The plural offers no clue, sense "endings" could mean the endings of lines or the endings of Alleluia psalms.

There is an indirect clue in the anonymous *Homily on the Psalms*, when it describes the performance format used by David and his fellow singers. When one had finished singing, the others intoned "Alleluia" in response.[6] Since this picture of Davidic psalmody has no basis in the psalms themselves and is not mentioned in ancient Jewish literature (which makes no reference to either the use of Alleluia by David and his fellow singers or to such a practice in Jewish psalmody), one suspects that the homilist was influenced by Christian custom. The same goes for the two similar descriptions of the Davidic composition process that have come down under the name of Eusebius, although one of them is not independent but shows cribbing from the anonymous *Homily*.[7] In any case, between the evidence in Tertullian and these descriptions, we have good reason to think that, by the third century, Christians in some places in both the East and the West had begun using Alleluia as a psalm response. The indirect testimony from the Christian descriptions of the original inspired psalm composition suggests a final Alleluia, not a refrain.

No other references to psalmody in Christian writings from the second and third century refer to responses, not even Cyprian's *Letter to Donatus*, which envisions Donatus taking up the duty of psalm-singing at a private Christian dinner party.[8] Formats of psalmody at Easter vigils may be implied by Eusebius when he claims that the singing described in Philo's account of certain festive vigils of the Therapeutae closely resembles the singing of the church at the Paschal vigil. Eusebius paraphrases Philo as follows: "while one chants with regular rhythm, the others, listening to the hymns in silence, join in by sounding forth the endings."[9] This probably means that the people chimed in by singing refrains at the end of each line or group of lines.[10] Eusebius thought

5. Tertullian, *Orat.* 27 (*clausulis respondeant*).

6. See the discussion of the anonymous *Homily on the Psalms* in chapter 3. The same interpretation is given by the author of the short essay, "Eusebius of Caesaria Concerning the *Diapsalma*," which may depend on the anonymous homily (PG 23: 76).

7. Again, see the discussion in chapter 3.

8. Cyprian, *Don.* 16 (also discussed in chapter 3).

9. Eusebius, *H.E.* 2.17.22.

10. See below under "Endings."

the Therapeutae must have been Christians because the church of his own time sang in the same fashion.

Formats of Psalmody in the Fourth and Fifth Centuries

Evidence for psalmody increases in the latter half of the fourth century, and detail about its formats becomes more abundant, too. Significantly, to the extent that the sources are explicit about formats, they indicate that the responsorial method was common for group psalmody in both churches and certain monasteries. Direct psalmody by a group is not explicitly attested.[11] Dual-chorus psalmody is well-attested for vigils, but antiphonal dual-choir singing with the choirs trading verses is nowhere expressly attested. It is important to keep in mind that dual choral psalmody with the groups trading the verses would have been a form of trading by direct psalmody, in which case each group had to be capable of singing the psalm *in directum*. In other words, both direct psalmody and antiphonal psalmody would have required the same competence—knowing the psalm by heart and how to sing it in unison according to the same melody (or the same melodic formula). That would have required choir practice. Significantly, in passages in fourth- and fifth-century literature where dual-choir Christian singing is described, a responsorial format is always an interpretive possibility.

Psalm Verses as Refrains

After Eusebius's remarks about the Therapeutae, which he penned in the early fourth century, the next reference to psalm responses appears in Athanasius's account of his flight from Alexandria in 356. When soldiers surrounded the church during a vigil, Athanasius instructed the deacon "to read a psalm and the people to answer, 'For his mercy is forever.'"[12] This is the first explicit reference to the use of a psalm verse as a response. Athanasius may have meant Psalm 135, where the words he quotes are repeated three times at the beginning and then after every line. But it is possible that the line, which appears in several lyrical contexts in the Jewish Bible, was used by Christians as a generic refrain, suitable for use with many psalms.

A number of John Chrysostom's sermons suggest that congregational responses were standard for psalmody in Antioch and/or Constantinople during the years 386 to 407. In one sermon, John criticizes the complacency of Christians who, "after responding to two or three hymns and performing the

11. The evidence is examined below under "Direct Choral Psalmody."

12. Athanasius, *Apol. pro fug.* 24 (SC 56: 234).

customary prayers carelessly and thoughtlessly," leave church thinking they have done "what suffices for salvation."[13] In a homily on Psalm 41, he mentions that the people had just sung Psalm 41:1 as the response to the psalm lesson.[14] In a homily on Psalm 117, he speaks of verse 24 as the people's "verse of responding."[15] In a Palm Sunday sermon, he refers to Psalm 145:2 and invites the congregation to "cry out these words, which we sang today."[16] And in a homily on Psalm 144, he identifies verse 15 as a Communion refrain, "which those initiated into the mysteries continuously sing in response."[17] These sermonic remarks provide explicit evidence of psalmody with repeated congregational responses, that is, refrains as opposed to final responses.

John further recommends what appears to be responsorial psalmody for households at mealtime. Husbands, he says, should teach psalmody to their children, and families should sing psalms before and after dining.[18] He gives an example: "And let us stand and say, 'You have made us happy, Lord, in your work, and in the works of your hands we will rejoice'" (Ps 90:5).[19] The specification of a verse that is not the first line (which might have been used to name the psalm) probably implies a refrain. John goes on to draw a contrast between this after-supper psalmody and what other men do by hiring "mimes, dancers, and female prostitutes." This shows that his comments are directed especially to educated men of means, those who could afford not only professional home entertainment but books, including a psalter. It is notable that John pictures the family standing to sing at the conclusion of the meal, which implies that the singing is not a form of leisurely after-supper recreation. It is a final act before departure, like an after-supper prayer.

---

13. John Chrysostom, *In Matt.*, Hom. 11.7 (PG 57: 200; Field, *Hom. in Matt.* 1: 149).

14. *In psalm. 41* 1 (PG 55: 155). This example and those quoted below can be conveniently reviewed in English translation in *MECL* §§163, 170, 172, 175 on church psalmody, together with §166, and §167 on domestic psalmody.

15. *In psalm. 117* 1 (PG 55: 328).

16. *Hom. hab. in magn. Hebd.* 2 (PG 55: 520).

17. *In psalm. 144* 1 (PG 55: 464).

18. *In psalm. 41* 2 (PG 55: 157). "It is necessary to erect a defense from the psalms against [the devil] both before and after the meal, and, after rising from the banquet (συμποσίου) with one's wife and children, to sing sacred hymns to God." The example he goes on to give shows that by "hymns" he means "psalms." The plural may be stylistic (see the discussion of the rhetoric of plurals in chapter 6). Regarding the Hellenistic and Roman eras, συμπόσιον, while still a term for a post-supper drinking party, was also quite commonly used to designate the social meal as a whole.

19. *In psalm. 41* 2 (PG 55: 158).

I have been giving examples from Eastern Christianity. The traditional view about when responsorial psalmody reached the West depends on an oft-quoted passage in Augustine's *Confessions.* In Book 9, he rehearses his recollections about song at Milan and what it meant to him during the days after his baptism (at Easter in 387). First, he describes how moved he was by the singing of the church. Then he backtracks, remarking that "not long ago, the Milanese church began to practice (*celebrare*) that type of consolation and encouragement of brothers and sisters singing with great zeal in voice and heart." He amplifies this statement by recalling the "Arian crisis"[20] in Milan (385/386), when Empress Justina, mother of the youthful king Valentinian, "persecuted" Ambrose. The conflict culminated in a contest over one or more basilicas. Justina had sent troops to claim a building, and pious members of Ambrose's congregation "camped out in the church, ready to die with their bishop." Augustine's own mother was there, he says, "having a chief share of the anxiety and wakeful watchings (*vigiliarum*)."[21] Augustine mentions the congregational singing, expanding on his earlier comment about his own experience of song at Milan:

> At that time, it was established that hymns and psalms should be sung according to the *morem* of the eastern regions, so that the people might not grow weary with sorrow and tedium. [The practice[22]] has been retained from then until today and has been imitated by many, indeed by almost all your congregations throughout the rest of the world.[23]

Augustine does not define the Eastern form of singing, and his only clues are the vague term "*more,*" the historical situation in Milan, the worldwide spread of the custom, and its particular purpose in relation to the situation in Mila, which he states twice: for "consolation and encouragement" and so that "the people might not grow weary with sorrow and tedium." Both expressions aptly describe what psalm-singing offered people who were camped out in a basilica and had to endure tedious hours of waiting, punctuated by moments of high anxiety. As for the meaning of "*morem* of the eastern regions," the word *morem* (from "*mos*") means "manner/way" or "custom/practice," and its use in this passage

20. The framing of the event by Ambrose and others on his side (including Augustine) as an attack fomented by Arians may distort the facts. See Michael S. Williams, "No Arians in Milan? Ambrose on the Basilica Crisis of 385/6," *Historia* 67 (2018): 346–365.

21. Augustine, *Conf.* 9.7.15.

22. The subject of this sentence is unexpressed.

23. Augustine, *Conf.* 9.7.15.

has often been understood as referring to the "manner"[24] of the singing, whether "antiphonal," as some historians of liturgy have thought, or "responsorial," as others have argued.[25]

It is very unlikely that the novelty in Milan was antiphonal psalm-singing. If there was a prevailing Eastern format of psalmody in this period, it was responsorial, not antiphonal. As for the West, none of the Western writers speak explicitly of antiphonal singing, while they do make unambiguous references to responsorial psalmody. Ambrose himself does.[26]

Was the novelty, then, simply congregational psalmody? Probably not. In a commentary on the psalms composed in around 365, Hilary of Poitiers refers to church psalmody at morning and evening prayer, writing as if it were a well-known practice.[27] With respect to evidence of congregational singing in works of Ambrose that predate the battle over the basilicas, there happens to be at least one. In his homiletic treatise *Cain and Abel*, composed shortly after 375, Ambrose addresses those who enjoy banquet songs, saying, "Listen to *the voice of the church*, which (exhorts us) not only in songs but in the Song of Songs, 'Eat, friends, and drink and get intoxicated, my brothers and sisters' [Song 5:1]."[28] Although it would be over-reading to infer that Ambrose's church sang Song of Songs at Communion or anywhere else, the first, general part of the assertion, the church exhorting "in songs," suggests practices of congregational singing.

The term *morem* in the expression "according to the *morem* of the eastern regions" need not be interpreted as "manner" in the sense of how a psalm was sung congregationally, but can be taken very naturally to mean "custom,"[29] in which

---

24. James McKinnon translates "manner" (*MEC*L no. 351); so does Maria Boulding in *The Confessions*, ed. John Rotelle (New City Press, 1997), 221.

25. In a thorough study of references to psalmody in Ambrose, Helmut Leeb concludes that Augustine's remark—*hymni et psalmi ut canerentur secundum morem orientalium partium*—probably refers to the introduction of responsorial psalmody at Milan. See Helmut Leeb, *Die Psalmodie bei Ambrosius* (Herder, 1967), 111 (summarizing the results of his study). For general discussions of liturgical song/psalms in Ambrose, see also Josef Schmitz, *Gottesdienst im altchristlichen Mailand* (Hanstein, 1975), 303–315; H. J. Auf der Maur, *Das Psalmenverständnis des Ambrosius von Mailand* (Brill, 1977), 326–328.

26. Ambrose, *Expl. psalm. 45* 15 (PL 14: 1140-1141; CSEL 64: 340); *Expos. euang. Luc.* 7.238 (PL 15: 1763; CSEL 32/4: 388); *Hex.* 3.5.23 (PL 14: 165; CSEL 32/1: 75); *Ep.* 76.20 and 24 (CSEL 82: 120 and 123). See Leeb, *Die Psalmodie bei Ambrosius*, 53–62.

27. See chapter 9 n. 96.

28. Ambrose, *Cain et Ab.* 1.5.19 (CSEL 32/1: 355).

29. Henry Chadwick, for example, translates *morem* as "custom" in *Saint Augustine, Confessions: A New Translation* (Oxford University Press, 1991), 165.

case the custom may have been the song-filled vigils of the East. Paul Bradshaw points out that vigils of this sort met resistance as novelties in the late fourth and early fifth centuries.[30] According to Basil, the clergy of Neocaesarea objected to "the psalmody and a type of singing" in his church, which, they said, departed from customs that had prevailed since the time of Gregory Thaumaturgis (bishop of Neocaesarea in the mid-third century).[31] It is not clear what they objected to in the singing, perhaps that it was not austere enough. Basil clarifies the dispute when he goes on to characterize the practices as "the staying up all night and the prayers and the psalmody in common," which had become nearly universal in the East, he insists.[32] Niceta of Remesiana (c. 335–c. 414) was similarly compelled to defend vigils that lasted "for part of the night" on Saturdays and Sundays, because certain people "consider sacred vigils . . . filled with prayers, hymns, and holy reading, to be superfluous, otiose, or, what is worse, unbecoming."[33] It is worth noting that the city of Remesiana stood on "the main highway between Western Europe and Constantinople"[34] and was thus situated in a border district between East and West, where Niceta's Latin-speaking church counted itself as Western and was closely affiliated with Italian Christianity.[35] Niceta's defense of vigils suggests that they were first introduced when he was bishop in Remesiana, perhaps in the final decades of the fourth century.[36]

In a letter to his sister Marcellina, Ambrose commented about events that occurred during his extended conflict with Empress Justina. The year of the

---

30. Paul F. Bradshaw, *Daily Prayer in the Early Church: A Study of the Origin and Early Development of the Divine Office* (Oxford University Press, 1982), 113–114.

31. Basil, *Ep.* 207.2 and 207.4. See the discussion in chapter 7.

32. *Ep.* 207.3.

33. Niceta of Remesiana, *Vig.*1; tr. Gerald G. Walsh, "Writings of Niceta of Remesiana," in *The Fathers of the Church: A New Translation*, vol. 7 (The Catholic University of America, 1949), 56. Niceta goes on to mention Saturday and Sunday as the vigil days (*Vig.* 3).

34. Andrew E. Burn, ed., *Niceta of Remesiana: His Life and Works* (Cambridge University Press, 1905), xix.

35. Burn points this out: "The Illyrian bishops, through their metropolitans and primate, acknowledged the patriarchal authority of the bishops of Rome. The personal relations of Niceta himself with Italy are a proof of the solidarity of Latin-speaking Illyricum with the cities of Latin Christianity. And in one passage of his *de psalmodiae bono* [*Util. hymn.* 2] he speaks of the Easterns [*sic*] in a phrase which proves that he classed [*sic*] his hearers with the Western Church." Burn, *Niceta of Remesiana*, xxii.

36. Burn estimates Nicetas's lifespan as circa 335–414 (*Niceta of Remesiana*, xxxv). He notes that a copy of Niceta's *On Vigils* was preserved among the letters of Jerome "and may have come to his notice when he was staying in Constantinople in 381 or later on in Rome" (which Jerome left in 385) (*Niceta of Remesiana*, lxxxv).

letter is disputed, however, the two most plausible possibilities being 386 (the time of the first crisis precipitated by Justina) and Holy Week of the year prior (when a similar contest for one or more basilicas may have taken place).[37] The letter pictures the people loyal to Ambrose spontaneously going to basilicas to hold them against the attempts of soldiers to lay claim to them. While Ambrose preaches at one of the churches, the people occupying a different basilica demand his presence.[38] At one point he leads a morning service where the people sing a politically apt psalm responsorially.[39] On the succeeding day, when soldiers surround one of the basilicas in question, he performs psalms with the faithful in a small chapel of that church.[40] This last description must be an instance of what Augustine heard from his mother about "that type of consolation and encouragement of brothers and sisters singing with great zeal in voice and heart," whether Ambrose's letter refers to events of 386 or of the prior year. In either case, it is easy to imagine that the congregants who staged the spontaneous vigils were emotionally sustained by the singing and that the experience was so galvanizing and successful that, once the immediate crisis was over, song-filled vigils became a tradition in Milan.

A last witness to the subject is Paulinus, Ambrose's biographer. Paulinus writes that during the struggle with Justina, "antiphons,[41] hymns, and vigils first began to be practiced in the Milanese church,"[42] a "practice" (*celebritatis*), he says, that spread to other parts of the West. Evidently, Paulinus understood that vigils were part of the novelty.

Although Paulinus may not have been living in Milan in the mid-380s, he assisted Ambrose during the final years of the bishop's life,[43] and he was present in 395/396 when Ambrose had the relics of a certain martyr removed from a

37. The debate over the question of the letter's date is rehearsed in Michael S. Williams, *The Politics of Heresy in Ambrose of Milan: Community and Consensus in Late Antique Christianity* (Cambridge University Press, 2017), 227–232. Against the current consensus, Williams sides with Barnes's 385 dating.

38. Ambrose, *Ep.* 76.4, 20 (CSEL 82:109–110, 119).

39. *Ep.* 76.20 (CSEL 82: 120). The psalm lesson was either fortuitous, in light of the circumstances, or chosen in the moment. The response was "O God, the heathen (*gentes*) have come into your inheritance," which he took to be prophetic, commenting to his sister, "In fact, the heathen did come."

40. *Ep.* 76.24 (CSEL 82: 123).

41. Regarding the meaning of the term "antiphon," see chapter 11.

42. Paulinus, *Vit. Ambr.* 13.3 (PL 14: 31; Navoni, 71, 73).

43. Paulinus, *Vit. Ambr.* 42 (PL 14: 42; Navoni, 124).

grave and interred in a church.[44] Moreover, when he composed his biography of Ambrose he was with Augustine. He may have learned about the vigils from Ambrose or Augustine or from Augustine's *Confessions*.[45]

Augustine's sermons show evidence of responsorial psalmody—not in the 380s but in the surviving body of his sermons from the period of his episcopate (395–430) and possibly from his initial service as a priest (391–395). In a number of his sermons (few of which can be dated even approximately), he happens to mention that the congregation responded to a psalm reading, and in almost every instance he quotes the refrain. The relevant passages are the following:[46]

Sermon 20: "We have just now responded: 'Hear my prayer and my petition, O Lord!' etc. [Ps 38:13]."[47]

*Sermon 22A: "We have responded, 'My God, save me. . .' [Ps. 71:4]. Perhaps each of you, when you hear these words from the reader or respond yourself. . ."[48]

Probably Sermon 25A: "We have sung to the Lord, 'Blessed is the one whom you instruct, Lord, and whom you teach from your law. . .' [Ps 93:12–13]."[49]

---

44. Paulinus, *Vit. Ambr.* 32.3 (PL 14: 38; Navoni, 108).

45. Paulinus's account is very similar to that of the *Confessions* and manifests the same structure. He states that the practice first arrived in Milan at the time of the conflict with Justina; then he adds that it spread from Milan throughout the West.

46. I owe my examples to McKinnon's assiduous search of Augustine's sermons. See James McKinnon, "Liturgical Psalmody in the Sermons of St. Augustine: An Introduction," in *The Study of Medieval Chant: Paths and Bridges, East and West: In Honor of Kenneth Levy*, ed. Peter Jeffery (Boydell, 2011), 10 (7–24) and Table 1.3, pp. 20-24. McKinnon identifies nine sermons in which Augustine explicitly mentions a verse that the congregation sang in response to a psalm reading, and he lists ten additional places where contextual evidence makes it likely that Augustine quotes such a response verse ("Liturgical Psalmody in the Sermons of Augustine," 10 with tables 1.1a and 1.1b). He does not include Augustine's sermon on Psalm 119 in Table 1.1a because it mentions responding but not the verse. For some reason, the Alleluia response mentioned in Augustine's sermon on Psalm 113 does not appear in his tables, but McKinnon notes this passage in his "Preface to the Study of the Alleluia," *Early Music History* 15 (1996): 219.

47. *Serm.* 20 1 (Denis) (PL 46: 898).

48. *Serm.* 22A (Mai 13) 1 (CCL 41:303). For clarity, I have translated the generic third-person language following *Fortasse unusquisque uestrum* into the second person.

49. *Serm.* 25A (Morin 12) 1 (CCL 41: 341). The psalm quotation consists of four cola. Questioning whether the congregation would have sung all of it as a refrain, McKinnon omits this instance from his lists of certain or probable quotations of congregational responses and points to it as a reason for caution against assuming that in each case where Augustine says,

Sermon 29A: "What the Holy Spirit has counseled us in the voice of the psalm [Ps 117], to which we have responded 'Alleluia' with one mouth and heart. . ."[50]

Sermon 30: (ca. 412-416): "Let us see, then, when it is that iniquity masters a person, so that we may understand what we heard him praying for, and what we too have been praying for ourselves, by making the response. We all, I imagine, responded (*respondimus*) with devout and truthful minds to the holy psalm, as we prayed and said to the Lord our God, 'Direct my steps according to your word, and let not any iniquity master me' [Ps 118:133]."[51] Later in the same sermon and referring to the same verse, Augustine asks, "Did you sing these words today or not?"[52]

*Sermon 81 (on Matt 18:7-9): ". . . what, listening and responding, we have sung (*etiam quod audiendo et respondendo cantauimus*): 'Yet the meek shall possess the earth as an inheritance and shall delight in abundance of peace' [Ps 36:11]."[53]

Sermon 153 (on Rom 7:5-13; delivered October 13, 419): "We have listened, and we have responded in one accord, and we have sung to our God with resounding voice, 'Blessed is the one whom you discipline, O Lord; and you teach him from your law' [Ps 93:12]."[54]

Sermon 306: "As we heard and sang, making the response, 'Precious is the death of the saints' [Ps 115:15]."[55]

"we have sung," a refrain is implied ("Liturgical Psalmody in the Sermons of Augustine," 11). I imagine that the people sang the first pair of cola (which I have quoted) and that Augustine added the next pair of lines for sermonic reasons. The sermon's CCL editor, Cyril Lambot, interpreted all four cola as a response, but the heading in his edition, which categorizes them in that way, is not in the ninth-century manuscript. Compare CCL 41: 341 with G. Morin "Deux nouveaux sermons retrouvés de saint Augustin," *Revue Bénédictine* 36 (1924): 187.

50. *Serm.* 29A 1 (CCL 41: 378).

51. *Serm.* 30.1 (PL 38: 187-188; CCL 41: 382); tr. adapted from Edmund Hill, tr., *The Works of Augustine for the Twenty-First Century,* Part 3/2: *Sermons (20-50) on the Old Testament,* ed. John E. Rotelle (New City Press, 1990), 123. On the date of the sermon, see Hill 3/2: 129 n. 1.

52. *Serm.* 30.8 (CCL 41: 387).

53. *Serm.* 81.1 (PL 38: 499).

54. *Serm.* 153.1 (PL 38: 825). On the date, see Edmund Hill, *The Works of Augustine for the Twenty-First Century: Sermons on the New Testament,* Part 3/5: *Sermons 148–183,* ed. John E. Rotelle (New City Press, 1992), 57 and 66 n. 1.

55. *Serm.* 306.1 (PL 38: 1400) in a sermon delivered at a martyr feast.

*Sermon 352 (on Ps 50; ca. 396-400): "The voice of the penitent is recognized in the words that we have responded to the singer (*uerbis quibus psallenti respondimus*): 'Turn your face from my sins, and expunge all my iniquities' [Ps 50:11] . . . In fact, we did not command the lector to sing this psalm; but that one, in his young boy's heart, judged what would be valuable for you to hear and commanded it."[56]

*Sermon on Psalm 40: "First, what we sang, when we responded to the reader, although it is in the middle of the psalm, we will nevertheless take up in the beginning of our sermon: 'My enemies have said evil things about me: when will he die and when will his name perish?' [Ps 40:6]."[57]

Sermon on Psalm 113: ". . . this psalm [Ps 113] to which we have now responded by singing 'Alleluia.'"[58]

Sermon on Psalm 119: "The psalm [Ps 119] that we have just now heard sung and have responded to in singing is short and beneficial."[59]

The sermons marked with * make very explicit that the response was taken from the psalm lesson. In some cases, a reference to congregational singing of a certain verse and the congregation's *hearing* of a different verse from the same psalm implies that the refrain was taken from the psalm lesson. For example, in Sermon 47 Augustine refers to Psalm 94:6 as the verse that the congregation has just sung, and later, in the same sermon, he reminds them of a different verse from Psalm 94 that they had heard (v. 2).[60] In other words, they had heard the lector sing this verse. Moreover, it is likely that in other sermons where Augustine mentions a verse that the congregation sang but does not speak explicitly of "responding," that verse, too, was a refrain. And while it cannot be ruled out that occasionally the refrain was taken from a psalm that was not the lesson or that the refrain was a nonpsalmic formula, Augustine gives no evidence of that.

---

56. *Serm.* 352.1 (PL 39: 1549-1550). On the date, see Edmund Hill, *The Works of Augustine for the Twenty-First Century*, Part 3/10: *Sermons 341–500*, ed. John E. Rotelle (New City Press, 1995), 149 n. 1 (citing Fischer, Kunzelmann, and van Bavel). In his translation, Hill takes *ille* ("that one") as a reference to God who commands the boy lector, inwardly, to choose the psalm (p. 137).

57. *Enarr. in psalm. 40* 1 (PL 36: 453; CCL 38: 447).

58. *Enarr. in psalm. 113* 1 (CCL 41: 1635).

59. *Enarr. in psalm. 119* 1 (PL 37: 1596; CCL 40: 1776).

60. *Serm.* 47 1, 8 (CCL 41: 572, 579).

Selecting the refrain from the psalm lesson itself may not have been as common in other locales. The line that Athanasius chose as a refrain during the vigil where the soldiers besieged the old church of Alexandria appears at various places in the Jewish Bible and might have been treated as a freestanding refrain, suitable to multiple psalms. And in a sermon on Psalm 45, Ambrose says, "What was sung today as a response to the psalm greatly strengthens our point, 'With anticipation I waited for the Lord, and he was attentive to me.'"[61] This verse is from Psalm 39, not Psalm 45. It is difficult to imagine that Psalm 45 was not sung as a lesson for a service at which Ambrose preached on Psalm 45. Either there were two psalm lessons that day, or Psalm 39:2 was used as the response for Psalm 45. Moreover, the Armenian Lectionary, although it was compiled much later, shows the use of a single refrain for a set of psalms (see below).

It is possible that psalm lessons were sometimes performed by the lector *in directum* (that is, without refrains), depending on the setting. McKinnon speculates that this might have been customary on penitential occasions, including the somber period of Lent, when a responsorial format could have seemed too festive to some bishops.[62] Yet he points out in an earlier essay that "the overwhelming impression created by the evidence from the patristic period" is that psalm lessons were sung responsorially, "even on penitential occasions."[63] The same is true for the psalmody of the daily office at church. By contrast, solo psalmody *in directum* was practiced at certain corporate services in monasteries of Egypt, according to John Cassian.[64]

"Endings"

The *Apostolic Constitutions* uses the word *akrostichia* for what the people say in response to psalms: "After two readings, let someone else sing the hymns of David; let the people sing the endings (*akrostichia*) in response."[65] In the history of the Greek language, *akrostichion* is a late word and occurs at least once as an alternate spelling (or misspelling) of the word "acrostics."[66] It is likely that the

61. Ambrose, *In psalm. 45* 15 (PL 14: 1140-1141; CSEL 64: 340).

62. McKinnon, "Liturgical Psalmody in the Sermons of Augustine," 14.

63. McKinnon, "Preface to the Study of the Alleluia," 223.

64. John Cassian, *Inst.* 2.10–12.

65. *Const. ap.* 2.57.5–6.

66. The feminine noun ἀκροστιχίς meant "acrostic," and *Sib. Or.* 8.249 uses the dative plural ἀκροστιχίοις to mean "acrostics;" compare also Eusebius's reference to *Sibyllene Oracles'* ΙΧΘΥΣ-acrostic (Eusebius, *Constantini imper. orat.* 18.2).

AC uses the term functionally, referring to the responses that the people make as "endings" to the verses sung by the lector. That is, the placement is what makes these responses "endings."[67]

A different but etymologically related term, *akroteleution*, appears in Philo's account of the Therapeutae's singing, where he writes that while a member of the sect is singing a hymn at the sect's festive banquet, the rest keep silent, except when it is necessary for them to sing "the endings (*akroteleutia*) and responses (*ephymnia*)."[68] In the contexts of rhetoric and poetry, *akroteleution* was sometimes used for the end of a speech, letter, oracle, poem or section of a poem, or even of a line.[69] Just what Philo meant is uncertain, but when Eusebius—who believed that the Therapeutae were Christians and that this passage describes festive church song—paraphrases Philo's sentence, he reduces "*akroteleutia* and *ephymnia*" to simply "*akroteleutia*," which makes pretty clear that he took the two words to be synonyms.[70] And more than a century later, Sozomen uses the expression in describing Arian song. They would add "endings (*akroteleutia*) composed to their view,"[71] which, again, could mean refrains.

Alleluia

The word "Alleluia" (*Allēlouia*) is a Greek transliteration of a Hebrew expression. Fourth-century divines offered opinions about its meaning. Eusebius defines Alleluia as "Praise the Lord" and says that when this word appears in a superscription, it means that what follows (the body of the psalm) should lead to

67. The *AC* passage is the earliest instance of a use of the term for responsorial singing and may reflect churchly coinage, which evolved to where the neuter term was supplanted by ἀκροστιχίς, with which it was easily confused (see n. 66), as a word for "response/refrain." Note that in the sixth century, a vita of Marcel the Archimandrite uses ἀκροστιχίς as a term for a response; there are additional similar examples in other Byzantine literatures.

68. Philo, *Contempl.* 80.

69. Philo uses the word in another place for the closing sentences of God's speech to Abraham in Genesis 26 (Philo, *Quis rer.* 8). Eusebius uses it for a closing declaration of one of Paul's letters (Eusebius, *Comm. in psalm.*, on Ps. 103 [PG 23: 1293], quoting 1 Cor 16:22). A commentary on the psalms dubiously attributed to Origen uses ἀκροτελεύτιον for the last verse of a biblical psalm ("Lord of the powers, happy is the person who hopes in you"—Ps 83:13). See Origen, *Frag. in psalm.*, on Ps. 83:13 (Pitra 2: 145). The grammarian Phrynichus says that "the ἀκροτελεύτιον of verse is the last part of a poetical section" (Phrynichus, *Praep. Soph.*, *fr.* 14). The orator Aelius Aristides (or an interpolator) uses the word for the end of a Homeric line (*Od.* 4.386). See Aelius Aristides, *Or.* 2(Πρὸς Πλάτωνα περὶ ῥητορικῆς).426 (Lenz and Behr; Dindorf, 107).

70. Eusebius, *H.E.* 2.17.22.

71. Sozomen, *H.E.* 8.8.1–3.

glorifying God.[72] Gregory of Nyssa, also defining Alleluia as "Praise the Lord," notes that psalms with this title are found in the last part of the Psalter (Book 5), where praise is the theme.[73] Athanasius says that Alleluia means "praise to the Eternal."[74] The fact that these interpreters deem it necessary to explain the word implies either that their audiences were not familiar with it as a common liturgical expression or, more probably, that they were accustomed to its liturgical use but did not know what it meant.

It is not clear what first inspired Alleluia responses, and there may have been more than one impetus. Christians who studied the places where Alleluia appears in the Psalter would have noticed its presence in quite a few superscriptions and once at the close of a psalm.[75] The only other instances in the Septuagint occur in Tobit and 3 Maccabees. In Tobit, the word appears in a description of public exultation, preserved in two versions.[76] Neither represents Alleluia as a response to a song. Instead, both versions characterize it as a cry or shout of jubilation:

> Short version (Vaticanus, Alexandrinus, and most other major manuscripts): "And all her streets will say 'Alleluia,' and will utter praise and will say 'Blessed be God, who has exalted all the ages!" Tob 13:18

> Long version (Sinaiticus): "And the gates of Jerusalem shall sing songs of exultation, and all her houses shall say "Alleluia, Blessed be the God of Israel!" And the blessed shall bless his holy name forever." Tob 13:18

Presumably the author of Tobit was familiar with "Alleluia" as a praise shout.[77]

---

72. Eusebius, *Comm in psalm. 104* (commenting on the superscription of Psalm 104) (PG 23: 1296).

73. Gregory of Nyssa, *Inscr. psalm.* 2.7 (GNO 5: 89-91). Some of Gregory's phrasing appears to come directly from Eusebius.

74. Athanasius, *Expos. in psalm. 104* (PG 27: 441). Athanasius interprets the word according to a supposed Hebrew etymology where *Al* means "God," *ēl* means "strength," and *ouia* means "might."

75. The Septuagint shows Alleluia as a superscription for 20 psalms. Athanasius counts 19 and specifies which: Pss 104–106, 111–118, 134–135, and 145–150. This list agrees with the Septuagint except for the omission of Psalm 110. Athanasius, *Ep. Marc.* 25 (PG 27: 37).

76. Both versions are given in Rahlfs's edition of the Septuagint.

77. A similar use of Alleluia appears at the end of a story in 3 Maccabees about favor shown to the Jews by King Ptolemy Philopator. According to the author, when a set of letters between the king and his generals was communicated to the Judeans at a mass gathering, the good news caused them to extol the king and then depart with a shout of "Alleluia!" 3 Macc 7:13.

In a hymn of a heavenly liturgy depicted in Revelation 19, the seer hears "the loud voice of a large crowd in heaven saying, 'Alleluia. Salvation and glory and power to our God because his judgments are true and just.'" It goes on to describe God's vindication of the righteous. Then a second voice cries, "Alleluia. Her smoke goes up for ever and ever." In response, the seer says, "the twenty-four elders and four creatures fell down and worshiped God, who was seated on the throne, saying, 'Amen, Alleluia.'" The Jewish-Christian composer of these scenes treated Alleluia as a shout that could begin or end a statement of praise. The word also appears in the *Life of Adam and Eve* (*Apocalypse of Moses*), a Jewish work that was redacted by Christians. The angel Gabriel, after instructing Seth, departs into heaven, "glorifying and saying, 'Alleluia!'"[78] In this example, too, the word is probably to be understood as a cry of praise.

Alleluia does not figure as a refrain in the passages cited so far. Its first appearance with that function is in a praise song in the third-century *Acts of Xanthippe and Polyxena*. The song is placed in the mouth of the holy Xanthippe, who, after a long fast in preparation for death, sings as follows:

> *Praise God, O sinners, because he welcomes your prayers. Alleluia.*
> *Praise the Lord, you who have given up hope for me, because his mercies are many.*
> *Alleluia.*
> *Praise him, O ungodly ones, because he was crucified because of you. Alleluia.*
> *Praise him, you who fight for the salvation of sinners, because God loves you. Alleluia.*
> *Praise him, you who rejoice at the restoration of sinners, because you are fellow citizens of the saints. Alleluia.*[79]

In this instance, the Alleluia refrain is a structural feature of the poem itself. Although a group of responders might have intoned the Alleluia in response to a soloist when performing a song of this form, the context in *Acts of Xanthippe and Polyxena* implies that Xanthippe herself says the refrain.

The date of *Acts of Xanthippe and Polyxena* and its Christian provenance could suggest a connection between its conception of Alleluia as a refrain and Christian liturgical uses of Alleluia. The alternative is that the author was guided solely by literary models. If so, they were probably not Jewish. No earlier instance of Alleluia in a Jewish writing shows Alleluia as a refrain. Moreover, the earliest reference to Alleluia as a response by a group to a song performed

---

78. Greek *Vit. Ad. et Ev.* [*Apoc. Mos.*] 43.

79. *Act. Xanth. et Polyx.* 19 (James, 71).

by a solo singer appears in Christian writings from around the same period—Tertullian's mention of a group Alleluia in response to Alleluia psalms in prayer meetings and the fictional depiction in the anonymous *Homily on the Psalms*, which describes David and his fellow singers responding with Alleluia to each singer's solo psalmody. In Tertullian, the Alleluia may not have been a refrain but a terminal response; it is very clearly a terminal response in the anonymous *Homily*. But in an Easter sermon on Psalm 117, Augustine refers to "Alleluia" as the people's *refrain*, which suggests a development or at least a different tradition.[80]

In a much more direct association with Christian liturgy than is typical in apocryphal literature, the *Passion of Matthew* pictures what it calls "Alleluia" as part of a Communion service conducted by a bishop with participation by a singer. A certain verisimilitude to ecclesial practice is likely. The Communion ritual occurs at the height of the story. The king of a certain city has just executed the Apostle Matthew, and the Christians have kept an all-night vigil. In the morning, a voice from heaven addresses the bishop as follows: "Taking the Gospel and the Psalter of David, go to the east side of the palace, together with the crowd of brothers and sisters, and sing Alleluia and read the Gospel and offer holy bread as Communion."[81]

The ensuing service in the scene features responsorial psalmody with psalm-verse refrains. After four psalms have been sung in this way, the people "cry" Alleluia. This Alleluia is clearly not a refrain. Several hours later in narrative time, when the bishop is granted a vision of the risen Matthew standing far out on the sea, two angels mark the moment by saying, "Amen, Alleluia."[82] This is the form of one of the heavenly praise-shouts in Revelation 19 (see above). Although the bishop's vision of the two angels does not depict a Christian liturgy, it describes angels doing something close to what the author has already treated as an essential part of Communion liturgy.

The *Passion of Matthew* was probably written (or at least edited) before the end of the fourth century.[83] One telltale sign is the fact that the author does not use the expression "the singer" for the one who stands on the rock and sings the psalms. Instead, the author's expression reflects Eastern usage in descriptions of liturgical psalm-singers during an era of transition, when it was common to use either *ho psallōn* ("the one who sings," an expression formed

80. Augustine, *Serm.* 29A 1 (CCL 41: 378). The statement is quoted above in the list of Augustine's references to psalm responses.

81. *Pass. Matth.* (*Mart. Matth.*) 25 PF text.

82. *Pass. Matth.* (*Mart. Matth.*) 26.

83. See the discussion of the Communion scene in the *Passion of Matthew* in chapter 5.

with a participle[84]) or a noun, *psaltēs* or *psaltōdos*.[85] By the fifth century, the substantival participle was no longer in general use for the liturgical singer,[86] and the standard term for that person and his office was *psaltēs*.[87] The author of the *Passion of Matthew* uses a common fourth-century designation for the one who sang the psalm lesson.

A Greek tractate, *Discourse on Salvation to a Virgin*, falsely attributed to Athanasius, gives direction for private singing of psalms and "Alleluia" during nightly prayer:

> When you get up, sing this verse first: "In the middle of the night I have arisen to acknowledge you for your righteous judgments." (Ps 118:62) Then pray and say the whole fiftieth psalm, up to the end. Let these things be daily requirements for you. Say the psalms, as many as you can say standing. And for each psalm let a prayer and genuflection be completed, confessing your sins to the Lord with tears and asking that they be forgiven to you. And after three psalms, say Alleluia.[88]

The *Discourse* was probably composed in the fourth century.[89] It depicts Alleluia as a terminal response following a series of responsorial psalms.

Adding a terminal Alleluia to a series of psalms was also the practice of the monks "throughout all Egypt and the Thebaid," Cassian says, referring to monastic adherence to the Rule of the Angel. The monks adopted this Rule,[90] whose model dictated that one monk should recite while the rest remain silent.[91] Cassian describes the community practice as follows: "When, therefore, they assemble to perform the rites just mentioned [vespers and nocturns], which they call synaxes, such silence is shown collectively—despite the fact that so great a

---

84. ὁ ψάλλων. John Chrysostom, *In I Cor.*, Hom. 36.6 (PG 61: 315; Field, *Interp. omn. epist. Paul.* 2: 461); *Const. ap.* 2.58.4; 8.14.1.

85. See *Const. ap.* 8.28.8 and 8.47.43 for ψάλτης; 2.28.5 and 6.17.2 for ψαλτῳδός.

86. The substantival participle remained a common description of David as composer-performer of psalms. The term ψάλτης probably seemed unfitting as a title for a king who happened to compose psalms.

87. Regarding the terminology, see chapter 4 under "Clerical Readers and Cantors."

88. Ps.-Athanasius, *Virg.* 20. On this work and the question of its authorship, see David Brakke, "The Authenticity of the Ascetic Athanasiana," *Orientalia* 63 (1994): 44–47.

89. See Brakke, "The Authenticity of the Ascetic Athanasiana," 45.

90. Cassian, *Inst.* 2.6.

91. *Inst.* 2.5.5.

number of brothers are gathered together—that it might be thought that, besides the one who performs the psalm, standing in the middle, no other person is present within."[92] An Alleluia was said in *responsione* after the final psalm, which was always a psalm marked with Alleluia in its superscription.[93] This probably means that it was the reciter who said the Alleluia, not the rest of the monks, since that is what the Rule of the Angel implies: the angel says Alleluia after finishing his twelfth psalm.[94] The form of the angel's recitation was singing.[95] One need not accept Cassian's claim about the universality of the practice in Egypt, much less the myth of the angel's revelation of the rule, to see here a use of Alleluia that was probably practiced by monks known to Cassian or one of his sources.

The Rule of the Angel was interpreted differently by two young brothers who visited Abba Macarius at Scetis. According to an anecdote about this pair, their custom was to sing "five psalms of six lines and one Alleluia," then another such set.[96]

Alleluia is also discussed in a work of questions and answers that was doubtfully attributed to Theodoret:

> Question 63: Since long ago the children sang Hosanna, and now we sing Alleluia, what is the meaning of these? Answer: The meaning of Alleluia is "Hymn the Being with melody," and the meaning of Hosanna is "placed high above."[97]

The children's Hosanna is a shout in the Gospel of Matthew, an acclamation repeated by children in the temple after the Triumphal Entry.[98] Although that acclamation is a four-word shout, the passage attributed to Theodoret means the single word "Hosanna," since it is the *word* that he defines. The same goes for his reference to Alleluia. He gives no clue about the contexts or formats in which Alleluia was sung by the church in his day.

---

92. *Inst.* 2.10.1.

93. *Inst.* 2.11.3.

94. *Inst.* 2.5.5.

95. Note *cantat* in *Inst.* 2.8.

96. Ps.-Macarius, *Apoph.* 33 (PG 34: 256) // *Apoph. patr.*, *Collectio alphabetica* 33 (PG 65: 277). This passage is quoted more fully in chapter 8.

97. The question is given in the *pinax* and then repeated in a garbled way in the body of the work, where it stands with its answer. I have paired the *pinax* form with the answer. See [Theodoret,] *Quaest. et resp.* 63 (Papadopoulos-Kerameus, 6 and 65).

98. Matt 21:15.

From a study of the Psalter, Christian divines would have found only a single instance of Alleluia outside a superscription, namely the Alleluia at the close of Psalm 150, where it is either an ending to that psalm or, more likely, an editorial ending to the last section of the Psalter or the Psalter as a whole. Eusebius, who knew a Psalter composed of 150 psalms,[99] writes that the book of Psalms is divided into five parts, each of which has a concluding blessing, and that "the fifth section ends in Alleluia, with which the whole book is concluded."[100] Eusebius says nothing about Christian use of Alleluia, but in at least two sermons, Augustine refers to Alleluia as a congregational response to the psalm lesson. In each case, the lesson was a psalm with an Alleluia superscription.[101] Alleluia psalms must have been regarded as especially festive in the West, since they were sung in Augustine's Hippo during the fifty days after Easter as songs of gladness, which followed the sorrowful period of Lent.[102]

In a sermon delivered in the late fourth or early fifth century, Severian of Gabala comments that when the cherubim of the vision in Isaiah 6 express their threefold Sanctus "one to the other," one cries "Holy," then the other cries "Holy," then the first one cries "Holy," "just as in psalmody the participants answer with Alleluias."[103] This implies the use of Alleluia as a refrain, just as Augustine's sermons attest; so, too, the Armenian Lectionary (see below).

Finally, there is the Alleluia mentioned in a fifth-century Western anecdote about a Vandal attack on an African church, which occurred sometime between 422 and 448. According to Victor of Vita, "a lector standing in the pulpit singing an 'alleluiatic melody' was shot in the throat by an arrow, while the people of God were listening and singing."[104] In chapter 5, I argued that the lector's Alleluia may have been a melismatic chant, that is, an extended singing of the word "Alleluia," to which the congregation responded with Alleluia.

The evidence as a whole shows considerable variety. In addition to being a term for a type of psalm in the Septuagint, Alleluia appears as an independent exclamation, the incipit of a praise song (sometimes paired with Amen), a terminal response to a praise song (sometimes paired with Amen), a terminal response to a set of psalms, and a refrain of psalmody. Christians believed that

---

99. Most manuscripts of the Septuagint have 151 psalms. The Septuagint labels Psalm 151 "outside the number."

100. Eusebius, *In psalm. 71*, discussing verses 18–20 (PG 23: 820).

101. See Augustine, *Enarr. in psalm. 113* 1 (CCL 41: 1635); *Serm.* 29A 1 (CCL 41: 378).

102. Augustine, *Enarr. in psalm. 110* 1 (PL 37: 1463; CCL 40: 1620–1621). See the comments in McKinnon, "Preface to the Study of the Alleluia," 222.

103. Severian of Gabala, *In mund. creat.*, Hom. 2.5 (PG 56: 445).

104. Victor of Vita, *Hist. pers. Afr. prov.* 1.41 [1.13] (CSEL 7: 18) (*alleluiaticum melos*).

angels sing Alleluia,[105] which implies that they conceived their own singing of Alleluia as an imitation of angelic song. Although there is no unambiguous evidence that Alleluia was sung in a melismatic form with psalm verses attached, as a predecessor to the Alleluia chants of the Byzantine liturgy and the later Roman rite, the anecdote in Victor of Vita's history suggests that some form of melismatic Alleluia may have developed in Africa in the first half of the fifth century.

Perhaps an independent song is also meant by "Alleluia" in an anecdote about an incident that occurred in Alexandria in the late fourth century. According to Sozomen, when Christians were about to seize the Serapion in Alexandria, its Christianization was foreshadowed by a sign. While pagans were guarding the temple, a certain Olympius heard someone singing Alleluia inside. Since Olympius heard only one voice, not a soloist and chorus, the Alleluia was not a refrain. Sozomen calls it "a melodious song (*psalmos*)," whether that means one of the Alleluia psalms of the Septuagint or a melismatic Alleluia.[106]

Refrains in the Armenian Lectionary

The Armenian Lectionary specifies a variety of types of congregational responses to psalms and canticles. Although the lectionary was compiled in the fifth century, perhaps as late as the 450s to 470s,[107] it derived its liturgy from Jerusalem and a good deal of what it prescribes correlates with what Egeria reports for Jerusalem in the late fourth century. There are also differences, to be sure, which reflect developments over the course of the generations between her visit to Jerusalem and the time of the AL.

The Armenian Lectionary uses designations of the following types for liturgical song:

> *Psalm 22, response: "The Lord is my shepherd."*
> *Alleluia. 79: "Give heed, Shepherd of Israel, you who leads."*
> *Psalm 2, response: "The Lord said to me, 'You are my son; today I have begotten you.'"*

105. In addition to the examples already mentioned, I will cite two more. According to Athanasius, "it is said that the angels praise God with this word." *Expos. in psalm. 104* (PG 27: 441). In Pachomius's vision of a dead monk's soul being carried to heaven in a sheet by three angels, one of the angels sings to the soul in a heavenly language that includes only one word that Pachomius understands—Alleluia (*Pach. vit. Boh.* 82).

106. Sozomen, *H.E.* 7.15.9.

107. See Hugo Méndez, "Revising the Date of the Armenian Lectionary of Jerusalem," *Journal of Early Christian Studies* 29 (2021): 61–92.

These examples from the first service in the lectionary[108] are typical. When the AL specifies an Alleluia, it gives the number of the psalm and then, in most instances, the first words of the psalm.[109] Two details make clear that Alleluia was the refrain for the psalm. First, the psalms labeled Alleluia in AL do not correspond to the psalms in the Septuagint that carry Alleluia in their superscriptions. Second, unlike the listings for the lectionary's nonAlleluia psalms, the lectionary always quotes the first verse of each of these psalms, after the number, which are clearly psalm titles, not refrains. For example, for the services of Epiphany (January 6) and the third day of Epiphany, the lectionary includes Psalm 109 (110 MT) among the assignments: "Alleluia, Psalm 109 'The Lord said to my Lord, Sit at (my) right.'"[110] The choice of Psalm 109 must have been for the sake of verse 3, "In the splendor of your holy ones, before the Morning Star, I have begotten you." But since the first verse is quoted and not the third, Alleluia must be the response, which explains why it is mentioned, while the words of the first verse serve to name the psalm.

In the case of nonAlleluia psalms, the stated refrain derives from a psalm verse. Moreover, sometimes a group of three biblically consecutive psalms, termed a "gobala," was sung with the same refrain for each psalm, the refrain being a verse or combination of verses. For example, the AL specifies the following five gobalas for the evening office and vigil of Good Friday, numbering each gobala and directing that kneeling and prayer should follow, presumably to symbolize Christ's three prayers in Gethsemene:

> *For the first gobala: Psalms 2–4 with Psalm 2:2b as the response.*
> *For the second gobala: Psalms 40–42 with Psalms 40:9/37:22 as the response.*
> *For the third gobala: Psalms 58–60 with Psalm 58:2 as the response.*
> *For the fourth gobala: Psalm 78–80 with Psalms 87:6b/78:13 as the response.*
> *For the fifth gobala: Psalms 108–110 with Psalm 108:2b–3a as the response.*[111]

---

108. AL 1 (an assembly on Jan. 5 at the tenth hour, the eve of Epiphany). Athanase Renoux, *Le codex arménien Jérusalem 121*, vol. 2: *Édition compare du texte et de deux autres manuscrits* (Brepols, 1971), 210–215 [72–77].

109. Renoux, *Le codex arménien Jérusalem 121*, vol. 2, 176 [38].

110. AL 2 and 4; Renoux, *Le codex arménien Jérusalem 121*, vol. 2, 216 [78]–219 [81].

111. AL 39.3, mss. J and P (Renoux, *Le codex arménien Jérusalem 121*, vol. 2, 268 [130]–273 [135]. In each case, the AL mentions only the first psalm of the gobala, the other two being implied.

Thus, the Armenian Lectionary shows that in Jerusalem, by at least the latter half of the fifth century, some psalms were sung with Alleluia refrains and others with psalm-verse refrains, the latter style having developed for certain feasts into the gobala format. The AL also specifies refrains for biblical canticles, specifically for the Song of the Sea (Exod 15) and the odes of Azarias and the Three Young Men (from the expanded Greek version of Daniel 3).

Egeria's vague references to hymns, psalms, and antiphons could be shorthand for the types of psalmody we see in the AL. She does refer to responsorial song, and the AL illustrates the principle of "suitability to the day" in its psalms and readings that Egeria notes about the Jerusalem liturgies. She nowhere mentions an Alleluia or gives any hint of groupings like the gobala.

Doxologies

In a passage quoted in chapter 7, John Cassian mentions the monastic practice of concluding a psalm with a doxology at vespers and nocturns: "one sings the psalm, at the close of which all are standing and sing *Gloria patri et filio et spiritu sancto* with a loud voice."[112] This was the practice in Gaul, he says, but from what he knew of "the East," all kept silent while the singer moved directly from the psalm to the prayer.[113] More specifically, the Twelve Psalms series was concluded with Alleluia by the soloist (see above).

The monks of Eastern monastic communities sang the *Gloria patri* only after an *antiphona*, according to Cassian, whatever he means by that term.[114] Cassian claims that the particulars of the Eastern communal psalmody he rehearses for his audience in Gaul was the norm in monastic communities throughout the East.[115] It was probably the norm in at least some places.

According to John Chrysostom, the monks who lived in the desert mountains east of Antioch sang the *Gloria in excelsis* at matins.[116] This neither confirms

---

112. *Uno cantante in clausula psalmi omnes adstantes concinant cum clamore "gloria Patri et Filio et Spiritui sancto."* Cassian, *Inst.* 2.8 (CSEL 17: 24; SC 109: 72).

113. *Nusquam per omnem Orientem audiuimus* [referring to the practice in Gaul], *sed cum omnium silentio ab eo, qui cantat, finito psalmo orationem succedere. Inst.* 2.8 (CSEL 17: 24; SC 109: 72).

114. *hac uero glorificatione Trinitatis tantummodo solere antiphona terminari. Inst.* 2.8 (CSEL 17:24; SC 109: 72). On Cassian's use of the term *antiphona*, see chapter 11.

115. See *Inst.* 2.1 and 3.1. Taft notes that the Gallic practice of singing the *Gloria patri* after each psalm, instead of after each unit of psalms, "still distinguishes eastern and western monastic psalmody." Robert F. Taft, *The Liturgy of the Hours in East and West: The Origins of the Divine Office and Its Meaning for Today* (Liturgical, 1986), 97.

116. John Chrysostom, *In Matt.*, Hom. 68.3 (PG 58: 644; Field, *Hom. in Matt.* 2: 297).

nor disconfirms Cassian's generalization, since John says nothing about the placement of this *Gloria*, which is also a different form of doxology. (It is clear that John has a communal synaxis in view, not a monk's private matins in his cell, for he speaks of the monks "singing with one voice," and he uses third-person-plural verbs.)

A west-Syrian form of the *Gloria in excelsis* is given in the *Apostolic Constitutions*, and one manuscript refers to it as a morning canticle.[117] Although this last remark is probably not original to the late fourth-century edition of the *Apostolic Constitutions*, it attests a tradition of church psalmody that fits with what John Chrysostom says about monastic psalmody in his day.

I noted in chapter 4 that John sought to combat "Arian" hymnody in Constantinople by having some of his own people perform hymns with Nicene Trinitarian language.[118] Although this probably included doxologies, the sources are not clear about that or whether the Nicene Christians sang composed hymns or biblical psalms or both. Sozomen, describing singing at Antioch a generation earlier, tells how the people and the clergy "used to gather in choruses" (at vigils, presumably), "which was their custom when they sang odes to God; and they indicated their opinion *at the end* of the songs. Some praised the Father and Son as equally worthy of honor; while others praised the Father in the Son, making the Son appear secondary by the addition of the preposition."[119] The implication is that each hymn, probably a psalm in most instances, concluded with a doxology. This conflicts with Cassian's generalization about the East, unless Cassian meant only what was done in monasteries or unless Cassian and Sozomen were both talking only about Christian hymns, in Cassian's case a type of hymn that he called an antiphon.[120]

Antiphons

The term "antiphon" and related words are discussed in chapter 11. To anticipate, some have suggested that antiphon originally referred to a bit of ecclesiastical poetry used as a response and that subsequently it came to be used for a psalm with such a response.[121] These two usages are not clearly documented for the

117. *Const. ap.* 7.47, ms. e (Funk, 455, note to 7.47). Metzger's edition does not even list this witness in his apparatus, but he does assume, presumably based on external evidence, that the *Gloria in excelsis* mentioned in 7.47 is a morning hymn (Metzger 2: 71, § 352).

118. Socrates, *H.E.* 6.8.4.

119. Sozomen, *H.E.* 3.20.8 (FS 73/2: 423).

120. See chapter 11 regarding the possibility that Cassian used "antiphon" for a type of hymn that easterners ended with a doxology.

121. See Taft, *The Liturgy of the Hours in East and West*, 54 and 95.

fourth and fifth centuries, although there are hints that the term was used in the one way or the other by certain groups of Christians. The word appears to have been used in diverse ways.

Psalmody with Two Choruses

The use of two choirs for psalmody is documented by a letter of Basil composed in about 375. I have already discussed certain aspects of it. Writing to clergy at Neocaesarea who object to what they denigrate as a new form of psalmody or perhaps the novelty of a psalm-filled popular vigil, Basil defends what his church does and claims that their practice is nearly universal in the East. Here is the passage (numbering added for subsequent reference):

> (1) Among us, the people get up at night and go to the house of prayer. In pain, distress, and anguish of tears, they make confession to God. (2) Finally, rising from their prayers, they begin the psalmody. (2a) And now, divided in two, they sing back and forth to each other (*antipsallousin allēlois*), maintaining a focus together on the words and directing the attention and the concentration of their hearts together to the words. (2b) Then again, leaving it to one to lead the songs, the rest respond.[122]

Did the two choirs first take turns singing the psalm verses antiphonally (2a), then shift to a responsorial format (2b)?[123] Or were both formats responsorial? The language and immediate context support the second possibility. The Greek expression *epeita palin*, here translated "then again" (2b), typically introduces a repetition, which in the present context would imply that after the choirs sang one psalm (2a), taking turns responding to the psalm leader, they then sang another psalm in the same manner (2b).[124] The alternative, which assumes that they first sang antiphonally, would have required that everyone had the psalm memorized, since the choirs would have been responsible for the verses. While that is not out of the question, especially if the psalms chosen for these vigils

122. Basil, *Ep.* 207.3. On the nature of this vigil, see chapter 7.

123. There is a long scholarly tradition of interpreting Basil's description of the choral alternation as direct choral antiphony, not a responsorial format with two choirs. See, for example, Taft, *The Liturgy of the Hours East and West*, 40; Everett Ferguson, "Congregational Singing in the Early Church," *Acta Patristica et Byzantina* 15 (2004): 146–147.

124. Although the adverb πάλιν is sometimes a "marker of contrast or an alternative aspect" (BAGD s.v. πάλιν), a search of the TLG shows that this is not its usual sense, especially in the common expression ἔπειτα πάλιν.

were very familiar and the vigils were frequent, nothing in the passage requires the inference that the vigil featured an antiphonal format; whereas the passage clearly refers to a responsorial style when it mentions a leader (2b).

Dividing a congregation into alternating choirs was an innovation that probably began at Antioch and spread more widely. According to Theodoret of Cyr, the laymen Flavian and Diodore were the "inventors" of a new kind of psalmody, which they introduced during the Arian conflicts at Antioch when Leontius was bishop (344–358). Flavian and Diodore "first taught [the church] to sing Davidic song in alternation by dividing the choirs of singers in two, a practice that, having first begun in Antioch, spread everywhere and reached the ends of civilization. And gathering the lovers of divine things at the tombs of the martyrs, they passed the nights with them hymning God."[125] The expression "in succession" refers to some kind of alternation. Theodoret uses this same term in remarks about a monastery in the vicinity of Zeugma, where a certain Pouplios assembled a community of Greek-speaking monks in roughly the same era. This original group was later joined by men whose only language was the local tongue.[126] When the resultant, linguistically diverse monastery held morning and evening prayer, the brothers performed psalmody "divided in two, each using their own language and sending up the song in succession."[127] Leclercq calls this "antiphonie" and opines that the two groups "alternated the verses, each in its own language."[128] But it may have been simply a case of successive singing of the refrain. Since neither Basil's account nor Theodoret's nor any other of the era expressly describes antiphonal psalmody, there is no basis for concluding that either passage refers to antiphony, the format of which is explained for the first time in surviving literature by Isidore of Seville in the seventh century.[129]

125. Theodoret, *H.E.* 2.24.8–11. He places Flavian and Diodore in the context of conflicts under bishop Leontius over Arianism, implying that their antiphonal psalmody played a salutary role in the defense of orthodoxy. See Wendy Mayer and Pauline Allen, *The Churches of Syrian Antioch (300–638 CE)* (Peeters, 2012), 191–192, 200–201.

126. Theodoret of Cyr, *H.R.*, *Vit.* 5.1–5. Theodoret mentions Publius in *H.E.* 4.28.1, doing so just after referring to Christian defenders of the faith such as Flavian and Diodore in the time of Julian the Apostate (*H.E.* 4.27.1–4a; note that 4.27b–5 on Constantius II is a brief, backtracking paragraph).

127. Theodoret, *H.R.*, *Vit.* 5.5: διχῇ μὲν διῃρημένοι καὶ τῇ οἰκείᾳ ἕκαστοι κεχρημένοι φωνῇ, ἐκ διαδοχῆς δὲ τὴν ᾠδὴν ἀναπέμποντες (SC 234: 336; PG 82: 1353).

128. Henri Leclercq, "Antienne (Liturgie)," in *Dictionnaire d'archéologie*, vol. 1, part 2, ed. Fernand Cabrol and Henri Leclercq (Letouzey et Ané, 1907), col. 2288.

129. Isidore, *Etym.* 6.19.7–8. In another place, Isidore traces the first use of antiphons in the West to Ambrose (Isidore, *Eccl. off.* 1.7; PL 83: 743–744), but he probably relied on Augustine and Paulinus for this idea, projecting his own understanding of antiphons onto that earlier history.

Assuming that Theodoret's information is accurate regarding the essentials of the innovation and the time period, the tracing of divided choirs to two laymen of Antioch in the 340s or 350s pushes the origin of this format back to two or three decades prior to Basil's letter of 375. As for how to correlate the two, Basil's letter could be read as implying that alternating psalmody with two choirs was relatively new but had quickly spread. Or else it was not so new, and the Neocaesareans who criticized it were behind the times. The tone and claims of Basil suggest the latter.

Direct Choral Psalmody

Did Christians sing whole psalms in unison on certain occasions?

Speaking of Psalm 140, the evening hymn of the cathedral office, John Chrysostom remarks that "in one sense,[130] everyone knows the words of this psalm, and they continue singing them through every stage of life. Yet they do not understand the meaning of the words."[131] The psalm was completely familiar to them because it was sung every evening. The same would have been true for the morning psalm, Psalm 62. Moreover, when Basil defends the psalmodic vigils of his church and describes alternating psalmody, he also says that when daybreak arrives, "all in common, as if in a single voice and a single heart, lift up the psalm of confession to the Lord, each making his own words of repentance."[132] This description implies the familiar pairing of a psalm with prayer, in this case group psalmody and individual prayers. Basil's use of the definite article ("*the* psalm of confession") suggests that churches in Cappadocia used a particular psalm for this purpose, probably Psalm 50. Wherever Psalm 50 was the standard psalm of confession, regular church attenders could have come to know it by heart, just as they could have learned Psalms 62 and 140 by heart where these were the regular psalms of the morning and evening office. Not only that, Basil celebrates the fact that Christians, having participated in psalmody in church, "sing the words of the psalms at home and carry them even to the marketplace."[133] Ambrose says something similar.[134] It is fair to assume, then, that many regular church attenders memorized, simply through frequent hearing, the verses of the fixed psalms of the morning and evening services, as well as any fixed psalm of

---

130. More literally: "so to speak" (ὡς εἰπεῖν). My functional-equivalent translation, "in one sense," interprets the expression in light of John's next sentence.

131. John Chrysostom, *In psalm 140* 1 (PG 55: 426).

132. Basil, *Ep.* 207.3.

133. Basil, *Hom. in. Psalm. 1* 1 (PG 29: 212).

134. *Domi psalmus canitur, foris recensetur.* Ambrose, *Expl. psalm. 1* 9 (PL 14: 925; CSEL 64: 8).

frequent vigils and any fixed Communion psalm. Hence, it is conceivable that they would have been capable of singing the verses of those psalms in unison during the liturgy.[135]

But did they? In the case of Psalm 144, a regular Communion psalm mentioned by John Chrysostom, there is direct evidence that they did not, since John comments that the people sang verse 15 continuously in response.[136] Moreover, in a statement about what was probably the morning and evening office, he speaks about Christians who imagine they have fulfilled their obligations "after responding to two or three hymns and performing the customary prayers."[137] Clearly, responsorial psalmody was the norm for the daily office and Communion in John's church, even if many people knew the fixed psalms of these services by heart. This is not surprising. Bishops had reason to ensure that the steady stream of newcomers, as well as any of the baptized who did not attend regularly, could participate with ease by singing refrains rather than have to struggle to recall verses or else not participate at all.

At least one interpreter has suggested that a passage in Ambrose's psalms commentary might refer to congregational singing of whole psalms in unison: "What an effort it is in church to remain silent when the lessons are read. When one speaks, everyone makes noise. If a psalm is read, it is itself the effecter of silence. All speak and no one makes noise."[138] Does this imply that the verses were sung in unison by the congregation?[139] Or is the point rather that responsorial psalmody was so preoccupying, with refrains being intoned after every colon, that the activity eliminated extraneous noisemaking, since everyone had to pay attention when not singing so that they would sing the refrain at the right moments? The envisioned liturgical moment has direct bearing on this question. Ambrose

---

135. According to a number of scholars, Psalms 62 and 140 were indeed sung by the congregation *in directum*. See for example Reiner Kaczynski, *Das Wort Gottes in Liturgie und Alltag der Gemeinden des Johannes Chrysostomus* (Herder, 1974), 108. Paverd suggests that these psalms were sung *in directum* or antiphonally. Frans van de Paverd, *Zur Geschichte der Messliturgie in Antiocheia und Konstantinopel gegen Ende des vierten Jahrhunderts: Analyse der Quellen bei Johannes Chrysostomos* (Pontificium Institutum Orientalium Studiorum, 1970), 117–118.

136. John Chrysostom, *In psalm. 144* 1 (PG 55: 464).

137. John Chrysostom, *In Matt.*, Hom. 11.7 (PG 57: 200; Field, *Hom. in Matt.* 1: 149). The description suggests a prayer gathering, since there is no reference to the people listening to a sermon or receiving Communion.

138. Ambrose, *In psalm. 1* 9. *Quantum laboratur in ecclesia ut fiat silentium, cum lectiones leguntur! Si unus loquatur, obstrepunt uniuersi; cum psalmus legitur, ipse sibi est effector silentii; omnes loquuntur et nullus obstrepit.* PL 14: 925; CSEL 64: 8.

139. Ferguson cautiously cites this passage as evidence of unison congregational singing of entire psalms ("Congregational Singing in Early Christianity," 148–149).

is talking about the psalm lesson of the service of the word. As we have already seen, there is direct evidence elsewhere in Ambrose that these psalm lessons were performed responsorially.[140] That is the only kind of singing that would have been practical for a lesson, since the lessons varied from service to service. To have sung them in direct unison would have required that the congregation know the entire Psalter by heart. That is extremely unlikely.

Moreover, any congregational singing in unison would have required not only knowing the words by heart but knowing their melody or how to sing them to a melodic formula with everybody intoning in the same way. It is difficult to judge how common it was to sing the verses of a given fixed psalm to the *same* melody or melodic formula week after week at a vigil or the daily office so that the congregation became familiar with a particular matching of words to tune. Lectors may not have sung even fixed psalms in the same way week by week.

What about monks who engaged in group psalmody? Did their devotion to Scripture memorization make direct singing in unison both feasible and attractive to them? It may seem surprising, but there is precious little evidence that when monks gathered for daily prayer or the Eucharist, they sang all the verses in unison. The expectation in Pachomian monasteries was for each brother to learn as much of the Psalter by heart as possible. Yet a significant number of monks, especially those who were new to the discipline, knew only a limited number of psalms.[141] During funeral rites, the Pachomians sang or recited responsively.[142] At their two daily liturgical gatherings, they took turns reciting "sections," passages of Scripture that included psalms, followed by prayer. Whether those not reciting responded is not mentioned.[143]

Cassian makes no explicit reference to direct unison singing in the monasteries with which he was familiar. When he describes psalmody at vespers and

---

140. See Ambrose, *Expl. psalm. 45* 15 (PL 14: 1140-1141; CSEL 64: 340). Ambrose also refers to responsorial psalmody at a morning service in *Ep.* 76.20 (CSEL 82: 120) and at a vigil-like gathering in the daytime during one of the conflicts with Empress Justina over the basilicas (*Ep.* 76.24; CSEL 82: 123). In two other places, he mentions responsorial psalmody without clearly implying the setting for it. See *Expos. euang. Luc.* 7.238 (PL 15: 1763; CSEL 32/4: 388); *Hex.* 3.5.23 (PL 14: 165; CSEL 32/1: 75).

141. A Pachomian rule refers to monks who do not memorize much and insists that they should learn at least "ten sections along with a section of the Psalter" (*Reg. Hor.* 16; tr. Armand Veilleux, tr., *Pachomian Koinonia*, vol. 2 [Cistercian, 1982], 202). Another rule implies that it was common for a monk to have his own set pieces for his personal synaxis (*Reg. Hor.* 17). See chapter 8.

142. Compare *Pr.* 127 and 128; perhaps also for the Sunday synaxis (see *Pr.* 15–17), although Jerome may have added the references to psalmody to the precepts about the Sunday synaxis (see chapter 8).

143. See chapter 8.

nocturns, he implies turn-taking by singers.[144] In an account of the Friday vigil in one or more monasteries at Bethlehem, Cassian or an interpolator says that the monks first sing three "antiphons"[145] standing, then sit on low benches and chant three "psalms" responsorially, taking turns reciting the verses. Whatever the antiphons were, the manner of their performance is not stated. Cassian's rather limited remarks about the formats of monastic psalmody mention only solo and responsorial singing.

There happens to be evidence for psalmody by organized choirs. The choirs must have sung their repertoire by heart. Some of it could certainly have been unison song, since they could have practiced their songs in advance. Fourth-century redaction of the *Apostolic Tradition* prescribes an after-supper vesper liturgy where virgins and children sing chorally.[146] Egeria refers to a choir of children singing *Kyrie eleison* at vespers in Jerusalem.[147] The *Testament of Our Lord*, which may have been written as late as the latter part of the fifth century, speaks of a choir of boys who sing psalms and hymns at vespers.[148] There is also good reason to think that in the mid-fifth century, the orphanage at Constantinople had a children's choir that performed public concerts. We are told that crowds flocked to the orphanage to hear songs composed by Timocletus, the brother of the presbyter Acacius, who ran the orphanage.[149] The songs, probably hymns, were sung chorally at these concerts, which leads one to think that the orphanage had a children's choir. Whether their repertoire included the singing of biblical psalms in unison is not known.

The Wider Culture

What was the relation of the formats of Christian corporate psalmody to patterns of performance in the wider culture, including the Jewish world?

Refrains are documented for an early period among the Babylonians and Assyrians, and some of these Eastern traditions were embraced in archaic Greece,

---

144. Cassian, *Inst.* 2.3.1 (the hours in question) and 2.7–11 (how the monks practiced the Rule of the Angel at these hours). See the preceding discussion under "Alleluia."

145. *antiphona tria concinuerint* in *Inst.* 3.8.4.

146. *Trad. ap.* 25/29C 11.

147. Egeria, *Itin.* 24.5.

148. *T. Dom.* 2.11.

149. Ps.-Zachariah Rhetor, *Chron.* 4.11 (discussed in chapter 4).

as is evident from the nonGreek etymologies of certain ritual refrain-cries.[150] The ancient Eastern refrains preserved in texts show a good deal of variety. Most are not regularly periodic throughout the whole of a hymn and may have been performed not responsorially but by a solo singer (or a trained chorus) who performed both the verses and the refrain.[151] Even in the case of songs that contain refrains, there are no hints in the records of them that they were sung with a division of performance between a soloist and choir.[152]

A direct reference to responsorial performance of the Israelite *ḥesed* refrain appears in a narrative in the book of Ezra about the rebuilding of the Jerusalem temple. Temple musicians performed in a grand ceremony after the foundations were laid. Their song is not quoted in full, but the narrator says that "they answered with praise (*hallēl*) and thanksgiving, 'Because he is good, for his steadfast love (*ḥesed*) endures forever.'"[153] The verb "answered" is clear evidence of a responsorial format. The account is modeled on the story about the dedication of Solomon's temple in 2 Chronicles, and there are allusions to this same refrain in the Maccabean literature. The words of the same refrain also appear in Hebrew Psalms 100, 106, 118, and 136 (Ps 118 being the final psalm of the Hallel psalms and Ps 136 being the Great Hallel). One or more of these psalms (or hymns like them) were probably sung with a *ḥesed* refrain at the festivals of Booths and Hanukkah in the late Hellenistic era by ad hoc choirs organized

150. See Martin L. West, *The East Face of Helicon: West Asiatic Elements in Greek Poetry and Myth* (Clarendon, 1997): 43–45.

151. For example, lines 1–7 of a 21-line lament to the Goddess of Širpurla (CT XV 22) have a repeated narration phrase at the end of each line, which was probably sung by the same performer who sang the first half of each line. The lament can be found in Stephen Langdon, *Sumerian and Babylonian Psalms* (Geuthner, 1909), 284–287 (no. xxx). The same probably applies to the repeated words that close each of the first 20 lines in a 34-line psalm to Enlil (CT XV 13). See Langdon, *Sumerian and Babylonian Psalms*, 292–295 (no. xxxii).

152. A prayer to Nintud, Goddess of Creation, consists of eight sections, each of which concludes with the same refrain. See Stephen Langdon, *Babylonian Liturgies* (Geuthner, 1913), 86–93 (no. 197). A Babylonian hymn to the Moon God is disposed in sections where lines 1 and 3 of each section are the same, which might suggest a responsorial or antiphonal cult performance. See Langdon, *Babylonian Liturgies*, 2–4 (no. 1). In a discussion of Assyrian hymns with refrains, Cumming points out that it is often difficult to determine whether the refrain was sung by anyone except the singer(s) who performed the verses. See Charles G. Cumming, *The Assyrian and Hebrew Hymns of Praise* (Columbia University Press, 1934), 72. In the case of hymns with half-line refrains, he speculates that a choir sang the refrains to a priest soloist (p. 76). This seems more likely for the intercalated one-line refrain of a hymn to Nergal (pp. 77–78).

153. Ezra 3:11.

for the occasion.[154] Moreover, the Mishna and Tosefta attest the singing of the Hallel at Jewish festivals in the Roman era,[155] and Rabbi Akiba refers explicitly to responsorial singing of the Hallel (see further below).

As for group singing in the wider culture during the Roman period, Greco-Roman sources make clear that it had a place in a variety of settings, both public and private.[156] There was "a real burst in celebratory ritual initiatives" in the second and third centuries, and inscriptions at sanctuaries "attest to the proliferation of choral singing" in these rites.[157] Hymns for public rituals at imperially sanctioned festivals were typically performed by trained choirs, both during the procession and at the sanctuary.[158] An inscription from Claros, for example, inscribed in 132/133 CE, states that a certain Philopappianos, a "prophet" of the temple of Apollo Pythios in Laodicea-on-the-Lycus, went to Claros to sing a hymn at Apollo's temple there with a choir of boys and young women.[159]

Some of the inscriptional evidence suggests that temples and other sites of worship conducted schedules of *daily* hymnody. According to an inscription from Stratonicea (Caria) that has been dated to the end of the second century CE, the city council ordained that Zeus, Panamarus, and Hecate should be honored every day by a chorus of thirty boys in the *bouleuterion*, where the

---

154. See Charles H. Cosgrove, *Music and Social Meals in Greek and Roman Antiquity: From the Archaic Period to the Age of Augustine* (Cambridge University Press, 2023), 286–290.

155. See chapter 1.

156. See the survey of both fictional representations and literal references, including inscriptional evidence, for the Greco-Roman era in Ewen Bowie, "Choral Performances," in *Greeks on Greekness: Viewing the Greek Past under the Roman Empire*, ed. David Konstan and Suzanne Saïd (Cambridge University Press, 2006), 65–92.

157. Giambattista D'Alessio, "Performance, Tradition, and the Loss of Hellenistic Lyric Poetry," in *Imagining Reperformance in Ancient Culture: Studies in the Traditions of Drama and Lyric*, ed. Richard Hunter and Anna Uhlig, (Cambridge University Press, 2017), 258.

158. See the discussion in Jan M. Bremer, "Greek Hymns," in *Faith, Hope, and Worship: Aspects of Religious Mentality in the Ancient World*, ed. H. S. Versnel (Leiden: Brill, 1981), 197–203 (pp. 193–215). In addition to the evidence cited below, a few additional pieces are IPph Ia 18d 11–19 and IPerg 374; IGRom 4:1608c = IEph VII 2 3801, as cited in S. R. F. Price, *Rituals and Power: The Roman Imperial Cult in Asia Minor* (Cambridge University Press, 1984), 118 and 105; inscriptions that mention boy hymn-singers at Herakleia Salbake in the first and second centuries CE in Jeanne Robert and Louis Robert, *La Carie: histoire et géographie historique avec la recueil des inscriptions antiques*, vol. 2 (Paris: Librairie d'Amerique et d'Orient, 1954), no. 132, 7; no. 135, 10 (by implication); no. 136, 13–14; no. 137, 20; no. 138, 4–5; no. 146, 7–8; no. 194, 9–11; 195, 9–11; no. 196, 12–14; Julian, *Ep.* 109, as cited in Bremer, "Greek Hymns," 215.

159. IGR IV 1587 (132/133 CE) (Greek text quoted in Bremer, "Greek Hymns," 202 n. 41).

statues of those gods had been carried in procession.[160] Since the chorus performed daily, it was probably a standing choir, perhaps composed of slaves. In 363, as part of his attempt to revive pagan religion, Emperor Julian wrote a letter of instruction to a priest named Theodorus, whom he had made inspector of all the sanctuaries of Asia Minor, specifying the details of his administration, including the hymnody to be performed at the temples. The priests were to learn the traditional hymns and sing them daily as part of their own personal devotion and their duties in public worship.[161] Unfortunately, Julian makes no mention of whether this singing was choral or not. Nor is it obvious how the prophet of Apollo, Pythios, performed hymns with the chorus of boys and young women at Claros—whether he sang the stanzas and they the refrain or some other type of format was followed.

Although most of the entertainment songs of the stage were probably solos performed by citharodes, tragic and comic singers, and singing mimes, choruses occasionally figured in plays[162] and were a standard part of Pyladic pantomime.[163] Children's choirs were sometimes kept or otherwise procured for home banquets by certain wealthy aristocrats,[164] and some of the voluntary associations put on entertainments that required choirs composed of their members.[165]

In *Table Talk*, Plutarch's persona mentions his own social set's customary singing of a group paean at symposia.[166] This refers to an old custom of the aristocratic symposion of classical Athens. Since that custom died out in the early Hellenistic period, either the paean was revived by elites of Plutarch's time (who wished to imitate certain habits of classical aristocrats) or else Plutarch has given his literary dialogue an Attic look, tongue-in-cheek, which most of his elite readers would have recognized.[167] Plutarch also describes himself and his

---

160. IStr 1101 = CIG 2715 = Franciszek Sokolowski, *Lois sacrées de l'Asie Mineure* (Boccard, 1955), 162 (no. 69).

161. Julian, *Ep.* 89b (Bidez 1/2: 169–170).

162. The evidence for choruses in plays, old and new, in the Roman era suggests a diminishment from the central role of the chorus in the classical age. See Cosgrove, *Music and Social Meals in Greek and Roman Antiquity*, 210–211.

163. See Eusebius's *Chronicle*, in Jerome's annotated translation, *Chron.*, *Ol.* 189.3 (Schoene, 143); Macrobius, *Sat.* 2.7.18.

164. This is implied by a remark in a sympotic scene in Aulus Gellius, *N.A.* 19.9.3.

165. See Cosgrove, *Music and Social Meals in Greek and Roman Antiquity*, 191–193.

166. Plutarch, *Q.C.* 7.8.4 (*Mor.* 712f–713a) and 9.14.1 (*Mor.* 743c).

167. See the historical analysis in Cosgrove, *Music and Social Meals in Greek and Roman Antiquity*, 188–190.

friends singing "Birth of the Muses," the prefatory hymn to Hesiod's Theogony. They are accompanied on the lyre by a musician-guest named Erato.[168] Details of this scene, too, sound anachronistic or otherwise implausible.[169] In neither story does Plutarch describe the format of the singing, but the old Attic paean was sung in unison by the diners. In another scene, Philo's Therapeutae offer songs before their festive supper, various members singing individually with the group responding.[170] Questions of historicity aside, the account shows that Philo and his readers were familiar with the responsorial format.

Aulus Gellius paints a scene in *Attic Nights* where a wealthy host brings in a choir of boys and girls to sing Greek poetry.[171] He makes no comment about the format. In *Hieroi Logoi*, Aelius Aristides mentions performances by children's choirs, boys' choirs, and men's choirs.[172] His descriptions are very general. The subject of a given verb for performance is always "the boys" or "the children" (etc.) and in one case a certain "Macedonian man," never specifically a choir with a leader. He reports that he dreamed that a boys' choir sang his hymns in a school at Alexandria[173] and that he himself maintained a choir of boys and staged performances of his songs with men's and boys' choirs, evidently in competitions in 147 CE.[174] He himself did not participate in these performances.[175]

Twice Aristides refers to a hymn's refrain. In one case, he heard a hymn in his sleep, a paean sent by Dionysus whose refrain was "Greetings, O ivy-crowned Dionysus."[176] When the Macedonian man sang one of Aristides's own hymns, the refrain was "*Iē Paian*, Heracles Asclepius."[177] The implication is that the man sang both the verses and the refrain.

In only one passage does Aristides describe what worshipers typically did when a paean was sung at the temple. They stood inside near the statue of the

---

168. Plutarch, *Q.C.* 9.14.1 (*Mor.* 743c).

169. See Cosgrove, *Music and Social Meals in Greek and Roman Antiquity*, 187–188.

170. Philo, *Contempl.* 80.

171. Aulus Gellius, *N.A.* 19.9.3–4

172. Aelius Aristides, *H.L.* 3.4; 4.38; 4.43–48.

173. *H.L.* 3.4.

174. *H.L.* 4.43–48.

175. *H.L.* 4.43

176. *H.L.* 4.39.

177. *H.L.* 4.42. Aristides calls this invocation a "greeting," but in *Heracles*, he refers to it as the ἐπᾳδόμενον of this hymn (*Her.* 21 [Jebb, 36]).

god.[178] Aristides makes no mention of the worshipers joining in by singing a refrain. Nor do other literary and inscriptional sources from the Roman era speak of visiting worshipers participating in choral hymnody at temple rituals by singing refrains.[179]

Refrains are found in surviving texts of poems, including some that date to the imperial era. It is important to keep in mind that refrains in poems are a structural feature, not direct evidence of a performance format. The late-republican *Eclogue* 8 of Virgil,[180] for example, and the second-century (CE) *Vigil of Venus* (*Pervigilium Veneris*) attributed to Florus have refrains. The latter is disposed in rough stanzas, each of which is followed by the words, "Tomorrow, the one who has never loved and the one who has loved—tomorrow let them both love."[181] If *Eclogue* 8 or the *Vigil of Venus* was set to music, as some of Ovid's poems were,[182] as well as some of Pliny's[183]—a soloist may have sung everything, or a chorus may have. The same goes for the surviving texts of cult hymns inscribed at sanctuaries, some of which show refrains.[184]

---

178. *H.L.* 4.50.

179. In my own searches in the sources and in scholarly literature on the subject, I have found no evidence for participation in the choral hymns by any worshipers besides the cult choir. Christopher Faraone discusses a particular cult hymn to Asclepius, which was inscribed at different temples in slightly different versions—the earliest from the Asclepion at Erythrae, dating to 380–360 BCE, and the others dating to the first and second centuries CE. Faraone suggests that "punctuation in two of the inscriptions and spacing on a third point to some kind of pause, perhaps to allow a larger group of worshippers to sing the refrain." Faraone does not, however, shore up the plausibility of this guess by citing explicit evidence from Roman-era literature or inscriptions for that kind of participation. Christopher Faraone, "An Athenian Tradition of Dactylic Paeans to Apollo and Asclepius: Choral Degeneration or a Flexible System of Non-Strophic Dactyls?" *Mnemosyne* 64 (2011): 209 n. 7 and 208–215. For the texts, see William D. Furley and Jan M. Bremer, *Greek Hymns: Selected Cult Songs from the Archaic to the Hellenistic Period*, vol. 1 (Mohr Siebeck, 2001), 211–214.

180. Virgil, *Ecl.* 8. The refrain, "Bring my songs home from town, bring Daphnis home," is sung by the character Aphesiboeus in the poem. Virgil's use of a responsorial format imitates the bucolic poetry of Theocritus in *Idylls* 1 and 2, which in turn may have been influenced by an even older literary tradition.

181. *cras amet qui numquam amavit quique amavit cras amet.*

182. See the autobiographical remark in Ovid, *Trist.* 2.509–20, which states that Ovid's poems were danced on the stage. This implies that they were set to melodies and used as librettos for some kind of narrative dance, perhaps pantomime, with a solo singer or a chorus. See Alessandra Zanobi, *Seneca's Tragedies and the Aesthetics of Pantomime* (Bloomsbury, 2014), 34–35.

183. Pliny boasts that Greeks set his verse to music and that his wife sings his poems—presumably for a small company of diners at private dinner parties. Pliny, *Ep.* 7.4.9 and 4.19.4.

184. Examples are found in the collection of hymns assembled by Furley and Bremer. An inscription from Crete that sets forth a hymn to Zeus-Kouros, for example, gives the refrain

Among the possible clues to a responsorial format in archaic-classical hymnody is the use of the verb *exarchein* (initiate, take the lead, etc.). When used of a chorus leader, it may sometimes describe what he or she does as a performer—singing strophes or other sections of a song to which the chorus responds.[185] If this performance style was current in the Roman age, it would have provided a cultural model for the church. Examples of *exarchein*-formulations for responsorial song-leading in Greek writings of the Roman era include a reference by cultural-geographer Pausanias and one by the church historian Sozomen. Although these authors are separated by centuries, their use of the verb without explanation in nontechnical works suggests its enduring currency for the type of song they describe. Pausanias describes a certain scene on a large chest in the temple of Hera at Olympia, which showed "the Muses singing" with "Apollo leading (*exarchōn*) the song."[186] The phrasing differentiates Apollo's role from theirs, meaning that Pausanias saw a familiar choral format in the picture, on the basis of which he inferred that Apollo was singing the verses in this scene, with the Muses responding. The passage in Sozomen describes a crowd of processing Christians who responded with refrains to singers who "were leading (*exērchon*) the psalms."[187]

Evidence for responsorial singing also appears in a novel by Longus, whose narrator observes that it was common for the boatswain to sing sea shanties while the rowers shouted in time to his voice.[188] Nearly as clear and direct is Clement of Alexandria's criticism of Christians who hymn God in church but "outside" recant their hymns and enjoy godless musical entertainments. "Those who sing this way and sing in response," he says, are the very ones who hymned

---

at the beginning, then repeats it after each stanza. See the text in William D. Furley and Jan M. Bremer, *Greek Hymns: Selected Cult Songs from the Archaic to the Hellenistic Period*, vol. 2 (Mohr Siebeck, 2001), 1–3; also the diplomatic transcriptions and photographs in Robert C. Bosanquet, "The Palaikastro Hymn of the Kouretes," *The Annual of the British School at Athens* 15 (1908/1909): 339–356.

185. Regarding the use of this verb for performance in classical times, see Ian Rutherford, *Pindar's Paeans: A Reading of the Fragments and a Survey of the Genre* (Oxford University Press, 2001), 66–68.

186. Pausanias 5.18.4. Because Apollo is traditionally represented as a lyre-player, it should not be inferred that he leads the Muses only instrumentally while they sing the verses of the hymn. Lyre-players were singers, who accompanied themselves on the lyre, and Apollo's singing is often mentioned in antiquity. See, for example, Euripides, *Her.* 349–351 and *Ion* 881–886; Plato, *Resp.* 383a–b; Statius, *Theb.* 6.355–364; Propertius, *El.* 2.1.3–4.

187. Sozomen, *H.E.* 5.19.19.

188. Longus, *Daphn. et Chlo.* 3.21.2.

immortality before."[189] The expression "singing and singing in response" could refer to responsorial song.

Responsorial song as a recreational cultural habit is also implied by reports that Christians adopted popular song forms of that type to purvey their message in appealing ways. We hear that the "Arians" did so, and our only description of an Arian song-format appears to refer to odes with refrains.[190] Moreover, when Augustine decided to try his hand at composing a hymn in a popular verse form, he wrote *Psalm against the Donatists*, which featured a one-line refrain.[191]

Augustine's description of his song throws light on the whole subject. He composed his poem for the "simple" and "uneducated," he says, so that they would find it easy to memorize. Each stanza of stichic verse began with a different letter of the alphabet in alphabetical order.[192] The hymn also had a one-line refrain, stated at the beginning of the poem and repeated after each stanza. This refrain was sung as a response (*quod respondetur*), he says, which implies a differentiation between the performer of the stanzas, most likely a solo singer who could read, and everyone else, the so-called simple people who could not read.

To review, group song of various kinds was common in the Greco-Roman world. While its formats are rarely described, the ancient sources occasionally refer to the use of refrains. And while the appearance of repeated material in a poem is not in itself evidence of a responsorial *performance* format, that format must have been common, since it is so very convenient. It must also have been highly esteemed as a format for ceremonial song, since we learn from Pausanias that the Greeks imagined that when Apollo and the Muses sang together, they did so responsorially.

Since responsorial song was part of Greco-Roman culture, the church's adoption of it is in some respects an unremarkable example of a group using

189. Clement of Alexandria, *Paed.* 3.11.80.4.

190. Socrates quotes what appears to be a refrain of one of these hymns (*H.E.* 6.8.4) and later refers to them as "antiphonal," which probably means "responsorial" (6.8.10). Sozomen speaks of songs "in the manner of antiphons," which have "endings" and certain lines "mixed in" (*H.E.* 8.8.1–3). These passages are discussed in chapter 11. "Arian" may be an anachronistic term for a group of Homoeans in the accounts.

191. Augustine, *Retract.* 1.20.

192. See the edition in Cyril Lambot, "Texte complété et amendé du <<Psalmus contra partem Donati>> de Saint Augustin," *Revue Bénédictine* 47 (1935): 312–338. The manuscript tradition suggests that medieval editors or copyists made efforts to regularize the rhythm as meter, a tendency found in modern editions of the hymn as well. Much of this may be misguided if Augustine sought to imitate the unmetrical style of the biblical psalms. See Vincent Hunink, "Singing Together in Church: Augustine's Psalm against the Donatists," in *Sacred Words: Orality, Literacy and Religion*, ed. A. P. M. H. Lardinois, J. H. Blok, and M. G. M. van der Poel, (Brill, 2011), 389–403.

a familiar song-format for its own purposes. Yet one characteristic of the Christian style of responsorial psalmody is not documented for song in the wider culture, namely, the way Christians selected refrains. The only known Jewish models for selection of refrains in psalmody are the performances of the Hallel and the Great Hallel. Some or all of the psalms that came to be known by these names had long been sung responsorially at Jewish festivals, and a rabbinic discussion about the Song of the Sea shows that the custom continued into the Roman era. Rabbi Eleazar ben Yose the Galilean speculates that when the Israelites of Moses's time sang the Song of the Sea, they would have followed the method used for singing the Hallel in the synagogue: Moses would have sung the verses, and the people would have sung the first line as the refrain. Rabbi Nehemiah offers the recital of the Shema as the clue. The Shema was performed responsorially in the synagogue between the leader and the people, who took turns intoning the successive phrases. Rabbi Akiba offers a different possibility. He suspects that the Song of the Sea would have been sung according to the lining-out method used for the Hallel in school settings.[193]

These differences of opinion, along with the fact that only the Hallel and the Shema are cited as guides, show that responsorial singing of the Hallel in the synagogue, which occurred at festivals, followed a well-established responsorial custom, where the first line served as the refrain. There is additional evidence that the old *ḥesed* refrain was also used in festival psalmody.[194] In other words, in the few references to responsorial Jewish song in ancient Jewish literature, we hear of first-line refrains and a certain traditional refrain.

When Christians began singing psalms chorally, adopting the convenient responsorial format, they had to decide which words to use as refrains. This was not obvious for most psalms, and whatever Christians may or may not have known about how Jews sang the Hallel, there is no evidence that Christians took their cue from Jewish festival psalmody.

Some Christians inferred that psalms with "Alleluia" in their superscriptions should be sung with that word as a final response or refrain. As for the rest of the Psalter, it is a peculiarity of the Christians' method that they did not treat the first line of a psalm as its implied refrain. They felt free to designate any verse as a refrain, making their choices on thematic grounds. This method is not attested elsewhere.

---

193. *T. Soṭa* 6.2–3.

194. The old *ḥesed* refrain is repeated three times at the beginning of the Great Hallel (MT Psalm 136) and then after every verse. It is also the first line of MT Psalm 118, the final psalm of the six-fold Hallel. The earliest references to it in Hebrew narrative are in 2 Chronicles and Ezra (see above).

Concluding Observations

Two formats of psalmody are explicitly documented for the church of the first several centuries: solo psalmody and responsorial psalmody. Responsorial singing was typically led by a soloist, but it is possible that on certain occasions, a small group of singers sang the verses to which the people responded. For example, it is conceivable that for a special event, such as a martyr procession, a group of young cantors sang together, having memorized the psalm to a fixed melody, so as to ensure a rendering of the verses in a volume that could be clearly heard by a mass of people in an outdoor setting. There is a clue to this sort of psalm-leading in a sentence in Sozomen's account of the translation of Babylas. "The accomplished among them led the psalms," he says, and the crowd chanted a refrain.[195] Sozomen's use of a plural noun for the leadership of the psalms suggests a small group, presumably persons with strong voices. Since Sozomen himself had not witnessed the parade, he probably relied on his personal knowledge of how psalms were sung in large public processions during the first half of the fifth century.

Responsorial psalmody made group singing of any psalm an accessible practice. First, the majority of people were not in a position to learn all 150 psalms by heart, since they did not possess their own personal copies of the Psalter and could not read in any case. Second, memorizing all the words of the psalms, which some monks did accomplish, was insufficient for group singing, unless the group also knew the melodies or how to sing them in unison to a formula. In this respect, there was an important difference between psalmody and the other sorts of song-learning in popular culture. In the case of folk songs, work songs, and musical entertainments of the theater, a song's melody was more or less fixed and came with the words. Hence the process of learning the words entailed learning the melody, and the two were mutually reinforcing. With psalmody, it was different. The psalms that Christians most often heard in liturgy were, originally, individual renditions by church members at Christian suppers. Later, by the fourth century, they heard and responded to psalms sung by readers at services of the word and at morning and evening church services. Reader-singers composed, improvised, or adapted a melody for every psalm assigned to them, when it was assigned. Hence, the singing of a given psalm varied from one reader to the next, and even when a psalm was sung on different occasions by the same reader, that reader had no compelling reason to sing it to the same melody. Moreover, even if readers used model melody forms, these "psalm tones" had to be fitted to unmetrical lines of varying lengths and groupings. The reader, who needed to practice all the lessons beforehand so that he would be able to read the

195. Sozomen, *H.E.* 5.19.19. Regarding the translation "the accomplished," see chapter 9, n. 36.

handwritten texts fluently, worked out how to fit a model melody to each line of the assigned psalm. The congregation, however, was not part of this rehearsal. By contrast, choirs, such as a children's choir that sang at a liturgy, would have been taught their song through rehearsals and could have sung in unison. The difference between a choir's preparation and the experience of a congregation explains why the congregation's part in psalmody was not the whole psalm but only a refrain and why refrain-singing was introduced into church psalmody in the first place.

The reader-cantor probably intoned the refrain at the beginning. A passage in the *Mystogogical Catecheses* is suggestive. Explaining to the catechumens how their participation in their first Communion would proceed, the author tells them that they will hear "the singer urging you with a divine melody into the communion of the holy mysteries, and saying, 'Taste and see that the Lord is good.'"[196] These words from Psalm 33 were probably a signal for the distribution to begin and the Communion psalm to be sung, the line intoned by the singer being an initial prompt for the people's response.

In the case of the prehomily lessons, where the psalms were often much less familiar, the reader-singer may have sung the refrain line with the congregation through the course of the performance to reinforce its pattern and keep the people together. This would have been especially helpful in settings where the congregation was composed of multiple language groups and not everyone had facility in the language spoken in liturgy.[197] There is no direct evidence, however, that readers followed this practice.

An alternative to responsorial psalmody with a refrain would have been for the reader to sing each line and the congregation to repeat it after him. As already noted, this method was used for the Hallel in Jewish schools as a teaching aid. Centuries later a form of it, called "lining out," appeared in the hymnody of early Protestantism, when congregational hymn-singing became popular but literacy was low and churches were not in a position to provide congregations with costly hymnals for individual use in any case. Someone who could read (the preacher or an educated layperson) sang the lines of the hymn from a book, and after each line the congregation sang it back. If this method was used by some ancient churches, there is no mention of it.

Indeed, there is no clear evidence that Christians engaged in any form of congregational psalmody other than the responsorial form. While

---

196. [Cyril of Jerusalem], *Myst. Cat.* 5.20.

197. According to Egeria, for example, the Jerusalem Christians spoke Greek and Syriac, and pilgrims also spoke these languages, as well as Latin. For that reason, she says, interpreters were present to explain the Greek services to the people who did not know Greek well. Egeria, *Itin.* 47.3–4.

psalm-singing with two choruses is mentioned a few times and entailed some kind of alternation, turn-taking in singing the refrain is more likely to have been the type of alternation than antiphonal singing of verses. It is true that formats that are not mentioned cannot be ruled out, given all the gaps in our knowledge of the early church. But silence is not evidence, and I have explained why singing in a format that required the entire congregation to know psalms by heart would have been impractical. If it did occur, it was probably rare.

CHAPTER ELEVEN

Antiphons and Antiphonal Singing

Patristic writers use the Greek noun *antiphōnon* and related forms—adjective, adverb, and verb—to describe elements of musical activity. Transliterations of this word group are also found in writings by Latin Christians. The liturgical use of the word has proven particularly difficult to define. A short and very selective history of interpretation will help map out the interpretive terrain, which tends to be revisited periodically by liturgical historians without definitive results, especially regarding the earliest liturgical uses of the language in the late fourth and fifth centuries.

Throughout the medieval period and during most of the twentieth century, it was widely held that alternating singing by two choirs trading parts of the body of the song was a very old format of the Eastern church, which entered the Western church through Ambrose.[1] In 1907, the *Catholic Encyclopedia* included an article by Andrew Shipman, who defined "antiphon" as both a form of singing and a type of song, where versicles are sung alternatingly by two choirs, with responses and a final doxology.[2] The same dictionary also included an article on antiphon by the renowned liturgical historian Henri Leclercq, who summarized research he published that same year in a much more extensive essay on "antienne" in *Dictionnaire d'archéologie*. Leclercq set forth a variety of two-choir formats that, according to him, ancient Eastern Christian writers called "antiphonal."[3] Meanwhile, the Latinized word *antiphona* acquired a distinct meaning in the West, Leclerq argued, as illustrated by Egeria's use of this term

1. This view has been subjected to trenchant criticism. In *Antiphon and Psalm in the Ambrosian Office*, Bailey provides a wide-ranging criticism of the traditional conception of antiphonal psalmody in the early centuries, both East and West (see below with n. 7). Before him, Helmut Leeb had offered a comprehensive study showing that psalmody with two choirs trading verses was not introduced by Ambrose and that psalmody in his church was responsorial: a reader or singer performed the verses and the people responded with a refrain. See Helmut Leeb, *Die Psalmodie bei Ambrosius* (Herder, 1967).

2. Andrew J. Shipman, "Antiphon. In the Greek Church—," *Catholic Encyclopedia*, vol. 1, ed. Charles G. Herbermann et al. (Appleton, 1907), 575.

3. Henri Leclercq, "Antiphon, In Greek Liturgy," *Catholic Encyclopedia*, vol. 1, ed. Charles G. Herbermann et al. (Appleton, 1907), 576; Leclercq, "Antienne (Liturgie)," in *Dictionnaire d'archéologie chrétienne et de liturgie*, vol. 1, part 2, ed. Fernand Cabrol and Henri Leclercq (Paris: Letouzey et Ané, 1907), cols. 2282–2319.

for an independent song, distinct from a psalm but, like psalms, sung responsorially.[4] According to Leclercq, an antiphon lasted longer than a psalm, perhaps because it had a different melodic or rhythmic style.[5]

Writing two generations after Leclercq, Robert Taft opined that in Egeria's usage the word "antiphon" meant a psalm response—"a trope or refrain, that is, a piece of ecclesiastical poetry," as distinguished from a psalm-verse or other biblical refrain or Alleluia—and that (by synecdoche) the word came to refer to a psalm to which such a response was sung.[6] Several years later, Terence Bailey set forth a detailed study of passages containing words of the *antiph** family, as well as passages describing various formats of group psalmody. Bailey concluded that the meaning of the term evolved. It was originally a designation for a psalm response. In some places, this response was a nonbiblical refrain or a doxology.[7] The word also came to be used for a psalm or set of psalm-verses sung with various kinds of refrains and was used in some communities for a responsorial psalm, sung standing, that closed with a doxology.[8]

In Greek, the adjective *antiphōnos* meant something done "in response." In technical ancient Greek musicology, the adjective described concordant intervals, and the neuter noun formed from the adjective meant "octave" or "sounding at the octave."[9] Singing in octaves occurred in choral song when those with higher vocal ranges (generally women and prepubescent boys) sang an octave above those with lower ranges (generally men, including older adolescents). The resulting sound was regarded as richly harmonious, even a kind of unison.[10]

Surviving ancient Christian literature contains no uses of antiphon in the sense of octave concordance. But Christian writers did use *antiphōnos* to mean an act of responding, and they used its cognate verb *antiphōnein* for "sound in

4. Leclercq, "Antienne (Liturgie)," cols. 2291–2292.

5. Leclercq, "Antienne (Liturgie)," col. 2292.

6. Robert Taft, *The Liturgy of the Hours in East and West: The Origins of the Divine Office and Its Meaning for Today* (Liturgical, 1986), 54.

7. Terence Bailey, *Antiphon and Psalm in the Ambrosian Office* (Institute of Mediaeval Music, 1994), 55–108 and the conclusions set forth on p. 123.

8. Bailey, *Antiphon and Psalm in the Ambrosian Office*, 73–75, 77–79, and 102–103 (where he draws his inferences).

9. Gaudentius, *Isag.* 20; Ps.-Aristotle, *Probl.* 19.17, 19.18, and 19.39. See Solon Michaelides, *The Music of Ancient Greece: An Encyclopedia* (Faber and Faber, 1978), *s.v.* antiphonon; *GMW* 1: 193–195 (Ps.- Aristotelian *Problems* 19.16–18 and the translator's commentary in notes 27 and 30), 200 (Ps.-Aristotelian *Problems* 19.39 with the translator's comments in n. 72).

10. See Ps.-Aristotle, *Probl.* 19.17–18; Ptolemy, *Harm.* 1.7.9–11 (Düring).

answer" or "respond."[11] These were common uses of the words by Greek-speaking people generally.

Gregory of Nazianzus refers to a "symphonious, antiphonous double arrangement of angels, set above and below, a hymnody of divine dignity and nature."[12] This passage led nineteenth-century scholars to conclude that patristic divines were familiar with antiphonal singing—two choirs trading verses back and forth.[13] A later specialist, noting that Isaiah 6 depicts seraphim crying a sanctus "one to the other," opines that Gregory must have had that passage in view.[14] Gregory's language certainly does bring Isaiah 6 to mind. The relation of his words to church psalmody is less clear. His double choir is not a divided chorus of angels in heaven, since one of his choirs (the one "set below") is composed of "angelic" virgins on earth. Hence, the earthly choir answers a heavenly choir, not another earthly choir.

In another poem, Gregory hymns "the great God who rules on high . . . the great clear-voiced hymns of angelic choirs standing nearby, the harmony of the world from (their) opposed voice."[15] Given the plural "choirs" in this last passage, the expression "opposed voice" (*opos antithetou*) probably means singing back and forth, but Gregory does not go into the specifics of the alternation: it could be choral antiphony or dual-choir responsorial singing.[16] Nor does Gregory use the term "antiphon" in this context. He does use that word in another poem: "Cast a light sleep upon my eyelids / that my hymnic tongue might not perish for long. / Let not the antiphon of the angels be silent about your creation."[17]

---

11. Hippolytus, for example, uses the term for one person responding to another in speech (*In cant. cant.* 14.1 [the Greek paraphrase]). Eusebius uses it for responding in a letter (Eusebius, *Vit. Const.* 4.34.1).

12. Gregory of Nazianzus, *Carm.* 1.2.10 (*Carm. mor.* 10 [*De virt.*]), lines 920–925 (PG 37: 746–747).

13. See, for example, Joseph Bingham, *The Works of the Rev. Joseph Bingham*, vol. 5 [= *Origines ecclesiasticae; or, the Antiquities of the Christian Church*, vols. 14 and 15] (Oxford University Press, 1855), 13.

14. Peter Jeffery, "Philo's Impact on Christian Psalmody," in *Psalms in Community: Jewish and Christian Textual, Liturgical, and Artistic Traditions*, ed. Harold W. Attridge and Margot E. Fassler (Society of Biblical Literature, 2003), 179–180.

15. Gregory of Nazianzus, *Carm.* 2.1.34 (*Carm. de se ipso* 34: *In silent. ieiunii*), line 80 (PG 37: 1313). Jeffery's article alerted me to this passage ("Philo's Impact on Christian Psalmody," 180).

16. Gregory also uses the expression ὀπὸς ἀντιθέτου in another place in application to singers, again without any clue to the format of their singing. Gregory of Nazianzus, *Carm.* 2.1.16 (*Carm. de se ipso* 16: *Somn. de anastas. eccl.*), line 84 (PG 37: 1260).

17. Gregory of Nazianzus, *Carm.* 1.1.32 (*Carm. dog.* 32: *Hymn. uesper.*), 33–38 (PG 37: 513; TLG lineation 11–19).

Does "antiphon" in these verses refer to angelic praise in a certain choral format, such as singing back and forth? Or does it mean a praiseful "response" to God's works? There is no way to know.

The noun "antiphon" also appears in a commentary on the Psalter by Diodore of Tarsus (d. circa 390).[18] In a set of comments on Psalm 23:7–10, Diodore concludes that the Israelites must have sung these words in two choruses, since the verses are a set of questions and answers:

> Since it was necessary to say utterances of this sort by antiphon (*ex antiphōnou*), another part answers, as it were, replying, "Who is the King of Glory?" Then the other part responds, "The Lord strong and mighty, the Lord strong in war." Then the others take up the same words (as before) and say, "Lift up, O gates." Then, it says, let this be: "And be lifted up, eternal gates, and the King of Glory will enter." Again, the ones who asked before ask in response and say, "Who is this King of Glory?" Then, naturally, those who have the witness of experience shout together, "The Lord of powers. He is the King of Glory."[19]

Here the expression *ex antiphōnou* is a shorthand. Diodore's verbs tell us what it means. After one group of singers has uttered the command, "Open, gates etc.," the other group responds (*apokrinetai*). Then the first singers respond (*antiphtheggontai*). Hence, *ex antiphōnou* means "by response." As for the antiphonal format, where the groups trade the singing of the verses, Diodore neither confirms nor disconfirms whether Christian psalmody ever took that form. It is not his topic.

In an anonymous Christian romance, the apocryphal saint Xanthippe, delighting in the birdsong she hears in a garden, marvels that "not only among human beings has God established myriad languages but also among birds, diverse voices, as if, by antiphons and responses, to receive tuneful and heart-piercing hymns from his own works."[20] The expression "antiphons and responses"

---

18. Louis Mariès has demonstrated that the commentary was written by Diodore of Tarsus in Antioch or at least reflecting Antioch's exegetical traditions. Louis Mariès, "Études préliminaires à l'édition de Diodore de Tarse 'Sur les Psaumes'—La tradition manuscrite," *Recherches de science religieuse* 22 (1932): 385–408 and 513–540. Mariès's arguments are rehearsed and affirmed by Olivier in his edition of the commentary for the CCSG series. Jean-Marie Olivier, ed., *Diodori Tarsensis commentarii in psalmos*, vol. 1: *Commentarii in psalmos I–L* (CCSG 6; Turnhout: Brepols, 1980), CIII–CVIII.

19. Diodorus of Tarsus, *Comm. in psalm. 23* 7.

20. *Act. Xanth. et Polyx.* 6.

refers to how birds seem to answer one another, which is here interpreted as their way of hymning God. Since birds sing individually, not in unison chorus, the description does not picture birds as antiphonal choirs.

In a sermon given around 400, roughly speaking, Severian of Gabala uses the expression "by antiphon" in comments on the vision of Isaiah 6, where the cherubim, as already mentioned, cry the threefold sanctus "one to the other." According to Severian, one cries "Holy," then the other cries "Holy," then the first one cries "Holy."[21] He adds that "just as in psalmody the participants answer with Alleluias, so, too, the powers above sing chorally to one another, even as they answer back by melodious antiphon with the doxology." Here, "by antiphon" refers to a repeated response by turn-taking singers, not to trading verses of a song.

In a lost work of Theodore of Mopsuestia (circa 350–428), quoted by the twelfth-century historian and theologian Nicetas Choniates (in his *Thesaurus of Faith*), Theodore offers a version of the story told by Theodoret of Cyr concerning two laymen of Antioch named Flavian and Diodore who invented some form of alternating hymnody. The Mopsuestian makes no mention of divided choirs. He does use the word "antiphon," whereas Theodoret of Cyr's account uses no term from the *antiph** word-group.[22] Now, Theodore of Mopsuestia was a Syrian who served as a presbyter in Antioch before being made bishop of a city in Cilicia. He traces "antiphons" to Syrian church song, said to have been introduced to Antioch by the aforementioned Flavian and Diodore. They brought over "from the Syrian language into the Greek the form of the antiphons of psalmody," he says, "and while the heretics were saying 'Glory to the Father through the Son in the Holy Spirit', Flavian was the first to say, 'Glory to the Father and to the Son and to the Holy Spirit.'"[23] Theodore associates an antiphon with a use of

21. Severian, *In mund. creat.*, Hom. 2.5 (PG 56: 445).

22. For the passage in Theodoret of Cyr, see above and compare Bailey's careful analysis of the passages in Theodoret of Cyr and Theodore of Mopsuestia (Bailey, *Antiphon and Psalm in the Ambrosian Office*, 76–79).

23. As quoted in Nicetas Choniates, *Thes. pist.*, Vat. Reg. gr. 67, f. 27v: καὶ ὥς φησι Θεόδωρος ὁ Μοψυεστίας, τὸ τῶν ἀντιφώνων τῆς ψαλμῳδίας εἶδος [Φλαβιανὸς καὶ Διόδωρος] ἐκ τῆς Σύρων εἰς τὴν Ἑλλάδος γλῶτταν μεταβίβασαν. The manuscript has not been edited and does not appear to be available in photographs, but it was examined by Terence Bailey, who quotes the passage (*Antiphon and Psalm*, 79). A version of the same has often been cited from a Latin translation of Nicetas's *Thesaurus* by Pierre Morel, based on a Greek manuscript at Mount Athos and republished in Patrologia Graeca. Morel's translation seems to interpret the type of psalmody as antiphons: *Atque ut Theodorus Mopsuestenus scribit, illam psalmodiae speciem, quas antiphonas dicimus, illi* [*Flavianus et Diodorus*] *ex Syrorum lingua in Graecam transtulerunt* (*Thes. orth. fid.* 5.30; PG 139: 1390). There is reason to believe that Nicetas did indeed have books by Theodore of Mopsuestia that have otherwise been lost to history. Uwe Lang, observing that Richard Vaggione has identified fragments of Theodore of Mopsuestia's *Contra Eunomium* in Nicetas

the doxology in psalmody. An "antiphon of psalmody" was either the doxology itself or a psalm sung with a doxology.

Socrates, a contemporary of Theodore of Mopsuestia, uses the *antiph** language in describing a conflict waged through hymnody between "Arians" and orthodox Christians in Constantinople in the closing years of the fourth century (398–400). Socrates, a native of Constantinople who completed a church history in the 430s, says that the Arians, whose regular gathering place was outside the city, went into the city on Saturdays and met "within the gates of the city near the portico." There they would sing "antiphonous odes, fitting them to the Arian view."[24] The Arians did this for most of the night, and "in the morning, saying these same sorts of antiphons, they would go through the middle of the city and outside the gates and would occupy the places where they used to assemble."[25] Meanwhile, the orthodox also had antiphonous hymns. Socrates purports to give an account of their origin:

> One should also tell from where the custom of antiphonous hymns in the church received its beginning. Ignatius the third bishop in Antioch in the succession from the Apostle Peter . . . saw a vision of angels hymning the Holy Trinity through antiphonous hymns (*tōn antiphōnōn hymnōn*), and he transmitted to the church at Antioch the manner (*tropon*) of the vision, whence the same tradition spread to all the churches. This, then, is the report concerning antiphonous hymns.[26]

Even though Socrates's Antiochene etiology cannot be credited, it implies that he believed that Christians had been singing antiphonous hymns for centuries. Moreover, he uses the noun "antiphons" to describe the antiphonous songs of the Arians and gives an example of one of them: "Where are they who say that the three are one power?"[27] This was probably the refrain of one of the songs. If

---

Choniates, comments that "Nicetas, who has until now not been studied extensively, seems to be a storehouse for extracts from Patristic writings which have not come down to us otherwise." Uwe M. Lang, *John Philoponus and the Controversies over Chalcedon in the Sixth Century: A Study and Translation of the* Arbiter (Leuven: Peeters, 2001), 22 n. 80.

24. ᾠδὰς ἀντιφώνους πρὸς τὴν Ἀρειανὴν δόξαν συντιθέντες. Socrates, *H.E.* 6.8.2. The next sentence (see n. 25), where Socrates uses the plural noun ἀντίφωνα, shows that ᾠδὰς ἀντιφώνους is a synonym for antiphons.

25. ὑπὸ δὲ ὄρθρον τὰ τοιαῦτα ἀντίφωνα λέγοντες διὰ μέσης τῆς πόλεως ἐξῄεσαν τῶν πυλῶν καὶ τοὺς τόπους, ἔνθα συνήγοντο, κατελάμβανον. Socrates, *H.E.* 6.8.3.

26. Socrates, *H.E.* 6.8.10–6.9.1.

27. Socrates, *H.E.* 6.8.4.

Arian antiphons had refrains, then Socrates, writing in the 430s, used the word "antiphon" for a song with a refrain. (It is probably no accident that he uses the term "songs" for the Arians' music but switches to "hymns," a common word for psalms, when he describes the antiphonous songs of the orthodox.) Socrates does not clarify whether antiphonous means simply responsorial or had a more specific meaning. The conflict in song between the Arians and the orthodox was one chapter in a debate that often focused on doxologies. But Socrates does not say that the two sides at Constantinople contended by formulating competing doxologies. His one example (quoted above) looks like a refrain, and it does not have the form of a doxology.

Sozomen, who used Socrates as his primary source, writes as follows in the 440s:

> And dividing into groups, [the Arians] would sing in the manner (*tropon*) of antiphons, adding endings (*akroteleutia*) composed to their view. . . . And to finish up, they added odes for the sake of provocation, mixing into their hymns (the line), "Where are the ones who call the three a single power?" and others like it. John [Chrysostom], being worried that some of those who congregated with him might go with them, encouraged his people to perform the same manner of psalmody.[28]

This account is clearly an expansion of Socrates's description and may rely on an additional source or sources. Sozomen interprets the line "Where are those who say. . .?" as a refrain. He also embellishes Socrates's account by saying that the Arians "added endings fitted to their doctrine," which were sung in "the manner of antiphons." If the endings were doxologies, why is he not more explicit? Perhaps he means that they used a variety of provocative refrains to mock the orthodox and their beliefs. He construed the expression "manner of antiphons" to mean a style of singing that included refrains. The orthodox applied this to their own "psalmody," whether that word refers in this context to hymns or psalms.

Sozomen does not retell the story about Ignatius's vision of singing angels, perhaps because he did not credit it. Instead, he contends that John Chrysostom's effort to protect his flock against Arian recruitment inaugurated a new form of hymnody among the orthodox. The Nicene Christians paraded through the streets at night, carrying silver crosses and tapers as they sang psalms or hymns (or both) in "the same manner (*tropon*)" as the Arians. And at the end of his account, when Sozomen tells how the Arians were compelled to give up meeting together, he writes that "the Catholics, having for such a cause begun to hymn

28. Sozomen, *H.E.* 8.8.1–3.

in the manner (*tropon*) mentioned, have continued to do the same right up to the present."[29] Clearly, "manner" is a shorthand for "the manner of antiphons."

What was new, as Sozomen conceived it? Was it Nicene adoption of responsorial singing or of some kind of dual-choir format? Or was it Nicene composition and performance of hymns in the manner of antiphons, meaning responsorial hymns with explicitly Nicene doctrine? It is very doubtful that Sozomen would have imagined that the manner of antiphons adopted by the Nicene Christians was simply responsorial song, since, in that case, Sozomen, who was born around 400, would have had to imagine that responsorial psalmody was invented during his parents' generation as the outcome of a particular conflict between the orthodox and the Arians in Constantinople near the beginning of the reign of Theodosius II, that is, around 379–381. Yet Sozomen himself gives an account of public psalmody with the use of refrains, which took place in the 360s. He does so when he rehearses the story of the translation of the relics of Babylas from Daphne back to Antioch. He even quotes one of the refrains.[30]

What about a dual-choir format? Sozomen does speak of the Arians dividing into groups. But his language is vague. His word for groups (*systēmata*) is not a common term for choirs, and he does not say that the Arians divided into *two* groups. Hence, the division may not have been a double-choir format but a distribution of the Arians into several groups around the city.[31]

If the new type of song adopted by "the Catholics" was not responsorial singing as such (which they already practiced in their psalmody) or dual-choir singing (which is probably not mentioned in Sozomen's account), that leaves the third option—responsorial Trinitarian hymnody, that is, the application of the familiar responsorial style used for psalmody ("the manner of antiphons") to explicitly Trinitarian hymnody, making it possible for Catholic composers of such hymns to introduce them into settings such as a vigil or procession as people's song.

Another bit of information about the use of the word "antiphon" comes from Palladius's description of a monastic community on the Mount of Olives to which Palladius belonged in the 380s. Every morning, he says, Abba Adolius used to make the rounds of the brothers, knocking on the door of each cell, "gathering them to the houses of prayer and singing the first or second antiphon

29. Sozomen, *H.E.* 8.8.5.

30. Sozomen, *H.E.* 5.19.17–19.

31. Bailey infers that the wording does not refer to a double-choir format but to a division of the Arians into singing groups spread around the city (*Antiphon and Psalm in the Ambrosian Office*, 75–76). Polybius uses the word σύστημα for a band of soldiers (see LSJ, *s.v.* σύστημα 2). Perhaps Sozomen calls the groups of Arians συστήματα to suggest the combative nature of their song as they challenged the orthodox.

with them in each house, and praying with them."[32] Palladius does not describe the format, but the word "antiphon" must refer to a psalm recited in a certain way, since monks would not have begun their day singing nonbiblical hymns. The numbering of the antiphons implies that they were fixed psalms of the morning office.

In the same locale a generation later (the early 430s), Melania Junior and Rufinus of Aquileia founded monasteries on the Mount of Olives, one for men and one for women. A friend named Gerontius, who knew Melania during this period, composed a biography of her a decade or two after her death in 439.[33] This account contains a description of the hymnody of the night office of the sisters in the 430s, together with what they sang at matins. At night there were "three *hypopsalmata*, three readings, and in the morning fifteen antiphons."[34] The word *hypopsalma* originally referred to a psalm refrain. "I heard the *hypopsalma*," declares Gregory of Nyssa in an address at the Synod of Constantinople in 381, "which we all added, singing together, 'Great is our Lord and great is his might, and of his understanding there is no limit' (Ps 146:5)."[35] Later examples show that refrains designated by this term could be bits of nonbiblical poetry.[36] But they could also be free-standing lines that were not always used as refrains. An instance that is more-or-less contemporary with Gerontius's' *Life of Melania* appears in the mid-fifth-century *Life of Hypatius* by Callinicus of Rufinianae, who tells how the dying saint gave a blessing to the monks gathered around him, saying the *hypopsalma*, "Come, let us rejoice in the Lord!" And the brothers sang the same words.[37] Melania called for just three *hypopsalmata* as the hymnody for nocturns but as many as fifteen antiphons for the morning office, the two offices being separated by a short period of sleep. Perhaps *hypopsalmata* were repeated over and over in her monastery. In any case, Melania's community distinguished *hypopsalmata* from antiphons, which were also independent songs of some type. Since we expect to see psalms in these services, it is odd that Melania assigns only *hypopsalmata* to nocturns, three of them. Something must be assumed here that

32. Palladius, *L.H.* 43.3 (Recension G; ed. Bartelink).

33. See Elizabeth A. Clark, *Melania the Younger: From Rome to Jerusalem* (Oxford University Press, 2021), 7.

34. Gerontius, *Vit. Melan. Jun.* 2.47.

35. Gregory of Nyssa, *De deitate adversus Evagrium* (GNO 9/1: 339).

36. In a general description of the use of this word in the Byzantine church, Egon Wellesz describes a ὑποψάλμα as a short phrase said after each psalm verse; the phrase was not taken from the psalm itself. See Egon Wellesz, *A History of Byzantine Music and Hymnography*, 2nd ed. (Clarendon, 1961), 35 n. 2.

37. Callinicus, *Vit. Hypat.* 51.2–3.

is not spelled out. As for the morning service, perhaps the word "antiphon" had acquired the sense it possessed in the later Byzantine era: verses selected from a psalm, each of which was answered with a recurring nonbiblical expression.[38]

The earliest known Latin-speaking writer to use the term "antiphon" is Egeria in her description of liturgical customs of the Eastern church in the late fourth century. Egeria uses three terms for song, usually in the plural: psalms (*psalmi*), hymns (<*h*>*ymni*), and antiphons (*antiphonae*). At the predawn daily service in Jerusalem (with monks, cloistered women, and laity in attendance), "psalms are recited, and hymns are responded to, and antiphons in a similar manner (*similiter et antiphonae*)."[39] This makes clear that antiphons were songs to which responses were made. In the same passage, Egeria reports that there was prayer by the clergy "with each hymn." A few lines later, she repeats this observation, using the expression "after each hymn or (*uel*) antiphon." She uses similar phrasing to describe the predawn Sunday service, where the attendees sang "hymns and antiphons," and prayers were again recited "after each hymn or antiphon."[40]

At the tenth hour (*licinicon*) of the daily office, Egeria says, "vesper psalms and antiphons" were sung.[41] When the bishop arrived and sat down with his clergy, "hymns or antiphons" were sung. During the eight weeks of Easter, after the midday meal, a service was held, where "hymns are said and prayers are made,"[42] a service to which Egeria subsequently refers using a slightly varied phrasing, writing "after the psalms are said and prayer is made."[43] The equivalence of these two phrases suggests that Egeria used the words "psalms" and "hymns" interchangeably. But if so, why did she write of the predawn service that "psalms are recited, and hymns are responded to, and antiphons in a similar manner"?

Egeria's most frequent term for a song is "hymn," and this word often stands alone. Notably, Egeria never uses the word "antiphon" by itself; that word is always the second element in a pair or trio of terms. By my count, the word "psalms" is paired with "antiphons" seven times in the *Itinerary*, and the word "hymns" is paired with "antiphons" seventeen times.[44] Twice Egeria uses the terms "psalms" and "hymns" in the same sentence in a fashion that seems to

38. Wellesz, *A History of Byzantine Music and Hymnography*, 35 n. 2.

39. Egeria, *Itin.* 24.1.

40. *Itin.* 24.8.

41. *Itin.* 24.4.

42. *Itin.* 39.3.

43. *Itin.* 39.4.

44. The expressions "psalms *et* antiphons" and "psalms *uel* antiphons" appear, and sometimes a verb or other term intervenes, e.g., "hymns are sung and antiphons."

differentiate them. These instances are perhaps best explained by prior church usage. Both words derive from Greek. Greek Christians used the words "psalms" and "hymns" interchangeably for the songs of David, probably under the influences of the Septuagint, which uses both terms (occasionally even together in superscriptions[45]), as well as under the influence of their reading of Jewish literature and the New Testament.[46] John Chrysostom, for example, says that "David, learning all these things, writes the psalm, lifting up thankful hymns to God."[47] Sozomen, speaking of the Therapeutae (and accepting Eusebius's claim that they were Christian monks of earliest times), writes that they worshiped God "with psalms and hymns," an expression that is surely a pleonasm for biblical psalmody.[48] Perhaps psalms and hymns were more or less synonyms for Egeria, too, as they probably were for Augustine, when he used the expression *psalmi et hymni* to describe the chants of prayer.[49]

In any case, Egeria uses her three terms loosely, appearing at times to have three different types of song in mind by using the three terms in a series, but, in practically the same breath, also using the word "hymns" as a catchall, which encourages one to infer that the three words are essentially synonyms for her: "hymns are said and psalms are responded to and similarly antiphons; and with each hymn prayer is made."[50] Another example of her imprecision is her description of the singing of a single psalm with a response on Palm Sunday. After a gospel lesson on the Triumphal Entry, which is read at the Imbomon, the bishop and the people process down to the city "with hymns and antiphons," carrying palm branches and "continually responding" with the words of Psalm 117:26.[51] Here the plural expression "hymns and antiphons" refers to a single responsorial psalm.[52]

---

45. The terms "psalm" and "hymn" are associated in the superscriptions of Psalms 6, 66, and 75.

46. Surviving Hellenistic Jewish literature tends to call biblical psalms "hymns," but the books of Luke and Acts use the terms "psalms" and "book of Psalms." See chapter 2.

47. John Chrysostom, *In psalm.* 73 (PG 55: 83).

48. Sozomen, *H.E.* 1.12.10.

49. Augustine, *Praec.* (*Reg. ad serv. Dei*) 2.3.

50. Egeria, *Itin.* 24.1. Some interpreters have concluded that Egeria uses the terms "psalms," "hymns," and "antiphons" interchangeably. See, for example, Anne McGowan and Paul F. Bradshaw, *The Pilgrimage of Egeria: A New Translation of the Itinerarium Egeriae with Introduction and Commentary* (Liturgical, 2018), 74.

51. *Itin.* 31.2.

52. Renoux claims that this statement proves that an antiphon is a response to a psalm, but he does not compare this instance of the word to other examples in Egeria. Renoux, *Le codex arménien Jérusalem 121*, vol. 2, 174 [36].

To summarize the evidence for antiphons in Egeria, she always pairs this word with one or more of the other two terms; she never uses it by itself. She never places the word "antiphon" first in a series of the terms. On certain occasions, she comments that prayers were said between hymns and antiphons, which implies that antiphons were not responses, whether intercalated or terminal. Moreover, in the passage where she makes separate statements about all three song-types, she seems to imply that the antiphons were responded to.[53] This passage makes clear that antiphon in her usage is not a general term for responsorial songs and also does not refer to responses.

The modern editor and translator of the Armenian Lectionary, Athanase Renoux, translates the term *kcʻurd* (sometimes transliterated as *kçowrd*) as "antienne" (antiphon), because he assumes that Egeria used the word "antiphon" for a psalm response.[54] In the AL, the word *kcʻurd* refers to a psalm-verse sung as a refrain to the psalm from which the verse was taken. *Kcʻurd* is obviously not a transliteration of the Greek word *antiphōnon*. It derives from an Armenian root for uniting/joining.[55] Renoux defines *kcʻurd* as "refrain," "response," or "hymn."[56] It is not clear what stood in the Greek original of the lectionary. Renoux guesses that it was *antiphōnon*, but the original word might have been one of the other common Greek words for a response. None of these observations clarify Egeria's much earlier use of *antiphona*.

According to Egeria, "vesper psalms are recited but also (*sed et*) antiphons for a longer time (*diutius*)" at the evening office.[57] Both the conjunction *sed* and the comparative *diutius* imply a distinction between the psalms and the antiphons as liturgical songs. The same goes for Egeria's very specific statement that at a particular service there was "one hymn" and "one antiphon."[58]

Was the distinction between a psalm/hymn and an antiphon one of content, antiphons being liturgical poems? It does not seem likely that vespers or other services in Jerusalem in the early 380s featured numerous nonbiblical hymns. Evidence from other sources from the same era suggests that the sung portion of the daily office was taken mostly from the Psalter. Moreover, a comparison of Egeria's implied lectionary with the very precise and comprehensive Armenian

53. Egeria, *Itin.* 24.1 (quoted above).

54. Renoux, *Le codex arménien Jérusalem 121*, vol. 2, 174 [36].

55. Louis Mariès and Ch. Mercier, ed. and tr., *Hymnes de Saint Ephrem conservées en version arménienne* (Firmin-Didot, 1961), 7–8.

56. Renoux, *Le codex arménien Jérusalem 121*, vol. 2, 174 [36] n. 11.

57. Egeria, *Itin.* 24.4.

58. *Itin.* 29.4.

Lectionary, which reflects Jerusalem practice about a century later,[59] shows that at every point where Egeria describes the same liturgical service as the lectionary does, the only songs mentioned by the lectionary are biblical psalms. In fact, the Armenian Lectionary mentions only two biblical odes and no nonbiblical hymns. No doubt there had been development in the Jerusalem liturgy between Egeria's time and the period reflected in the AL. Yet it is difficult to imagine that a large corpus of nonbiblical hymns, central to the services in Egeria's day, were eliminated from the liturgy in later decades. Assuming some degree of stability in the tradition between Egeria's time and that of the AL, it is reasonable to conclude that Egeria used the word "antiphons" not for nonbiblical hymns but for psalmody of a certain type, whether the refrains of antiphons differed from those used for other psalms or the distinction was a matter of format or performance style.

If Egeria used the word "antiphon" for a certain type of psalmody, then "the vesper psalms" were the fixed psalms of that hour and the antiphons were additional psalms, sung responsively, perhaps with a type of refrain or melody (or both) that distinguished them from other psalms. Egeria does not explain why the antiphons at vespers were sung "for a longer time," whether it was because their refrains were longer or for some other reason.

In his *Institutes*, Cassian uses the term "antiphon" in three places. One passage concerns the proper conduct of nocturns: "Some have judged that every night twenty or thirty psalms should be said and that these should be prolonged by the melodies of antiphons (*antiphonarum protelatos melodiis*) and by the addition of certain rhythms (*quarundam modulationum*)."[60] This statement distinguishes psalms from antiphons, making clear that in Cassian's usage, "antiphon" is not simply a general term for a responsorial psalm.

A second passage in the *Institutes* concerns the use of the doxology at monastic vespers and nocturns:

> The custom that we have observed in this province [Gaul]—that one sings the psalm, at the close of which all are standing and sing *Gloria patri et filio et spiritu sancto* with a loud voice—this we have never heard in the whole of the east. There, all keep silent while the singer, after he concludes the psalm, adds a prayer. Only an antiphon is concluded with this true glorification of the Trinity.[61]

59. On the date of the Armenian Lectionary, see Hugo Mendez, "Revising the Date of the Armenian Lectionary of Jerusalem," *Journal of Early Christian Studies* 29 (2021): 61–92.

60. Cassian, *Inst.* 2.2.1.

61. Cassian, *Inst.* 2.8: *Illud etiam quod in hac prouincia uidimus, ut uno cantante in clausula psalmi omnes adstantes concinant cum clamore 'gloria patri et filio et spiritui sancto', nusquam per*

This passage describes a difference between psalmody *in directum* at vespers and nocturns in the East, where there is no use of a closing doxology, and a Western custom where the psalms of those services were each concluded with a corporate doxology. In the East, only antiphons were concluded in that way. So, what was an antiphon? We have already seen that it was not a type of psalm for Cassian. It is theoretically possible that he used the word for the refrain of responsorial psalmody, but that would mean that Eastern monks sometimes performed responsive psalmody by adding the doxology to each instance of the refrain, something Cassian never mentions and which is never mentioned in any other descriptions of late-antique or medieval psalmody.[62] (My focus here is Casian's word-usage as a guide to the meaning of antiphon in his circles, not his reliability as a describer of the history of monastic customs.)

It is also clear that Cassian does not use "antiphon" to designate a terminal response to a psalm (or to a group of psalms), such as an amen, doxology, Alleluia, or similar final formulation. The only psalm-concluding termini that Cassian mentions are the doxology and the Alleluia. Obviously, the doxology is not meant in the passage just quoted, since the doxology is what Eastern monks say after an antiphon. The Alleluia, as Cassian describes it, was probably said by the solo reciter of the final psalm of the twelve-psalm cursus. Cassian never calls this Alleluia an antiphon. Moreover, in his lengthy discussion of the twelve-psalm cursus, he says nothing about a doxology. When he describes the angel's twelve-psalm cursus, he makes clear that the Alleluia was the end of the psalmody.[63] When he goes on to describe the Egyptian monks' practice of the angel's rule, he mentions no concluding doxology after the Alleluia.[64] In fact, had the Egyptian fathers sung a

---

omnem Orientem audiuimus, sed cum omnium silentio ab eo, qui cantat, finito psalmo orationem succedere, hac uero glorificatione trinitatis tantummodo solere antiphona terminari (CSEL 17: 24).

62. Joseph Dyer suspects that Cassian means refrains sung after each psalm verse and that the same practice is implied by two sixth-century monastic orders, the *Rule of the Master* 55.7 and the *Rule of Benedict* 17.6. See Joseph Dyer, "The Singing of Psalms in the Early-Medieval Office," *Speculum* 64 (1989): 540 (535–578). Both passages describe a more protracted form of psalmody, which they distinguish from singing the psalms *in directum*. The *RB* refers to this shorter pattern as "without an antiphon" (*sine antefana*). Neither the *RM* nor the *RB* refers to any intoning of doxologies after each psalm refrain. Moreover, elsewhere in the *RM*, an antiphon appears to be a type of psalm (see esp. 46.1), distinguished from a responsory. It is possible but by no means certain that "antiphon" was used by synecdoche in *RM* for a psalm paired with an antiphon (hymn), a psalm that might have included a refrain when performed corporately (see *RM* 22.13–14), and that "responsory" was used by synecdoche for a psalm with a refrain and no antiphon. See *RM* 45.1–2, 8, 12. These are mere guesses.

63. Cassian, *Inst.* 2.5.5.

64. *Inst.* 2.6–8. Taft arrives at a different conclusion by interpreting "antiphon" in 2.8 very dubiously as "the whole psalmody" (*The Liturgy of the Hours in East and West*, 59, in his translation,

doxology at the end, their custom would have resembled that of the monks of Gaul, who sang a doxology after each psalm or section of psalms. The impression Cassian gives is that the Gallic introduction of a doxology was an aberration, a departure from the original psalmody of the angel and the Egyptians, who were the angel's perfect imitators. We are left, then, with the possibility that Cassian uses the word "antiphon" for an independent hymn sung as an "answer" to a psalm, a definition that has the advantage that it agrees with later Western usage. Such a hymn was not used during nocturns in Egypt, Cassian says. But in certain settings in the East, monks sang antiphons and concluded them with doxologies, something they did not do for psalms. This seems to be the implication of the contrast Cassian draws between the innovation in Gaul and what he says was typical in the East.

The third passage in Cassian uses the word "antiphon" in a description of monastic psalmody at communal Friday vespers, with vigils, in Palestine: "When they have sung three antiphons while standing (*nam cum stantes antiphona tria concinuerint*), after this, sitting on the ground or on low benches, they respond to three psalms with one intoning (*tres psalmos uno modulante respondent*), which are offered successively by the brothers, one by one."[65] If the passage is original, then the psalmody of the vigil differed from regular nocturns and included much more singing by the monks. Moreover, Bailey reasons that if doxologies were typically sung standing, out of respect for the Trinity, that would explain why the three antiphons of the vigil were performed standing: they must have concluded with doxologies.[66] This in turn would explain why the monks were permitted to sit for vespers and nocturns (out of consideration for their weariness from work and perhaps their lack of sleep) but were nonetheless expected to stand for the three antiphons of the vigil.[67] That said, the section of the *Institutes* in which this statement is found has been judged to be an interpolation.[68]

---

taken from NPNF; see also the *ordo* as he reconstructs it, pp. 60–61). Hence, he sees a distinction between a custom in Gaul where a corporate doxology followed each psalm and a custom in the East where the doxology came only at the end of all twelve psalms.

65. *nam cum stantes antiphona tria concinuerint, humi post haec uel sedilibus humillimis insidentes tres psalmos uno modulante respondent, qui tamen singuli a singulis fratribus uicissim succedentibus sibi praebentur. Inst.* 3.8.4. The noun *antiphona* must be a neuter plural here, representing a variant Latin spelling of this loanword.

66. Bailey, *Antiphon and Psalm in the Ambrosian Office*, 103–104 with back-reference to an observation about the monks of Palestine standing for three psalms at vigils (p. 93, quoting *Inst.* 3.8).

67. This is how Bailey works out the relation of 3.8.4 to what Cassian says in 2.8 (which he inadvertently cites as 2.2) (*Antiphon and Psalm in the Ambrosian Office*, 104). Bailey, writing before Goodrich (see n. 68), assumed that 3.8.4 is part of the original *Institutes*.

68. See the detailed analysis in Richard J. Goodrich, *Contextualizing Cassian: Aristocrats, Asceticism, and Reformation in Fifth-Century Gaul* (Oxford University Press, 2007), 246–273.

Egeria's use of the word "antiphon" probably reflects Latin usage, but she applies the word in describing an Eastern style of worship. Cassian also uses the term for Eastern practices. The first example of the term in Latin for specifically Western psalmody appears in the biography of Ambrose composed by Paulinus of Milan between 411 and 422. I quoted his statement in chapter 10 regarding an innovation in Milan in the 380s. Paulinus, who is the only one to speak of "antiphons" in describing this innovation, may use the word anachronistically when he writes that in those days "antiphons, hymns, and vigils first began to be practiced in the Milanese church."[69] If Augustine's *Confessions* is his source, then Paulinus turned Augustine's "hymns and psalms"[70] (by which Augustine probably meant responsorial psalmody) into "antiphons" and "hymns." Perhaps Paulinus meant Ambrosian hymns and responsorial psalms, but the context provides no clue.

Writing in Latin, perhaps in North Africa in the early to mid-fifth century, the unknown but well-educated author of the *Ordo monasterii* uses the terms "psalms" and "antiphons" as follows:

> We now describe how we ought to pray or sing (*psallere*). In the morning, three psalms should be said—the sixty-second, the fifth, and the eighty-ninth. At terce, first a responsorial psalm (*psalmus ad respondendum*) should be said, then two antiphons (*antiphonae*), a reading, and a conclusion [i.e., dismissal]; likewise at sext and none. At the time following *lucernarium*, however, it is proper to say one responsorial psalm, four antiphons, one further responsorial psalm,[71] a reading, and a conclusion . . . Regarding the nocturnal prayers, in the months of November, December, January, and February: twelve antiphons, six psalms, three lessons; in March, April, September, and October: ten antiphons, five psalms, three lessons; in May, June, July, and August: eight antiphons, four psalms, two lessons.[72]

On the basis of internal inconsistencies and uncharacteristic terminology, Goodrich contends that 3.4–6 and 3.8 were added by someone whose views were more closely aligned with those of the sixth-century *Rule of the Master*. Owen Chadwick had already suggested that 3.4–6 might be an interpolation. Owen Chadwick, *John Cassian* (Cambridge University Press, 1968), 76–77.

69. Paulinus of Milan, *Vit. Ambr.* 13.3.

70. Augustine, *Conf.* 9.7.15. On the history of responsorial psalmody at Milan, see chapter 10.

71. Reading *item psalmus unus responsorius, lectio et completorium* without de Bruyne's comma after *unus*. On this comma, see Odilo Heiming, "Zum monastischen Offizium von Kassianus bis Kolumbanus," *Archiv für Liturgiewissenschaft* 7 (1961): 111.

72. *Ord. monast.* 2 (de Bruyne, 318–319).

The distinctions here must concern different types of psalmodies, since it is very unlikely that terce and none featured a single biblical psalm followed by two canticles or nonbiblical hymns, or that the nocturnal office typically had more hymns than psalms. If responsorial psalms used a psalm-verse for a refrain, perhaps antiphons were psalms with nonbiblical refrains or psalms that concluded with a doxology.

Finally, I will mention Porphyrios from Pisidia, a member of an association that dedicated a church to St. George, probably in 419. The inscription that records this information calls him a "singer of antiphons."[73] This usage suggests freestanding songs, hymns, or psalms of some special type.

Conclusion

The evidence for the use of "antiphon" from its first appearances as a word for church song in the late fourth century through its use in the fifth century is not sufficiently explicit to permit a precise definition or, better, precise definitions of different liturgical uses of the word over time and geography. A handful of conclusions are nonetheless possible, some firm, others more tentative.

Since the word "antiphon" meant "response" in fourth-century secular Greek, the Christian use of the word for a type of liturgical singing probably began with the use of the word "antiphon" to designate a response. We find unambiguous examples in the use of the expression "by antiphon" in three Christian writers of the third and fourth centuries, one of whom applies the expression to the Alleluia refrains of psalmody (in a homily from around 400).[74] All three are Greek-speaking Christians. Another Greek-speaking Christian (Theodore of Mopsuestia), writing in the late fourth or the early fifth century, uses the term "antiphon" for a doxology in psalmody or a psalm sung with a doxology. If the latter is meant, this is an early instance in an Eastern Christian writing where the word "antiphon," originally a term for a response, is used by synecdoche for a psalm sung with a response.

At least four Christian writings from the late fourth to the first half of the fifth centuries use the word "antiphon" for a type of psalmody: Egeria's *Itinerary*, Palladius's *Lausiac History*, Gerontius's *Life of Melania*, and the *Ordo monasterii*.[75] Egeria used "antiphon" for a type of responsorial psalmody.[76] Cassian says

73. See chapter 4 with notes 86 and 87.

74. *Act. Xanth. et Polyx.* 6 (third century perhaps); Diodore of Tarsus (d. circa 390), *Comm. In psalm.* 23 7; Severian, *In mund. creat.*, Hom. 2.5 (circa 400) (PG 56: 445).

75. See the preceding discussions of the term "antiphon" in these writings.

76. Egeria, *Itin.* 24.1.

that antiphons lengthened psalms, which could mean that they were hymns added to psalms or refrains that lengthened the psalmody.[77]

If in some places an antiphon was a type of responsorial psalm, what distinguished it? The association of antiphons with doxologies suggests one possibility but perhaps not a defining characteristic. Only two writers speak explicitly about antiphons and doxologies. According to Cassian, in the monastic East, only antiphons were concluded with a doxology. But he may have used the word "antiphon" for a type of hymn. Theodore of Mopsuestia uses the expression "the antiphons of psalmody" ambiguously with reference to doxologies. Antiphons of psalmody were either the doxologies themselves or psalms with doxologies. Whatever he meant, he does not imply that all antiphons in psalmody were doxologies or that all antiphons concluded with doxologies. Sozomen implies that antiphons were *hymns* with explicitly Trinitarian phrasing, whether in their refrains or in a concluding doxology. It may have been common in some communities to conclude an antiphon with a doxology or incorporate doxological language into the refrain, whether that antiphon was a psalm or a hymn.

It is also possible that in some places, at least in the late fourth century, what distinguished antiphons *as psalms* from other psalms was the content of the refrain. Hence, a plausible explanation for the distinction between psalms and antiphons in one trajectory of the history of the antiphons is that Christians began using the word "antiphon" for a psalm sung with a nonpsalm-derived refrain.[78]

The evidence as a whole shows that the word was used in different ways across time and from one place to another, so that not only can it not be assigned a single definition as a type of liturgical song, it cannot be given a single history of development. Moreover, it is very possible that certain early-Christian writers used the word very imprecisely, especially when the format of Christian singing was not their topic.

77. Cassian, *Inst.* 2.2.1 (discussed above).

78. Compare Bailey's not identical but somewhat similar set of conclusions in *Antiphon and Psalm in the Ambrosian Office*, 123, nos. (3) and (4).

CHAPTER TWELVE

Melody

THE PRECEDING CHAPTERS have identified various settings and formats in which Christians sang psalms during the first several centuries of the church. Thus far, I have given only hints about the musical character of psalmody. It is now time to take a close look at the specific evidence for melodic delivery of psalms and the nature of the melodies.

Clement of Alexandria on Music Ethos

The earliest references to the musical aspects of Christian song appear in Clement of Alexandria. In *Paedagogus*, Clement tells his readers to avoid certain deleterious musical modes, and he commends "temperate" modes.[1] A passage in his *Stromata* reveals that he regarded Dorian as a temperate mode. David's psaltery, Clement claims, was a model for the famous Greek musician Terpander, who composed a hymn to Zeus in a style that Clement praises as solemn, thanks to the character of the Dorian.[2] In the same passage he implies that he regarded the Phrygian as also a temperate mode. Clement was probably influenced by Plato's selection of only these two modes for the ideal state.[3]

Rhythm, too, lent character to song. The words of Terpander's *Hymn to Zeus*, the first lines of which Clement quotes, are composed of all long syllables, a rhythm that Dionysius of Halicarnassus calls "lofty and dignified."[4] When Clement says that the *Hymn to Zeus* displays "melodic solemnity," he probably means that both the Dorian mode and the rhythm of the hymn to Zeus produced this character.

Perhaps there was already a well-established Christian custom of intoning psalms in a calm, unhurried manner, treating all the syllables as more or less equal in length. Modal selection, however, is likely to have been a choice that singers made without realizing that the patterns of their melodies implied a certain scale-type. *Conscious* modal selection in psalmody during this era would

1. Clement of Alexandria, *Paed.* 2.4.40.1–2.4.44.5. See the discussion in chapter 2.

2. Clement of Alexandria, *Str.* 6.11.88.1–2.

3. Plato, *Resp.* 3.10 (399a–c).

4. Dionysius of Halicarnassus, *Comp.* 17.8.

have been necessary only where the singer performed a psalm to the lyre, which would have necessitated a modal tuning. The average person did not know what a mode was, and even educated people who recalled their school introduction to technical aspects of music would probably not have been able to sing a Dorian or Phrygian scale on command or to say what mode a popular song was in.

How, then, could Clement have expected his readers to avoid intemperate modes and embrace temperate ones? The answer is probably that he associated intemperate modes with erotic music, especially the popular erotic music of the stage and upper-class dinner party, for it is the music of debauchery that he attacks. Moreover, his language about modes was intended to invoke a moral-philosophical tradition of music criticism that went back to Plato. If Christians avoid erotic music, they will avoid unsuitable modes. That seems to be the logic.

Clement probably did not realize that modes, which Greeks termed *harmoniai*, were melody-types in Terpander's time and Plato's, melody-types defined not only by their implicit scales but by other features,[5] whereas *harmoniai* were purely scale-types and tunings by Clement's time.[6] Scale-types were not decisive for determining the character of a melody,[7] but perhaps Clement thought they were and, more specifically, believed that they imbued music with *moral* qualities. In any case, the modal names in his discussion are ciphers for music associated with certain kinds of settings and moral character, Dorian and Phrygian standing for music he regarded as both dignified and morally salubrious.

The Christian singing Clement had in mind was soloistic, not choral and not necessarily even responsorial. Christians passed around "toasts of song," he says, using a figure of speech that harked back to the fifth-century aristocratic symposion. As we saw in chapter 2, some of these Christian song-toasts were probably psalms, just as some of the singing "from Scripture" at Christian suppers in Tertullian's Carthage was probably psalmody. Did Christians of this era *improvise* melodies as they sang psalms? Or did they develop repertoires of a certain number of psalms for which they created through-composed melodies, that is, melodies that did not repeat for various segments of the lyrics, whether for lines or "stanzas"? Or did they use adaptable formulas, perhaps their own or a common chant? Improvisation, precomposition and rehearsal, and use of formulas—all these approaches are possible. Given Clement's defense of

5. See the detailed discussion in Charles H. Cosgrove, *Music at Social Meals in Greek and Roman Antiquity: From the Archaic Period to the Age of Augustine* (Cambridge University Press, 2023), 46–48.

6. See Martin West on the "denaturing" of the old modes in the post-classical eras. Martin L. West, *Ancient Greek Music* (Clarendon, 1992), 85.

7. West, *Ancient Greek Music*, 186; Charles H. Cosgrove, *An Ancient Christian Hymn with Musical Notation: Papyrus Oxyrhynchus 1786* (Mohr Siebeck, 2011), 180–181.

lyre-playing in Christian music-making,[8] one can imagine that a few Christians sang psalms to their own string accompaniment and either improvised a melody or worked it out in advance. They would have been exceptional.

Conventions for Intoned Reading of Psalms

Athanasius advises Marcellinus to make lyrical reading of the psalms part of his daily discipline.[9] And the late fourth-century *Apostolic Constitutions*, in its restatement of the *Didascalia*'s guidance about private reading, contains the instruction, "Sing the hymns [i.e. the psalms]."[10] In many churches during the fourth century, the psalms were also sung when read as Scripture lessons. Canon 15 of the Canons of Laodicea implies that reading by singing (instead of performance by memory) was also the practice of the lectors/cantors who led the psalmody of vigils and/or the daily office.[11]

How did Christians read by singing? Did they improvise a melody as they read, whether very creatively or by using melodic phrases that had become part of their own personal psalm-singing repertoire? The alternative to free melodizing or the use of one's own idiosyncratic melodic phrases would have been to sing to a more-or-less fixed formula, a formula commonly used by other psalm-singers, probably one designed to facilitate clarification of the sense through the musical marking of phrases.

Reading by Singing in Antiquity

How difficult would it have been to make up a melody as one read? There are almost no explicit references in ancient literature to melodic improvisation, although classicists who study ancient music posit its use and ethno-musicologists regard it as a common form of music-making in many traditional cultures. With respect to Greek antiquity, much of this improvisation is understood to have been an exercise of freedom in performing a flexible body of poetry, such as Homeric epic, or of fixed poems, such as solo performance of Pindar's poems at symposia by men who followed a common approach to melodizing the words. As reconstructed by specialists, the common approach of poets and singing aristocrats during the archaic and classical eras was to express the inherent rhythm of the quantity-based poetry, singing according to tune-types (*harmoniai*) and

8. Clement of Alexandria, *Paed*. 2.4.43.3. See chapter 2.

9. Athanasius in his *Letter to Marcellinus*.

10. *Const. ap*. 1.5.

11. See chapter 4.

shaping the improvised melody to the contour of the pitch accents of the words.[12] Moreover, nonelites could certainly have sung in similar ways, using tune-types and improvising melodies in a fashion that respected the word accents.[13]

As for melodic *reading*, there are few explicit references in the literature of the archaic, classical, or Hellenistic periods to methods of *reading* poetry, whether melodically or not. In the late Hellenistic period, poetry was read aloud in school using school-taught styles of recital. Students exhibited their skill in recital in school competitions, and inscriptional evidence for these competitions reveals that special terms were used for recital. The terms are not words for singing.[14]

The earliest author to comment on how poetry should be read aloud in school, as part of a boy's foundational preparation for oratory, cautions against turning expressiveness into anything that sounds like singing. Speaking of poetry (probably both Greek and Latin), the Roman rhetorician Quintilian states that a poetry reading should be "manly with sanctity and gravity, and certainly not like prose, for poetry is also song (*carmen*) and the poets claim to sing (*canere*)."[15] Yet one should not ruin the reading by using "songs or effeminate inflections, which is common these days." He is probably referring to a tendency of young men to render poetry as if they were performing songs in the theater.[16] Quintilian then quotes a snarky remark attributed to a young C. Caesar, probably Julius Caesar

---

12. Fashioning a melody according to the contour of the verbal pitch accent meant not having the melody descend on a syllable that a speaker would have raised tonally. See the summary of these conventions in Charles H. Cosgrove and Mary C. Meyer, "Melody and Word Accent Relationships in Ancient Greek Musical Documents: The Pitch Height Rule," *Journal of Hellenic Studies* 126 (2006): 66. On the operation of this convention in archaic and classical antiquity, see below with n. 26.

13. Habits of melodic improvisation in rendering ancient poetry did not exclude the composition and preservation of songs with their "fixed" melodies, although transmission almost certainly reshaped those melodies through reperformance.

14. See Cosgrove, *Music at Social Meals in Greek and Roman Antiquity*, 136 with n. 118.

15. Quintilian, *Inst.* 1.8.2.

16. There are many references in literature from the time of the late Roman republic through the third century to orators approaching song in their delivery or outright singing at certain points. See Quintilian, *Inst.* 11.3.57; Cicero, *Orator* 8.27 and 8.57 (referring to an "Asiatic" style of oratorical singing, particularly in the peroration, a style that Cicero distinguishes from the more restrained lyricism he approves, which does not become literal song); Plutarch, *Q.C.* 1.5.2 (*Mor.* 623b); Pliny, *Ep.* 2.14.13; Dio Chrysostom, *Or.* 32.68 (regarding orators in his time: "they all sing, both orators and sophists"); Lucian of Samosata, *Rhet. praec.* 19 (satirical depiction of a professor of rhetoric advising would-be orators that when it seems to be the moment for singing in a speech, one should sing everything); Philostratus, *Vit.* 1.20 (Olearius, 513); 2.10 (Olearius, 589); 2.28 (Olearius, 620).

mocking a classmate: "If you are singing, you are singing badly; if you are reading, you are singing (*si cantas, male cantas: si legis, cantas*)."[17] Evidently in the era of the late republic and the early imperial period, there was a fashion of reading or reciting poetry in a musical way, a style cultivated by young aristocrats.

Ancient people, like modern people, had no difficulty intoning their speech melodically when they wished, without relying on a precomposed melody or other preparation. Aristoxenus, a musicologist of the early Hellenistic period, remarks that "in conversing we avoid vocal standstill, except that we are sometimes compelled to go into such a movement because of emotion."[18] Vocal standstill is Aristoxenus's technical term for the nature of singing: the voice pauses on the pitches of the melody, however briefly, to define them, as opposed to moving across tonal space without marking intervals, which is characteristic of ordinary talking. His observation is that emotion sometimes impels people to sing a nonpoetic utterance for expressive reasons.

A somewhat similar observation is made by Nicomachus of Gerasa. Writing around 200 CE and commenting on Aristoxenus' distinction between the continuous movement of the voice in talking and its intervallic movement in singing, Nicomachus makes the following observations:

> The continuous is that by which we converse with one another or read, having no need to make clear the pitches of the notes and the distinctions between them, and uttering the speech to the end of what we are saying. For if a person—whether conversing or recounting something or reading—makes the magnitudes clear between each note, dividing and shifting the voice from one to the next, he or she is said not to speak or read but to melodize.[19]

Making "magnitudes" clear through shifts from one note to the next is a clear reference to melodic singing.[20] Exactly when someone might shift to melodizing

---

17. Quintilian, *Inst.* 1.8.2.

18. Aristoxenus, *Harm.* 1.9 (da Rios, 14) (ἂν μὴ διὰ πάθος ποτὲ εἰς τοιαύτην κίνησιν ἀναγκασθῶμεν ἐλθεῖν).

19. Nicomachus, *Harm. Ench.* 2.1.

20. The word μελεάζειν occurs only here in extant preByzantine literature, other instances in the TLG being from twelfth-century writers. According to Timothy Moore, Nicomachus uses μελεάζειν for an intermediate vocalization between speaking and singing. See Timothy J. Moore, *Music in Roman Comedy* (Cambridge University Press, 2012), 96 with n. 58. But Nicomachus, a music theorist, is clearly talking about melodic singing, not something short of it. He speaks of making "the magnitudes" (τὰ μεγέθη) clear, which invokes Aristoxenus's concept of magnitude

when conversing, recounting, or reading, Nicomachus does not say. It is significant that he does not speak in the subjunctive ("if someone were to make the magnitudes clear") but uses the present tense ("if/when someone makes the magnitudes clear"). This suggests that he means to describe something actual: people in his day sometimes did shift into singing when engaged in conversation or recounting something or reading.

An ability to read with melody was assumed by ritual experts in therapeutic and protective formulas when they instructed their clients to sing a formula. Cato the Elder knew examples of this and cites one in his book on agriculture, introducing a certain formula with the words, "Begin to chant (*incipe cantare*)."[21] Cato says nothing about the melody to be used. In chanting a formula, people must have done what was usual. There may have been familiar magical chant forms, but none are mentioned. Perhaps a specific sequence of melodic intervals was not important to the effectiveness of the chant.

The *Art of Grammar* (which has come down under the name of Dionysius Thrax) assumes that one should *read* certain texts melodically, namely texts of melic poetry.[22] Two late-antique scholiasts comment on this passage, which they understood to refer to the poetry of the old nine lyric poets. One scholiast says that singing these lyric poets is now impossible:

> [Dionysius] said "melodically" because it is necessary to sing lyric poems with melody, which is impossible with us now. For if one wished [to do so] according to the ancient music, as it was written (composed), it is impossible, since ancient music is different from modern music. For ancient music was divided into three (modes): Dorian, Phrygian, Lydian. Modern music has ten. How then could one sing melodies composed according to the old modal system using the modern system? Therefore, this is impossible in literature, due to the change that has taken place in harmony. Nevertheless, the manner of reading shall not be completely unclear. But there is some particular difference

as the measure of an interval: τῇ μὲν γὰρ ἀκοῇ κρίνομεν τὰ τῶν διαστημάτων μεγέθη (Aristoxenus, *Harm.* 33; Da Rios, 42); cf. also Aristides Quintilianus: ἰδίως δὲ κατὰ μουσικὴν γίνεται διάστημα μέγεθος φωνῆς ὑπὸ δυεῖν φθόγγων περιγεγραμμένον ("the interval in the peculiarly musical sense is a magnitude of the voice bounded by two notes") (*Mus.* 1.7; Winnington-Ingram, 10).

21. Marcus Porcius Cato, *Agr.* 160. The ritual instruction is quoted fully in chapter 13.

22. Dionysius Thrax, *Ars gramm.* 1.1 (under "Concerning Reading"). The author uses the word ἐμμελῶς, which is shown by a remark by Dionysius of Halicarnassus to mean "melodic." Dionysius refers to the difference between the pleasing intonations of the voice in speaking and singing, speaking being "mellifluous" (εὐμελὲς) but not melodic (ἐμμελές)" (*Comp.* 11.24 in Aujac and Lebel 3: 96 = Radermacher and Usener 6: 43).

> concerning this, the reading by the voice respecting the melodies in their being directed.[23]

The last statement is very confusing. That comment aside, the scholiast seems to imply that the best thing one can do is to sing in a modern mode (*harmonia*) on the assumption that the result will be at least somewhat similar to the original, presumably thanks to the words and their inherent rhythm, as well as the fact that one sings at all. The other scholiast asserts simply that "it is necessary to read this lyric poetry with melody, even if [or "even though"] we have not received or have not remembered their melodies."[24]

The passage in *Art of Grammar* is a school text, and the scholiasts just quoted probably had school instruction especially in mind. The tradition they endorse was not universal, since references to recital of old and new poetry at school contests in the latter part of the Hellenistic age speak of a nonmelodic delivery style (see above). Moreover, a number of Roman-era writers refer to a custom of reciting in a semi-lyrical way that was neither ordinary reciting nor melodic singing but something in between.[25]

In any case, the scholiasts' position on the Thrax passage seems to be that when the melody for a given lyric text is not known, which is usually the case, the student should make up a tune, a practice that the teacher would have modeled, improvising a melody, probably conforming it in an old-fashioned way to the general contours of the archaic-classical pitch accent (as Alexandrian scholarship defined it), which was the Platonic standard for ensuring that the melody served the words.[26]

Psalm Tones or Melodies?

We know that by a certain point in church history, a common method for performing a psalm was to use a psalm tone that facilitated communication through melodic inflection by marking the beginnings and ends of cola and thus phrasing the words through use of a formula. Figure 12.1 shows a standard example from the seventh of the eight Western psalm tones:

---

23. Heliodorus, *Schol. Londinensia* (Hilgard, 476.29–477.3).

24. ταύτην οὖν τὴν λυρικὴν ποίησιν δεῖ μετὰ μέλους ἀναγινώσκειν, εἰ καὶ μὴ παρελάβομεν μηδὲ ἀπομεμνήμεθα τὰ ἐκείνων μέλη. Melampodis (or Diomedis) (Hilgard, 21.19–21).

25. See the postscript at the end of this chapter.

26. Plato, *Resp.* 3.398d; cf. *Leg.* 2.669d. See Cosgrove, *Music at Social Meals in Greek and Roman Antiquity*, 47, 87–88; Armand D'Angour, "The New Music—So What's New?" in *Rethinking Revolutions through Ancient Greece*, ed. Simon Goldhill and Robin Osborne (Cambridge University Press, 2006), 279–280.

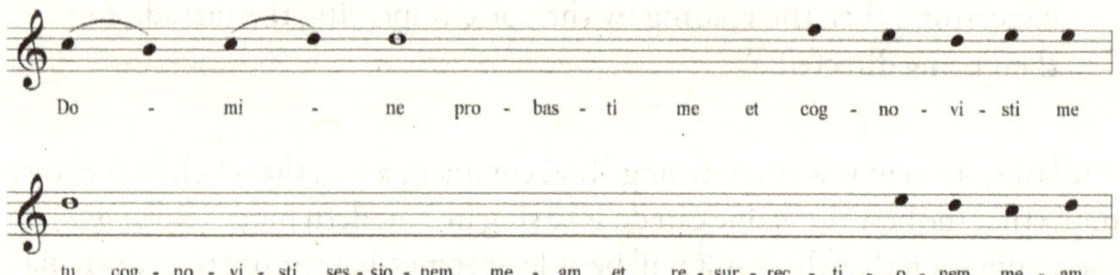

Figure 12.1. Psalm tone with the words of Psalm 138:1–2, based on an example in David Hiley, *Gregorian Chant* (Cambridge University Press, 2009), 46.

It is very unlikely that a method of this sort was already in use in late antiquity. First of all, psalm tones are not expressly documented before the ninth century.[27] Second, no one would have spoken of psalm tones the way Augustine, for example, speaks of psalm *tunes* when he refers to "all the melodies of the sweet little songs to which the Psalter of David is repeated."[28] A psalm tone composed of incipits and cadences linked by monotone chanting on a reciting tone hardly fits the repeated patristic characterizations of the melodies as "sweet"[29] or Basil's remark that the people find them irresistible, so that they sing them in daily life, just as they do theater songs.[30]

If fourth- and fifth-century lectors did not use psalm tones of the medieval type, they did not simply improvise either. They used melodies, as Augustine says. Moreover, the expression "to which (*quibus*)" in Augustine's phrasing implies that the melodies existed independently of the psalms themselves, that is, that a given melody served more than one psalm.[31] It is reasonable to infer that when Augustine made this statement in his *Confessions* at the close of the fourth century, lectors in the church of Hippo were using a collection of psalm melodies.

27. The earliest evidence for psalm tones in the West is a tonary from Metz that dates to around 835. See *Der karolingische Tonar von Metz*, ed. Walther Lipphardt (Achendorff, 1965).

28. *Melos omnes cantilenarum suauium, quibus Dauiticum psalterium frequentatur.* Augustine, *Conf.* 10.33.50.

29. Gregory of Nyssa, *Inscr. psalm.* 1.2 and 1.3 (GNO 5:28–29 and 5:32 and 34); Basil, *Hom. super psalm. 1* 1 (PG 29: 212); and John Chrysostom, *In psalm. 150* (PG 55: 497–498); see further the references to the pleasure of psalmody in John Chrysostom, *In psalm. 41* 1 (PG 55: 157); Niceta of Remesiana, *Util. hymn.* 5; and Augustine, *Conf.* 10.33.50. On the sweetness of psalm melodies, see also chapter 13.

30. Basil, *Hom. super psalm. 1* 1 (PG 29: 212).

31. Also of interest is Augustine's reference in his commentary on the psalms to "this pleasant melody" (*ista suauis melodia*), referring to a particular psalm-verse (probably the refrain). Augustine, *Enarr. in psalm. 132* 2 (PL 37: 1729; CCL 40: 1927).

Presumably, the lector chose a melody for a given lesson. They would have been taught how to adapt a melody to a given psalm.

What about elsewhere? John Chrysostom extols the monks who reside in the desert outside Antioch for rising in the middle of the night to stand and sing "prophetic hymns with much harmony, with well-crafted melodies."[32] The expression "well-crafted" implies that the monks' psalm-melodies were precomposed. A statement by Basil is further evidence that lectors of the late fourth century drew from a common pool of psalm melodies. The Holy Spirit mixed the sweetness of melody into the Psalter, he says, and "these harmonious melodies of the psalms were conceived for us," so that people "might educate their souls in truth while seeming to educate themselves in song."[33] The divine passive in the first clause might imply that, as Basil imagined it, the Spirit composed the melodies, which were eventually passed down to the church. But Basil may mean no more than that God intended the church to sing the psalms, for the purpose stated, and that, therefore, the church developed psalm melodies to fulfill that divine intention. In either case, the expression "these melodies" implies a definite body of tunes.

Phrasing and Lineation

Biblical psalms are not metrical poems, and they exhibit no regularity of stanzas, being composed of sense groupings of cola of varying length. The melodic phrases of psalm melodies had to be adapted to these variable lines if the melodies were to serve the sense. Christian psalm manuscripts show accommodations for readers that would have assisted ancient lectors in the task of singing psalm lessons. Before examining this evidence, it is helpful to recall that the fourth-century Council of Laodicea issued a rule that permitted no one "except the canonical psalmers to sing in church, ascending the platform and singing from the parchments."[34] The reference to parchments implies that it was standard practice to provide psalm readers with parchment texts, fine books whose pages were made of processed leather. Books of this kind were expensive. Hence, we can assume that great care was taken in the design and scribal transcription of the texts copied into parchment scrolls and books. If so, the handful of examples of surviving parchment Bibles produced in the fourth and fifth centuries probably give us a good impression of standard ways in which psalms were written out in Bibles or Psalters meant for church reading.

---

32. Chrysostom, *In 1 Tim.* 5, Hom. 14.4 (PG 62: 576).

33. Basil, *Hom. super psalm.* 1 (*PG* 29.212).

34. Council of Laodicea, Canon 15.

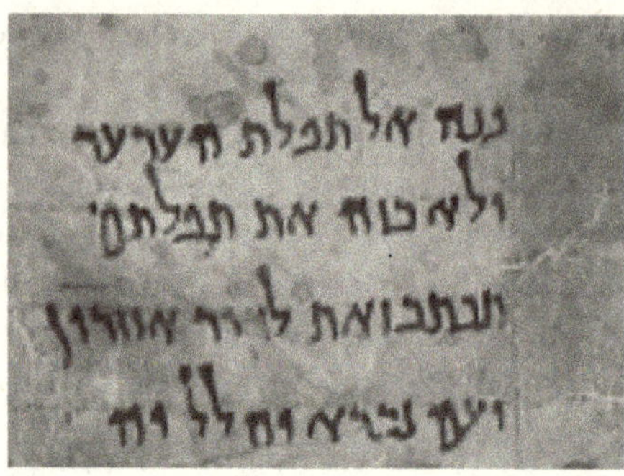

Figure 12.2. 4QPs^{b} col. xxi, Heb Psalm 102:17–18. Source: Israel Antiquities Authority, B-298388.

In parchment books, psalm texts are disposed in formats that differ from the way prose texts were treated. This differentiation clearly implies a conception of the psalms as poems,[35] and it has antecedents in papyri psalm collections. Not only that, Christians like Jerome, who examined Hebrew psalm scrolls, would probably have seen at least some examples where psalms were written out in formats that differed from the disposition of historical narratives, for example, specifically in lineation of various types,[36] as illustrated by Figure 12.2.

He will regard the prayer of the destitute
    and will not despise their prayer.
Let this be recorded for a generation to come,
    so that people yet unborn may praise the Lord. (NRSV)

---

35. Disposing Greek poetry with one κῶλον per written line was established by the Hellenistic grammarian Aristophanes of Byzantium (3rd/2nd century BCE). This method was subsequently extended to texts of oratory, notably to Demosthenes (in Latin also to Cicero), and was called κατὰ κῶλα καὶ κόμματα, where κῶλα carried no metrical implication and κόμματα was essentially its synonym. To write out an oration "according to the members and parts" was to display the speech in sense units, one unit per line. Jerome was aware of this exception to the general practice of disposing only poetic texts κατὰ κῶλα καὶ κόμματα (see below with n. 41). Incidentally, the Psalter itself does not refer to the songs of David as poems, but patristic authors would have found an application of that genre designation (τὰ ποιήματα) to David's songs in Reg 1 LXX 19:4.

36. See Emanuel Tov, *Scribal Practices and Approaches Reflected in the Texts Found in the Judean Desert* (Brill, 2004), 168, Table 8; F. W. Dobbs-Allsopp, "Space, Line, and the Individual Written Poem in Texts from the Judean Desert," in *Puzzling Out the Past: Studies in Northwest Semitic Languages and Literatures in Honor of Bruce Zuckerman*, ed. Marilyn. J. Lundberg, Steven Fine, and Wayne T. Pitard (Brill, 2012), 19–61; also Dobbs-Allsopp, *On Biblical Poetry* (Oxford University Press, 2015), 14–94.

This type of lineation in a psalm text from Qumran would not have been motivated by the needs of cantors, since a tradition of singing psalms in liturgy is not attested for the Qumran sect or for Jewish practice more widely during the Second Temple period.[37] The layout in lines (stichs) might have been intended as an aid to reading aloud or simply to guide the eye and facilitate easier reading comprehension. Yet it was not common in antiquity to use lineation or other visual markings (such as slash marks or dots) in prose texts (except in school texts for beginning readers).[38] Moreover, lineation is not found in Hebrew narrative texts from Qumran. It is found only in texts of Biblical songs, specifically in certain psalm texts. It also appears in other ancient Mediterranean song texts. Taken together, the evidence suggests that lineation was used for poetry in particular.[39]

There are a few exceptions to what I have just said, but they prove the rule. When Jerome produced his Latin translation of the Bible, he decided to apply a stichic approach to Isaiah and Ezekiel, whose prose he regarded as especially difficult. He had seen stichic layouts in texts of the orations of Demosthenes and Cicero, he explains, and thought that this sort of lineation made the syntax clearer to readers. No one should infer, he emphasized, that because he had disposed Isaiah and Ezekiel "in lines" (*versibus*) that the Hebrew originals of these prophets were in meter (*metro*) or that they were at all similar to the book of Psalms or the works of Solomon (Song of Songs, presumably[40]).[41] Jerome's comment presupposes that stichic dispositions typically signaled poetry, which is just what we see in certain psalm manuscripts from Qumran and also in copies of psalm texts produced elsewhere, including a number of early Greek psalms papyri and the three earliest Christian Bible codices—the fourth-century Sinaiticus and Vaticanus, and the fifth-century Alexandrinus.

---

37. Not all psalm manuscripts from Qumran display lineation. See the varieties listed in Tov, *Scribal Practices and Approaches Reflected in the Texts Found in the Judean Desert*, 161. On the subject of the singing of psalms in ancient Judaism, see my discussion in chapter 1.

38. See Raffaella Cribiore, *Writing, Teachers, and Students in Graeco-Roman Egypt* (Scholars Press, 1996), 48–49.

39. This is one of the important points made by Dobbs-Allsopp regarding special layouts in ancient graphic representations of ancient Mediterranean song/verse texts, the special layouts being confirmatory in the Judean tradition that the psalms and like texts were regarded as poetry (see the citations to Dobbs-Allsopp in n. 36 above).

40. In his preface to the writings of Solomon, however, he says nothing about any of them being in verse.

41. Jerome, *Praef. in Isai.* (PL 28: 771); *Praef. in Ezech.* (PL 28: 938–939). These passages are pointed out in M. B. Parkes, *Pause and Effect: An Introduction to the History of Punctuation in the West* (University of California Press, 1993), 15 with notes 86 and 87.

Figure 12.3. Greek P. Add. 1287. Source: Image no. JRL21071289, John Rylands Research Institute and Library, University of Manchester.

Among the Greek psalms papyri, too, are a number that display lineation. At least two forms were used. In one type, the scribes used flush-left indentation to start each line and indented any words of the line if they ran out of room at the right margin. In another type, they used spacing to separate individual lines. An early second-century papyrus fragment from Montserrat shows this second type.[42] The first type appears in a third- or fourth-century fragment of Ps 19:7–8, held by the John Rylands Library, as illustrated in Figure 12.3.

7b He will listen to him [from his holy heaven.]
7c In mighty deeds is the sal[vation of his right hand.]
8a [The]se in char[iots, those with horses,]
8b [but we] in the name of our Lord God exult.

This fragment (Figure 12.3) is thought to be from a school text or an amulet. Its style of lineation is also found in Hebrew psalms texts from Qumran, with right-hand line endings (as illustrated in Figure 12.2).

Lineation in a psalms manuscript represents its poetic character, but it does not imply the purpose or use of the manuscript. Yet the psalters in Bible codices such as Sinaiticus, Vaticanus, and Alexandrinus undoubtably illustrate some of the text forms that psalm readers encountered, whether these codices themselves

42. In the fragment, containing Psalm 14:4–5, the three lines of verse 4 are separated by spaces, as are those of 14:5. See P.Mont.Roca inv. No. 2 = LDAB 3082. See *Greek Papyri from Montserrat (P.Mont.Roca IV)*, ed. Sofía Torallas Tovar and Klaas A. Worp (Abadia de Montserrat, 2014), 83–84. (In Ps 14:5, one of these space separators is a marginal break.)

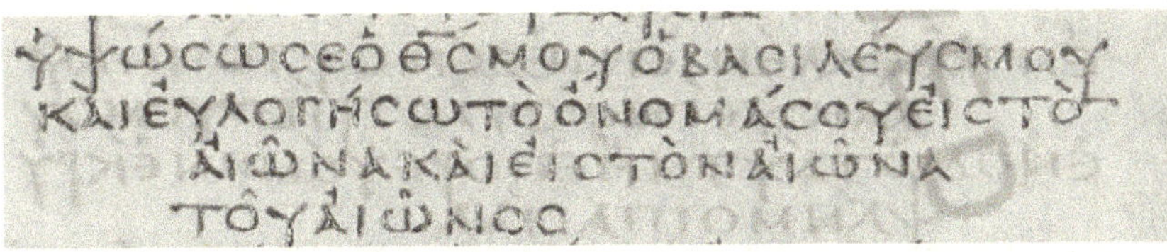

Figure 12.4. Psalm 144:1 Codex Vaticanus gr. 1209, f. 710. Source: Biblioteca Apostolica Vaticana.

Figure 12.5. Psalm 144:1b Codex Sinaiticus Quire 63, f. 8r. Source: The British Library Board, the British Library Collection. (Verse 1a is not shown because it happens to be on the preceding page.)

were used in liturgy or served only as masters for the production of liturgical Bibles. Codex Sinaiticus is a large, cumbersome deluxe codex with marginalia. It was probably kept in a library. But it would have provided an excellent exemplar for the making of liturgical Bible manuscripts. Codex Vaticanus, a more manageable codex, suitable for liturgical use, may have been produced in the same scriptorium as Sinaiticus, which could have served as its master copy.[43]

Sinaiticus, Vaticanus, and Alexandrinus provide information about the sort of text layout that a fourth- or fifth-century reader-cantor would have seen on the page. Lineation in the psalms sections of these codices would have guided the reader's execution of the lines as sung poetry. Consider an example from Psalm 144 in Codex Vaticanus, as shown in Figure 12.4.

> *1a I will exalt you, my God, my king,*
> *1b and I will bless your name for*
> *ever and for ever*
> *and ever.*

The lineation in Figure 12.4 marks the beginnings of the poetic lines at flush left, and the indentation indicates that the second poetic line continues past the right margin onto the next two manuscript lines.

Codex Sinaiticus also divides Psalm 144:1 into two poetic lines by indenting to accommodate a long line, as Figure 12.5 illustrates for verse 1b.

43. See the sage comments in Christfried Böttrich, "Codex Sinaiticus and the Use of Manuscripts in the Early Church," *The Expository Times* 128 (2017): 475.

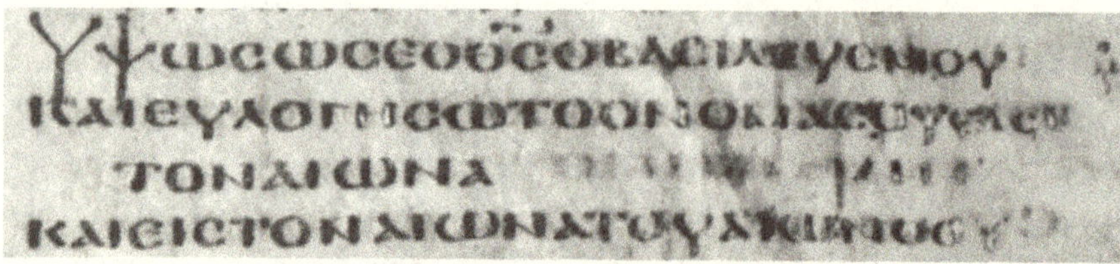

Figure 12.6. Psalm 144:1 Codex Alexandrinus p. 563v. From: *Facsimile of the Codex Alexandrinus*, vol. 3, *Old Testament: Psalms–Ecclesiastes* (British Museum, 1883). (The marks in the space after TONAIΩNA are bleed-through from the recto.)

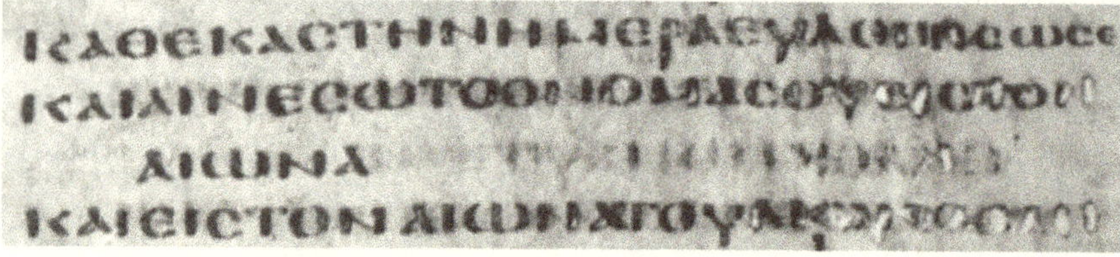

Figure 12.7 Psalm 144:2 Codex Alexandrinus p. 563v. From: *Facsimile of the Codex Alexandrinus*, vol. 3, *Old Testament: Psalms–Ecclesiastes* (British Museum, 1883).

1b and I will bless your name for
ever and for ev-
er and ever.

Here, too, the codex tells the reader not to mark a sense pause at mid-line, say, after the first "for ever."

Lineation is used in Codex Alexandrinus, as illustrated in Figure 12.6 for the same verse.

1a I will exalt you, my God, my king,
1b and I will bless your name for
ever
1c and for ever and ever.

This layout divides Psalm 144:1 into seemingly three poetic lines. Yet the resulting disposition is not according to sense clauses, since 1c belongs to 1b as a matter of sense phrasing. The only framework in which 1c could conceivably function as a separate line is a performance framework. Nor is this the only place where a sense line is divided into two poetic lines in Alexandrinus. It happens again in the same psalm at verse 2 (Figure 12.7).

2a Every day I will bless you,
2b and I will praise your name for
ever
2c and for ever and ever.

Here, too, Alexandrinus disposes the text in a way that suggests performance lines. Of course, that might not always have been the scribe's purpose, particularly since Alexandrinus is not consistent in its treatment of similar compound "for ever" phrases. The reader was not bound to phrase according to the book layout in any case. Although the reader's recognition of sense groupings was assisted by the page layout, he had the final say in performance decisions, specifically, where to mark sense phrases. Since he could adapt the melody to the words in any way he chose, he had the option of phrasing by breath-pause, syllable-lengthening, cadence, or some combination of these.

Since the congregation did not know what to sing in response until they were told, it must have been the reader who gave them the refrain in a musical form. A statement in Theodoret's account of the psalm-accompanied translation of the relics of Babylas suggests that one format was for the people to respond after every line. The paraders, Theodoret writes, escorted the martyr "en masse, stepping and singing the Davidic song, and after each colon they responded, 'Let all who worship graven images be put to shame.'"[44] The term "colon" (*kōlon*) designated a metrical unit in poetry, consisting of "no more than about twelve syllables or less."[45] Here it does not designate a metrical form but probably means simply a line. The psalm leader(s) sang out a colon, and the crowd responded with their designated colon as a refrain.

Frequent repetition of the refrain is also suggested by John Chrysostom's comment that the words of the refrain for Psalm 144, a traditional Communion psalm, were "sung continually in response."[46] If church leaders took their cues from the Psalter itself, Psalm 135 would have provided them with an encouragement to sing refrains after every line, following the pattern of the intercalated refrain in this psalm.[47]

44. Theodoret of Cyr, *H.E.* 3.10.3.

45. M. L. West, *Greek Metre* (Clarendon, 1982), 5.

46. John Chrysostom, *In psalm 144* 1 (PG 55: 464).

47. Most psalms do not exhibit repetitions of any sort. With the exception of Ps 135 (MT 136) and perhaps 106 (MT 107) (which repeats the formulation introduced at verse 8 with a certain regularity in verses 15, 21, 31), repetitions in the psalms lack the periodicity of a refrain. Ps 41:4b repeats with modest variation at 11b; Ps 45:8 repeats exactly at verse 12; Ps 48:13 repeats exactly 21; Ps 58:10b-11a repeats with a variation at 18b-c; Ps 61: 3 repeats with a variation at 7; Ps 66: 4 repeats exactly at 6; Ps 79:8, which varies 4, repeats exactly at 20; Ps 106:8 repeats

I pointed out in chapter 10 that frequent singing of the refrain would explain the following remark by Ambrose. "What an effort it is in church to remain silent when the lessons are read. When one speaks, everyone makes noise. If a psalm is read, it is itself the effecter of silence. All speak and no one makes noise."[48] The format was almost certainly responsorial. Hence, Ambrose's observation implies a continual engagement of the congregation in the singing of the psalm lesson, that is, a frequent singing of the refrain. Such a custom would also explain some phrasing used by Augustine when he refers to a certain congregational response as "the words of the psalm that we have just now sung."[49] The relative pronoun "that" is singular and refers to the psalm, not to the plural term "words."[50] This shows that Augustine conceived the congregation's responsorial participation as singing the psalm itself, even though what they sang was only the refrain. If they repeated the refrain frequently, their participation would have been so substantial that it would have been natural for Augustine to have said that they sang "the psalm."

There is a further, practical reason for frequent repetition of the refrain. When the reader gave the congregation its refrain, they had to remember it in order to perform it at the appropriate points. Since psalm lessons changed in services of the word from one gathering to the next, the refrain was new each time. Even though a given psalm was usually repeated from time to time with the same refrain in the course of text-selections for the lessons throughout the year, the congregation would have preserved only a vague recollection of it, if any, and would scarcely have remembered how it had last been melodized, assuming that readers in prior services even used the same melody for it from one instance to the next. Hence, frequent singing of the refrain after it was first intoned by the reader would have helped the congregation keep it fresh in mind through the course of the psalm performance.

Finally, reports of people's great pleasure in psalmody[51] are difficult to explain if their own participation was merely a handful of responses per psalm. A response after every colon would have given them the enjoyment of substantial engagement in the singing.

---

exactly at 15, 21, and 31; "Holy is he!" repeats in Psalm 98 at the end of verses 3 and 5, and is echoed at the end of the psalm.

48. Ambrose, *Expl. psalm. 1* 9. PL 14: 925; CSEL 64: 8.

49. Augustine, *Serm.* 33A (CCL 41: 418).

50. *De uerbis istius psalmi quem modo cantauimus.* The psalm is Psalm 145, and in the next sentence Augustine quotes these *uerba* (v. 2) as the refrain.

51. See above with notes 28 and 29; also chapter 13.

Melody-Making

The psalm reader had to perform sense-phrases as musical phrases, doing so in ways that were musically coherent. He had to create or adapt a melody to poetic lines of unequal length that lacked any metrical framework. And he had to accommodate responders, ensuring that when he crafted the melodic ending of a clause that was directly followed by the response, he did so in a way that made the responders' starting note clear. In time, common conventions for lyrical psalm reading must have developed. Readers who were new to the task imitated others and may have received some training.[52]

Since the psalms were texts without melodies, melodizing them was a practice that Christians carried out as people formed by the wider musical song culture. It is difficult to speculate how the nature of lyric song in late antiquity might have influenced methods for melic reading of psalms, but one source is a small body of texts that preserve Greek lyric with musical notation.

The Roman-era portion of the scores of Greek music are an invaluable guide to trends in music in the Roman period. Centuries of Greek emigration and Hellenization had established the Greek poetic-musical tradition throughout the Mediterranean world. No doubt other ethnic musical traditions survived locally, especially folk traditions, but the sources show that Greek entertainment traditions were pervasive. The Roman-era scores document mostly entertainment music and give us an idea of the popular music that people of all classes heard on stage, as well as the professional musical entertainment that the wealthy provided at their private banquets.

Nevertheless, certain aspects of the scores reflect conservative tendencies, probably because they emanate from educated musicians. One clear indicator of that is that all the lyrics in the scores, right through to the end of the third century, show rhythm based on traditional ("classical") quantitative metrical schemes. Meanwhile, the spoken language was becoming increasingly less differentiating in the pronunciation of syllabic lengths (quantity).[53] Moreover, Greek verse of the era, outside the scores, reveals that other poets who hewed to the old ways of measuring syllables also exercised freedom or were uncertain about quantity in certain instances;[54] or else they anticipated that the melody would fix any rhythmic infelicities. It stands to reason, however, that a good deal of the music of the imperial age was composed by musicians who had no classical education and did not treat syllables as having defined lengths for the purposes

---

52. On training for lyrical psalm reading, see chapter 4.

53. See Geoffrey Horrocks, *Greek: A History of the Language and Its Speakers*, 2nd ed. (Wiley Blackwell, 2010), 169–170.

54. West, *Greek Metre*, 163 and West, *Ancient Greek Music*, 132 n. 11.

of expressing metrical rhythm in poetry. They lengthened and shortened at will and they, too, used melisma for effect and to help out the meter.

The scores also show an increasing tendency toward rhythmic values beyond the old "long," as well as an increasing fondness for melisma (the setting of a single syllable to more than one note).[55] The former was not a feature of classical poetry and the latter is nearly absent from the scores of the Hellenistic era. They probably reflect an assimilation on the part of educated Roman-era songwriters of trends in the music of the wider culture.

Another feature of the scores is melodic contouring for the accent. The tonal accent in spoken Greek had been widely replaced by a stress accent by the mid-second century BCE, a development that was concomitant with the breakdown of syllabic quantity.[56] Yet the scores that date to the Hellenistic period and the first two centuries of the Roman era exhibit melodic contouring for the accent, as if the accent were tonal. Since the tonal accent had disappeared from conversational pronunciation, melodic contouring that respected the accent was another bit of Atticizing by the songwriters represented by the scores of the first and second centuries.[57] There is no reason to imagine that this was widespread in the Roman period, however, since most songwriters were not educated and were, therefore, not taught the old Greek pronunciation. And even the educated musicians seem to have abandoned the convention by the third century.

Liturgical psalmers who served Greek-speaking churches in the fourth and fifth centuries *were* educated, and many of the older lectors, especially those from wealthy families, would have learned in school how to read classical poetry aloud by observing the classical quantities so as to bring out the rhythm and to express the tonal accent. Depending on their teachers, they were instructed to do the latter either by improvising melodies (see the discussion of two scholia to the *Ars grammatica* above), probably melodies that respected the old Greek tonal accent, or by reciting the poems using a studied, old-Attic *speaking* intonation.[58] But many of the melodies of the songs they heard in the theater or odeon and at private social gatherings would not have been influenced by the tonal accent

55. The evidence can be conveniently examined in the section of Roman-era scores in Egert Pöhlmann and Martin L. West, eds., *Documents of Ancient Greek Music: The Extant Melodies and Fragments* (Clarendon, 2001).

56. See Horrocks as cited in n. 53.

57. The evidence in the scores for melodic contouring to the accent is analyzed in detail in Cosgrove and Meyer, "Melody and Word Accent Relationships in Ancient Greek Musical Documents."

58. See Charles H. Cosgrove, "Semi-Lyrical Reading of Poetry in Late Antiquity," *Studies in Classical Philology* 111 (2021): 463–482. See the discussion in the postscript to the present chapter.

and would have shown freedom in their quantity-based schemes of rhythm, if they paid attention to quantity at all.

Liturgical psalmers would have had no reason to shape the melody-line to a tonal accent that was practically gone from everyday speech and had never been part of the Hebraic tradition from which the poetry sprang. Gregory of Nyssa was aware of these things. In a book on the superscriptions of the psalms, he suggests that David received "thoughts" from the Holy Spirit and interpreted them, "weaving the words into the melody."[59] Elsewhere in the same writing, Gregory distinguishes David's method of composition from that of the Greek lyric poets:

> But we should not pass by without noticing that these songs are not composed in the fashion of the lyric poets, which lie outside our wisdom. For the melody does not lie in the pitch of the words, as is seen in them, with whom, in a certain kind of prosodic combination—the pitch of the notes being made lower or higher, and shortened or lengthened—the rhythm is brought into being. But he (David), having woven, without artifice or design, the song into the divine words, wants to interpret the meaning of what is said by means of the melody, revealing as far as possible the implied sense of the words by a kind of disposition of the vocal pitch (melody) to the words. Such, therefore, is the dessert of the meal, by which the nourishment of the teachings is sweetened just as with some spices.[60]

As these comments show, Gregory knew that the poems of the lyric poets, who lived in the seventh through fifth centuries, were sung to melodies that respected the tonal accents of the words. Gregory was also aware that David, composing in Hebrew, did not use a method of that sort. David, Gregory says, used melody to interpret the words (and sweeten them), not to express "natural" speech intonation. Unfortunately, Gregory does not go into the specifics of David's method. Perhaps he simply posited that David, as the original and master psalm-singer, must have sung in the fashion that Gregory describes, using the melody to assist communication and to make what he communicated attractive to the ear. But Gregory must have believed that David's sense-sensitive method or something comparable to it should be the church's method. In fact, he may have projected a churchly way of singing psalms onto David.

As for rhythm in psalmody, it is doubtful that liturgical psalmers sought to produce metrical rhythms by lengthening particular syllables. Psalmers sang to

59. Gregory of Nyssa, *Inscr. psalm.* 2.10 (GNO 5: 108–109).

60. *Inscr. psalm.* 1.3 (GNO 5: 34).

no musical instrumental accompaniment that might have required regularity of line lengths, and the psalms themselves implied that they were not intended to express rhythm in the manner of Greek poetry. Moreover, regularizing line lengths would have required a somewhat challenging compositional effort, even if one sought to impose no more than a simple rhythmic scheme such as anapests or dactylic hexameters, which were common meters of the era. These sorts of regularization could not have been easily improvised. Singing psalms in anapests or hexameters would have required careful treatment of syllable lengths and probably a good deal of rehearsal.

Since readers were almost certainly not expected to engage in metricizing execution of the rhythm, they probably gave nearly all syllables the same time value and sang the stress accents gently so as not to insinuate syncopation in places where a particular accentual pattern might otherwise have caused that effect. Nonrhythmic singing and a gentle treatment of accents would have given each psalm line a certain floating or fluid quality. Arguably, it was such an approach that gave psalm-singing a quality that reappears in the later chant style, its undifferentiated rhythm and lack of marked rhythmic pulse.

It has been suggested that early Christian psalmody was a kind of "heightened speech or semi-musical recitative."[61] I gather that those who apply the term "recitative" to ancient psalmody use the word in its modern sense and mean it only by way of analogy.[62] Recitative is a serviceable word for ancient psalmody if used in the sense of melodic singing that reflects the phrasing of ordinary speech and avoids rhythmic and melodic complexity. Other senses of the term may be less apt, including the idea that church psalmody was a semi-melodic form of heightened speech, since the references to psalmody as singing and as melodic in form are so frequent in the ancient sources.

Historians of Christian liturgy have not, as far as I know, considered whether an ancient type of recitative might provide a closer parallel. A brief history of the use of the term will help clarify the possibilities. A traditional scholarly view, formulated in the nineteenth century, is that recitative was invented by Florentine composers who wanted to create a new form of opera inspired by what they believed to have been the musical style of ancient Greek drama, a style

---

61. John A. Smith, *Music in Ancient Judaism and Early Christianity* (Ashgate, 2011), 211. Cf. Ewald Jammers, "Der Choral als Rezitativ," *Archiv für Musikwissenschaft* 22 (1965): 143–168 (discussing the degree to which traditional chant forms as attested by later sources reflect features of recitative).

62. Dyer applies the word "recitative" to ancient psalmody and is careful to qualify the application as "anachronistic." See Joseph Dyer, "The Singing of Psalms in the Early-Medieval Office," *Speculum* 64 (1989): 539.

of singing that was more like speech in its free rhythms and intonation range.[63] Modern classicists subsequently borrowed the word "recitative" and applied it not to solo song generally in Greek drama but to certain parts, typically verses in stichic meters in contrast to lyric strophes.[64] Opinions vary about how melodic these recitative passages were, since all that survives are the texts, not the music. The same applies to putative recitative in Roman drama.[65]

It is also regularly asserted in the field of classics that the Greek word *parakatalogē* was a special ancient term for dramatic recitative.[66] The word *parakatalogē* appears only twice in ancient Greek literature, and only one of those references associates it explicitly with dramatic delivery, calling it "tragic." That sole mention does not characterize its intonation. But there is a clue in the form of the word. It ought to mean "near recitation" by comparison with the term *katalogē*, which means recitation of poetry without singing.[67] Hence *parakatalogē* could mean a style of singing that was more speech-like than other styles. That said, no Christian writer applies the word *parakatalogē* to psalmody, which is not surprising. All the recitative of Greek and Roman drama was metrical poetry, whereas psalmody's rhythms would have sounded like prose rhythm to people of the Greco-Roman era.

Finally, there is the question of tonality in ancient Christian psalmody. The psalm reader needed to sing in such a way that the congregation had no difficulty finding the starting note of its refrain. This called for keeping the melody's tonal center(s) clear and ensuring that at the end of each unit (usually a colon) the psalmer's final note clearly implied, in its tonal context, the starting note of the refrain. The simplest way to facilitate a smooth transition from verse-colon to refrain would have been for the psalmer to end each verse-colon on the refrain's starting note, although familiar cadences might have been just as serviceable.

The Roman era scores exhibit diatonic melodies organized around pitch centers, which composers established by frequency of occurrence and duration. The pitch center belonged to a scale implied by the melody. Complex melodies

63. See, for example, David Ewen, *The New Encyclopedia of Opera* (Hill and Wang, 1971), 491. The historical narrative of the traditional view is now regarded as too simplistic. See, for example, Carolyn Abbate and Roger Parker, *A History of Opera: The Last Four Hundred Years* (Penguin, 2012), 37–44.

64. Amy M. Dale, *The Lyric Metres of Greek Drama* (Cambridge University Press, 1948), 4, 11, 28, and passim.

65. See the survey of scholarly discussion in Timothy J. Moore, *Music in Roman Comedy* (Cambridge University Press, 2012), 92–104.

66. See, for example, Dale, *The Lyric Metres of Greek Drama*, 4 n. 1.

67. Ps.-Plutarch, *Mus.* 28 (*Mor.* 1141a); Ps.-Aristotle, *Probl.* 19 (918a); regarding καταλογή, see Hesychius, *Lex.*, *s.v.* καταλογή (τὸ τὰ ᾄσματα μὴ ὑπὸ μέλει λέγειν).

often moved away from their pitch centers and then returned.[68] Sometimes they introduced contextually novel scale notes. To increase the likelihood of surefooted transitions from psalm lines to the refrain, a psalmer had reason to orient his melody to one pitch center, without any shift to a new tonal center midline or from one verse to the next, and to keep to a simple note-palette "based on" or implying a familiar scale, for which the pitch center was the orientation point. (These are things an ordinary person with a good ear could have done intuitively, based on his or her cultural shaping; just as a modern person is able to improvise a melody that happens to be "based" on a major or minor scale, having been shaped by contemporary musical culture.) Any deviation of the reader's melodization of the verses from the tonality established by the refrain would have risked the possibility that the congregation ended up shifting into a different tessitura or suffering pitch confusion about the melodic pattern of the refrain. No doubt mishaps occurred, even when readers were careful, since strong voices in a congregation, if they belonged to people with a weak sense for tonality, could have occasionally led a group in the wrong direction.

Modes

A story set in the fourth century but invented perhaps two or more centuries later features an unnamed monk who tells Abba Silvanus that when he is alone he follows the "canon" and the "hours" and sings "the hymns of the *oktaēchou*."[69] Silvanus replies, "You know the great fathers, how they were unskilled and not trained, except in a few psalms. And they knew neither modes (*ēchous*) nor troparia." Nor do the many choirs in heaven "sing with the *oktaēchou*."[70] Troparia and the *oktaēchos*[71] or "eight-mode system" were urban musical conventions of the storyteller's own time, perhaps the seventh century. With respect to the melodies of psalmody in an earlier period, the question is when modes became standard musical forms for Christian song and whether they were melody types.

---

68. On these features of ancient Greek music, see the appendix on pitch centers and the tonal structure of ancient Greek melodies in Cosgrove, *An Ancient Christian Hymn with Musical Notation*, 157–179.

69. The expression is simply τὰ τῆς ὀκταήχου.

70. *Jean Rufus Évêque de Maïouma, Plérophories: Témoignages et révélations contre le Concile de Chalcédoine, version syriaque et traduction française*, ed. François Nau (Firmin-Didot, 1911), 180 [580].

71. The word ὀκταήχος, usually spelled ὀκτώηχος, is a late-antique Christian term for an eight-mode system. It is not formed from the standard Greek term for mode—ἁρμονία.

The Greek word *ēchos* has no pre-Christian history as a specifically musical term.[72] The noun—found in masculine, feminine, and neuter forms that were more or less synonymous—meant "sound," its cognate verb meant "to sound," "make noise."[73] People used the noun and verb to refer to sounds of all sorts—the sound of the sea, the sound of musical instruments, the noise of a crowd, and so forth.[74] The church fathers were perfectly familiar with the phrase "sound of the trumpet" in Psalm 150:3, of course, a verse that Paul quotes in 1 Corinthians 15:52. But ancient trumpets were not melodic instruments like citharas, harps, and pipes. They were mostly used as signal and annunciatory instruments, being employed in military actions, gladiatorial spectacles, and processions. It is very unlikely that the image in Psalm 150:3 and 1 Corinthians 15:52 of a trumpet sounding a signal inspired the church's use of *ēchos* for a musical form, whether of psalmody or hymnody. Nor, for obvious reasons, would the following negative examples in the Greek Bible have been a source of a term for melody forms in Christian music: Paul's statement that to speak in tongues without love is just "sounding brass" (*chalkos ēchōn*) (1 Cor 13:1); the derisive statement in Amos 5:23, "Take away from me the sound/noise (*ēchon*) of your songs," and the line, "their memory was destroyed with sound" (*met' ēchous*, presumably a loud one), which fourth-century Christian writers liked to quote from Psalm 9. These passages illustrate how unusual the church's adoption of the word *ēchos* was as a term for an element of Christian music.

At first sight, a more plausible linguistic precedent appears in the following phrasing in the Wisdom of Solomon, which speaks of "the elements modulating their natures with each other, just as in a harp the strings change the form of their rhythm, while always remaining in *ēchō*."[75] The author uses this analogy because he wants to make clear that the creatures were still recognizable as themselves, even though they changed their natures, like strings that remain the same while expressing different rhythms. Here, the expression "*ēchō*" (simply a dative with no preposition) refers to each string having the same pitch throughout the

72. An etymologically related word, ἠχεῖον, referred to a thing that made sound (sometimes a tone) when struck, such as a drum, tambourine, or gong. This provides no clue to the Christian use of ἦχος as an abstract concept, whether a scale or melody-pattern.

73. See BAGD, s.v. ὁ ἦχος, τὸ ἦχος, and ἡ ἠχώ.

74. The masculine form was also used idiomatically to mean "news," "a public report." BAGD, s.v. ὁ ἦχος, no. 2.

75. Wis 19:18 (LXX). The simile is an analogy for the way living creatures and natural elements supposedly exchanged habitats and behaviors as portents during the period leading up to the exodus, land animals going into the sea, sea creatures taking up residence on land, fire surviving in water.

performance of a tune.[76] That is, it means "in tune," and this instance is as close as any examples of the word come to expressing a technical musical idea; but it is not "mode," which Greeks called *harmonia*.

There is no clear evidence of transitional development between such non-modal senses of *ēchos* and the use of the term for a mode in the eight-mode Byzantine system called the Octoechos, where each *ēchos* consisted of a set of melodic formulas based on a scale type. Under this system, a given hymn, such as a troparion, was composed in a specific mode, for which there were many traditional melodic formulas available to a hymn composer. The eight modes were organized as four pairs of modes. Analysis of the modes suggests that the members of a pair had the same scale notes but differed in their internal tonal structure, their "base" notes (which were usually their finals) and their standing notes (or dominants) which functioned as pitch centers.[77] It would be a mistake to imagine that when the term and the concept of singing with a mode first appeared in the Greek church, all these features of tonal organization and compositional process were in place, much less that the Octoechos system was developed early on as a way to organize the modes. Liturgical manuscripts show that by the seventh century and perhaps as early as the late sixth century, the word *ēchos* had entered the Eastern church as a musical term, modes being designated by number and assigned to psalms and troparia. This evidence implies the existence of some kind of system. But modes may not have been developed in church music until the sixth century, and the Octoechos system not until some time after that.[78]

Tellingly, the earliest story to mention troparia does not mention modes. The story concerns instruction in how to sing troparia, which a fifth-century monk named Auxentius[79] gave to the crowds of pilgrims who visited him at

---

76. ἐν ψαλτηρίῳ φθόγγοι τοῦ ῥυθμοῦ τὸ ὄνομα διαλλάσσουσιν, πάντοτε μένοντα ἤχῳ. The subject of μένοντα almost has to be the plural φθόγγοι, but that word is not a neuter plural. Variants address the problem by reading πάντα for πάντοτε, but πάντα does not agree with its putative antecedent.

77. There was a parallel development in the West, where the eight modes of Gregorian chant were organized in four pairs, each pair consisting of a plagal and an authentic mode.

78. Peter Jeffery suspects that church liturologists invented the eight-mode system and imposed it on existing chant practices, doing so both interpretively and prescriptively. That is, they "discovered" eight abstract scales implicit in the chants, took note of associated musical formulae, and called the combination of scales and melodic formulae *ēchoi*, which facilitated the use of modal signatures as a lectionary shorthand. Jeffery opines that it was these ancient liturologists who first assigned a specific musical sense to the word *ēchos*. Peter Jeffery, "The Earliest Oktōēchoi: The Role of Jerusalem and Palestine in the Beginnings of Modal Ordering," in *The Study of Medieval Chant, Paths and Bridges, East and West: In Honor of Kenneth Levy*, ed. Peter Jeffery (Boydell, 2001), 149–161.

79. Auxentius was born in Syria around 400 CE. After becoming a monk, he lived as a solitary in Bithynia near Chalcedon, first at Mount Oxia and later on Mount Scopus, gaining a reputation and attracting seekers. He died near Chalcedon in the latter part of the fifth century.

Mount Oxia. The anecdote appears in a *Life of Auxentius* composed not long after his death:

> Therefore, having prescribed certain troparia of two or three very pleasing and useful statements of sincere and simple character, he prepared all of them [the pilgrims] to sing. The first [troparion] was said frequently in succession, and again, according to the direction of the blessed one, they passed on to the second one. And then in the same way from the second to the third, and the rest in order [seven troparia are quoted]. The crowd of those present, both the ill-prepared and the well-prepared, men and women, slaves and free, sang these [the troparia] with good rhythm according to the blessed one's prescribed unpretentious melody (*melos*).[80]

At the point noted in brackets, the biographer quotes the words of seven troparia that Auxentius taught the pilgrims. A curiosity is that according to the anecdote, these troparia consisted of two or three phrases; yet the quoted troparia consist of five to seven phrases or lines. In fact, only one of the seven troparia exhibits as few as three phrases; none has two. This suggests that an earlier version of the original story may have concerned simpler and more uniform troparia. If so, it would be easier to understand how a single melody could have been used for them, with modest melodic adaptation.

An alternate explanation is that *melos* here means *ēchos*-mode in the sense of a collection of musical formulae all based on the same scale. In that case, each troparion was set to a different formula or set of formulae. While this solution is attractive in the way it accounts for the poetic diversity of the quoted troparia, there is no instance in ancient Christian literature where *melos* is clearly used as a synonym for *ēchos* as mode. Moreover, since *melos* is not defined by a number in this passage,[81] the anecdote provides no hint that a modal system informs the description.

Since modes in the East and the West were used to facilitate transitions between psalms and hymns by ensuring melodic affinity between the two, it is likely that the need for modes did not become pressing until psalms (or psalm verses) were paired with hymns that had fixed melodies and especially when a verse of a psalm was sung with a hymn (as in the East) or a psalm was paired with an antiphon (as in the West) and one or both parts of such two-part musical units

80. *Vit. s. Auxent.* 46–47.

81. Regarding the earliest evidence for modal numbering, see Christian Troelsgård, "A New Source for the Early *Octoechos*? Papyrus Vindobonensis G 19.934 and Its Musical Implications," presented at the First International Conference of Byzantine Musical Culture, American Society of Byzantine Music and Hymnology, Peania, Attica, 2007.

were sung in choral unison.[82] In the East, the use of modes, *ēchoi*, may have first developed in the sixth century, when the first slight evidence of modes appears. In the West, the use of modes appears to be associated with the replacement of solo psalmody, with or without responses, by choral psalmody *in directum*, a shift that took place in the latter part of the eighth century into the ninth century.[83]

Postscript

"Semi-Lyrical" Psalm Reading?

The only instance where an ancient writer draws a *contrast* between different styles of reading psalms is a comment in a well-known passage in Augustine's *Confessions*, where he recalls an anecdote about the performance of psalm lessons in Alexandria. Augustine had "often heard" that when Athanasius was bishop there, he "made the lector vocalize the psalms with so modest a modulation of the voice (*tam modico flexu vocis*) that it was more like *pronuntianti* than *canenti* (singing)."[84] If Augustine had "often" heard this anecdote, it was probably told by more than one person, apparently by people who were familiar with a style of psalm lesson that was more like song and who noted that Alexandrian psalm lessons were less melodic.

But the anecdote is problematic. It is unclear whether the observer(s) compared a style in Athanasius's church to psalm-singing elsewhere in Athanasius's day or to psalm-singing in a later period. James McKinnon suggests the latter possibility, reasoning that since Augustine was baptized fourteen years after the death of Athanasius, his anecdote about Athanasius's lector amounts to a comparison of "the melodious psalmody of the late fourth century with the drier type of several years earlier."[85] This theory requires the assumption that one or more people who spent time in Athanasius's church in Alexandria between 328 and 373 lived into the last decades of the century and witnessed the evolution

82. For the East, see the seminal article by Oliver Strunk, "Intonations and Signatures of the Byzantine Modes" (1945), in Oliver Strunk, *Essays on Music in the Byzantine World* (Norton, 1977), 19–44; see also Egon Wellesz, *A History of Byzantine Music and Hymnology*, 2nd ed. (Clarendon, 1961), 300–309.

83. Regarding the rise of choral psalmody *in directum*, I am informed by the historical reconstruction in Joseph Dyer, "The Singing of Psalms in the Early-Medieval Office," *Speculum* 64 (1989): 542–546.

84. Augustine, *Conf.* 10.33.50 (*tam modico flexu vocis faciebat sonare lectorem psalmi ut pronuntianti vicinior esset quam canenti*). Translators of Augustine often render *pronuntianti* as "speaking," which probably does not capture the sense, as I go on to point out.

85. James McKinnon, "The Fourth-Century Origin of the Gradual," *Early Music History* 7 (1987): 105.

of psalm readings from an earlier "drier" style into the melodic style familiar to Augustine. There is nothing unreasonable about this assumption. Yet the anecdote does not say that in an earlier age, readers rendered psalms in a less melodic way. It says that Athanasius directed the reader to perform the psalm with a certain reduced intonation. In other words, the anecdote implies that, had Athanasius not intervened, lectors in Alexandria would have sung psalms more melodically than Athanasius approved. That in turn implies that it was common to sing psalms melodically in Athanasius's day.

Then there is the question of the verbs in the comparison. According to Augustine's rendering of the anecdote, Athanasius demanded a style that was "more like elevated speaking (*pronuntianti*) than singing (*canenti*)." The verb *pronuntiare* was often used for the heightened speech of dramatic performance, such as that of actors delivering lines of dialogue. For example, Aelius Donatus (fourth century), writing about the second-century comedies of Terence, distinguishes the performance of the speaking parts from that of the singing parts. "The actors would declaim (*pronuntiabant*) the dialogue," he explains, whereas "the songs were truly regulated by melody, composed not by a poet but by an expert in the art of music."[86] Now, the dialogue parts of drama were not spoken conversationally. Cast in iambic senarii, they were performed as poetry, no doubt in a way that brought out their rhythm and entailed a stylized modulation of the voice.[87]

The verb *pronuntio* was not used exclusively for delivery of poetry,[88] but the contrast between *pronuntio* and *modus* in an anecdote about delivering biblical poetry suggests that the storyteller meant to compare a stylized kind of recitation with melodic singing, just as Aelius Donatus did. Hence, the anecdote's use of *pronuntianti* instead of, say, *loquendi* (the ordinary verb for speaking) implies that the reader was instructed to perform the psalm lesson in a style that was more like reciting or declaiming poetry than like singing a song.

---

86. *Deuerbia histriones pronuntiabant, cantica uero temperabantur modis non a poeta sed a perito artis musicae factis*. Aelius Donatus, *Com.* 8.9. As applied to music, *modus* means the measure of tones or rhythm or the two together as melody. In the present context, the distinction between the *deuerbia*, which had poetic rhythm, and the *cantica*, whose *modi* were composed by a musician, makes clear that *modis* here means melody. See the discussion in Moore, *Music in Roman Comedy*, 136–139.

87. Iambic scenarii means iambic trimeter—three metra each, consisting of two iambs.

88. See the wide range of uses listed in the *OLD*, s.v. *pronuntio*. In Latin, at least since the time of the republic, the words *cantare, recitare, pronuntiare,* and *legere* overlapped in meaning, and *pronuntiare* was often used for delivery of words to an audience. It did not specify a specific type of vocalization, and it was not a technical term for reciting poetry, inasmuch as it was also used for making public announcements and for many other types of declaration.

It has been suggested by at least one scholar that Athanasius likely instructed the reader to render the psalm with a "middle" vocalization that was sometimes used for poetry.[89] In late antiquity, elite boys were taught in school how to read old Greek poetry aloud (notably Homer, probably the lyric poets as well) with an affected intonation that was meant to approximate the old Greek tonal accent. This intonation sounded like a "middle" intonation between speaking and singing. That same intonation would not have sounded that way in the archaic and classic periods, when the tonal accent was part of everyday speech. But in late antiquity, when the verbal accent of everyday speech was no longer tonal, to pronounce Greek poems using the old-fashioned tonal accent sounded semi-lyrical.[90]

That said, this school tradition cannot be what Athanasius approved for liturgical psalm reading. For in *Letter of Marcellinus* he says that the psalms are to be read *melodically*, since "the Lord prescribed that the canticles be sung melodically and the psalms be read with song."[91] The expression "with song" was commonly used for delivering a poem by singing it.[92] Moreover, Athanasius's explanation of the reason for the divine mandate was so that the orderliness of music would be expressed as a symbol of the good order of the soul.[93]

Presumably, Athanasius derived his opinion from the book of Psalms itself, where a good deal of praise is pictured as musical, and where the psalmist uses the expression "with song" in the command, "Praise the name of the Lord with song" (Ps 68:31). Moreover, in another place in *Letter to Marcellinus*, Athanasius distinguishes between the parts of Scripture that should be read as

89. Joseph Dyer, "The Desert, the City and Psalmody in the Late Fourth Century," in *Western Plainchant in the First Millennium: Studies in the Medieval Liturgy and Its Music*, ed. Sean Gallagher et al. (Ashgate, 2003), 29–30. In what follows, I explain why I disagree with Dyer's suggestion that the tradition of a middle vocalization explains the anecdote about Athanasius and his readers.

90. This is how I interpret the idea of the middle intonation in Aristides Quintilianus, *Mus.* 1.4; Boethius, *Inst. mus.* 1.12; Albinus, as quoted in Boethius; Martianus Capella, *De nuptiis Philologiae et Mercurii* 9.937. See Cosgrove, "Semi-Lyrical Reading of Poetry in Late Antiquity."

91. ὁ Κύριος τετύπωκεν ἐμμελῶς τὰς ᾠδὰς ψάλλεσθαι καὶ τοὺς ψαλμοὺς μετ' ᾠδῆς ἀναγινώσκεσθαι. *Ep. Marc.* 28 (PG 27: 40). Cf. ἡ τῶν ψαλμῶν ἐμμελὴς ἀνάγνωσις in the same context. The adjective ἐμμελής/ές means melodic. Note the remark of Dionysius of Halicarnassus about the difference between the pleasing intonations of the voice in speaking and singing, speaking being "mellifluous" (εὐμελὲς) but not "melodic" (ἐμμελές). *Comp.* 11.24.

92. Numerous examples can be found in the TLG, and Athanasius himself illustrates the meaning of the expression when he refers to biblical poems that Christians regarded as biblical odes by saying, "Moses writes an ode, Isaiah sings, and Habbakuk prays with song (μετ' ᾠδῆς)." *Ep. Marc.* 9 (PG 27: 17).

93. Athanasius, *Ep. Marc.* 27–29. See the further discussion of this aspect of Athanasius's views of singing psalms in chapter 13.

prose and the parts that should be sung. "It is fitting," he says, "for the divine Scripture to hymn God not only in the continuous (*tē synecheia*) but also in the broad (*kata platos*) voice."[94] The law, prophets, historical books, and the New Testament should be spoken in the continuous fashion (*kata synecheian*), he says, the psalms and odes broadly (*kata platos*).[95] Athanasius had already used very similar phrasing earlier in the letter, when he explained that the book of Psalms "has the distinctive character of being a book of songs," and "sings with melody in broad (*kata-platos*) voice."[96] There are two things to observe in these formulations. First, the expression *kata synecheian* was used by Greek musicologists to distinguish speaking from singing. They characterized the movement of the speaking voice as *synechēs* and the movement of the singing voice as *diastēmatikē*.[97] Athanasius uses *synecheia* for the movement of the voice in nonmelodic reading of Scripture prose. When referring to the movement of the voice in reading the lyrical parts of Scripture, he does not use the musicologist's expression *diastēmatikē*. Yet it is clear from the context that the expression he does use, *kata platos*, describes singing; for he states that the book of Psalms "has the distinctive character of being a book of songs" and "sings with melody in a *kata-platos* voice."[98]

Athanasius's characterization of the singing as *kata platos* ("broadly," "in extension") is perhaps to be explained by a comment in Boethius. Quoting a certain Albinus, Boethius says that singing exhibits a "sustained and slow manner of voice." Significantly, Albinus contrasts the "sustained and slow manner of singing" to both ordinary speaking and the middle intonation of

---

94. *Ep. Marc.* 27 (PG 27: 39).

95. *Ep. Marc.* 27 (PG 27: 40).

96. ἡ τῶν ψαλμῶν βίβλος, ἔχουσα τὸ ἴδιον τῶν ᾠδων. . . τῇ κατὰ πλάτος φωνῇ μετὰ μέλους ψάλλει. *Ep. Marc.* 9 (PG 27: 20).

97. These distinctions and the terminology go back to Aristoxenus, *El. Harm.* 1.8–10 and 1.18 (da Rios, 13–15 and 24). Aristoxenus was a student of Aristotle. His book on music was a standard in antiquity, and his terminology for the movements of the voice is used by Aristides Quintilianus (*Mus.* 1.4, Winnington-Ingram, 6) and, in Latin equivalents, by Vitruvius (*De arch.* 5.4.2) and Boethius (*Inst. mus.* 1.12).

98. ἡ τῶν ψαλμῶν βίβλος, ἔχουσα τὸ ἴδιον τῶν ᾠδῶν. . .τῇ κατὰ πλάτος φωνῇ μετὰ μέλους ψάλλει. *Ep. Marc.* 9 (PG 27: 20). Given the information that Dyer had gathered, it was perfectly reasonable of him to have concluded that Athanasius's expression κατὰ πλάτος refers to the intermediate vocalization that Aristides Quintilianus and Boethius placed between speaking and singing, a vocalization that was used for reading or reciting poetry (see Dyer as cited in n. 89). Yet there is no evidence in Greek musicology or in other Greek literature that κατὰ πλάτος was used for the middle movement of the voice. Regarding the cultural-linguistic context for the use of the middle vocalization, see Cosgrove, "Semi-Lyrical Reading of Poetry in Late Antiquity."

poetry recital.[99] Athanasius may have used the expression "broadly" because he was thinking of the slower pace of song as compared to conversational speech, a broadening of each syllable in performing them to defined pitches.[100]

No fewer than four intellectuals of late antiquity mention the middle intonation for reciting poetry—Aristides Quintilianus, Albinus, Boethius, and Martianus Capella.[101] By contrast, when Augustine repeats the anecdote about Athanasius and the lector, he does not use the term *medium*, and he does not even hint that the anecdote concerns a well-known way of reciting epic and other poetry composed in the archaic and classical eras. Nor does the poetry to which he refers (biblical poetry) belong to the type that was vocalized in a "middle" way.

Finally, there is the question of the linguistic history of the anecdote. The anecdote claims that Athanasius told readers to read the lessons with a form of delivery that the anecdote calls *prununtianti*. When this Latin word is used by a Latin speaker in a story about reading biblical poetry, it could very naturally refer to the intonation used by Latin speakers when they recited Latin poetry. Which term a Greek speaker may have used for it, if the anecdote started out in Greek, is anyone's guess. But if we knew what that word was, we might be able to achieve a better understanding of the story in its original setting. In any case, as it stands, the anecdote flatly contradicts Athanasius's own emphatic instructions about how biblical poetry should be read. Either Athanasius had a change of mind, or, by the time that Augustine first heard the anecdote, the story had become garbled. Or else there was confusion about which bishop it concerned, a real possibility, since it was not at all uncommon in antiquity for a free-floating anecdote to become attached to someone other than its original subject.

---

99. Boethius, *Inst. mus.* 1.12. The Latin expression used by Boethius for the full singing mode is *suspenso segniorique modo vocis*.

100. It happens that certain ancient music theorists claimed that a musical note has "breadth" (πλάτος). Since a note's duration is a matter of rhythm, other theorists thought it wrong to attribute anything but pitch or scale position to a note. Aristoxenus writes, "So as not to suffer the conclusion that Lassus and certain followers of Epigonus suffer, who thought it [a note] has breadth (πλάτος), it is necessary to speak about it a little more precisely" (*El. Harm.* 1.3 [da Rios, 7]. Later writers in the Aristoxenian tradition also state that a note is a single indivisible sound with no breadth (Nicomachus, *Harm. Ench.* 12 [Jan, 261]; Cleonides, *Isag.* 2.4–5 [Solomon, 115]). The defenders of the idea that notes have breadth may have meant that they do so when performed, which is a common-sense perception of a musical tone.

101. See the citations in n. 90.

CHAPTER THIRTEEN

Purposes and Pleasures

SEVERAL LATE FOURTH-CENTURY bishops make a point of saying that the Psalter includes all the content and speech forms found in the rest of the Bible, including law and commandments, historical narrative, and prophesy, making the Psalter eminently practical.[1] To quote Basil, "The prophets teach some things, the historians others, the law still others, and the type of the proverbial exhortation yet further things," but "the Book of Psalms embraces the benefit of all of them. It prophecies what is to come. It recalls history. It legislates for life. It sets forth practical advice. And it is a general, common storehouse of good instructions."[2] Ambrose speaks in similar terms. "History instructs," he writes, "the law teaches, prophecy proclaims, reproof disciplines, and moralizing persuades; in the Book of Psalms there is the successful accomplishment of all of this along with a kind of balm of human salvation."[3] Without making observations of this sort about genres, Athanasius goes into great detail about the benefits of psalmody, setting forth various classes of human needs and interests and citing the psalms that suit each one.[4] Niceta of Remesiana speaks in briefer compass, declaring that the psalms contain everything needed for "the benefit, edification, and consolation of the human race, whatever one's circumstance, gender, or age."[5]

The benefits of the psalms were not communicated solely through singing them, of course, since the psalms were also studied, meditated, quoted for illustration or proof-texting, and preached on for their edifying instruction. It is beyond the scope of the present chapter to examine all the lessons that Christian writers and preachers extracted from psalms. The focus here is primarily on the ways in which the musical aspect was understood to contribute to the purposes and pleasures of psalmody.

---

1. Athanasius, *Ep. Mar.* 3–10; Basil, *Hom. in psalm. 1* 1 (PG 29: 209, 212); Ambrose, *Expl. psalm. 1* 7 (PL 14: 923; CSEL 64: 6).

2. Basil, *Expos. in psalm.*, *In psalm. 1* 1 (PG 29: 212).

3. Ambrose, *Expl. in psalm. 1* 7 (PL 14.923; CSEL 64: 6). H. J. Auf der Maur concludes that these remarks, which are part of a larger encomium to the psalms, are dependent on Basil's encomium in the opening of his own commentary on Psalm 1. H. J. Auf der Maur, *Das Psalmenverständnis des Ambrosius von Mailand* (Brill, 1977), 24.

4. Athanasius, *Ep. Mar.* 2–9.

5. Niceta of Remesiana, *Util. hymn.* 5 (Turner, 235).

Tears

Common sense, based on experience, convinces most of us that music expresses emotions and also stimulates them.[6] It appears that psalmody was often performed with tears, which suggests that it was often accompanied by strong emotions, emotions that some writers regarded as a direct effect of the psalms. "How greatly I wept at your hymns and songs," Augustine writes, "being deeply moved by the voices of your sweetly singing church! The voices flowed into my ears and the truth was poured out into my heart, from which a rush of piety surged and my tears overflowed."[7] Tearful expressions of love for God, aroused by psalm-singing, is also the theme of John Chrysostom's description of the nighttime psalmody of the monks who lived in the wastelands outside Antioch:

> And they sing prophetic hymns with much concord, with rhythmical melodies. No lyre or pipe or any other musical instrument releases such a sound as one hears from those holy men singing in the deep silence and in the desert. And the songs themselves are fitting and full of love for God. "In the night," he*[8] says, "lift your hands to God;" and again, "My spirit rises early in the night to you, O God, because your ordinances are light upon the earth." And the Davidic songs provoke fountains of tears. For when he* sings—saying, "I have grown weary in my groaning, I drench my bed every night, I will water my couch with tears;" and again, "Because I ate ashes as bread;" and again, "What is a human being that you would remember him?" "A human being is like vanity, and our days pass by like a shadow;" and "Do not be afraid when a person becomes rich and the glory of his house increases;" and [five more quotations]—he* shows their burning love for God.[9]

6. The expression or communicative power of melody and rhythm has been the subject of a good deal of philosophical debate. Leaving aside the question of whether music possesses intrinsic communicative powers, it is perhaps not controversial to say that in a given cultural setting people are socialized to experience melody and rhythm in certain ways and tend to think of music as both expressive and affecting.

7. Augustine, *Conf.* 9.6.14.

8. Here and in the other instances where I have marked "he" with *, the grammatical subject is not expressed and could be either David or "Scripture." On this aspect of the passage, see chapter 8.

9. John Chrysostom, *In epist. I ad Tim., Hom.* 14.4 (PG 62: 576). The twelve quotations in the long sentence are Pss 6:7; 101:10; 8:5; 143:4; 48:17; 67:7; 118:164; 118:62; 48:16; 22:4; 90:56; 43:23.

John sets forth a diverse sampling of psalm verses here to illustrate the monks' love for God when they sing what David once sang. John first speaks of psalms that stimulate a tearful response, then of the words of various psalms that express love for God. The implication is that the act of singing stimulates or reawakens the emotion of love for God, which provokes tears.

Since John cites some twelve passages on different topics from various psalms, he clearly means to illustrate how the psalms as a whole function in the nighttime devotions of the monks, who probably sang through the entire Psalter over the course of several nights. Since the many different topics of the psalms would not have caused the same response unless they were all interpreted in a particular framework and for a particular purpose, it must have been the monks' way of using the psalms that caused their tears.

A clue is found in another of John's sermons. Commenting on Jesus's statement, "I have come to cast fire on the earth," John explains that Jesus means "spiritual fire," which enters into the soul and drives out spiritual insensitivity to one's own sin. As a result, the repentant person "remains continually in compunction, releasing constant fountains of tears and reaping much pleasure from it; for nothing so binds and unites us to God as tears of this sort."[10] This state of continual compunction is emotionally complex, combining sorrow for sin with gratefulness for God's mercy, which engenders ardent love for God and feelings of release and peace. John mentions this last element when he adduces the example of the "sinful woman" who wept at Jesus's feet. The woman wept in repentance, and "just as the sky becomes clean when a violent rain comes down, so tranquility and peace arise from falling tears, and the darkness caused by sins vanishes."[11]

Although John does not mention psalmody in the passage just quoted, his conception of the connections between compunction, tears, relief, love for God, and a feeling of unity with God suggests a framework for understanding how he and other Christians approached psalm-singing. They were taught to use psalm recitation as an occasion to ponder their own sinfulness, doing so with a self-searching and repentant spirit, and, at the same time, to cultivate feelings of gratefulness to God for forgiveness and salvation, which engendered the emotion of love-filled unity with God that John prized as a great pleasure. This conception and practice of psalmody was also current in the West. "The singing of psalms

---

10. John Chrysostom, *In Matt.*, Hom. 6.5 (PG 57: 68; Field, *Hom. in Matt.* 1: 80). Note that for some reason the English translation of this homily in NPNF 10 fails to represent a large section of material at this point, including this passage, omitting everything from καὶ τὸ πνεῦμα διὰ τοῦτο ἐν πυρὶ φαίνεται (Field, 79) through οὕτω τὰ κατὰ θεὸν δάκρυα χαρὰν βλαστάνει διηνεκῆ καὶ ἀμάραντον (Field, 80).

11. John offers this example of the tears of the sinful woman (Luke 7) at a later point in the same sermon. *In Matt.*, Hom. 6.5 (PG 57: 69; Field, *Hom. in Matt.* 1:81).

and hymns," writes Augustine, "is so useful for moving the soul devotionally and igniting an affection of divine love."[12]

In monasteries, novices experienced communal psalm recitations and occasional psalm-singing in which senior monks routinely wept. This must have conditioned the novices to respond in the same way. An anecdote in the *Life of Pachomius* is suggestive. A certain Theodore, who was one day to become an abbot, approached Pachomius, seeking assurance that he would eventually "see God."[13] Pachomius noticed that he was weeping, which was characteristic of him but surprising since "he was so new." In other words, weeping was typically an acquired habit of those who entered the monastery, something learned. This is also evident from an anecdote of unknown date. An unnamed monk asks an unnamed abba, "Why do tears sometimes come of themselves but sometimes only with great effort?" The abba answered by comparing tears to the unpredictability of rain.[14] It is notable that he does not tell the brother that tears are unnecessary for the experience of contrition. His answer assumes that weeping is desirable and that the brother is right to cultivate it.

Other Christian divines also understood psalms as an occasion for repentant tears.[15] "A psalm offers medicine for all who would receive it," says Niceta of Remesiana, "not disdaining the sinner, to whom it contributes a health-giving remedy through weeping penitence."[16] Basil declares that "a psalm summons tears from a stony heart."[17] In another place, he describes an occasional vigil, where the people say prayers of confession "with suffering and affliction and tearful distress," then rise and sing psalms, presumably also with weeping.[18] His sister Macrina told the women of her monastery that the only proper time for

---

12. Augustine, *Ep.* 55.34 (PL 33: 221; CSEL 34: 208–209). See the previous section.

13. *Vit. Pach.* Boh. 33. Translation from Armand Veilleux, tr., *Pachomian Koinonia*, vol. 1: *The Life of Saint Pachomius and His Disciples* (Cistercian, 1980), 58.

14. Anonymous story in the collection compiled by Paul Evergetinus, *Synagoge* 2.32, as quoted in Irénée Hausherr, *Penthos: The Doctrine of Compunction in the Christian East* (Cistercian Publications, 1982), 75–76.

15. On the broader topic of the role of compunction in a Christian's progress in virtue, see Jeremy Driscoll, "Penthos and Tears in Evagrius Ponticus," *Studia Monastica* 36 (1994): 147–163; Andrew Mellas, "Tears of Compunction in John Chrysostom's On Eutropius," *Studia Patristica* 83 (2017): 159–172; Hausherr, *Penthos*; Ilaria Ramelli, "Tears of Pathos, Repentance and Bliss: Crying and Salvation in Origen and Gregory of Nyssa," in *Tears in the Graeco-Roman World*, ed. Thorsten Fögen (De Gruyter, 2009), 367–396.

16. Niceta of Remesiana, *Util. hymn.* 5.

17. Basil, *Hom. in psalm. 1* 2 (PG 29: 213).

18. Basil, *Ep.* 207.3.5-8.

tears is prayer, which meant the time of prayer and psalmody.[19] And like John Chrysostom and Augustine, some Christian leaders also associated tearful contrition with love for God. Theodoret of Cyr writes, "Fervent ardor for God gives birth to tears."[20] Antony is said to have declared that "the very praise of the psalms is a lament," which makes sense only if lament for one's sin and praise for divine salvation are understood as the essence of the proper mindset to be cultivated in psalmody.[21] Later stories about the desert fathers sound a similar note. For example, a monk who had "continual compunction" is said to have practiced psalmody all day long, "ceaselessly shedding tears."[22]

There was, therefore, a nexus of ideas connected with compunction that Christian divines discussed in different ways. Compunction, cultivated through prayer and psalmody, leads to positive emotions such as gratefulness to God for mercy, love for God, unity with God, release, hope, and so on. For if sorrow for sin is not connected with these positive things, it is merely despair, as Cassian points out when he says that sorrows (*tristia*) are useful only for repentance, desire for perfection, and contemplation of the blessed future life, since these forms of sorrow lead to reformative action, whereas despair over one's sin does not.[23] Cassian advocates the *decantatio* of psalms to cultivate compunction.[24] The noun *decantatio* can mean chant but also suggests frequent repetition, whatever the exact mode of delivery. Repetitive meditative psalm recitation is probably the main idea.

In daily prayer, as practiced both privately and communally, psalms and prayers were intercalated. Since the prayers focused on confession, the psalms must have been understood as conducive to contrition. A particularly clear example is found in a Greek tractate titled *Discourse on Salvation to a Virgin*, dubiously attributed to Athanasius, which provides instructions to celibate ascetic women who live at home.[25] The author assigns confession of sin to the prayer that follows each set of psalms. Presumably, the purpose of the psalms was to create feelings of contrition in preparation for the prayer of confession: "Let these things be daily requirements for you. Say the psalms standing, as many as

19. According to Gregory of Nyssa, *Vit. Macr.* 27.

20. Theodoret of Cyr, *Historia religiosa* 30(*Domnina*).2.

21. *De vitis patrum* 7(*Verba seniorum*).38.1 (PL 73: 1055) (*ipsa laudatio psalmorum planctus est*).

22. Paul Evergentinus, *Synagoge* 4.37, as quoted in Hausherr, *Penthos*, 78.

23. Cassian, *Inst.* 9.9–10.

24. Cassian, *Conlat.* 1.17.2.

25. The envisioned readership is a celibate, ascetic woman living in a private household, a household that sometimes but not always included some number of other women like herself.

you can. And for each psalm let a prayer and genuflection be completed, confessing your sins to the Lord with tears and asking that they be forgiven to you."[26] In another place, the author urges prayer at the ninth hour, "again in hymns and doxologies with tears, confessing your sin,"[27] which suggests that psalms at this hour and the preceding hour (the sixth), perhaps all the hours, were to be recited or sung[28] with penitential weeping.

Augustine describes a Christian singing with tears during a service. He offers the example to show how ostensibly devout outward behavior in psalmody can serve a shameful ulterior purpose. Commenting on Psalm 71:4—"Lord, deliver me from the hand of the sinner, and from the hand of the wrongdoer and the bully"—Augustine warns his flock against applying these words to their own worldly troubles and making "the sinner" a person they know and regard as a threat in some worldly matter. Instead, they should construe "sinner" as a reference to anyone, including themselves. He then pictures a person who engages in the bad kind of self-serving interpretation of the psalm-verse:

> You see him singing, and singing with deep feeling, even fitting his expression to the words of the psalm, sometimes also watering his cheeks with tears, and sighing between the words of the tune. Anyone without experience in assessing expressions of feeling will now praise that man and say, "He listens to the reading with such great feeling. Oh how he groans, how he sighs!" But he is thinking of that enemy of his . . . and with all his heart and soul, with voice, expression, he sighs, "Lord, deliver me from the hand of the sinner . . ." Anyone singing like that, it is the old man [Adam] singing and trying with his materialist, literal-minded understanding to sing the new song even while he is old.[29]

This illustration shows that Augustine was familiar with people's weeping during psalmody, some of it very demonstrative.

At least some of the passages examined thus far suggest that melody was thought to play a role in stimulating compunction during psalmody or providing

26. Ps.-Athanasius, *Virg.* 20.

27. ἐνάτῃ ὥρᾳ πάλιν ἐν ὕμνοις καὶ δοξολογίαις μετὰ δακρύων ἐξομολογουμένη τὰ παραπτώματά σου. Ps.-Athanasius, *Virg.* 12.

28. The author uses verbs for "saying," "hymning," and "psalming" (forms of λέγειν, ὕμνειν, and ψάλλειν in §20 and elsewhere).

29. Augustine, *Serm. de Vet. Test.* 22A, on Ps. 70:4 (CCL 41: 303); tr. from *The Works of Saint Augustine: A Translation for the Twenty-First Century*, ed. John E. Rotelle: Sermons, Part 3/2: (20–50) on the Old Testament, tr. with notes by Edmund Hill (New City Press, 1990), 51.

an expression for it. It is difficult to judge whether this was a widespread view or only the opinion of a handful of divines. In one respect, it is a problematic idea, given the apparently pervasive view of Eastern bishops that melody serves as a sweetener to make psalms attractive to the average person, who find it hard to attend to divine teachings. Moreover, Athanasius taught that melody is proper to psalmody but only as a symbol of harmony in the soul. Furthermore, in certain monastic traditions, the melodic rendering of psalms was restricted to particular occasions, and these did not always or even usually include the daily synaxis or the monks' private recitation in their cells. Not only that, some Christians regarded melody as a distraction or temptation. The urban monk Isidore of Pelucium (born c. 360) complained that people in his day "do not suffer contrition from the divine hymns but use them for the stimulation of passions with the pleasure of melody," treating them like theater songs.[30] An interesting passage in the writings of the fifth-century ascetic Diodochus of Photice (b. c. 400) is less negative but likewise distinguishes the function of melody in psalmody from the process of compunction. "When the soul is in a state of physical wellbeing,"[31] Diodochus writes, "it performs the psalmody more loudly and wants to pray with the voice. But when it is acted upon by the Holy Spirit, it sings and prays with complete relaxation and sweetness with the heart alone. In the former state it is busy conceiving joy; in the latter, spiritual tears, and after these a certain delight of solitude."[32] This analysis implies that singing is the soul's own expression of joy in God, while tearful compunction is a work of the Spirit and produces no sound, since it takes place silently, in the heart alone.

Moral Formation and Soul Therapy

If some fourth- and fifth-century Christians doubted that melody in psalmody was an aid to cultivating proper emotions and attitudes, others celebrated the beneficial power of song. "Nothing," exclaims John Chrysostom, "nothing so lifts the soul, gives it wings, sets it free from the earth, liberates it from the chains of the body, causes it to love wisdom and to scorn all the things of this life, as does a concordant melody and sacred song composed in rhythm."[33] He says something similar in another sermon, specifying various benefits of a psalm as speech addressed to God:

---

30. Isidore of Pelusium, *Epistulae*, *Lib.* 1, *Ep.* 90 (PG 78: 245).

31. The Greek expression is a bit curious: ὅταν ἐν εὐθηνίᾳ ᾖ ἡ ψυχὴ τῶν φυσικῶν αὐτῆς καρπῶν.

32. Diadochus of Photice, *Capita centum de perfectione spirituali* 73.

33. John Chrysostom, *In psalm. 41* 1 (PG 55: 156).

> In addition, [psalmody] possesses, through melody, much pleasure and a certain comfort and relief, and it dignifies the one singing. That it effects these sorts of things is evident from the translators [of the words, "Sing to the Lord because it is *kalon*"], one who translates 'because it is appealing' and another 'because it is pleasing'. What both say is true. And even if the singer might be licentious a thousand times over, by singing the psalm he subdues the tyranny of his licentiousness. And if he is burdened by countless troubles and weighed down by discouragement, when he is captured by the spell of the psalm's pleasure, he relieves his mind, gives wings to his understanding, and makes his soul feel light.[34]

The pleasure of melody does not operate independently. Indeed, John criticizes those who think that Psalm 140, which they sing daily, is "just a song," with the result that they pay no attention to the words, when the words are what make it "a medicine of salvation and a cleansing of sins."[35] He goes on to call Psalm 140 a "spiritual charm-song" (*epōdēs pneumatikēs*) through which we are stripped [of our sins]."[36] Psalm 62, the regular morning psalm, is similar, he says. These psalms work sacramentally[37] and not only through their words but also thanks to "concordant melody and sacred song composed in rhythm," as John says in a sermon on Psalm 40. The words of the psalms "cleanse the soul" and "the Holy Spirit flies swiftly to the soul who sings them."[38] He speaks in similar terms in another sermon, where he describes public psalmody following an earthquake that the Christians of the city and John himself interpreted as a divine judgment. The Christians' penitential[39] singing, he tells them, had a sanctifying effect on others. "If someone is licentious, that person hears the voice [of psalmody] and their mind is changed. The song, and their impiety is changed. The passions of

---

34. *In psalm. 134* 1 (PG 55: 388). "The singer" is grammatically masculine in Greek but semantically generic.

35. *In psalm. 140* 1 (PG 55: 427).

36. *In psalm. 140* 1 (PG 55: 427).

37. See Harald Buchinger, "Psalmodie als Sakrament: Johannes Chrysostomus über den täglichen Abendpsalm 140(141)," in *Wort des lebendigen Gottes:Liturgie und Bibel*, ed. Alexander Zefaß and Ansgar Franz (Naar/Francke/Attempto, 2016), 226.

38. John Chrysostom, *In psalm. 40* 1 (PG 55: 157).

39. John conceives the psalmody as restraining God's wrath and saving the city. Hence, he states at one point, "We have need of nothing but repentance, tears, and wailings. And all things were dissolved. God appeared, and we dissolved his wrath." *De terrae motu* (PG 50: 716).

licentiousness flee."[40] Moreover, the people's singing, as they processed through the streets, sanctified the public spaces, John says, and made the whole city holy.[41]

The idea that psalmody calms and cures the troubled soul appears in comments by various early Christians about David's use of music to cure the madness of Saul (1 Sam 16:23). By singing, David banished the demons and healed Saul, writes Clement of Alexandria.[42] David sang and put Saul's soul at peace, says Athanasius.[43] Basil connects the story with a similar tale about Pythagoras, who "when he encountered some drunken revelers, it is said, commanded the piper who was leading their revel to change the mode and pipe the Dorian for them. Thus, they were brought to their senses by the melody, so that they tore off their garlands and returned home ashamed."[44]

Clement, Athanasius, and Basil do not make clear whether they thought that the particular melodies of David's psalmody possessed special curative powers or simply that David used the general curative power of music to heal Saul. In addition to folklore about music's power, a connection was made between music and emotions, specifically between musical modes and emotional states.[45] Certain forms of music or modes were thought to be expressive of certain kinds of activity or suitable for people who engage in those activities, and also to be formative of character, whether good or bad. These ideas were advanced by Plato and Pythagoras, whose opinions on the subject were widely embraced in later

40. *De terrae motu* (PG 50: 714). John's statement is the last in a sequence of four sentences structured with syntactical parallelism, where the first three have the subject at the end. Hence, John almost certainly meant—and his audience would have been conditioned by the parallelism to hear—the last term of the fourth sentence, τὰ πάθη, as the grammatical subject (neuter plural taking the singular verb). Moreover, the subject of this fourth sentence is compared to beasts (τὰ θηρία) in the very next sentence, which is a further reason to interpret the plural τὰ πάθη as the subject. Finally, in cases where fleeing from something is stated with the verb δραπετεύειν, the preposition ἐκ is typically used; and this usage is found elsewhere in John, e.g., ἐδραπέτευσεν ἐκ τῆς ἡμετέρας ψυχῆς in *In illud: Vidua eligatur* (PG 51: 334) and τὸν θάνατον ἐξ αὐτῆς δραπετεῦσαι ἐποίησαν in *In Gen.* (PG 54: 484).

41. In the sermon preached after an earthquake (see above), John praised the common people, the poor, for their nighttime processions and vigils, their ceaseless singing of psalms as they moved through the streets and marketplace, cleansing the city with their "holy feet" (thanks to their virtue) and sanctifying the air with their singing, "for the air becomes holy through psalmody." *De terrae motu* (PG 50: 714).

42. Clement of Alexandria, *Protr.* 1.5.4.

43. Athanasius, *Ep. Marc.* 29.

44. Basil, *Leg. gent.* 9. This story also appears in Iamblichus's *Life of Pythagoras* (*V.P.* 25.112).

45. See the sources and discussion (together with the cited scholarly literature) in Francesco Pelosi, "Music and Emotions," in *A Companion to Ancient Greek and Roman Music*, ed. Tosca A. C. Lynch and Eleonora Rocconi, eds. (Wiley, 2020), 337–349.

generations, particularly by Stoics and Neopythagoreans. In the *Republic*, Plato has Socrates say that Dorian is the proper mode for representing the courage of the soldier in war and that Phrygian is the mode for the peacetime activities of prudent men who engage in such things as discussion, persuasion, and petition, including religious petition in hymns.[46] He does not say that these modes should *accompany* the activities they suit, only that they are the modes for the entertainment of men who engage in the activities. In the case of hymns, however, it seems implied that the activity of petitioning the gods in song should be performed in the Phrygian mode. Moreover, in addition to approving Dorian and Phrygian for inclusion in the ideal state, Plato proposes that other modes be excluded, namely, those that express softness, luxury, drunkenness, idleness, and grief.[47] Furthermore, he suggests that the modes not only express certain states but stimulate them and shape character.[48] This must have been apparent to Strabo and his source, Posidonius, when they remarked that according to Plato and Pythagoras, "the universe is constructed according to a mode" and these philosophers "assign moral formation to music."[49]

The idea that modes not only express but also conduce to particular emotional states was taken up by certain Hellenistic intellectuals. Writing around 200 BCE, the Athenian Stoic Diogenes of Babylon recommended the singing of "Homer and Hesiod and the other poets of meter and melody,"[50] but not the lyric poets, whose melodies, he claimed, exert a corrupting influence on young men. Diogenes's book survives only in excerpts quoted in a study of music by the Epicurean philosopher Philodemus (*fl.* first century BCE[51]), who offers a rebuttal. Regarding the allegedly corrupting influences of the lyric poets "Ibycus, Anacreon, and the like," all that Diogenes manages to prove, Philodemus says,

46. Plato, *Resp.* 310.399a–c.

47. Plato, *Resp.* 310.398e–399a; 399c.

48. Plato, *Leg.* 653e–656c (esp. 656b–c); *Tim.* 36e–37b with 47c–e, and 90c–d. Plato's views are astutely analyzed in Tosca Lynch, "Tuning the Lyre, Tuning the Soul: Harmonia, Justice and the Kosmos of the Soul in Plato's Republic and Timaeus," *Greek and Roman Musical Studies* 8 (2020): 111–155.

49. Strabo, *Geog.* 10.3.10 (quoting Posidonius). The expression for what I have translated "moral formation" is τὴν τῶν ἠθῶν κατασκευὴν.

50. Τὸν Ὅμηρον καὶ τὸν Ἡσίοδον καὶ τοὺς ἄλλους ποητὰς τῶν μέτρων καὶ μελῶν. Diogenes as quoted in Philodemus, *Mus.* 4, fr. 131.9–11. Diogenes uses the plural μέτρων but may mean simply "verses" and not a variety of meters beyond epic. I have translated μέτρων καὶ μελῶν with singular nouns to express the ambiguity.

51. Philodemus was born about 110 BCE; his death date is uncertain. See David Sider, *The Epigrams of Philodemos: Introduction, Text, and Commentary* (Oxford University Press, 1997), 7, 11–12.

is that these poets corrupted young people "with their *thoughts*: for the *words* caused corruption in them . . . if even that."[52] Disputing the claims of Diogenes and other Hellenistic philosophers who believed that music both expresses and shapes emotions, Philodemus contended that melody is meaningless, nonmimetic sound. It adds nothing useful to poetry as a form of communication and has no "ethical" or other effect on the soul.[53] People find melody pleasurable and that is its chief value. But the pleasure of melody is a lowly and ultimately unnecessary enjoyment.[54]

Music-ethos theories persisted into the Roman age and probably had more adherents than detractors, since later references do not hint at any debate about the subject. Galen touted music therapy as a matter of countering emotional extremes with music that stimulates the opposite state, so that the person is brought into balance.[55] One of his illustrations is a story about the fifth-century philosopher Damon applying a change of mode to calm a group of inebriated young men who were overstimulated by the music they were listening to.[56] Plutarch has one of his characters remark that certain experts know how to use melodies and modes to mold character and soothe emotions.[57] Iamblichus's *Life of Pythagoras* claims that Pythagoras used his musical knowledge to cure emotional ills, "cleverly mixing certain diatonic, chromatic, and enharmonic melodies through which he easily led and circulated the contentious passions of the soul"—"griefs, angers, compassion, unreasonable jealousies, and fears," etc.—"correcting each of them for virtue

52. Οὐδὲ τοὺς νέους τοῖς μέλεσι διαφθείροντας παρέδειξεν τὸν Ἴβυκον καὶ τὸν Ἀνακρέοντα καὶ τοὺς ὁμοίους, ἀλλὰ τοῖς διανοήμασι· καὶ γὰρ ἃ Περσαῖος ὀνόματ' ἔλεγε, τούτοις ἔθρυπτεν, εἴπερ ἄρα. Philodemus, *Mus.* 4.128.8–15. On the subject of Diogenes's and other Stoics' reception of Plato's views on music, see Linda Woodward, "Diogenes of Babylon Reading Plato on Music," in *Aristotle and the Stoics "Reading" Plato*, ed. Anne D. R. Sheppard et al. (Institute of Classical Studies, 2010), 233–253. Philodemus implies that Diogenes embraced some version of Plato's teaching about musical ethos; but for whatever reason, Diogenes did not share Plato's concern about myth in Homer.

53. See, for example, Philodemus, *Mus.* 4.140.14–16; 143.12–43. On the topic in general, see Spencer A. Klavan, "Melody and Meaning: The Semiotics of Ancient Greek Music in the Late Classical and Early Hellenistic Eras" (D.Phil. dissertation; Oxford University, 2019), 200–201, 218, and passim.

54. Philodemus, *Mus.* 4.151.29–39.

55. See Galen, *Plac. Hipp. et Plat.* 5.6.20.

56. *Plac. Hipp. et Plat.* 5.6.21. This is a version of the same story that others told about Pythagoras, as cited above (see n. 44).

57. Plutarch, *Sept. sap.* 13 (*Mor.* 156c). Cf. Posidonius's statement about Plato and Pythagoras, quoted by Strabo, as cited in n. 49.

through suitable melodies as through some curative mixed medicines."[58] The second-century polymath Claudius Ptolemy asserts that "our souls are quite plainly affected in sympathy with the actual activities of a melody, recognizing the kinship, as it were, of the ratios belonging to its particular kind of constitution, and being moulded by the movements specific to the idiosyncrasies of the melodies." This influence, he says, leads our souls into different emotional states—"sometimes into pleasures and relaxations, sometimes into griefs and contractions; [our souls] are sometimes stupefied and lulled to sleep, sometimes invigorated and aroused; and they are sometimes turned towards peacefulness and restraint, sometimes towards frenzy and ecstasy, as the melody itself modulates in different ways at different times, and draws our souls towards the conditions constituted from the likenesses of the ratios."[59] The third-century (or fourth-century) music theorist Aristides Quintilianus writes that there is "a fitting style of treatment through music" that brings a person who is subject to extreme emotion "into a proper state" without their own awareness.[60] Hence, music is able to treat emotions, which are irrational, where reasoning fails.[61]

Not everyone read or was otherwise familiar with the opinions about modes espoused by mathematicians and specialists in music theory, but most educated people of the Roman era were probably familiar with certain commonplaces about modes, such as the ones that Lucian of Samosata recites when he has a musician in one of his dialogues speak of "the frenzy of the Phrygian, the Bacchic wildness of the Lydian, the dignity of the Dorian, and the elegance of the Ionian."[62]

One of the few early-Christian thinkers to invoke elements of music-ethos theory is Clement of Alexandria, who, like Plato, appears to have believed that modes both express and shape character. In *Paedagogus*, he writes as follows:

---

58. Iamblichus, *V.P.* 15.64.

59. Ptolemy, *Harm.* 3.7; tr. from *GMW* 2: 379. Ptolemy echoes Plato's idea of a correlation between the cosmic order and the mundane musical order, which makes soul-tuning possible through music; but he does not repeat Plato's specific opinions about modes.

60. Aristides Quintilianus, *Mus.* 2.5 (Winnington-Ingram, 58.21–23); tr. *GMW* 2: 462. Antonietta Provenza concludes that Aristides's and Ptolemy's discussions reflect Aristotle's theory of catharsis. See Antonietta Provenza, "Music and Medicine," in Tosca A. Lynch and Eleonora Rocconi, eds., *A Companion to Ancient Greek and Roman Music* (Wiley, 2020), 354–355 (351–363).

61. Aristides Quintilianus, *Mus.* 2.5 (Winnington-Ingram, 58.6–18). Galen says the same thing. Galen, *Plac. Hipp. et Plat.* 5.6.22.

62. Lucian of Samosata, *Harm.* 1.

> Temperate modes are admissible, but let the truly pliant modes ride off as far away as possible from our sound minds. These modes by the turns of their notes debase the (musical) art to weakness (debauchery) and lead to foolishness. Let the grave and temperate songs have nothing to do with the revelries of drunkenness. One must leave behind, then, the chromatic modes with their shameless drinking songs and their florid and meretricious music.[63]

In *Stromata*, Clement declares that "excessive music is to be rejected that weakens the soul and leads into complexity, then mourning, then intemperance and luxury, then Bacchic frenzy and madness."[64] Elsewhere in *Stromata* he appears to recommend the Dorian and the Phrygian, which Plato favored.[65]

Perhaps Clement thought that Christians should sing hymns and psalms in the Dorian and Phrygian modes.[66] Yet it is difficult to imagine that he intended his technical observations as practical advice. Presumably, the rare Christian who played the lyre or cithara could have done so, tuning his instrument to the Dorian or Phrygian mode, as he understood these terms. But it is doubtful that the average Christian who took a turn in the rounds of singing at Christian symposia held by men of Clement's set was prepared to compose a song, much less improvise one, in Clement's preferred modes. Furthermore, the music of the Roman age was overwhelmingly diatonic, while the old-fashioned enharmonic genus, which Clement purports to recommend for the Dorian mode, was no longer common and would have been very difficult for the average person to have sung, since it entailed a quarter-tone interval.[67] Finally, the idea that a particular ethos goes with each mode was minted by Plato in a time when modes were tune-types associated with particular scales. By Clement's time they were only scales. It is unclear whether Clement was aware of this historical evolution. In any case, since his remarks are not very practical as advice to nonmusicians, whether for people who sang at Christian social meals or who hired professional entertainers for their private dinner parties, it may be best to interpret his use of technical musical terms as ciphers, as I suggested in chapter 12, that is, as a

---

63. Clement of Alexandria, *Paed.* 2.4.44.5.

64. *Str.* 6.11.90.2–3.

65. *Str.* 6.11.88.1–2. I discuss this passage in chapter 12.

66. The setting Clement envisions for hymns and psalmody is the Christian dinner party. See the discussion in chapter 2.

67. See Charles H. Cosgrove, *Music at Social Meals in Greek and Roman Antiquity* (Cambridge University Press, 2023), 320.

Christian intellectual's way of referring to music that he associated with certain sorts of settings and moral behaviors.

With the exception of Clement, no Christian intellectual of antiquity is known to have embraced a version of the Greek music-ethos theory. Any Christian thinkers who may have delved into the available late-antique literature on music and soul therapy would soon have realized that the topic is dense and quite technical, at least if one moves beyond Plato into the writings of the late-antique music theorists who connect music with moral philosophy. In a long speech in Ps.-Plutarch's *On Music*, for example, a symposiast named Lysias, apparently quoting the early-Hellenistic musicologist Aristoxenus, states that music as expressive of ethos is a combination of mode, genus, and rhythm in melody, according to the creative skill of a composer.[68] It is not enough to know "harmonics" (the technical matters of genera, modes, rhythms, etc.), since achieving proper ethos requires more knowledge than harmonics and is a "task of the practitioner (composer)."[69] For example, "the person who is familiar with the Dorian mode but lacks the judgement to understand the fittingness of its usage [in a particular application in a piece of music] does not know what he is doing. In fact, he will not even preserve the ethos of the mode."[70]

The same difficulty applied to music therapy, which was understood as a case-specific practice.[71] It is telling that Aristides Quintilianus's remarks on the subject rarely reach the level of particular recommendations or case examples to show how a certain combination of mode, genera, rhythmic style, and note choices could be an effective cure for a person suffering from a particular extreme passion. As an expert in harmonics but not a music therapist, Aristides probably possessed little knowledge of the specific applications that the music therapists used.[72] Hence, it is not surprising that Christian intellectuals did not enter into discussions about music therapy in their efforts to guide, exhort, and encourage in their sermons, commentaries, moral and theological treatises, hagiographies, and letters.

---

68. Ps.-Plutarch, *Mus.* 33 (1142f–1143e). The borrowing from Aristoxenus seems to begin at 31. Aristoxenus relies heavily on Plato. See *GMW* 1: 238 n. 210 and the notes in the Loeb edition.

69. Ps.-Plutarch, *Mus.* 33 (1143a).

70. Ps.-Plutarch, *Mus.* 33 (1143c).

71. See Aristides Quintilianus, *Mus.* 2.16 (Winnington-Ingram, 85.21–86.1); Iamblichus, *Vit. Pyth.* 15.64.

72. Aristides does get specific in describing different types of rhythms and their effects on emotional states (*Mus.* 2.15 [Winnington-Ingram, 82–84]), but not in discussing other aspects of music.

In fact, the debate about the alleged power of melody to influence character may not have held more than passing interest for the typical Greco-Roman intellectual. For one thing, it was widely agreed that reason is sufficient to deal with the passions. Even Aristides Quintilianus, a convinced advocate of music therapy, holds that wise people have no need of it, since they do not become debilitated by extreme emotions.[73] Christian writers and homilists tended to think that Christ-formed reason, tutored by Scripture, was sufficient for gaining control of unruly passions. Moreover, they touted the Psalter as Scripture's most comprehensive body of instruction for soul therapy. Hence, when Christian intellectuals of late antiquity gave advice about the use of the psalms in the moral struggle, they usually had in mind the *words* of the psalms. They wrote and preached voluminously about these words. They singled out the efficacious properties of psalmodic *melody* only occasionally.

Psalmody, Cosmic Music, and the Symbolization of Virtue

Although Clement of Alexandria is the only ancient Christian on record as espousing Greek philosophical ideas about music and ethos, two Christian thinkers besides Clement accepted versions of Plato's concept of cosmic music. That notion was the basis of Plato's teaching about soul-tuning through music. Yet it was not any idea of soul-tuning that Athanasius and Gregory of Nyssa embraced when they drew on the Greek tradition to develop their own idiosyncratic views about musical order and the moral life.

In a treatise on the inscriptions of the psalms, Gregory poses the following question: "What explains the indescribable divine pleasure that the great David has poured over the teachings [meaning the psalms], through which the instruction has become readily acceptable to the nature of human beings?"[74] For most people, he says, the obvious answer is melody,[75] a sensory enjoyment, which Gregory himself calls a "sweetener" that makes "severe and manly virtue" palatable as a medicine for "infants."[76] But while it may seem obvious that sensory musical pleasure is the great enticement of psalmody, "one must not overlook

73. Aristides Quintilianus, *Mus.* 2.5 (Winnington-Ingram, 58.6).

74. Gregory of Nyssa, *Inscr. psalm.* 1.3 (GNO 5:30).

75. *Inscr. psalm.* 1.3 (GNO 5:30).

76. Before even mentioning melody, Gregory refers to the sensory type of pleasure of psalm-singing as a "sweetener" of bitter medicine, calling psalmodic medicine "the severe and manly aspect of virtue to be made pleasurable for the infants when sweetened by something of the things that cheer our sensory perception" (*Inscr. psalm.* 1.2; GNO 5:28–29). His reference to melody as a sweetener in 1.3 shows that these earlier references (in 1.2) inform and anticipate the later one.

what is not obvious;" for something hidden and greater lies behind the pleasure people have in singing.[77]

To explain that hidden source of pleasure, Gregory rehearses a well-known Greek theory of cosmic music. "The concord and affinity of all things with one another . . . is the primal, archetypal, and true music."[78] This musical order, which is a form of cosmic hymnody,[79] controls everything; and through it, all the parts of the cosmos have an affinity for each other.[80] This affinity applies to human beings in a special way, since human "nature" is a microcosm of the cosmos, thanks to the creation of human nature in the image of God.[81] Hence, "in the microcosm, that is, in human nature, all the music seen in the whole is perceived, being proportional (analogical) to the whole through the part, inasmuch as the whole is contained by the part."[82] Moreover, since everything in accord with nature is a "friend" to nature (making for sympathy and attraction) and since "the music that is in us has been shown to be in accord with nature," David "mixed singing into the philosophy of virtue, pouring a certain sweetness of honey over the lofty things." This is the second time that Gregory uses the pouring metaphor, and it repeats the first instance in a clarifying way. Singing, he writes, melodizing, is "the indescribable divine pleasure" that David "mixed into" the philosophy of virtue and "poured over" the lofty teachings. Hence, what makes psalm-singing a divine pleasure is the fact that it occasions a noetic hearing of the sublime, inaudible music of the cosmos, the intelligent order of "musical harmony 'whose author and maker is God.'"[83] This hearing is possible thanks to human nature's affinity for things that are "in accord" with it. In other words, the intellectual perception of virtue, which Gregory conceives as a "natural" pleasure of the soul, is the hearing of the natural order of cosmic music. He also uses a visual figure for this, when he describes the human being as a microcosm that mirrors the macrocosmos, which melody in singing symbolizes through mirrored reflections.[84] Hence, Gregory speaks of the perception of cosmic music

77. *Inscr. psalm.* 1.3 (GNO 5: 30).

78. ἡ πρώτη τε καὶ ἀρχέτυπος καὶ ἀληθὴς ἐστι μουσική. *Inscr. psalm.* 1.3 (GNO 5:32).

79. *Inscr. psalm.* 1.3 (GNO 5:32).

80. *Inscr. psalm.* 1.3 (GNO 5:30–32). Ronald Heine points out the Stoic framing of this thought, citing studies by J. Daniélou and K. Reinhardt. See Ronald E. Heine, *Gregory of Nyssa's Treatise on the Inscriptions of the Psalms* (Clarendon, 1995), p. 90 n. 16.

81. Gregory states this twice in *Inscr. psalm.* 1.3 (GNO 5:30 and 32).

82. *Inscr. psalm.* 1.3 (GNO 5:32–33).

83. *Inscr. psalm.* 1.3 (GNO 5:32). The quoted words cite Heb 11:10.

84. *Inscr. psalm.* 1.3 (GNO 5:32). See below.

as an intellectual hearing and an intellectual seeing, but these are not two different modes of perception but only two different ways of talking about noetic perception of the cosmic order.

Gregory's entire train of thought implies that the indescribable beauty of the music of the cosmos is heard by the mind in psalm-singing. Yet since the cosmos "makes the music of this all-harmonious melody in everything" and since "the mind 'hears' not by using hearing but by transcending the sense-perceptions of the flesh and being above,"[85] what is unique about psalmody that makes it the occasion for perceiving it? In fact, Gregory does not say that psalmody is the unique occasion. He speaks of mundane melody as such. That said, one would think that Gregory, who believed that cosmic music is available to people everywhere and in all situations and activities, would have assumed that people could detect it in all situations, whether through music or not, so long as they had the capacity of mind to do so, as David did.[86] Why does Gregory seem to restrict the perception of cosmic music to events of mundane melody? The answer may be that, although cosmic music is the order in everything, the mind "hears" it only in audible music, where it is uniquely available.

Gregory does not say that only the virtuous hear cosmic music in mundane music. Instead, he maintains that those on the journey to virtue are assisted by psalm-singing. The words of the psalms help them, and that help is the primary topic of Gregory's treatise. Yet the melody helps, too. A full quotation of one of the passages in which the preceding ideas are tied together should now make good sense:

> Since everything that accords with nature is a friend to nature, music is revealed to be a friend to us. For this reason, the Great David mixed melody into the philosophy concerning the virtues, which [referring to melody] he poured in as a certain honeyed pleasure of the higher things, through which nature examines itself in a certain way and cures itself. And this cure of nature is the good rhythm of life, which the melody seems to symbolize through mirrored reflections. For this itself—that the character of those living in virtue should not be unmusical and out of tune and unharmonious—may become an encouragement to the establishment of the higher life.[87]

---

85. *Inscr. psalm.* 1.3 (GNO 5:31).

86. *Inscr. psalm.* 1.3 (GNO 5:31). "Thus one hears the hymnody of the heavens. And it seems to me that the great David—when an artful and all-wise movement was perceived by him in them [the heavens]—listened to them telling the glory of God, who causes these things in them."

87. *Inscr. psalm.* 1.3 (GNO 5: 33). With respect to the expression δι' αἰνιγμάτων, Gregory has just said that the human being, as a microcosm, reflects the macrocosm in a mirror-like way

Gregory goes on to adduce the example of David's use of music to calm a raving Saul:

> For this reason, the history [1 Samuel] bears witness to the right orderings of this divine music by David. For when madness overtook Saul and caused a change of his understanding, he thus healed him completely, singing over[88] his passion, with the result that his mind returned to him to be in accord with nature. It is clear from these things what the mirrored reflection looks toward, that it symbolizes the bringing about of a subjugation of the passions, which arise in us variously from life circumstances.[89]

The wider framework of Gregory's discussion of music in psalmody is his conception of the goal of virtue and the Psalter's role in progress toward that goal. The purpose (*telos*) of "a virtuous life" is "happiness (*makariotēs*)," Gregory says,[90] specifically happiness as a divine state, possessed above all by God.[91] Hence, "the definition of human happiness is likeness to God."[92] Progress in virtue makes human beings more and more like God, giving them a greater share in the divine happiness. The Psalter— "the divine Scripture of the psalmody" —"points the way to this for us through a certain skillful and natural sequence . . . prescribing the method for acquiring happiness."[93] The very division of the Psalter—its "sequence"—expresses a progressive ascent by stages that culminate in praise (Book 5 of the Psalter). As the ultimate stage of virtue, praise is itself an

---

(1.3; GNO 5:32). The word παρηχημένον is puzzling. The verb παρηχέομαι means "resemble in sound," and παραχέω means "pour on." Later in the treatise, Gregory pairs παρηχημένος with a word that means "unrhythmical": ὡς ἂν μή τις ἄρρυθμός τε καὶ παρηχημένος. . .τύχοι (2.3, GNO 5:76). Hence, it must mean "unharmonious" or the like.

88. Κατεπᾴδων. The verb κατεπᾴδω was used for singing a magical formula over someone. Gregory means that the words of the song charmed Saul's intellect, assisting his reason to overcome his passion.

89. Gregory, *Inscr. psalm.* 1.3 (GNO 5:33–34).

90. *Inscr. psalm.* 1.1 (GNO 5:25).

91. Gregory cites 1 Tim 6:15 as a prooftext for this, but it was already a truism of Greek myth and religion that the state of the gods is happiness. *Inscr. psalm.* 1.1 (GNO 5:25–26).

92. *Inscr. psalm.* 1.1 (GNO 5:26).

93. *Inscr. psalm.* 1.1 (GNO 5:26).

experience of blessedness, the soul's condition being like that of the angels, a state of constant laudation.[94]

Somewhat analogous to Gregory's conception of musical order is Athanasius's idea of melody as a symbol of order in the soul, which he describes in his *Letter to Marcellinus*. When Christians behave properly, Athanasius writes, they govern their passions through reason, which is essentially "the mind of Christ" in them. As a result, they enjoy "an undisturbed and calm state." Melodic reading of the psalms is "an image and a type" of that state.[95] Athanasius does not speak of mundane music's relation to the cosmic order, but many of his educated readers would have taken for granted that the order of the created universe is a divine music that mundane music reflects.

Athanasius's focus is the way melody expresses what the words of the psalms aim to achieve. While melody in a lyrical reading of the psalms symbolizes an ordered state of the soul, the words of the psalms help restore that state when the soul is out of balance. To illustrate this, Athanasius quotes three passages from the psalms. "Thus, the disturbances and roughness and disorder in the soul are smoothed out, and we heal our grief, when we sing, 'Why are you grieved, my soul, and why do you trouble me?' [Ps 41:6]. And when something threatens to bring us down, we can sing, 'My feet were nearly shaken' [Ps 72:2]. And we can deal with fear by saying, 'The Lord is my helper, and I will not fear what a human being may do to me' [Ps 117:6]." Given Athanasius's understanding of the relation of the mind to the passions, these examples must be meant to show that the words inform the mind, and that the mind, responding, brings about a calm order and cheerful state,[96] which is symbolized by melody as a cheerful musical orderliness. Moreover, "those who do not read the divine songs in this way," Athanasius continues, "do not sing wisely but (only) please themselves."[97] Wise singing is "singing well," which he defines in two very similar passages within his larger discussion. Comparing them can help us clarify his meaning and avoid erroneous inferences based on certain ambiguous phrases:

---

94. *Inscr. psalm.* 1.9 (GNO 5:68).

95. Athanasius, *Ep. Marc.* 28 (PG 27: 40).

96. Athanasius shows that he thinks of the calm unperturbed state of the soul not as an impassive condition but as a disposition of good cheer: "The desire of the soul is this—to be disposed well (καλῶς), as it is written, 'Is anyone among you cheerful, let them sing (ψαλλέτω)' [Jas 5:13]." *Ep. Marc.* 28 (PG 27: 40).

97. *Ep. Marc.* 29 (PG 27: 40).

> For just as we understand and signify the thoughts through the words that carry them, so, too, the Lord, wanting *the melody from the words* to be a sign of spiritual harmony in the soul, prescribed that the canticles should be sung melodically and the psalms read with song.[98]

> Those who sing in the aforementioned way—so that *the melody of the words* is brought out from the rhythm of the soul and symphony with the Spirit—these people sing with the tongue, but by singing with the mind, too, they greatly benefit not only themselves but also those who wish to hear them.[99]

Does the expression "melody from the words" in the first passage, which must have the same meaning as "melody of the words"[100] in the second passage, refer to melody that is in some way inherent in the words? Or does it refer to melody that is imposed on the words by the singer? Melody imposed by the singer is the only interpretation that fits the near and wider contexts. In the second passage, Athanasius's expression "in the aforementioned way" refers to singing in such a way that reason controls the passions when it is informed by the instructive and encouraging words of the psalms. Moreover, "the melody of the words" is said to be "brought out from the rhythm of the soul and symphony with the Spirit." The melody is not inherent in the words; it comes from the singer's own soul and is imposed by the singer onto the words.

Athanasius does not specify which sorts of melodic choices express the approved order but instead goes on to restate his idea that the singer imposes the order.[101] "Melodic reading" is "a symbol of the mind's good order (*eurythmou*)

98. Ὥσπερ γὰρ τὰ τῆς ψυχῆς νοήματα γνωρίζομεν καὶ σημαίνομεν δι' ὧν προφέρομεν λόγων, οὕτως, τῆς πνευματικῆς ἐν ψυχῇ ἁρμονίας τὴν ἐκ τῶν λόγων μελῳδίαν σύμβολον εἶναι θέλων, ὁ κύριος τετύπωκεν ἐμμελῶς τὰς ᾠδὰς ψάλλεσθαι καὶ τοὺς ψαλμοὺς μετ' ᾠδῆς ἀναγινώσκεσθαι. *Ep. Marc.* 28 (PG 27: 40).

99. Οἱ δὲ κατὰ τὸν προειρημένον τρόπον ψάλλοντες, ὥστε τὴν μελῳδίαν τῶν ῥημάτων ἐκ τοῦ ῥυθμοῦ τῆς ψυχῆς καὶ τῆς πρὸς τὸ πνεῦμα συμφωνίας προσφέρεσθαι, οἱ τοιοῦτοι ψάλλουσι μὲν τῇ γλώσσῃ, ψάλλοντες δὲ καὶ τῷ νοΐ, οὐ μόνον ἑαυτούς, ἀλλὰ καὶ τοὺς θέλοντας ἀκούειν αὐτῶν μεγάλως ὠφελοῦσιν. *Ep. Marc.* 29 (PG 27: 40–41).

100. The expressions (already quoted in the preceding notes) are τὴν ἐκ τῶν λόγων μελῳδίαν and τὴν μελῳδίαν τῶν ῥημάτων, respectively.

101. Along the way, Athanasius adduces biblical examples. He first cites David, who "was pleasing to God" [hence well-ordered in his soul] and soothed the madness of Saul by "psalming at" him. Then he mentions the priests of Israel, who, by psalming, "summoned the souls of the people into serenity and into the concord of the choral singers of heaven." *Ep. Marc.* 29 (PG 27: 41).

and undisturbed condition."[102] He elaborates this in terms that explain how psalm-singing figures as both a symbol of the soul's good order and an instrument of the process that brings that order about:

> For praising God with the euphonious cymbals and cithara and ten-string *psalterion* was again a symbol and sign of the regulated members of the body situated together like strings, the reasonings of the soul becoming like cymbals, and the rest, by the sound and sign of the Spirit, all being moved and living. Thus, according to what is written, "the person who lives by the Spirit shall put to death the deeds of the body." So, too, the one singing well (*kalōs*) rhythmicizes (orders) his soul and similarly leads it from disequilibrium to equilibrium . . . And being disposed by the melody of the words, it forgets the passions, and, rejoicing, looks to "the mind which is in Christ," contemplating finer things.[103]

Singing, demanded by God for its symbolic function, is the occasion or medium of the ordering of the soul that the mind brings about. This occurs when the psalm-singing Christian looks to the mind of Christ and brings a music-like order to his or her soul.

Psalmody and Ritual Power

In addition to the philosophical traditions about music's moral-psychological powers, there were also para-philosophical traditions that attributed magical powers to music. Clement of Alexandria rehearses Greek claims about musicians of yore who used music to attract fish, tame beasts, and transplant trees.[104] Many well-educated people were familiar with the representations of magical uses of music in classical drama.[105] Moreover, general cultural knowledge acquainted ordinary people with the custom of chanting magical spells.[106]

---

102. Athanasius, *Ep. Marc.* 29 (PG 27: 41).

103. *Ep. Marc.* 29 (PG: 27.41).

104. Clement of Alexandria, *Protr.* 1.1.1.

105. Andrew Barker collects examples in *GMW* 1: 87–90.

106. For example, the verbs ἐπᾴδειν and κατεπᾴδειν are used in the magical papyri and other texts for chanting a magical formula.

Probably many Christians accepted as reliable cultural knowledge that in the hands of certain people music has "magical" power, whether for good or ill. Ancient Christian recourse to magical rituals for healing and other forms of help appears to be documented by the papyri, although scholars are by no means united in their interpretations of the function of the putatively Christian magical texts.

The word "magic" is itself a problematic term, since it has traditionally been used ideologically to differentiate inferior or otherwise suspect rituals from "religion."[107] In the present context, I have in view something very specific: the intoned chanting of words to avoid a harm or to receive a release from a malignant power, where the benefit is achieved not through effects of the meaning of the words on the chanter's own understanding or of the melody on his or her emotions but solely through the chant's effects on the external threat through apotropaic protection, binding, or liberation. It was not only psalms that were used by Christians in this way. Other biblical texts figured in magical rituals as well.

The ancient belief that melody could be an essential element in a healing ritual is evident from a passage in Cato the Elder's book on agriculture, which gives the following instructions for mending a broken bone:

> Any kind of dislocation may be cured by the following charm (*cantione*): Take a green reed four or five feet long and split it down the middle, and let two men hold it to your hips. Begin to chant (*incipe cantare*): "*motas uaeta daries dardares astataries dissunapiter*" and continue until they meet. Brandish a knife over them, and when the reeds meet so that one touches the other, grasp with the hand and cut right and left. If the pieces are applied to the dislocation or the fracture, it will heal. And nonetheless chant (*cantato*) every day and, in the case of a dislocation, in this manner, if you wish, "*huat haut haut istasis tarsis ardannabou dannaustra.*"[108]

Here the intoning of the words appears to be an essential part of the ritual. That said, it is it is not clear that people were routinely instructed to chant the magical formulas they purchased or otherwise acquired. Practices undoubtedly varied.

107. See the editors' introduction in Marvin W. Meyer and Richard Smith, eds., *Ancient Christian Magic: Coptic Texts of Ritual Power* (Princeton University Press, 1999), 1–6.

108. Marcus Porcius Cato, *Agr.* 160; tr. from *Marcus Porcius Cato, On Agriculture; and Marcus Terrentius Varro, On Agriculture*, with an English translation by William D. Hooper, rev. Harrison B. Ash (Harvard University Press, 1935; Heinemann, 1935), 153.

A number of psalm texts—occasionally whole psalms but more often excerpts, usually embedded in other material—have been preserved in forms and contexts that suggest they were used in apotropaic ways.[109] The texts are late. Some date to the fifth or sixth century, most to later centuries. The evidence includes psalm material in various media: papyrus and parchment texts, so-called *bous* amulets (usually wooden), and armbands.[110] Psalm 89 (MT 90), with its reference to God as a "refuge," was a favorite source of excerpts for apotropaic formularies.[111]

The presence of Christian terms and symbols in amulets and incantations offers indirect evidence of Christian magical use. Direct evidence is found in remarks by John Chrysostom and Augustine. In an exhortation about the benefits of alms-giving, John refers to the "gospel" that members of his congregation hang by their beds or around their necks.[112] Commenting on the Gospel of John, Augustine expresses qualified approval of Christians who place the gospel against their heads when they have a headache, since that is better than using an amulet as a remedy.[113] Of course, Christians who pressed a gospel against their foreheads to get rid of a headache were treating the gospel as an amulet.

The gospels that Christians hung from their beds and necks and pressed against their heads may have been miniature single-gospel codices. Moreover, a recent exhaustive study of such practices makes a persuasive case that "gospels" in John's and Augustine's remarks refers to the gospel stories as preserved in shorthand, that is, in texts containing incipits that stand for whole narratives that are not themselves written out. Texts containing such incipits are a well-documented type of many papyri snippets that appear to have been prepared for use as amulets.[114]

Texts used as amulets were understood to be protective in themselves and not in need of being chanted or recited aloud by their wearers to become effective.

---

109. A seminal study is Paul Collart, "Psaumes et amulettes," *Aegyptus* 14 (1934): 463–467.

110. A survey of the apotropaic use of biblical texts, including psalm texts, can be found in Joseph E. Sanzo, *Scriptural Incipits on Amulets from Late Antique Egypt: Text, Typology, and Theory* (Mohr Siebeck, 2014), passim.

111. See Thomas Kraus, "Septuaginta-Psalm 90 in apotropäischer Verwendung: Vorüberlegungen für eine kritische Edition und (bisheriges) Datenmaterial," *Biblische Notizen* 125 (2005): 39–73.

112. John Chrysostom, *In 1 Cor.*, Hom. 43.4 (PG 61: 373; Field, *Interp. epist. Paul.* 2: 542) and John Chrysostom, *Ad pop. Antioch.* 19.4 (PG 49: 196). In the first passage, John rejects this popular belief. The physical artifact does nothing, he says; but alms are a defense against the devil and give wings to prayer, etc.

113. Augustine, *In ev. Ioan.* 12.7 (PL 35: 1443).

114. Sanzo, *Scriptural Incipits on Amulets from Late Antique Egypt*, 161–164.

Moreover, since most wearers were probably illiterate, the assumption must have been that God reads the amulets as petitions and responds with aid or that the demons are directly repelled by the words. Of course, people may have had different ideas about how amulets worked, and many may have simply accepted that they were efficacious, without having a theory about it.

That said, those who created textual amulets treated them as messages, and the semantic aspect of Scripture amulets is evident from the choice of texts and especially from the occasional use of "etc." in them.[115] An example is an amulet text that includes Psalm 89:1 in combination with the beginning of Mark 1:1; Luke 1:1; perhaps John 1:23; and the beginning of the Lord's Prayer in Matthew 6:9. An explicit "etc." appears after the incipits of Psalm 89 and the Lord's Prayer; and an implicit "etc." is almost surely implied by the citations of the gospel openings.[116] The use of incipits in amulet texts (see above) and especially the occasional instance of "etc." are clear evidence of an intention to communicate a message, since the abbreviations imply that God and/or the threatening powers, such as demons, "know the rest."[117]

The use of biblical excerpts in Christian amulets establishes the premise for comparable oral uses as well, including apotropaic chanting of psalm verses, whether this was thought of as prayer or apotropaic speech (incantation).[118] Basil's *Longer Rules* instructs that one should say Psalm 90 at the sixth hour "so that we may be delivered from assault and from the noonday demon."[119] This psalm (91 in the MT) had a long history in Judaism as an apotropaic prayer

---

115. On the use of "etc." (καὶ τὰ ἑξῆς), see Sanzo, *Scriptural Incipits on Amulets from Late Antique Egypt*, 136–137, 166, and 169–171.

116. PSI VI 719 = PGM 2: 207–208, no. 19. The *editio princeps* (not available to me) is Giramo Vitelli, ed., *Papiri greci e latini*, vol. 6 (Florenz: Ariani, 1920), 151–152, no. 719.

117. As far as I know, the question of whether users of amulets believed that demons can read, which the use of texts in amulets seems to assume, is a neglected topic in the study of amulets. I myself know of no express assertion in ancient literature that demons are literate. Tertullian assumes that they are not, when he says that demons know Scripture because they heard the prophetic utterances when they were first made orally and because they "gather" Scripture's messages when the Scripture lessons are "sounding," that is, being read aloud (*lectionibus resonantibus carpunt*) (*Apol.* 22.9).

118. In a discussion of adaptations of biblical texts at Qumran, including psalm texts, for apotropaic purposes, Esther Eshel makes a distinction between apotropaic prayers, which request God's help against evil powers, and apotropaic magical formulas, which directly address those powers. See Esther Eshel, "Apotropaic Prayers in the Second Temple Period," in *Liturgical Perspectives: Prayer and Poetry in Light of the Dead Sea Scrolls*, ed. Esther G. Chazon (Brill, 2003), 69–88.

119. Basil, *Reg. fus. tract.* 37.4 (Silvas, 246; PG 31: 1013–1016).

against evil powers,[120] including defense against special assaults by demons at specific hours of the day.[121]

Evagrius of Pontus (b. circa 345) also advises monks about the apotropaic power of psalmody. In *Antirhētikos*, he writes that "the melody of the psalms alters the condition of the body and drives away the demon that touches it on the back, chills its sinews, and troubles all its members."[122] Since Evagrius writes for monks, he must have heard accounts from them about the feeling of being touched from behind by a malevolent power. He may have had such an experience himself. In any case, he regarded the body as the primary point of attack by demons.[123]

If we could be certain that the Syriac term for "melody" in the passage just quoted is grammatically definite, Evagrius's formulation would suggest that psalms were sung to a particular effective melody, since "melody" is singular, while "psalms" is plural. But the Syriac term is in the emphatic state, which means that it could be definite or indefinite. Moreover, the term could also mean "the singing."[124] It is not clear, then, that Evagrius meant to claim that a *particular* melody had a demon-banishing effect, only that singing the psalms did.[125]

According to the *Canons of Hippolytus*, when the priests go behind the veil at Communion, they must sing psalms "because of the powers of the holy place."[126] The context is the special care to be taken to ensure that nothing alien gets into the cup, that no drop or morsel of the Communion gifts falls to the floor, where

---

120. See the studies of apotropaic uses of Psalm 91 in ancient Judaism cited in Abraham J. Berkovitz, *A Life of Psalms in Jewish Late Antiquity* (University of Pennsylvania Press, 2023), 224 n. 170.

121. See *Targum Pseudo-Jonathan* to Num 6:24, quoted in Eshel, "Apotropaic Prayers in the Second Temple Period," 71.

122. Evagrius, *Antirrhētikos* 4.22; tr. from David Brakke, tr., *Evagrius of Pontus, Talking Back: A Monastic Handbook for Combating Demons* (Liturgical Press, 2009), 104.

123. See the discussion in Luke Dysinger, *Psalmody and Prayer in the Writings of Evagrius Ponticus* (Oxford University Press, 2005), 120–121.

124. I owe these observations about the Syriac to David Brakke (personal correspondence).

125. In a different work, titled *Praktikos*, Evagrius describes the effectiveness of psalmody in a monk's struggle with the *passions*. In this case his focus is entirely on the words: "The demonic songs set our desire in motion and cast the soul into shameful fantasies, but 'psalms, hymns, and spiritual songs' [Eph. 5:19] call the mind to the constant remembrance of virtue, cooling our boiling irascibility and extinguishing our desires." Evagrius, *Prakt.* 71. Translation from Sinkewicz, *Evagrius Ponticus*, 109.

126. *Canons of Hippolytus* 29; tr. Carol Bebawi in Paul F. Bradshaw, ed., *The Canons of Hippolytus*, with an English tr. by Carol Bebawi (Grove Books, 1989), 30.

demons might take control of it, and that nothing be said or done except what is prescribed. The author of the *Canons* adds that psalms sung behind the veil are "to replace for them the bells that were on the garment of Aaron."[127] Tinkling bells were widely thought to have apotropaic power.[128] Since the author of the *Canons* did not deem it sufficient that sacred words be spoken behind the veil to protect the holy place but insisted that psalms be sung as well, he must have regarded the musical element of psalmody as an important part of the ritual actions that keep the demons at bay.

Niceta of Remesiana describes an apotropaic use of a *symbol* in a biblical musical scene. David, "singing sweetly yet strongly to his cithara," Niceta says, "subdued the evil spirit that was working in Saul." But it was not the strength (*uirtus*) of the cithara that worked this effect, he explains, "but the figure (*figura*) of the cross of Christ itself, which was mystically carried in the wood and the stretching of the strings, [and] which was sung, that subdued the spirit of the demon at that time."[129] This parallels the use of cross symbols in apotropaic texts.

Niceta's reference to David's cithara is part of a series of proofs that the Bible commends singing, and a chief purpose of the sermon in which he offers these proofs is to defend psalm-singing. Moreover, Niceta refers to the cithara as a symbol of the cross "mystically carried" in the instrument because he has already declared that the principal boon of psalmody, among its many benefits, is "singing the mysteries of Christ."[130]

In a sermon on Psalm 141, John Chrysostom urges fathers to sing psalms with their families, doing so especially at meals, since the devil finds opportunities for attack in convivial situations. This makes it advisable "to set up a security of psalms against him" by singing "before and after the meal."[131] Psalmody protects the meal on each end, as if the meal were a space and the psalms were a protective wall.

Finally, the *Physiologus*, a didactic Christian bestiary,[132] attributes an apotropaic power to the song of Christian virgins, comparing them to a flock of doves:

---

127. *Canons of Hippolytus* 29; tr. Bebawi in Bradshaw, *The Canons of Hippolytus*, 31; see also the French translation in Georges Coquin, *Les canons d'Hippolyte* (Firmin Didot, 1966), 401 [133].

128. Evidence about cultic and magical uses of bells is presented in Margaret A. Schatkin, "Idiophones of the Ancient World: Description, Terminology, Geographical Distribution, Functions," *Jahrbuch für Antike und Christentum* 21 (1978): 147–172.

129. Niceta of Remesiana, *Util. hymn.* 4.

130. *Util. hymn.* 6.

131. John Chrysostom, *In psalm. 41* 2 (PG 55: 157).

132. The *Physiologus* has been dated to the second or third century, perhaps the fourth. Alan Scott, "The Date of the Physiologus," *Vigiliae Christianae* 52 (1998): 430–441; Horst Schneider,

> The Physiologus has written that if all the doves fly to one place, the hawk is not at all brave enough to go near any one of them, because of the resonant sound of their wings. . . . The same is understood of a group of virgins. For when they have come together as a flock in the church, sending up a euphonious hymn with concordant voice through prayers and psalmody to God, their adversary the devil is not at all brave enough to go near any one of them, because he is afraid of their loud prayer and psalmody.[133]

It is clearly the sound that frightens the hawk, since there is no suggestion that the doves fend off the hawk physically through their strength in numbers. Likewise, it is the virgins' loud psalmody that frightens the devil. The author goes on to suggest that all Christians find safety in the gathered community so that they do not become "prey of the evil one," which shows that the author did not mean to claim that psalmody alone protects the church. Yet the statement about the psalmody of the women suggests that the corporate singing of psalms provides an especially effective defense.

An Alternative to Heretical Hymns?

It has been suggested by some that psalmody became more and more pervasive as bishops became more and more suspicious of composed hymns, which were sometimes used as vehicles of heresy.[134] There is in fact no express evidence of general opposition to hymns during the first several centuries. The self-styled orthodox do occasionally criticize heterodox Christian hymns (as well as pagan

---

"Introduction to the Physiologus," in *The Multilingual Physiologus: Studies in the Oldest Greek Recension and Its Translations*, ed. Caroline Macé and Jost Gipper (Brepols, 2021), 31–47.

133. *Physiologus* 35a.

134. Robert Taft, *The Liturgy of the Hours in East and West: The Origins of the Divine Office and Its Meaning for Today* (Liturgical, 1986), 28; Calvin R. Stapert, *A New Song for an Old World: Musical Thought in the Early Church* (Eerdmans, 2007), 159; Reiner Kaczynski, "Die Psalmodie bei der Begräbnisfeier," in *Liturgie und Dichtung: Ein interdisziplinäres Kompendium*, vol. 2, ed. Hansjakob Becker and Reiner Kaczynski (EOS, 1983), 804 (suggesting that clergy began replacing composed funeral psalms with biblical psalms because of the heretical use of hymnody). According to Martin Hengel, from the second to the fourth century the self-styled catholic church increasingly banned hymns from worship, because of the influence of heretical hymns, and made biblical psalms nearly exclusive as the repertoire of church song. See Martin Hengel, "The Song about Christ in Earliest Worship," in Martin Hengel, *Studies in Early Christology* (T. & T. Clark, 1995), 241–246.

songs), but they do not say that people should not sing composed Christian hymns, restricting themselves to biblical psalms.

Tertullian, for example, who drew a contrast between the hymns of Valentinus and the psalms of David, speaks positively of Christians who sing personal hymns in church.[135] In the mid-third century, Paul of Samosata, then Bishop of Antioch, forbade hymns to Christ at Easter in favor of biblical psalms, which, his critics claimed, he had arranged to be sung "to him" by a choir of women.[136] Paul's rationale—which was presumably designed to appeal to shared convictions, since it was meant to persuade his congregation and to defend against his detractors—was that the hymns to Christ were newly composed poems, not that they were heretical. Moreover, the conflict shows that Christ hymns were well-established in Antioch when Paul tried to bar them and that the bishops who criticized Paul approved of hymns.

The Syrian author of the third-century *Didascalia* encourages Christians to read Scripture songs instead of pagan ones. His advice does not mention Christian hymns, heretical or otherwise.[137] In mid-fourth-century Alexandria, Arius used songs to disseminate subordinationist Christology. When Athanasius composed a series of orations against the Arians, he criticized Arius's song *Thalia*, classifying it with shameless drinking songs.[138] But he did not disparage Christian hymns generally or warn against their use.

The only explicit evidence of an effort to control the use of hymns is canons from two church councils. One is a rule promulgated by a council held in Laodicea sometime between 345 and 381.[139] In Canon 59, the attending bishops prohibited the use of "personal hymns" in church. The context is the regulation of liturgical readings, not Christian use of books or hymns generally. Similarly, Canon 18 of the Canons of Athanasius prescribes that singers and readers are to read only from the catholic (or perhaps "canonical") books, and Canon 12 directs them to sing only "in the Spirit" and not perform the writings of Meletius or other ignorant persons. The Muratorian Canon also bans certain literature from church lessons. The councils and the Muratorian Canon do not reject all use of writings or poems not counted as Scripture. In fact, while the Muratorian Canon

135. Tertullian, *Carn.* 20.3 (criticizing the hymns of Valentinus) and *Apol.* 39.18 (speaking positively of personal Christian hymnody).

136. Eusebius, *H.E.* 7.30.10. See chapter 3.

137. *Didasc.* 2 // *Const. ap.* 1.5–6.

138. Athanasius, *Or. contra Arianos* I.4.1–2.

139. On the dating of the Council of Laodicea, see chapter 4 n. 10.

excludes the *Shepherd of Hermas* from the category of proper church lessons, it approves private use of the *Shepherd* as edifying literature.[140]

The church historian Socrates recounts an event in Constantinople, during the episcopate of John Chrysostom, when Nicene Christians combatted the influence of Arian street hymnody by singing against the Arians in public demonstrations.[141] John's congregation sang either psalms with Trinitarian responses or Trinitarian hymns or both.[142] Sozomen recounts the same story.[143] Neither Socrates nor Sozomen refers to any Nicene wariness about hymns or makes it a point to say that John's people sang biblical psalms *instead of* hymns.

Meanwhile east-Syrian Christians were singing the madrasas of Ephrem (d. 373), some of which were intended to combat the heretical hymnody of Bardaisan.[144] Here it is hymn against hymn, not psalm against hymn. And in the West, Hilary of Poitiers (circa 315–367), Ambrose of Milan (circa 339–397), and Prudentius (circa 348–413) were celebrated for their hymnody. Even Augustine dabbled in the genre, composing his *Psalm against the Donatists* in a popular verse-form and supplying it with a one-line refrain.[145] And Gregory of Nazianzus composed many poems, hoping that some of them would be taken up by young people instead of the "songs and lyre-tunes" they usually enjoyed.[146]

Finally, although it is difficult to determine the extent to which nonbiblical hymns were used in the liturgies of the fourth- and fifth-century church, Ambrose's hymns must have been regularly used in Milan, particularly at vigils. Moreover, it is unlikely that the extensive liturgical hymnody of the Byzantine church would have developed as it did, had the hallowed fourth-century Greek fathers opposed the use of composed Christian hymns.

The preceding considerations do not exclude the possibility that in certain times and places, one or more church leaders expressed opposition to composed hymnody as such, out of a combination of reverence for biblical songs and anxiety

---

140. *Canon Muratori* 73–80.

141. Socrates, *H.E.* 6.8.1–9.

142. See the discussion in chapter 9.

143. Sozomen, *H.E.* 8.8.1–5.

144. Ephrem's hymns were collected under the title *Hymns against Heresies*. See Sidney H. Griffith, "Setting Right the Church of Syria: Saint Ephraem's Hymns against Heresies," in *The Limits of Ancient Christianity: Essays on Late Antique Thought and Culture in Honor of R. A. Markus*, ed. William E. Klingshirn and Mark Vessey (University of Michigan, 1999), 100.

145. Augustine, *Retract.* 119 (PL 32: 617; CSEL 36.96–97).

146. Gregory of Nazianzus, *Carm. de se ips.* 37–44 (PG 37.1332.3–10).

about misuse of hymns. We simply do not find any clear examples of that, much less any sustained effort to ban hymns as such. It is nonetheless true that leading fourth-century bishops touted the efficaciousness of the Psalter as a prayer-book and songbook of the church's liturgies and the individual Christian's private devotion. They do not encourage hymn-singing in the same way, which is not at all surprising, since composed Christian hymns were not Scripture.

Honeyed Songs

In a little encomium to the psalms, Basil notes that the only thing some Christians retain from church services is the psalmody. "For not one of the many indifferent people ever leaves (church) easily retaining in memory an apostolic or prophetic precept, but they do retain the words of the psalms. And they sing them at home and carry them to the marketplace."[147] It may be helpful to consider this remark within a wider cultural context. There happen to be a substantial number of references to the singing that both elites and nonelites, male and female, did in a wide range of settings, including home, work, social gatherings, the public streets and baths, travel, and open-air congregating at festivals.[148] In cases where the format is stated or implied, it is almost always solo singing. A vivid scene from a fine domestic dining room in Pompeii depicts four reclining diners at an elite social gathering. One declares—according to words written above the diners' heads—"Make yourselves comfortable! I'm going to sing." Another responds, "So it is, do well!"[149] Although none of the four diners is shown with an open mouth—it being typical for visual artists to depict closed mouths on speaking persons—two of the diners are shown making gestures that draw the viewer's attention to them, and the words appear to start above the heads of these two diners, respectively. Hence, the painting seems to suggest that the woman on the far left, who is in the process of pouring a stream of wine into her mouth from a drinking horn held in her upraised hand,[150] is about to sing. And whether she is

147. Basil, *Hom. in psalm. 1* 1 (PG 29: 212).

148. See a discussion of this subject with special attention to music-making at social gatherings in Cosgrove, *Music at Social Meals in Greek and Roman Antiquity*, 177–193 and 223–238.

149. Museo Archeologico Nazionale di Napoli inv. 120031. The words shown in the painting are also documented by CIL IV.3442a and 3442b.

150. In commenting on this scene in *Music at Social Meals in Greek and Roman Antiquity* (pp. 181–183), I suggested that the woman's tilted head is a singing pose. Upon subsequent examination of a fine photograph, enlarged, I now see that a thin red line runs from her uplifted drinking vessel to her mouth, indicating that she is in the act of drinking, which explains her pose.

the would-be singer or not, the scene suggests a friendly sympotic environment, in which diners sometimes sang spontaneously.

People of high and low status did a good deal of recreational singing. Aelius Aristides remarks that "women and little boys and everyone else" learn the songs of a certain bawdy stage comedy and sing them "in the baths, alleyways, market-place, and at home."[151] Hence, when Christians learned psalms by heart and sang them for pleasure in both private and public settings, singing them "at home" and in "the marketplace," as Basil observes, they were using biblical songs in a fashion that was similar to how people in the wider culture used songs of the stage.

Basil placed the church's love for psalmody in a framework of divine design. It was the Holy Spirit, he said, who mixed melody into the psalms. For the Spirit knew that it is "hard to lead the human race to virtue," since "we neglect the upright life due to our inclination toward pleasure." Therefore, the Spirit added a sweetener to the psalms, making it pleasurable to learn the teachings about virtue, mixing melody into David's poems the way physicians "smear the cup with a little honey" when they give their patients bad-tasting medicines to drink.[152] In another place, Basil describes the monastic life at his retreat in Cappadocia, where he and the other monks added psalms to their work like "salt" to a dish, which more than relieved their tedium, he says. The "encouragements of the hymns bestowed happiness and a state of inner freedom from care."[153] John Chrysostom took a similar view. Without melody, psalm recitation could seem like work. "But God, seeing that many people are unserious and dislike a reading about spiritual things and do not endure the labor of it gladly, and wanting to make the effort more desirable and to prevent the impression of work, mixed melody into the prophecy, so that everyone, beguiled by the rhythm of melody, might send up the holy hymns to him with great eagerness."[154] He makes the same observation in another place, commenting that reading is hard work, which is why the apostle Paul "did not lead you to history but to psalms [Col 3:16–17], so that by singing you might delight your soul and remove the burden (of reading as labor)."[155]

The idea of melody or verse as a sweetener was a well-worn trope. Plato compared the mnemonic chants taught in school to the sweeteners physicians

151. Aelius Aristides, *Or.* 29.30.

152. Basil, *Hom. in psalm. 1* 1 (PG 29: 212).

153. Basil, *Ep.* 2.2.

154. John Chrysostom, *In psalm. 41* 1 (PG 55: 156).

155. John Chrysostom, *In Col.*, Hom. 9.2 (PG 62: 362–363).

put in medicines.[156] The Roman poet Lucretius said that he composed his *De rerum natura* in verse form because just like physicians who smear the honey on the cup of a bad-tasting medicine, he decided to mix the honey of poetry into his philosophical discourse, since many people find philosophy bitter.[157] The Roman-era sophist Maximus of Tyre used a variation of this simile when he compared the poets of old to physicians who hide bitter medicine in pleasant food.[158] Dio Chrysostom applied the same analogy to the comic poets, comparing them to nurses, who, when they need to make children drink something unpleasant, "offer them the cup smeared with honey."[159] One of Basil's contemporaries, the philosopher Themistius, says of his own speechifying that "we must imitate the more knowledgeable of the physicians, who administer bitter medicines, having smeared the cup with honey."[160]

When Basil and John Chrysostom suggest that the melody is a divine concession to human weakness, designed to get their attention but not possessing an intrinsic value, inasmuch as the "honey" is not the "medicine," they seem to trivialize the melodic aspect of psalmody.[161] In fact, in one place Basil seeks to distance the musical aspect of psalmody from melody generally, opining that Davidic psalmody transcends ordinary melody and its carnal pleasures. "This psaltery [of David]," he declares, "possesses occasions for harmonic rhythms from above, so that we, too, might take care to seek the things above and not be carried down by the pleasure of melody to the things of the flesh."[162] Whether the church's psalmody has the same quality, Basil does not say.

Other fourth-century Christian intellectuals spoke about the pleasure of melody without trivializing it or qualifying it as unlike any other kind of mundane melody. Without invoking the medicinal trope, Gregory of Nyssa refers to

---

156. Plato, *Leg.* 659e.

157. Lucretius, *Rer. nat.* 1.930–950 // 4.8–25.

158. Maximus of Tyre, *Diss.* 4.6.

159. προσφέρουσι μέλιτι χρίσασαι τὴν κύλικα. Dio Chrysostom, *Or.* 33.10.

160. τοὺς σοφωτέρους μιμητέον τῶν ἰατρῶν, οἳ τὰ πικρότερα τῶν φαρμάκων μέλιτι τὴν κύλικα περιχρίσαντες πίνειν διδόασι. Themistius, *Protr. ad. Nic.* (*Or.* 24).

161. John also disparages his congregation's appetite for song in another sermon. Speaking of stage music, he asks, "Do you wish to hear beautiful songs? Assuredly, you were not bound to [want beautiful songs]. But if you want them, I will *make allowances*—not that you should listen to satanic songs, but rather to spiritual ones." *In Col.*, Hom. 12.7 (PG 62: 389).

162. Basil, *Hom. in psalm.* 1 2 (PG 29: 213): τὸ ψαλτήριον δὲ τοῦτο τῶν ἁρμονικῶν ῥυθμῶν ἄνωθεν ἔχει τὰς ἀφορμάς, ἵνα καὶ ἡμεῖς τὰ ἄνω ζητεῖν μελετῶμεν καὶ μὴ τῇ ἡδονῇ τοῦ μέλους ἐπὶ τὰ τῆς σαρκὸς πάθη καταφερώμεθα. This sentence also appears in a commentary on the psalms spuriously attributed to Hippolytus: *Frag. in psalm.* 10 (GCS 1.2 140–141).

psalmodic melody as "a sweetness of honey," "the dessert of the meal by which the nourishment of the teachings is sweetened, just as with species,"[163] and Niceta of Remesiana, who does allude to the medicinal trope, makes melody part of the medicine, declaring that "the Lord prepares a potion for human beings that is sweet by virtue of its melody," giving humanity "a remedy *in* the sweetness of these songs."[164] Moreover, he writes, "our soul rightly enjoys this kind of pleasure for that purpose," and "God erected the psalms" as a defense against the temptation of licentious song, "so that [the psalms] would be an occasion for both pleasure and profit."[165]

Some fathers regarded the sound of melody as sensual in a morally dangerous sense. To enjoy a sensual pleasure for its own sake, not as a concomitant of satisfying a bodily necessity (such as nourishment), was to succumb to temptation, they thought, which inhibited the soul's progress toward its goal, the blessed life to come. Augustine, who happens to be one of the most direct witnesses in antiquity to the beauty and emotionally moving power of music, analyzes his own experience of song as a moral test. The pleasure of song was so intense for the young Augustine that he found himself in thrall.[166] Even church music became a trap for him, a "carnal pleasure" (*delectatio carnis*).[167]

What Augustine meant can be illustrated from a comment he makes about temptation through another physical sense—taste. While we are in the body, food is necessary, he writes, and God has taught us to treat food as a medicine for health, not a pleasure.[168] Yet Augustine found that when he passed from the discomfort of hunger to the tranquility of satisfaction, the transition itself was a pleasure. There was no sin in that pleasure per se, he remarked, and there was also no avoiding it. The trap lay in seeking the pleasure for its own sake[169] and

---

163. Gregory of Nyssa, *Inscr. psalm.* 1.3 (GNO 5:33 and 34).

164. Niceta of Remesiana, *Util. hymn.* 5 (Turner, 235–236).

165. John Chrysostom, *In psalm. 41* 1 (PG 55: 157). In another sermon, he addresses people's difficulty in keeping nighttime prayer hours by explaining that melody is God's method "to rouse them to do with pleasure the things that make for profit." Thus, "God contrived to wake [people] up by this cleverness, mixing the pleasure of melody with the pain of diligence." *In psalm. 150* in PG 55: 497–498.

166. Augustine, *Conf.* 10.33.49. "The pleasures of the ear held me even more tightly and subjugated me."

167. *Conf.* 10.33.49.

168. *Conf.* 10.31.44.

169. When he takes nourishment for his health, Augustine explains, pleasure often overtakes that motivation and becomes the real reason or motive (*causa*) for what he purports to be doing. *Conf.* 10.31.44.

not as a collateral effect of taking nourishment for the sake of bodily health. Likewise in the case of hearing: "When it happens to me that the singing moves me more than the thing (*res*) that is sung, I confess to sinning punishably."[170] And in another place, Augustine orders various types of pleasure in a hierarchy, affirming the pleasure of the singing voice but counseling that one should not be more delighted by lesser pleasures—food that satisfies hunger, a sunrise, a lovely song—than by greater ones, such as righteousness.[171]

It is in the context of ruminating about the pleasures of psalmodic melody in *Confessions* that Augustine relates an anecdote about Athanasius discussed in chapter 12—how Athanasius instructed readers to deliver psalm readings in a way that was more like declamation than singing. I have pointed out the problems with the anecdote. Those problems aside, Augustine's use of the story shows that for him the chief temptation of song, its carnal seductiveness, was sung melody as such, whether in secular song or church song. Although the spellbinding blend of melody, rhythm, and euphonious, image-evoking, and story-telling words, sometimes accompanied by graceful dancing, is what people in antiquity generally thought of as "music," Augustine is very clearly focused here on only one of these elements, namely, melody as sung by the human voice: "All the diverse emotions of our spirits have their various modes [*modos*: measures/melodies] in voice and chant appropriate in each case, and are stirred by a mysterious inner kinship."[172] Melodic inflection was the element of the psalm reading that Augustine believed Athanasius had directed lectors to reduce and practically eliminate, thus removing the carnal temptation of lyrical psalm readings. He adduces the anecdote in order to confess that when his pleasure in melody becomes too much of a temptation, the Athanasian practice looks attractive to him.

Augustine did not demand that his own lectors reduce the style of the psalm lesson so that it lacked melody altogether. But he did endorse a style that was less rhythmic or energetic than what he understood the Donatist style of composed hymnody to be. For in a comment about how singing differs from one church or Christian communion to the next,[173] he remarks that "many members of the African church are slower (*pigriora*),[174] with the result that the Donatists criticize us because we sing the divine songs of the prophets soberly in church, while

170. *Conf.* 10.33.50.

171. *Serm.* 159.2 (PL 38: 868–869).

172. *Conf.* 10.33.49; tr. Owen Chadwick, *Saint Augustine, Confessions* (Oxford University Press, 1991), 207–208.

173. The singing of psalms and hymns *varia consuetudo est.* Augustine, *Ep.* 55.18.34.

174. The term "slower" (*pigriora*) is probably the Donatists' term for Augustine's flock, which Augustine reinterprets positively.

they ignite their own drunken rites to a singing of psalms composed by human invention, as if by a call to trumpets."[175]

As for Athanasius, he declared that melodic delivery of psalms was ordained by God.[176] Yet, like Augustine, he insisted that the pleasure of melody in psalmody should not be enjoyed for its own sake.[177] In fact, he does not even value it for its usefulness in easing the burden of hours-long devotional reading, drawing a congregation into more attentive engagement with a psalm lesson, lifting the spirit, evoking tears of compunction, or moving the soul to greater ardor for God. At least he does not mention any of these benefits of melody in psalmody. According to Athanasius, melody's sole and proper function is to symbolize the good order of a Christian's soul.[178]

In a very different context, a book of practical counsel for monks, Evagrius of Pontus gives the following advice about the discipline of psalmody in a monk's private synaxis. I noted this passage in chapter 8. It, too, concerns the pleasure of melody:

> Sometimes one must speak a psalm in a whisper in the synaxis, and sometimes to persevere in the psalmody is the proven method. For it is necessary to adapt ourselves in accord with the trickery of the opponent. For sometimes he teaches the tongue to hurry when listlessness (acedia) circles the soul. And sometimes, when self-pleasure (*autareskia*) poses an impediment to the soul, he provokes (the tongue) to sing the words.[179]

This guidance recalls some analogous remarks by Antony about demons using psalmody in cunning attacks.[180] In Evagrius's example, they seek to alter the

175. Augustine, *Ep.* 55.18.34. The meaning of the final phrase is uncertain. Perhaps the sense is "as if militantly."

176. Athanasius, *Ep. Marc.* 28 (PG 27: 40); see chapter 12.

177. "Some of the simple among us . . . think that psalms are sung melodically for the sake of good sound and the pleasure of the ear. But this is not so." Athanasius, *Ep. Marc.* 27 (PG 27: 37).

178. See the discussion of Athanasius in the section above, "Cosmic Music and the Path to Virtue."

179. Πῇ μὲν ῥοίζῳ τὸν ψαλμὸν ἐν τῇ συνάξει λεκτέον, πῇ δὲ ἐνδελεχεῖν τῇ ψαλμῳδίᾳ δοκιμαστέον. Evagrius, *Eulog.* 9, following Lavra Γ 93 in Robert E. Sinkewicz, *Evagrius of Pontus: The Greek Ascetic Corpus* (Oxford University Press, 2003), 315 (Greek text, long recension). The short recension in PG has ἐν τῇ νήψει ("in sobriety"?) instead of ἐν τῇ συνάξει, as well as an editorial emendation of ἐνδελεχεῖν to ἀδολεσχεῖν ("meditate").

180. Athanasius, *Vit. Ant.* 25 (discussed in chapter 8).

monk's own psalmody in ways that undermine it. Evagrius identifies two demonic stratagems and gives advice, in reverse order, for how to deal with each. When the demon causes the reciting tongue to sing for pleasure, one should speak "in a *rhoizō*." Elsewhere, Evagrius uses *rhoizos* for the whoosh of an arrow, a common usage.[181] The term is also used by Roman-era writers for the rush of the wind, the whizz of a rope being pulled from a spindle, and the sound of whistling.[182] It happens that some examples of *rhoizos*, but not the very loud ones, are the sorts of sounds that a person makes or imitates without engaging the voice-box. In other words, to resist the temptation to sing, the monk is to whisper, perhaps so that the voice box, the organ of singing, is not engaged.[183]

When the soul suffers acedia, the demon urges the monk to hurry up and finish the psalms. Acedia (listlessness) was a special affliction of solitaries. Evagrius comments that "when a spirit of acedia falls over you, it tells the soul that psalmody is burdensome." To combat acedia, the monk should resist the temptation to hurry (to "drive") and should "persevere," that is, keep to the regular pace.

In another place, Evagrius describes how singing can keep away a demon.[184] But in the present context, his focus is how singing through the psalms can become burdensome, because it takes so long, or can pose a sensual pleasure to be avoided by whispering the psalms.

Honor and Praise

According to John Chrysostom, the purpose of funeral psalmody is "to honor the departed."[185] Sozomen makes the same assumption when he describes the funeral procession for Bishop Meletius, writing that he was "honored by turns with psalmody" as his cortege moved from city to city.[186] Martyrs were likewise

181. Evagrius, *De octo spiritibus malitiae* 12; see also Claudius Aelianus, *Nat. animal.* 17.21.

182. Heliodorus, *Aeth.* 2.3.2 (ashes being carried away by the wind "in a whoosh"); [Hippolytus,] *Ref.* 4.32.1 (the sound of the quick pull of a thin cord); Longus, *Daph. et Chlo.* 2.10.2 (whistling). A ῥοῖζος was not inherently loud, and when writers had in mind a loud ῥοῖζος, they tended to use a modifier, such as a river moving along with "a great ῥοίζῳ" (Ps.-Plutarch, *Fluv.* 25.1).

183. Sinkewicz suggests that the expression implies "a low voice, effectively a soft, rhythmic, lightly voiced whisper" (*Evagrius of Pontus*, 239 n. 20, commenting on his translation on p. 35).

184. Evagrius, *Antirrhētikos* 4.22 (discussed above under "Psalmody and Ritual Power" and also in chapter 8).

185. John Chrysostom, *In Heb.*, Hom. 4.5 (PG 63: 44).

186. Sozomen, *H.E.* 7.10.5.

honored by psalmody. Speaking to a crowd at a martyr festival, who had sung psalms for hours, Basil commends them for valuing "honor to the martyrs[187] and worship of God above sleep and rest."[188] And when martyr relics or bishops were honored with public processions that included the trappings and receptions of an adventus, psalmody was a distinctive feature of the event.[189]

Other dignitaries were also honored by psalmody in public processions. When John Chrysostom recalled how Empress Eudoxia had joined a martyr procession and made a public display of her humility, he did not have to explain his remark that the people's processional psalmody was a kind of crowning of the empress herself.[190] Everyone understood that ceremonial actions conducted with great pomp and circumstance spread an aura of magnificence over the event's chief subjects and officiants.

Psalms addressed to God honored God directly, of course, and some were praise songs, while others contained praise statements or otherwise described God's character and activities in ways that were implicitly laudatory. Moreover, both Jews and Christians often called the psalms "hymns" (*hymnoi*), a Greek term for praising a deity in song, the term "praises" (*tehillim*) being the traditional Hebrew designation for the Psalter as a book.

Jews and Christians did not call the Psalter a book of hymns or praises in a form-analytical sense. They knew very well that the Psalter contains a variety of literary types and that not all its poems praise God in the ordinary sense of hymnic laudation. Jews and Christians used the words "hymns" and "praises" as loose catchalls for the Psalter as a body of literature that includes a goodly number of praise poems, together with poems that contain instances of praise and thanksgiving, along with other types of verse that do not, although some of those contained characterizations of God that could be treated as implicit praise.

In the ancient Christian sources, the first unambiguous reference to biblical psalms as hymns is found in Eusebius, who also interprets the act of psalmody as praise. In festive gatherings at churches throughout the world, he says, there is "one hymn of praise from all," meaning the psalmody of the morning and evening office.[191] Elsewhere he writes that "after the death of Moses and Joshua,

---

187. τὴν εἰς τοὺς μάρτυρας τιμὴν.

188. Basil of Caesarea, *Hom. in ps. 114* 1 (PG 29: 484).

189. All of this is described in chapter 9.

190. Again, see the discussion in chapter 9.

191. Eusebius, *H.E.* 10.3. This passage refers to two different types of service, one with psalmody and readings, the other with the Eucharist. See the discussion in chapter 6, "The Psalmody of Daily Cathedral Prayer."

and after the Judges, David . . . first delivered to the Hebrews a new way, that of psalmody, by which he removed the legislation of Moses concerning sacrifices and brought in the new way of serving God through hymning and exulting."[192] Eusebius describes David's own practice as follows:

> He used to send up the first hymn in accord with the saying, "In the night my soul rises to you, O God" [Isa 26:9b] and "Oh God, my God, I rise early to you" [Ps 62:2]. Then with the onset of day, at the first hour, likewise early, he brought the second sacrifice to God, similarly the third at the third (hour), and again the fourth at the sixth, the fifth at the ninth, and the sixth at the twelfth. Then at vespers, after care for the body, he used to offer the seventh hymn when he was about to go to bed. And in this way, he used to fulfill the saying, "Seven times a day I praised you."[193]

This rich passage conceives daily psalmody as a spiritual sacrifice of praise. Moreover, Eusebius gives the impression that this is no novel idea but a commonplace one, shared by his readers, something he can take for granted as a presupposition of the points he wants to make about the value and times of the daily office. Eusebius simply assumes that whatever the words of a given psalm happen to be, in subject matter or form, they are approved and perfect words of spiritual sacrifice, a pleasing offering that can be categorized as "praise" or "hymning and exulting." One of Eusebius's main prooftexts for the idea of evening prayer as spiritual sacrifice is Psalm 140. This psalm refers to the psalmist's words as his prayer and praise, comparing them to incense and an evening sacrifice. Eusebius quotes these lines in another place, where he celebrates daily psalmody in the churches.[194]

A further clue to Eusebius's understanding of daily psalmody is his idea that David's songs are musical offerings that *delight* God, a very old belief, inasmuch as Israelites, Greeks, and others thought of hymns as pleasing musical offerings to a deity. Eusebius describes psalms in these terms when he comments on Psalm 64:9, "Those who dwell at the ends of the earth shall be made afraid by your signs. You shall gladden the early and evening outgoings." As noted in chapter

192. Eusebius, *Didascalia*, in Bandt, 120 = *Fragmenta in psalmos*, fr. 6 in H. Achelis, *Hippolyt's kleinere exegetische und homiletische Schriften* (Hinrichs, 1897), 136. The passage is also included, without a title, as part of the introduction to Eusebius's psalms commentary in PG 23: 76 (ὡς ἡ βίβλος τῶν ψαλμῶν κ.τ.λ.). See the discussion of the text in Bandt, 119.

193. Eusebius, *In psalm. 118* (PG 23: 1392).

194. *Comm. in psalm. 64* (PG 23: 640) (discussed in chapter 6).

6, Eusebius interprets *terpseis* ("you shall gladden") not as a verb but as the noun "delights" (v. 9c), and he equates these delights with the "signs" God performed by establishing the universal church and its morning and evening office. He also exploits the differences in the Greek translations, seizing on Symmachus's use of the word "hymnologies" for *terpseis* and Aquila's use of the word *ainopoiēseis*, another verb that he construes as a plural noun, "praise-makings." These interpretive decisions allow him to conclude that God established the universal morning and evening office as delights, which Eusebius defines as the "hymnologies" and "praise-makings" of those hours.[195] Hence they are spiritual offerings that delight God, even if the church also finds it delightful to sing them.

The idea of morning and evening prayer as a form of spiritual sacrifice seems to have influenced Ambrose's conception of the church's psalmody as hymns and praise. When Ambrose borrows from Basil's encomium to the psalms, he adds additional references to psalms as praise, and it has been suggested that for him and his audience the psalms were more or less identified with the church's daily office, understood as morning and evening praise.[196] Augustine, who sometimes refers to psalms as hymns, defines a hymn as sung praise of God[197] but does not explain how the psalms in their literary diversity all qualify as hymns. Nor does John Chrysostom, when he uses "praise" as a synonym for "sing psalms."[198] But John shows that he takes Eusebius's framework for granted when he says that God "accepted [Israel's] sacrifices without needing them," but rather "to urge human beings toward the honor of him," and "so, too, he accepts hymns not because he needs fine speech from us but because he desires our salvation."[199]

John's comments reinterpret the old idea of hymns as a means of delighting God by construing them as opportunities for God to offer a gift to human beings. Yet the gift of salvation, as John describes it, entails honoring God, which the church does in multiple ways, including in its hymnody.

"See whether there can be any doubt that such songs [the psalms] please God," says Niceta of Remesiana, "when everything advanced (in them) looks

---

195. Eusebius, *Comm. in psalm.* 64 (PG 23: 640). See the discussion of this passage in chapter 6.

196. Ambrose, *Expl. psalm. 1* 9 (PL 14: 924–925; CSEL 64: 7–8). See Auf der Maur, *Das Psalmenverständnis des Ambrosius von Mailand*, 25–26.

197. Augustine, *Enarr. in psalm. 72* 1 (PL 36: 914; CCL 39: 986). Augustine overlooks literary hymns, including prose hymns, which were post-classical developments; all the earliest hymns were forms of melic poetry.

198. John Chrysostom, *In psalm. 41* 2 (PG 55: 157), encouraging the men of his congregation to sing psalms at mealtimes and telling them, "I say these things not so that you alone *sing praise* (ἐπαινῆτε) but so that you teach your wives and children to sing such songs."

199. John Chrysostom, *In psalm. 7* 15 (PG 55: 104).

to the glory of the Creator."[200] Like Eusebius, Niceta regarded the psalms as a "spiritual sacrifice" offered to God instead of blood sacrifices, and he conceived this spiritual offering as "a sacrifice of praise," quoting exhortations to praise from the Psalter.[201]

The tendency to think of psalmody as praise continued in later centuries.[202]

Singing Well

Two Christian intellectuals purport to know something about David's achievement as a poet. One is Gregory of Nyssa, whose remarks on this subject are described in chapter 12. The other is Jerome, who celebrates David's artistry while at the same time rejecting any idea that Christians should sing psalms skillfully. Jerome calls David "our Simonides, Pindar, and Alcaeus, our Flaccus, too, Catullus, and Serenus."[203] David composed in Hebrew meter, Jerome claims,[204] although the metrical-poetic rhythm of the psalms did not survive Greek and Latin translation:

> In fact, what can be more musical than the Psalter? Like the writings of our Flaccus and the Greek Pindar, it now flows in iambics, now resounds in alcaics, now swells into sapphics, now uses half a metrical foot. What can be lovelier than the hymns of Deuteronomy and Isaiah? What is more solemn than Solomon, what more perfect than Job? All these works, as Josephus and Origen wrote, were composed in hexameters and pentameters and circulated among their own people. When they are read in Greek their sound is different; when in Latin they are utterly incoherent. But if anyone thinks that the grace of the language does not

200. Niceta of Remesiana, *Util. hymn.* 7 (Turner, 236–237).

201. See the wider context of Niceta's statement just quoted from *Util. hymn.* 7.

202. Bradshaw observes that in later centuries (i.e., the fifth century and beyond), monastic psalmody, which had generally been practiced as meditative reflection, came to be regarded as an act of praise as well. Paul F. Bradshaw, *Reconstructing Early Christian Worship* (Liturgical Press, 2009), 124. A passage in the sixth-century *Rule of the Master* is illustrative when it stipulates the proper posture for psalmody: "The one singing should stand with body unmoving and head bowed down and should sing praises to the Lord with composure, since one is in fact performing one's service before the Godhead, as the prophet [David] teaches when he says, 'In the presence of angels I will sing your praise.'" *Reg. mag.* 47.

203. Jerome, *Ep.* 53(*Ad Paulum. presb.*).8.17.

204. *Chron., praef.* (GCS 47: 3); *Praef. Job.* (PL 28: 1081–1082).

> suffer through translation, let him read Homer word for word in Latin. I will go further and say that, if he will translate this author into the prose of his own language, the order of the words will seem ridiculous, and the most eloquent of poets [will seem] almost mute.[205]

With these remarks, Jerome defends the poetry of the Bible against the inevitable impression of unmetrical verse that well-educated readers received when reading the psalms in the Septuagint or the Old Latin version.

Yet nothing in Jerome's comments is meant to suggest that he valued aesthetic beauty in Christian psalm-singing or that he would have thought that the unrecoverable fine rhythms of Hebrew psalmody should be honored by fine melodies and fine singing on the part of Christians. Although he took for granted that psalms should be sung daily in the church and in the monastery,[206] he placed no value at all on the aesthetic quality of Christian psalmody. He tells a certain Rusticus that one of the virtues of life in the monastery at Bethlehem is that "sweetness of voice" (*dulcedo uocis*) is not required for performing the psalm lessons, only "an ardor of mind" (*mentis affectus*), since Paul says, "I will sing with the Spirit, I will sing with the mind, too."[207] When Jerome describes the sort of female companion a consecrated virgin ought to have, he advises that she should not be a pretty young girl "who manipulates a song with a sweet throat."[208] And when he inserts a bit of advice to adolescent cantors in comments on Ephesians 5:19, he tells them that "God is to be sung not with the voice but with the heart (*Deo non voce sed corde cantandum*)," meaning "more with the spirit than with the voice" (*magis animo quam voce*).[209]

Obviously, the cantors of this last admonition were not supposed to perform the psalms silently. They were to sing out loud with the right attitude and not imitate stage singers, Jerome says, "smearing the throat and larynx with a sweet

205. *Chron., praef.* (GCS 47: 3–4); tr. from Stefan Rebenich, *Jerome* (Routledge, 2002), 77.

206. Jerome refers to "Psalm 9, which was sung (*cantantus est*) by you to the Lord" (*Tract. psalm.* 9; CCL 78: 28). He says that the women of Paula's monastery, which was the sister monastery to Jerome's, "sang (*canebant*) the Psalter in sequence at night" (*Ep.* 108[*Epitaph. s. Paulae*].20; PL 22: 896; CSEL 55: 335). He advises that a girl consecrated to virginity should have a mature female companion, who "by example will accustom her to rise for prayers and psalms at night and to sing (*canere*) hymns in the morning" (*Ep.* 107[*Ad Laet.*].9 [PL 22: 875; CSEL 55: 300]).

207. Jerome, *Ep.* 125 *Ad Rust. monach.*).15 (PL 22: 1081; CSEL 56.134).

208. Jerome, *Ep.* 107(*Ad Laet.*).9 (PL 22: 875; CSEL 55: 300).

209. *Comm. in ep. ad Eph.* (PL 26: 528). In the interests of English style, I have reversed the order in which the complementary phrases happen to appear in this passage.

medication in the manner of tragic singers, so that melodies and songs of the theater are heard in church."[210] Elsewhere, Jerome refers to singers, including church cantors, who wear their hair long and curled, and dress in a certain way.[211] Apparently, at least some of these youthful cantors[212] sought to imitate the tragic singers of the stage in dress, manner, and musical style. Penning these comments in Bethlehem, where he had established a monastery in the 380s with a handful of friends from Rome, Jerome may have been recalling church lectors in Rome, where there was a long history of fandom for entertainers of all sorts—gladiators, charioteers, pantomimes, and actors, including singing actors of the theatrical and concert stage.[213] That said, Roman Palestine also had theaters in late antiquity, and adolescent boys and young men of wealthy families in Bethlehem could have attended public entertainments in nearby Jerusalem, becoming socialized into the cult of stage celebrity.[214] Jerome seeks to disabuse young cantors and their parents of the notion that style is what counts. On the contrary, what matters is the message. In fact, since the spiritual meaning of the words is more important than the "bodily" sound,[215] someone who is a bad singer, a so-called *kakophōnos*,

---

210. *Comm. in ep. ad Eph.* (PL 26: 528) (*nec in tragoedorum modum guttur et fauces dulci medicamine colliniendae* [correction of *colliniendas*] *sunt, ut in ecclesia theatrales moduli audiantur et cantica*).

211. Jerome, *Ep.* 52.5; 54.13; and 128.4 (excerpted in *MECL*, nos. 319, 320, and 330). The long and/or curled hair and other forms of dress must have referred to the way famous singing actors dressed in presenting a certain public persona and style (preseumably off-stage, when they were not masked and costumed for a particular role). The first of the cited passages refers specifically to church lectors, acolytes, and cantors who sported long hair and a certain clothing style. The other two passages refer to long-haired singers generally, without differentiating cantors and stage singers.

212. Jerome addresses them as *adolescenti*, a term with a broad range of application; it was used for children, adolescents, and young men in their twenties.

213. Both literary and epigraphic evidence (inscriptions and graffiti) document the avidity of the populace of Rome and other cities of the empire for performers—gladiators, charioteers, pantomimes, and actors (a category that included the singing actor of the theatrical and concert stage)—as well as the public honors that were bestowed on entertainers of various kinds. "From Gades to Dura Europos, with a particular concentration at Pompeii, fans scratched on walls sketches of their favourite athletes, charioteers, actors, or gladiators . . . or briefer tags in street-Latin praising particular actors and gladiators." Michael J. Carter and Jonathan Edmondson, "Spectacle in Rome, Italy, and the Provinces," in *The Oxford Handbook of Roman Epigraphy*, ed. Christer Bruun and Jonathan Edmondson (Oxford University Press, 2015), 555.

214. On the theater in Roman Palestine in late antiquity, see Zeev Weiss, *Public Spectacles in Roman and Late Antique Palestine* (Harvard University Press, 2014).

215. In immediately preceding comments, Jerome interprets the expression "psalms, hymns, and spiritual songs" (in Eph 5:19) as implying a distinction between the spiritual and bodily aspects

can sing a psalm lesson well, Jerome says. For it is the lector's moral character and knowledge of Scripture, not his singing ability, that makes him a "sweet singer," one who pleases with the words he utters, not with the sound of his voice.[216] In short, Jerome assigned no value to musical skill in psalm-singing or to aesthetic enjoyment of the melodic element in psalmody. But obviously other Christians *did*, or else Jerome would not have voiced his concern.

Something like Jerome's opinion was shared by the abbas of the Pachomian community of Tabennisi in Upper Egypt, whose writings Jerome translated. The Pachomians incorporated psalm recitation into their daily routine as nonlyrical meditation; they *sang* psalms only for ceremonial purposes during processions (e.g., funeral processions and processions for visiting bishops) and perhaps at Sunday worship (although there are reasons to doubt that their Sunday gatherings featured lyrical psalmody).[217] But their elders taught them that it was a sin to sing for the enjoyment of song, for the devil declares, "I am the one who is at work in those who sing for pleasure."[218]

Monks who had to be taught not to sing for pleasure would have come to the monasteries from churches where psalmody was prized. Church psalmody was probably executed with increasing skill in the late fourth century, especially in the larger churches, which could be selective about choice of lector-singers and had the wherewithal to train them. Even if we assume that the adolescent lector who imitated stage singers was not typical and that Jerome's picture of him is somewhat exaggerated, the fact that Jerome witnessed young people who in any way approached what he describes suggests that adolescent cantors were encouraged to sing well and that people valued the beauty of a fine young voice singing the psalm verses artfully to "pretty little melodies" (to borrow Augustine's expression).

The training of church singers is a further indication that the church valued skillful psalmody, which presumably included both good diction and good execution of a melody. Explicit evidence for this training first appears in the fifth century and refers not to lectors but to choirs. Choral training probably had its beginnings in the fourth century, however, when choirs of children and virgins were already a regular part of certain liturgies.[219]

---

of psalmody: "psalms" refers to the bodily aspect, he writes, and "songs" to the spiritual aspect (*Comm. in ep. ad Eph.*; PL 26: 328). Psalm-singing entails both.

216. *Comm. in ep. ad Eph.* (PL 26: 528).

217. See the discussion in chapter 8 of the Pachomians' use of psalms.

218. *Pach. vit. Boh.* 64; tr. Veilleux, *Pachomian Koinonia*, vol. 1, 85.

219. See chapter 4.

From the standpoint of communication, the rationale for good singing would have been to ensure that people understood the words, which demanded good articulation and phrasing on the part of the singer(s), just what Gregory of Nyssa commends as David's art of psalmody. From the standpoint of psalmody as worship, the rationale for skillful singing would have been the duty to praise well. "God is worthy of the most magnificent praise of which humans are capable," Augustine writes.[220] Although he does not make this statement about psalmody, the assertion expresses a proposition on which an aesthetics of music in worship might be predicated. Yet there is no discussion of the aesthetics of worship in patristic writings, and only Niceta of Remesiana hints at the idea, doing so just briefly in some instructions about good singing.

Niceta's remarks appear in a sermon he delivered at a vigil, sometime between 370 and his death in 410. He notes that psalmody is the principal activity at a vigil, and his topic is the benefits of psalmody, which he defends against certain Christians who hold that singing has no place in church. As advice to his audience (an urban congregation or possibly a community of monks), his instructions about how to sing well must concern the refrains in psalmody, which were probably frequent, performed after every line.[221]

Singing psalms should be decorous, Niceta says, "not florid in the manner of the euphonious theatrical voice."[222] The "sound and melody should be suitable to holy religion; it must not express theatrical distress but should rather demonstrate Christian simplicity in its own movement (*in ipsa etiam modulatione*); it must not smack of anything theatrical but should rather create compunction in the hearers."[223] There are quite a few references to theatrical style in these remarks. Does Niceta mean to curb any individual inclination to distinguish oneself, or is he merely reassuring his readers that his endorsement of singing is not advocacy of anything worldly? When he gets into specifics about the difference between

---

220. *Institutor tamen earum deus praeclarissime pro humana facultate laudandus est.* Augustine, *Lib. arb.* 3.5.12 (44); tr. from Simon Harrison, *Augustine's Way into Will: The Theological and Philosophical Significance of De libero arbitrio* (Oxford University Press, 2006), 172. A more literal translation would be something like, "God is to be praised most magnificently in accord with human ability."

221. On the frequency of refrains, see the discussion in chapter 12. All the *explicit* evidence for the styles of group psalmody in the fourth and fifth centuries indicates responsorial formats, not singing *in directum*. See chapter 10.

222. Niceta of Remesiana, *Util. hymn.* 2. I have translated *garriendum* "florid" instead of "chattering" since the latter word does not fit a description of euphonous theatrical singing. Note that *garrio* was used for the sound of nightingales.

223. *Util. hymn.* 13.

proper and improper singing, his chief point is that good congregational singing is a harmonious blend:

> Our voice should not be discordant (*dissona*) but concordant (*consona*): one person extends (*protrahat*), another compresses (*contrahat*); one lowers (*humiliet*), another elevates (*extollat*). Instead, let each person seek to integrate his voice within the sound of the harmonious (*concinentis*) chorus, not extending externally (*extrinsecus protrahens*) in the manner of a cithara, as if to make an indecent display. Everything should be conducted as if in the sight of God, not from an eagerness to please other people or oneself. . . . But one who is unable to equalize (*aequare*) or adapt (*aptare*) to the others—it is better (for him) to sing in a soft (*lenta*[224]) voice than to make a lot of noise, for thus he performs his liturgical function and does not disturb the singing fraternity. Not everyone possesses a flexible or melodious voice (*uocem flexibilem uel canoram*).[225]

The words *non dissona*, *consona*, and *concinentis* describe the varying qualities of good unison singing, that is, the degree to which people's voices all conform to the same rhythmic timing and pitch. It is possible that *protrahat* and *contrahat* imply slowing and quickening, so that the voices go out of sync. It is possible that the words "lowers" (*humiliet*) and "elevates" (*extollat*) refer to pitch, which would imply that some singers made up their own melodies in singing the responses. But that seems implausible on its face. Moreover, Latin speakers, following the usual Greek way of speaking about musical sound, tended not to use the metaphors of "high" and "low" for pitch; they usually spoke of pitch as "sharp" (*acutus*) or "heavy" (*grauis*). Hence, Niceta's words probably refer to varying intensities of volume, which cause imbalance in the blending of voices. The proper task of each singer is to "equalize and adapt" his or her voice to the others and avoid self-display by not singing too loudly or following one's own tempo. Some people, however, are incapable of equalizing and adapting—whether because of the quality of their voices or their inability to sing in tune. These he encourages to sing softly. For it is important that the psalmody sounds sweet, not discordant, since "there is something attractive about religious sweetness"—here he refers to

224. *Lentus* often means "pliant" but here seems to be the opposite of "loud." Note the use in Pliny, *Ep.* 2.14.10, where it describes a dignified mode of pleading in court—*grauiter et lente*—in contrast to crowd-pleasing "noise" (*clamorem*).

225. *Util. hymn.* 13.

Cyprian's remark to Donatus[226]—"and those who sing well have a certain grace that encourages the souls of those who hear toward religion."[227]

Singing psalms well serves several purposes, Niceta says. With an allusion to cymbals as instruments of praise in the psalms, he concludes his exhortation by telling his audience that "our voice, if it is fluid and harmonizes well with the cymbals, will delight ourselves and edify our listeners, and our praise will be pleasing (*suauis*) to God."[228] The insinuation that pleasing God with psalmodic praise requires that the church sing well is perhaps as close as any early Christian writer comes to asserting a premise for a liturgical aesthetic of psalmody.

226. Niceta had just quoted from Cyprian, *Don.* 16 (on which, see chapter 3).

227. *Util. hymn.* 13.

228. *Util. hymn.* 13.

BIBLIOGRAPHY

ANCIENT WRITINGS

Acts of Paul. Schmidt, Carl, ed. *Acta Pauli aus der Heidelberger Koptischen Papyrushandschrift Nr. 1*. Leipzig: Hinrichs, 1904; Schmidt, Carl and Wilhelm Schubart, eds. Πράξεις Παύλου. *Acta Pauli nach dem papyrus der Hamburger Staats- und Universitäts-Bibliothek*. Glückstadt: Augustin, 1936.

Acts of Thomas, Greek. *Acta Apostolorum Apocrypha*, vol. 2/2, edited by Maximilian Bonnet, pp. 99–291. Leipzig: Mendelssohn, 1903. Reprint Darmstadt: Wissenschaftliche Buchgesellschaft, 1959.

Acts of Xanthippe and Polyxena. *Apocrypha Anecdota: A Collection of Thirteen Apocryphal Books and Anecdota*, edited by M. R. James, pp. 43–85. Cambridge: Cambridge University Press, 1893.

Aelius Aristides. *P. Aelii Aristidis Opera quae exstant omnia*, *Orationes 1–16*, ed. Friedrich W. Lenz and Charles A. Behr. 2 vols. Leiden: Brill, 1976 and 1980. *Aelii Aristidis Smyrnaei quae supersunt omnia*, vol. 2: *Orationes 17–53*, edited by Bruno Keil. Berlin: Weidmann, 1898 (repr. 1958).

Aelius Donatus. *Aeli Donati quod fertur commentum Terenti*, vol. 1. Leipzig: Teubner, 1902.

Ambrose. *Sancti Ambrosii opera*, Part 5: *Expositio Psalmi CXVIII*, 2nd ed. and Part 6: *Explanatio Psalmorum XII*, 2nd ed., edited by Michael Petschenig and Michaela Zelzer. CSEL 62 and 64. Vienna: Verlag der Österreichischen Akademie der Wissenschaften, 1999. *Sancti Ambrosii opera*, Part 10: *Epistula et Acta*, edited by Michaela Zelzer. CSEL 82. Vienna: Hoelder-Pichler-Tempsky, 1982. *Ambroise de Milan, Hymnes*, edited by Jacques Fontaine et al. Paris: Cerf, 1992. *De virginibus*, edited by Egnatius Cazzaniga, translated by Franco Gori. Milan: Biblioteca Ambrosiana, 1989.

Aphrahat. *Aphraatis Sapientis Persae, Demonstrationes*, edited and translated by Jean Parisot. 2 vols. Patrologia Syriaca 1/1 and 1/2. Paris: Firmin-Didot, 1894 and 1907.

Apocalypse of Paul/Visio Pauli. Latin: *Apocrypha Anecdota: A Collection of Thirteen Apocryphal Books and Fragments*, edited by Montague R. James, pp. 1–42. Cambridge: Cambridge University Press, 1893. Greek epitome: *Apocalypses apocryphae Mosis, Esdrae, Pauli, Iohannis: item Mariae dormitio, additis Evangeliorum et actuum Apocryphorum supplementis*, edited by Constantine Tischendorf, pp. 34–69. Leipzig: Mendelssohn, 1866.

Apostolic Church Order. Alistair Stewart-Sykes, *The Apostolic Church Order: The Greek Text with Introduction, Translation, and Annotation*. Strathfield: St. Paul's, 2006.

Apostolic Constitutions. Marcel Metzger, ed. *Les constitutions apostoliques: introduction, texte critique, traduction et notes*, 3 vols. SC 320, 329, 336. Paris: Cerf, 1985–1987; Franz X. Funk, ed., *Didascalia et Constitutiones Apostolorum*, vol. 1. Paderborn: Schoeningh, 1906.

Apophthegmata patrum. Jean-Claude Guy, ed. *Les apophtegmes des pères, Collection systématique*. 3 vols. SC 387, 474, and 498. Paris: Cerf, 1993, 2003, 2005.

Apophthegmata patrum, Collectio anonyma. François Nau, "Histoires des solitaires égyptiens." In *Revue de l'Orient Chrétien* 12 (1907): 48–68, 171–181, and 393–404; 13 (1908): 47–57 and 266–283; 14 (1909): 357–379; 17 (1912): 204–211 and 294–301; 18 (1913): 137–146.

Apostolic Tradition. Botte, Bernard, ed. *Hippolyte de Rome: La Tradition apostolique d'après les anciennes versions*. Paris: Cerf, 1968. *Der aethiopische Text der Kirchenordnung des Hippolyt*, ed. Hugo Duensing. Göttingen: Vandenhoeck & Ruprecht, 1946. Alessandro Bausi, "La nuova versione etiopica della Traditio apostolica: edizione e traduzione preliminare." In *Christianity in Egypt: Literary Production and Intellectual Trends: Studies in Honor of Tito Orlandi*, edited by Paola Buzi and Alberto Complani, pp. 19–69. Rome: Institutum Patristicum Augustinianum, 2011. Gregory Dix and Henry Chadwick, eds., *The Treatise on the Apostolic Tradition of St. Hippolytus of Rome*, revised. London: SPCK, 1968. Erik Tidner, ed. *Didascaliae apostolorum, Canonum ecclesiasticorum, Traditionis apostolicae versiones latinae*. Berlin: Akademie, 1963.

Appian. *Appiani historia Romana*, vol. 1, edited by A. G. Roo, P. Viereck, and Emilio Gabba. Leipzig: Teubner, 1962.

Aristides Quintilianus. Reginald P. Winnington-Ingram, ed. *Aristidis Quintiliani De Musica libri tres*. Leipzig: Teubner, 1963.

Aristotle. *Aristotelis, Ars Rhetorica*, edited by Rudolf Kassel. Berlin: De Gruyter, 1976. Ps.-Aristole: *Aristotle, Problems, Books 1–19*, edited and translated by Robert Mayhew. Cambridge: Harvard University Press, 2011 (based chiefly on the critical editions by G. Marenghi).

Aristoxenus. Rosetta da Rios, ed. *Aristoxeni elementa harmonica*. Rome: Typis Publicae Officinae Polygraphicae, 1954.

Armenian Lectionary. *Le codex arménien Jérusalem 121*, vol. 2: *Édition comparée du texte et de deux autres manuscrits*, edited by Athanase Renoux. Turnhout: Brepols, 1971.

Arnobius the Younger. *Arnobii iunioris Commentarii in psalmos*, edited by Klaus-D. Daur. CCL 25. Turnhout, 1990.

Assumption of the Virgin (*Liber de Dormitione Mariae*) (Greek). In Constantin von Tischendorf, ed., *Apocalypses Apocryphae*, pp. 95–112. Leipzig: Mendelssohn, 1866.

Asterius the Sophist. *Asterii sophistae commentariorum in Psalmos quae supersunt*, edited by Marcel Richard. Oslo: Brøgger, 1956.

Athenaeus Naucratites. *Athenaeus Naucratites, Deipnosophistae*, edited by S. Douglas Olson. 5 vols. Berlin: De Gruyter, 2019–2022.

Athanasius. *Athanasius Werke*. 2/1, fasc. 6: *Die Apologien*, edited by Hans-Georg Opitz. Berlin: De Gruyter, 1938. *Athanasius Werke* 1/1: *Die dogmatischen Schriften*, 2nd ed., edited by Karin Metzler and Kyriakos Savvidis. Berlin: De Gruyter, 1998. *Athanase d'Alexandrie, Deux apologies: A l'empereur Constance, Pour sa fuite*, edited by Jan-M. Szymusiak. SC 56. Paris: Cerf, 1987. *Athanase d'Alexandrie, Vie d'Antoine*, ed. Gérard J. M. Bartelink. SC 400. Paris: Cerf, 2004. *The Canons of Athanasius of Alexandria: The Arabic and Coptic Versions*, edited and translated by Wilhelm Riedel and W. E. Crum. London: Williams and Norgate, 1904. *Discipline Générale antique*, vol. 2: *Les canons des pères grecs (IVe–IVe s.)*, edited by Périclès-Pierre Joannaou. Grottaferrata (Rome): Italo-Orientale "S. Nilo," 1963. *Histoire "acephale" et index syriaque des lettres festales d'Athanese d'Alexandrie*, edited by Annick Martin, translated by Micheline Albert. SC 317. Paris: Cerf, 1985. David Brakke and David M. Gwynn, *The Festal Letters of Athanasius of Alexandria, with the Festal Index and the Historia Acephala*. Liverpool University Press, 2022. Ps.-Athanasius, *De virginitate*: E. von der Goltz, ed., Λόγος σωτηρίας πρὸς τὴν παρθένον. Leipzig: Hinrichs, 1905.

Augustine. *Aurelii Augustini Hipponiensis episcopi Epistulae*, Part I: *Prefatio, Ep. I–XXX*, edited by Alois Goldbacher CSEL 34/1. Vienna: Tempsky, 1895. *Sancti Aurelii Augustini Retractionum libri 2*, edited by Almut Mutzenbecher. CCL 57. Turnhout: Brepols, 1984. James J. O'Donnell, *Augustine: Confessions*, vol. 1: *Introduction and Text*. Oxford: Clarendon, 1992. *Enarrationes in psalmos*, edited by Eligius Dekkers and Jean Fraipont. 3 vols. CCL 38, 39, and 40; Turnhout: Brepols, 1956. *Sancti Aurelii Augustini Sermones de Vetero Testamento*, ed. Cyril Lambot. CCL 41; Turnhout: Brepols, 1961. *Sancti Aurelii Augustini Hipponensis episcopi Sermones inedit*, edited by Michael Denis. Vienna: Trattner, 1792; reprinted in PL 46. *Sancti Aurelii Augustini Hipponensis episcopi Operum tomus*, vol. 5: *Sermones* [Maurist edition]. Paris: Muguet, 1683; reprinted in PL 38 and 39. *La Règle de saint Augustin*, vol. 1: *Tradition manuscrite*, edited by Luc Verheijen, 417–437 (*Praeceptum*). Paris: Études Augustiniennes, 1967. *De libero arbitrio libri tres*, edited by William M. Green. CSEL 74. Vienna: Hoelder-Pichler-Tempsky, 1956. Cyril Lambot, "Texte complété et amendé du <<Psalmus contra partem Donati>> de Saint Augustin." *Revue Bénédictine* 47 (1935): 312–330.

Aulus Gellius. *Auli Gelli Noctes Atticae*, edited by Leofranc Holford-Strevens. 2 vols. Oxford: Clarendon, 2020.

Auxentius. See *Life of Auxentius*.

Avitus of Braga. See Lucian the Priest.

Babylonian Talmud. *The Hebrew-English Edition of the Babylonian Talmud*, edited by Maurice Simon, Isidore Epstein, and Joseph Herman. London: Soncino, 1965–1989.

Basil of Caesarea. Yves Courtonne, ed. *Saint Basile, Lettres*. 3 vols. Paris: Les Belles Lettres, 1957–1966. ET and subsection numbering for the *Longer Rules* (*Asceticon magnum sive quaestiones/Regulae fusius tractate* in PG 31): Anna M. Silvas, *The Asketikon of St. Basil the Great*. Oxford: Oxford University Press, 2005.

Boethius. *Boetii De institutione arithmetica libri duo / De institutione musica libri quinque*, edited by Gottfried Friedlein. Frankfurt a. M.: Minerva, 1966 (orig. Leipzig 1897).

Breviarium Hipponense. Concilia Africae A. 345–A. 525, edited by C. Munier, pp. 30–46. CCL 149. Turnhouts: Brepols, 1974.

Caelius Aurelianus. *On Acute Diseases and On Chronic Diseases*, edited and translated by Israel E. Drabkin. Chicago: University of Chicago Press, 1950.

Callinicus of Rufinianae. *Callinicos, Vie d'Hypatios*, edited by G. J. M. Bartelink. SC 177. Paris: Cerf, 1971.

Canon Muratori. Clare K. Rothschild, *The Muratorian Fragment: Text, Translation, Commentary*. Tübingen: Mohr Siebeck, 2023.

Canons of (Ps.-)Basil. Translation in Wilhelm Riedel, ed. Die Kirchenrechtsquellen des Patriarchats Alexandrien. Leipzig: Deichert, 1900.

Canons of Hippolytus. René-Georges Coquin, ed. Les Canons d'Hippolyte. Paris: Firmin-Didot, 1966.

Cassian, John. *De institutis coenobiorum, De incarnatione contra Nestorian*, edited by Michael Petschenig, rev. Gottfried Kreuz. CSEL 17. Vienna: Verlag der Österreichischen Akademie der Wissenschaften, 2004. *Collationes XXIIII*, edited by Michael Petschenig, rev. Gottfried Kreuz. CSEL 13. Vienna: Verlag der Österreichischen Akademie der Wissenschaften, 2004. *Institutions cénobitiques*, 2nd ed., edited by Jean-Claude Guy. Paris: Cerf, 1965.

Cassius, Dio. See Dio Cassius.

Cedrenus. See Georgius Cedrenus.

Chronicon paschale. Ludwig Dindorf, ed. *Chronicon Paschale*. 2 vols. Bonn: Weber, 1832.

Claudian. *De Consulatu Stilichonis*. In John B. Hall, ed. *Claudii Claudiani Carmina*. Leipzig: Teubner, 1985.

Claudius Ptolemy. *Die Harmonielehre de Klaudios Ptolemaios*, edited by Ingemar Düring. Göteborg: Elanders, 1930.

Clement of Alexandria. Otto Stählin and Ursula Treu, eds. *Clemens Alexandrinus*, vol. 1: *Protrepticus und Paedagogus*, 3rd ed. GCS 12; Berlin: Akademie-Verlag, 1972. Otto Stählin, Ludwig Früchtel, and Ursula Treu, eds., *Clemens Alexandrinus*, vol. 2: *Stromata Buch I–VI*, 4th ed. Berlin: Akademie-Verlag, 1985. Otto Stählin, Ludwig Früchtel, and Ursula Treu, eds., *Clemens Alexandrinus*, vol. 3: *Stromata Buch VII und VIII*, 2nd ed. Berlin: Akademie-Verlag, 1970.

Cleonides. Jon Solomon, "Cleonides: ΕΙΣΑΓΩΓΗ ΑΡΜΟΝΙΚΗ: Critical Edition, Translation, and Commentary." Ph.D. diss. University of North Carolina, 1980.

Council of Carthage. *Sacrorum conciliorum nova, et amplissima collectio*, vol. 3, edited by Giovan Domenico Mansi. Florence: Zatta, 1759. Reprint Paris: H. Welter, 1901.

Council of Elvira, Canons of. *Concilios visigóticos e hispano-romanos*, edited by José Vives. Barcelona: Consejo Superior de Investigaciones Cientificas, Instituto Enrique Flórez, 1963.

Council of Laodicea, Canons of. *Fonti*, fasc. 9: *Discipline générale antique (IVe–IX s.)*, vol. 1/2: *Les canons des synodes particulieres*, Périclès-Pierre Joannou. Grottaferratta, Rome: Italo-Orientale "S. Nilo," 1962; vol. 2: *Les canons des Pères Grecs*, edited by Périclès-Pierre Joannou. Grottaferratta, Rome: Italo-Orientale "S. Nilo," 1963.

Cyprian. *Sancti Cypriani Episcopi Opera*, edited by Robert Weber et al. Turnhout: Brepols, 1972–.

Cyril of Alexandria. *Sancti patris nostril Cyrilli archepiscopi Alexandrini in xii prophetas*, ed. Philip E. Pusey. 2 vols. Oxford: Clarendon, 1868.

Cyril of Jerusalem. *Catéchèses mystagogiques*, Auguste Piédagnel, SC 126. Paris: Cerf, 1966. Maxwell E. Johnson, ed. and trans., *Lectures on the Christian Sacraments: The Procatechesis and the Five Mystagogical Catecheses Ascribed to St. Cyril of Jerusalem: Text, Translation, and Introduction*. Yonkers, NY: St. Vladimir's Seminary Press, 2017. *Catecheses ad illuminandos* in W. C. Reischl and J. Rupp, eds. *Cyrilli Hierosolymorum archiepiscopi opera quae supersunt omnia*. 2 vols. Munich: Leitner, 1848 and 1860; reprint Olms, 1967.

Dead Sea Scrolls. *The Dead Sea Scrolls Study Edition*, edited and translated by Florentino García Martínez and Eibert J. C. Tigchelaar. 2 vols. Leiden: Brill, 1997 and 1998.

Diadochus of Photice. *Capita centum de perfectione spirituali*. In *One Hundred Practical Texts of Perception and Spiritual Discernment from Diadochus of Photike*, vol. 8, edited and translated by Janet E. Rutherford. Belfast: Institute of Byzantine Studies, 2000.

Dialogues of Zacchaeus and Apollonius. *Questions d'un païen à un chrétien: Consultationes Zacchei christiani et Apollonii philosophi*, edited by Jean L. Feiertag. 2 vols. SC 401 and 402. Paris, Cerf, 1994.

Didascalia. *Didascalia Apostolorum: The Syriac Version Translated and Accompanied by the Verona Latin Fragments*, edited and translated by R. Hugh Connolly. Oxford: Clarendon, 1929; *The Didascalia Apostolorum in Syriac*, edited by Arthur Vööbus. 2 vols. Louvain: Secrétariat du CorpusSCO, 1979. *Didascalia apostolorum, fragmenta ueronensia latina*, edited by Edmund Hauler. Leipzig: Teubner, 1900.

Didymus the Blind. *Didymos der Blinde, Psalmenkommentar (Tura-Papyrus)*, edited by Michael Gronewald. 5 vols. Bonn: Habelt, 1968–1970. *Didyme l'Aveugle sur Zacharie*, edited by L. Doutreleau. 3 vols. SC 83, 84, 85. Paris: Cerf, 1962.

Dio Cassius. Earnest Cary, trans., and Herbert B. Foster, ed., *Dio's Roman History*. 8 vols. Cambridge, MA: Harvard University Press; London: Heinemann, 1914–1927.

Dio Chrysostom. *Dionis Prusaensis quem vocant Chrysostomum quae exstant omnia*, edited by J. von Armin. 2 vols. Berlin: Weidmann, 1893 and 1896 (repr. 1962).

Diodorus of Tarsis. *Diodori Tarsensis commentarii in psalmos*, vol. 1, edited by Jean-Marie Olivier. *Commentarii in psalmos I–L*. Turnhout: Brepols, 1980.

Dionysius of Alexandria. *The Letters and Other Remains of Dionysius of Alexandria*, edited by Charles L. Feltoe. Cambridge: University Press, 1904.

Dionysius of Halicarnassus. *Denys d'Halicarnasse*, vol. 3: *Opuscules rhétoriques*, 2nd ed., edited by Germaine Aujac and Maurice Lebel. Paris: Les Belles Lettres, 2003. *Dionysii Halicarnasei quae exstant*, vol. 6, edited by L. Radermacher and H. Usener. Leipzig: Teubner, 1929.

Dionysius Thrax. *Ars grammatica in Grammatici Graeci*, vol. 1.1, edited by G. Uhlig, pp. 5–100. Leipzig: Teubner, 1883. Reprint Hildesheim: Olms, 1965.

Egeria. *Égérie, Journal de voyage (Itinéraire): Introduction, texte critique, traduction, notes et cartes*, 2nd ed., edited by Pierre Maraval. SC 296. Paris: Cerf, 2002. Bound with *Lettre de Valérius du Bierzo sur la bienheureuse Égérie: Introduction, texte, und traduction*, edited by Manuel C. Díaz y Díaz.

Ephrem Syrus. S. P. N. *Ὁσίου Ἐφραίμ τοῦ Σύρου ἔργα*, vols. 3 and 5, edited by K. G. Phrantzolas. Thessalonica: To Perivoli tis Panagias, 1990 and 1994.

Epiphanius. *Epiphanius*, edited by Karl Holl. 3 vols. in 4. GCS 25, 31, 37. Leipzig: Hinrichs, 1915–1933.

Epistula apostolorum. Ethiopic and Coptic. C. D. G. Muller [Müller], trans. *Epistula Apostolorum* in *New Testament Apocrypha*, vol. 1: 249–284, edited by Wilhelm Schneemelcher, translated by R. McL. Wilson. Louisville: Westminster John Knox Press, 1991. *Epistula apostolorum nach dem äthiopischen und koptischen* [German trans.], translated by Hugo Duensing. Bonn: Marcus and Webster, 1925.

Eusebius. *Die Kirchengeschichte*, 2nd ed., edited by Eduard Schwartz and Theodor Mommsen. 3 vols.; GCS n.s. 6. Berlin: Akademie-Verlag, 1999. *Die Demonstratio evangelica*, edited by I. A. Heikel. GCS 23. Leipzig: Hinrichs, 1913. *Über das Leben des Kaisers Konstantin*, edited by F. Winkelmann. Berlin: Akademie, 1975. *Eusebius Werke*, vol. 7: *Die Chronik des Hieronymus*, part 1, 2nd ed., edited by R. Helm. GCS 47; Berlin: Akademie, 1956. Cordula Bandt, "Eusebius, Didascalia," in *Die Prologtexte zu den Psalmen von Origenes und Eusebius*, edited by Cordula Bandt, Franz Xaver Risch, and Barbara Villani, pp. 117–121. Berlin: De Gruyter, 2018. Cordula Bandt, "Eusebius, Periochae," in *Die Prologtexte zu den Psalmen von Origenes und Eusebius*, 122–141. Cordula Bandt, "Eusebius, *De divisione psalterii et psalmorum*," in *Die Prologtexte zu den Psalmen von Origenes und Eusebius*, 162–169. Cordula Bandt, "*De diapsalmate*," in *Die Prologtexte zu den Psalmen von Origenes und Eusebius*, 273–277. *Quaestiones évangéliques*, edited by Claudio Zamagni. SC 523. Paris: Cerf, 2008. *Eusebi Chronicorum*, vol. 2, edited by Alfred Schoene. Berlin: Weidmann, 1875.

Evagrius of Pontus. *Eulogios*—Text of Lavra Γ93 in Robert E. Sinkewicz, *Evagrius of Pontus: The Greek Ascetic Corpus*. Oxford University Press, 2003, pp. 310–333 (Appendix 2). *Évagre le Pontique. Sur les pensées*, edited by Antoine and Claire Guillaumont and Paul Géhin. SC 438. Paris: Cerf, 1998.

Galen (med.). Galen, *On the Doctrines of Hippocrates and Plato*, edited by P. H. De Lacy. Berlin: Akademie, 1978.

Gelasius of Caesarea Maritima. M. Heinemann and G. Loeschcke eds., *Gelasius, Kirchengeschichte*. GCS 28. Leipzig: Hinrichs, 1918.

Georgius Cedrenus. *Georgius Cedrenus, Compendium historiarum*, edited by Immanuel Bekker, vol. 1. Bonn: Weber, 1838.

Gerontius. *Vie de Sainte Mélanie*, edited by Denys Gorce. SC 90. Paris: Éditions du Cerf, 1962.

Gospel of Bartholomew. See *Questions of Bartholomew*.

Greek Anthology. Beckby, Hermann, ed. *Anthologia Graeca*, 2nd ed. 4 vols. Munich: Heimeran, 1965.

Gregory of Nazianzus. *Discours funèbres en l'honneur de son frère Césaire et de Basile de Césarée*, edited by F. Boulanger. Paris: Picard, 1908.

Gregory of Nyssa. *Grégoire de Nysse, Vie de Sainte Macrine*, edited by Pierre Maraval. Paris: Cerf, 1971. *Gregorii Nysseni opera*, vol. 8, Part 1, edited by Werner Jaeger, Johann P. Cavarnos, and Virginia Woods Callahan. Leiden: Brill, 1963. *Gregorii Nysseni opera*, vol. 5: *In inscriptiones psalmorum; In sextum psalmum; In ecclesiasten homiliae*, edited by James A. McDonough and Paul Alexander. Leiden: Brill, 1962. *Gregorii Nysseni opera*, vol. 9: *Sermones*, Part 1, edited by Günther

Heil, Adrian Van Heck, Ernest Gebhardt, and Andreas Spira. Leiden: Brill, 1967. *Gregorii Nysseni Opera*, vol. 10/1: *Sermones*, Part 2, edited by Günther Heil, Johann P. Cavarnos, and Otto Lendle. Leiden: Brill, 1990. Friedhelm Mann, *Die Weihnachtspredigt Gregors von Nyssa: Überlieferungsgeschichte und Text*. Diss. Münster, 1975.

[Hephaestion.] *Peri poiēmatōn*. In *Hephaestionis Enchiridion*, edited by Maximilian Consbruch, pp. 62–73. Leipzig: Teubner, 1906.

Hexapla. See Origen.

Hilary of Poitiers. *Sancti Hilarii Pictaviensis Episcopi Tractatus super Psalmos*, edited by Jean Doignon. 3 vols. CCL 61, 61A, 61B; Turnhout: Brepols, 1997–2009.

Hippolytus. *Hippolyt's kleinere exegetische und homiletische Schriften*, edited by H. Achelis. GCS 1.2; Leipzig: Hinrichs, 1897. See also *Homily on the Psalms*; *Apostolic Tradition*.

Historia acephala. See Athanasius.

Homily on the Psalms. Pierre Nautin, ed., *Le dossier d'Hippolyte et de Méliton dans les florilèges dogmatiques et chez les historiens modernes*. Paris: Cerf, 1953.

Iamblichus. *Iamblichi de vita Pythagorica*, edited by L. Deubner, edited and corrected by U. Klein. Stuttgart: Teubner, 1975.

Ignatius. *Ignace d'Antioche; Polycarpe de Smyrne; Lettres; Martyre de Polycarpe*, edited by P. T. Camelot. Paris: Cerf, 1969. Pseudo-Ignatius (*recensio longior*): *Patres apostolici*, vol. 2, 2nd ed., edited by Franz Diekamp and Franz X. Funk. Tübingen: Laupp, 1913.

Index to the Festal letters of Athanasius. See Athanasius.

Isidore of Seville. *Isidori hispalensis episcopi Etymologiarum sive originum*, edited by Wallace M. Lindsay. Oxford: Clarendon, 1911.

Jerome. *Sancti Eusebii Hieronymi Opera*, sect. 1, part 1: *Epistolae I–LXX*, edited by Isidor Hilberg. CSEL 54. Vienna: Tempsky, 1910. [Jerome], *Opera exegetica* 2: *Commentariorum in Esaiam*, edited by M. Adriaen. 2 vols. CCL 73; Turnhout: Brepols, 1963. *Préfaces de la Bible latine*, edited by Donatien de Bruyne. Namur, Belgium: Godenne, 1920.

John Chrysostom. *Sancti patris nostri Joannis Chrysostomi . . . Interpretatio omnium epistularum Paulinarum*, edited by F. F. [Frederick Field]. 7 vols. Oxford: Parker, 1845–1862. *Sancti patris nostri Joannis Chrysostomi . . . Homiliae in Matthaeum*, edited by Frederick Field. Oxford: Parker, 1839. [Johannes Chrysostomos] *À Théodore*, edited by Jean Dumortier. SC 117. Paris: Éditions du Cerf, 1966. *Jean Chrysostom, Discours sur Babylas; Homélie sur Babylas*, edited and translated by Margaret A. Schatkin, Cécile Blanc, Bernard Grillet, and Jean-Noël Guinot. Paris: Cerf, 1990.

Julian ("the Apostate"). *L'Empereur Julien, Oeuvres complètes*, edited by J. Bidez, vol. 1, part 2: *Lettres et fragments*, 3rd ed. Paris: Les Belles Lettres, 1972.

Justin Martyr. *Justin, Philosopher and Martyr: Apologies*, edited by Denis Minns and Paul Parvis. Oxford: Oxford University Press, 2009.

Letters to Virgins. See Pseudo-Clementine *Letters to Virgins*.

Liber Pontificalis. *Le Liber Pontificalis: Texte, Introduction et Commentaire*, vol. 1, 2nd ed., edited by Louis Duchesne. Paris: Boccard, 1955.

Life of Adam and Eve (*Apocalypse of Moses*). *La Vie grecque d'Adam et d'Eve*, edited by D. Bertrand. Paris: Adrien Maisonneuve, 1987.

Life of Auxentius. BHG 199. *Vita sancti Auxentii*, ed. Paolo Varalda. Allessandria: Edizioni dell'Orso, 2017.

Life of Macarius (Bohairic). *Histoire des monastères de la Basse-Égypte*, edited by Émile Amélineau. Paris: Leroux, 1894.

Life of Pachomius. Coptic: *Sancti Pachomii vita bohairice scripta*, edited by L. Théophile Lefort. 2 vols. CSCO 89 and 107. Paris: Reipublicae, 1925 and 1936. Greek: *Sancti Pachomii vitae Graecae*, edited by François Halkin. Brussels: Société des Bollandistes, 1932. *Le corpus athénien de saint Pachôme*, François Halkin. Geneva: Cramer, 1982.

Liturgy of Saint James. *The Greek Liturgies, Chiefly from Original Authorities*, edited by Charles A. Swainson. Cambridge: Cambridge University Press, 1884.

Livy. *Titi Livi Ab urbe condita*, edited by Robert S. Conway et al. Oxford: Clarendon, 1955–.

Longus. *Longus, Pastorales (Daphnis et Chloé)*, edited by Georges Dalmeyda. Paris: Belles Lettres, 1934.

Lucian the Priest (and Avitus of Braga). S. Vanderlinden, "Revelatio Sancti Stephani (BHL 7850–56)." *Revue des Études Byzantines* 6 (1946): 178–217.

Lucian of Samosata. *Luciani Opera*, edited by M. D. Macleod. 4 vols. Oxford: Clarendon, 1972–1987.

Lucretius. *Titus Lucretius Carus, De rerum natura, libri VI*, edited by Marcus Deufert. Berlin: De Gruyter, 2019.

Macarius, life of. See *Life of Macarius*.

Mark the Deacon. *Marc le Diacre, Vie de Porphyre, évêque de Gaza*, edited by H. Grégoire and M.-A. Kugener. Paris: Les Belles Lettres, 1930.

Martial. *M. Valerii Martialis, Epigrammaton liber quintus*, edited by Alberto Canobbio. Naples: Loffredo, 2011.

Martianus Capella. *Martianus Capella*, edited by James Willis. Leipzig; Teubner, 1983.

Maximus of Tyre. *Maximus Tyrius, Dissertationes*, edited by Michael B. Trapp. Stuttgart and Leipzig: Teubner, 1994.

Mishnah. *Mishnayoth* 2nd ed., edited by Philip Blackman. 7 vols. Hebrew with English translation. New York: The Judaica Press, 1963.

Muratorian Fragment (Canon). See Canon Muratori.

Niceta of Remesiana, *De utililitate hymnorum*. C. H. Turner, "Niceta of Remesiana II: Introduction and Text of *De psalmodiae bono*," *Journal of Theological Studies* 24 (1923): 225–252.

Nicomachus of Gerasa (math.). *Harmonicum enchiridion* in *Musici scriptores graecae*, edited by Karl Jan, pp. 235–265. Hildesheim: Olms, 1962 (reprint of 1895 edition).

Ordo monasterii. Donatien de Bruyne, "La première règle de saint Benoît," *Revue Bénédictine* 42 (1930): 316–342.

Ordo romanus primus (I). Andrieu, Michel, *Les ordines romani du haut moyen age*, vol. 2: *Les textes (Ordines I–XIII)*. Louvain: Spicilegium Sacrum Lovaniense, 1948.

Origen. *Origène: Homélies sur les Nombres*, edited by W. A. Baehrens, revised by Louis Doutreleau. 3 vols. SC 415, 442, 461. Paris: Cerf, 1996–2001. *Origenis*

Hexaplorum quae supersunt, edited by Frederick Field. 2 vols. Oxford: Clarendon, 1875. *Origenes Werke*, edited by Paul Koetschau et al. GCS 2–3, 6, 10, 22, 29–30, 33, 35, 38, 40, 41; Leipzig: Hinrichs, 1899–1955. *Origène, Commentaire sur saint Jean*, edited by Cécile Blanc. 5 vols. SC 120, 157, 222, 290, 385. Paris: Cerf, 1966–1992. *Origenes Werke*, vol. 13: *Die neuen Psalmenhomilien: Eine kritische Edition des Codex Monacensis Graecus 314*, edited by L. Perrone et al. GCS NF 19. Berlin: De Gruyter, 2015. Dubious: *Fragmenta in Psalmos 1–150* in J. B. Pitra, ed., *Analecta sacra spicilegio Solesmensi parata*, vol. 2 (pp. 444–483) and vol. 3 (pp. 1–364). Paris: Tusculum, 1883 and 1884.

Pachomian literature. *Oeuvres de S. Pachôme et de ses disciples*, edited by L. Théophile Lefort. 2 vols. CSCO 159 and 160. Louvain: Durbecq, 1956. Amand Boon, ed., *Pachomiana latina: Règle et Épitres de s. Pachome, Épitre de s. Théodore et 'Liber' de S. Orsiesius, texte latin de S. Jérôme*. Louvain: Bureaux de la Revue, 1932.

Pachomius, life of. See *Life of Pachomius*.

Palladius. *Palladio, La storia Lausiaca*, edited by G. J. M. Bartelink; introduction by Christine Mohrmann; Italian translation by Marino Barchiesi. Milan: Valla, 1974. *Palladii Dialogus de vita S. Joannis Chrysostomi*, edited by Paul R. Coleman. Cambridge: Cambridge University Press, 1928.

Passion of Matthew (*Passio Matthaei/Martyrium Matthei*). *Acta Apostolorum*, vol. 2/1, edited by Maximillian Bonnet, pp. 217–262. Leipzig: Mendelssohn, 1898.

Paul Evergetinus. Παύλος Ο *Ἑυεργετινός, Συναγωγή των θεόφθογγων ῥημάτων και διδασκαλίων των ἁγιων και θεοφόρων και ἁγίων πατέρων* [Paul Evergetinus, *A Collection of Inspired Words and Teachings of the Holy and God-bearing Fathers*], edited by Demetrios G. Takos. Venice, 1783; reprint, Athens, 1900. This work was unavailable to me; I quote it from Hausherr, *Penthos*.

Paulinus of Milan (Paulinus the Deacon). Marco Navoni, ed. and trans., *Paolino di Milano, Vita di Sant'Ambrogio: La prima biografia del patrono di Milano*. Milan: Edizione San Paolo, 1996.

Paulinus of Nola. *Sancti Pontii Meropii Paulini Nolani carmina*, 2nd ed., edited by Wilhelm Hartel and Margit Kamptner. CSEL 30. Verlag der Österreichischen Akademie der Wissenschaften, 1999.

Pervigilium Veneris. *Pervigilium Veneris*, edited and translated by Laurence Catlow. Brussels: Latomus, 1980.

Petronius Arbiter. Konrad Müller, ed., *Petronii Arbitri Satyricon reliquiae*, 4th ed. Berlin: De Gruyter, 1995.

Philodemus. *Philodème de Gadara, Sur la musique, Livre IV*, edited and translated by Daniel Delattre. 2 vols. Paris: Les Belles Lettres, 2007.

Philostratus. *Flavii Philostrati Opera*, edited by Carl L. Kayser. 2 vols. Leipzig: Teubner, 1870–1871. Olearius page numbers: *Philostratorum quae supersunt omnia*, edited by Gottfried Olearius. Leipzig: Fritsch, 1709.

Phrynichus Arabius (soph.). *Phrynichi sophistae praeparatio sophistica*, edited by Jean de Borries (Johann von Borries). Leipzig: Teubner, 1911.

Physiologus (*redactio prima*). *Physiologus*, edited by Francesco Sbordone. Milan: Dante Alighieri-Albrighi, Segati, 1936. Reprint Hildesheim: Olms, 1976.

Plato. Simon R. Slings, ed., *Platonis Rempublicam*. Oxford: Oxford University Press, 2003.

Pliny. *C. Plini Caecili Secundi Epistularum libri decem*, edited by R. A. B. Mynors. Oxford: Clarendon, 1963.

Plutarch. *Plutarchi moralia*, vol. 4, edited by Kurt Hubert. Leipzig: Teubner, 1938.

Pseudo-Clementine *Letters to Virgins*. Franz Diekamp, ed. *Patres apostolici*, vol. 2/2, pp. 1–49. Tübingen: Laupp, 1913. Jan Theodoor Beelen, ed., *Sancti patris nostri Clementis Romani Epistolae binae de virginitate*. Leuven: C. J. Fonteyn, 1856.

Pseudo-Ignatius. See Ignatius.

Pseudo-Zachariah Rhetor. *Historia ecclesiastica Zachariae rhetori vulgo adscripta*, edited by Ernest W. Brooks, ed. (Syriac) and trans. (Latin). CSCO 83–84 and 87–88. Paris: Reipublicae, 1919–1924. *The Syriac Chronicle Known as That of Zachariah of Mitylene*, translated by F. J. Hamilton and E. W. Brooks. London: Methuen, 1899. *The Chronicle of Pseudo-Zachariah Rhetor: Church and War in Late Antiquity*, edited by Geoffrey Greatrex, translated by Robert R. Phenix, Cornelia Horn, with Sebastian P. Brock and Witold Witakowski. Liverpool: Liverpool University Press, 2011.

Ptolemy. See Claudius Ptolemy.

Questions of Bartholomew (*Gospel of Bartholomew*). G. Nathanael Bonwetsch, "Die apokryphen Fragen des Bartholomäus," *Nachrichten von der königlichen Gesellschaft der Wissenschaften zu Göttingen, Philologisch-historische Klasse*, pp. 1–42. Göttingen: Horstmann, 1897. Latin version: Umberto Moricca, "Un Nuovo Testo dell' 'Evangelo di Bartolomeo'," *Revue biblique* 30 (1921): 481–516; "Un Nuovo Testo dell' 'Evangelo di Bartolomeo' (fin.)," *Revue biblique* 31 (1922): 20–30.

Rufinus of Aquileia. In *Eusebius Werke*, vol. 2/2: *Die lateinische Übersetzung des Rufinus* [pp. 957–1040]; *Die Bücher VI–X über die Märtyrer in Palästina*, edited by Eduard Schwarz. Leipzig: Hinrichs, 1908.

Rule of the Master (*Regula magistri*). Adalbert de Vogüé, *La règle du maître: texte, traduction et notes*. 2 vols. SC 105 and 106. Paris: Cerf, 1964.

Rule of Paul and Stephen. *Regula Pauli et Stephani: Edició critica i comentari*, edited by J. Evangelista Vilanova. Montserrat: Abadia de Montserrat, 1959.

Sextus Empiricus. *Sexti Empirici opera*, vol. 3: *Adversus mathematicos, libros I–VI*, 2nd ed., edited by Jürgen Mau. Leipzig: Teubner, 1961.

Sibylline Oracles. *Die Oracula Sibyllina*, edited by Johannes Geffcken. Leipzig: Hinrichs, 1902.

Sidonius Apollinarus. *Sidonius, Letters: Books 3–9*, translated by W. B. Anderson. Cambridge: Harvard University Press, 1965.

Sozomen. Günther C. Hansen, ed. and trans., *Sozomenos, Historia ecclesiastica / Kirchengeschichte*. 4 vols. FS 73. Turnhout: Brepols, 2004; *Sozomenus Kirchengeschichte*, edited by Joseph Bidez and Günther C. Hansen. GCS 50. Berlin: Akademie, 1960.

Socrates of Constantinople. *Sokrates, Kirchengeschichte*, 2nd ed., edited by Günther C. Hansen and Manja Širinjan. GCS NF 1. Berlin: Akademie, 1995.

Statuta ecclesiae antiqua. *Concilia Galliae, A. 314–A. 506*, edited by Charles Munier, pp. 162–188. CCL 148. Brepols: Turnhout, 1963.

Strabo. *Strabons Geographika*, edited by Stefan Radt. Göttingen: Vandenhoeck & Ruprecht, 2002–2010.

Suetonius. C. *Suetonii Tranquilli Opera: Editio minor*, vol. 1. edited by Maximilian Ihm. Stuttgart: Teubner, 1908.

Syrian martyriology. See William Wright under Modern Literature and Translations.

Terullian. *Quinti Septimi Florentis Tertulliani Opera*, edited by Eligius Dekkers et al. 2 vols. CCL 1 and 2. Brepols: Turnhout, 1954.

Testament of the Lord. The Synodicon in the West Syrian Tradition, edited by Arthur Vööbus. CSCO 367–368 and 375–376. Louvain: Secrétariet du CorpusSCO, 1975–1976. *Le Testamentum Domini éthiopien*, edited by Robert Beylot. Louvain: Peeters, 1984.

Themistius. *Themistii orationes quae supersunt*, vol. 2, ed. H. Schenkl, G. Downey, and A. F. Norman. Leipzig: Teubner, 1971.

Theodoret of Cyr. *Theodoret, Kirchengeschichte*, 3rd ed., edited by Léon Parmentier, Felix Scheidweiler, and Günther C. Hansen. GCS NF 5. Berlin: Akademie, 1998. *Théodoret de Cyr. Histoire des moines de Syrie: Histoire Philothée.* 2 vols., edited by P. Canivet and Alice Leroy-Molinghen. SC 234 and 257. Paris: Cerf, 1977 and 1979. *Théodoret de Cyr, Thérapeutique des maladies helléniques*, edited by P. Canivet. 2 vols. SC 57. Paris: Cerf, 1958. *Θεοδωρήτου ἐπισκόπου πόλεως Κύρρου πρὸς τὰς ἐπενεχθεἰσας αὐτῷ ἐπερωτήσεις παρά τινος τὸν ἐξ Αἰγύπτου ἐπίσκοπον ἀποκρίσεις*, edited by A. Papadopoulos-Kerameus. St. Petersburg: Kirschbaum, 1895.

Theodosian Code. Theodor Mommsen and Paul M. Meyer, eds. *Theodosiani libri XVI cum constitutionibus Sirmondianis et leges Novellae ad Theodosianum pertinentes.* Berlin: Weidmann, 1905.

Varro, Marcus Terrentius. *Marcus Porcius Cato, On Agriculture; Marcus Terrentius Varro, On Agriculture*, with an English translation by William D. Hooper, revised by Harrison B. Ash. Cambridge: Harvard University Press, 1935.

Virginitate (De virginitate). Separate works by Pseudo-Athanasius and Ambrose, not to be confused with *De virginibus* by Ambrose.

Vulgate. *Biblia Sacra iuxta vulgatam versionem*, 2nd ed., edited by Boniface Fischer, revised by Robert Weber. 2 vols. Stuttgart: Würtembergische Bibelanstalt, 1969.

Zachariah Rhetor/Zachariah of Mitylene. See Pseudo-Zachariah Rhetor.

MODERN LITERATURE

Abbate, Carolyn, and Roger Parker. *A History of Opera: The Last Four Hundred Years.* Penguin, 2012.

Albrecht, Ruth. *Das Leben der heiligen Makrina auf dem Hintergrund der Thekla-Traditionen.* Vandenhoeck & Ruprecht, 1986.

Allen, Pauline, and Wendy Mayer. "The Thirty-Four Homilies on Hebrews: The Last Series Delivered by Chrysostom in Constantinople?" *Byzantion* 65 (1995): 309–348.

Attridge, Harold W. "Giving Voice to Jesus: The Use of the Psalms in the New Testament." In *Psalms in Community: Jewish and Christian Textual, Liturgical, and Artistic Traditions*, edited by Harold W. Attridge and Margot E. Fassler. Society of Biblical Literature, 2003.

Auf der Maur, H. J. *Das Psalmenverständnis des Ambrosius von Mailand*. Brill, 1977.

Bailey, Terence. *Antiphon and Psalm in the Ambrosian Office*. Institute of Mediaeval Music, 1994.

Barker, Andrew. *Greek Musical Writings*, vol. 1: *The Musician and His Art*. Cambridge University Press, 1984.

Barker, Andrew. *Greek Musical Writings*, vol. 2: *Harmonic and Acoustic Theory*. Cambridge University Press, 1989.

Barnes, Timothy D. *Tertullian: A Historical and Literary Study*. Oxford University Press, 1971.

Barnes, Timothy D. *Constantine and Eusebius*. Harvard University Press, 1981.

Barnes, Timothy D. *Athanasius and Constantius: Theology and Politics in the Constantinian Empire*. Harvard University Press, 1993.

Bauckham, Richard. *The Jewish World around the New Testament*. Mohr Siebeck, 2008.

Beard, Mary. *The Roman Triumph*. Harvard University Press, 2007.

Berger, Albrecht. "Imperial and Ecclesiastical Processions in Constantinople." In *Byzantine Constantinople: Monuments, Topography, and Everyday Life*, edited by Nevra Necipoğlu. Brill, 2001.

Bergmeier, Roland. "Der Stand der Gottesfreunde: Zu Philos Schrift 'Über die kontemplative Lebensform'." *Bijdragen: International Journal in Philosophy and Theology* 63 (2002): 46–70.

Berkovitz, Abraham J. *A Life of Psalms in Jewish Late Antiquity*. University of Pennsylvania Press, 2023.

Bidez, Joseph. *La vie de l'empereur Julian*. Belles Lettres, 1965.

Boddens Hosang, F. J. E. *Establishing Boundaries: Jewish-Christian Relations in Early Council Texts and the Writings of Church Fathers*. Brill, 2000.

Bosanquet, Robert C. "The Palaikastro Hymn of the Kouretes." *The Annual of the British School at Athens* 15 (1908/1909): 339–356.

Bowes, Kim. *Private Worship, Public Values, and Religious Change in Late Antiquity*. Cambridge University Press, 2008.

Binder, Donald D. *Into the Temple Courts: The Place of the Synagogues in the Second Temple Period*. Press, 1999.

Boersma, Hans. *Embodiment and Virtue in Gregory of Nyssa: An Anagogical Approach*. Oxford University Press, 2013.

Bovon, François, and Pierre Geoltrain, eds. *Écrits apocryphes chrétiens*, vol. 1. Gallimard, 1997.

Bowie, Ewen. "Choral Performances." In *Greeks on Greekness: Viewing the Greek Past under the Roman Empire*, edited by David Konstan and Suzanne Saïd. Cambridge University Press, 2006.

Bradshaw, Paul F. *The Apostolic Tradition Reconstructed: A Text for Students*. [London]: Alcuin Club and the Group for the Renewal of Worship, 2021.

Bradshaw, Paul F., ed. *The Canons of Hippolytus*, with an English translation by Carol Bebawi. Grove Books, 1989.

Bradshaw, Paul F. *Daily Prayer in the Early Church: A Study of the Origin and Early Development of the Divine Office*. Oxford University Press, 1982.

Bradshaw, Paul F. "The Origins of Easter." In *Passover and Easter: Origin and History to Modern Times*, edited by Paul F. Bradshaw and Lawrence A. Hoffman. University of Notre Dame Press, 1999.

Bradshaw, Paul F., Maxwell E. Johnson, and L. Edward Phillips. *The Apostolic Tradition: A Commentary*. Fortress, 2002.

Bradshaw, Paul F., and Maxwell E. Johnson. *The Origins of Feasts, Fasts, and Seasons in Early Christianity*. SPCK, 2011.

Brakke, David. "The Authenticity of the Ascetic Athanasiana." *Orientalia* 63 (1994): 17–56.

Brakke, David, trans. *Evagrius of Pontus Talking Back: A Monastic Handbook for Combating Demons*. Liturgical Press, 2009.

Braun, Joachim. *Music in Ancient Israel/Palestine: Archaeological, Written, and Comparative Sources*, translated by Douglas W. Stott. Eerdmans, 2002.

Bremer, Jan M. "Greek Hymns." In *Faith, Hope, and Worship: Aspects of Religious Mentality in the Ancient World*, edited by H. S. Versnel. Brill, 1981.

Brent, Allen. *Hippolytus and the Roman Church in the Third Century: Communities in Tension before the Emergence of a Monarch-Bishop*. Brill, 1995.

Brown, Peter. *Augustine of Hippo: A Biography*. University of California Press, 2000.

Brown, Peter. *The Cult of the Saints: Its Rise and Function in Latin Christianity*. University of Chicago Press, 2015.

Brennecke, Hanns Christof. *Studien zur Geschichte der Homöer: Der Osten bis zum Ende der homöischen Reichskirche*. Mohr Siebeck, 1988.

Brightman, Frank E. *Liturgies Eastern and Western*, vol. 1, *Eastern*. Oxford: Clarendon, 1896.

Brubaker, Leslie. "The Chalke Gate, The Construction of the Past, and the Trier Ivory." *Byzantine and Modern Greek Studies* 23 (1999): 258–285.

Buchinger, Harald G. "Die älteste erhaltene christliche Psalmenhomilie: Zu Verwendung und Verständnis des Psalters bei Hippolyt (Zweiter Teil)." *Trierer Theologische Zeitschrift* 104 (1995): 272–298.

Buchinger, Harald G. "Early Eucharist in Transition? A Fresh Look at Origin." In *Jewish and Christian Liturgy and Worship: New Insights into Its History and Interaction*, edited by Albert Gerhards and Clemens Leonhard. Brill, 2007.

Buchinger, Harald G. "Die Bedeutung der Auferstehung für Termin, Gestalt und Gehalt der ältesten Osterfeier." In *"If Christ has not been raised. . .": Studies on the Reception of the Resurrection Stories and the Belief in the Resurrection in the Early Church*, edited by Joseph Verheyden, Andreas Merkt, and Tobias Nicklas. Vandenhoeck & Ruprecht, 2016.

Buchinger, Harald G. "Psalmodie als Sakrament: Johannes Chrysostomus über den täglichen Abendpsalm 140(141)." In *Wort des lebendigen Gottes: Liturgie und Bibel*, edited by Alexander Zefaß and Ansgar Franz. Naar/Francke/Attempto, 2016.

Buchinger, Harald G. "Breaking the Fast: The Central Moment of the Paschal Celebration in Historical Context and Diachronic Perspective." In *Sanctifying*

Texts, Transforming Rituals: Encounters in Liturgical Studies: Essays in Honour of Gerard A. M. Rouwhorst, edited by Paul van Geest, Marcel Poorthuis, and Els Rose. Brill, 2017.

Buchinger, Harald G. "Psalm (liturgisch)." In *Reallexikon für Antike und Christentum*, vol. 28, edited by Georg Schöllgen, Heinzgerd Brakmann, and Therese Fuhre. Hiersemann, 2017.

Buchinger, Harald, David Hiley, and Sabine Reichert, eds. *Prozessionen und ihre Gesänge in der mittelalterlichen Stadt: Gestalt, Hermeneutik, und Repräsentation*. Schnell und Steiner, 2017.

Burgess, Richard W. "The Passio S. Artemii, Philostorgius, and the Dates of the Invention and Translations of the Relics of Sts. Andrew and Luke." *Analecta Bollandiana* 121 (2003): 5–36.

Burn, Andrew E. *Niceta of Remesiana: His Life and Works*. Cambridge University Press, 1905.

Burns, Paul C. *A Model for Christian Life: Hilary of Poitiers' Commentary on the Psalms*. The Catholic University of America Press, 2012.

Burrus, Virginia. "Is Macrina a Woman? Gregory of Nyssa's Dialogue on the Soul and the Resurrection." In *The Blackwell Companion to Postmodern Theology*, edited by Graham Ward. Blackwell, 2001.

Cain, Andrew. *Jerome and the Monastic Clergy: A Commentary on Letter 52 to Nepotian, with an Introduction, Text, and Translation*. Brill, 2013.

Cameron, Alan. *The Last Pagans of Rome*. Oxford University Press, 2011.

Carter, Michael J., and Jonathan Edmondson. "Spectacle in Rome, Italy, and the Provinces." In *The Oxford Handbook of Roman Epigraphy*, edited by Christer Bruun and Jonathan Edmondson. Oxford University Press, 2015.

Cavallera, Ferdinand. *Le schisme d'Antioche (IVe–Ve siècle)*. Picard, 1905.

Cerrato, J. A. *Hippolytus between East and West: The Commentaries and the Provenance of the Corpus*. Oxford University Press, 2002.

Chadwick, Owen. *John Cassian*. Cambridge University Press, 1968.

Chaniotis, Angelos. "Acclamations as a Form of Religious Communication." In *Die Religion des Imperium Romanum: Koine und Konfrontationen*, edited by Hubert Cancik and Jörg Rüpke. Mohr Siebeck, 2009.

Chase, Nathan. "Another Look at the Daily Office in the 'Apostolic Tradition.'" *Studia Liturgica* 49 (2019): 5–25.

Chatterjee, Paroma. "Iconoclasm's Legacy: Interpreting the Trier Ivory." *Art Bulletin* 100 (2018): 28–47.

Clark, Elizabeth A. *Melania the Younger: From Rome to Jerusalem*. Oxford University Press, 2021.

Clarke, G. W. "An Illiterate Lector?" *Zeitschrift für Papyrologie und Epigraphik* 57 (1984): 103–104.

Clarke, M. L. *Higher Education in the Ancient World*. Routledge and Kegan Paul, 1971.

Claussen, M. A. "Pagan Rebellion and Christian Apologetics in Fourth-Century Rome: The Consultationes Zacchaei et Apollonii." *Journal of Ecclesiastical History* 46 (1995): 589–614.

Colish, Marcia L. "Why the Portiana? Reflections on the Milanese Basilica Crisis of 386." *Journal of Early Christian Studies* 10 (2002): 361–372.

Collart, Paul. "Psaumes et amulettes." *Aegyptus* 14 (1934): 463–467.

Connolly, R. Hugh. "The Use of the *Didache* in the *Didascalia*." *Journal of Theological Studies* 24 (1923): 147–157.

Corcoran, Simon, and Benet Salway. "The Newly Identified Greek Fragment of the Testamentum Domini." *Journal of Theological Studies* 62 (2011): 118–135.

Cosgrove, Charles H. "Clement of Alexandria and Early Christian Music." *Journal of Early Christian Studies* 14 (2006): 255–282.

Cosgrove, Charles H. "Song at the Christian Cena in Tertullian's Carthage (Apologeticum 39.18)." *Ephemeides Liturgicae* 131 (2017): 162–182.

Cosgrove, Charles H. "Word and Table: The Origins of a Liturgical Sequence." *Vigiliae Christianae* 74 (2020): 357–373.

Cosgrove, Charles H. "Semi-Lyrical Reading of Greek Poetry in Late Antiquity." *Harvard Studies in Classical Philology* 111 (2021): 463–482.

Cosgrove, Charles H. *Music at Social Meals in Greek and Roman Antiquity: From the Archaic Period to the Age of Augustine*. Cambridge University Press, 2023.

Cosgrove, Charles H., and Mary C. Meyer. "Melody and Word Accent Relationships in Ancient Greek Musical Documents: The Pitch Height Rule." *Journal of Hellenic Studies* 126 (2006): 66–81.

Cribiore, Raffaella. *Writing, Teachers, and Students in Graeco-Roman Egypt*. Scholars Press, 1996.

Cribiore, Raffaella. *Gymnastics of the Mind: Greek Education in Hellenistic and Roman Egypt*. Princeton University Press, 2001.

Cumming, Charles G. *The Assyrian and Hebrew Hymns of Praise*. Columbia University Press, 1934.

Dale, Amy M. *The Lyric Metres of Greek Drama*. Cambridge University Press, 1948.

D'Alessio, Giambattista. "Performance, Tradition, and the Loss of Hellenistic Lyric Poetry." In *Imagining Reperformance in Ancient Culture: Studies in the Traditions of Drama and Lyric*, edited by Richard Hunter and Anna Uhlig. Cambridge University Press, 2017.

D'Angour, Armand J. "The New Music—So What's New?" In *Rethinking Revolutions through Ancient Greece*, edited by Simon Goldhill and Robin Osborne. Cambridge University Press, 2006.

Davril, Anselme. "La psalmodie chez les Pères du desert." *Collectanea Cisterciensia* 49 (1987): 132–139.

de Santos Otero, Aurelios. "Later Acts of Apostles." In *New Testament Apocrypha*, vol. 2: *Writings Relating to the Apostles, Apocalypses, and Related Subjects*, revised edition, Wilhelm Schneemelcher, English translation edited by R. Mcl. Wilson. Clarke, 1992.

de Vogüé, Adalbert. "Psalmodier n'est pas prier." *Ecclesia Orans* 6 (1989): 7–32.

Dickey, Eleanor. *The Colloquia of the Hermeneumata Pseudodositheana*, 2 vols. Cambridge University Press, 2012 and 2015.

Dix, Gregory. *The Shape of the Liturgy*, 2nd ed. Dacre, 1945.

Dobbs-Allsopp, F. W. "Space, Line, and the Individual Written Poem in Texts from the Judean Desert." In *Puzzling Out the Past: Studies in Northwest Semitic Languages and Literatures in Honor of Bruce Zuckerman*, edited by Marilyn J. Lundberg, Steven Fine, and Wayne T. Pitard. Brill, 2012.

Dobbs-Allsopp, F. W. *On Biblical Poetry*. Oxford University Press, 2015.

Downey, Glanville. "The Shrines of St. Babylas at Antioch and Daphne." In *Antioch-on-the-Orontes*, vol. 2: *The Excavations, 1933–1936*, edited by Richard Stillwell. Princeton University Press, 1938.

Duchesne, Louis. *Origines du culte chrétien: Étude sur la liturgie latine avant Charlemagne*, 3rd ed. Fontemoing, 1902.

Duensing, Hugo, ed. "Die dem Klemens von Rom zugeschriebenen Briefe über die Jungfräulichkeit." *Zeitschrift für Kirchengeschichte* 63 (1950/1951): 166–188.

Driscoll, Jeremy. "Penthos and Tears in Evagrius Ponticus." *Studia Monastica* 36 (1994): 147-163.

Duncan, Julie A. "Excerpted Texts of 'Deuteronomy' at Qumran." *Revue de Qumran* 18 (1997): 43–62.

Dugmore, Clifton W. *The Influence of the Synagogue upon the Divine Office*. Oxford University Press, 1944.

Dunn, Geoffrey D. *Tertullian*. Routledge, 2004.

Dunn, James D. G. *The Epistles to the Colossians and to Philemon: A Commentary on the Greek Text*. Eerdmans, 1996.

Dyer, Joseph. "Augustine and the 'Hymni ante oblationem': the Earliest Offertory Chants?" *Revue des études Augustiniennes* 27 (1981): 85-99.

Dyer, Joseph. "The Singing of Psalms in the Early-Medieval Office." *Speculum* 64 (1989): 535–578. Reprinted in *Chant and Its Origins*, edited by Thomas F. Kelly. Routledge, 2009.

Dyer, Joseph. "The Introit and Communion Psalmody of Old Roman Chant." In *Chant and Its Peripheries: Essays in Honour of Terence Bailey*, edited by Bryan Gillingham and Paul Merkley. The Institute of Medieval Music, 1998.

Dyer, Joseph. "The Desert, the City and Psalmody in the Late Fourth Century." In *Western Plainchant in the First Millennium: Studies in the Medieval Liturgy and Its Music*, edited by Sean Gallagher et al. Ashgate, 2003.

Dyer, Joseph. "*Psalmi ante sacrificium* and the Origin of the Introit." *Plainsong and Medieval Music* 20 (2011): 91–121.

Ehrman, Bart D. *Forgery and Counterforgery: The Use of Literary Deceit in Early Christian Polemics*. Oxford University Press, 2013.

Engberg-Pedersen, Troels. "Philo's De vita contemplativa as a Philosopher's Dream." *Journal for the Study of Judaism* 30 (1999): 40–64.

Elliott, J. K., trans. *The Apocryphal New Testament: A Collection of Apocryphal Christian Literature in an English Translation Based on M. R. James*. Oxford University Press, 1993.

Elm, Susanna. *'Virgins of God': The Making of Asceticism in Late Antiquity*. Clarendon Press, 1994.

Eshel, Esther. "Apotropaic Prayers in the Second Temple Period." In *Liturgical Perspectives: Prayer and Poetry in Light of the Dead Sea Scrolls*, edited by Esther G. Chazon. Brill, 2003.

Flint, Peter W. *The Dead Sea Psalms Scroll and the Book of Psalms*. Brill, 1997.

Foley, Edward. "The Cantor in Historical Perspective." *Worship* 56 (1982): 194–213; revised in Edward Foley, *Ritual Music: Studies in Liturgical Musicology*. Pastoral, 1995.

Fortescue, Adrian. "Gradual." In *The Catholic Encyclopedia*, vol. 6, edited by Charles G. Herbermann. Encyclopedia Press, 1913.

Franz, Ansgar. "Die Tagzeitenliturgie der Mailänder Kirche im 4. Jahrhundert: Ein Beitrag zur Geschichte Kathedraloffiziums im Westen." *Archiv für Liturgiewissenschaft* 34 (1992): 23–83.

Frøyshov, Stig Simeon R. "The Cathedral-Monastic Distinction Revisited. Part 1: Was Egyptian Desert Liturgy a Pure Monastic Office?" *Studia Liturgica* 37 (2007): 198–216.

Frøyshov, Stig Simeon R. "The Early Development of the Liturgical Eight-Mode System in Jerusalem." *St. Vladimir's Theological Quarterly* 51 (2007): 139–178.

Füglister, Notker. "Die Verwendung und das Verständnis der Psalmen und des Psalters um die Zeitenwende." In *Beiträge zur Psalmenforschung: Psalm 2 und 22*, edited by Josef Schreiner. Echter, 1988.

Furley, William D., and Jan M. Bremer. *Greek Hymns: Selected Cult Songs from the Archaic to the Hellenistic Period*, vol. 1: *The Texts in Translation*. Mohr Siebeck, 2001; vol. 2: *Greek Texts and Commentary*. Mohr Siebeck, 2001.

Garitte, Gérard. "Un fragment grec attribué à S. Antoine l'Ermite." *Bulletin de l'Institut historique belge de Rome* 20 (1939): 165–170.

Goodrich, Richard J. *Contextualizing Cassian: Aristocrats, Asceticism, and Reformation in Fifth-Century Gaul*. Oxford University Press, 2007.

Gnilka, Joachim. *Der Epheserbrief*. Herder, 1971.

Griffith, Sidney H. "Setting Right the Church of Syria: Saint Ephraem's Hymns Against Heresies." In *The Limits of Ancient Christianity: Essays on Late Antique Thought and Culture in Honor of R. A. Markus*, edited by William E. Klingshirn and Mark Vessey. University of Michigan Press, 1999.

Gwynn, David M. *The Eusebians: The Polemic of Athanasius of Alexandria and the Construction of the 'Arian Controversy'*. Oxford University Press, 2007.

Gwynn, David M. *Athanasius of Alexandria: Bishop, Theologian, Ascetic, Father*. Oxford University Press, 2012.

Habinek, Thomas N. *The World of Roman Song: From Ritualized Speech to Social Order*. Johns Hopkins University Press, 2005.

Hagel, Stefan, and Tosca Lynch. "Musical Education in Greece and Rome." In *A Companion to Ancient Education*, edited by W. Martin Bloomer. Wiley, 2015.

Halporn, James W., Martin Ostwald, and Thomas G. Rosenmeyer. *The Meters of Greek and Latin Poetry*. Bobbs-Merrill, 1963.

Harnack, Adolf von. "Die pseudoclementinischen Briefe de virginitate und die Entstehung des Mönchtums." *Sitzungsberichte der königlich-preussischen Akademie der Wissenschaften zu Berlin* 21 (1891): 361–385.

Harrison, Simon. *Augustine's Way into Will: The Theological and Philosophical Significance of De libero arbitrio*. Oxford University Press, 2006.

Hausherr, Irénée. *Penthos: The Doctrine of Compunction in the Christian East*, translated by Anselm Hufstader. Cistercian Publications, 1982.

Heine, Ronald E. *Gregory of Nyssa's Treatise on the Inscriptions of the Psalms*. Clarendon, 1995.

Hengel, Martin. "The Song about Christ in Earliest Worship." In *Studies in Early Christology*. T. & T. Clark, 1995.

Hickson Hahn, Frances. "Triumphal Ambivalence: The Obscene Songs." In *Ancient Obscenities: Their Nature and Use in the Ancient Greek and Roman Worlds*, edited by Dorota M. Dutsch and Ann Suter. University of Michigan Press, 2015.

Hiley, David. *Western Plainchant: A Handbook*. Oxford University Press, 1993.

Hiley, David. *Gregorian Chant*. Cambridge University Press, 2009.

Hilgard, Alfred. *Scholia in Dionysii Thracis Artem grammaticam*. Teubner, 1901.

Hill, Edmund, trans. *The Works of Augustine for the Twenty-First Century: Sermons*, Part 3/2: *(20–50) on the Old Testament*, edited by John E. Rotelle. New City Press, 1990.

Hill, Edmund, trans. *The Works of Augustine for the Twenty-First Century: Sermons*, Part 3/5: *Sermons on the New Testament, Sermons 148–183*, edited by John E. Rotelle. New City Press, 1992.

Höeg, Carsten, and Günther Zuntz, eds. *Prophetologium*, vol. 1, fasc. 1: *Lectiones nativitatis et epiphaniae*. Munksgaard, 1939.

Horrocks, Geoffrey. *Greek: A History of the Language and Its Speakers*, 2nd ed. Wiley Blackwell, 2010.

Huglo, Michel. "The Cantatorium: From Charlemagne to the Fourteenth Century." In *The Study of Medieval Chant: Paths and Bridges, East and West: In Honour of Kenneth Levy*, edited by Peter Jeffery. Boydell, 2001.

Huglo, Michel, and Joan Halmo. "Antiphon." In *The New Grove Dictionary of Music and Musicians*, 2nd ed., vol. 1, edited by Stanley Sadie and John Tyrrell. Grove, 2001.

Hunink, Vincent. "Singing Together in Church: Augustine's Psalm against the Donatists." In *Sacred Words: Orality, Literacy and Religion*, edited by A. P. M. H. Lardinois, J. H. Blok, and M. G. M. van der Poel. Brill, 2011.

Hunter, David G. *Marriage, Celibacy, and Heresy in Ancient Christianity: The Jovinianist Controversy*. Oxford University Press, 2007.

Huttner, Ulrich. *Early Christianity in the Lycus Valley*. Brill, 2013.

Idelsohn, Abraham Z. *Jewish Music in Its Historical Development*. Holt, 1929.

Jastrow, Marcus. *Dictionary of Targumim, the Talmud Bavli and Yerushalmi, and the Midrashic Literature*. 2 vols. Luzac, 1903.

Jeffery, Peter. "The Earliest Oktōēchoi: The Role of Jerusalem and Palestine in the Beginnings of Modal Ordering." In *The Study of Medieval Chant, Paths and Bridges, East and West: In Honor of Kenneth Levy*, edited by Peter Jeffery. Boydell, 2001.

Jeffery, Peter. "The Introduction of Psalmody into the Roman Mass by Pope Celestine I (422-432): Reinterpreting a Passage in the *Liber Pontificalis*," *Archiv für Liturgiewissenschaft* 26 (1984): 148–153.

Jeffery, Peter. "Philo's Impact on Jewish Psalmody." In *Psalms in Community: Jewish and Christian Textual, Liturgical, and Artistic Traditions*, edited by Harold W. Attridge and Margot E. Fassler. Society of Biblical Literature, 2003.

Jensen, Robin M. "Altar Veils: Concealing or Displaying the Holy in Early Church Architecture." In *Why We Sing: Music, Word, and Liturgy in Early Christianity*, edited by Carl J. Berglund, Barbara Crostini, and James A. Kelhoffer. Brill, 2023.

Kaczynski, Reiner. "Die Psalmodie bei der Begräbnisfeier." In *Liturgie und Dichtung: Ein interdisziplinäres Kompendium*, vol. 2, edited by Hansjakob Becker and Reiner Kaczinski. EOS, 1983.

Kedar, Benjamin. "The Latin Translations." In *Mikra: Text, Translation, Reading and Interpretation of the Hebrew Bible in Ancient Judaism and Early Christianity*, edited by Martin J. Mulder. Van Gorcum, 1988.

Kelly, Christopher. "Stooping to Conquer: The Power of Imperial Humility." In *Theodosius II: Rethinking the Roman Empire in Late Antiquity*, edited by Christopher Kelly. Cambridge University Press, 2013.

Klavan, Spencer A. "Melody and Meaning: The Semiotics of Ancient Greek Music in the Late Classical and Early Hellenistic Eras." D.Phil. diss., Oxford University, 2019.

Kohlbacher, Michael. "Wessen Kirche ordnete das Testamentum Domini Nostri Jesu Christi? Anmerkungen zum historischen Kontext von CPG." In *Zu Geschichte, Theologie, Liturgie und Gegenwartslage der syrischen Kirchen*, edited by Martin Tamcke and Andreas Heinz. LIT, 2000.

Kraeling, Carl H., and Lucetta Mowry. "Music in the Bible." In *Ancient and Oriental Music*, edited by Egon Wellesz. Oxford University Press, 1957.

Kraus, Hans-Joachim. *Psalms 1–59: A Commentary*, translated by Hilton C. Oswald. Augsburg, 1988.

Kritzinger, Peter. "The Cult of the Saints and Religious Processions in Late Antiquity and the Early Middle Ages." In *An Age of Saints? Power, Conflict, and Dissent in Early Medieval Christianity*, edited by Peter Sarris, Matthew Dal Santo, and Phil Booth. Brill, 2011.

Kruse, Thomas. "The Magistrate and the Ocean: Acclamations and Ritualised Communication in Town Gatherings in Roman Egypt." In *Ritual and Communication in the Graeco-Roman World*, edited by Eftychia Stavrianopoulou. Presses universitaires de Liège, 2006.

Lamb, John A. *The Psalms in Christian Worship*. Faith, 1962.

Lang, Uwe M. *John Philoponus and the Controversies over Chalcedon in the Sixth Century: A Study and Translation of the Arbiter*. Peeters, 2001.

Lázaro Sánchez, Miguel J. "L'état actuel de la recherche sur le concile d'Elvire." *Revue des sciences religieuses* 82 (2008): 517–546.

Leclercq, Henri. "Antienne (Liturgie)." In *Dictionnaire d' archéologie chrétienne et de liturgie*, vol. 1, part 2, edited by Fernand Cabrol and Henri Leclercq, cols. 2282–2319. Letouzey et Ané, 1907.

Leclercq, Henri. "Antiphon, In Greek Liturgy." In *Catholic Encyclopedia*, vol. 1, edited by Charles G. Herbermann et al. Appleton, 1907.

Leclercq, Henri. "Communion (Rite et Antienne de la)." In *Dictionnaire d'archéologie chrétienne et de liturgie*, vol. 3, part 2, edited by Henri Leclercq and Fernand Cabrol. Letouzey et Ané, 1914.

Leeb, Helmut. *Die Psalmodie bei Ambrosius*. Herder, 1967.

Lewis, Charlton T., and Charles Short. *A New Latin Dictionary*. Oxford: Clarendon, 1879.

Lipphardt, Walther, ed. *Der karolingische Tonar von Metz*. Achendorff, 1965.

Lipsius, Richard A. *Die apokryphen Apostelgeschichten und Apostellegenden: Ein Beitrag zur altchristlichen Literaturgeschichte*. 2 vols. (1, 2/1, 2/2). Schwetschke, 1883–1887.

Lynch, Tosca. "Tuning the Lyre, Tuning the Soul: Harmonia, Justice and the Kosmos of the Soul in Plato's Republic and Timaeus." *Greek and Roman Musical Studies* 8 (2020): 111–155.

MacCormack, Sabine. "Change and Continuity in Late Antiquity: The Ceremony of 'Adventus.'" *Historia* 21 (1972): 721–752.

McGowan, Andrew B. "Rethinking Agape and Eucharist in Early North African Christianity." *Studia Liturgica* 34 (2004): 165–176.

McGowan, Andrew B. *Ancient Christian Worship: Early Church Practices in Social, Historical, and Theological Perspective*. Baker Academic, 2014.

McGowan, Anne, and Paul F. Bradshaw. *The Pilgrimage of Egeria: A New Translation of the Itinerarium Egeriae with Introduction and Commentary*. Liturgical, 2018.

Machabey, Armand. *Histoire et évolution des formules musicales der Ier au XVe siècle de l'ère chrétienne*. Payot, 1928.

Mackie, Gillian V. *Early Christian Chapels in the West: Decoration, Function, and Patronage*. University of Toronto Press, 2003.

McKinnon, James W. "On the Question of Psalmody in the Ancient Synagogue." *Early Music History* 6 (1986): 159–191.

McKinnon, James W., ed. *Music in Early Christian Literature*. Cambridge University Press, 1987.

McKinnon, James W. "The Fourth-Century Origin of the Gradual." *Early Music History* 7 (1987): 91–106.

McKinnon, James W. "Desert Monasticism and the Later Fourth Century Psalmodic Movement." *Music and Letters* 75 (1994): 505–521.

McKinnon, James W. *The Advent Project: The Later-Seventh-Century Creation of the Roman Mass Proper*. University of California Press, 2000.

McKinnon, James W. "Liturgical Psalmody in the Sermons of St. Augustine: An Introduction." In *The Study of Medieval Chant: Paths and Bridges, East and West: In Honor of Kenneth Levy*, edited by Peter Jeffery. Boydell, 2001.

MacMullen, Ramsay. "The Preacher's Audience (AD 350–400)." *Journal of Theological Studies* 40 (1989): 503–511.

MacMullen, Ramsay. *The Second Church: Popular Christianity A.D. 200–400*. Society of Biblical Literature, 2009.

Maier, Johann. "Zur Verwendung der Psalmen in der synagogalen Liturgie (Wochentag und Sabbat)." In *Liturgie und Dichtung: Ein interdisziplinäres Kompendium I:*

Historische Präsentation, edited by Hansjakob Beker and Reiner Kaczynski. EOS, 1983.

Maier, Johann. "Zu Kult und Liturgie der Qumrangemeinde." *Revue de Qumrân* 14 (1990): 543–586.

Maraval, Pierre. *Lieux saints et pèlerinages d'Orient: Histoire et géographie des à la conqête arabe.* Cerf, 1985.

Mariès, Louis. "Études préliminaires à l'édition de Diodore de Tarse 'Sur les Psaumes'—La tradition manuscrite." *Recherches de science religieuse* 22 (1932): 385–408 and 513–540. Republished as the first two chapters of Louis Mariès, *Études préliminaires à l'édition de Diodore de Tarse "Sur les Psaumes."* "Les Belles Lettres," 1933.

Markschies, Christoph. "Wer schrieb die sogenannte *Traditio Apostolica*? Neue Beobachtungen und Hypothesen zu einer kaum lösbaren Frage aus der altkirchlichen Literaturgeschichte." In *Tauffragen und Bekenntnis*, edited by Wolfram Kinzig, Christoph Markschies, and Markus Vinzent. De Gruyter, 1999.

Martinez, David G. "Epiphany Themes in Christian Liturgies on Papyrus." In *Light from the East: Papyrologische Kommentare zum Neuen Testament*, edited by Peter Artz-Grabner and Christina M. Kreinecker. Harrassowitz, 2010.

Mateos, Juan. "La vigile cathédrale chez Égérie." *Orientalia christiana periodica* 27 (1961): 381–312.

Mateos, Juan. "L'office monastique à la fin du IVe siècle: Antioche, Palestine, Cappadoce." *Oriens Christianus* 47 (1963): 53–88.

Mateos, Juan, ed. *Le Typicon de la Grand Ėglise*, vol. 1: *Le cycle des fêtes mobiles.* Pontificum Institutum Orientalium Studiorum, 1963.

Mateos, Juan. "Quelques anciens documents sur l'office du soir." *Orientalia christiana periodica* 35 (1969): 347–374.

Mayer, Wendy. "Who Came to Hear John Chrysostom Preach? Recovering a Late Fourth-Century Preacher's Audience." *Ephemerides Theologicae Lovanienses* 76 (2000): 73–87.

Mayer, Wendy. *The Homilies of St. John Chrysostom—Provenance: Reshaping the Foundations.* Pontificio Istituto Orientale, 2005.

Mayer, Wendy, and Pauline Allen. *The Churches of Syrian Antioch (300–638 CE).* Peeters, 2012.

Mayer, Wendy, and Bronwen Neil. *St. John Chrysostom: The Cult of the Saints: Select Homilies and Letters.* St. Vladimir's Seminary Press, 2006.

Meier, Mischa. "Die Demut des Kaisers: Aspekte der religiösen Selbstinzenierung bei Theodosius II (408–450 n.Chr.)." In *Die Bibel als politisches Argument: Voraussetzungen und Folgen biblizistischer Herrschaftslegitimation in der Vormoderne*, edited by Andreas Pečar and Kai Trampedach. Oldenbourg, 2007.

Mellas, Andrew. "Tears of Compunction in John Chrysostom's On Eutropius." *Studia Patristica* 83 (2017): 159–172.

Méndez, Hugo. "Revising the Date of the Armenian Lectionary of Jerusalem." *Journal of Early Christian Studies* 29 (2021): 61–92.

Menn, Esther M. "Sweet Singer of Israel: David and the Psalms in Early Judaism." In *Psalms in Community: Jewish and Christian Textual, Liturgical, and Artistic*

Traditions, edited by Harold W. Attridge and Margot E. Fassler. Society of Biblical Literature, 2003.

Merkelbach, Reinhold. *Steinepigramme aus dem griechischen Osten*, vol. 2: *Die nordküste Kleinasiens (Marmarameer und Pontos)*. Saur, 2001.

Meyer, Marvin W., and Richard Smith, eds. *Ancient Christian Magic: Coptic Texts of Ritual Power*. Princeton University Press, 1999.

Michaelides, Solon. *The Music of Ancient Greece: An Encyclopedia*. Faber and Faber, 1978.

Mihálykó, Ágnes T. *The Christian Liturgical Papyri: An Introduction*. Mohr Siebeck, 2019.

Miller, Timothy S. *The Orphans of Byzantium: Child Welfare in the Christian Empire*. The Catholic University of America Press, 2003.

Moore, Timothy J. *Music in Roman Comedy*. Cambridge University Press, 2012.

Morin, G. "Deux nouveaux sermons retrouvés de saint Augustin." *Revue Bénédictine* 36 (1924): 187–199.

Muller, C. Detlef G., trans. "Epistula apostolorum." In *New Testament Apocrypha*, vol. 1, revised edition, edited by Wilhelm Schneemelcher, translated by R. Mcl. Wilson. Clarke, 1991.

Neusner, Jacob. *The Mishnah: A New Translation*. Yale University Press, 1988.

Niewöhner, Philipp. "Historisch-topographische Überlegungen zum Trierer Prozessionselfenbein, dem Christusbild an der Chalke, Kaiserin Irenes Triumph im Bilderstreit und der Euphemiakirche am Hippodrom." *Millennium* 11 (2014): 261–288.

O'Brien, Peter T. *Colossians, Philemon*. Word, 1982.

Oesterley, William O. E. *The Jewish Background of the Christian Liturgy*. Clarendon, 1925.

Osborn, Eric. *Tertullian: First Theologian of the West*. Cambridge University Press, 1997.

Page, Christopher. *The Christian West and Its Singers: The First Thousand Years*. Yale University Press, 2010.

Page, Christopher. "The Magnificence of a Singer in Fifth-Century Gaul." In *Magnificence in the Middle Ages*, edited by C. Stephen Jaeger. Palgrave MacMillan, 2010.

Parkes, M. B. *Pause and Effect: An Introduction to the History of Punctuation in the West*. University of California Press, 1993.

Pelosi, Francesco. "Music and Emotions." In *A Companion to Ancient Greek and Roman Music*, edited by Tosca A. C. Lynch and Eleonora Rocconi. Wiley, 2020.

Pervo, Richard I. *The Acts of Paul: A New Translation with Introduction and Commentary*. Clarke, 2014.

Pietersma, Albert, trans. *A New English Translation of the Septuagint and Other Greek Translations Traditionally Included Under That Title: The Psalms*. Oxford University Press, 2000.

Pietersma, Albert. "Exegesis and Liturgy in the Superscriptions of the Greek Psalter." In *Proceedings of the Xth Congress of the International Organization for the Septuagint and Cognate Studies, Oslo July-August 1998*, edited by Bernard A. Taylor. Scholars Press, 2001.

Pöhlmann, Egert, and Martin L. West, eds. *Documents of Ancient Greek Music: The Extant Melodies and Fragments*. Clarendon, 2001.

Powell, Douglas. "Tertullianists and the Cataphrygians." *Vigiliae Christianae* 29 (1975): 33–54.

Price, R. F. *Rituals and Power: The Roman Imperial Cult in Asia Minor*. Cambridge University Press, 1984.

Provenza, Antonietta. "Music and Medicine." In *A Companion to Ancient Greek and Roman Music*, edited by Tosca A. Lynch and Eleonora Rocconi. Wiley, 2020.

Quasten, Johannes. *Music and Worship in Pagan and Christian Antiquity*, revised edition, translated by Boniface Ramsey. National Association of Pastoral Musicians, 1983.

Rabinowitz, Louis I. "The Psalms in Jewish Liturgy." *Historia Judaica* 6 (1944): 109–122.

Raffa, Massimo. "Music in Greek and Roman Education." In *A Companion to Ancient Greek and Roman Music*, edited by Tosca A. C. Lynch and Eleonora Rocconi. Wiley, 2020.

Ramelli, Ilaria. "Tears of Pathos, Repentance and Bliss: Crying and Salvation in Origen and Gregory of Nyssa." In *Tears in the Graeco-Roman World*, edited by Thorsten Fögen. De Gruyter, 2009.

Rankin, David. *Tertullian and the Church*. Cambridge University Press, 1995.

Rapp, Claudia. "The Elite Status of Bishops in Late Antiquity in Ecclesiastical, Spiritual, and Social Contexts." *Arethusa* 33 (2000): 379–399.

Ravolainen, Kaija. "The Singer in the Ecclesiastical Hierarchy: The Early History of the Order." Doctoral diss., University of the Arts Helsinki, 2014.

Rebenich, Stefan. *Jerome*. Routledge, 2002.

Rebillard, Éric. *The Care of the Dead in Late Antiquity*, translated by Elizabeth Trapnell Rawlings and Jeanine Routier-Pucci. Cornell University Press, 2009.

Rebillard, Éric. *The Early Martyr Narratives: Neither Authentic Accounts nor Forgeries*. University of Pennsylvania Press, 2021.

Robert, Jeanne, and Louis Robert. *La Carie: histoire et géographie historique avec la recueil des inscriptions antiques*. Vol. 2: *Le Plateau de Tabai et ses environs*. Librairie d'Amerique et d'Orient, 1954.

Rouwhorst, Gerard A. M. *Les hymnes pascales d'Ephrem de Nisibe: Analyse théologique et recherche sur l'évolution de la fête pascale chrétienne à Nisibe et à Edesse et dans quelques Églises voisines au quartrième siècle*. 2 vols. Brill, 1989.

Rutherford, Ian. *Pindar's Paeans: A Reading of the Fragments and a Survey of the Genre*. Oxford University Press, 2001.

Sanders, E. P. *Judaism: Practice and Belief, 63BCE–66CE*. SCM, 1992.

Sanzo, Joseph E. *Scriptural Incipits on Amulets from Late Antique Egypt: Text, Typology, and Theory*. Mohr Siebeck, 2014.

Schatkin, Margaret A. "Idiophones in the Ancient World: Description, Terminology, Geographical Distribution, Functions." *Jahrbuch für Antike und Christentum* 21 (1978): 147–172.

Scheidweiler, Felix. "The Questions of Bartholomew." In *New Testament Apocrypha*, vol. 1, revised edition, edited by Wilhelm Schneemelcher, translated by R. Mcl. Wilson. Clarke, 1991.

Schmitz, Josef. *Gottesdienst im altchristlichen Mailand: Eine liturgiewissenschaftlichen Untersuchung über Initiation und Messfeier während des Jahres zur Zeit des Bischofs Ambrosius (obit. 397)*. Hanstein, 1975.

Schneemelcher, Wilhelm. "Acts of Paul." In *New Testament Apocrypha*, vol. 2: *Writings Relating to the Apostles; Apocalypses and Related Subjects*, edited by Wilhelm Schneemelcher, and R. McL. Wilson, translated by Ernest Best et al. Westminster, 1963.

Schwartz, Daniel R. *2 Maccabees*. De Gruyter, 2008.

Schwartz, Eduard. "Überschriften und Kephalaia." In *Eusebius Werke*, vol. 2.3, edited by Eduard Schwartz. Akademie, 1999 (orig. 1903).

Shipman, Andrew J. "Antiphon. In the Greek Church—." *Catholic Encyclopedia*, vol. 1, edited by Charles G. Herbermann et al. Appleton, 1907.

Sider, David. *The Epigrams of Philodemos: Introduction, Text, and Commentary*. Oxford University Press, 1997.

Silvas, Anna M. *The Asketikon of St. Basil the Great*. Oxford University Press, 2005.

Silvas, Anna M. *Macrina the Younger, Philosopher of God*. Brepols, 2008.

Smith, Jannes. "The Meaning and Function of Ἀλληλουϊά in the Old Greek Psalter." In *XII Congress of the International Organization for Septuagint and Cognate Studies, Leiden, 2004*, edited by Melvin K. H. Peters. Society of Biblical Literature, 2006.

Smith, John A. "The Ancient Synagogue, the Early Church and Singing." *Music and Letters* 65 (1984): 1–16.

Smith, John A. *Music in Ancient Judaism and Early Christianity*. Ashgate, 2011.

Sokolowski, Franciszek. *Lois sacrées de l'Asie Mineure*. Boccard, 1955.

Stapert, Calvin R. *A New Song for an Old World: Musical Thought in the Early Church*. Eerdmans, 2007.

Stein, S. "The Liturgy of Hanukkah and the First Two Books of Maccabees–II." *Journal of Jewish Studies* 5 (1954): 148–155.

Stewart, Columba. *Cassian the Monk*. Oxford University Press, 1998.

Stewart-Sykes, Alistair C. *The Didascalia Apostolorum: An English Version with Introduction and Annotation*. Brepols, 2009.

Stewart-Sykes, Alistair C. *The Canons of Hippolytus: An English Version, with Introduction and Annotation and an Accompanying Arabic Text*. SCH, 2021.

Strunk, Oliver. "Intonations and Signatures of the Byzantine Modes" (1945). In *Essays on Music in the Byzantine World*, edited by Oliver Strunk. Norton, 1977.

Swancutt, Diana M. "Christian 'Rock' Music at Corinth?" In *Psalms in Community: Jewish and Christian Textual, Liturgical, and Artistic Traditions*, edited by Harold W. Attridge and Margot E. Fassler. Society of Biblical Literature, 2003.

Tabory, Joseph. *The JPS Commentary on the Haggadah: Historical Introduction, Translation, and Commentary*. Jewish Publication Society, 2008.

Taft, Robert F. *The Liturgy of the Hours in East and West: The Origins of the Divine Office and Its Meaning for Today*. Liturgical, 1986.

Taft, Robert F. "The Frequency of the Eucharist Throughout History?" In *Between Memory and Hope: Readings on the Liturgical Year*, edited by Maxwell E. Johnson. Liturgical, 2000; reprinted from Robert F. Taft, *Beyond East and West: Problems in Liturgical Understanding*, 2nd ed. Pontifical Oriental Institute, 1997.

Taylor, Joan E. *Jewish Women Philosophers of First-Century Alexandria: Philo's 'Therapeutae' Reconsidered.* Oxford University Press, 2003.

Teitler, Hans C. *The Last Pagan Emperor: Julian the Apostate and the War against Christianity.* Oxford University Press, 2017.

Tov, Emanuel. "Excerpted and Abbreviated Biblical Texts from Qumran." *Revue de Qumrân* 16 (1995): 581–600.

Tov, Emanuel. *Scribal Practices and Approaches Reflected in the Texts Found in the Judean Desert.* Brill, 2004.

Treu, Kurt. "Varia Christiana." *Archiv für Papyrusforschung* 24/25 (1976): 113–127.

Trevett, Christine. *Montanism: Gender, Authority and the New Prophecy.* Cambridge University Press, 1996.

Trigg, Joseph W. "Introduction." In *Origen, Homilies on the Psalms: Monacensis Graecus 314*, translated by Joseph W. Trigg. Catholic University of America, 2020.

Troelsgård, Christian. "A New Source for the Early Octoechos? Papyrus Vindobonensis G 19.934 and Its Musical Implications." Presented at the First International Conference of Byzantine Musical Culture, American Society of Byzantine Music and Hymnology, Peania, Attica, 2007.

van Bekkum, Wout J., ed. *A Hebrew Alexander Romance according to MS London, Jews' College no. 145.* Peeters, 1992.

Van Nuffelen, Peter. "Playing the Ritual Game in Constantinople (379–457)." In *Two Romes: Rome and Constantinople in Late Antiquity*, edited by Lucy Grig and Gavin Kelly. Oxford University Press, 2012.

Veilleux, Armand. *La liturgie dans le cénobitisme pachômiene au quatrième siècle.* Herder, 1968.

Veilleux, Armand, trans. *Pachomian Koinonia.* Vol. 1: *The Life of Saint Pachomius and His Disciples.* Cistercian, 1980. Vol. 2: *Pachomian Chronicles and Rules.* Cistercian, 1982.

Versnel, Hendrik S. *Triumphus: An Inquiry into the Origin, Development, and Meaning of the Roman Triumph.* Brill, 1970.

Visonà, Giuseppe, ed. *Cronologia Ambrosiana, Bibliografia Ambrosiana (1900–2000).* Biblioteca Ambrosiana, 2004.

Vitelli, Giramo, ed. *Papiri greci e latini*, vol. 6. Ariani, 1920.

Vitringa, Campegius. *De synagoga vetere libri tres.* Gyzelaar, 1696.

Volp, Ulrich. *Tod und Ritual in den christlichen Gemeinden der Antike.* Brill, 2002.

Vööbus, Arthur. "Ein merkwürdiger Pentateuchtext in der pseudo-klementinischen Schrift De virginitate." *Oriens Christianus* 43 (1959): 54–58.

Wagner, Peter. *Einführung in die gregorianischen Melodien: Ein Handbuch der Choralwissenschaft*, vol. 1, 2nd ed. Universitäts-Buchhandlung, 1901.

Walsh, Gerald G. "Writings of Niceta of Remesiana." In *The Fathers of the Church: A New Translation*, vol. 7. Catholic University of America, 1949.

Weiss, Zeev. *Public Spectacles in Roman and Late Antique Palestine*. Harvard University Press, 2014.

Wellesz, Egon. *A History of Byzantine Music and Hymnography*, 2nd ed. Clarendon, 1961.

Werner, Eric. *The Sacred Bridge: The Interdependence of Liturgy and Music in Synagogue and Church during the First Millennium*, vol. 1. Dobson, 1959.

Wessely, Othmar. "Die Musikanschauung des Abtes Pambo." *Anzeiger der philosophisch-historischen Klasse der Österreichischen Akademie der Wissenschaften* 89 (1952): 46–62.

West, Martin L. "The Singing of Homer and the Modes of Early Greek Music." *Journal of Hellenic Studies* 101 (1981): 113–129.

West, Martin L. *Ancient Greek Music*. Clarendon, 1992.

West, Martin L. *The East Face of Helicon: West Asiatic Elements in Greek Poetry and Myth*. Clarendon, 1997.

Wilkinson, John. *Egeria's Travels*, revised and corrected. Oxbow, 2002.

Williams, Frank, trans. *The Panarion of Epiphanius: Book I*, 2nd ed. Brill, 2009.

Williams, Michael S. *The Politics of Heresy in Ambrose of Milan: Community and Consensus in Late Antique Christianity*. Cambridge University Press, 2017.

Winkler, Gabriele. "The Appearance of Light at the Baptism of Jesus and the Origins of the Feast of Epiphany: An Investigation of Greek, Syriac, Armenian, and Latin Sources." In *Between Memory and Hope: Readings on the Liturgical Year*, edited by Maxwell E. Johnson. Liturgical, 2000.

Woodward, Linda. "Diogenes of Babylon Reading Plato on Music." In *Aristotle and the Stoics 'Reading' Plato*, edited by Anne D. R. Sheppard, Mary M. McCabe, R. W. Sharples, and Verity Harte. Institute of Classical Studies, 2010.

Wortley, John. "How the Desert Fathers 'Meditated.'" *Greek, Roman, and Byzantine Studies* 46 (2006): 315–328.

Wright, William. "An Ancient Syrian Martyriology [Syriac]." *Journal of Sacred Literature* 8/15 (1865): 45–56.

Wright, William. "An Ancient Syrian Martyriology [English translation]." *Journal of Sacred Literature* 8/16 (1866): 423–432.

Wright, William. *A Short History of Syriac Literature*. London: Black, 1894.

Zanobi, Alessandra. *Seneca's Tragedies and the Aesthetics of Pantomime*. Bloomsbury, 2014.

Zinonos, Timotheos. "Homilia in divini corporis sepulturam: An Examination of Its Language, Style and Authorship (Epiphanios of Salamis and Other Candidates)." M.A. thesis, University of Edinburgh, 2020.

INDEX OF ANCIENT SOURCES

Codices

Alexandrinus, British Library Royal 1 D VII, fol. Llv [532v]: 165n38
Vat. gr. 1579, f. 200r-v: 183n129
Vat. gr. 1970 (Rossanensis): 83n29
Vat. gr. 2089: 112n79

Inscriptions

ArchEph (1929) 151, 6: 70n89
CIL
IV.3442a: 348n149
IV.3442b: 348n149
VIII 453: 69n82
XI 1709: 69n82
XI 4629: 140n105, 202n14, 218n98
FGLIBulg 243: 71n90
IC 489: 70n89
IG
II2 13547: 70n89
VII 2692: 70n89
X
2 1 1030: 70n89
2 2 151: 70n89
IGChEg 2: 71n90
IGLSyr2 270: 70n89
IGR IV 1587: 261n159
ILCV II 4711: 140n106, 218n97
IStr 1101 = CIG 2715: 262n160
IvO 657: 70n89
PSI VI 719 = PGM 2: 207–208, no. 19; 342n116
RIChrM
225: 70n89
242: 70n89
SEG
39: 515: 70n89
49: 728: 70n89
SGLIBulg 223: 70n89

Papyri

P. Berol. 16595: 127n19, 127n20
P. Heid.
51–52 (Schubart, 44*–45*): 22n22
52, line 16 [Schmidt, 44*]: 21n27
P.Oxy 41 (= W. Chr. 45): 222n116
P.Oxy. 3555: 72n97

Ancient Literature

Achilles Tatius, *Leuc. et Clit.* 2.1.1: 72n97
Acts of Paul
4.2: 95n7
12: 48n61
Acts of Thomas
9–15: 95n8
169: 95n9
Acts of Xanthippe and Polyxena
6: 274n20, 287n74
19: 245n79
Aelius Donatus, *Com.* 8.9: 315n86
Ambrose
Cain et Ab., 1.5.19: 236n28
De obit. Theodos. 17: 145n137
Ep.
40.16: 178n102
76 (Maur. 20): 151n165
764: 238n38

76.20: 236n26, 238n38, 238n39, 258n140
76.24: 151n168, 236n26, 238n40, 258n140
771–2: 214n82
772: 215n84
773–4: 218n99
773–13: 214n81
774: 216n89, 218n98
777: 219n101
77.12: 217n95
77.12–13: 216n90
77.13: 217n94
77.15–23: 214n81
77.17: 215n84
77.23: 216n90
Exc. frat. Satyr.
1.61: 68n75
1.70: 142n116
Expl. psalm. 1 7: 319n3
Expl. psalm. 1 9: 114n90, 152n175, 223n118, 256n134, 257n38, 304n48, 357n196
Expl. psalm. 45 15: 236n26, 242n61, 258n140
Expos. euang. Luc. 7.238: 236n26
Expos. psalm. 118
8.48: 111n75, 115n103
19:28: 175n83
19:30: 175n83
19.30: 175n83
19.32: 113n89
Hex. 3.5.23: 236n26
Hymn. 10 (*Victor, Nabor, Felix pii*).32: 215n86
Interpel. Job et Dauid 4.6.24: 56n18, 67n70
Myst. 58: 89n49
Virginibus, 1.60: 152n173
Ammianus Marcellinus
Res gest.
16.10.6: 210n63
21.10.1: 199n3
229.14: 204n31
22.13.2: 206n39
22.13.3: 206n38
232.3: 205n31
Aphrahat, *Dem.* 12.13: 124n4
Apocalypse of Paul
29: 85n38, 85n39
30: 88n48
Apophthegmata patrum
Collectio alphabetica: 164n31, 164n32
Collectio anonyma 229: 164n30
Collectio systematica 10.150: 164n31
Apostolic Constitutions
1.5: 291n9
1.5.6 // *Didasc.* 2.: 34n2
2.26.3.: 64n53
2.28.5: 64n52
2.57.5–6: 56n15, 64n48, 242n65
2.58.4: 247n84
2.59: 155n190
2.59.2: 113n87
2.60.6–62.4: 107n64
3.11.1: 65n54
5.13.1: 133n57
6.17.2: 64n52, 69n83
6.30.2: 139n100, 141n109
6.30.3: 146n140
7.47–48.3: 112n79
7.48:4: 112n79
8.12.3: 90n56
8.12.4: 90n56
8.13.14: 64n51
8.13.15–8.14.1: 79n11
8.14.1: 64n50, 247n84
8.28.7–8: 64n51, 65n54
8.34.1: 111n77
8.34.7: 155n190
8.34.8–10: 55n11, 111n78
8.34.10: 118n113
8.42.1: 139n100, 141n108
8.47.26: 64n51, 65n54
73.47, ms. e: 253n117
Apostolic Tradition
11: 71n91

21.27: 90n56
25/29C: 136
25/29C 11: 73n101, 259n146
Appian, *Lyb.* 395 [66]: 219n104
Aristides, Aelius
H.L.
3.4: 263n172, 263n173
4.38: 263n172
4.39: 263n176
4.42: 263n177
4.43: 263n175
4.43–48: 263n172, 263n174
4.50: 264n178
Or., 29.30: 349n151
Aristides Quintilianus
Mus.
1.4: 316n90
25: 330n60, 330n61, 333n73
2.15: 332n72
2.16: 332n71
Aristophanes, *Sept.* 636: 117n109
Aristotle, *Rhet.* 3.6.4 (1407b26–35): 114n92
[Aristotle]
Prob.
19.17: 272n9
19.17–18: 272n10
19.18: 272n9
Aristoxenus
El. Harm.
13: 318n100
18–10: 317n97
19: 293n18
1.18: 317n97
Armenian Lectionary
1: 127n23, 128n30, 129n33, 251n108
1*bis*: 128n25
2: 128n26, 128n30, 251n110
3: 129n33
4: 128n30, 251n110
5: 128n30, 129n33
6: 129n33
7: 129n33
8: 129n33
9: 129n33
34: 131n42
38: 20n22
39: 20n23
39.3: 251n111
43: 131n45, 132m47, 132n47, 132n48
Asterius the Sophist
Comm. in psalm., Hom. 18.20: 9n45
In psalm., Hom. 25.24: 134n62
Athanasius
Apol. contra Arianos, 3–19: 149n158
Apol. pro fug. sua
24: 64n45, 149n157, 233n12
24.4: 55n13
Ep. enc.
2.2: 200n9
4.1: 200n9
Ep. Marc.
2–9: 319n4
3–10: 319n1
9: 316n92, 317n96, 317n98
11: 55n12
25: 24n40, 244n75
27: 317n94, 317n95, 353n177
27–29: 316n93
28: 192n167, 316n91, 337n95, 337n96, 338n98, 353n176
29: 327n42, 337n97, 338n99, 338n101, 339n102, 339n103
31: 120n125
Expos. in psalm.: 132n47, 132n48
Expos. in psalm. 33: 80n16
Expos. in psalm. 104: 244n74, 250n105
Expos. in psalm. 117 1: 80n18
Hist. Ar., 81: 150n160
Or. contra Arianos I.4.1–2: 346n138

Vit. Ant.
  2–3: 191n158
  3: 95n11
  3–4: 191n160, 191n162
  3.5: 191n159
  25: 353n180
  25.1: 182n123
  25.1–3: 172n72
  39–40: 171n70, 191n163
  39.5: 171n70
  44.2: 171n69, 192n164
  54: 95n11
  55.3: 171n68, 192n165
  71: 172n73
[Athanasius]
  De sancte trinitate, Dial. 1.12: 104n50
  Virg.
    12: 324n27
    20: 97n28, 112n79, 247n88, 324n26
Augustine
  Conf.
    4.12.19: 134n65
    5.9.17: 90n54
    7.1.1: 69n80
    96.14: 320n7
    97.15: 152n170, 152n171, 235n21, 235n23, 286n70
    97.16: 215n85
    9.12.31: 146n141
    10.33.44: 351n168, 351n169
    10.33.49: 351n166, 351n167, 352n172
    10.33.50: 55n14, 296n28, 314n84, 352n170
  De opere monach. 17.20: 9n45
  Enarr. in psalm. 40 1: 241n57
  Enarr. in psalm. 72 1: 357n197
  Enarr. in psalm. 110 1: 249n102
  Enarr. in psalm. 113 1: 241n58
  Enarr. in psalm. 119 1: 241n59
  Enarr. in psalm. 132 2: 296n31
  Ep.
    29.10–11: 55n11, 113n83
    55.18.34: 352n173, 353n175
    55.34: 322n12
    111.8: 90n54
    158.2: 141n107, 202n15
  In ev. Ioan., 12.7: 341n113
  Lib. arb. 3.5.12 (44): 362n220
  Praec. (*Reg.ad serv. Dei*) 2.3: 281n49
  Reg. 2.3: 120n127
  Retract.
    1.20: 266n191
    2.11.37: 89n50
    119: 347n145
  Serm.
    20.1 (Denis): 239n47
    22A (Mai 13) 1: 239n48
    25A (Morin 12) 1: 239n49
    29A 1: 240n50, 246n80
    30.1: 240n51
    30.8: 240n52
    33A: 304n49
    47 1, 8: 241n60
    811: 240n53
    153.1: 240n54
    159.2: 352n171
    184.1: 133n60, 135n71
    185.1: 133n60
    187.4: 134n64, 135n71
    188.2: 134n64
    189 (*In nat. dom.* VI): 133n59
    189.1: 136n81
    189.2: 133n60
    190.4: 136n81
    191.2: 133n60, 134n64
    192.1: 133n60
    192.3: 134n64
    193.2: 133n60
    194.4: 134n64
    195.3: 134n64
    196.1: 135n71
    252.9: 88n46
    306.1: 240n55
    352: 67n71
    352.1: 241n56
  Serm de Vet. Test. 22A: 324n29

Basil of Caesarea
Ep.
2.2: 349n153
46.2: 97n27
204.6: 96n15
207.2: 153n176, 237n31
207.3: 153n177, 153n178, 175n83, 237n32, 254n122, 256n132
207.3.5–8: 322n18
207.4: 237n31
223.3: 96n15, 197n190
Expos. in psalm., In psalm. 1: 319n2
Hom. in psalm. 1: 296n30, 297n33
Hom. in. psalm. 1 1: 256n133, 319n1, 348n147, 349n152
Hom. in psalm. 1 2: 121n130, 350n162
Hom. in psalm. 7 3: 104n50
Hom. in psalm. 37: 132n48
Hom. in psalm. 114 1: 148n153, 202n18, 355n188
Leg. gent. 9: 327n44
Reg. fus. tract.
5: 176n89
37.3: 176n86
37.3–4: 176n90, 196n185
37.3–5: 176n85
37.4: 176n89, 342n119
37.5: 176n88
38: 176n91
Spir. Sanct. 29 [73]: 107n62
[Basil of Caesarea], *Canon* 97: 115n101, 115n102
Bible

Old Testament
Exod
13:19: 229n142
15:20–21: 125n9, 229n142
Josh 24:32: 229n142
1 Sam, 16:23: 327
2 Chron
5:13: 4n20
7:3: 4n20
7:6: 4n20
Ezra, 3:11: 4n20
Song 5:1: 236
Isa
26:9: 110n75, 173, 174
26:9-25: 175
26:9b: 104, 356
50:4: 179n105
52:13: 129n32
62:6: 92
148:1: 173, 174
Ps
2:2b: 251
2:7: 128n27, 128n31
3:6: 84
5:4: 111n76
6:7: 173
8:5: 173
11:6: 84
17:50: 17
18:6: 134
19:7–8: 300
21:19: 131n46
21:27: 24n39
22:4:173
22:5: 80–1
22:5a: 81
22:5c: 81
22:27 MT: 24n39
23:7–10: 274
30:6a: 131n46
32:1: 29
33:9: 79–80
36:11: 240
37:22: 251
38:13: 239
39:2: 242
40:6: 241
40:9: 84, 251
41:6: 337
43:3: 173
48:17: 173
50:11: 241

58:2: 251
62:2: 111n76, 356
64:6–9: 100
64:9: 102, 356
64:98: 110n75
67:7: 173
68:22: 131n46
68:31: 316
71:4: 239, 324
71:21: 15
72:2: 337
78:13: 251
84:12: 133
87:6b: 251
89:1: 342
90:5: 234
90:5–6: 173
93:12: 240
93:12–13: 239
94:6: 241
95:1–2: 136
99: 88n47
101:10: 173
103:34: 102n43
108:2b–3a: 251
109:1: 128n31, 129, 129n32
113: 19, 241
113:12: 98n30
115:6: 84
115:15: 240
117:1: 17, 18n17
117:6: 337
117:24: 80, 135
117:26: 224
117:26–29: 127
118:27 MT: 4n24
118:62: 247
118:113: 240
118:148: 110n75
118:161–164: 104
133:2: 173, 174
134:1a: 24n39
134:3: 24n39
134:15: 98n30
135:1b MT: 24n39
135:3 MT: 24n39
138:11–12: 211
140:2: 102n43, 111n76
140:2a: 102
140:2b: 102
143:4: 173
145:2: 234
148:1: 176
150:3: 311
Amos 5:23: 311
Dan
3:24: 8n42
3:51: 8n42
3:91: 8n42

New Testament
Matt
6:9: 342
6:9–13: 93n1
12:30: 108
18;7–9: 240
21:8: 130n41
21:15: 130n41, 224n125, 248n98
22:41–46: 17n9
27:35: 131n46
27:48: 131n46
271–56: 131n46
Mark
1:1: 342
14:26: 11n58
15:1–41: 131n46
26:30: 11n59
Luke
1:1: 342
2:14: 173
2:15: 128n24
11:2–4: 93n1
20:42: 16
22:66–23:49: 9n46
23:46: 131n46
24:44: 16
John
1:23: 342

19:16b–3: 131n46
20:19: 129
Acts
1:14: 93n3
1:16: 17n9
1:20: 16
2:34–35: 129n31
2:42: 93n3
3:1: 93n1
10:2: 93n1
10:9: 93n1
10:30: 93n1
12:5: 93n3
13:33: 129n31
16:25: 9n43, 18n18, 118n117
Rom
7:5–13: 240
14:6: 26n52
15:9–12: 18n14
1 Cor
1:4: 26n52
10:30: 26n52
11:23–32: 20
11:24: 26n52
14:13–18: 18n18
14:15–17: 18n15, 27n54
14:16: 231n1
14:16–17: 18n16
14:26: 18n18
15:52: 311
2 Cor
1:11: 26n52
1.11: 26n52
8:16: 26n52
Eph
5:4: 26n52
5:19: 343n125, 359, 360n215
5:20: 26n50, 26n52
5.18–19: 18n19
5.19: 18n18
Phil
1:3–5: 26n52
4:6: 26n52
Col
1:3: 26n52
1:12: 26n52
2:7: 26n52
3:16: 18n18, 18n19, 20, 30
3:16–17: 349
3:17: 26n52
4:2: 26n52
1 Thess
1:2: 26n52
3:9: 26n52
4:13: 142n115
5:17: 93n1, 190
5:17–18: 26n52
5:18: 26n50
2 Thess
1:3: 26n52
2:13: 26n52
1 Tim, 2:1: 26n5
Phlm 1:4: 26n52
Heb
1:3: 128n31
1:5: 128n31
1:13: 128n31
Jas 5:13: 9n44, 18n18, 142, 337n96
Rev
19:1: 41n33
19:3: 41n33
19:4: 41n33
19:6: 41n33
Boethius, *Inst. mus.* 1.12: 316n90, 318n99
Callinicus, *Vit. Hypat.* 51.2–3: 279n37
Canon Muratori 73–80: 347n140
Canons of Athanasius 16: 126n16, 126n17
Canons of Hippolytus, 29: 343n126, 344n127
Cassian, John
Conlat.
1.17.2: 323n24
24: 160n15
25.5: 161n16, 178n103

2.10–12: 242n65
2.11.1: 161n18
2.11.3: 161n20
2.13.10: 179n105
32: 160n14
34.1: 158n5
36: 110n72, 153n179, 159n7
38: 159n7
38.1–3: 160n12
38.4: 159n10, 160n11
3.12.3: 179n105
3.15.4: 179n105
8.16.1: 179n105
9.36.1: 179n105
10.10.14: 179n105
10.10.15: 179n105
10.11.4: 121n1312, 179n105
10.11.5: 179n105
10.13.2: 179n105
11.9.2: 179n105
14.9.2: 179n105
16.15: 179n105
23.5.9: 179n105

Inst.
22.1: 283n60, 288n77
23.1: 259n144
25.5: 247n91, 248n94, 284n63
26: 161n17, 247n90
26–8: 284n64
27–11: 259n144
28: 248n95, 252n112, 252n113, 252n114, 283n61
2.10.1: 248n92
2.11.3: 248n93
38.4: 259n145, 285n65
9.9–10: 323n23

Cassius Dio, 74.2.3: 219n103
Cato, Marcus Porcius, *Agr.* 160: 294n21
Chron. Pasch.: 209n60, 228n141
Chrysostom, John *see* John Chrysostom
Claudian, *VI cons.* 551: 210n65

Clement of Alexandria
Paed.
1.6.25.2: 128n28
2.4.40.1–2.4.44.5: 289n1
2.4.43.1–2.4.44.1: 30n64
2.4.43.3: 291n8
2.4.44.3: 31n69, 231n3
2.4.44.5: 331n63
3.11.80.4: 266n189
Protr.
1.1.1: 339n104
1.5.4: 327n42
Str.
1.21.146.1–3: 125n11
6.11.88.1–2: 289n2, 331n65
6.11.90.1: 231n3
6.11.90.2–3: 331n64
6.16.145: 135n72
7.7: 191n161
7.7.49.4: 118n118, 192n166

Clement of Rome, *Ep. 1 ad Cor.*
36.4–5: 129n31

[Clement]
De virg. [*Ep. virg.*]
2.6.1–2: 42n36
2.6.3–4: 42n37

Codex Theodosius
9.7.17: 217n92
16.1.4: 216n91

Consultationes Zacchaei et Apollonii
3.6: 185n135
3.6.2: 186n136
3.6.3: 186n137, 186n138
3.6.4: 186n138
3.6.5: 121n131, 186n139, 186n140
3.6.5–9: 186n141
3.6.10: 186n142

Cyprian
Dom. orat.
35: 111n76, 135n73
36: 191n161
Don.
16: 35n5, 232n8
[= *Ep.* 1] 1: 35n4

Ep.
1.2: 84n36
12.2: 84n36
27.1.2: 68n74
29: 71n94
38.1.2: 68n74
39.3: 84n36
39.4.3: 68n74
39.5.2: 68n74
63.16.1: 35n7, 36n9, 78n6
63.9: 86n41
Mort., 21: 142n115
Cyril of Alexandria
Comm. in XII proph. minor. 1.43: 135n77
Expos. in psalm.: 132n47, 132n48
Glaph. in pent.: 135n79
[Cyril of Jerusalem]
Myst. cat.
4.7: 81n20
5.20: 78n9, 269n196
14:8: 132n47
De vitis patrum 7 (*Verba seniorum*).38.1: 323n21
Diadochus of Photice, *Capita centum de perfectione spirituali* 73: 325n32
Didascalia
2: 346n137
9: 128n29
9.3: 128n28
12.6: 90n56
13: 100n38
21: 43n41, 44, 47n56, 50n68, 50n69
Didymus the Blind
Comm. in psalm.: 132n47
Comm. in psalm. 26: 153n178
Comm. in psalm. 40 7: 132n47
Comm. in Zach. 4.110: 135n78
Dio Chrysostom
Or.
33.10: 350n159
46.3–4: 114n94
Diodore of Tarsus, *Comm. in psalm. 23* 7: 274n19, 287n74
Dionysius of Alexandria, *Ep.*, 14.1: 48n63, 49n66
Dionysius of Halicarnassus
Ant. Rom
2.34.2: 221n112
7.72.11: 220n106
Comp., 17.8: 289n4
Dionysius Thrax, *Ars gramm.* 1.1: 72n96, 294n22
Egeria
Itin.
6.3: 148n154
10.7: 148n153
24: 195n181
24–25: 195n179
241: 106n56, 118n114, 154n188, 196n183, 280n39, 281n50, 282n53, 287n76
242: 106n57
243: 106n58, 195n182
244: 106n59, 280n41, 282n57
245: 73n100, 106n60, 138n95, 259n147
248: 280n40
248–9: 115n98, 154n188
248–12: 114n97
249: 65n59
24.10: 115n99, 155n189, 155n191
24.11: 115n100, 155n192
251: 114n97
256: 127n21
256–7: 224n123
257: 127n22
277–8: 129n34
291–2: 129n34
292: 129n35
29.40: 282n58
302: 130n41
30.10: 130n39
311: 133n55

312: 114n91
31.1: 224n124
31.2: 281n51
31.3: 224n125
31.4: 225n126
321: 133n55
351: 82n22
353: 133n55
371: 129n36, 130n37
374: 131n45
375: 131n43
376: 133n55
38: 124n5
391: 132n49
393: 280n42
393–4: 224n122
394: 224n121, 280n43
395: 132n50
401: 132n50
402: 132n50, 224n121
41–43: 132n52
433: 225n128
435: 132n53, 133n54, 133n55
436: 132n53
436–7: 225n129
475: 132n51

Epistula apostolorum 15 (26): 48n62

Ephrem Syrus, *De psalm.*, lines 5–7: 121n128

Epiphanius
Fid., 24: 105n53, 106n54, 113n88
Pan., 30.13.6 Holl 1: 350: 128n28

[Epiphanius], *Hom. in laud. Mar.*: 135n68

Eusebius
Comm. in psalm.: 37n17, 39n21, 120n122, 132n47
Comm. in psalm. 23: 119n121
Comm. in psalm. 33: 80n15
Comm. in psalm. 64: 99n35, 100n39, 102n42, 111n76, 356n194, 357n195
Comm. in psalm. 91: 135n74
Comm. in psalm. 104: 244n72
Comm. in psalm. 118: 104n51, 104n52
Comm. in psalm. 142: 104n49, 111n76
Comm. in psalm. (on v. 11): 132n47

Dem. ev.
1.10.28: 81n19
9.18.7: 135n76
10.1.25: 132n47

Didascalia, fr. 6: 356n192

H.E.
2.16–17: 45n44
2.17.16: 45n46
2.17.21–22: 45n45
2.17.22: 45n48, 123n2, 232n9, 243n70
5.23–24: 43n39
6.34: 45n49
6.43.11: 64n43
7.30.10: 51n71, 73n99, 138n94, 346n136
7.30.11: 51n73
7.30.12: 95n10
89.4: 226n135
89.5: 226n135
8.17.3–10: 226n132
9.1.10: 226n133
9.1.11: 226n134
9.9.9: 220n110
10.2.1: 99n32
10.3: 355n191
10.3.1–4: 99n32
10.3.3: 99n33
28.5: 51n75

In psalm. 71: 249n100

In psalm. 84: 134n61

In psalm. 118: 356n193

Periochae: 118n120

Quaest. ev. ad Marinum 2.2: 47n55

Vit. Const.
1.39.2: 220n110
4.22: 124n7

Evagrius Ponticus
Antirrhētikos 4.22: 188n147, 343n122, 354n184
De octo spiritibus malitiae 12: 354n181
Eulog. 9: 187n144
Orat. 82: 188n146
Prakt. 71: 343n125
Galen
Plac. Hipp. et Plat.
5.6.20: 329n55
5.6.21: 329n56
5.6.22: 330n61
Gaudentius, *Isag.* 20: 272n9
Gelasius of Caesarea Maritima, *H.E.* 2.31.7: 132n47
Gellius, Aulus
N.A.
19.9.3: 262n164
19.9.3–4: 263n171
Georgius Cedrenus, *Comp. hist.*: 209n58
Gerontius, *Vit. Melan. Jun.* 2.47: 279n34
Gregory of Nazianzus
Carm.
1.1.32 (*Carm. dog.* 32: *Hymn. uesper.*), 33–38: 273n17
1.2.10 (*Carm. mor.* 10 [*De virt.*]), lines 920–925 (PG 37:746–747): 273n12
2.1.16 (*Carm.de se ipso* 16: *Somn. de anastas. eccl.*), line 84: 273n16
2.1.34 (*Carm. de se ipso* 34: *In silent. ieiunii*) line 80: 273n15
2.1.37–44 (*Carm. de se ipso* 37–44): 347n146
Or.
Fun. in laud. Bas. Magn. (*Or.*43) 52: 126n13
Fun. in laud. Bas. Magn. (*Or.*43) 80.3: 144n128
Funebris oratio in partem (*Or.* 18).28: 124n8, 124n9
In laud. Athan. (*Or.* 21) 28: 200n4
In laud. Athan. (*Or.* 21) 29: 199n1, 199n2
In laud. Caesarii fratris (*Or.*7) 15.5: 140n104, 144n127
In sanct. bapt. (*Orat.* 40) 40: 104n50
Gregory of Nyssa
De deitate adversus Evagrium: 279n35
Encom. in xl mart. ii: 148n152
Inscr. psalm.
1.1: 336n90, 336n91, 336n92, 336n93
1.2: 333n76
1.2 and 1.3: 296n29
1.3: 307n60, 333n74, 333n75, 334n77, 334n78, 334n79, 334n80, 334n81, 334n82, 334n83, 334n84, 335n85, 335n86, 335n87, 336n89, 351n163
1.9: 337n94
27: 244n73
2.10: 307n59
Or. 1: 125n10
Oration in diem nat. Christi: 135n80
Vit. Macr.
1.15–17: 143n125
3: 96n14, 177n93
3:19–26: 177n94
5: 96n18
6: 198n192
7: 96n18
10: 143n125
10.6–10: 144n126
11: 96n18, 97n22, 143n125

11–35: 97n21
12: 143n125
22: 97n23, 177n95
26.23–29: 143n121
27: 323n19
27.3–7: 143n124
27.4–9: 143n122
27.9–11: 143n123
33: 144n129
33.6–8: 148n151
HAAureliani
6.5: 220n109
7.2: 220n109
HAClodiusAlbinus 13.5: 114n96
Heliodorus
Aeth., 2.3.2: 354n182
Schol. Londinensia: 295n23
Hilary of Poitiers
Tract. in psalm. 64 12: 102n44, 217n96
Hippolytus
In cant. cant. 14.1: 273n11
In Dan. 3.29.3: 22n29
Ref., 8.17.3–4: 134n67
Homily on the Psalms (Anon.)
3: 37n14
4: 38n19
5: 37n16, 39n22
6: 37n15
Iamblichus
Vit. Pyth. 15.64: 332n71
V.P. 15.64: 330n58
Ignatius, *Ep. Polycarp* 1.3: 191n161
[Ignatius], *Ep.* 9(*Ad Antioch.*) 12.2: 65n55
Index to the Festal Letters of Athanasius 28: 150n161
Isidore, *Etym.* 6.19.7–8: 255n129
Isidore of Pelusium, *Epistulae, Lib.* 1, *Ep.* 90: 325n30
Jerome
Chron., *Ol.* 189.3: 262n166
Chron., *praef.*: 358n204, 359n205
Comm. in ep. ad Eph.: 359n209, 360n210, 361n216
Comm. in ep. ad Eph., 3: 67n68, 69n80
Comm. in Esai., 2.5.20: 79n12
Contra Vigilantium, 1.5: 202n19
Ep.
21.26–27: 79n14
52.5: 360n211
52.5.6: 57n19, 67n66
53 (*Ad Paulum. presb.*).8.17: 358n203
54.13: 360n11
71.6: 79n14
107 (*Ad Laet.*). 9: 359n206, 359n208
108.29: 144n131, 144n132
125 *Ad Rust. monach.* 15: 359n207
128.4: 360n11
Praef. in Ezech.: 299n41
Praef. in Isai.: 299n41
Praef. Job.: 358n204
Tract. psalm. 9: 359n206
V. Pauli 16: 140102
John Chrysostom
Ad pop. Antioch. 19.4: 341n112
Ad Theodor. [2] 3:60: 174n79
Adv. ebr. et de res. dom. 2: 81n21
Ann., Hom. 4.5–6: 112n80
Cat. bapt., 8.17–18: 112n80
De Bernice et Prosdoce 3: 145n138
De Laz., Hom. 5.3: 142n116
De terrae motu: 9n45, 326n39, 327n40, 327n41
Disc. sur Bab.
5: 205n32
67: 204n26
67–69: 204n27
80–81: 205n32
93–94: 206n37
Expos. in psalm. 140, 1 and 3: 112n80
Hom. dicta post. reliq. martyr.
2: 212n72, 212n73
3: 211n68, 211n70, 211n71, 229n142

Hom. in diem nat. Jes. Chr.: 133n58
Hom. hab. in magn. Hebd. 2: 234n16
Hom. sur Bab.
8: 206n37
10: 205n34, 207n46, 208n51
In 1 Cor.
Hom. 36.6: 56n16, 56n17, 65n57, 247n84
Hom. 43.4: 341n112
In 1 Tim.
Hom. 14.4: 178n101
Hom.6.1: 112n80
In 1 Tim. 4, Hom. 14.4: 196n184, 320n9
In 1 Tim. 5
Hom. 14.4: 173n75, 175n80, 194n177, 297n32
Hom. 14.5: 140n103, 201n12
In Col.
Hom. 9.2: 349n155
Hom. 12.7: 350n161
In Heb. 2
Hom. 4.5: 141n110, 141n112, 142n117, 145n134, 145n135, 145n136, 146n139, 201n11, 354n185
Hom. 4.5–6: 145n133
In Joann., Hom. 62.4: 141n111, 141n113, 142n118
In Matt. 21, Hom. 68.3: 173n74, 178n100
In Matt.
Hom. 6.5: 321n10, 321n11
Hom 11.7: 113n85
Hom. 11.7: 234n13, 257n137
Hom. 31.4: 142n119, 143n120
Hom. 68.3: 252n116
In nat. Jes. Chr: 134n63
In psalm. 7
3: 281n47
15: 357n199
In psalm. 40 1: 326n38
In psalm. 41
1: 56n16, 234n14, 325n33, 349n154
2: 234n18, 234n19, 344n131, 357n198
In psalm. 117, 1: 56n16, 125n10, 234n15
In psalm. 134 1: 326n34
In psalm. 140, 1: 107n61, 109n69, 113n86, 256n131, 326n35, 326n36
In psalm. 144 1: 234n17, 257n136, 303n46
Laz., Hom. 5.3: 141n114
Pan. Juv 1: 204n26
Terr. mot.: 120n126, 226n131
[John Chrysostom], *Poen.*: xiiin1, 87n43
Josephus
Ant.
6.214: 16n5
7.305: 16n5
7.364: 16n5
8.984: 16n5
12.323: 2n7
Ap. 1.140: 16n5
Julian (emp.), *Ep.* 89b: 262n161
Justin (hist.), *Epit. hist. Philipp.* 9.8.15–16: 114n95
Justin Martyr
1 Apol.
37.3: 54n6
40.1–4: 134n66
65: 23n33
65–67: 78n8
67: 23n33
67.5: 90n56
Dial.
41.3: 17n12
70.4: 86n40
88.8: 128n28

97.1: 17n12
103.6: 128n28
Liber pontificalis
9: 59n31, 60n34
34: 60n34, 60n35
39: 61n40
48.11: 225n130
Livy, *Ab urb. cond.* 4.53.11–12: 219n104
Longus, *Daphn. et Chlo.* 3.21.2: 265n188
Lucian of Samosata, *Harm.* 1: 330n62
Lucretius, *Rer. nat.* 1.930–950 // 4.8–25: 350n157
[Macarius], *Apoph.* 33: 164n33, 182n124, 248n96
1 Macc
4:24: 2n7, 3n17, 5n26
4:52–59: 3n18
4:54: 2n7
2 Macc
2:11: 5n26
10:1–8: 4n22
10:6–7 NRSV: 4n23
10:7: 2n7
3 Macc
6:35: 2n7
7:13: 24n41, 244n77
7:16: 2n.7
4 Macc.
10.21: 10n51
18:15: 16n6
18.10–19: 10n48
18.15: 10n49
Mark the Deacon, *Vit. Porph.* 58: 201n10
Martial, *Ep.* 7.8.9: 220n107
Martyrdom of Polycarp 14: 86n42
Maximus of Tyre
Diss. 4.6: 350n158
Diss. 7.1: 117n109
Methodius, *Symp.*, 8.9: 128n28
Mishnah
m. Bik., 3.4: 13n65
m. Meg.
4.1: 2n4
4.2: 2n4
m. Pesaḥ
5.7: 2n9, 12n64
9.3: 210
9.3D–E: 2n10
10.5: 210
10.5E 24n41
10.6: 12n61
10.6–7: 3n12
10.8: 210
10.9: 12n61
m. Rosh ha-Shanah 4.7: 3n15
m. Sukk. 3.9: 3n13
m. Ta'anit, 4.5K 3n14
m. Tam. 7.4: 12n63
m. Ter. 11.10: 9n46
Niceta of Remesiana
Util. hymn.
1: 154n182
2: 154n184, 362n222
4: 344n129
5: 319n5, 322n16, 351n164
6: 344n130
7: 358n200
12: 154n186
13: 154n183, 154n187, 362n223, 363n225, 364n227, 364n228
Vil. 1: 154n185, 237n33
Nicetas Choniates, *Thes. pist.*: 275n23
Nichomachus, *Harm. Ench.* 2.1: 293n19
Opusculum de passione ac translatione sancti Saturnini, 1 [Prolog.]: 147n144
Ordo monasterii 2: 110n73, 286n72
Ordo Romanus I 85: 90n57
Origen, *Comm. in ev. Joann.* 1.31.220: 132n47
Origen
Hex.: 101n40, 101n41
In Num., Hom. 27.1.4: 54n9

In psalm. 67, Hom. 1.1: 118n119
Orat.
12: 111n76
12.2: 103n48, 191n161
31.1: 103n48
[Origen], *Frag. in psalm. 34:11*: 132n47
Ovid
Fast. 3.535: 9n45
Met. 4.763: 114n93
Trist. 2.509–20: 264n182
Pachomian Writings
Exc.
1: 169n57
2: 170n59
7: 170n63
17: 180n110
Inst. 1–12: 166n41
Inst. 14: 166n40, 166n41
Leg. 10: 166n41
Pachomii vita Bohairice
3–8: 193n168
9–10: 193n169
10: 193n170
27: 181n122
28: 168n48
33: 322n13
35: 169n54
64: 182n128, 361n218
82: 167n44, 250n105
83: 167n46
93: 140n103, 168n52
123: 140n103, 168n52
181: 167n47
201: 168n49, 180n112, 200n6
204: 168n51
205: 140n103, 168n52
206: 163n26
207: 140n103, 168n52, 181n120
Pachomii vita graeca 1
103: 140n103, 168n52
116: 140n103, 168n52
117: 140n103, 168n52
143: 200n7
147: 181n121
Pachomii vita graeca 3 32: 162n23
Pr.
3–14: 169n55
6: 169n56
8: 169n58
15: 170n60, 201n115
15–18: 169n55
16: 170n61
17: 170n62
49: 170n65
116: 181n118, 181n119
121: 166, 166n41
126: 166n41
139: 170n65
140: 171n66
Reg. Hor.
16: 171n67, 258n141
17: 170n64, 258n141
17 (CSCO 159: 86.33): 179n109
44: 181n117
45: 181n117
Palladius
Dial. 5: 194n176
L.H.
7.5: 188n148
22: 164n29
22.6: 162n21, 182n127
22.8: 162n21, 182n124
32.6: 162n21
43.3 (Recension G; ed. Bartelink): 279n32
Pass. Matth. (*Mart. Matth.*): 84n35, 246n81, 246n82
Paul Evergetinus
Synagoge
2.32: 322n14
4.37: 323n22
Paulinus of Milan
Vit. Ambr.
13: 151n167
13.3: 152n172, 238n42, 286n69

14.2: 215n83
32.3: 239n44
42: 238n43
Paulinus of Nola, *Carm.* 19(*Natal.* 11).329–342: 209n56
Pausanias 5.18.4: 265n186
Philo
Agr. 50: 16n4
Conf.
39: 16n4, 117n110
52: 16n4
Deus 74: 16n4
Flacc.
121: 2n7
122: 2n7
Gig. 17: 16n4
Migr. 157: 16n4
Mut. 115: 16n4
Plant.
29: 16n4
39: 16n4
Somn.
2.245: 16n4
2.246: 16n4
Spec. 1.272: 10n52
Spec. leg. 2.148: 11n57
Vit. contempl.
25: 11n53
29: 7n34, 7n35
30–33: 2n6
34: 45n46
64–89: 45n47
80: 7n34, 7n35, 243n68, 263n170
Philodemus
Mus. 4
fr. 131.9–11: 328n50
fr. 151.29–39: 329n54
Physiologus 35a: 121n129, 345n133
Plato
Leg.
653e–656c (esp. 656b–c): 328n48
659e: 350n156
Resp.
3398d: 295n26
310.398e–399a: 328n47
310.399a–c: 289n3, 328n46
399c: 328n47
Tim. 36e–37b with 47c–e, and 90c–d: 328n48
Pliny
Ep.
4.19.4: 264n183
7.4.9: 264n183
10.96: 231n2
Plutarch
Q.C.
7.14.1 (*Mor.* 743c): 263n168
7.8.4 (*Mor.* 712f–713a): 262n166
9.14.1 (*Mor.* 743c): 262n166
Sept. sap, 13 (*Mor.* 156c): 329n57
[Plutarch]
Mus.
28 (*Mor.* 1141a): 309n67
33 (1142f–1143e): 332n68
33 (1143a): 332n69
33 (1143c): 332n70
Psalms of Solomon 6.4: 8n40
Ptolemy
Harm.
1.79–11: 272n10
3.7: 330n59
Questions of Bartholomew
4.69: 41n34
4.70: 41n34
Quintilian, *Inst.* 1.8.2: 292n15, 293n17
Qumran Writings
1QH[a]XIX:5–6: 6n31
1QS X:9–10: 6n28
1QS X:23 (= 4Q260 V:5–6): 6n29
4Q397, frs. 14–17, col. 1 (= 4QMMT[d] =4QHalakhic Letter[d]): 16n8
4Q491(4QM[a]) fr. 17.4: 15n1

11QPs[a] (11Q5): 6n32
11QPs[b] (11Q6): 6n32
11QPs[c] (11Q7): 6n32
Regula magistra 47: 358n202
Revelatio sancti Stephani
rec. A 44–50: 213n77
rec. A 48: 214n80
rec. B 42–48: 213n77
rec. B 48: 214n80
Rufinus
H.E.
10.28: 207n49
10.31: 207n51
10.36: 205n35, 206n42, 207n47
10.37: 206n40
Severian of Gabala, *In mund. creat.*, Hom. 2.5: 249n103, 275n21, 287n74
Sibylline Oracles
3.726: 8n40
8.249: 242n66
Sidonius Apollinaris, *Ep.* 4.11.6: 73n106
Sirach 39:13, 14–15: 8n38
Socrates (hist.)
H.E.
35: 207n49
39: 207n50
3.18.1–2: 205n32
59.3–4: 208n53
5.22: 150n164
68: 227n137
68.1–9: 347n141
68.2: 276n24
68.3: 276n25
68.4: 253n118, 266n190, 276n27
68.10: 266n190
68.10–6.9.1: 276n26
88.1–3: 266n190
Soferim 18.1: 2n5
Sozomen
H.E.
1.12.10: 281n48
3.20.8: 253n119
4.3.1: 65n58
5.19.12–13: 204n26
5.19.12–17: 205n32
5.19.17–18: 207n48
5.19.17–19: 278n30
5.19.19: 205n36, 265n187, 268n195
71.21.4–5: 209n60
7.10.5: 201n13, 208n51, 208n54, 354n186
7.15.9: 250n106
7.21.1–3: 209n59
88: 227n137
88.1–3: 243n71, 277n28
88.1–5: 347n143
88.5: 227n138, 278n29
Strabo
Geog.
10.3.10: 328n49
16.2.6: 205n33
Suda, E 3819: 117n108
Suetonius, *Div. Iul.* 51: 220n105
T. Job, 14.1–3: 8n37
Tertullian
Adv. Marc. 5.8.12: 28n57
An. 9.4: 27n55, 28n61, 54n8, 117n112
Apol.
22.9: 342n117
39: 54n7, 78n8
39.1–4: 27n56
39.18: 21n25, 23n35, 231n4, 346n135
Bapt. 17.5: 22n28, 22n29
Carn. 20.3: 19n21, 28n59, 346n135
Cor.
3: 84n36
3.3: 35n8, 77n2, 77n3, 77n4
Didasc. 6.22: 84n36
Orat.
12.2: 25n45

19.1–4: 35n8, 77n2
23: 191n161
25: 25n45, 94n5, 103n47, 197n187
27: 23n36, 26n48, 94n4, 232n5
28.4: 26n49
Pat. 9.1–3: 142n115
Praescr. haer. 41.8: 63n42
Spec. 29.4: 23n34
Str. 7.7.40: 25n45
Ux.
2.5: 77n4
2.8.8: 94n4, 190n155
Testaments of the Twelve Patriarchs
T. Dom. 2.11: 73n102, 138n96, 259n148
T. Jos., 8.5: 8n41
Themistius, *Protr. ad. Nic.* (*Or.* 24): 350n160
Theodoret of Cyr
H.E.
2.24.8–11: 255n125
2.24.9: 147n147
2.24.10: 147n148
3.10.1–2: 205n32
3.10.2: 204n26
3.10.3: 207n48, 303n44
3.12.1: 206n39, 207n44
3.19.1–6: 98n29
4.28.1: 255n126
Historia religiosa
2.15: 207n51
30(*Domnina*).2: 323n20
Vit.
5.1–5: 255n126
5.5: 255n127
Interp. in psalm. 40 7: 132n47
Interp. in psalm. 117 v. 24: 135n75
Theodosius, *De situ terrae sanctae* 7: 130n38
Theognis 943–944: 117n109
Tobit 13:18: 24, 41n32, 244
Tosefta
t. Pesah, 10.8: 3n11
t. Sanh., 12.10a: 9n46
t. Soṭa
5.4d–e: 41n28
6.2–3: 41n29, 267n193
6.3: 41n30
6.3B: 3n16
Victor of Vita
Hist. pers. Afr. prov.
1.41 [1.13]: 70n88, 87n45, 249n104
3.34 [5.9]: 70n88
3.39 [5.10]: 74n109
3.40 [5.13]: 74n110
Virgil, *Ecl.* 8: 264n180
Vita Adae et Evae (a.k.a. *Apoc. Mos.*)
43: 245n78
43.4: 41n32
Vita sancti Auxenntii 46–47: 313n80
Wisdom 19:18: 311n75
[Zachariah Rhetor], *Chron.* 4.11: 73n103, 259n149

SUBJECT INDEX

Page numbers in *italics* are for figures.

accent 306–8
acedia 184, 187, 353–4
Acts of Andrew and Matthew 83
Acts of Cyprian 140102
Acts of the Martyrdom of St. Saturninus 146–7
Acts of Paul 20, 32, 149
  ascetic households 95
  community suppers 21–3, 77
  fasts/fast-breaking 48
Acts of Thomas 95
Acts of Xanthippe and Polyxena 245–6
Adolius, Abba 278–9
adventus 219–23, 228
Aelia Capitolina 13
age, clerical singers 68–71
Akiba, Rabbi 9, 41
akrostichia 242–3
Albinus 317–18
Alexandrians 48–9, 150n162, 295
Alleluia 23–7, 33, 267
  Cassian on 284–5
  and Communion 85, 87–9
  formats 243–50
  in *Homily on the Psalms* 37, 38–42
  and responsorial psalmody 243–50, 251
altars 92
Amalar 58
Ambrose of Milan
  Aeterne rerum conditor 49n65
  and antiphons 271
  biography by Paulinus of Milan 286
  Cain and Abel 236
  direct choral psalmody 256, 257–8
  and funerals 142, 145
  hymns 347, 357
  on prayers in church 110, 113–14
  prelude to Communion 115
  purpose of psalms 319
  and responsorial psalmody 235–9, 304
  on singers 56, 67, 68–9
  on singing 178
  translation of relics of Gervasius and Protasius 214–19
  and vigils 150–1, 152
Ammianus Marcellinus 206, 210
amulets 341–3
Anastasis (Jerusalem)
  daily prayer 106, 195
  Epiphany 127
  Holy Week 131
  Lenten vigils 129–30
  preludes to Communion 114–15
  public liturgical processions on feast days 223–5
  Sunday vigil 154–5
Andrew, St., translation to Constantinople 209
angels
  Alleluia 245–50
  and antiphons 273–4, 276, 277, 284–5
  in the *Apocalypse of Paul* 85, 87–9
  in the Bohairic *Life of Pachomius* 167–8, 169
  monks singing with 173–6
  Rule of the Angel 161–6, 178–9, 247–8

ante sacrificium 57–63
"antiphons and responses" 274–5
antiphons/antiphonal singing 159n10, 253–4, 271–88
Antony 171–2, 183
  and daily psalmody 190–3
  and demons 171, 353–4
  emotions and psalms 323
  and Paul the Hermit 140
  and the twelve psalms/prayers 164
Aphrahat, *Demonstrations* 123–4
Apocalypse of Paul (*Visio Pauli*) 85, 87, 88, 92
Apophthegmata Patrum 164
Apostolic Constitutions 33–4, 56
  Christmas 133
  church prayers 107–10, 111–12, 113
  funerals 139, 141
  and the *Gloria* 253
  Psalm 33 79
  psalmody as prayer 117–18
  on readers and cantors 63–5, 69–70
  response to psalms 242–3
Apostolic Tradition
  community suppers 136–7
  readers and singers 71, 73
  virgins and children's choirs 259
Appian 219n104
Aquila 101, 357
Arcadius Augustus, Emperor 228
Arians 74, 147, 211, 227, 235, 266, 276–7, 346
Aristides, Aelius 263–4, 349
Aristides Quintilianus 318, 332–3
Aristophanes of Byzantium 298n35
Aristotle, *The Art of Rhetoric* 114
Aristoxenus 293, 332
Arius, *Thalia* 346
Armenian Lectionary 74, 81
  antiphons 282–3
  on Epiphany 127–8
  Holy Week 131–2
  on the Last Supper 20
  public processions 223
  and refrains 250–2
  responsorial psalmody 242, 250–2
Ars grammatica (Dionysius Thrax) 72
Asaph 37, 39
ascetics 25
  households 94–9
  and tears 323–4
  traveling 42
  women's monastery at Annisa 95–7
  see also monastic life
Assyrians 259
Asterius the Sophist 2, 9n45, 134
Athanasius
  Alleluias in psalms 24n40, 244
  and the bishop in Egypt 180
  on bread 80
  Defense against the Arians 149–50
  expulsion of 149–50
  on fast-breaking 49
  Letter to Marcellinus 55, 337–8
    how to read Scripture 316–17
  Life of Antony 171–2, 181–2, 191–3
  lyrical vocalization 314–18
  On His Flight 55
  and Pachomius 168–9
  procession 199–201
  purpose of psalms 319, 325, 327, 337
  on readers 64
  responsorial psalmody 242
  lyrical vocalization 314–18
  speech-types in the Psalter 120
  see also Ps.-Athanasius
Augustine 53
  on age of *adulescentia* 69n80
  on Alleluia 88, 246, 249
  amulets 341
  on birth of Christ 135
  on Christmas 133–6
  Confessions 286
    on Athanasius 55, 352
    on melodies 296, 314–15
    responsorial psalmody 235
  and funerals 140–1, 202
  pleasure and temptation 351–2

on prayers in church 113
Psalm against the Donatists 266, 347
psalm lessons 57, 67–8
psalms and hymns as prayer 281, 357
purpose of psalms 320, 322, 324
responsorial psalmody 235, 238, 239–41
Retractions, on Hilary and psalms *ante oblationem* 89–90
Rule of Augustine 120
singing well 362
theater songs 9n45
on translation of relics of Gervasius and Protasius 216
on tunes 296
on the vigil in Milan 151–2
Auxentius 312–13
Azarias 252

Babylas 147, 194, 203–8, 229, 268, 278
Babylonians 259
baptism, of Jesus 128–9
Bardaisan 347
Basil of Caesarea 95–7, 349
and direct choral psalmody 256
on Epiphany 126
and formats of psalmody 237
and funerals 144, 202
Longer Rules 176–7, 196, 197, 342
and martyr feasts 148
melodies 296, 297
personal psalmody 194
prayer 121
purpose of psalms 319, 322, 327
Shorter Rules 197
two choirs 254
Basil the Elder 96n17
basilicas
Athanasius's escape 149
conflict between Justina and Ambrose 150–2, 216–17, 229, 235–6, 238
Basilides 49, 125, 125–6
bells 344
benefits of psalms *see* purposes of psalmody
Bethlehem, monasteries 158–9
Bible
Acts 9, 103, 118, 149
Amos 311
2 Chronicles 4, 260
Colossians 18, 30, 349
1 Corinthians 18, 20, 311
2 Corinthians 85
Ephesians 18, 26
Exodus 7, 148, 252
Ezekiel 185
Ezra 260
Isaiah 92, 104, 110, 173, 173–5, 249, 273, 275
James 9, 142
John 79, 80, 129, 341
Luke 127, 173
Mark 11
Matthew
Hosanna 248
John Chystostom's sermons on 142–3, 172–3
and Paschal gatherings 46, 47
Passover 11, 248
Numbers 54
Psalms
2 128, 250
3 84
5 110, 111
10 119
11 84
14 119
15 119
18 119, 134, 218
19 300, *300*
22 20, 80–2, 127, 146, 250
30 12, 117
30 MT 30
31 146
33 78–80, 83, 269
35 119
40 84, 326

41 234
44 119
50 110, 153, 158, 159, 256
62
daily psalmody 103–4, 108–11, 194
direct choral psalmody 256
monastic life 159
as soul therapy 326
64 99, 102, 103, 110
67 98
68 316
71 15, 119
79 127
81 (MT) 12
82 (MT) 12
84 133–4
89 110, 159, 342
90 176, 342
91 342
95 136
96:7 205
109 17, 128
109 (110 MT) 251
110 (MT) 17
112 218
113 19
113 (MT) 19
114 12, 145–6, 146
114 (MT) 12, 19
115 84, 146
117
and the birth of Christ 135
and Communion 80
and Easter 125
and Epiphany 127, 224
and Holy Week 130
homily on 234
and Palm Sunday 114, 130, 131
and responses 281
118 3, 104, 110, 115
133 173–5
135 303
136 3–4
138 211
140
daily psalmody 102–3, 106–7, 108–9, 111, 194
direct choral psalmody 256
as soul therapy 326
spiritual sacrifice 356
141 344
142 103, 104
144 80, 234, 257, 303
145 15, 234
148 158, 159
149 158, 159
150 159, 249, 311
Revelation 245, 246
Romans 17
Song of Songs 236
1 Thessalonians 26, 190–1
1 Timothy 173
Boethius 317–18
Booths, festival of 3, 4, 260
bread from heaven 79–80

Callinicus of Rufinianae, *Life of Hypatius* 279
canonical singers (term) 71
Canons of Athanasius 66–7, 82–3, 92, 126, 346
Canons of Hippolytus 82, 91, 112–13, 136, 343–4
Canons of Laodicea *see* Council of Laodicea
cantors *see* singers
Cappadocia, monastic life in 176–7, 349
Carthage 54
Communion 77
community suppers 27–8
household prayer 94
morning service 35
readers and singers 70, 71, 73–4
Cassian, John 110
Conferences 121, 178–9
direct choral psalmody 258–9
direct psalm lessons 242
doxologies 252

Institutes 121, 157–61
antiphons 283–5, 287–8
on prayer 196
purpose of psalms 323
Rule of the Angel 247–8
on the singing angel 178
Cassius Dio *see* Dio Cassius
cathedral prayer 99–113, 196
cathedral psalmody 10–11, 100, 103
Cato, Marcus Porcius (the Elder) 294, 340
Cedrenus, Georgius 91n57, 209
Celestine I 57–63, 89n52
chants 294
adventus 219–23, 228
and magic 340, 342–3
chariots 210
children
choirs 107, 137, 138, 259, 262, 263
as clerical singers 68–71, 75
Hosanna 248
martyrs 147
translation of relics 204
processions 224
vandalism by 151
choirs 8, 73–5, 95, 107, 137, 138, 259, 269
angelic 273, 275
format using two 254–6
Jewish 260–70
and John Chrysostom 227, 229
psalmody with two 254–6, 278
Roman period 221, 262, 263
Christ hymns 51, 95, 346
Christian hymns 30, 51, 105, 107, 190, 253, 345–6
Christmas 133–6
Chronicon Paschale 228
Chrysostom, John *see* John Chrysostom
Church of the Holy Sepulcher (Jerusalem) 115, 223–4
Church of the Resurrection *see* Anastasis
churches *see* cathedral prayer
citharas 30, 38, 211, 219n104, 339, 344
class, Gregory of Nyssa on 143
Claudian 210
cleansing, and Communion 92
Clement of Alexandria 20, 28–9, 32, 36
and Christmas 135
on Epiphany 125–6, 128
magical uses of music 339
and monasteries 197
Paedagogus 29–31, 289–91, 330–1
psalmody as prayer 118
purpose of psalms 327, 330–1
responsorial psalmody 265–6
Stromata 31, 289, 331
codices 299, 300–3
Alexandrinus 112n79, 165, 299, 303
Bezae (D) 128
Sinaiticus 299
single-gospel 341
Vaticanus 112n79, 299
Commodus 219
communication, and good singing 362
Communion 77–91
and Hallel psalms 20
and Levitical song 13
morning Eucharists and community suppers 136–9
preludes to 114–16
purposes of Communion psalmody 91–2
and responsorial psalmody 257
community suppers 20–1, 32, 48–50, 75, 77
in *Acts of Paul* 21–3
and morning Eucharists 136–9
see also dinner parties
compunction 121, 183–5, 321–5, 362
confession, psalm of 153
Constantine 129, 208–9, 210, 220
Constantinople, processions of martyr relics 208–12
Constantius, Emperor 149, 200, 210
cosmic music 333–5
Council of Alexandria 149–50
Council of Constantinople 107
Council of Laodicea 54–5
church prayers 105

on readers and singers 63, 64, 71
reading by singing 291
singing in church 297
use of hymns 346
cross symbols, in apotropaic texts 344
cult hymns 264
curative powers 327, 329–30, 332, 335, 336, 351
cymbals 38, 339, 364
Cyprian 33
and Christmas 135
on Communion 86
on community meals 78
and funerals 142
Letter to Donatus 34–6, 364
on readers 64
Cyril of Alexandria 135
Cyril of Jerusalem, *Mystagogical Catecheses* 78–9, 81–2

Damasas, Pope 60–2
Daniel 8
David 358
in *Apocalypse of Paul* 85
author of the Psalms 16–19, 119–20
and Communion 87, 88
confession 153
in *Homily on the Psalms* 36–42
John Chrysostom on 281
in *Passion of Matthew* 84
and Saul 188, 327, 344
Dead Sea Scrolls 15
delighting God 8, 101–2, 356–8
demons 187–8, 342, 342–4
and Antony 171, 353–4
Dialogues of Zacchaeus and Apollonius 121, 185–6, 188
diapsalma 37–8, 40
Didascalia 108
against heretical hymns 346
Communion 90n56
daily cathedral prayer 100, 108
on Epiphany 128
melodic reading 33–4
Paschal gatherings 43–7, 50
private reading 291, 346
Didymus the Blind 153
and Christmas 135
dinner parties, Christian 28–31, 33, 36
Dio Cassius 219
Dio Chrysostom 114, 350
Diodochus of Photice 325
Diodore and Flavian 255
Diodore of Tarsus 274
Diogenes of Babylon 328–9
Dionysius of Alexandria 48–9
Dionysius of Halicarnassus 220, 289
Dionysius Thrax, *Ars grammatica* 72, 294–5
direct psalmody (*in directum*) 231, 233, 242, 256–9
Domatius and Maximus 165
Donatists 266, 347, 352
Donatus, Aelius 315
Dorian mode 289–90, 294, 327–8, 330, 330–2
doves 344–5
doxologies 252–3, 283–5, 288
dress, for singing 360
dual choirs 254–6, 278

earthquakes 120, 213, 226, 326–7
Easter 43
vigils *see* Paschal vigils
Easter Octave 131, 132–3, 224
ēchos 311–14
Edict of Milan 99–105, 180
Edict of Recantation 226
Edict of Thessalonica 107
Eduthun (Jeduthun) 37, 39
Egeria
on antiphons 271–2, 280–3, 287
choirs 139
on Communion 81–2
Easter vigil 124
on Epiphany 127, 128
Holy Week/Easter Octave/Fifty Days of Easter 130–3
Lenten vigils 129–30

- monastic use of psalms 195–6
- preludes to Communion 115
- on psalm lessons 65, 73
- psalmody at the daily office 107, 189
- psalmody as prayer 118
- public processions 223–5
- Sunday vigils 103, 110, 114, 154–5

eight-mode system 310, 312
Eleazar ben Yose 41, 267
emotion 320–5
- *see also* soul therapy

endings 242–3
Ephrem Syrus 121, 347
epinicia 220–1
Epiphanius
- birth of Christ 135
- on church prayers 113
- *On the Faith* 105–6

Epiphany 125–9, 224, 251
Epistula apostolorum 48
Ethan 37, 39
Ethiopic I/II 137–8
Eucharist *see* Communion
Eudoxia, Empress 210–11, 227, 228–9, 355
Eusebius 33
- on bread 80
- and Christmas 135
- on daily prayer 93–4
- on Edict of Milan 99
- "Eusebius of Caesaria Concerning *Diapsalma*" 37–9
- on hymns 355–8
- ministerial offices 63–4
- on Paschal vigils 45–7
- on Paul of Samosata 51
- on Psalm 22 80–1
- psalmody as prayer 118–19
- on the Psalter 249
- public processions 226
- responses 243
- spread of psalmody 194, 197
- victory chants 220–1
- on when to pray 100–5
- *see also* Ps.-Eusebius

Evagrius Ponticus 158
- *Antirrhētikos*, apotropaic power 343
- pleasure of melody 353–4
- *Treatise to Eulogius* 186–7

exarchein 265

fast/fast-breaking 46–50, 124, 125
Felix (martyr) 203n23, 214, 215, 218
festivals, and Jewish psalm-singing 2–5
Fifty Days of Easter 132, 249
First Greek Life of Pachomius 163
Flavian and Diodore 255
Florus, *Vigil of Venus* (*Pervigilium Veneris*) 264
formats 231–3, 268–70
- Alleluia 243–50
- antiphons 253–4
- direct choral 256–9
- doxologies 252–3
- endings 242–3
- refrains 233–42
  - and the Armenian Lectionary 250–2
- two choruses 254–6, 270
- and the wider culture 259–67

funerals 139–46, 201–2, 229
- and Pachomians 168, 181, 182

Gabriel (angel) 245
Galen 329
Galerius, Emperor 226
Gallus Caesar 204
Gellius, Aulus 263
gender, Gregory of Nyssa on 143
Gerontius, *Life of Melania* 279, 287
Gervasius, translation of relics of 214–19, 229
gifts
- Paschal gatherings 50
- *see also* sacrifice

Gloria in excelsis 59, 105, 112n79, 173, 252
gobalas 251
Good Friday 131–2

Gospel of the Ebionites 128
Gospel of Matthew 248
Greco-Roman world 261–6, 333
Greece 259–60
  music 305, 309, 333–4
Greek acclamation 221–3
Gregory of Nazianzus
  and antiphons 273–4
  on Athanasius's return from exile 199–200, 201
  on Epiphany 126
  and funerals 140, 144
  Paschal vigils 124
  poetry 347
Gregory of Nyssa 95–7, 197
  on Alleluia 244
  and Christmas 135
  on David 307, 358, 362
  and funerals 143–4
  hypopsalma 279
  Life of Macrina 177, 198
  and martyr feasts 147–8
  on melody 350–1
  personal psalmody 194
  sensory musical pleasure 333–6
Gregory Thaumaturgis 96n15

Hallel 2–5, 11–12, 19–20, 40–1, 50, 260–1, 267, 269
Hallelujah 2n10, 24, 40
Hanukkah 3, 4, 5
harmoniai 290, 291–2
harmonics 332
harps 5–6, 38, 311
Heman 37, 39
heretical hymns 345–8
Hermogenes 134
hesed 3–4, 260, 267
Hesiod, Theogony 263
Hilarius, Pope 225
Hilary (layman of Carthage) 89, 91
Hilary of Poitiers 102, 217, 236, 347
Hillites 12, 19
Hippolytus of Rome 36
Historia Augusta 114
Hodayoth (1QH) 5
  The Thanksgiving (Hodayoth) Scroll 6
holy sites, pilgrim rites 148
Holy Week 130–1
Homily on the Psalms (Anon.) 24, 36–42, 120, 246
Homoeans 206–7, 227
honor, as purpose of psalmody 354–8
horns 38
Horsiesios 163, 168, 193
Hosanna 248
households 25
  daily prayer 93–9, 111
  Jewish practices 7–12
  responsorial psalmody at meals 234
hymnbook, book of Psalms as 190
hymnos (Greek term) xxx, 15–16, 116–17
hymns 355
  Christ 95
  Christian 30, 51, 105, 107, 190, 253
  cult 264
  Eusebius on 355–8
  heretical 345–8
  term 7, 15, 17, 46, 280–1
  see also Christ hymns
hypopsalma 279

Iamblichus, *Life of Pythagoras* 329
improvisation 291, 295, 296
incipits 249, 296, 342
Index to the Festal Letters of Athanasias 150
introit 57–9, 60, 89
Irenaeus 86
Isidore of Pelucium 325
Isidore of Seville 255

Jeduthun (Eduthun) 37, 39
Jerome 57
  on Antony 140
  on David 358–9
  and forged letters to Pope Damasus 60–2

and funerals 144–5
and martyr feasts 202–3
Psalm 33 as a Communion psalm 79
and psalm scrolls 298
readers and singers 67, 69, 72
and the Rule of the Angel 163
on singing well 359–61
stichic approach in Bible translation 299
translation of Pachomius's *Precepts* 163, 167, 169, 170, 180–1
translation of the *Rule of Pachomius* 161

Jerusalem *see* Egeria
Job, in the *Testament of Job* 7–8
John the Baptist 209–10
John Chrysostom
amulets 341
and antiphons 277, 281
on Christmas 133
Communion psalms 80, 81
on David 281
and formats of psalmody 233–4, 256, 257
and funerals 139, 140n103, 141–2, 145, 201–2, 354
on the *Gloria* 252–3
lineation 303
melody 297, 325–6, 349, 350
monastic use of psalms 194–5, 196
on Paschal vigils 125
on prayers 109, 112, 113, 120
psalm lessons 56, 65
purpose of psalms 357
moral formation and soul therapy 325–7
tears 320–1
on singing 178, 186, 344, 347
spontaneous public song 226, 227
Syrian monasticism 172–6
theater songs 9n45
on translations of relics 204, 207, 208, 228–9, 230

John II of Jerusalem 79, 212–13
Josephus 2, 16
Judaism 117, 269
apotropaic prayer 342–3
daily prayer 93
hymns and praises 355
psalm-singing 1–2, 14
festivals 2–5
household/recreational/work settings 7–12
Levitical psalmody 12–13
sectarian psalmody 5–7
responsorial performance 260–1, 267

Julian, Emperor ("the Apostate") 98, 204–7, 255n126, 262
Justin (historian) 114
Justin Martyr 23, 54, 86
on birth of Christ 134
and Epiphany 128
offertory 90n56

Justina, Empress 151, 216–17, 235, 237–8, 258n140

kinnor 8
Kyrie eleison 107, 138, 259

Last Supper 19–20
lectors *see* readers/lectors
Lenten vigils 129–30
Leontius, bishop of Antioch 147, 204, 206–7, 255
lessons
"before the sacrifice" 57–63
clerical readers and cantors/singers 63–8
age of singers 68–71
training 71–5
history of sung psalm readings 53–7, 75

Levitical psalmody 12–13
Liber pontificalis 57, 59–63, 223, 225
Life of Auxentius 313
Life of Pachomius 166–9
on Athanasius 200
and emotions 322

funerals 140
recitation 180–2
lineation 297–304, *298*, *300–2*
lining out 269
Liturgy of Saint James 83
Longus 265
Lord's Prayer 93
Lucernarium see vespers
Lucian the Priest, *Revelation of Saint Stephen* 212
Lucian of Samosata 330
Lucifer, Bishop 207
Lucretius, *De rerum natura* 350
Luke, relics of, translated to Constantinople 209
Lydian mode 294, 330
lyres 30, 263, 290

Macarius 164–5, 182
see also Ps.-Macarius
3 Maccabees 24
4 Maccabees 10, 14, 16
Maccabeus, Judas 3, 4
Macrina the Elder 96, 197
Macrina the Younger 95–6, 143–4, 176–7, 197–8
and martyr feasts 148
and tears 322–3
magical powers 339–45
Mamertus Claudianus 73–4
Marcion 27–8
Mark the Deacon, *Life of Porphyry* 201
marriage
encratic 95
and lectors and singers 69–70
Tertullian on 25
Martial 220
Martianus Capella 318
Martyrdom of Polycarp 86
Martyrdom of Saint Theodotus of Ancyra 95
martyria 147–8
Martyrium (Jerusalem) 20, 82n22
Epiphany 128
Paschal vigil 124
martyrs
feasts of the 146–8
honored by psalmody 354–5
translation of relics 201–3, 228
Babylas 203–8
Constantinople 208–12
Gervasius and Protasius 214–19
Stephen 212–14
Masoretes 15
matins 110, 113, 159
Matthew
in *Passion of Matthew* 83–4, 246–7
see also Gospel of Matthew
Maximus and Domatius 165
Maximus of Tyre 350
Melania Junior 279
Meletius 66n64, 201, 207–8
melismatic Alleluias 88, 249–50
melodic inflection 295–7, 352
melodic reading 33–4, 45, 292, 337, 338–9
see also reading by singing
melodic singing 180, 181, 183, 188, 293–4, 308, 315
melody
and compunction 324–5
and healing 340
and intoned reading 291
melody-making 305–10
modes 310–14
as morally dangerous 351
music ethos 289–91
phrasing and lineation 297–304, *298*, *300–2*
reading by singing 291–5
and semi-lyrical reading 314–18
as a sweetener 348–54
and tones 295–7, *296*
melos 313
middle vocalization 316–18
Mishnah 2, 3, 5, 11, 41, 261
modal selection 289–90
modes 310–14, 327–8, 329–32
monastic life 121, 279
Cappadocia 176–7, 349

John Cassian 157–61
and the Pachomian community 166–72
Rule of the Angel 161–6
singing or reciting 177–89, 322–3, 361
spread of psalm-singing to the wider Church 189–98
Syrian 172–6
and the wider church 189–98
women's monasteries 95–7, 279
Monica 146, 151
monks
group psalmody 258
and processions 200, 201, 224, 229
see also monastic life
moral formation 325–33
morning service 35
Muratorian Canon 346–7
music ethos 289–91, 329–32, 333
musical instruments 6, 29
citharas 30, 38, 211, 219n104, 339, 344
cymbals 38, 339, 364
harps 5–6, 38, 311
horns 38
kinnor 8
lyres 30, 263, 290
psalteries 30
psalterion 339
strings 38
trumpets 311
Mystogogical Catecheses 78–9, 81–2, 269

Nabor (martyr) 203n23, 214, 215, 218
Nehemiah, Rabbi 267
Nicene Christianity 107, 207–8, 227, 347
and antiphons 277–8
Constantinople 211, 253
Niceta of Remesiana
apotropaic symbols 344
delighting God 357–8
on formats of psalmody 237
melody as medicinal 351
On the Usefulness of Hymnody 154
purpose of psalms 319, 322
on singing well 362–4
on vigils 237
Nicetas Choniates 275
Nicomachus of Gerasa 293–4

oblation 89–91
Octoechos 312
odes, Israelite 9
offertory 89, 90
Ordo monasterii 110, 286, 287
Origen 33
Hexapla 101
Homilies on Ezekiel 128
sermon on Numbers 54
when to pray 103
Ovid 9n45, 114, 264

Pachomians 158
group psalmody 258, 361
literature 179–80
Pachomius 167–72
Precepts 163, 167, 169–70, 180
and the Rule of the Angel 161–3, 166
pagan rites/cults 107–8, 116, 262
see also unbelievers
Palladius 182, 278–9
Lausiac History 161, 162, 164, 165, 287
on monastic psalmody 188
Palm Sunday 130
public 224–5
Pambo, Abba 183–4
Pamphilus 209
Paschal gatherings 43–51
processions 226
Paschal vigils 123–5
Passion of Matthew (or *Matthias*) 83–4, 246–7
Passover 11–12, 19, 43
Paul (Apostle)
in *Homily on the Psalms* 39
on mourning 142

on prayer as thanksgiving 18, 26–7
on prayer without ceasing 93
singing 349
and vigils 149
Paul the Hermit 140
Paul of Samosata 51, 73, 95, 138, 346
Paul the Simple 164
Paula, abbess 144–5
Paulinas of Nola 209
Paulinus of Milan 151n167, 152
Life of Ambrose 215, 238–9, 286
Pausanias 265, 266
Peace of Constantine 197
Pentecost 129, 132
persecutions, of Christians 203, 226, 235
personal psalmody 190n155, 194
Philo 117
On the Contemplative Life 5, 45, 243, 263
on psalm-singing 2, 7, 10–11
Philodemus 328–9
phrasing 295, 297–304, 308, 362
Phrygian mode 289, 290, 294, 328, 330–1
Physiologus 121, 344–5
pilgrim rites, holy sites 148
Plato 327–8, 331, 349–50
pleasures, and music 326–30, 333–6, 348–54
Pliny 264
plurals 113–14, 174, 176
Plutarch 262–3, 329
Pompeii 348–9
popular songs 266, 268, 290, 349
Porphyrios 287
Posidonius 328
praise 15, 26, 40–1, 354–8
prayer
daily 93
cathedrals 99–113
households 25, 94–9
psalmody as 116–22
term 45–6
pre-anaphoral rites 90
preludes to Communion 114–16
processions 227–30
and adventus chants 219–23, 228
episcopal 199–201
martyr relics 201–3, 208–12
public, on feast days 223–6
spontaneous public 226–7
pronuntio 315
prophesy 16–17, 22, 119–20, 134
Protasius, translation of relics of 214–19, 229
protest psalms 206, 229
Prudentius 347
Ps.-Athanasius
Discourse on Salvation to a Virgin 247, 323
Ps.-Basil 115
Ps.-Clement, *Letters to Virgins* 33, 42
Ps.-Ignatius 65
Ps.-Macarius, *Apophthegmata* 164
Ps.-Plutarch, *On Music* 332
psalmos (Greek term) 15–16
psalms, Egeria's use of the term in Latin 280–1
psalteries 30
psalterion 339
Ptolemy, Claudius 330
Publia 97–8
purposes of psalmody 319
honor and praise 354–8
moral formation/soul therapy 325–33
spiritual ardor 321, 323
tears and compunction 320–5
see also pleasures
Pythagoras 327, 328, 329

Quartodecimans 20, 43–4, 47, 49, 50
Questions of Bartholemew 41n34
Quintilian 292–3
Qumran community 5–6, *298*, 299, 300
quotation formulas 103, 175

readers/lectors 53, 63–8, 306
age of 68–71
moral character 361

and refrains 242
training 71–5
Vandal attack 249
see also reading by singing
reading by singing 291–5
recitative 308–9
reciting, and monastic life 177–89
refrains 233–42, 250–2
and Alleluias 243–50
Regulations of Horsiesios 166, 170–1, 179
responsorial psalmody 231–42, 268–70
and Alleluias 243–50
antiphons 253–4
in the Armenian Lectionary 250–2
definition 231
direct choral psalmody 256–9
doxologies 252–3
endings 242–3
wider culture 259–67
see also antiphons/antiphonal singing
rhoizos 354
rhythm 289, 307–8
ritual power 339–45
Roman period
acclamations/chants 219–23
music 305–6, 309–10, 331
music-ethos 329–30
song during 261–2, 266, 360
Rosh ha-Shanah 3
Rufinus of Aquileia 279
on translation of relics 204, 205, 206–7
Rule of the Angel 161–6, 247–8

sacrifice
and Communion 85–7, 92
spiritual 256, 356, 357
Samuel (prophet) 228
Saul 16n5, 98, 188, 327, 344
Scripture readings 44, 50, 53–4, 55n11, 59
Athanasius on 316–17
self-pleasure, and singing 187–8
Severian of Gabala 249, 275
Shammaites 12, 19
Shema 267
Shepherd of Hermas 347
Sibylline Oracles 8
Sidonius Apollinaris 73–4
Silvanus, Abba 184, 310
singers, liturgical 55–7, 63–8
age of 68–71
dress 360
terms 56
training 71–5, 361
singing well 358–64
Sirach (Hebrew book) 8
"six sections" 166
social meals *see* dinner parties
Socrates (historian) 206, 276–7, 347
Sofer Tehillim ("Book of Praises") 15, 117
solo psalmody 231, 242, 245–6, 259, 260, 262, 264, 266, 268, 348–9
and doxologies 252
processions 218, 222, 230
Song of Moses (Ex 15) 7, 148
Song of the Sea (Exod 15) 7, 41, 252, 267
Song of Songs 9
song-passing 30, 31, 36
songs *see* singing
soul therapy 325–33
Sozomen 65, 347
on Alleluias 250
antiphons 277–8, 281, 288
on doxologies 253
funeral of Bishop Meletius 201, 354
psalm endings 243
translation of Babylas 205, 206, 268
translation of John the Baptist 209–10
translation of Meletius 208
spiritual sacrifice 256, 356, 357
stage songs *see* theater songs
stational liturgy 225–6
Stephen 212–14
stichic approach 299
Strabo 328
strings (musical instrument) 38
Suda 116–17
Suetonius 220

suppers 190, 268
  see also community suppers; symposia
Sylvester, Pope 60
symbols
  and magical power 344
  singing as 339
Symmachus 101, 357
symposia 31, 262, 349
  Christian community 23–8, 331
  see also community suppers
Syria, monasticism 172–6
Syrianus 149

taste, as temptation 351
tears 320–5
Telesphorus, Pope 59
temptation, and taste 351
Terpander, *Hymn to Zeus* 289
terpseis 101, 357
Tertullian 32
  Against Marcion 28
  Alleluia responses 24, 246
  on Christian community symposia/suppers 20–1, 23–8
  on Communion 77–8
  on David 19
  Exhortation to Chastity 25
  and funerals 142
  household prayer 94, 197
  on hymns in church 346
  liturgical order 54
  On the Incarnation 28
  On Prayer 24, 25–6
  On the Soul 27
  prayer in church 103
  psalmody as prayer 117
  on readers 63–4
Testament of Job 7–8
Testament of Joseph 8
Testament of the Lord (*Testamentum Domini*) 73, 138
thanksgiving 26
  community suppers 21, 77
  Jewish psalm-singing 4–5, 6
  and martyr translation 216
  Paul on church songs as 18
  Philo on 10
theaters 9, 262, 268, 290, 349, 360
Thecla 94–5
Themistius 350
Theodore of Mopsuestia 275–6, 287, 288
Theodoret of Cyr
  and Alleluia 248
  and antiphons 275
  on ascetic female households 97–8
  and martyr feasts 147, 303
  tears 323
  two choirs 255–6
Theodosius, Emperor 107, 145
Theodosius (pilgrim) 130
Theodulus 209
Therapeutae 2, 5n27, 7, 10–11, 33, 123, 243, 281
  and Paschal gatherings 45, 46
therapy, music 332–3
Theucarius of Carthage 73–4
Third Council of Carthage 57, 67
Third Greek Life of Pachomius 162
Three Young Men 252
Timocletus 259
toasting 31, 290
Tobit 24, 244
tonal accent 306–7
tonality 309–10
tones 295–7, *296*
Tosefta 2, 3, 9, 11, 19, 41, 261
training, readers and singers 71–5, 361
translation of martyr relics *see* martyrs
Trier ivory 215n88
Trinitarian hymnody 227, 278, 288, 347
triumph, and martyrs 216–17
Triumphal Entry 130, 224–5, 248, 281
troparia 312–13
trumpets 311
turn-taking in song 39, 259, 270, 275, 331
Twelve Prayers and Twelve Psalms 121, 161–6

unbelievers 111–12
unison song 222–3, 233, 256–9

Valens, Emperor 126, 207, 209
Valentinian II, Emperor 150–1, 216–17
Vandals 87–8, 249, 250
vespers 97, 104, 106, 113, 137, 286
Victor (martyr) 203n23, 214, 215, 218
Victor of Vita 70n88, 74, 87–8, 249, 250
vigils
  and Basil of Caesarea on 153–4
  Sunday in Jerusalem 154–5
  unscheduled 149–52
  see also Lenten vigils; Paschal vigils
Virgil, *Eclogue* 8 264
virgins
  and apotropaic power 344–5
  ascetic women 95
  choirs of 137, 259
virtue 333–7
vocal movement in singing 293

whispering 187
Wisdom of Solomon 311–12

Xanthippe 274

Zachariah of Mitylene, *Syrian Chronicle* 73